Charles Lawson

Jubilee Of Queen Victoria Empress Of India

Charles Lawson

Jubilee Of Queen Victoria Empress Of India

ISBN/EAN: 9783742831934

Manufactured in Europe, USA, Canada, Australia, Japa

Cover: Foto ©ninafisch / pixelio.de

Manufactured and distributed by brebook publishing software (www.brebook.com)

Charles Lawson

Jubilee Of Queen Victoria Empress Of India

NARRATIVE OF THE CELEBRATION

OF

The Jubilee

OF

HER MOST GRACIOUS MAJESTY

Queen Victoria, Empress of India

IN THE

PRESIDENCY OF MADRAS.

COMPILED BY

SIR CHARLES LAWSON

Delegate of the Right Honourable the Governor of Fort St. George; Honorary Secretary, Madras Central Jubilee Committee; Editor of the "Madras Mail"; Secretary of the Madras Chamber of Commerce; and Fellow of the University of Madras.

SECOND EDITION.

LONDON:

MACMILLAN AND CO.

1887.

Dedicated by Permission

TO HER MOST GRACIOUS MAJESTY

Queen Victoria, Empress of India,

IN TOKEN OF

THE LOYALTY TO THE THRONE, AND THE DEVOTION TO

HER MAJESTY'S PERSON AND FAMILY

OF HER

EUROPEAN, HINDU, MOHAMMEDAN, AND OTHER SUBJECTS

IN

The Presidency of Madras.

PREFACE.

With a population almost as numerous as that of the United Kingdom, Madras may yield in importance to other portions of the British Empire; but in respect to the grateful appreciation of the blessings which have, under Providence, flowed from Her Majesty's beneficent sovereignty, she claims to be second to none, and her people have rejoiced at being afforded, by the auspicious completion of the fiftieth year of Her Majesty's reign, an opportunity for giving enthusiastic expression to the feelings towards Her Majesty which animate all their hearts.

Not, however, by race, by creed, or by caste, but as a great multitude united by a touching emotion, did they do what they could to pay homage to Her Majesty; and they cherish the hope that it will be a source of gratification to Her Majesty to possess the assurance which this Volume affords of the affection of Madras for the Mother of her People.

Never before was an Address of loyal congratulation to a Sovereign adopted by one hundred and ninety-one towns on behalf of thirty-one millions of subjects. The harmony which produced this result in the Presidency of Madras is attributable to the amiable characteristics of the people, the diffusion of education, and the sympathetic administration of the country during Her Majesty's reign.

The Compiler having most respectfully submitted that it would be exceedingly gratifying to the people whom he had the honour to represent, to possess a *fac-simile* of the signature which Her Majesty inscribed at the head of her reply to their Address, Her Majesty was graciously pleased to accord to him her permission to introduce into this Volume that token of her appreciation of the loyalty and attachment of her subjects in Madras.

The portrait of Her Majesty which forms the frontispiece was engraved for the *Illustrated Sporting and Dramatic News*, from a life-like photograph recently taken at Windsor Castle, by Mr. Alexander Bassano, of Bond Street, London. It has been inserted by permission of Mr. Bassano, and of the proprietors of that journal. The sketch of the Madras Address Casket was engraved for the *Illustrated London News* from a photograph by the London Stereoscopic Company, and is also republished by permission.

The narratives of the celebration were in most instances communicated by the Honorary Secretaries of the Jubilee Committees whose proceedings are recounted. The exigencies of space have necessitated condensation, but the reports in their present form give a faithful account of the measures which were taken throughout the Presidency to observe the Jubilee in a way that would impress the significance of the event on the minds of the present, and on the memories of the rising generation.

The Appendix contains a concise notice of the Madras Presidency, extracted, by permission of Mrs. Duncan, from the late Mr. George Duncan's *Geography of India*. This is followed by a series of sketches illustrative of the progress of Madras during Her Majesty's reign, which were contributed for the purposes of this record, by Colonel F. H. Tyrrell, M.I., Colonel W. M. Scharlieb, I.V.G., Surgeon-General G. Bidie, C.I.E., Mr. T. Venkaswami Rao Dewan Bahadur, Mr. H. Bradley, C.S., Mr. R. W. Barlow, C.S., Mr. G. Hamnett, C.I.E., Mr. H. Farrer, B.C.S., Mr. E. Dowson, Captain W. L. C. Baddeley, R.E., Major W. H. Coates, R.E., Mr. F. N. Thorowgood, M.I.C.E., Mr. J. P. Davidson, Mr. J. R. Hunter, Captain J. H. Taylor, R.N.R., Mr. C. G. Douglas, Mr. M. A. Lawson, M.A., Mr. J. Steavenson, B.A., Mr. H. S. Thomas, C.S., F.Z.S., Mr. H. T. Ross, M.A., LL.B., Colonel T. Weldon, M.S.C., Colonel W. S. McLeod, M.S.C., Rai Bahadur Ranganadha Mudelliar, M.A., Mr. C. Michie Smith, B.Sc., Captain H. D. Love, R.E., Mr. N. R. Pogson, C.I.E., Archdeacon J. F. Browne, B.D., the Rev. W. Relton, M.A., the Rev. E. Sell, B.D., Bishop Caldwell, D.D., LL.D., Bishop Sargent, D.D., Archbishop Colgan, D.D., the Rev. E. H. de Silva, Mr. F. Gainsford, B.A., Mr. Ahmad Mohindin Khan Bahadur, Mr. V. Ramiengar, C.S.I., and Mr. T. Govinda Menone. To these gentlemen the Compiler begs to offer publicly as he has already done privately, his cordial thanks for their invaluable assistance.

London, 1st August, 1887.

CONTENTS.

REPORTS OF THE CELEBRATION IN THE MADRAS PRESIDENCY—(*continued*):—

REPORTS OF THE CELEBRATION IN THE MADRAS PRESIDENCY—(*continued*):—

TO HER MOST GRACIOUS MAJESTY,

Victoria,

OF THE UNITED KINGDOM OF GREAT BRITAIN AND IRELAND, QUEEN: EMPRESS OF INDIA.

MAY IT PLEASE YOUR MAJESTY:

WE, the undersigned, representing Your Majesty's subjects of every race and every creed throughout the Presidency of Madras, do unanimously desire on the auspicious occasion of Your Majesty's Jubilee, to approach Your Majesty with our loyal congratulations.

Your Majesty's assumption of direct Sovereign supremacy over the Empire of India is accepted as the most glorious event in the annals of this ancient land. In Madras it heralded the dawn of a new era of progress and prosperity. Education has been encouraged and sanitation promoted; roads have been made, rivers bridged, railways opened, telegraphs constructed, and irrigation extended; a system of local self-Government has been introduced, industries have been stimulated, and the resources of the country largely developed.

During the fifty years of Your Majesty's reign the Presidency of Madras has conspicuously enjoyed the blessing of tranquillity, the result of the wisdom and impartiality which have pre-eminently characterised Your Majesty's Government.

The even tenour of events in this Presidency was disturbed in 1877 by a famine of unprecedented severity, which evoked from Your Majesty's subjects in the United Kingdom a response, unparalleled in its munificence, to the appeal made for help in our great extremity. Your Majesty's personal sympathy on that occasion is not the least of Your Majesty's many claims on our gratitude.

In profound thankfulness for the noble words of Your Majesty's Proclamation that in our prosperity is Your Majesty's strength, in our contentment Your Majesty's security, and in our gratitude Your Majesty's great reward, we earnestly pray for the long continuance of Your Majesty's beneficent reign, and for the welfare of Your Majesty and the Royal Family.

With sentiments of the deepest loyalty and attachment we subscribe ourselves,

Your Majesty's most obedient and devoted subjects:

TOWN SIGNATORIES

City of Madras.—Robert Bourke; P. P. Hutchins; G. M. J. Moore; C. A. Lawson; J. Colgan; F. Madras; P. S. Ramasawmy; P. Chentsal Rao; Arthur Collins; T. Madava Row; C. G. Master; and 354 others.

Adirampatnam (*Tanjore*).—F. W. Montague Stone; M. Subbaraya Pillai.

Adoni (*Bellary*).—D. Ananthaya; W. Peddoo Chetty; N. Venkoba Row; Bellalli Iyappa; Badshasaib Sultan; H. Gurupaddappa; S. Basalingappa; M. Latchmayya; V. Moddappah; &c.

Alamur (*Godavery*).—Sankaranarachi Narasa; V. Ramayya; B. Vencatakrishnayya; B. Subbarayudu; B. Narayudu; M. Nagayya.

Amalapur (*Godavery*).—K. Venkata Narasaiah; C. V. Krishna Row; and a few others.

Anantapur (*Anantapur*).—B. Teperumall Chetti; C. Audikesavulu Naidu; V. C. Gopala Charriar; P. Subba Row; G. Bundappa; K. Venkatasawmy Chetti; V. Venkatasawmy Chetti; H. Sitarama.

Anjengo (*Malabar*).—D. Kunyan; Bagavathi Ramen; Narayanan Pulpan; George Gomez; Domingo Antony Pereira; Ahamad Allar; S. Velaidhum.

Arcot (*North Arcot*).—M. Krishnasawmy Iyer; S. E. Camul Singh; A. Vurthuraja Moodelliar; A. Padmanabha Moodelliar; Hajee Moideen Ghattala Sahib; N. Dorasawmy Iyer; P. Vijiaraghava Charlu; &c.

Ariyalur (*Trichinopoly*).—H. Subberaya Aiyar; A. Sami Ayar; K. V. Rungacharry; T. Sadasiva Iyer; S. P. Ragunatha Doray; A. Chengalvarayya Raju; Balakristna Pillay; Doresawmy Chetty; &c.

Arkonam (*North Arcot*).—G. K. Winter; E. W. Stoney; A. Gnanasawmy Mudali; J. Gnanaprakasam; C. D. Theobald; J. Andrews; A. A. Edwards; J. W. Read; D. Coomarappen.

Arni (*North Arcot*).—M. G. Visvanadham Shastri; B. S. Sesha Aiyengar; Syed Mohceddeen; E. C. Scudder; B. Virasamiah; V. Murgasastri.

Arupakota (*Madura*).—M. D. Manikum Pillai; Z. S. Taylor; A. Meenakshisoondram Pillai; A. Pirmydeen Sahib; S. Krishnasamier; K. Abdool Rahiman Sahib; T. Athmanath Row; Kondiena; &c.

Aska (*Ganjam*).—F. J. V. Minchen; K. Paupiah; L. Kollmann; M. Visvanatha Aiyar; A. Fletcher; V. Narsaiah; &c.

Atmakur (*Kurnool*).—B. Subba Row; R. Koneti Aiyar; Hajla Khaj Hussain; Rama Rau; M. Subraya Mudaliar; Kishen Singh; M. Nagireddy.

Atur (*Salem*).—Dawood Khan Nabi Sahib; A. Gooroosawmien; A. S. Muthuvenkatrama Chetty; M. Muttoosawmy Naiker; N. Saahachella Naidu.

Bapatla (*Kistna*).—V. Subramanyam; A. Pundarikakshudu; M. Jagannadham; S. Venkateswami; J. Mohammad Fazlullah; E. Bullard.

Bellary (*Bellary*).—A. Sabapathy Modeliar; M. Vasudeva Naidu; K. Narasinga Row; B. Ramchondru Rao; Kareem Sahib; Ebrahim Sait; Godigi Mareppa; Mutiyala Seenappa; P. C. Anuntha Charlu; &c.

Beltangady (*South Canara*).—Manjaya Hidgle; V. Rama Rao; Narayana Paduvetnaya.

Berhampore (*Ganjam*).—J. Thompson; A. Gurumurthy Naidu; P. Narasimha Row; Sri Venkateswaro; N. Ramadoss Puntalu; Abdul Karim Sahib Bahadur.

TOWN	SIGNATORIES

Bezwada (*Kistna*).—P. Ramachendra Row; S. Lingayya; W. A. Benson; T. G. F. Gundain; Erra Subbarayadu; Meer Shamsuddeen; C. H. Venkatachellem; P. Veerasawmy.

Bhadrachellam (*Godavery*).—P. Tirumal Rau; K. Sadasiva Rau; V. Kristnamurty Naidu; Y. Rangaiah Naidu; S. Kamayya; K. Ramasawy Naidu.

Bhavani (*Coimbatore*).—T. Appagiah; B. T. Sangaranarayana Chetti; T. Karuppi Chetti; Pullayar Pillai; Pattabi Iyengar; Velayuda Chetti; Gurunada Pillai; G. Venkataranga Chetti.

Bhowanagiri (*South Arcot*).—R. V. Rengacha Ayar; B. Streenevasa Row; Dwanaga Pillai; Rajagopal Pillai; Shaik Kadur Sahib; M. Krisnasawmy Ayar.

Bimlipatam (*Vizagapatam*).—V. Anantha Row Puntulu; W. J. Evans; W. A. P. Greenfield; T. Kipping; T. A. D. MacDougall; R. Minto; R. P. O'Hearn; D. G. Roberts; K. Ramadoss Puntulu; &c.

Bobbili (*Vizagapatam*).—V. S. Runga Row, Rajah of Bobbili; G. Ranganayakulu; A. Ramakrishnayya; G. Narasimhaswamy, T. S. Narayana; S. S. Subrahmanyam; &c.

Bodynyakaner (*Madura*).—T. B. Kamaraja Pondia Naiker; Vellia Rowther; J. D. Sylvester; M. Kumaruswami Chetty; S. Peerana Rowther; E. Seymour; B. M. Varadaraga Aiyar; &c.

Calicut (*Malabar*).—W. S. Gantz; D. Maneckjee; C. M. Raruchan; A. Subba Row; W. Logan; F. R. Wilkinson; Mana Vikrama Zamorin Maharajah Bahadur; C. Kunhi Raman Menon; &c.

Cannanore (*Malabar*).—S. C. Sarkies; W. P. Schoenthal; E. Gadsden; Maneckjee Dassabhoy; B. D'Rozario; O. Koyamoo; C. Coonjee Ellaya; L. B. Rego.

Chagalmarri (*Kurnool*).—A. Latchmana Row; B. Venkoba Row; M. Patcha Saib; D. Soobba Row; B. Vankara Setti; M. Venkatasubbanna; J. Garudachalam; A. Raja Row.

Chatrapur (*Ganjam*).—H. L. Howell; J. Hargreaves; J. Norman; W. Venkatapiah; D. Streenevasa Row; S. L. Narasinga Row; C. Poornayya; D. Venkata Sastri.

Chicacole (*Ganjam*).—P. Suryanarayana Row; T. Venkat Row; T. V. Siva Row; P. J. Fox; S. Goonniah; V. Guraviah.

Chidambaram (*South Arcot*).—C. Varaha Iyengar; P. N. Ramachandra Row; Ambalavana Pillai; Syed Sha Mayinuddin, Parch Jahagirdar; V. Malhari Row; G. A. W. Velloma.

Chingleput (*Chingleput*).—Evans C. Johnson; Abdul Ghani Khan; C. Valoidum; P. Streenevasa Charry; Mir Serajudin; M. Bhashica Charlu; V. Ragava Charlu.

Chingleput (*District*).—C. Sury Iyer; P. Ramasawmy Iyer; C. V. Ramanuja Chariar; M. Ramanaja Charriar; N. Streenevasaragavacharry; Rathna Chetty; Muthusawmy Chetty.

Chirala (*Kistna*).—B. D'Prater; N. Venkata Row; M. Ramayya; Meer Kariymoddeen; R. Venkata Subbiah; P. Venkataramame; D. Sadasiva Row; &c.

Chittoor (*North Arcot*).—T. S. Narasinga Row; V. Gopalacharriar; Z. S. Anthony; N. Sreenivasavarada Charry; C. V. Sreenivasa Charlu; C. Masilamoney; V. D. Arunachella Moodr.

Cochin (*Malabar*).—George Brunton; N. Black; J. H. Boyer; J. E. Winckler; M. A. Platel; Mani Mani; Krishnasawmy Iyer; A. F. Sealy; Dharsey Khetsy; G. Badenoch; E. H. Black; &c.

TOWN SIGNATORIES

Cocanada (*Godavery*).—W. A. Happell; V. M. G. Rama Row; T. H. Baker; G. Vencataratnam; J. M. Bryce; G. H. White; V Janakeramiah; G. V. Krushnayya; M. Ramanneh; B. Vencataratnam; &c.

Coimbatore (*Coimbatore*).—A. Periyasawmy Mudaliar; N. Annasawmy Rao; I. Bashiakarloo; C. Vencatesiah; Mahomed Caseim Meracoir; Mahomed Cudarathulla Sahib; N. Roody; &c

Coonoor (*Nilgiris*).—W. N Carey; A. Allan; K. A. Sashiengar; Soomar Sait; C. F. Keyser; and W. L. Edmiston.

Cuddalore (*South Arcot*).—H P. Gordon; S. Devanayaga Moodelliar; A. B. Fortune; M. Arumuga Pillai; C. H. Creswell; Y. Seshachellum Naidu; S. Doraisawmy; Geo. Gouge; Mahomed Murath Merkair; &c.

Cuddapah (*Cuddapah*).—Lewis Moore; Gabriel Stokes; Max. Ward Elliot; M. Iyasawmy Pillai; J. C. Johnston; I. Kotilingam Naidu; S. Srinivasa Chariar; C. Jumbulingam Moodelliar; K. Seshia Chetti; &c.

Cumbum (*Kurnool*).—Syed Aly; K. Kristna Seng; A. Goodwin; D. Therumal Rao; C. Sivayya; M. Pitchayya; Syed Ahmed Sahib.

Dachepalle (*Kistna*).—Kola Pitcheredde; D. Brahmanandam; E. A. White; C. V. Chinniah Modaliar; T. K. Rajoo; C. John; P. Ragoonatha Sastri; P. Sivaramiah; D. Venkatasoobiah; &c.

Denkanikota (*Salem*).—P. A. Ramaswami Iyer; P. Bhowani Sankara Rau; Krishna Sastri Sankara Aiyar; Syed Mustappa Sahib; Samuel Stendy; P. Aamachier; Seshagiri Rau; Ramacharriar; &c.

Deva Shola (*Nilgiris*).—J. W. B. Money; Louis J. Creed; J. B. Barclay; R. Macfeat; V. Kunnusawmy; and V. Paul.

Dharmavaram (*Anantapur*).—H. Ragavendra Row; P. Veerasawmy Naidu; J. J. Smith; Khasim Saib; Chindaloor Nagappa Chetty.

Dharapuram (*Salem*).—M. S. Beleghary Row; H. D. Ramachandra Naidu; Syed Moortoza Sahib; R. Kunthappa Chetti; Venugovinda Oodyan.

Dindigul (*Madura*).—C. H. Mounsey; J. E. Evans; Geo. S. Hickey; J. Heimpel; Lavathiere; A. Ayasami Sastri; A. Kareem Khan; M. Sundram Iyer; R. Subbier; A. Authmanatha Iyer; &c.

Ellore (*Godavery*).—L. C. Miller; E. Kachapeswara Sastry; Venkatarangayer; M. Browne; Mahomed Vaizulla Khan Sahib; O. Sevarama Kristnamma.

Erode (*Coimbatore*).—Tiruvencata Dorasawmy Pillai; K. R. Lakshminarayan Aiyar; Royapoli Kalyanasundramiah; Khadir Alla-ud-din Saib; S. Subbu Chetti.

Ganjam (*Ganjam*).—J. G. Horsfall; H. L. Howell; F. J. V. Minchin; T. Sivaramayya; Rajah Sri Rajamani; M. Sri Lakshminarayana Ananga; Sri Narayana; Sri Kisorachevdra; &c.

Gingee (*South Arcot*).—C. S. Kristnasawmy Iyengar; T. Velayuda Mudaliar; C. Narasimmacharriar; C. Venkata Rao; V. Narayanasawmy Nynar; H. A. Aslem Sahib; T. S. Gabbilet; &c.

Gooty (*Anantapur*).—T. Ramachendra Row; S. E. Carrapiett; P. T. Rajagopaul; J. Sreenivasa Row; P. Kesava Pillai; Y. Chandapa; S. Ambajee Row; R. Seshiah.

Gudivada (*Kistna*).—V. Lakshmaji Row; F. C. Rodrigues; S. Bhagyanadha Pillai; D. Sobhanadri; V. Venkatasubbayya; A. Subramanyam.

TOWN — SIGNATORIES

Guntur (*Kistna*).—C. M. Mullaly; J. Douglas; W. B. Taylor; J. W. Webster; J. A. Narrain Row; N. Venkoba Row; D. Dhurma Row; V. Krishnayya; C. V. Subramania Sastri; &c.

Harpanhalle (*Bellary*).—C. Guru Row; V. Kodandarama Iyer; K. Padmanabha Ayar; H. Rama Row; N. Mukappa; Ragha Venkappa; I. Bommanna; Bhimasaina Row; Venkoba Row; &c.

Hindapur (*Anantapur*).—K. Gundanja; C. Gopal Row; M. Seenlah; B. Munisawmy Mudelliar; K. Beemannah; K. Bhaskarappa; K. Nagiah; D. Gangadhariah; S. Chennappa.

Hospett (*Bellary*).—G. Campbell; Y. Hanumanta Row; Krishna Avadhuta Pandit; Virupakshamarigalu; Kalcabalu Sinappa; Devasikhamany Mudaliar.

Hosur (*Salem*).—H. Subba Row; P. A. Ramaswami Aiyar; G. Venkatarama Chetti; Kotha Rangappa Chetti; Ramalinga Aiyar; Kotha Subbu Chetti.

Idayangudi (*Tinnevelly*).—S. Guanamuttu; P. Gnanakan Nadar; P. Simon Nadar; G. James Nadar; K. Annayah Rajoo; D. S. David; M. Cornelius Devar; M. Samuel Nadar; K. Soobiah Pillay.

Illapudi (*Godavery*).—T. V. Ramiah; D. Raghavendra Rao; H. A. Walford; P. Sriramulu.

Iskipalle (*Nellore*).—J. M. Mitchell; H. M. Bond; J. V. Cherry; O. A. Luza.

Jagayyapet (*Kistna*).—T. Vasudeva Murti; W. A. Pascal; J. L. Kelly; D. Narayanam; Sreeram Jayaramudu; Peruri Venkatareddi; Genugentla Ramanna; Sreeram Sreeramulu; &c.

Jamalamadugu (*Cuddapah*).—Pular Subba Row; P. Ratnam Mudaliar; P. Parthasarathy Naidu; Syed Shah Badruddin; M. Venkatareddy Jaghirdar.

Kalahastri (*North Arcot*).—Rajah Murthoo Venkatappah Naidu Bahadur Varuo; Mysore Tiruvenkata Charlu; Rajah D. K. Thimmanayanim Bahadur Varoo; D. Ramanayanim Varuo; P. Sashachellapathe.

Karakal (*South Canara*).—Andar Syed Hyder Saib; K. Rama Heggade; K. Anantha Kampti; M. Mundappa Baugera; V. Rama Row; X. Krishna Row; B. Raghavendra Row; H. Annappaya; J. B. Lobo.

Karur (*Coimbatore*).—A. David Pillai; M. Muthuviranna Chetty; Putty Ramier; T. S. Subba Row; Henry Little; N. C. Kuppanaiyangari; V. Varada Raju Mudeliar; A. Krishna Row.

Kodavasel (*Tanjore*).—Kaliyanaramier; S. Swaminathier; Alagusingaiyangar; Ramabadracharriar; R. Sreenivasa Iyengar; Annasami Iyengar; Saminadier; T. Subbier.

Kollegal (*Coimbatore*).—M. Sashachellum Naidu; Rahimtollah Ahamed Set; Rama Chetty; Matam Seshadri Chetty; C. B. Franks; P. A. Pires; K. E. Subbarayer; D. Ramakrishnaiya; &c.

Kotagherry (*Nilgiris*).—W. L. Edmiston; F. R. Griffith; Fitz Roy Sherman; J. H. Strange; M. J. Redmond; D. S. Appaji Aiyer.

Kulitalai (*Trichinopoly*).—V. Krishnasawmy Aiyar; M. S. Narayanasawmy Iyar; P. Moses Pillai; V. Rengarathnam Iyer; S. Annamalai Pillai; M. Aziulla Saib; V. Nilakanta Iyer; R. Kristnamacharyar.

Kullakurchi (*South Arcot*).—T. Rudrachellam Pillai; V. Krishnaswami Aiyar; P. Subba Row; C. Duraisawmi Mudeliar; V. Vydhianadha Mudeliar.

c

TOWN	SIGNATORIES

Kumbaconam (*Tanjore*).—G. Ramasawmiah; S. Seshayya; V. Krishnaier; P. Thambisawmy Moodelliar; A. Ramalinga Chettiar; A. C. Narayanasawmy Iyer.

Kundapur (*Malabar*).—R. Ramayya; N. Babu Row; Nagappa Holla; D. Vencata Row; and P. Venkatramanayya.

Kungundikupam (*North Arcot*).—N. Narrainsawmy Moodelliar; G. Kistnasawmiah; Y. Alikhan; S. Govindarajulu Naidu; V. Davasegumoney Pillai; P. C. Subramiah; J. Bhagavuntha Row; S. Soobbaroyadu

Kurnool (*Kurnool*).—A. Subba Row; H. Saint M. Rencontre; C. Somasundra Sastri; L. Chandulal; Madam Soobbanah Chetty; Mehomed Abbas Allykhan; K. Narsinasawmy Naidoo; &c.

Kuttuparamba (*Malabar*).—Kottal Uppi Haji; Parapravan Kunji Ahmed Haji; Randapurayil Kunji Koppar; Kottal Kunjalikutti; Ottayerayil Pakkar Haji; Ninkilary Kunjamboo Nambiar; &c.

Madakasira (*Anantapur*).—M. Vijayraghavalu Naidu; M. Narayana Rau; Bunder Nanjundappa; Jilla Dasanna.

Madura (*Madura*).—E. Turner; L. Narasimha Charriar; R. Venkatasaiyer; Ramasawmy Chetty; T. Sevakamiah; R. Venkoba Row; T. Weir; John French; M. K. Ramasawmy Aiyer; &c.

Madurantakam (*Chingleput*).—J. Rhenius Pillai; M. Sanjevi Naidu; Moothoobauboo Reddy; C. Kumarasawmy Mudaliar; D. Kesavulo Naidu; &c.

Malapuram (*Malabar*).—S. Ramiah; A. A. Visvanath; K. M. Naraina Menon; V. Paramaswara Iyar; L. Ramunni; M. Kunnar; Kalappada Munian.

Manantoddy (*Malabar*).—T. R. Richmond; P. Mathel Sooben Puttur; L. Ramachandra Iyer; Vamooth Nambier; C. F. Wilkins; M. Krishna Nair; J. W. Wooldridge; &c.

Mangalore (*South Canara*).—Manjayya Hegada; T. M. Rama Row; Amirudeen Saib; W. Arnot; N. Sheva Rau; T. Kontappa; N. Goonda Row; K. Narna Chetti; J. C. Coelho; Hadgee Ayoob Noor; &c.

Manjeri (*Malabar*).—T. Manavikraman; T. Narayanan Nair; Karanamulpad; Tenayancheri Eliad; K. Sankara Paniker; Ahamad Gurukal; K. Kunholenkutti; N. K. Chamu Menon.

Mannargudi (*Tanjore*).—Sambasiva Iyer; Rajappa Iyer; N. Gopalakrishnasunia Chettiar; R. Naragausawmy Naidu; Gopala Iyer; Mahathava Chettiar; Thiruvaugadatha Iyengar; Singaravelu Odyar.

Masulipatam (*Kistna*).—R. Sewell; C. A. Bird; J. V. Subbaroyadu; F. L. Haleman; G. D. Wybrow; J. H. Fletcher; W. G. Peel; C. Nagoji Rau; A. Subbarayudu; Nawab Hassan Alikhan; &c.

Mayaveram (*Tanjore*).—T. A. Alaga Pillai; Thiruvengadasami Pillai; T. Durasami Pillai; T. G. Suntharesa Iyer; Sivarama Chettiar; Syed Abdul Aziz; D. Krishna Row.

Melur (*Madura*).—C. Kristna Row; B. Vencatakristnaiengar; M. Tirumalai Pillai; A. Vythlingam Moodelliar; George Rowland; Kadarkani Maniagaran; T. Vencataramaiah; Gurusawmy; &c.

Mettapolium (*Coimbatore*).—D. B. Gamble; V. Rungasawmy; C. S. Ranga; T. N. Soobrayaloo Naidu; D. Samuel; J. Ephraim; S. V. Ramachendram; T. A. Mooroogiah Pillai; Sitaramier; &c.

TOWN — SIGNATORIES

Mulki (*South Canara*).—Paulloth Kalappa Shetti ; Bhadrachary ; D. Hamma Biari ; B. Keshava Kamti ; Vode Pujari ; P. Ramakrishnanja ; M. Bhavani Row.

Muttupet (*Tanjore*).—P. V. Lakshmanasami Naidu.

Namakal (*Salem*).—T. N. Suba Ramaiya Sastri ; T. Ramaswami Iyengar ; S. T. Venkatapathier ; P. Subramanya Iyer ; N. Narasimma Pillai ; P. Aiyavier ; P. Rajagopala Charriar ; Venkataravana ; &c.

Nandyal (*Kurnool*).—C. Vencatajugga Row ; K. Seshadri Aiyengar ; P. Sambayya ; Abdalla Sait ; P. Krishnama Charry ; L. Subba Row ; Hanumanta Row ; V. Vencata Row ; Mammuth Khan ; &c.

Narsapur (*Godavery*).—F. R. C. Carr ; C. Stewart ; K. Vencatachalam ; G. Pattabbiramayya ; Y. Naracinga Row ; K. Subba Rao ; A. Kristnayya ; C. Rungayya ; Thomas Heelis ; S. Sambasiva Row ; &c.

Narsipatam (*Vizagapatam*).—V. Jagannadham ; G. Vijaya Ramamurty ; C. Mangaya ; T. Appalavarasaya Chetty ; K. Koormaya.

Nazareth (*Tinnevelly*).—Arthur Margoschis ; Moses Kolipillai ; J. Canagarayan Chettiar ; David Periansyakam Pillai ; P. Peter Samuel ; Y. V. Jacob ; V. Simon ; J. Vedomuthu ; A. Abraham.

Negapatam (*Tanjore*).—Charles E. Crighton ; P. Rutnasabapathy Pillai ; M. Ganapathy Pillai ; J. Adamson ; V. Chinnamaricar ; V. Srinivasa Charlu ; M. A. Gopala Iyer ; M. Mutia Chetty.

Nellore (*Nellore*).—L. A. Campbell ; H. M. Bhamtulla ; Syed Davood Alikhan ; A. Venkaya ; Joseph Smith ; P. Rama Reddy ; D. Downie.

North Arcot (*North Arcot*).—W. H. Glenny ; Rajah of Kalahastri ; Zemindar of Punganur ; Jaghirdar of Arnee ; Shree Mahant ; Rajaratna Moodelliar ; Shu a Kaji ; Hasrat Sayyid ; Ruhhamudin Khadir ; &c.

Nundalore (*Cuddapah*).—Doddi Yogappah ; C. Aananthacharlu ; A. Kristniah ; T. Venketsawmy Naidu.

Omalur (*Salem*).—S. A. Subramani Aiyar ; C. Ramaswami Aiyar ; Pacha Miyan Sahib ; Venkatappa Chettiyar ; A. Venkatachella Mudaliar ; Aiyaswami Sastri.

Ongole (*Nellore*).—W. J. Tate ; N. Vencata Rangacharlu ; V. Ananda Row ; John Everitt Clough ; Gurram Pitchayya ; Ahamad Hussain Saib ; D. Markandayya Sastri.

Ootacamund (*Nilgiris*).—H. Prendergast ; C. E. Plunkett ; Jacob Samuel ; Dadabhai Eduljee ; Abdool Rahiman Hajee ; Fakeer Mohamed Sait ; W. E. Schmidt ; Gool Mahomed Sait ; &c.

Pakala (*Nellore*).—J. M. Mitchell ; D. Holman ; V. Subba Row ; Hochur Pitchaya ; S. Raghava Reddi ; S. Ramalinga Reddi ; A. Veeranna ; A. Bhadraya ; A. Govinda Row ; J. Venkata Subbaya ; &c.

Palladam (*Coimbatore*).—C. Seetha Ramiah ; Mahomed Sibgathulah Chidak ; Appa Naikenpatty Ganga Naiker ; Rangasamudram Komarasamy Goundan ; Muthusawmy Goundan ; &c.

Palghat (*Malabar*).—Sekari Varma Valia Rajah ; C. S. Swaminatha Pattar Kaiakar ; Syed Ismail Khan ; V. P. D'Rozario ; O. Raman ; T. A. Ramakrishna Iyer.

Palmanair (*North Arcot*).—K. Krishna Row ; E. Venkataramiah ; Guntai Lingayya ; V. Ramasami ; C. Appasawmy ; Gopala Krishnappa.

TOWN	SIGNATORIES

Palni (*Madura*).—H. C. Hasen; J. Samuel Pillai; C. Runga Row; S Goosmiah Sahib; T. Krishna Row; Krishnasawmi Naidu; Ramanathan Chetty; Chethambaram Chetty; &c.

Pambam (*Madura*).—John P. James; C. Raja Retnum Pillay; Patrick B. Gibbons; J. E. P. Steel; A. S. Penagapany Mudelliar; J. Venkatrayloo Nayudu.

Panruti (*South Arcot*).—M. Parthasarathy Raju; M. Ramaswami Iyer; A. Sivakahma Mudeliar; P. Coopoosawmy Odyar; D. Venkat Row; M. Subba Row; Mavil Rama; B. Nagappa Holla; &c.

Paramathi (*Salem*).—P. Raja Gopalacharyar; A. Mukti Chidambara Mudelliar; T. Rama Sesha Aiyer; C Manickam Muduliyar; T. Mahomed Kasim Sahib; Venkata Rama Reddiar; &c.

Paramakudi (*Madura*).—V. Cooppoosawmy Iyer; M. Nagalingam Pillai; G. T. Ananthanarayana Pillai; V Mohanarungum Naidu; S. Mahomed Hussan; Malarmyar Saib; &c.

Parla Kimidi (*Ganjam*).—Sri Sri S. Gajapaty; W. Taylor; M. Srinivasa Rao; P. Jagannadham.

Paravatipore (*Vizagapatam*).—E. A. Elwin; M. Ninganlooloo; V. A. Narasimluraz; K. Narasimha Row; A. Appadu; S. C. White; C. S. Morton; N. Jaya Rao; K. Seshagiri Row; Narayana Bakshi; &c.

Pattikonda (*Kurnool*).—G. Khande Row; J. Goondoo Row; T. Poonarungam Pillai; C. Coopoosawmy Aucharry; C. Venkataramiah; M. Sankar Row; N. Sevayya; K. Narayanappa; &c.

Patukota (*Tanjore*).—J. Venkatramiah; T. Vydealingam Pillai; V. R. Soondrum Iyer; N. Streenivasa Pillai; S. Moothoosawmy Iyer; M. Ramanathier; D. Asirvadham; &c.

Peapully (*Kurnool*).—Syed Mushar Ali; N. Panchanadham Pillay; R. Lakshmanarasu Pantulu; N. Varadachariar; D. Cotilingum Devara; V. Kristappa; C Subba Sastri; Subba Sastri; &c.

Penukonda (*Anantapur*).—Bannatyne Macleod; H. Krishnaier; G. Narasing Row; Abdool Wahab; E. Hanumiah; K. Narasappa; P. Subby Reddy; Nagasa Row.

Pentapadu (*Godavery*).—D. Venkata Seva Row; D. Venkatarathnam; S. Subba Row; V. Sreenivasa Chary; V. Janakiramayya.

Peravkolam (*Madura*).—K. Narayana Iyer; P. Rengasawmy Iyer; T. Soonder Row; V. P. Rajem Iyer; C Sangaralingam Pillai; C. F. Peter Sebastian; N. Alamelu Chetty; Chinnasawmy Asari.

Pollachi (*Coimbatore*).—S. Kristnaiyar; M. R. Kalingaraya Kavandar; M. Yerrappa Kavandar; Subbaraya Devaya Nayakar; R. Somasundra Mudaliar; S. M. Ponnoosawmy Pillai; &c.

Ponnani (*Malabar*).—K. Shangara Menon; P. J. Itteyerah; E. Ambu Nair; Seyd Aythross Imbichi Koya Thangal; M. Kouthi Menon; E. Krasto Menon; P. Vydanatha Iyer; &c.

Ponery (*Chingleput*).—P. Jaganada Lala; Murugusawmy Chettiar; P. Panchappakesa Iyer; C. Latchmiya Naidu; Namasivaya Mudaliar; Kariappa Moodelliar.

Polur (*North Arcot*).—Patel Hoosman Saheb; Snoberoyer; S. Ragava Charlu; B. Venkatapathy Naidu; V. Masalamoney Moodelliar; Krishnier.

Poonamallee (*Chingleput*).—T. Chellappah Naicker; S. Kristnaswamy Iyer; K. S. Prakasarau Moodelliar; P. Raghunatha Nayanar; R. Nadaraaui Aiyangar.

TOWN SIGNATORIES

Produttur (*Cuddapah*).—S. Subba Row; B. Tirumala Row; H. Ramiah; M. Dhormalingam Pillai; S. Ramiah Chetti; M. V. Kamakshi Row; C. P. Gurumoorth.

Pudukota (*Trichinopoly*).—A. Sashiah Sastri; D. Ruthnam Moodelliar; Thathachariar; K. Vasudeva Iyengar; A. Thandavoroya Pillai; G. A. Salisbury; Jamied Shah; Jacob Gnanaolion; &c.

Pullampett (*Cuddapah*).—P. Dhonda Row; N. Venkojee Row; T. N. Govinda Rajulu Naidu; M. Govindasawmy Pillai; P. Varda Charry; S. K. Anna Pillai.

Pundalur (*Malabar*).—J. W. Minchin; J. L. Large; H. Punnet; H. Lyon; A. W. L. Smith; A. Brown; C. Brown; A. Montelro; W. J. D'Costa; J. R. D'Lima; G. Towers; A. M. D'Lima.

Rajahmundry (*Godavery*).—Ahmed Ullakhan Amiruddin; B. Gavarraus; R. Harris; Kamarasu; Narayanasawmy; Runga Charriar; Seshagiri Row; Subba Rao; Sundara Rao; Venkatasubba Row; &c.

Ramachendrapur (*Godavery*).—S. Narasingaier; B. Ramalingaswarappa; Rajah K. Ramachendrarju; G. P. Walch.

Remnad (*Madura*).—P. Rutnaswamy Daver; P. Sivagnanaswamy Daver; T. Rajaram Row; G. Pandithorey Daver; Spencer A. Shaile.

Ranipet (*North Arcot*).—C. Balakisna Moodelliar; R. G. Morrison; V. Ranganatha Row; A. Soobramanya Iyer; A. Ramoogapala Chetdar.

Repalli (*Kistna*).—K. Anandarow; P. V. Hanumanta Row; K. Nageswara Row; B. Ramaswamy.

Royachote (*Cuddapah*).—T. Sreenevasa Row; A. Ramanuja Charry; C. Subbaroyalu Naidu; C. Nagi Reddi; Y. Ramiah Chetty; Nagi Reddi; S. Michael; C. Mohiyeddeen Khan.

Salem (*Salem*).—C. Prichard; J. Bertho; M. Suryamurthy Pillai; T. Appajee Row; P. Venkataramaiyya; W. Visuami Ayer; K. V. Lakshman Row; R. C. Narayanasami Naidu; &c.

Sandur (*Bellary*).—R. Vitthal Row; J. F. Firth; Bala Sahib; K. Abdul Rahim; Venkata Row; Bhema Row.

Sankaranarkoil (*Tinnevelly*).—C. Mukunda Row; T. Ramiengar; Venkataram Aiyar; S. V. Sankaranarayana Aiyar; S. Subramania Pillai; Suriyanarayana Pillai; S. Tirumalaikolundu Pillai; &c.

Sattanapalle (*Kistna*).—Raja Vasiredi Vencata Lakshmi Narasimha Naidu, Bahadur Manne Sultan; K. Sri Ramalu; V. Subramanyam; Mahomey Rahamatulla; C. Buchiragavayya.

Satyamangalam (*Coimbatore*).—J. Ramasamiah; Kamashi Sastri; Venkatarama Chetty; Nanjappa Chetty.

Sevagunda (*Madura*).—T. Venkataramiah; Perianna Oodyar Taver; M. Alagirisawmy Naidu; S. Sankara Iyer; K. Pattabiramiah; E. Cavary Pillai; M. Krishna Row, A. Narayana Chetti; &c.

Sivagiri (*Tinnevelly*).—S. V. P. Chinnatambiyar; Senthalikalai Pandiyan; A. Ganapathy Ayer; and Somayagi Ayar.

Shiyali (*Tanjore*).—T. Audinarayana Chetty; R. Chakrapani Row; K. Seshaiya; R. A. Sundram Pillai; S. Vadamalai Pillai; Ramanuja Charri; R. S. Sundrappiar.

TOWN SIGNATURIES

Shalingur (*North Arcot*).—P. V. Rangacharlar; K. Narasimha Charry; C. Subbiah Naidu; N. Vencata Row; M. Balachendra Iyer; A. Varada Charry; C. Soobaroya Pillai.

Srirangam (*Trichinopoly*).—L. Kristnlengar; S. Kristniengar; S. Kristnama Charry; T. R. Kuppusawmy Iyengar; C. Thirumallay Naidu, &c.

Sriperumbudur (*Chingleput*).—G. Ramasawmy Chettiar; Sri. M. Veera Ragava Charriar; Shaik Meeran Saib; Damudara Mudeliar; Sriram Baahlakadoo Naidu; Venkataragava Reddiar.

St. Thomas Mount (*Chingleput*).—W. W. Elwes; J. P. Fitzpatrick; J. Chesny; Pierre E. Messinier; Thomas Mellor; W. C. Lewis.

Tadpatri (*Anantapur*).—J. Walls; M. Gopala Row; S. Parker; A. Omer Khan; Kalavalah Chencheyya.

Taliparamba (*Malabar*).—J. F. Pereira; P. W. Chacko; K. Raman; T. H. Rama Potuval; E. P. Narayanen Nambudiri; P. Kunhen Mayen; M. Othena Menon; Tayyil Govindan; Kottai Mayan; &c.

Tungacherry (*Malabar*).—F. John; A. Nanoo Menon; J. P. Rodrigues; J. N. Martin; M. R. Consalves; F. Rodrigues; J. Moreira; J. C. Surrao; S. S. Bous; S. Neves; G. Abraham; &c.

Tanjore (*Tanjore*).—E. Gibson; H. V. Cobb; K. Govinda Row; M. Kamakshiamba Boyisaheb; M. Sieulba Boyisaheb; M. Deepamba Boyisaheb; M. Ramakumarumba Boyisaheb, &c.

Tanuku (*Godavery*).—R. Hanumanta Row; V. Vijaya Ramiah; A. Ramachandra Row.

Tellicherry (*Malabar*).—H. Sewell; R. Tathan; O. Mayen Ally; A. Thompson; J. J. D'Rosario; M. Kunhi Ramen Vydiar; Coroth Ramuni; Cheruvari Mannen; C. Keloth Bavachee; &c.

Tinnevelly (*District*).—J. Lee-Warner; Rajah Jagaviira Ramakumara Ettappa Nayakar; P. Rattari; P. Rowther; J. C. Hughesdon; Edwin Sargent, Bishop; A. Soomasundram Pillai, &c.

Tinnevelly (*Town*).—T. Muzier; T. Ramalingum Moodaliar; M. Appadorai Aiyar; Krishna Row; T. S. Muthia Pillai; E. Muthia Pillai; T. Jesudasem; Thirumall Ayengar; Muhammad Husain; &c.

Tirukoilur (*South Arcot*).—E. A. A. Ihle; C. J. Stuart; K. Subba Row; V. Narayana Row; Thiruvenkataramanuja Charriar; Abdul Kareen Sahib; V. Strinevasa Rao; &c.

Tirumangalam (*Madura*).—M. Gurusawmy Sastri; N. Vasudeva Pillai; G. Narayana Row; S. Jackson; P. Soobramania Iyer; V. Subaraya Devai; V. Rathnaswami Moopanar; I. Appavoo Pillai; &c.

Tirupati (*North Arcot*).—Sri Mahant Bhagavan Dasji; V. V. Ranga Charloo; K. Narasimha Charloo; C. Sunthara Charloo; P. Munesawmy Chetty; C. Seshagiri Rau; C. Krishnama Chari; K. Ramiah.

Tirupatur (*Salem*).—C. Annamalai Chetty; C. Runganadam; O. Subba Row; C. Perumal Nadar; Mahomed Hussein Sahib; K. V. Karthikeya Pillay; V. Krishnier; Choteba Sahib.

Tirushali (*Madura*).—P. Venkatswarah; M. Vythilingam Pillai; G. Loganathen Pillai; Sundram Iyer; Gopalakristnien.

TOWN SIGNATORIES

Tiravady (*Tanjore*).—Latchmana Mudaliyar; R. Rengasami Naidoo; S. Rajagopala Iyer; Seenubala Bhattugosami; Kothandarama Iyer; Muttukumara Tharabiran; Narayanasami Chetty; &c.

Tiruvallur (*Chingleput*).—P. Shithambra Row; Demingala Naidu; P. Allagusengara Naidu; T. E. Beabiyagam; C. Srinivasa; A. Kunthapa Chetty.

Tiravalore (*Tanjore*).—N. R. Narasimmiah; T. Narayanasami Iyer; M. Krishna Row; T. Krishna Row; P. R. Kothandaramier; M. K. Subramanier; T. Dorasawmy Pillai; &c.

Tiruvadamandur (*Tanjore*).—K. Colundasawmy Pillai; L. Sreenevasa Aiyar; D. Krishnasawmy Aiyar; R. K. Ramachandru Aiyar; Kasnadu Thambiran.

Tiruvannamalai (*South Arcot*).—G. R. Middleton; M. Srinivasa Charri; S. Venkatachella Puntalu; T. Appasami Naidu; Arunagiri Moodelliar; Sundra Rajalu; Kassim Sahib; Bavudeen Sahib.

Tiruvur (*Kistna*).—Rajah V. Venkata Ramarow; Rajah V. Ramakristna Row; Rajah V. L. Venkayyamma Row; Rajah G. V. Subbar Row; K. Venkatarayanim; K. Ramayya; M. Sitaramayya; &c.

Tittakudi (*South Arcot*).—A. Venkatakrishniah; T. Shunmoogam Pillai; T. Kumaraswami Pillai; T. L. Ramasawmy Pillai; Periathamby Mudaly; Kaudar Meera Hossan Rowther; &c.

Tranquebar (*Tanjore*).—K. Pamperrian; A. S. Daniel Pillai; M. Appasawmy Chetty; A. Pakyam Pillai; N. W. Subbaraidu Naidu; A. S. Ayasawmy; Ramasawmy Naidu; R. Vasudeva Naidu; &c.

Trichengode (*Salem*).—Paramasiva Coundan; C. S. Chockalingam Pillai; C. Ramalinga Iyer; V. Sethachellam Iyer; T. Athmaram Davay; K. C. Arunachellam Pillai; R. Mahalinga Ayer; &c.

Tuticorin (*Tinnevelly*).—J. A. Sharrock; R. Caldwell; P. Iyemperumall Pillai; P. Soobaraya Pillay; J. B. Roche; G. A. Phipps; &c.

Udamalpet (*Coimbatore*).—T. Ramasawmi Iyer; K. Vencatakrishnier; Syed Deavan; Syed Fakurdeen Sahib; V. Moonea Pillai; Ramier; Ramasawmy Pillai; Ramasawmy Chetty; &c.

Udayarpalaiyam (*Trichinopoly*).—Zemindar of Udayarpalaiyam; K. U. Kalakka Thola Udayar; Chidambara Reddear; &c.

Udipi (*South Canara*).—A. Butterworth; K. Ganapaiya; K. Krishna Row; G. Gascoyne; K. Santappa; G. Ritter; Haji Harum Shet; Manki Hassan Sahib; G. Mohedin Sahib; Purna Acharya; &c.

Usalampatti (*Madura*).—T. Panchampigasier; S. Krishnasawmy Aiya; P. D. A. Andaperumal Pillai; T. Thyriam Pillai; Ally Hussain Khan; Venkatapathi Aiyar; Chockalingam Pillai; &c.

Uttankere (*Salem*).—V. Munisawmy Pillai; M. Sevarama Iyer; D. Narasinga Row; K. Vithiya Natha Iyer; Varatharajulu Chettiar; A. Ellappa Mudeli; T. Paul Pillai; Balagi Singh.

Uttramallur (*Chingleput*).—T. Alwar Pillai; T. Tulasinga Mudaliar; A. Rangaiyar; M. Kasthuri Aiyangar; V. Govindarajulu Naidu; U. A. Thirumalai Aiyangar; A. S. Krishnasawmy Reddiar.

Vallum (*Tanjore*).—T. Raja Row; N. Subba Row; Mahommad Abdul Hie; Baksha Routher; Venkataramier; Ibramsa Routher; Travaman Chettiar.

TOWN SIGNATORIES

Vanyambady (*Salem*).—C. Suriyappa Charri; M. Sayilaputheri Saib; Hajee Abdul Hamed Saib, B. Narasinga Lala; N. Jaffer Saib; T. M. Suveseaba Muttu Pillai; Syed Adam Sahib; &c.

Vayitri (*Malabar*).—W. E. Underwood; V. Bathur; S. Ananta Pattar; P. Damodaran; C. V. Sankara Menon; P. Theagaraja Moodelliar.

Vedarniam (*Tanjore*).—D. Jaganatha Pillai; W. J. Woodhouse; P. Narainasawmy Sastri; J. R. Wilson; V. Veloyudham Moodelliar; K. Nuturaja Pillai; &c.

Velanganni (*Tanjore*).—Deva Sarguna Nadar; Manicam Mudelly.

Vellore (*North Arcot*).—G. W. Fawcett; V. Subramania Moodelliar; G. Narasimha Charriar; K. Abdul Rhyman Sahib; V. Dorasamy Moodelliar; R. Pemberton.

Vennkonda (*Kistna*).—Rodnam Sooria Row; P. V. Narasimha Row; W. Subbaroyadu; V. Venkataroyadu; G. Lakseminarayana; M. Lakshim Narasimham; J. Subbaramaya.

Virdachellam (*South Arcot*).—R. Franklin; C. Murugisem Pillai; M. Muregesa Modeliar; C. Sreenevasier; R. Govendaraju Aiengar; Nataraja Pillai.

Vizagapatam (*Vizagapatam*).—John Kelsall; G. N. Gajputtee Row; H. G. Turner; C. Runga Row; R. Ramalinga Sastri; N. C. Narisimhuloo; F. G. M. Pascal; P. Jagannadham; T. Ramamurti; &c.

Vizianagram (*Vizagapatam*).—P. Jaganath Row; H. G. Puckle; V. Jagannadha Row; B. Narayana Murti; U. V. O. Gopolaraju; C. Chandrasekharam; M. V. L. N. Somayajulu; K. Venkanna; and others.

Wallajapett (*North Arcot*).—V. V. Bashika Charlu; S. Swaminatha Aiyar; V. Subbarayien; C. Venkatakrishna Moodelly; A. Parthwasthina Saib.

Walwanad (*Malabar*).—V. M. Ranavarma Rajah; K. K. Kasi Ayar; K. Ukkandunni Muppil Wariyar; O. M. Paramasvaram Nambudripad; T. Coonjambu; K. V. Chappunl Nair.

Wandiwash (*North Arcot*).—T. Ramaswami Aiyar; T. Vencoba Row; Thamboo Chetty; Vinayaga Moodelliar; Mirakhader Sahib; Vellaya Mercayer; K. Moideen Sahib; Alla Pechai Routher; &c.

Wynaad (*Malabar*).—G. Romilly; W. F. Gooding; V. Puenricex; E. Trollope; E. A. Tanqueray; A. Malcolm; J. W. Little; E. C. Mitchell; R. Lamb; M. D. Taylor; E. J. Winterbotham; &c.

Yercaud (*Salem*).—J. Shortt; C. F. McMahon; C. G. Lechler; F. D. H. Shortt; E. A. Smith; K. M. Cherry; B. R. Bowes Daly; A. G. Nicholson.

PRESENTATION OF

THE MADRAS PRESIDENCIAL ADDRESS TO HER MAJESTY

THE QUEEN EMPRESS.

On the 30th June 1887 a Court was held by the Queen Empress in Windsor Castle. At three o'clock Her Majesty entered the Green Drawing Room, accompanied by their Royal Highnesses the Duke and Duchess of Connaught and Strathearn, Prince and Princess Henry of Battenberg, and her Grand Ducal Highness Princess Alix of Hesse.

Her Majesty was attended by the Duchess of Buccleuch, Mistress of the Robes; the Dowager Duchess of Roxburghe, Lady in Waiting to Her Majesty; the Hon. Evelyn Moore and the Hon. Harriet Phipps, Maids of Honour in Waiting to Her Majesty; the Earl of Mount-Edgcumbe, Lord Steward; the Earl of Lathom, Lord Chamberlain; the Duke of Portland, Master of the Horse; General Viscount Bridport, K.C.B., Lord in Waiting; Viscount Templetown, Gold Stick in Waiting; Lord Burghley, Groom in Waiting; General the Right Hon. Sir H. F. Ponsonby, G.C.B., Private Secretary and Keeper of the Privy Purse; Major-General Sir F. I. Edwards, K.C.B., Major-General C. T. Du Plat, C.B., and Lieutenant-Colonel Hon. W. Carington, Equerries in Waiting; Colonel Sterling, Field Officer in Brigade Waiting; Colonel R. A. J. Talbot, Silver Stick in Waiting; the Hon. Sir S. Ponsonby Fane, K.C.B., Comptroller in the Lord Chamberlain's Department; Sir Albert Woods, Garter; Lieutenant F. C. Fredericks, Adjutant in Brigade Waiting. Maharaj Sir Pertab Singh, K.C.S.I., Aide-de-Camp to his Royal Highness the Prince of Wales, was on duty with Her Majesty. Viscount Cross, G.C.B., Secretary of State for India, and Mr. Seymour Vesey FitzGerald, C.S.I., Political Aide-de-Camp to the Secretary of State for India, were also present.

The following officers of the Indian Contingent were on duty in the Green Drawing Room:—Captain C. W. Muir, Captain G. A. Money, Subadar Sheik Imdad Ali, Ressaldar Major Nurul Hussun, Ressaldar Lall Singh, Ressaldar Hafiz Muhammad Nawaz Khan, Ressaldar Major Nadir Ali Khan, Ressaldar Major Iari Singh, Ressaldar Sher Singh, Sirdar Bahadoor, Ressaldar Major Zafar Ali Khan,

d

Sirdar Bahadoor, Ressaldar Major Mozuffer Khan, Woordie Major Lena Singh, Subadar Ibrahim Khan, Jemadar Kanchan Singh, and Ressaldar Muhammed Buksh.

The Madras Presidential Address had been beautifully engrossed on vellum by Mr. Alexander Barren, of St. Thomé, Madras, a retired Government official. The elaborate border was of an Indian pattern, somewhat after the style of the ornamentation at Tirumal Naick's palace in Madura; the outer filigree border was worked in gold, on a pale pink ground; and the heavier foliage of the adjoining border on a pale blue ground. The style of the lettering throughout was

Church text. The central word "Victoria" looked very beautiful in gold on a pale blue ground. The words "Empress of India" were also in gold, interspersed with filigree lines of delicate blue; while the word "Queen," in gold was thrown up with pink ornamental lines circling about it. The body of the Address was worked up in black, red, and gold, the first word in each paragraph being ornamented, and between each paragraph an elaborate dash was inserted.

Mr. Lawson having been announced to Her Majesty by the Political Aide-de-Camp, placed the Address in Her Majesty's hand, and was invited by Her Majesty to show to her the Casket which had been made in Madras for its reception, and which had been placed on the opposite side of the room.

This Casket had been manufactured by Messrs. P. Orr and Sons, from the design of Mr. R. F. Chisholm, late Madras Government Architect. The chief feature of it is a very beautifully modelled and well-proportioned oxydised silver elephant, standing ten inches high. The elephant is richly caparisoned, with jewelled frontlets, breastplate, and howdah cloth. On the lower part of the howdah cloth the badge in gold of the Order of the Crown of India is shown. The elephant bears a richly gilt embossed howdah, that supports a very handsome cylindrical, fluted, beaded, and jewelled silver-gilt casket, decorated with mythical three-headed cobras, and richly embossed end-pieces. The elephant, and a finely modelled mahout, or keeper, in oxydised silver, at its side, stand upon a richly gilt silver case, seventeen inches long by ten inches broad, decorated with embossed corner-pieces, and set with malachite, bearing the inscription, "Jubilee Address from the Presidency of Madras, 1887." This again rests upon a slab of Malabar rosewood.

Her Majesty having expressed her admiration of the Address Casket, was then shown the Casket of sandalwood, overlaid with silver, which had been executed in Madras for the Memorial Volume by Mr. Framjee Bhaumgara, from a design prepared by himself and Mr. Lawson. The upper side of the lid of this Casket shows the badge of the Order of the Crown of India in the centre; the lotus and the rose in medallions at the upper left and right hand corners respectively; the rose and the lotus at the lower corners; and very artistic details. The under side of the lid is most tastefully carved, and bears in the centremost position an ivory tablet, encircled by a chased silver frame, bearing the following inscription in black and gold characters :—

Presented, with a
Narrative of the Celebration
of Her Majesty's Jubilee in Madras, to
Queen Victoria, Empress of India,
on behalf of the Thirty-One Millions of Her
Loyal Subjects in that Presidency.
June 1887.

The sides and bottom of the Casket are lined with pale blue satin, puffed.

The Memorial Volume is bound in scarlet and blue morocco, lined with pale blue moiré silk, and illustrated with a photographic portrait of Her Majesty as a frontispiece, and thirty-four large photographs of towns, buildings, and Princes in Southern India. The book as it reposed in the Casket was covered by a thin quilted pillow, illustrative of Madras needlework, made for the purpose by the girls of the Gordon Refuge, Madras, under the superintendence of Mrs. E. J. Firth, the Honorary Secretary. This pillow repeated on one side, in an exquisite manner, the general features of the design on the lid of the Casket, and on the cover of the Volume.

Her Majesty exclaimed as she examined these tokens of the fidelity and regard of her people in Southern India, "Most beautiful! Most beautiful!" She then returned to the position in the room from which she had advanced with Mr. Lawson, and gave to him the following gracious reply to the Address which he had presented:—

"*It gives me great pleasure to receive this expression of the sentiments of loyalty and attachment from my subjects in the Presidency of Madras.*

"*That Presidency, as stated in the Address, has been blessed with peace throughout my reign, and I am rejoiced to know that it has made steady progress in prosperity, and in the happiness of its people.*

"*The famine which visited the Presidency in 1877 was a source of deep grief to me; but my officers did all in their power to mitigate its effects. I pray that it may please God to avert such another calamity from my people.*"

Mr. Lawson was now requested by Viscount Cross to kneel, and Her Majesty was pleased to confer upon him the honour of Knighthood. Sir Charles Lawson then kissed Her Majesty's hand, arose, and withdrew.

On the 7th of July Her Majesty intimated to Sir Charles Lawson, through the India Office, that she wished to sign her reply to the Madras Address, and upon the document being returned to her she was pleased to inscribe at the head of it her sign manual of

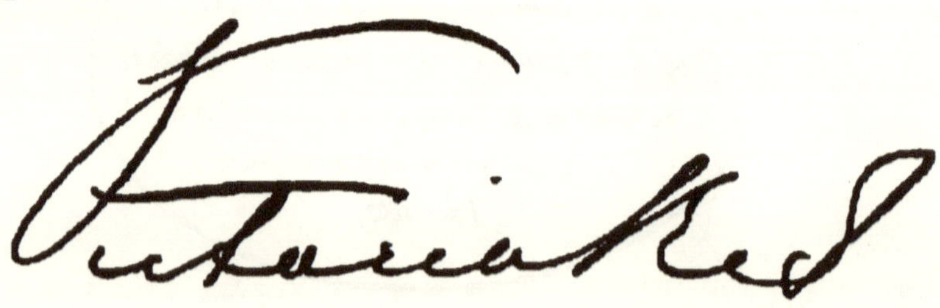

PRESENTATION OF

A COPY OF THE MEMORIAL VOLUME TO H.R.H.

THE PRINCE OF WALES.

On the morning of the 4th July Sir Charles Lawson received a note from Sir Francis Knollys, K.C.M.G., C.B., Private Secretary to the Prince of Wales, stating that it would afford His Royal Highness "much pleasure to accept from you in person" a copy of the Narrative of the Celebration of the Jubilee in the Presidency of Madras. Sir Francis Knollys proceeded to say that if Sir Charles Lawson would call with the book at Marlborough House at 3.30 P.M. "His Royal Highness will have great satisfaction in receiving you."

The Madras Delegate obeyed the Royal command, and having arrived at Marlborough House, was met by Sir Francis Knollys, and conducted to the Prince's private room. Sir Francis Knollys mentioned Sir Charles Lawson's name, and His Royal Highness immediately rose from his chair, and accorded to the Delegate a cordial greeting. His Royal Highness said that he was glad to have an opportunity of personally assuring the Delegate that he had derived much pleasure from hearing of the liberality with which the Presidency of Madras had responded to the invitation to support the scheme of the Imperial Institute. Sir Charles Lawson in reply adverted to the ceremony of the laying, by Her Majesty, of the foundation stone of the Institute three hours previously, and respectfully offered His Royal Highness congratulations on the success that had so far rewarded his efforts. After some further conversation His Royal Highness opened the blue cloth case (ornamented with the star and badge, in gold, of the Order of the Star of India), containing the fac-simile of the book that had been presented to the Queen Empress on the 30th June. The Prince commented in a very appreciative manner on the beauty of the book, and then examined the photographs, many of which he recognised as illustrative of towns of Southern India that he had visited in 1875. He came to the picture of Ootacamund, and said it must be a beautiful place, and that he was sorry that he was unable to see it. The Delegate explained that the book was devoid of literary pretensions, but that it would probably interest His Royal Highness, as it was devoted to the record of a demonstration of loyalty which for unanimity and extent was probably unparalleled. The Prince said he was very glad to receive the book, and he would be happy to place it in his library. He was good enough to speak in complimentary terms of the Delegate's services: and after the Delegate had suitably acknowledged His Royal Highness's kindness in receiving him, the Prince shook hands, and the interview terminated.

The copy of the book that was presented to the Heir Apparent contains the following inscription:—

> *Presented to His Royal Highness Albert Edward, the Prince of Wales, &c., on behalf of His Excellency Lord Connemara, G.C.I.E., the Governor, and the Public of the Presidency of Madras.*
>
> *Charles Lawson.*
>
> *London, 4th July, 1887.*

PRESENTATION OF

A COPY OF THE MEMORIAL VOLUME TO

THE PRIME MINISTER.

In accordance with his instructions, the Delegate addressed the Marquis of Salisbury, K.G., on the 25th June, and, on behalf of the Governor and the Public of Madras, begged his acceptance of a copy of the Memorial Volume. His Lordship replied on the 28th idem:—

"I have to acknowledge your letter of the 25th instant, and to thank you much for having forwarded to me the magnificent Volume of which the authorities of the Presidency of Madras have been kind enough to present me with a copy. It is a very fitting and valuable remembrance of a most interesting occasion."

NARRATIVE OF THE CELEBRATION

OF

The Jubilee of Her Majesty the Queen Empress

IN THE PRESIDENCY OF MADRAS.

INCEPTION OF THE CELEBRATION.

ON the morning of the 16th September, 1886, a Public Meeting was held at the People's Park, in the City of Madras, to inaugurate a Christmas Fair for 1886-7, the ninth of the annual series. After various preliminaries had been arranged, Mr. C. A. Lawson suggested that the Queen's Jubilee might be appropriately celebrated on the 1st January, 1887, the last day of the Fair, which would be the tenth anniversary of the Proclamation of Her Majesty as Empress of India. He submitted that the demonstration of loyalty might be made by the capital in conjunction with the whole Presidency; that Collectors of Districts might be asked to convene meetings at their head-quarters, for the adoption of a uniform Address of Congratulation to the Queen; that such Address might be signed by representative persons at each meeting at which it was adopted; that one unanimous expression of loyalty to the Queen might thus be made in Southern India; and that a subscription list might be opened for the purpose of obtaining a suitable Casket for the reception of the Address. The meeting expressed its cordial approval of these proposals.

At the first meeting, on the 23rd September, of the General Committee of the Fair Committee, Mr. Lawson complied with the invitation to submit the outlines of the scheme which he had sketched at the previous meeting. Having reminded the meeting that there were insuperable climatic objections to the celebration of the Jubilee in India on the 20th June, the anniversary of Her Majesty's Accession, and having mentioned the advantages offered in India by the 1st January, he again urged that arrangements should be made for the adoption of one Address to Her Majesty throughout the Presidency. He also proposed that a Volume, containing a narrative of the celebration of the Jubilee in the City and Provinces of Madras, interspersed with Photographs illustrative of the people, the scenery, and the edifices of the Presidency might be prepared, and offered for Her Majesty's gracious acceptance. The meeting thereupon unanimously requested the following gentlemen to form themselves into a Sub-Committee for the purpose of making arrangements for the celebration of the Queen's Jubilee throughout the Presidency of Madras on New Year's Day, viz.:—The Honourable Mr. Justice Brandt, the Honourable Mr. J. A. Boyson, Rajah Sir T. Madhava Row, K.C.S.I., the Honourable Mir Humayun Jah, C.I.E., Colonel H. McLeod, R.A., Lieutenant-Colonel W. M. Scharlieb, M.V.C., Mr. B. H. Chester, M.A., Mr. P. S. Ramasawmy Mudelliar, C.I.E., Mr. Vijiarungam Mudelliar, Dr. Moaleen Sheriff, and Mr. Lawson as Honorary Secretary.

This Committee held its first meeting on the 28th September, and resolved to address a circular letter to the Collectors and Judges, inviting them to co-operate in concerting measures for the celebration of the Jubilee in their Districts. This initiative was cordially responded to at Salem, Ootacamund, North Arcot, Pennukonda, Cumbum, Mangalore, Kurnool, Trichinopoly, Chittoor, Mercara, Trichengode, Nellore, and elsewhere. The Committee was led, however, to apprehend, from communications which reached it from various quarters, that the 1st of January would not be as convenient a day for the celebration in the Mofussil as it would be in the City of Madras, since numerous public functionaries would then be absent from their Districts spending the Christmas vacation elsewhere; and, at its second meeting, it was resolved that, before proceeding further with the scheme before the Committee, it was desirable to ascertain the wishes of the Government of India as to the choice of a day for the celebration. A communication was thereupon made to H.E. the Right Honourable Sir M. E. Grant Duff, G.C.S.I., Governor of Madras, who expressed cordial approval of the Committee's objects, and undertook to make the proposed reference to H.E. the Earl of Dufferin, G.M.S.I., &c., Viceroy and Governor-General of India. The Madras Government accordingly enquired by telegraph whether it would be in accordance with the wishes of Her Majesty, and the intention of the Government of India, that the celebration should take place on the 1st January. The Government of India replied that it knew nothing about the date fixed for the Jubilee, but "thought it very doubtful that it would be so early as January 1st." Shortly afterwards the Municipal Corporations of Calcutta and Bombay resolved that the question of celebrating the Jubilee in those Cities was a proper matter to be taken up by the local authorities. The Committee therefore invited the Municipality of Madras to move in the matter; and that body agreed to do so.

PROCLAMATION OF THE JUBILEE DAY.

About the middle of January the following letter was addressed to all Local Governments and Administrations by the Government of India:—

"His Excellency the Governor-General in Council having taken into consideration the loyal desire of the people of India that, in the fiftieth year of the reign of Her Majesty the Queen Empress, their devotion to her person and Throne should be manifested throughout the Empire on a specially appointed day of public rejoicing, and having regard to the conditions of the season, which are adverse to the selection for this purpose of the anniversary of Her Majesty's birth, or that of Her Accession, is pleased to designate Wednesday, the 16th of February, for adoption throughout India as the day of Her Majesty's Jubilee. The 16th of February will be observed as a holiday in all public offices. The official ceremonial by which the occasion will be distinguished will be separately notified. In other respects His Excellency the Governor-General in Council confidently leaves to the discretion of the local Governments and Administrations, acting in concert with the people under their charge, and more especially to the deep and unaffected loyalty of Her Majesty's subjects, the measures which shall be undertaken to celebrate the day of Jubilee with appropriate honours. His Excellency in Council is assured that the executive authorities may on this occasion safely yield the initiative to the spontaneous action of Municipal Councils and of the community at large, and that the unanimous voice of the Empire will gratefully tender to Her Majesty the Queen Empress a homage worthy of the noble charity of her life, and the justice and benevolence of her reign."

Shortly after the publication of this letter the President and Members of the Municipal Commission, and about two hundred other citizens of Madras, addressed a requisition to the Sheriff, asking him to convene a Public Meeting to concert measures for the celebration. In pursuance of this requisition the Sheriff convened a Meeting at the Banqueting Hall, which was held on the 24th January, and was very largely attended. His Excellency the Right Honourable Robert Bourke, the new Governor of Madras, having complied with the invitation to take the chair, said:—

"Sir Madhava Row, my colleagues, and Gentlemen;—It gives me great pleasure to see so numerous an assembly on this occasion. I am quite certain that there is but one feeling in the hearts of all present, and that is that Madras should show her loyalty to Her Majesty, and should celebrate the Jubilee of her reign in a befitting manner. (Cheers.) Madras, though by no means the wealthiest of the communities in India, though she cannot, I am sorry to say, vie with the great wealth of Bombay and Calcutta, yet Madras has always shown herself in the van in the promotion of every object connected with education and charity, and we know that those two objects have always been most dear to the heart of Her Imperial Majesty. (Hear, hear.) Now, gentlemen, I am quite sure that we have only one object in view, and that is, that in celebrating this event, we shall do so in a way which will not only be pleasing and satisfactory to ourselves, but also pleasing and creditable to the great body of people in this Presidency. (Cheers.) We also wish to show, not only to India, but to foreign nations, to the Colonies, to the United Kingdom, and to the Queen herself, that we are acting in a manner worthy of this great occasion. (Hear, hear.) This is not an occasion when the chairman need descant on the great progress that has been made in India by the British during the reign of Her Majesty. This is not an occasion for entering upon any discussion of that kind, because what we are anxious to show upon this occasion is, that it is not only of the public works that have been done during Her Majesty's reign that we are so proud, but that we are proud of being ruled by a Sovereign who, by her own personal virtues, has recommended herself to her subjects. (Loud applause.) And therefore, gentlemen, it would be rather inappropriate, I think, on this occasion, to speak of those great advances in civilisation which have marked Her Majesty's reign. Gentlemen, I observe that in one of the Resolutions I shall have the honour of putting to you presently, mention is made of a Committee which will be appointed. I hope you will appoint a thoroughly representative Committee, so that every person who has an opinion on the subject of the celebration of the Jubilee will have an opportunity of making his influence felt. (Hear, hear.) I trust that the deliberations of that Committee will be harmonious, and that it will apply all its energies to extracting from the pockets of its friends as much money as possible. I hope that its labours, in that direction, will be as diffused as possible. If you begin with a poor Governor, I beg you will not forget the rich Vakil; and if you do not spare the rich Vakil, you must not spare the liberal Zemindar. (Laughter.) I have no doubt, however, that very little persuasion will be necessary; but if any is needed, I am sure there will be on that Committee men who, being noted for their eloquence, will be able to charm out of the pockets of the most penurious more money than we anticipate. (Hear, hear.) I shall now call upon your old friend, Sir T. Madhava Row to move the first resolution." (Prolonged applause.)

Rajah Sir T. Madhava Row, K.C.S.I., in moving the first Resolution, said: -

"I agree with His Excellency that it is gratifying to see so large an assembly in this Hall on such an occasion. That is a circumstance which testifies to the full appreciation of the importance of the present occasion. (Hear, hear.) The Jubilee to be celebrated is that of a Sovereign lady, who holds the sceptre of a mighty Empire—an Empire which is one of the largest, the most populous, and the most prosperous that the world has seen. (Hear, hear.) It is an Empire that enjoys the blessings of peace, order, liberty, and security beyond the dreams of antiquity. British rule has been the salvation of India, and India is the brightest gem in the British Crown. (Hear, hear.) Everybody is aware of the immense progress India has made during the last fifty years of Her Majesty's beneficent rule. His Excellency has well said that the present occasion was not the occasion on which to recount the history of that beneficent reign, and I may venture to say that any one who undertook to write a history of that reign would have to fill volumes. It is no wonder then that we regard our Empress with feelings of profound loyalty, love, devotion, and gratitude for the many benefits of incalculable value that have come to India during her rule. In the whole of the world's history, there has not been found a ruler proclaiming, as Her Majesty has done, to the people of India, that her security and peace, and reward, lies in the happiness and well-being and good of her subjects. The people should therefore greatly rejoice now that they are afforded the rare opportunity of giving expression to the feelings which they cherish towards their beloved Empress, and they should generously vie with each other in celebrating the Jubilee with the utmost enthusiasm." (Hear, hear.)

He concluded by moving:—"That the 16th of February, having been designated by the Viceroy as the day to be observed throughout India in celebration of the Jubilee, a subscription list be opened for the purpose of celebrating the event on that day, and in any other manner in which the Committee may determine." Mr. E. Norton seconded the Resolution, which was put to the meeting, and carried unanimously.

Mr. G. G. Arbuthnot, of Messrs. Arbuthnot & Co., moved the next Resolution: —"That the following gentlemen do form themselves into a Committee for the purpose of collecting subscriptions, &c.":—

H. E. the Governor, the Members of Council (Executive and Legislative), the Judges of the High Court, the Heads of Departments, the General commanding the Eastern Division, the Officers commanding Corps in Madras, the Judges of the Small Cause Court, the Presidency Magistrates, the Commissioner of Police, the Municipal Commissioners, the Members of the Board of Revenue, Chamber of Commerce, Trades Association, and Port Trust, the Maharajah of Vizianagram, Bishop Gell, Archbishop Colgan, Rajah Sir T. Madhava Row, the Honourable Mr. Subramania Iyer, Dr. D. Duncan, Messrs. Gould, C. W. Wilson, Kristnama Chariar, W. R. Robinson, H. R. P. Carter, Moss, E. Norton, Willie Grant, W. T. Morgan, Soondaram Sastriar, Bashyam Iyengar, Cheotsal Rao, the Editors of the *Madras Mail*, *Madras Times*, *Madras Standard*, and *Hindu*, Messrs. Michie Smith, J. Adam, G. L. Chambers, H. A. Stewart, R. G. Orr, B. H. Chase, B. Lovery, J. H. Salisbery, G. D. Coleman, Appasami Chettiar, Ahppy Naidu, Abdul Raman Sayyed, Balaji Rao, Batcha Sahib, Gopal Nayar, Govinda Chetty, Haji Ismail Sayet, Iyava Iyer, Jugga Rao Pillai, Kistnasami Chettiar, Kuppusami Naidu, Kinna Doss Balamcundra Doss, Sashachellam Chetty, Mahadeva Chetty, Haji Alarak Sayet, Kusal Doss Khan Doss, Namberumal Chetty, Palney Aandy, Peremananda Doss, Ananda Doss, Rajarathna Chettiar, Ramalinga Pillay, Ramachendra Row Sahib, Rangiah Chetty, Sankara Nair, Sankara Menon, N. Subramaniem, Soomoondram Chettiar, Thakkiah Chetty, M. Veeraghavaiah, and Waljee Lalyee Sait. (*Subsequently added*), Archdeacon Browne, Captain H. D. Love, Messrs. E. B. Havell, the Editor of the *Muslim Herald*, Rev. P. Rajagopaul, Mahomed Monavarkhan Bdr., Haji Moulvie Zohoorooden Khan Bdr., Nizamoden Khan Bdr., Nazar Alikhan Bdr., Mahomed Ebadullah Khan Bdr., Anwarudin Khan Bdr., Ahmed Mohideen Khan Bdr., Abdul Ali Khan Bdr., Abdul Ghani Khan Bdr., Hussain Alikhan Bdr., Mahomed Maben Khan Saib Bdr., Sherfood Dowlah Bdr., Mirza Feroze Hossain Khan Bdr., Haji Pacha Saib Sayed, Hajee Abdullah Patcha Saib Sayed, Messrs. F. G. R. Branson, J. Carr, D. Grant, T. W. Laing, A. Champion, J. Short, P. S. Ramasawmy Modelliar, P. Ranganahda Modelliar, J. D'Rozario, Manickam Moodelly, Mandayam Singara Charry, Mooroogasa Moodely, Krishnasamy Naidu, Pragasa Moodelly, Arokasawmy Moodelly, Beaumont, Veeracotti Pillay, Rajah Eswara Doss, Bunsee Lal, Gopal Doss, Dhanmulal, Augurchand, Vullaba Doss, Krisna Doss, Bulamoogaada Doss, Nawab Nuzahmed Dowlah, Roostoomjah Bdr., Mahd Moonuwar Khan Bdr., Ghulam Ghouse Khan Bdr., Mahd Mahmood Khan Bdr., Nahammad Ishay Sahib, Abdul Jbara Khan Bdr., Hafiz Sudrat Islam Khan Bdr., Mohideen Ahmed Sahed Bdr., Haji Ibrahim Ahmed Saheb Bdr., V. Mahd Ghouse Sahib, Vellae

Abdul Rhyman Sahib, R. M. Khajah Mohideen Rowther, Ibrahim Sait, Haji Mahdi Isphahani, Abdush Shukoor, R. Badsha Sahib, Haji Mahmood Namazi Sherazi, Mullah Zafferjee Sahib, Abdul Kareem Sahib, Shivajee Nawaji, Abdul Rhyim Sahib, Nanmazi Shirazi, Haji Khader Mohideen Saib, and Haji Shaik Mohideen Sahib Btr.

The Honourable Mr. J. A. Boyson, of Messrs. Binny and Co., seconded the Resolution, which was put to the meeting, and carried unanimously.

His Highness the Maharajah of Vizianagram moved the next Resolution, "That a vote of thanks be passed to the Sheriff for kindly convening this meeting, and that another vote of thanks be passed to His Excellency the Governor for kindly presiding on the occasion." The Honourable Sir Arthur Collins, Q.C., Chief Justice of Madras, seconded the Resolution, which was carried unanimously with applause.

Mr. P. S. Ramasawmy Mudelliar, C.I.E., the Sheriff of Madras, said that in honour of the Jubilee he would give a treat to a large number of Poor Schools and institutions in the Madras Municipality, and would build a Female Medical Ward, to be called the Victoria Ward, at the Monegar Choultry, and endow it with Rs. 25,000. His Excellency then proposed :—"That this meeting records its grateful thanks for the munificent donation which the Sheriff has been kind enough to announce to us on this occasion." Mr. J. H. Garstin, C.S.I., Second Member of the Board of Revenue, seconded this Resolution, which was carried unanimously. Three hearty cheers were then given for Her Majesty the Queen Empress, and the meeting dissolved.

The General Committee held its first meeting on the 27th January. His Excellency the Governor presided, and the following Executive Committee was appointed :—

The Honourable Mr. C. G. Master, the Honourable Mr. P. P. Hutchins, Mr. G. G. Arbuthnot, Rajah Sir T. Madhava Row, the Honourable Mr. J. A. Boyson, the Venerable Archdeacon Browne, B.D., Mr. V. Ramiengar, C.S.I., Colonel C. J. Gunning, Mr. C. A. Lawson, Mr. J. W. Handley, Colonel T. Weldon, Colonel Carter, His Highness the Maharajah of Vizianagram, Mr. Hajee Mahomed Abdulla Badsha Sahib, Mr. V. Krishnama Chariar, Mr. C. Yecherajulu Naidu, Mr. P. S. Ramasawmy Mudelliar, Mr. R. G. Orr, Mr. G. L. Chambers, Mr. J. Adam, Mr. Teagaroya Chettyar, Mr. Ramasawmy Chettyar, Mr. Mir Ausuruddin Saib, Mr. P. Anandu Charlu, Mr. P. Soomasoondram Chettyar, Mr. B. H. Chester, Dr. Mohideen Sheriff, Mr. E. Dalakati, Mr. S. R. Turnbull, Mr. P. Rungunadha Mudelliar, Dr. D. Duncan, Mr. P. Vijiaranga Mudelliar, Mr. W. M. Scharlieb, the Honourable S. Subramanya Iyer, Mr. Soondram Sastry, Mr. J. A. Jones, Mr. C. Michie Smith, and the Rev. P. Rajagopaal.

His Excellency indicated three objects for which the money subscribed might be appropriated, namely, the Local Celebration, a Presidencial Memorial, and the Imperial Institute of London. He announced that the Government of Madras had resolved to subscribe Rs. 10,000 towards the Imperial Institute, and he expressed the hope that the Government might be able to subscribe to the Presidencial Memorial that was selected. Mr. Lawson then alluded to the tentative steps which had been taken in September to carry out the idea of the adoption of one Address for the whole Presidency, and proposed :—"That the Executive Committee do place itself in communication with Mofussil Committees, and do act as a Central Committee for an Address of loyal congratulation to Her Majesty from the Presidency of Madras." The Honourable Mr. Justice Muthusawmy Aiyar, C.I.E., seconded the proposition, and it was carried unanimously.

The Executive Committee met immediately after the General Committee meeting had dissolved, and unanimously invited the Honourable Mr. Hutchins, the Junior Member of Council, to accept the office of Chairman, and Mr. Lawson that of Honorary Secretary. It was resolved that the Presidencial Memorial should take the form of a Technical Institute for the benefit of the entire Presidency, and be called the Victoria Technical Institute. A Sub-Committee, with Mr. G. L. Chambers as Honorary Secretary, was appointed to give effect to this resolution. Another Sub-Committee, with Mr. B. H. Chester, M.A., as Honorary Secretary, was appointed to arrange for the local celebration. A third Sub-Committee, with Mr. Lawson as Honorary Secretary, was appointed to draw up an Address to Her Majesty.

On the following day the Chairman addressed a circular letter to the Collectors and Magistrates of the Districts, inviting their co-operation. The officers addressed lost no time in communicating with the chief towns in their Districts, and a large number of Jubilee Committees in the Mofussil immediately signified their intention of accepting the Central Committee's proposals, and of making a contribution to one or more of the objects for which that Committee had invited subscriptions. These Mofussil Committees subsequently communicated reports of their proceedings to the Central Committee.

The Technical Institute, the Local Celebration, and the Address Sub-Committees had meanwhile been at work. The draft of the Address which was submitted by the last-named Sub-Committee to the Executive Committee was approved, and it was accepted by the General Committee on the 4th February. It was then telegraphed to the more distant Collectors, for communication to local Committees, and despatched by post to the Districts comparatively near to Madras. It was eventually adopted by one hundred and ninety-one Committees in as many towns, as an expression of the loyalty of the thirty-two millions of Her Majesty's subjects in the Presidency of Madras.

THE OBSERVANCE IN THE CITY OF MADRAS.

The site of the City of Madras was ceded in the year 1639 to Mr. Francis Day, Chief of the East India Company's settlement at Armagaon, by the Rajah of Chandragiri. The factory which Mr. Day founded was made subordinate to the Chief of Bantam in Java; but in the year 1653 it was made independent, and named the Presidency of Fort St. George. The Fort was blockaded by Daud Khan, a general in Aurungzebe's service, in 1702; and again in 1741 by Mahrattas. In 1746 it was bombarded and captured by the French under La Bourdonnais. Two years afterwards it was restored to the British by virtue of the Treaty of Aix-la-Chapelle. In 1758 it was besieged by the French under Lally. After two months the beleaguered garrison was relieved by a British fleet. Hyder Ali threatened the town in 1769 and 1780. The town, with its suburbs, now covers an area of twenty-seven square miles. It contains a population of 405,848, occupying 48,386 houses. Of Hindus there are 315,527; of Mohammedans, 50,298; and of Christians, 39,631. The Europeans number 3,205, and the Eurasians 12,659. There are 993 males to 997 females. The town is the seat of the Government of Madras during the cool season. It is the head-quarters of the Eastern Division of the Madras Army, and of many military and civil Departments. The High Court of the Presidency is permanently located there. The garrison usually numbers 3,000 men, of whom one-third are Europeans. The City Police includes a Commissioner, a Deputy Commissioner, an Assistant Commissioner, and 960 subordinate officers and constables. The Municipality includes a President, appointed by the Government, and thirty-two Commissioners, of whom one-fourth are nominated by Government, and three-fourths are elected by ratepayers. It possesses a good water-supply, obtained chiefly from a reservoir or lake at the Red Hills, seven miles from the town. Madras has one Anglican Bishop, one Roman Catholic Archbishop, and one Roman Catholic Bishop. There are fifteen Anglican places of worship, including one Cathedral; four Roman Catholic places of worship, including two Cathedrals; three Scotch churches; eight Nonconformist chapels; and numerous meeting-houses, mission schoolrooms, &c. There are 495 educational institutions in the town, with 26,234 pupils. Over twenty-four per cent. of the total population can read and write. The death-rate and the birth-rate average about 40 per mille per annum. The former has declined considerably since the blessing of an abundant supply of good water was conferred upon the town. Madras holds the third place in commercial importance in India. The annual value of its imports and exports amounts to about nine millions sterling. The serious drawbacks to trade of an open roadstead are being overcome by the construction of an enclosed harbour, which will cost about one million sterling when completed. Madras is the eastern terminus of the Madras and South India Railways; and the trunk roads of the Presidency converge upon it.

RELIGIOUS SERVICES.

St. George's Cathedral.—At 7 o'clock on the morning of the 16th February, there was a Celebration of the Holy Communion, at which portions of the Office appointed for the Anniversary of the Queen's Accession were used. At 11 o'clock there was a grand Choral Service, when a large congregation assembled. Among those present were His Excellency the Governor and Lady Susan Bourke, C.I.; Major General A. C. Johnson, C.B., commanding the Eastern District, several of the Judges of the High Court, and numerous representatives of the Civil and

Military Services, of the Mercantile Community, and others. The service commenced with a Processional Hymn, "Now thank we all our God," which was sung with great heartiness by the choir, numbering about thirty voices, and congregation. The Canticle, "O Lord, our Governor," took the place of the *Venite exultemus Domino*, and Psalms xx. xxi. and ci. were chanted in place of those for the day of the month. The Lessons were Joshua i. 1-10, and Romans xiii. Garrett in F was the Service selected for the Canticles, and the Suffrages and Collects appointed for the 20th of June were used. The Venerable Archdeacon J. F. Browne, B.D., preached from Eccles. x. 17. In the course of his sermon he said:—

"On the 8th July 1837 there was laid to rest in the Royal vault of St. George's Chapel, Windsor, the mortal remains of William IV., known since in history as 'England's Sailor King.' And before the great officers of the Royal Household broke their staves of office, and the vast assembly left the Chapel, the Deputy to Garter Principal King of Arms pronounced over the grave an address, of which these were the concluding words:—'Let us humbly beseech Almighty God to bless and preserve with long life, health, and honour, and all worldly happiness, the most high, most mighty, and most excellent Princess, our Sovereign Lady Victoria, now, by the Grace of God, of the United Kingdom of Great Britain and Ireland Queen, Defender of the Faith, and Sovereign of the most noble Order of the Garter. God Save Queen Victoria.' Nearly fifty years have passed away since then, and the graceful maiden of eighteen has drawn close to the three score and ten years of the days of man; passed through a long life, in which the purest joy and bitterest sorrow have had their allotted part, and yet withal the prayer has been answered; and we, my brethren, assembled in God's house on this morning of Jubilee commemoration, are here to acknowledge the goodness and mercy of God; and to raise our *Te Deum* of grateful praise, that the fierce light that beats upon a throne has been bright with the rays of Divine favour, which from that as a centre has shone forth far and wide. Those whose duty it has been to attend upon the Queen in matters of business have noticed that Her Majesty, as a person well versed in the conduct of affairs, is wont to keep closely to the point at issue, and to speak of nothing but what is directly connected with the matter before her. But whenever there is an exception to this rule it arises from Her Majesty's anxious desire to make some inquiry about the welfare of her subjects, to express her sympathy with this man's sorrow, or that man's bereavement; to ask what is the latest intelligence about this disaster, or that suffering, and what can be done to remedy or assuage it; thus showing, unconsciously, that she is indeed the mother of her people, feeling the deepest interest in all that concerns them, without respect of persons, from the highest to the lowest. Our Queen's reign must for all future history be the symbol of progress. There have never been fifty years in which progress was so vast as it has been under her. Come what may, the progress which has been made in the last half century must be regarded as the key and symbol of whatever progress may be in store for us in the future; and the Queen herself is one who stands almost alone in the whole line of English Sovereigns—and some of them have been revered and great—for the extraordinary personal affection which has clustered around her Throne and herself. Still more, she has identified herself so much with the social, moral, and religious progress of the nation that almost every great movement has been carried forward under the shadow of Her Majesty, and she has herself, occasionally by word, and occasionally by her presence, here or there given a great stimulus to it. And any lasting memorials which will remain from this Jubilee commemoration will be memorials of marvellous activity and blessings during the reign of a Queen whom the Church and nation loves and honours more than any other Sovereign who has ever ruled. 'Not unto us, not unto us, O Lord, but unto Thy name give glory, for Thy mercy and for Thy truth's sake.' 'By Thee Kings reign and Princes decree justice.' God Save the Queen."

At the conclusion of the sermon the Collect for the Queen, the "supreme Governor" of the Church, was read, followed by the Benediction. The choir and congregation then united in a very impressive rendering of the National Anthem. The Hallelujah Chorus from the *Messiah*, performed on the organ as a concluding voluntary, brought the service to a close.

Roman Catholic Cathedral.—Pontifical High Mass, at which the Most Rev. the Archbishop Colgan officiated, was held at 7 A.M., in the presence of a very large congregation. The Deacons of Honour were the Rev. Messrs. Tenme and Walsh, and those at the altar were Rev. Messrs. de Silva and Mitchell, the Very Rev. T. Mayer having the duties of Assistant Priest assigned to him at the Throne and Altar. A Special Mass prepared for the occasion was effectively sung by the Cathedral choir. At the conclusion of the Mass the Benediction of the Holy Sacrament was given; and after the Gregorian *Te Deum* intoned by him and taken up by the choir had concluded, he sang the Versicles, and brought the service to a close with the Special Prayer assigned in the Roman Ritual for Her Majesty.

St. Thomé Cathedral (Portuguese Catholic Mission at Mylapore).—At 7.30 A.M. a Solemn High Mass was celebrated in the St. Thomé Cathedral by the Very Rev. J. B. Gonsalves, assisted by two other priests, at which all the clergy were present. It was followed by a *Te Deum* sung alternately by the clergy and the choir, and by the Benediction of the Most Holy Sacrament. At the conclusion of the service the choir sang "God Save the Queen."

St. Mary's Church, Fort St. George.—The first Jubilee Service of Thanksgiving in this the oldest Protestant Church in India (completed in 1680), was held on the evening of the 15th February, at 6 o'clock and was numerously attended. Major General A. C. Johnson, C.B., commanding the Eastern District, Colonel Westby, commanding the Bedfordshire Regiment, other officers, and a large number of soldiers, were present. His Excellency the Governor's Band played orchestral accompaniments to the Hymns, the Anthem, and the Chants, the Psalms alone being sung to the organ accompaniment. The Service commenced with the Processional Hymn, "Onward, Christian Soldiers," sung by the choir, who marched from the vestry to their seats followed by the band and the

Chaplain. The opening sentences, suffrages &c., from the Accession Service were then read, the special Psalms being xxi. and cxlv. The First Lesson was taken from 2 Samuel xxiii. to v. 6, and the Second Lesson from Romans xiii. That was followed by two special prayers for the Queen, a prayer for India (by the late Bishop Cotton, Metropolitan of India), and a prayer for Unity (from the Accession Service). Hymn 166 (Ancient and Modern) was then sung, followed by a short Anthem—"O Lord, save our Queen Victoria; and hear us in the day in which we call upon Thee." A prayer for the Queen Empress (from the Prayer Book) was then said, and the remaining part of the Accession Service was proceeded with. The next hymn was "God Save the Queen," which was taken up very heartily by the whole congregation. The Rev. A. C. Taylor, the Chaplain, then preached a short sermon, taking for his text, 1 Tim. ii. 1-2—"I exhort therefore, that first of all, supplications, prayers, intercessions, and giving of thanks, be made for all men: for Kings and all that are in authority; that we may lead a quiet and peaceable life in all godliness and honesty." A hymn, "Now thank we all our God," was next sung, after which a *Te Deum* was sung by the choir to the band accompaniment.

A second special Service of Thanksgiving was held in this church on the morning of the 16th, at 11 o'clock, when the same form of service was gone through, but there was no sermon. The Holy Communion was celebrated chorally, and the *Te Deum* was sung at the end of the service. Another Service of Thanksgiving was held at 7 o'clock on the morning of the 17th, when special prayers for the Queen were used.

The Kirk.—A Jubilee Service was held at 11 A.M. on the 16th. The service opened with a Jubilee hymn, by the Dean of Wells, and closed with a Jubilee version of the National Anthem by the same author. The *Te Deum* and Psalms xxix. and xxi. were also sung. The Rev. J. N. Ogilvie delivered an address on the life of the Queen Empress in relation to her home, the British nation, and the Church. There was a large congregation present.

Tucker's Church.—There was a Special Jubilee English Service at 7.30 on the 16th, conducted by the Rev. J. W. Foley, M.A. It was followed at 8.45 by a Tamil Service, which was conducted by the Rev. Samuel Paul, who preached a short sermon. Several of the prayers for the 20th of June were used. The service ended with the chanting of the *Te Deum*. At 10 A.M. a Children's Service was held, when all the school children, about 290 in number, attached to the church, were present with their banners. The service began with an opening hymn. The Litany was sung, and the Rev. S. Paul preached. The service ended with the singing of the *Benedictus*. Immediately after the service the children were marched to the church compound with their banners, and sang a song composed for the occasion in honour of the Empress, the Viceroy, the Governor, the Bishop of Madras, the Church Missionary Society, &c. After that sweetmeats &c., were distributed. Three hearty cheers were then given by the children.

St. Francis Xavier's Church.—At 7 A.M. the Rev. Father T. Doyle celebrated a Special Mass in honour of the Jubilee, at the conclusion of which a *Te Deum* was sung. The church was well filled. At noon the Eurasian school children attached to the church were treated to a dinner. The native children attending the Native Convent School of the church were also treated to a dinner of curry and rice, fruits, &c., under the superintendence of the native nuns. The children then gave three cheers for the Queen Empress, and three more for the Governor.

Perambore Railway Church.—At 7 A.M. there was a celebration of the Holy Communion with special Collect, Epistle, and Gospel. The service opened by the singing of hymn 165, "O God, our help in ages past," and after the Prayer for the Church Militant, the Prayer for "Unity" was offered. Hymn 166, "All people that on earth do dwell," was sung at the close of the Communion Service; after which, at 7.45, Matins, as appointed for the 20th day of June, was said, and was followed by a sermon preached by the Chaplain, the Rev. C. N. Bazely, who, taking for his text Rom. xiii. 1—"Let every soul be subject unto the higher powers; for there is no power but of God; the powers that be are ordained of God,"—dwelt on the subject of loyalty, and alluded to the most notable events in the reign of Her Majesty.

Baptist Chapel, New Town.—A Jubilee Service was held at 10 A.M. The service was conducted by Mr. R. E. Mackenzie, one of the Deacons of the Church, who preached a sermon appropriate to the occasion.

Methodist Episcopal Church.—The South India Conference of the Methodist Episcopal Church recorded the following Resolution:-

"The South India Conference of the Methodist Episcopal Church assembled at Madras in February, 1887, under the presidency of Bishop Ninde, are reminded that this year is the fiftieth of Her Majesty Queen Victoria's reign, the year of Jubilee, and deem it incumbent to place on record, and to express to Almighty God, their profound sense of the extraordinary blessings enjoyed under this reign by the widely-extended realms and peoples over whom Her Majesty has sway. We feel specially called upon to make mention of the enlarged measure of civil and religious liberty, the political and social reforms and ameliorations, the diffusion and promulgation of knowledge, the multiplication of educational facilities, all tending to further the opportunities of making known the Gospel of the grace of God to mankind. We leave it to others to dwell upon the marvellous expansion of commerce, the still more marvellous application of the powers of steam and electricity in binding together the remote nationalities of the Empire of Her Majesty the Queen Empress, so that the means of inter-communication between the members of the Empire equal, in the year of Jubilee, those which united the Kingdom of Great Britain in the first year of Queen Victoria's reign. We recognise the fact that by the superintending Providence of God these unprecedented material advantages have conspired with the development of the evangelistic spirit to place the priceless gift of salvation within the reach of all classes and conditions of this magnificent Empire. We recommend, therefore, that at all stations embraced in the South India Conference meetings be held on the day appointed for the celebration of the Jubilee, for the public recognition of these blessings of Divine Providence with the thanksgiving and prayer for the greater diffusion and appreciation of the blessings bestowed, and for the safety, health, and happiness of Her Gracious Majesty herself, and of all the members of the Royal Family."

THE JUBILEE PARADE.

The troops in garrison, including the Governor's Body Guard, the Madras Volunteer Guards, and the Madras Railway Volunteers, paraded in review order on the Island at 6.45 A.M. on the morning of the 16th of February. The force was drawn up in line at open order with twelve paces intervals, in the following order: —The Body Guard on the extreme right, with the wing of the Second Battalion Bedfordshire Regiment, under the command of Colonel Westby, on its left; then came the wing of the 4th Madras Pioneers, under the command of Colonel Blenkinsop; the 9th Regiment Madras Infantry, under the command of Colonel Richmond: the Madras Railway Volunteers, under the command of Colonel F. H. Trevithick, Locomotive Superintendent of the Madras Railway; and the Madras Volunteer Guards, under the command of Colonel J. McMullin, M.S.C., with the Mounted Company on the extreme left. Major-General A. C. Johnson, C.B., commanding the Eastern District, attended by Lieutenant-Colonel Shelley and several other officers, arrived on the ground shortly before 7 o'clock. The General rode up and down the line and inspected the troops, after which an Imperial salute of 101 guns was fired by the 4-1st N. I. Division Royal Artillery from the Saluting Battery. A *feu de joie* was fired by the Infantry and Volunteer Corps. The troops then presented arms, and the colours of the several corps were lowered. Three cheers for Her Majesty the Queen Empress were called for by the General, and were heartily given by the assembled troops. The Battalion formed up into quarter columns, and marched past in column of companies. They were then marched back to their quarters. The review was witnessed by an immense crowd of spectators. Both the Volunteer Corps mustered strong, the Madras Volunteer Guards having six companies, while the Railway Volunteers were about 500 or 600 strong. The march past was very creditably performed by all the troops.

The Royal Standard was hoisted at the flagstaff at Fort St. George at sunrise, and continued flying until sunset.

THE FEEDING OF THE POOR.

About 15,000 adult poor of various nationalities were fed at Vepery, Royapooram, and Triplicane, in honour of the Jubilee. The old parade-ground at Vepery was used as one of the principal centres for the purpose. From an early hour large numbers of people commenced to assemble, and by 11 A.M. 5,032 Hindus had been fed in the spacious shed attached to the long building formerly used as an armoury. The authorities of the Church of the Assumption, situated in Portuguese Church Street, Black Town, gave a dinner to about 300 poor people at noon; and in the evening, at 5 o'clock, sweets were provided for the Sunday School and other poor children of the district. At 5.30 P.M. a grand procession, with a banner, bearing the portrait of the Queen Empress, marched through the streets of the town singing an appropriate hymn, composed by S. M. T. Murrian Pillay, the Churchwarden; and at 7 o'clock there was a display of fireworks The church compound was very tastefully decorated for the occasion. The poor of the Mohammedan community were fed in the grounds of the Grand Mosque in Triplicane. 4,000 persons sat down in groups of 700 at a time. The meal consisted of *pillau* with curries, in the preparation of which there were used 28 maunds of rice, 22 maunds of ghee, and 8 maunds of vegetables, &c. Sixty-five sheep supplied the mutton, and three tons of fuel were used. Of the number of people fed, 100 were gosha women, whose portions of food were sent to their houses, as well as those of 50 other persons who, being infirm or blind, were unable to leave their residences. About 4,000 members of the Hindu community in Triplicane were fed in Parthasarathy Covil Garden, Ice House Road. They sat down 400 at a time. In the preparation of the various dishes there were used 1,000 measures of rice, 20 maunds of potatoes, 20 maunds of sweet potatoes, 100 green plantains, 100 calabashes, 20 pumpkins, 150 cucumbers, 150 bundles of greens, 125 measures of tyre, and 6 maunds of ghee. In addition to this there were prepared 4,000 cakes, 4,000 uplams, and wheat confectionery, in which were used 50 measures of milk, 10 viss of cashua-nuts, and 5 maunds of sugar. Three tons of fuel were used in cooking. Five thousand leaf platters were supplied with an equal number of leaf cups. At the conclusion of the meal each recipient was presented with a packet, containing betel nut, spice, &c.

From 4,000 to 5,000 of the poor of all classes were fed at the Robinson's Park.

In addition to their usual daily subsistence allowance, the inmates of the Friend in Need Society's Home, received at noon a substantial meal of rice and curry, roast meat and roast duck, vegetables and fruit. At 7 P.M. pudding, bread, coffee, and cigars were served out. The building was illuminated, and music having been provided, a large number of the younger folk enjoyed themselves by dancing.

At the New Town Prayer Meeting Hall over 100 adult poor were fed at 4 P.M.

A repast was given by Sir P. S. Ramasawmy Mudelliar, C.I.E., the Sheriff of Madras—who received the honour of knighthood on this day—to the paupers of the Monegar Choultry, the patients of the Native Infirmary, and the Leper Hospital. To the paupers of the Monegar Choultry this gentleman distributed cloths. The European and Eurasian patients of the Leper Hospital were also remembered. At the close of the entertainment three cheers were given for the Queen Empress, the Viceroy and Governor-General of India, the Governor of Madras, and Sir P. S. Ramasawmy Mudelliar respectively.

TREATS TO SCHOOLS.

15,990 children attending educational institutions in the City of Madras were entertained by the Celebration Committee, and 5,820 children attending poor schools were treated at the expense of Sir P. S. Ramasawmy Mudelliar.

PRESENTATION OF THE PRESIDENCIAL ADDRESS.

The hour fixed for the ceremony of the presentation of the Presidencial Address at the Banqueting Hall was 5.30 P.M., but long before that time carriages were seen hurrying along towards Government House, and very large numbers of people wended their way in the same direction. Before 5 o'clock the compound of the Government House in front of the Hall was crowded. The northern flight of steps to the Hall was covered with scarlet baize. The members of the Executive Committee were assembled on the top of the steps. Seats were arranged in the open space immediately in front of the Hall, while the space beyond looked like a sea of heads. A guard of honour, consisting of 100 rank and file of the Madras Volunteer Guards, under the command of Captain F. G. Heaven, with band and colours, was drawn up in review order immediately in front of the steps. His Excellency the Right Honourable the Governor, with Lady Susan Bourke, C.I., Lady Eva Quin, and the Government House staff, arrived at the foot of the steps at 5.30 P.M. His Excellency wore the scarlet and silver uniform of the Deputy Lord-Lieutenant of Lothian; while the Members of Council, the Chief Secretary, and a few other officers of Government appeared in diplomatic uniform. Among the Native Princes present were His Highness the Maharajah of Vizianagram, the Prince of Pudoocottah, the Kumara Rajah of Pittapur, and the Minor Zemindars of Ramnad. His Excellency and Lady Susan Bourke ascended the steps, and took the seats of state provided for them. The Honourable Mr. P. Hutchins, Chairman of the Executive Committee, then stepped forward, and said:—

"YOUR EXCELLENCY,—The deputation before Your Excellency comprises nearly all the members of the Executive Jubilee Committee for this City, which has also appointed a Central Committee to concert measures with our fellow subjects in the Provinces for the due celebration of Her Majesty's Jubilee. From the first it has been our anxious endeavour to enlist co-operation from every part of the Presidency, and our invitations have been received with the utmost cordiality everywhere. The Address which we prepared has been accepted and signed by every District or Local Committee of which we are aware, certainly by every District Committee, and by close upon 100 Committees of various subdivisions or towns. I therefore claim to be the mouthpiece on this great day of rejoicing, not merely of this deputation, nor yet of the 400,000 citizens of Madras alone, but of the 32,000,000 forming the entire population of this great Presidency. This unanimity indeed may be regarded as the distinctive feature of our Madras celebration. With Your Excellency's permission I will now proceed to read the Address in which we have sought, however feebly, to give expression to the ardent devotion with which these 32,000,000 regard their Most Gracious Sovereign Lady, the Queen Empress Victoria."

Mr. Hutchins then read the Presidencial Address:—

"MAY IT PLEASE YOUR MAJESTY:

"We, the undersigned, representing Your Majesty's subjects of every race and every creed throughout the Presidency of Madras, do unanimously desire, on the auspicious occasion of Your Majesty's Jubilee, to approach Your Majesty with our loyal congratulations.

"Your Majesty's assumption of direct Sovereign supremacy over the Empire of India is accepted as the most glorious event in the annals of this ancient land. In Madras it heralded the dawn of a new era of progress and prosperity. Education has been encouraged and sanitation promoted; roads have been made, rivers bridged, railways opened, telegraphs constructed, and irrigation extended; a system of local self-government has been introduced, industries have been stimulated, and the resources of the country largely developed.

"During the fifty years of Your Majesty's reign the Presidency of Madras has conspicuously enjoyed the blessing of tranquillity, the result of the wisdom and impartiality which have pre-eminently characterised Your Majesty's Government.

"The even tenour of events in this Presidency was disturbed in 1877 by a famine of unprecedented severity, which evoked from Your Majesty's subjects in the United Kingdom a response, unparalleled in its munificence, to the appeal made for help in our great extremity. Your Majesty's personal sympathy on that occasion is not the least of Your Majesty's many claims on our gratitude.

"In profound thankfulness for the noble words of Your Majesty's Proclamation that in our prosperity is Your Majesty's strength, in our contentment Your Majesty's security, and in our gratitude Your Majesty's great reward, we earnestly pray for the long continuance of Your Majesty's beneficent reign, and for the welfare of Your Majesty and the Royal Family.

"With sentiments of the deepest loyalty and attachment we subscribe ourselves, Your Majesty's most obedient and devoted subjects."

Mr. Hutchins continued :—

"Trusting that Your Excellency will be pleased to telegraph to Her Most Gracious Majesty the purport of what has been said, we now tender this Address to Your Excellency as Her Majesty's representative, and pray that it may be forwarded as soon as we can provide a suitable Casket, so as to reach Her Majesty's own hands on or about the 20th of June next."

A copy of the Address, enclosed in a small box, was then presented to His Excellency, who, after accepting it, replied as follows :—

"LADIES AND GENTLEMEN :—I deem it a great honour that it has fallen to my lot as Governor of Fort St. George to receive this remarkable and memorable Address. It has been my wish to do so in such a way, and in such conditions that all classes of the community can participate in the ceremonial. In the name of our Gracious Sovereign, the Queen Empress, I beg to thank the people of this Presidency, European and native, of every caste and creed, for the hearty expression of loyalty which their Address contains. It has been unanimously agreed to by the people of this Presidency, from the Chilka Lake to the Coast of Malabar. It is a worthy portion of that joyous and harmonious chorus of Thanksgiving which this day resounds from the Khyber Pass to Cape Comorin. It is in thorough accord with those prayers which since sunrise this morning have been offered up from church, mosque, and temple throughout the Indian Empire for the welfare of our Sovereign. It will be my duty to transmit it to the foot of the Throne, enclosed in a Casket, which I believe will be an exquisite specimen of Indian art and industry. It is not for me to presume to interpret the sentiments of Her Majesty upon receiving this respectful token of the homage of her Madras subjects. But the record of Her Majesty's daily life supplies striking and ample proof of the interest she takes in everything which affects the progress, prosperity, and security of her people. (Hear, hear.) I am therefore confident that Her Majesty will be gratified to learn that the people of Southern India are convinced that her reign has been distinguished by that glorious advance of civilisation which your Address so eloquently describes. It will be pleasing to her heart to know that the people of this Presidency remember with gratitude the efforts which her subjects at home made to alleviate suffering when this land was visited by a severe famine. Rest assured that these acknowledgments on your part will cement more closely than ever the hearts of the British people to their fellow-subjects in India. Your Address alludes to the peaceful triumphs of the past which have marked the reign of Her Majesty. Depend upon it the triumphs of the future will be no less conspicuous. The progress of the Victorian Era is not ephemeral. Great as the benefits are which that reign has conferred upon India, they are not only valuable in themselves but are valuable also for the wide foundation they have laid for future prosperity. Education, railroads, telegraphs, sanitation, water-supply are prolific parents, and will be productive of numerous blessings yet unborn. But if our prosperity here is still to increase, if the condition of the millions who are still very poor is to be ameliorated, the loyal people of Madras know full well that this can only be attained by the maintenance of that Paramount Power whose just and vigorous rule in India is the only guarantee the people have against the recurrence of the strife, misery, and oppression which the page of History painfully records. May those whose duty it is to serve the Queen Empress in India, both in high as well as subordinate office, ever remember this Jubilee day. May we recollect the devoted loyalty displayed upon this occasion by our native fellow-subjects, and may this thought inspire us all to do our best to promote their welfare, knowing that in devoting ourselves to that object we are fulfilling the wishes of our august Sovereign. (Hear, hear.) It is a great pleasure to me upon this occasion to acknowledge the munificence of many individuals, not only in Madras, but throughout the Presidency—who have subscribed large sums both to the celebration in their different localities, and to various useful objects which they have at heart, and which they wish to associate with the name of our Sovereign. I think we may well be proud of our Presidency, not only for the munificence of their gifts, but also for the sentiments by which that munificence was prompted. Large sums have also been collected, and have been given in feeding the poor this day. We are all the happier for knowing that their wants have been supplied; and while the benevolent have not forgotten the poor, the Queen on her Throne has not been unmindful of the prisoner and the captive. She has determined to exercise in a liberal spirit her prerogative of mercy—that attribute 'which becomes the throned Monarch better than his crown.' That great attribute will be exercised in this Presidency with no niggard hand, and I am glad to inform you that orders have gone out to-day for the release of more than 2,800 prisoners. (Hear, hear.) It has also been determined to partially remit the sentences of more than 2,200 others. (Hear, hear.) Her Majesty has also not forgotten the poor debtor—a class with which we all sympathise; and I am happy to say that all civil debtors owing Rs. 100, or less, will be released this day throughout the Presidency, and the decrees under which they are confined will be satisfied out of the public funds. There is another prerogative of the Queen that has been exercised on this occasion; and I am sure you will all be glad to hear that one of the first names I have to mention is the name of that distinguished Maharajah whose family and property have been for so long a time connected with the Presidency. The Maharajah of Vizianagram does not depend on his own merits alone for recognition by the British Government, but he inherits loyalty to the Throne through a long line of ancestors, and in announcing that he is appointed a Knight Commander of the Indian Empire, I can say that the honour has been worthily bestowed. (Applause.) The next name I have to mention is that of an old friend to all who have lived in Madras for many years. I mean Mr. Master. (Hear, hear.) I am sure it gives you as much pleasure to hear, as it does me to announce, that Her Majesty has been pleased to confer upon him the Companionship of the Star of India. There is one more name I should like to mention, because he is a very old friend of yours, and a friend of all who have taken part in the administration of this Presidency during many years. I mean the name of Mr. Chentsal Rao Pantulu, which has now become a household word among you (hear, hear), and from what I have heard of him I can say most truly that there is no more devoted servant of the Crown in this broad land—European or native. I have not quite exhausted the list. There is one gentleman known in Madras who has subscribed most munificently to its charities for a long time, and who has come forward on this occasion with his usual liberality. He has not only fed the poor, but has subscribed a large sum of money, both to the Imperial Institute and to that Technical Institute that we hope to establish in Madras. I am happy to be able to announce that in future Mr. Ramasawmy Modelliar will be known to us as Sir Ramasawmy Modelliar (applause), he having received the title of Knight Bachelor. There are native titles, all of which will be gazetted to-morrow; but I need not detain you this evening by going through the names. I will only mention that one gentleman has been made a Rajah, three have been made Dewan Bahadurs, thirteen Rai Bahadurs, and three Khan Bahadurs. Her Majesty has also thought it well to introduce a system of giving literary titles to those persons who have done good service to the cause of literature in India. There will be four gentlemen in this Presidency to whom will be given the title of Mahamahopadhyaya, and three others the title of Shams-ul-Ulema. I propose now, with your permission, that we shall sing that great National Anthem which conveys to every British subject, no matter what his creed or race may be, in beautiful and expressive words, the sentiments of that loyalty to the Throne which we are met here to celebrate." (Loud applause).

The National Anthem was sung by a special choir, under the direction of Mr. St. Leger, Organist of the St. George's Cathedral, accompanied by the Governor's Band, under Mr. Stradiot. The second verse was sung as a solo by Miss Edith Lawson. Three enthusiastic cheers were then given for Her Majesty the Queen Empress, and three more for His Excellency the Governor.

At the conclusion of the ceremonial of the presentation of the Presidential Address, Lady Susan Bourke planted a mahogany-tree in the Park of Government House, near the Hall, in the presence of a large assembly.

His Excellency the Governor gave a State Banquet at Government House at 7-30 P.M. in honour of the Jubilee. Lady Susan Bourke, C.I., and Lady Eva Quin were present. The guests included the Honourable the Chief Justice and Lady Collins; the Most Reverend the Archbishop Colgan; the Honourable Mr. C. G. Master, C.S.I., Senior Member of the Council, and Mrs. Master; the Honourable Mr. P. P. Hutchins, Junior Member of the Council, and Mrs. Hutchins; the Honourable Mr. Justice Kernan, Q.C., and Miss Kernan; the Honourable Mr. Justice and Mrs. Brandt; the Honourable Mr. Justice Parker; the Honourable Mr. R. W. Barlow, Collector of Sea Customs; the Honourable Mr. J. A. and Mrs. Boyson; the Honourable Mr. H. J. Stokes, Acting Chief Secretary to Government; Mr. H. S. Thomas, First Member of the Board of Revenue, and Miss Thomas; Surgeon-General Irvine, Army Medical Department; Surgeon-General G. Bidie, C.I.E., Madras Medical Department, and Mrs. Bidie; Major-General A. C. Johnson, C.B., commanding the Eastern District; Mr. J. H. Garstin, C.S.I., Second Member of the Board of Revenue; Mr. J. Grose, M.A., Acting Third Member of the Board of Revenue, and Mrs. Grose; Mr. F. Price, Acting Revenue Secretary to Government, and Mrs. Price; Colonel A. R. Kenney Herbert, Military Secretary to Government; Colonel C. J. Smith, R.E., Consulting Engineer and Local Secretary to Government Public Works Department; the Venerable J. F. Browne, B.D., Archdeacon of Madras, and Mrs. Browne; Colonel C. A. Carter, Controller of Military Accounts, Madras; Colonel T. K. Guthrie, Inspector-General of Police, Madras, and Mrs. Guthrie; Mr. H. O'C. Cardozo, Acting Superintendent Madras Surveys, and Mrs. Cardozo; Major G. M. J. Moore, President of the Madras Municipal Commission; Mr. W. A. Willock, B.A., Acting Commissioner of Salt and Abkari Revenue, and Mrs. Willock; Mrs. David Duncan, wife of the Acting Director of Public Instruction (absent on tour);

Mr. C. A. Lawson, Honorary Secretary Madras Central Jubilee Committee, and Mrs. Lawson.

THE DECORATIONS AND ILLUMINATIONS.

During the day the Mercantile Houses and Government Offices along the North Beach Road exhibited a brave display of bunting. The ships in the harbour were also gaily dressed, the *Wirrenbee*, *Manora*, *Clan Drummond*, and *Goalpara* being decked out from stem to stern, the last-named being especially noticeable with her flags in a "rainbow" from her foremost awning stanchion, over her mast-heads, to her taffrail, right aft. The Royal Standard floated from the Master Attendant's flagstaff; and the offices of the Messageries Maritimes and the Peninsular and Oriental Steam Navigation Company looked especially gay, the former with the tricolour arranged around the balcony, and the latter with the well-known flag of the Company flying from the mast-head, and at each yard-arm, surrounded with other flags. The flags of the various Consuls added to the attractiveness of the scene, while the Sailors' Home was appropriately decorated with the Mercantile Marine ensign and Jack surrounded by commercial code flags. The Custom House was adorned with the flags of all nations; the Union Jack flew at the head of the Pier; and the titan cranes on the breakwaters were gaily decorated. The Chamber of Commerce and the *Madras Mail* Offices were tastefully decorated with flags, festoons, and rosettes.

Shortly after 7 P.M. the beach illuminations commenced, the Post and Telegraph Offices bursting into bold relief with red, blue, green, and white lights burnt on the portico, and at the various windows of the two central and side towers. The front of Messrs. King and Co.'s premises was lit up with brilliant white lamps, and the Stamp Office was tastefully illuminated, the building being outlined. The central space between the columns of the verandah displayed a medallion transparency of Her Majesty, with a Malta Cross and a double triangle on either side, each forming a very effective star. The lamps used gave a mellow light that was very pleasant to the eye. An hour later the High Court, Custom House, Harbour Board Office, and Harbour Works buildings were illuminated, the three last named with plain white lights, outlining the buildings. The general effect along the beach was at this time incomplete, the mercantile firms (which had been munificent donors to the Jubilee Fund) having decided not to illuminate for prudential reasons connected with fire insurance. There was, however, one exception to this rule. Messrs. Gordon Woodroffe & Co.'s office was most tastefully decorated with festoons of Chinese lanterns, pendant from the various pillars of the upper and lower verandahs, their rich colours and soft, subdued light giving a most charming effect. Several of the Dubashes' godowns were also illuminated, and the Government Workhouse at Royapooram made a brilliant display. In the Harbour the *Clan Drummond* exhibited lights at her mast-heads and yard-arms; and the *Manora* was illuminated in the most approved nautical manner, the whole of her masts and yards being clearly defined, while red and green side-lights were displayed at her mast-heads and in her tops. The electric light, brightly shining along her rail, revealed the long outline of her hull to great advantage. The steamer *Clan Matheson* was illuminated from stem to stern with coloured and electric lights. For nearly an hour rockets, Bengal lights, &c., followed each other in quick succession. Not the least interesting of the various fireworks was the "Holmes' Patent Water Signals," an improved life-buoy appliance for saving life at sea at night.

At 8.30 P.M. a red light burst forth from the titan crane, on the north break-water. It was answered instantly by another at the south, and a third from the wave-breaker near Clive's battery, whilst others simultaneously burst forth from the whole length of both arms of the Harbour. The effect was marvellous, and the view from the T end of the Pier was very beautiful. A fresh breeze threw a considerable surf on to the beach, and this, reflecting back a warm roseate hue, was lovely. The ships stood out in clearly-defined relief, each rope and block being distinct. The Beach Road which, but a moment before, presented dark gaps, contrasting strongly with the brilliant appearance from the Pier of the illuminated buildings, leapt into view clear and bright; and from Carlton House at Royapooram on the north, to the Fort on the south, each building was defined in every detail with a delicate pink hue, while the illuminated buildings sparkled as though covered with myriads of fire-flies. Suddenly blue lights took the place of red along the arms of the Harbour, and the pink was turned to an appearance as of brilliant moonlight. Each house now stood out like a white marble palace, cool and calm; then the lights on the illuminated buildings grew dim, though still sparkling; and the Telegraph Office, distinct in every detail, re-assumed its commanding prominence. The surf sparkled snow-white: while the waves, as they rolled in before breaking, reflected the most delicate shades of green.

Upon the Mount Road, Messrs. Simpson and Co. exhibited three transparencies, one, the Royal Coat of Arms, flanked by the Mayo and the Dalhousie Coats of Arms, with the names "Mayo" and "Dalhousie" beneath. Messrs. Franck and Co.'s buildings and gateways were illuminated with white and coloured lanterns. Messrs. Nicholas and Co. exhibited a fine transparency, which occupied the whole frontage of their premises; in the centre was a full-length portrait of Her Majesty, with the motto "Vivat Regina" in large characters; and underneath the transparency was a row of lights. Messrs. T. Owen and Co. illuminated their premises with lamps and Chinese lanterns. The arrangements for the illumination of Messrs. P. Orr and Sons' artistic building by gas made on the premises were very elaborate, but the gas disappointed expectations. Messrs. Moses and Co., Syed Cassim and Co., and Syed Essack illuminated their premises with lamps. Messrs. W. Hawes and Co. displayed monograms of the Queen Empress, with the Prince of Wales' plumes above, in transparencies. The Oriental Bakery was illuminated with lamps and Chinese lanterns. The Moothi Mahal, the residence of the Kumara Rajah of Pittapur, were illuminated with lamps; and blue lights were burnt at intervals on the roof. Messrs. Duff and Co. illuminated with lamps, and decorated with foliage, the motto, "God bless our Empress." Messrs. C. Ponoosawmy Moodally and Co.'s premises were well illuminated. Mr. Ebrahim Adamally used tumbler lights of various colours, besides Chinese lanterns. The East India Art Manufacturing Co. showed an arch of lights. Mr. Framjee Pestonjee Bhatugara had lamps distributed over his premises, and the front of the building showed the words "Inform Empress we are happy." The *Guardian* Press had a portrait of the Queen, and lights. The proprietor distributed copies of the Jubilee version of the National Anthem, printed in gold. Messrs. Misquith and Co. exhibited two transparencies, with the Royal Coat of Arms, and a Crown. The *Hindu* Press and *Andhraprakasika* Office, on the Mount Road, was brilliantly illuminated with lanterns, and blue lights were burnt at intervals. Messrs. C. Appasooty Pillay and Co. illuminated with lamps, and had a motto, "God bless the Empress of India." Messrs. Rodgers and Co. had a transparency of the British Lion, foliage decorations, and a string of lights. Messrs. Vest and Co. had a transparency of the Royal Arms, and the motto, "God bless our Queen; Long may she reign." Messrs. Deschamps and Co.'s illuminations were very effective with lamps and Chinese lanterns. The building was decorated with French and English flags, and Roman candles were burnt at intervals. The building occupied by Mr. G. D'Angelis was excellently illuminated, and showed a transparency of the Royal Coat of Arms, with the motto, "*Salute e pace a le Grande Regina!*"

At each gateway of Messrs. Spencer and Co.'s premises was erected a castellated arch, with two towers to each, surmounted with six bannerets, and a string of flags across, with the Union Jack in the centre. At the apex was a large star with a portrait of the Queen Empress, and each angle of the arch was furnished with a Britannia shield. Each archway had a motto in large white letters on a red ground, one being "May Her Glory never wane," and the other "She reigns in our hearts." A crimson and gold curtain, or valance, ran the whole length of the building with flags and bannerets at every point. Surmounting the whole there were planted two large flags with the name of the firm in the centre. The verandah of the upper floor was hung with a curtain of red, white, and blue. Coloured lamps were profusely used for illuminating purposes, and in addition lamps were placed in the margins of the two large mottoes on the arches. On the second parapet of the main building was a large festoon of lamps. On the portico were two sun-lights of great brilliancy, and three others in the gables of the adjacent store. In the compound there were erected two large beacons, and on the summits of these structures blue lights were burnt at intervals. At the top of the building was the motto "Long live Victoria the Good."

Messrs. Waller and Co. illuminated their premises with lamps, and displayed the motto "God bless the Empress of India." Messrs. Barrie and Co. had lights, and the words "The Royal Jubilee, 1887—God bless our Empress," painted on their windows. The Madras Stable Co.'s gateway was decorated with foliage and flags. Mr. Chendra Khan Lallah illuminated his house with lamps of various descriptions. Messrs. Higginbotham and Co.'s illuminations were very effective. As the premises stand away from the road, only the gateway and bindery portions were illuminated, for which purpose white and coloured lamps were liberally employed. Across the gateway in large letters were the words "Royal Jubilee Year." Over this was a transparency of the Royal Coat of Arms, and underneath was a transparency of the name of the firm. To the right, and a little below, was a portrait of the Queen Empress, and to the left that of the Prince of Wales. There were also two large flags over the gateway. Messrs. W. E. Smith and Co. exhibited a transparency of the Royal Coat of Arms with the motto "God bless our Queen Empress." White and coloured lamps were used for illuminating purposes, and the premises were decorated with flags. Messrs. Norton and Co. exhibited an oil-painting of Her Majesty. The premises were illuminated with lamps, and decorated with flags. Mr. C. Chamberlain had lights, and the motto "The Queen Empress: Constitution and State for ever." On the top of the Eastern Castlet Messrs. Addison and Co. had placed a large flag of the Waterbury Watch Company, formed of a combination of the Union Jack and the Stars and Stripes. The frontage of the building was illuminated with small lamps, and there was a string of lights along the boundary wall. Mr. Hughes exhibited two transparencies, one a likeness of the Queen, and the other a likeness of the Maharajah of Vizianagram. Coloured lamps were artistically used in the illumination of this building.

Messrs. Runganathum and Co., and Garratt, Camille and Co., conjointly illuminated their premises with a very pretty effect. A large number of lamps were used, and numerous flags, including the Royal Standard, were planted on the top of the building. The pillars were draped with flags. In the verandah was an oil painting of the Royal Coat of Arms, at the left upper corner was the Star of India, and at the right the Royal monogram. On the shield were the words, "Queen Empress of India;" and above, "May peace and happiness surround her in life." Groups of foliage plants were arranged with Chinese lanterns. Messrs. Rungee Laul and Co., Moothea Pillay and Co., Ostheidier and Co., and Archer and Co. decorated their buildings with flags and illuminated them with lamps. The gateway of Nawab Mira Hoossain's residence was very prettily illuminated with devices picked out with lights, and on the compound wall Chinese lanterns were placed at intervals. Plants were also placed on the walls contiguous to the gates. The Begum's residence opposite was also illuminated. The Ameer Mahal Palace, the residence of the Prince of Arcot, and the Shadee Mahal, on the Triplicane High Road, the former residence of His Highness's ancestors, and now occupied by His Highness's nephew, Ghulam Mohummed Ghouse Khan Bahadur, were beautifully illuminated. The entrance of the Agri-Horticultural Gardens had a transparency with the words "Vivat Regina!" The gateways of some of the private residences in Teynampet were also illuminated.

Many places of business and private residences on the Poonamallee Road were decorated and illuminated. At each of the two gates of the Survey Office, opposite the Kirk, was erected a handsome triumphal arch, at the top of which was placed a crown of white lights. The house of Sir P. S. Ramasawmy Mudelliar, C.I.E., was decorated with flags and bunting, and some thousands of lamps were used in the illumination of it. The boundary walls were covered with small lamps, and the compound looked bright with Chinese lanterns suspended from the branches of trees or placed on the ground. Mr. V. Ramiengar, C.S.I., also illuminated his house in a very tasteful manner.

Looking towards the town from the summit of Government House Bridge the view was charming. The road was defined on each side by strings of lamps, and in the distance were to be seen several brilliant beacons, and the illuminations of the Central Station, and the Madras Medical College. The Chemical Examiner to the Government had the letters "V.I." and a Star of India worked in gas jets placed at the top of the Medical College building on the south face. The roads round the Fort and Esplanades were lit with small lamps on bamboo poles at intervals, and all the approaches to the Island were illuminated. Turning into

Esplanade Row a bright avenue was entered, with strings of lanterns on each side. The illumination of the fine Grecian frontage of Pacheappah's Hall was seen to great advantage. Messrs. West and Co. had their premises well illuminated with many lamps; a triumphal arch was erected at the gateway, on which was exhibited a transparency, which showed a portrait of the Queen, and the letters "V.I." Messrs. Fisher and Co. showed the words "God bless our Empress" in a transparency. Mr. Macartoom had a transparency showing the words "God bless our Queen Empress." Some of the shops in the Broadway were also illuminated. The *Madras Times* Office had an attractive transparency of the Royal Coat of Arms. Several of the native residents in town had their houses lit up, and numerous religious processions passed through the streets at night, in honour of the Jubilee.

The Government made a grant for the illumination of each of the Railway termini in this Presidency, but in consequence of there being very little time for preparations, the Madras Railway authorities decided upon devoting all their attention to illuminating the Central Station. A ball of light, four feet nine inches in diameter, was placed above the top of the centre tower of the station, with a crown of yellow lights at its base. The centre tower was outlined in white lights, and all the architectural details of the building were picked out in coloured lights. The green lights at the base of the building gave way higher up to red lights, which were surmounted by white lights. Besides the illuminations, the building was decorated with over 500 flags. Large flags were placed on the summit of the central tower, and on the tops of the side turrets, and to each pillar along the upstair verandah flags were fastened.

On the eastern portion of the Island, within the fireworks arena, a magnificent arch, about 40 feet in height, and bearing many lamps of all colours, had been erected. This was lighted up at 8 P.M. The arch was surmounted by a richly-jewelled crown, below which was the word "Jubilee;" and immediately underneath this was the inscription, "God bless the Empress." The letters "V.I." and the dates "1837—1887," were shown on each side.

THE FIREWORKS.

The eastern corner of the Island was reserved as the site for fireworks. The immense *maidan* afforded accommodation for the parking of over a thousand carriages in such a way that the occupants obtained a good view of everything that took place. More than 50,000 people found standing room in front of the carriages. The South Beach and Marine Villa Roads were also covered with spectators. His Excellency the Governor with his guests viewed the scene from the roof of Government House. The Island is reached by three bridges—one near Government House, another near St. Mary's Cemetery, and the third opposite the Wallajah Gate of Fort St. George. Each of these bridges was brilliantly illuminated by beacons towering to a great height. The summit of each was encircled by hundreds of lamps, and long lines of light ran from top to bottom. To add to the effect, blue, red, and green lights were burnt continuously from dusk to midnight, on the tops of the beacons, and on high poles placed in conspicuous places. The Mount Road, from the Wallajah Gate Bridge to the Mount Road Bridge, was lined on each side with poles 30 feet high. These were surmounted by the flags of all nations; and festoons of lamps extended from post to post, so that the whole roadway was flooded with light. The other roads on the Island were marked off by lamps at short intervals, which not only served as guides to the crowds of spectators, but also added considerably to the general effect. A novel feature in the evening's illuminations was the lighting up of the Cooum river by a fleet of catamarans, whose owners burnt lights of various colours while paddling round the Island. The countless lamps that bordered the river were reflected in the water.

Although the hour for the commencement of the pyrotechnic display was fixed for 9 P.M., a very large crowd assembled at an early hour in the evening, and in order to keep their attention occupied several large fire balloons were sent up at 8 o'clock. At 8.45 P.M., an Imperial salute of 101 detonating shells was fired. Shells were first exploded, followed by a *feu de joie* of crackers; then 34 more shells, and a second *feu de joie;* and thirdly, the remaining 33 shells, followed by a third *feu de joie.* The display of fireworks now took place. The set pieces were divided into sixteen sections, and the firing of each division was simultaneous with the discharge of maroons. When the set pieces were concluded, there was a grand simultaneous burst of maroons, immediately succeeded by the discharge of a large number of Roman candles. The words "Good night" were then suddenly displayed in letters of fire from the top of an arch, and the crowd gradually dispersed.

CONCLUDING PROCEEDINGS OF THE GENERAL COMMITTEE.

The concluding meeting of the General Committee was held on the afternoon of the 23rd March, 1887, in the Banqueting Hall, Madras, and was largely attended. His Excellency the Right Honourable R. Bourke, the Chairman of the Committee, presided. The proceedings were marked throughout with great enthusiasm. They commenced by the Honourable Mr. Hutchins, Chairman of the Executive Committee, requesting the Honorary Secretary to read the Report of that Committee. Mr. Lawson then read the following Report :—

REPORT OF THE EXECUTIVE COMMITTEE.

"To His Excellency the Chairman, and the Members of the Madras General Jubilee Committee.—The duty of receiving and publishing narratives of the celebration of Her Most Gracious Majesty's Jubilee in the provinces of the Presidency of Madras having now been fulfilled, it devolves upon the Executive Committee to submit a Report of the manner in which it has obeyed the instructions it received on the 27th of January from the General Committee, to 'place itself in communication with Mofussil Committees, and to act as a Central Committee for an Address of loyal congratulation to Her Majesty from the Presidency of Madras.'

"Immediately after the first meeting of the General Committee had dissolved, the Executive Committee addressed itself to the task assigned to it, and its earliest act was to unanimously invite the Honourable Mr. Hutchins to accept the office of Chairman. It was then agreed that the Presidency Memorial should take the form of a Technical Institute for the benefit of the entire Presidency, to be called the Victoria Technical Institute; and that subscriptions should also be invited for the Imperial Institute of London, as well as for the expense of the local celebration in Madras. On the following day, the 28th January, a circular letter was addressed by the Chairman, on behalf of the Committee, to the Collectors of Districts, soliciting them to make it known to District Jubilee Committees that the objects which the Executive Committee desired to promote included local rejoicings; an Address of Congratulation to Her Majesty from the whole Presidency; the provision of a suitable receptacle for that Address; the compilation of a Narrative of the celebration of the Jubilee for Her Majesty's information; the Victoria Technical Institute; and the Imperial Institute. The District Committees were at the same time invited to communicate to the Executive Committee accounts of their proceedings for publication previous to their being placed on record in the Memorial Volume.

"The features of the celebration at the Presidency town must be so well known to members of the General Committee that there can be no occasion to make more than a passing allusion to them. The appropriations that were made for special purposes by subscribers to the Jubilee Fund afforded the Executive Committee a safe guide to the wishes of the public as to expenditure of an ephemeral character, and justified the reasonable outlay that was incurred. The demands on the resources at the Committee's disposal were diminished by the liberality with which many firms and private individuals illuminated their premises; and the charge for school treats and for feeding and clothing the poor was reduced by the contribution of the Government, and the liberality of Sir Ramasawmy Mudelliar, Mr. Cunniah Chetty, and other gentlemen. Thus it was that 5,800 school children were entertained, and 15,000 poor people were fed in this city on the Day of Celebration. A pyrotechnic display suitably concluded the proceedings, which owed their success in a very great measure to the indefatigable energy which was displayed by Mr. B. H. Chester, the Honorary Secretary, in carrying out the wishes of the Local Celebration Sub-Committee.

"The response of District Committees to the overtures of the Executive Committee was gratifying in the extreme. The interval that elapsed between the receipt of the circular letter and the date fixed for the celebration was very brief, but the Districts vied with one another in the energy of their preparations, and the cordiality of their co-operation with the Madras Committee. The Collectors of Districts gave their hearty support to the local efforts that were made to honour the occasion; but, in conformity with the wishes of the Government, they scrupulously abstained from the exercise of an official influence that might detract from the spontaneity of the proceedings.

"The modes of acknowledging Divine blessings, and of showing homage to the Sovereign, that are time-honoured in India, were followed in most of the one hundred and seventy-six towns[1] which have been placed in communication with the Executive Committee. Houses and streets were decorated; salutes were fired; public prayers and thanksgivings were offered in places of worship; the poor were fed and clothed; children were feasted; mass meetings were held; processions were formed; marks of honour were shown to Her Majesty's portrait, or to her Standard; odes were composed, and recited; and the festivities concluded with illuminations and fireworks. In every instance, so far as the Executive Committee is aware, all classes of the community waived traditional differences, and associated in the most friendly manner in contributing to the success of the day.

"It is not possible to arrive at even an approximate idea of the number of people who took part in the celebration throughout the Presidency. Some towns have communicated rough estimates of the crowds that were attracted by local proceedings; but quite as many have omitted to do so, and have confined themselves to very general statements. It is, however, abundantly evident that unusually large numbers were collected, alike in small as in great towns, and that the aggregate must have been enormous. Yet from all quarters has been received the assurance that the proceedings were conducted in the most orderly, as well as in the most enthusiastic manner, and not an accident occurred to mar the happiness of the celebration.

"The acceptance by one hundred and twenty-nine[2] District, or local Committees, of the Address of Congratulation which the Executive Committee proposed for adoption, has conferred upon this Presidency the unique distinction of having united in an expression of grateful homage to Her Majesty. In now submitting that document for ratification by the General Committee, the Executive Committee may be permitted to say that it is proud of having been instrumental in concerting so remarkable a testimony to the loyalty and harmony that prevailed among the thirty-two millions of Her Majesty's subjects in Southern India.

"The District Committees have not been content with contributing towards the carrying out of the Presidential memorials mentioned in the programme of the Executive Committee, but have, in a large number of cases, resolved to secure a permanent local memorial of Her Majesty's reign and Jubilee. These local memorials include thirteen Chuttrams, or Choultries; nine lamps; eight wells; eight reading-rooms; six town halls; six scholarships; five hospitals, or dispensaries; five tanks; four technical institutions; three libraries; three museums; three water pandals; two markets; two school prizes; two tablets; two fountains; a playground; a tope; a temple; a Jubilee House; a Victoria Lodge; a portrait of Her Majesty; an Agricultural College; a provident fund; a clock tower; land for a poor-house; a garden; a flight of steps; a temple door; the diversion of a river to bring water to a town; the improvement of the water supply of another town; a memorial

[1] The number amounted eventually to 205.
[2] The number increased to 191 in the three weeks that followed the presentation of this Report.

tree; a tennis court; a Badminton court; a gong, &c.; and six schools, one club, and one public hall have been re-named in honour of Her Majesty. His Highness the Maharajah of Travancore has subscribed Rs. 50,000 for a memorial at Trevandum which has yet to be selected, and has been a generous contributor to the Madras Jubilee Fund. His Highness the Maharajah of Vizianagram made a princely donation to the Madras and the Imperial Institutes; and, in further celebration of the occasion, devoted a large sum towards the maintenance of temples, the support of poor families, and the embellishment of both temples and mosques on his estate, besides remitting nearly four lakhs of arrears of revenue due by his ryots. With similar munificence His Highness the Rajah of Venkatagherry has contributed Rs. 10,000 to the Committee fund, to be divided equally between the two Institutes.

"The cordial co-operation of District Committees was so largely conducive to the success of the celebration, that the Executive Committee desires to record its grateful acknowledgments of the assistance it has received from the Chairmen, Honorary Secretaries, and other Members of those Committees, as well as its warm appreciation of the support that the demonstration met with from the public at large. The knowledge that on so memorable an occasion the Presidency of Madras acquitted itself in a manner worthy of its reputation for loyalty, will, the Executive Committee believes, be a source of universal satisfaction.

"It is with much pleasure that the Executive Committee announces, both that the Presidency of Madras is now in a position to make a substantial contribution to the Institution in the Metropolis of the British Empire which has commended itself to Her Majesty as a peculiarly appropriate memorial of her reign, and that the occurrence of Her Majesty's Jubilee has bestowed upon the Presidency the nucleus of a fund for supplying a great want in the educational system of the country. The Committee entertains the confident expectation that the selection as a Presidencial Jubilee Memorial of the scheme for a Technical Institute will be peculiarly agreeable to the General Committee. The development of this important undertaking was delegated by the Executive Committee to a Sub-Committee, which has recently been greatly enlarged, and the acceptance of the office of Honorary Secretary of that Committee by Mr. G. L. Chambers is a guarantee that no pains or expenditure will be spared to speedily make the Victoria Institute an accomplished success.

"The Presidencial Casket, which has been designed by Mr. R. F. Chisholm, late Architect to the Government of Madras, will be executed by Messrs. P. Orr and Sons of Madras. Every effort is being made to complete it by the 15th May, in view to its being tendered for Her Majesty's gracious acceptance by the 21st June, the date on which the Jubilee will be celebrated in the United Kingdom.

"The Memorial Volume will be very handsomely printed and bound by Messrs. Macmillan and Co., of London, and will be enclosed in a silver and sandal-wood box of much artistic beauty, now being made by Mr. Framjee Pestonjee in Madras. It will commence with a copy of the Presidencial Address; then will come the narratives of local celebrations; and the book will conclude with an Appendix, containing a retrospect of progress in the Presidency of Madras during Her Majesty's reign, and other matters of interest to the student of the history of Madras. It will be illustrated by photographs. A facsimile copy of this Imperial quarto Volume will be presented to the Secretary of State for India, to H.E. the Viceroy of India, and to H.E. the Governor of Madras; and other copies, without photographs, will be presented to each of the Jubilee Committees in the Mofussil that has contributed not less than Rs. 50 to the funds of the Central Committee. As many gentlemen who have taken an interest in the recent celebration of the Jubilee may be glad to possess a record of the event, it is proposed to instruct Messrs. Macmillan and Co. to publish the same matter as will appear in the large volume in an octavo edition, moderately priced. Any profit arising from the sale of this edition will be given to the Victoria Technical Institute, Madras.

"The subscriptions that have been made to the Fund of which the Executive Committee has had charge amount to the very handsome sum of Rs. 1,48,023, to which additions are likely to be made. The appropriation to the Imperial Institute has been Rs. 62,428; to the Victoria Technical Institute Rs. 56,824; and to the Victoria People's Hall Rs. 1,005. The expenditure on the local celebration was Rs. 11,579, and Rs. 3,000 are held in reserve to be applied to rejoicings on the 20th June. The cost of the Address, Casket, and Memorial Volume is estimated at Rs. 8,000. The office charge for stationery and stamps is Rs. 328, and for clerical assistance Rs. 60. The Sheriff's bill for advertisements, the use of chairs, stationery, and postage is Rs. 265. The *Mail* Press has declined to make a charge for printing. A balance remains of Rs. 4,534, the appropriation of which will be duly notified."

The Honourable Mr. HUTCHINS then said:

"YOUR EXCELLENCY AND GENTLEMEN,—There is one point which could not be touched upon in the Report which was compiled, and had to be read by the Honorary Secretary, but which I, as Chairman, find it a pleasing obligation to bring prominently before this Committee. Every one who reads his *Mail*—and who does not?—can bear testimony to the persistent energy and ability with which Mr. Lawson has, during the past two months, laboured to sustain our enthusiasm, and to promote unity and co-operation throughout the Presidency in reference to the Jubilee. (Hear, hear.) No one can know, as I do, how much we are indebted to him. The Volume is entirely his own idea, and his own performance, and I trust it may prove a gratifying success, as I am sure he deserves it should be a success in every respect (applause). From within twenty-four hours of the first meeting of the General Committee when he enabled me to send round circulars to all parts of the Presidency, down to the present moment of his reading the Report, I have found his assistance invaluable. He has grudged neither his time nor his talents; neither the columns of his paper, nor the resources of his establishment; but has lavished them all freely on the great objects we have had in view. (Cheers.) He certainly deserves, and I am sure he will receive, your very cordial thanks, and hearty approbation." (Applause.)

Mr. H. S. THOMAS proposed, and Mr. P. RAMASAWMY CHETTY RAI BAHADUR seconded, that a hearty vote of thanks be given to the Executive Committee for their labours, accompanied by congratulations on their success. The proposition was put to the meeting by His Excellency, and carried amid applause.

Mr. ADAM proposed that a hearty vote of thanks be given to Mr. Hutchins, for his personal efforts as Chairman of the Executive Committee in carrying out the various portions of the Jubilee demonstration. Mr. RUNGANADHA MUDELIJAR RAI BAHADUR seconded the proposition, which was put to the meeting, and carried with acclamation.

Mr. HUTCHINS moved, "That the cordial thanks of the General Committee be given to Mr. Lawson for his great and valuable services." The proposition was seconded by Colonel GUTHRIE, and carried with much enthusiasm. The compliment was acknowledged by Mr. Lawson.

In compliance with the proposition of Mr. Adam, seconded by Mr. Ananda Charlu, it was unanimously resolved to invite the following gentlemen to form themselves into a Committee for the celebration, on the 20th June, of the conclusion of the fiftieth year of Her Majesty's reign, viz.:—

Lieutenant-Colonel G. M. J. Moore; Sir P. S. Ramasawmy Mudelliar, C.I.E.; Messrs. J. Adam; E. Norton; R. G. Orr; W. M. Scharlieb; B. H. Chester; P. Somasundram Chetty; C. Tetheragooloo Naidu Rai Bahadur; P. Ananda Charlu; C. V. Sundram Sastri; M. Veraraghava Chariar; M. Abbaye Naidu, &c. (*Subsequently added*) Messrs. P. Rungiah Naidu; P. Theagaroya Chetty; Hajee Mahomed Ismael Sait; Cowasjee Edulgee Pandy; C. V. Cunniah Chetty; and G. Mahadeva Chetty.

Sir P. S. Ramasawmy Mudelliar proposed that the Report of the Executive Committee be adopted. The Honourable S. Subramanya Aiyar having seconded this proposition, it was put to the meeting by His Excellency, and carried *nem. con.*

His Excellency then said:—

"Gentlemen,—The Executive Committee have crowned their work upon this occasion by bringing to the notice of the General Committee all they have done. If you look back at the proceedings since we last met in this Hall, I do not think that anybody can help feeling that the proceedings have been most remarkable, and that they will make a considerable mark in the history of Madras. The Report which we have heard has dealt with the whole subject, and it will therefore be unnecessary for me to go over the subjects dealt with by them. The Committee and the Report will go down to history, fortunately in a way which will be agreeable to all, and well worthy of the occasion. I am sure that it must be very gratifying to us in Madras to find that we have reflected the general opinion of all the Executive Committees throughout the Mofussil. It is unique in the history of this Presidency, and scarcely in the other Presidencies as well, that one hundred and twenty-nine Executive Committees in the Mofussil should have agreed to every word of an Address on such an occasion as the present. It is highly creditable to the Mofussil Committees that they have all united, and followed the lead of the Presidency town. You have all been so unanimous with respect to the exertions of Mr. Hutchins and Mr. Lawson, that I think I would be carrying coals to Newcastle if I were to say anything more with respect to those exertions. I wish, however, as Governor of this Presidency, to offer those gentlemen my most sincere thanks for the great amount of labour they underwent. They have acted not only like business men, but like prudent men in all the details of the arrangements, and as such they did what business men and prudent men should do. They have gauged public opinion very well and accurately. It is clear from the first meeting down to the last that they have carried the public opinion of thirty-two millions of Her Majesty's subjects heartily with them. I think also that I ought to acknowledge the great munificence of a vast number of private individuals; and as we represent the whole Presidency of Madras, I think we ought not to forget to acknowledge the munificence of a great number of natives in the Mofussil, who have shown munificence of a very great character. I observe that they have shown great patriotism in spending their money in a way which will be beneficial particularly to their fellow subjects. Gentlemen, I think there is no greater proof of the very great progress made during Her Majesty's reign than what we have heard read in the paragraph which alludes to the objects chosen by them to spend their money upon. I observe in that paragraph that some are for

Halls, some for Schools, some for Hospitals, some for Dispensaries, some for Technical Institutions, some for School Prizes, some for Fountains, some for Agricultural Colleges, some for Temple Doors, some for the diversion of water to towns, some for the improvement of the water supply of towns, and some for the re-naming of Schools and public Halls. If any of those great men whose portraits adorn this Hall, and who lived some sixty, seventy, or a hundred years ago, were to hear that the community of Madras had joined in one body for the purpose of promoting objects like those we have just listened to, they would imagine that the Millennium had arrived, and certainly that the country they knew in their time was very different to what we now find around us. I do not think any greater instance of the progress made by the country could have been exhibited by the natives than the promotion of those objects by which the people of Madras have celebrated this Jubilee. They may be said to be illustrative of all the signs of civilisation and advancement by which a rising community can be marked, and therefore, I recognise this fact as one which Her Majesty and every one interested in the country will mark with satisfaction. Now, gentlemen, we have done what we can to express our thanks and acknowledgments to Mr. Hutchins and Mr. Lawson, and to the munificent donors who fed the poor in this city on the day of the celebration. We have also done what we can to express our thanks to those munificent gentlemen who have fed the poor throughout the Presidency. It is proposed to send your Address and Book home. I am sorry that I cannot present them myself in person. There is, however, a gentleman who is going home, and who would take the Address with much appropriateness to the Secretary of State. I refer to Mr. Lawson, the Honorary Secretary, and I am sure if we request him at this meeting to take the Address home and if he undertakes to present it to the Secretary of State, we shall all be very pleased. (Cheers.) Some time ago I was asked to undertake to present it myself, and if you will allow me to delegate that duty, I shall be most happy to delegate it to Mr. Lawson, and I feel certain that it will be received by the Secretary of State with great satisfaction. The Address would have much greater importance attached to it by being sent by a special messenger than if it were merely to be transmitted by me. Under these circumstances I take the liberty of asking Mr. Lawson to undertake the duty. (Hear, hear.) I am sure we shall all be glad to see him on his return here again, and if he likes to take the opportunity of telling us what has happened with respect to the Address we shall be very grateful to him. I hope that what he will do for us will be a happy termination of the good work which he and his colleague, Mr. Hutchins, are engaged in. I hope also that what has taken place with respect to the Jubilee will be a good example to those who may take part in public affairs in future, not only to the governing, but also to the governed. The experience which we have gained upon this occasion will teach us all, that if we endeavour to carry the people of this Presidency with us, we shall always find them loyal and devoted to the Sovereign and the Crown." (Great applause.)

Mr. SOMASUNDRAM CHETTY proposed a vote of thanks to His Excellency the Governor for his conduct in the chair, for the courtesy he had shown during the celebration of the Jubilee, and for the kindness he had evinced since his arrival in Madras to all classes of the people. (Applause.) The Honourable Mr. SUBRAMANYA AIYAR seconded the proposition, which was carried with applause.

His Excellency the Chairman having acknowledged the vote in cordial terms, the meeting terminated with three cheers for Her Majesty.

THE CONCLUSION OF THE CELEBRATION.

MONDAY, the 20th June, the fiftieth anniversary of the accession of Her Majesty, was observed as a general holiday throughout the Presidency; and there were great rejoicings in the City of Madras, which were zealously directed by Colonel G. M. T. Moore the Chairman, Mr. B. H. Chester and Rai Bahadur P. Ananda Charlu the Honorary Secretaries, and the other members of the special Celebration Committee. The Royal Standard was kept flying at the Fort flagstaff from sunrise to sunset, and an Imperial salute was fired at 6 o'clock in the morning by the Royal Artillery from the saluting battery. The town assumed a gala appearance from an early hour, and the weather was propitious.

The decorations on the Mount Road were effective. Messrs. Spencer and Co. had their premises surmounted by large flags, banners, bannerets, and lines of streamers. Messrs. Runganadam and Co.'s premises, and several small shops on the Mount Road, were decorated, some of them displaying mottoes expressive of loyalty to the British Crown, as "God bless the Empress," "God save the Queen," "Long may she reign," "Vivat Regina," and the like. Messrs. Roberts and Co., Messrs. Ponnoosawmy and Co., and Messrs. Duff and Co., had floral arches erected in front of their buildings, on the faces of which were inscribed various mottoes. Messrs. Hawes and Co., and the *Guardian Press* exhibited transparencies, which, when illuminated at night, looked remarkably well. In front of the premises of Messrs. P. Orr and Sons, and Messrs. Moses and Co. there was a pretty arrangement of "Union Jacks." Venetian masts, from the tops of which streamers floated, lined the roadway at short intervals from the Government House bridge to the Round Tannah. In the Wallajah Road, the *Hindu* Office and *National Press*, the *Muslim Press* Office, and the Mohammedan Library were decorated. On approaching Black Town, from the Mount Road side, the premises of Messrs. W. J. Eales and Co. were seen to be decorated with about two hundred large flags and a number of small banners. In the Broadway, Messrs. Calli and Co., the *Madras Times* Office, the Volunteer Guards' Club, Messrs. T. Aroonachella Pillai and Co., and several other houses were decorated with bunting, and had mottoes placed over the entrances. The Steamer Offices on the Beach were decorated, as also were the Custom House and Master Attendant's Office. The vessels in the Harbour were dressed with flags, and the Royal Standard was hoisted at the Master Attendant's Office all day. On Esplanade Row, the premises of Messrs. Fischer and Co. and other firms were decorated.

The poor of the city were fed in large numbers at three centres by Sir Savalay Ramasawmy Modelliar, C.I.E., on behalf of Rajah G. N. Gajapati Rao, of Vizagapatam. About 4,000 poor men, women, and children, assembled in Manickam Moodelly's garden at Tondiarpett, and cooked food and sweetmeats were distributed among them. About 4,500 people were fed at Pereamattoo, in Chengalroya Naick's Orphanage. The Mohammedan poor of the city were also fed at the expense of the Rajah. Over 4,000 people assembled in the compound of the Great Mosque at Triplicane, and each of them received a measure of *pilau*. Owing to the season being the Ramazan the Mohammedans had to fast from sunrise to sunset, except in cases of absolute necessity. The Mohammedan poor therefore assembled at 3 o'clock in the afternoon, and food was distributed among them. The food was not eaten on the spot, but each person, after receiving his dole, retired, to partake of it after sunset. It was close upon 7 o'clock before the distribution of food was over. The Rajah also made arrangements to have prayers for Her Majesty offered in all the temples of the city, and the devotees were fed, and presented with new cloths and small sums of money.

The Jubilee Committee made grants for treats to various schools and to several charitable institutions in Madras, such as the Friend-in-Need Society's home, the Monegar Choultry, the Famine Orphanage, the Civil Orphan Asylum, &c.

A Jubilee Service was held at St. George's Cathedral at 11 o'clock in the forenoon, His Excellency Lord Connemara and Staff being present. The service opened with the processional hymn, 379, "Now thank we all our God," and the form of prayer appointed for the 20th June was read. The proper Canticle was sung instead of the *Venite*, and the proper Psalms were xx., xxi., and ci.; *Te Deum* and *Jubilate*, Porter in D. The Anthem selected was "The Lord is my strength" (Novello). Immediately before the Benediction the National Anthem was sung. At the conclusion of the service the Jubilee Hymn by Dr. Plumptre, Dean of Wells, was sung. The Revds. Alexander Jones, E. Gibson, and J. Brittain officiated, and Mr. W. D. St. Leger presided at the organ. At St. Matthias' Church, Vepery, there was full choral celebration at 7 o'clock in the morning, followed by a solemn *Te Deum*. The Rev. W. H. Hobart officiated. Special Services were also held in the other churches. In the Roman Catholic Cathedrals in Armenian Street and at Mylapore, High Mass was sung, followed by the *Te Deum*, after which the Benediction of the Blessed Sacrament was given. The Very Rev. Father Mayer officiated in Armenian Street, while at St. Thomé, the Bishop of Mylapore conducted the service.

UNVEILING OF THE QUEEN'S STATUE.

In February the Sheriff had intimated that Rajah Gajapati Rao had promised to present the City of Madras with a bronze Statue of Her Majesty, as a Jubilee gift. The statue—a replica of one at Windsor Castle—was executed in London by Mr. Boehm, with permission of Her Majesty, under the supervision of His Grace the Duke of Buckingham and Chandos, former Governor of Madras. Her Majesty is represented as seated on a high-backed Chair of State, wearing a small crown on her head, and bearing a sceptre in her right hand. The statue is placed in the centre of a small plot of ground opposite the south entrance of the Senate House, and to the north of the road between the Senate House and the Revenue Board Office. At the foot of the statue, on a basement of granite, with polished panels (erected under the direction of Honorary Assistant Engineer H. Stephens), is this inscription:—

Victoria, Queen Empress of India.
This statue is erected in token of his
loyalty, respect, and admiration
of Her Majesty's many virtues
by a faithful subject,
Rajah Goday Narrain Gajapatee Rao
of Sree Goday Family
Vizagapatam,
and presented to the City of Madras
in commemoration
of Her Majesty's Jubilee.
Unveiled by
The Right Hon'ble the Lord Connemara,
Governor of Fort St. George, June 20, 1887.

The ground in front of the statue was covered with a carpet and red cloth, and the Chepauk compound was gaily decorated. An arch was erected at the west gate of the Chepauk grounds, and another stood close to the small bridge that spans the Buckingham Canal in front of the Revenue Board Office. This latter arch bore the inscription "Long live our Empress," on its west face, with a painting of the Royal Coat of Arms above it, and the inscription "Victoria, the Light of India," on its east face. Venetian masts, from the tops of which large flags floated in the breeze, lined the roadway on both sides from the west gate of Chepauk, up to the Beach Road; and the South Beach Road from the iron bridge to the Presidency College looked very attractive. Strings of lamps were placed along each side of these roads. Opposite the Cricket Pavilion there was a grand display of bunting. The Revenue Board Offices were also prettily decorated. A Saracenic arch was erected at the gate leading from Government House into Chepauk, and over the top of this arch ran the inscription "The People thank their Governor." Two arches, built after the fashion of the old rock-cut Hindu temples, were placed on the roadway in front of the statue, on either side. The inscriptions on these arches were "God bless the Empress of India," and "Long live our beloved Sovereign."

A guard of honour, consisting of 100 rank and file of the Madras Volunteer Guards under command of Major Sherman, with band and colours, paraded in review order opposite the statue. By 5 P.M. several thousands of people were present. The terraces and verandahs of the Revenue Board and Public Works Offices were crowded. While the people were waiting the arrival of the Governor, pamphlets giving a short sketch of the life of Her Majesty were distributed. Messrs. Calastry Brothers distributed over 2,000 copies of the Queen's photograph among the crowd, while the *Hindu* newspaper circulated an "Extra" containing a poem in Her Majesty's honour. His Excellency the Governor, accompanied by Mr. J. D. Rees, Private Secretary, Major Stewart Mackenzie, Military Secretary, Viscount Marsham and Captain Wingfield, A.D.C.s, and escorted by the Body Guard under Lieutenant Kerrich, arrived at the Government House gate leading to Chepauk at 5.15 P.M., and was met there by a band of native musicians, and a large number of people. A procession then formed and marched towards the place where the statue was erected, the musicians preceding His Excellency's carriage. His Excellency was met at the west arch by Colonel Moore, the Chairman, and the members of the special Celebration Committee. The Guard of Honour presented arms, and the band played. His Excellency having taken his seat on a gilt chair placed at the foot of the statue, Sir Savalay Ramasawmy Mudelliar addressed His Excellency as follows :—

"MY LORD,—In the absence of Rajah Gajapati Rao, the duty of addressing your Lordship on this occasion has devolved upon me. While I consider it a very great honour to be allowed the privilege of taking such an important part in this evening's ceremony, I regret, and I have no doubt that all those present here also regret, that circumstances over which he had no control should have prevented that gentleman from being present on such an auspicious occasion as the celebration of the Jubilee of Her Most Gracious Majesty the Queen Empress of India. My Lord, the name of Rajah Goday Narayana Gajapati Rao is very familiar to the residents of Madras, both European and Native. He was a member of the Legislative Council of this Presidency for several years, and took an active part in all the public movements connected with it. Availing himself of such a rare opportunity as the Jubilee of our beloved Sovereign, the Rajah has undertaken, at his own cost, to get out from England this Statue of Her Imperial Majesty, through the kindness of His Grace the Duke of Buckingham and Chandos, and with the kind permission of Her Majesty, and to present the same to this City of Madras. The Rajah could not have selected a more appropriate object as a tribute from a faithful and loyal subject to undoubtedly the most beloved of all monarchs on the face of the earth, on whose dominion the sun never sets, and whom God has been pleased to ordain as the Ruler of this vast Indian Empire. Without taking up your Lordship's precious time with more preliminary remarks, I offer this Statue of Her Imperial Majesty on behalf of the Donor, and request that your Lordship, as the representative of such an illustrious Sovereign in this part of her dominions, will be graciously pleased to accept the same, and to unveil it."

His Excellency then proceeded to unveil the statue, which was covered with a scarlet cloth. On the statue being unveiled, the people clapped their hands, the Guard of Honour presented arms, and the band played the National Anthem. An Imperial Salute of 101 guns was then fired from the Saluting Battery by the Royal Artillery. Colonel Moore the President of the Municipality, then accepted the statue on behalf of the City. He said :—

"YOUR EXCELLENCY AND SIR S. RAMASAWMY MUDELLIAR,—The interesting ceremony which we have just witnessed places the City of Madras in possession of a lasting memorial of this auspicious day, the Fiftieth Anniversary of Her Most Gracious Majesty's accession to the Throne. For this memorial we are indebted to the liberality of one who has long been honourably connected with this city, Rajah Goday Narrayana Gajapati Rao. This Presidency is fortunate in having within its limits many of the most liberal-hearted and liberal-minded gentlemen of India, and amongst them the donor of this magnificent gift will ever hold an honourable place. And in choosing you, Sir, as his representative to-day, he has done well in selecting one to whom Madras is already indebted for many generous gifts. Madras has ever been pre-eminent in its loyalty and devotion to Her Most Gracious Majesty, and her image and the memory of her good works are already graven on all our hearts; yet are we none the less grateful to have this lasting memorial in our midst—a memorial which will be handed down to unborn generations, and be an abiding testimony of the sympathetic liberality of Rajah Goday Narayana Gajapati Rao. It is needless for me to dilate upon the operations connected with this anniversary. I am confident in only giving expression to the thoughts of all hearts when I say that in none of Her Majesty's world-wide dominions has she more loyal and devoted subjects than in this City and Presidency of Madras. Long may she be spared to rule over the peoples whom she has bound to herself by the strong bonds of undying affection. It now only remains for us, Sir, to accept at your hands this statue, and to beg you to convey the grateful thanks of the citizens of Madras, for his generous and most welcome gift, to Rajah Goday Narayana Gajapati Rao."

His Excellency replied:—

"I can assure you that it has afforded me the most extreme gratification to come down from the Hills to unveil this statue, and to take part in the unofficial and spontaneous festivities which the good people of Madras have thought fit to prepare in commemoration of the completion of the fiftieth year of Her Majesty's reign. It is a time of year at which the Courts of Law are taking their holiday, and when merchants and professional men are away, when many native gentlemen find it too hot to remain at Madras, and when the Government of the country can be more effectively conducted in a cool climate. It is therefore not surprising that we miss many familiar faces that are generally present on public occasions, and I think that H.E. the Viceroy exercised a wise discretion in fixing the date of the official Jubilee at a time when the greatest number of persons, official and unofficial, could attend the celebration. That celebration, we are all glad to remember, in this Presidency, was conducted with brilliant success, and in a measure which did great credit to the Presidency, and made us all proud to be connected with Madras. From a telegram in the papers I observe that the Prince of Wales has expressed himself much gratified with the interest shown by the Presidency in the Imperial Institute; and your respected townsman, Mr. C. A. Lawson, has been very cordially received by the Secretary of State, and I understand that the Address and the Casket which your

Committee confided to his care will be duly received in person by Her Gracious Majesty. I have already had occasion to speak of the ability with which the Committee presided over by Mr. Hutchins performed its labours, and how much the Presidency was indebted to Mr. Lawson, the Secretary, for his valuable services; and upon this occasion we must not forget that the Committee, recognising a very generally expressed wish, set apart a sum of money out of the General Fund for defraying the expenses of any festivities which might take place to-day. It is a very happy coincidence that the presentation of this statue to the town of Madras should synchronise with this day of general and spontaneous rejoicing. No more appropriate ceremony could have been chosen to form the central event of this remarkable occasion. Our official Jubilee proclaimed to the world by one unanimous Address that 30 millions of people joined with the rest of India in expressing their loyalty to the throne, and this statue of Her Majesty will be a lasting symbol of the respect and affection entertained for the person of the Sovereign by the people of Madras, and of their admiration of those great qualities and virtues which have adorned her life. At the official Jubilee we were reminded of the great progress the nation had made during the last fifty years. We dwelt on the great facts that our knowledge and our power had expanded; our literature had been brought within the reach of the poor and humble; our commerce had increased enormously, and our means of communication extended beyond the imagination of the last generation, while the limits of the Empire had vastly widened, and we thanked Almighty God for the blessings which had attended the reign. But to-day we are brought face to face with the very image of our Sovereign; and by the generosity of an eminent fellow subject, and the genius of a distinguished artist, are vividly reminded of the personality of that Queen who reigns in love over the hearts of her countless subjects. She is no stranger to her people, for no Sovereign ever laid bare for the benefit of her children the details of her private life in the way the Queen has done. We know from her private Journals not only what she is in Council, in times of State difficulty and danger, but we know what she is in the intimacy of private life, when she is surrounded by those most near and dear to her. And we know also the sympathy which she ever shows to those who are in suffering, and who have, like her, experienced the bitterness of affliction. In these personal qualities Her Majesty shows a noble example, not only to Sovereigns, but also to her Viceroys and Governors who wield power in her name. She exercises a personal influence never before possessed by a human being. The Journals of the Queen also show us her kindness of heart for all around her, and her love for everything beautiful, elevated, and good, combined with a deep and unaffected piety. And now, gentlemen, allow me to say a word about this beautiful statue. As a work of art, I believe it may be said to possess great merit. It is the work of a man of genius, Mr. Boehm, who has the reputation of being one of the most eminent artists in the Empire, and I think the generous Donor may be congratulated upon the care that has been taken in the execution of his wishes. His Grace the Duke of Buckingham, who continues to take the greatest interest in everything connected with this Presidency, has been most anxious that it should arrive safely, and receive a worthy site. He will be most glad, I am sure, to read the account of this ceremony. I hope the public will feel pleased with the locality selected. For myself, I think the front of the Senate House an appropriate place, a building dedicated to learning, progress, science, and civilisation, the characteristics which have especially marked the reign of Queen Victoria. Now, gentlemen, what shall I say of the public spirit, loyalty, and generosity which have induced Rajah Gajapati Rao to make this munificent gift to the Town of Madras? In taking this step Rajah Gajapati Rao is only acting consistently with his former life, and in conformity with the traditions of his family. The Rajah's grandfather, more than 100 years ago, earned the thanks of the Government of Fort Saint George for his zeal and assistance. Subsequently the same Rajah distinguished himself by various acts of charity to his fellow-countrymen and neighbours of the Vizagapatam, Ganjam, and Rajahmundry Districts, in which many a tank and well still bear his name. The Rajah's uncle, Godey Surya Prakasa Rao, was also a man of much distinction, not only in military matters, but in encouraging agriculture and horticulture in the neighbourhood in which he lived, and reports connected with Vizagapatam bear eloquent testimony to the improvements in agriculture, and in the general condition of the villages which the example of this gentleman very widely inspired. The Rajah's father, Goday Sooria Narayan Rao, followed in the footsteps of his father, founded various charitable institutions, and during the famine of 1833 fed a large number of poor in the neighbourhood of Nellore. He also contributed largely to various public works, and established an Observatory with a view of assisting the shipping on the coast. Rajah Gajapati Rao therefore is not only eminent for his good deeds, but also for the distinguished ancestry of which he is the worthy representative. I hope that the Municipal Commissioners of Madras who are now in possession of the statue of the Queen will take care that time deals lightly with it, and that it will be cared for and protected, not only as a work of art, but as the statue of her who, from the day she assumed the crown, determined to be good."

The son of Sir Savalay Ramaswamy Mudelliar now presented His Excellency with a bouquet of flowers in a handsome silver holder.

Colonel Moore read the following congratulatory telegram to Her Majesty, which had been adopted by the Madras and Mofussil Committees, and despatched to England:—

"We, your Majesty's loyal subjects in the Presidency of Madras, humbly desire to offer our congratulations to your Majesty on the fiftieth anniversary of your Majesty's Accession to the throne of this Empire. That your Majesty may be blessed with long life is the heartfelt prayer of your Majesty's loyal, affectionate, and devoted subjects."

Colonel Moore then said:—

"YOUR EXCELLENCY, LADIES, AND GENTLEMEN,—There yet remains one duty for me to perform—the duty of thanking Your Excellency for your presence in our midst to-day. The kindly response you have made to the wishes of the Committee for the celebration of the fiftieth anniversary of Her Most Gracious Majesty's accession to the throne, in leaving the cool and pleasant heights of your summer residence, to brave the burning heat of your Presidency Town at this most trying period of the year, but rivets another link in that chain of gratitude and affection by which you have so quickly bound to yourself those whom it is your high honour to rule over. Next to the approval of one's own conscience, perhaps the grateful appreciation of one's fellow-men is the greatest reward for self-denying labour. Your Excellency must possess the former, and it is now my most pleasing duty to assure you of the latter. I take this first opportunity, my Lord, of offering you, in the name of the people of Madras, their heartiest congratulations on the marks of her favour which Her Gracious Majesty has been pleased to bestow upon you, and to express the hope that you and Lady Connemara may long be spared to enjoy those well-merited honours. In the name of the Committee and of the people of Madras, I thank Your Excellency for performing this ceremony."

His Excellency thanked Colonel Moore for the cordial terms in which that gentleman had spoken of himself and Lady Connemara, and said that he sincerely hoped that the honour that Her Gracious Majesty had been pleased to bestow upon him would give Lady Connemara and himself more power and influence for doing good. It would be his utmost endeavour, as long as he was Governor, to show that he was not altogether unworthy of holding the place which Her Majesty had been kind enough to confer upon him.

After the ceremony was over, large crowds of people collected round the statue and remained there till darkness set in. The roadway was then lighted by strings of lamps on either side. The illuminations on the Mount Road were very good. The roadway from the Round Tannah to the Government House bridge and the Napier Park gate was lit with strings of little lamps, on both sides of the road. The Maharajah of Vizianagram's Fountain at the Round Tannah was brilliantly illuminated with a large number of variously coloured lamps. The roads from Government House bridge to the Fort, round by the west as far as the Broadway to the north, and the Central Station bridge to the west, were made bright with small lamps placed on poles fixed in the ground. The Chepauk grounds and the South Beach Road were also lit up. A few places of business on the Mount Road and Wallajah Road were illuminated. In Black Town Messrs. Eales and Co.'s premises were the centre of attraction. Over 2,000 lamps were used in illuminating the building, and the artistic arrangement of the red, white, and green lamps (the Austrian colours), produced a grand effect. Several other places of business in town were illuminated, as also were numerous private residences. The native inhabitants of Black Town generally had their premises lighted as during the Karthigai festival. In Mylapore, the St. Thomé Cathedral, the Roman Catholic Bishop's residence, the Seminary buildings, and numerous other buildings were illuminated.

The proceedings of the day concluded with a musical entertainment at the Banqueting Hall, which was honoured by the presence of His Excellency the Governor, and was attended by about 500 persons.

THE CELEBRATION IN THE PROVINCES OF MADRAS.

ADIRAMPATNAM (TANJORE).

The population of Adirampatnam, "The City of the great hero Rama," with its hamlets, is 9,755, of whom about seven-eighths are Mohammedans and the remainder Hindus. There are also a few Native Christians. The inhabitants are largely engaged in sea fisheries. The only Europeans in the town are the Officers of the Salt Department. An extensive salt marsh in the vicinity produces salt of superior quality. The town possesses a Local Union Board (recently formed), the Chairman of which is the Superintendent of Sea Customs. Rice in very considerable quantities is shipped to Ceylon. There is also a good trade in cocoa-nuts, and salt fish. The Salt Factory supplies a large portion of the Tanjore District with salt.

Jubilee Committee.—Messrs. F. W. MONTAGUE STONE, *Chairman*; M. SUBBARAYA PILLAY, *Secretary*; VARADARAJULU NAIDU; IYASSU NAINAR PILLAY; KHADIR MUHIDIEN MARIKAYAR; KAYAROGANA TEVAR; S. M. RAJANAIGAM PILLAY; RAMALINGA PILLAY; and others.

At sunrise on the 16th February the peons of the Salt Department were paraded. A few swivels had been obtained from neighbouring Hindu temples, and an Imperial salute of 101 guns was fired, in the intervals of which the Salt peons fired a *feu de joie*. Between the rounds a band of native musicians played the National Anthem. After the *feu de joie* a "march past" was gone through by the peons, and three hearty cheers were given for the Queen Empress, in which the large crowd present enthusiastically joined. Between 10 A.M. and 2 P.M. *pujahs* were performed in the Hindu temples; prayers were offered in the mosques; and a special Service for Christians was held in the bungalow of the Salt Inspector by a Catechist of the S.P.G. Mission, to invoke the blessing of the Almighty upon Her Majesty. The poor of the town, numbering 270 Mohammedans, 11 Brahmins, 400 other Hindus, and 50 Native Christians, were then fed. Great enthusiasm was displayed by the people, and blessings were invoked on Her Majesty. At 3.35 P.M. a troupe of gymnasts performed, and sports, consisting of racing, wrestling, &c., for which prizes were given, and which caused great merriment, were held. At about 8 P.M. there was a display of fireworks, which lasted about an hour. At its conclusion three cheers were called for Her Majesty, and were most heartily given by the people assembled. The proceedings terminated with a nautch, followed by a distribution of sandal and *pan supari*. The Presidencial Address was adopted.

ALAMUR (GODAVERI).

The population of Alamur is 2,455. There is a Local Fund School. Cloths of a coarse description are manufactured here.

Jubilee Committee.—Messrs. MANDAVITTI VENKATAPAYYA, Sub-Registrar, *Chairman*; SINKARAMANCHI NARASANNA PUNTALU, *Secretary*; NEKKANTI RAMAYYA; BALUSU VENKATAKRISHNIAH; S. LAKSHMANA ROW PUNTALU; M. NAGAYYA; A. SESHAGIRI ROW PUNTALU; BALUSU SUBBARAYUDU; and fourteen others.

A prettily decorated Pandal had been erected in a central position in the town, and here large numbers of people assembled to take part in the festivities of the day. The poor of all classes were fed, and a nautch party was held. The Hindu god was taken in procession, and followed by about 2,000 persons. At night the streets were illuminated, and there was a beautiful display of fireworks. *Abishekams* and *archanas* were performed in the several local temples for the continuance of the Queen's reign. The Committee resolved that, after defraying the expenses of the local festivities, and contributing to the Presidencial Casket, Memorial Volume, and Technical Institute at Madras, the balance of the subscriptions to the local Jubilee Fund should be given to the school at Ramachendrapur, the head-quarters of the taluk, and that the school should in future be known as the "Queen's Jubilee Middle School." The Presidencial Address was adopted.

ALVAR-TIRUNAGARI (TINNEVELLY).

Alvar-Tirunagari, an ancient town situated in the District of Tinnevelly, is about 18 miles from Palamcottah. It has a population of 5,956, namely, 5,799 Hindus, 16 Mohammedans, and 141 Christians. It has a large Temple devoted to Alvar. The town is one of the richest in the District. It contains a High School belonging to the S.P.G. Mission, Nazareth, and several Pial schools.

At about 4 o'clock on the afternoon of the 16th February, all the students of the High School, dressed in their best clothes, marched in procession, accompanied by an elephant, flags, and music. The procession was headed by the Head Master of the School, a graduate of the Madras University, wearing his gown and hood. Jubilee banners of the school were placed upon the elephant. The procession as it went on was joined by large crowds of people, and after going through the principal streets, it halted in the Mantapam in front of the Temple, where an address expatiating upon the merits of British Administration, and especially upon the good qualities of Her Majesty, was read in Tamil. The Sub-Magistrate made a long speech upon the same subjects, and a distribution of sandal, *pan supari*, rose-water, fruit, &c., took place. The meeting broke up with cheers for Her Majesty. At night *abishekams* and *archanas* were performed on a grand scale, and there was a torch-light procession of the god Authinathar. The temple and streets were illuminated, and there was a display of fireworks.

AMALAPURAM (GODAVERI).

The population of Amalapuram, "The Sinless City," is 8,623, including 8,176 Hindus, 440 Mohammedans, and 7 Christians. There are three Schools in which English and Telugu are taught—the Local Fund High School, the Hindu High School, and the Mission Middle School. Besides these there are two Girls' Schools, the Mission and the Local Fund, and two Results system Primary Schools. Cocoa-nut, betel nut, paddy and other grains, fruits, &c., are exported largely. Cocoa-nut oil is produced here. Various cloths are manufactured.

Jubilee Committee.—Messrs. Kokkonda Venkata Narasana Puntalu, *Chairman*; G. Jaganada Rao Puntalu; Ivanki Venkataramayya; Peri Virayya; Ivvagari Ramabhadrudu; Kasa Jogayya; Kanchella Narayana Naidu; Bodi Tirayya; and fifteen others.

On the morning of the 16th February rice and money were distributed to 150 poor people, and cloths were presented to 60 lame and blind persons, in a Pandal which had been erected in front of the temple in the Agraharam. The Pandal was beautifully decorated. The chief residents of the town met there at about 2 P.M., when there was a nautch, and a distribution of *pan supari*. At 5 P.M. prayers were offered in all the temples for Her Majesty's health, prosperity, and long life. At 7 P.M. there was a torchlight procession of the gods, and as it proceeded fireworks were let off at intervals. Over 5,000 people from Amalapuram and the adjoining villages took part in the procession. There were two nautch parties at night. The whole town, and all the villages in the taluk were illuminated as on the Deepavali festival. The procession returned to the Pandal at 1 A.M., when there was another nautch party, followed by a distribution of *pan supari*. A grand display of fireworks followed, and the festivities wound up at 4 A.M. At about 3 P.M. on the 17th the people again met at the Pandal. A nautch was held, *pan supari* was distributed, and the proceedings closed at 6 P.M. with hearty cheers for Her Majesty. The permanent Memorial of the event is to take the form of a "Chuttram." The Presidencial Address was adopted.

ANANTAPUR (TOWN).

Anantapur, or more accurately Handé Anantapuram, was originally called Anantasagaram. It was built A.D. 1364 by Chikkappa Wadeyar, Dewan to the Rajah of Vijiyanagar, to whom the site was granted in consideration of military services, and in whose family it remained till Hyder Ali seized it in 1775. It was the seat of Poligars until 1800, when Colonel (afterwards Sir Thomas) Munro, on the Districts being ceded, chose it for his residence, and for many years it was the Head Quarters of the ceded Districts. The place became the Head Quarters of the Sub-Division in 1830;

and in 1869, when a redistribution of the Division was made, the Sub-Collector was removed to Gooty. In 1882 the District of Bellary was divided into two, and Anantapur became the Head Quarters of a District of that name. It lies 62 miles to the south-east of Bellary, and contains 1,133 houses, with a population of 4,907, namely Hindus 3,488, Mohammedans 1,407, and 12 Christians. Being the Head Quarters of the District it contains the Chief Police and Magisterial Courts, a Sub-Jail, a Dispensary, the Municipal High School, Post Office, Telegraph Office, the Sub-Engineer's Office, and a Travellers' Bungalow. There is also a District Board, a Taluk Board, and Municipal Council. There is a large open square in the heart of the town called Robertson Square, with a beautiful Mantapam in its centre. Rice, cotton goods, grain, and vegetables form the chief articles of commerce.

Jubilee Committee.—Messrs. R. Tevenitmal Chetti, *Chairman*; F. A. Nicholson; T. M. Thomson; Captain Jackson; S. Kandaya Pillai; S. Vedoji Row; A. Durgachella Mudelliar; B. Hanumantha Row; and thirty-four others.

A large Pandal had been erected on the site of the proposed "Victoria Jubilee Park," which is to be the local permanent memorial of the happy event. A programme of the festivities had been circulated by the Committee, both in English and the vernacular of the district. The inhabitants of the town and district were invited to take part in the festivities, and they were requested to observe the 16th February as a local festival, and to plant a tree, or a number of trees, to be called the "Queen's Tree," or the "Queen's Tope," respectively, in commemoration of Her Majesty's Jubilee. The streets were decorated, and arches covered with evergreens were erected in many places. At 7 A.M. a deputation of the Committee waited on Mrs. Nicholson, the wife of the Collector, and requested her to lay the foundation stone of the proposed Park. She consented, and was conducted in procession from her bungalow to the entrance into the town, near the bridge on the Bellary road, where the party was met by a band of native musicians, and about 2,000 people. Opposite the Collector's Office a large Pandal had been erected. Here the procession halted, and the Presidencial Address to Her Majesty was read, and adopted. It was then handed to Mr. F. A. Nicholson, the Collector and Magistrate, as Her Majesty's chief representative of the district. The Police presented arms and fired a *feu de joie*, and the people gave three enthusiastic cheers for Her Majesty. The National Anthem—of which many copies had been distributed—was then sung by the boys of the Schools. The procession continued its march, and arrived at the Pandal at the site of the proposed Park at 8.15 A.M. The ceremony of laying the foundation stone of the Park was performed at 9.15 A.M. by Mrs. Nicholson, after which she planted the first tree, amid loud cheering. The children of the Girls' School sang a Telugu song, and some Pundits recited Canarese and Tamil verses, which they had composed in honour of the occasion. The Head Master of the Municipal High School gave a brief account of the many blessings that had been vouchsafed to India during Her Majesty's reign, after which there was a distribution of *pan supari*, flowers, and rose-water. At 10 A.M. Mr. and Mrs. Nicholson were conducted home in procession as far as the Collector's Office, where the assembly dispersed. The feeding of the poor commenced at 11 o'clock, and upwards of 500 people were fed, and most of them were also supplied with cloths. At noon Special Services were held in the temples, and soon after *prasadams* were distributed. At 3.30 P.M. there were sports, which attracted a very large crowd. Prizes were awarded to the winners. At 6.30 P.M. sweetmeats were distributed to the children of all the Schools, and at 7 P.M. there was a grand display of fireworks. The town was prettily illuminated at nightfall. The prayers and processions in the temples continued till very late in the night. The sports were continued on the 17th, on which date the local Theosophical Society fed the poor, who numbered about the same as on the previous day. The proceedings throughout were marked by great enthusiasm. The local permanent memorial of the occasion—namely, the "Victoria Jubilee Park," will include a Reading Room and Library, a Playground, and a small Economic Museum of the District. It is also intended to provide a large reservoir of water for bathing and swimming purposes, and to construct one or two large wells for drinking purposes. The site of the old Fort, adjoining Robertson Square, has been selected for the Park, and the Committee hope to have the Park opened on the 20th June.

ANJENGO (MALABAR).

This town is situated within the Native State of Travancore, but is under British jurisdiction, and is included in the District of Malabar. It was once a place of considerable mercantile importance, but is now only a fishing town. A Sub-Magistrate is stationed here. The East India Company occupied the site by permission of a petty local Chief, and erected a fortified Factory here in 1695. The chief of the Factory was also second in Council in Bombay. Robert Orme, the Indian Historian, was born here in 1728, his father being a physician in the Company's service.

At 6 o'clock on the morning of the 16th February a Royal salute was fired in the Cutcherry compound. The feeding of the poor commenced a little after 8 A.M., and nearly 800 poor people were entertained. Mr. Kurryan, the Chairman of the Jubilee Committee, explained to the poor before their repast, why they were fed on that day, and why there was cause for rejoicing. At 4 P.M. the people assembled in a grandly decorated Pandal, which had been erected at the beach, opposite to St. Peter's Church. Mr. Kurryan read aloud the Presidencial Address to Her Majesty, both in English and in Malayalam. He explained in both languages the importance of the Jubilee, and enumerated the blessings India had derived during the long reign of her good and noble Queen. The Address was received with hearty cheers. A procession was now formed, which marched from the beach to the site fixed for the erection of the "Victoria Jubilee Chuttrum," which will be the local permanent memorial of the happy event. The Anjengo band headed the procession. On arrival at the scene the foundation stone was laid by Mr. Kurryan with much ceremony. Fifty guns—a gun for each year of Her Majesty's reign—were then fired, and the procession returned to the beach, where arrangements had been made for sports. The sports, which afforded much amusement to the assembled crowds, commenced at 4.15 P.M., and lasted for nearly two hours. At 8 P.M. there was a display of fireworks. Three Native dramatic performances,—one Christian, and two Kathakali dramas,—were provided. More than 5,000 persons were present to witness the theatricals. Sports were held on the following morning at the beach. At 4.30 P.M. a small regatta took place, which created great excitement. Soon after 7 P.M. there was a grand display of fireworks on the beach, which wound up with the firing of fifty guns from the Cutcherry compound. Dramatic performances then commenced. The town was illuminated on both nights.

ARCOT (NORTH ARCOT).

Arcot, a town of great historical interest, lies on the southern bank of the Palar River. It was once the capital of the Carnatic under the Nababs of Arcot. Some of its ruined buildings bear witness to its former greatness. The town was occupied by Clive in 1751. The following public offices, &c., are located here:—2nd Class Taluk Cutcherry; Offices of the Inspector of Police D. P. W. Supervisor; Local Fund Overseer; Sub-Registrar; and Forester. The town contains a Middle School, and several Normal and other Schools; a Local Fund Dispensary; and Union Office. The population numbers about 10,000, consisting chiefly of Hindus and Mohammedans. Lace is the principal article of manufacture.

On the 16th February *abishekams* were performed in all the temples, and prayers were offered in the mosques for Her Majesty. From 10 to 3 o'clock nearly 1,000 poor people were fed, and 100 of them were clothed. At 4 P.M. a public meeting was held in the School House, which was admirably decorated for the occasion, and a native band was in attendance. The proceedings opened with a nautch, followed by a musical entertainment. An interesting narrative of the life of Her Majesty was then read aloud in English, at the close of which the National Anthem was sung. Mr. Kamal Singh, Secretary of the Jubilee Committee, then made a short speech in English, and dwelt upon the innumerable benefits the people of India had derived during the long reign of Queen Victoria. Messrs. Soondriah and Vijia Ragava Charlu, explained to the audience in Tamil the meaning and obligations of loyalty, and why it was that they were invited to celebrate the Jubilee in honour of Her Majesty. The school children were treated to fruits and sugar, and alms were distributed to poor Brahmins. At 8 P.M. there was a distribution of flowers and *pan supari*, and rose-water was sprinkled. The whole assembly then formed a procession, and, headed by the Tahsildar, marched through the principal streets of the town. Every house was illuminated, and fireworks were let off at intervals. The proceedings terminated shortly before midnight. They were characterised by the utmost enthusiasm. The Presidencial Address was adopted.

ARIVALUR (TRICHINOPOLY).

By 10 o'clock on the 16th February the town had been elaborately decorated, and several processions of Hindu gods, accompanied by large crowds, went around the town, which presented a very attractive appearance. Rice was served to the poor. In the evening the *élite* of the community met at the site chosen for the "Victoria Jubilee Choultry," the permanent memorial to be erected in this place. The foundation stone was laid amidst strains of native music, and cheers for the Queen Empress. A bottle was placed underneath the stone, containing current silver and copper coins, and a paper with the following record:—

"On Wednesday the 16th February, 1887, in the fiftieth year of Her Majesty Queen Victoria's reign, this foundation stone of the 'Victoria Jubilee Choultry' is laid. The humble building over this foundation is designed to mark the deep loyalty of the people, and the grateful appreciation of the manifold blessings they enjoy under Her Majesty's benign sway. May the God of all nations and creeds bless Her and Her Royal Household with long life and prosperity, and Her wide Empire with peace and contentment."

At the conclusion of this ceremony, sandal, sugar, and betel were distributed to those present. The company then marched in procession to the Kothandaramaswami's temple, where there was a musical entertainment and banquet, provided by S. Prasanna Regunatha Dorai Avergal. At the same time service was performed in the Christian churches, which were beautifully decorated. There were processions and prayers in the Mohammedan mosque. At 10 P.M. the temple processions began, and the town was beautifully illuminated. The gods of the two important Siva and Vishnu temples went together in procession. The festivities continued till 1 A.M.

On the same day the construction of the "Victoria Jubilee Tank" at Jeyamkondasholapuram was begun, and the foundation stone was laid of the "Victoria Jubilee School," at Kilapalur.

ARKONAM (NORTH ARCOT).

The rising town of Arkonam is the chief junction on the Madras Railway, and the northern terminus of the South Indian Railway. Its population is 3,280; of whom 2,575 are Hindus, 419

Mohammedans, and 296 Christians, including Europeans and Eurasians. The town contains the station buildings of the Madras and South India Railway Companies, Sub-Magistrate's and Sub-Registrar's Offices, Police Station, Post Office, Choultry, &c., Mission School Buildings, a Mosque, a Church, &c. Education is entirely in the hands of the Scotland Mission, which maintains a first grade Middle School with 106 boys, a large Primary School with 134 boys, and a Girls' School attended by 64 girls. There is also a Block School for station-masters under the supervision of the Telegraph Engineer of the Madras Railway, who resides here. The Railway Workshops and Offices give work to above a fourth of the population. Agriculture and merchandise form the chief occupation of the remainder. The town has no local manufactures. Rice, ground nuts, and indigo are the principal exports. Salt, liquor, piece goods, and kerosine oil are the chief imports.

The town assumed a holiday appearance on the 16th February. A large and handsome Pandal had been erected in front of the Choultry; and arches were placed at the four entrances into the town. The streets were decorated with flags and *thoranams*; and the houses were whitewashed, decorated, and illuminated. At 6 A.M. a band of musicians played at the Pandal; at 6.30 A.M. the Railway Volunteers paraded, fired a *feu de joie*, and then marched to the rifle range, where they competed for the "Jubilee Prizes" for which a collection had been made among themselves. At 8 A.M. a special Thanksgiving Service was conducted at the Protestant Native Church, and Mass was said in the Roman Catholic Chapel. At 10 o'clock musicians marched through the streets of the town. Between 10 A.M. and 2 P.M. above 800 poor people were fed, and some of them also received cloths. At 5 P.M. the teachers and boys of the Middle School marched in procession from their school, with music and banners, bearing the mottoes "*Vivat Regina et Imperatrix*," "God bless our Gracious Empress," &c. On the way they were joined by the teachers and children of the Primary and Girls' Schools. On arriving at the Pandal, where the chief residents of Arkonam were already assembled, the Middle School boys sang a Tamil lyric, which was followed by a *Mungalam*, sung by one of the native gentlemen present. A procession was then formed, with the school children in front, headed by the band. At 3.30 P.M. it started from the Pandal, moved on in good order over the long iron bridge that spans the Madras Railway and South Indian Railway lines, and arrived at the military camping ground, where preparations had been made for sports and fireworks. The sports commenced at 5 P.M., with much enthusiasm, several local gentlemen having offered extra prizes. The school children took part in the sports, which included chatty race, all-four race, three-legged race, wheelbarrow race, tug-of-war, &c. At 6.30 P.M., after sweets and fruits had been distributed to the children, the boys of the Middle School sang the National Anthem, the whole assembly standing. The fireworks then commenced, and lasted till 8 o'clock. There were upwards of 3,000 people of all ages present. At the conclusion of the fireworks the procession was reformed, and, returning by the same route, halted under the triumphal arch between the station and the town. After giving three hearty cheers for the Queen Empress, the assembly dispersed at 8.30 P.M. The Presidencial Address was adopted and signed.

ARNI (NORTH ARCOT).

Arni has a population of 4,812, namely, Hindus 4,177, Mohammedans 536, Christians 26, and "others" 73. It was formerly an important military station. It was stormed by Clive in 1751, after he had repulsed Raja Sahib from Arcot; and in 1782, under its walls, Sir Eyre Coote defeated the combined forces of Lally and Hyder Ali. It is now the centre of a large trade which forms the chief occupation of the inhabitants. There is a ruined Fort here, in which are located the offices of the Deputy Collector, the D. W. P. Sub-Divisional Officer, and the District Munsiff, &c., with a Sivite Temple in the north-west corner, dedicated to Kylasanadaswami. The muslin manufactured at this town is of exceptional excellence.

Jubilee Committee.—Messrs M. G. VISWANADHA SASTRIAR, RAO SAHIB, *Chairman*; B. S. SESHA AIYANGAR, *Secretary*; A. VYDINADHA AIYAR; W. P. CORNELIUS PILLAI; LINGAPPA NAYUDU; and EMAVATHUILA SHERIFF SAHIB.

The approach of the Jubilee was proclaimed to the people by beat of tom-tom throughout the town and the surrounding villages on the 13th, 14th, and 15th February; and, on the morning of the 16th, a messenger went round inviting the residents to decorate their houses and streets with *thoranams*, and to illuminate the town at night. 280 poor Mohammedans and a few Christians were fed in the forenoon, and rice was distributed among 1,420 Hindu poor. At 3 P.M. on the 16th the Kylasanadaswami god was taken to the Suria Kanta Tank, and floated in procession three times around it, attended by music and nautch girls. On the completion of the third round, the god was carried back, in the midst of a great crowd, to the temple in the Fort, the whole of which was splendidly illuminated, and a grand pyrotechnic display then took place in front of the Sub-Magistrate's Office. Then followed the distribution of *pan supari*, and the sprinkling of rose-water; and the whole assembly shouted "Long live our Gracious Queen Victoria." The Presidencial Address was adopted and signed. On the night of the 17th a floating festival was celebrated in the Streenivasa Perumal temple, in the presence of upwards of 6,000 people.

ARUPUKOTA (MADURA).

Arupukota has a population of about 10,831; of whom 10,365 are Hindus, 309 Mohammedans, and 157 Christians. It has about 1,928 houses. A good trade is carried on in cotton. It is a rising town, and has a Sub-Registrar's Office, a Post Office, an American Church, a Local Fund Dispensary, and about four Schools receiving grants from the Local Fund. The town was constituted a Union under the Local Fund Act. Weaving is carried on to a considerable extent.

Jubilee Committee.—Messrs. M. D. Manikam Pillay, *Chairman*, the Rev. Y. S. Taylor, *Secretary*; Mahomed Buran Said; Ambalam Sami Naicker; Varrappa Naicker; Patham Perumal Naicker; Nallaperomal Pillai; Muthalagu Pillai; and four others.

At daybreak on the 16th February the town assumed a very gay appearance, being dressed in flags and bunting. *Thoranams* and festoons overhung every street. A large number of the poor were fed in different places. Triumphal arches had been erected in the main streets by the people of different castes. Each of these arches bore an appropriate inscription in Tamil. A spacious Pandal had been erected in front of the Police Station, where a large number of people assembled to do honour to Her Majesty. A portrait of Her Majesty was placed in a conspicuous part of the Pandal, and was decorated with garlands of flowers. Native music played. The Rev. S. Taylor, the Secretary, made an interesting speech, in which he dwelt on the good government of Her Majesty, and the benefits derived by India from it. Three cheers were given for Her Majesty, and the meeting terminated with a distribution of sandal, betel, and sugar. The Presidential Address was adopted.

ASKA (GANJAM).

This town, with 3,909 inhabitants, is the head-quarters of the Zemindary of the same name. It possesses a Subordinate Court, a Police Station, Post Office, &c. It lies in a fertile tract of country, planted for the most part with sugar cane. The local sugar-works of Mr. Mincahn employ about 1,000 hands. All the latest improvements in machinery have been introduced from Europe.

Rice and cloths were distributed to 500 poor persons on the 16th February. Mr. Maluqdar Sundara Row fed 1,000 ryots. Special prayers were said in all the temples, the Roman Catholic church, and in the Mohammedan mosque, all of which were brilliantly illuminated. The house-owners illuminated the streets. In a large Pandal erected for the occasion, about 5,000 people assembled, and Messrs. Viswanathaiyar, Gopalrow, and Jaganadha Choudari addressed the meeting in English, Telugu, and Oriya. The Presidencial Address was read and adopted, and the Police fired three volleys, after which *pan supari*, fruits, and scents were distributed; and cheers were given for Her Majesty. There was a grand display of fireworks, and nautches were held throughout the night. On the 17th the Queen's portrait, in a beautiful frame of artificial flowers, accompanied by the temple gods, was carried in procession with music through the streets. A large crowd followed the procession, after which nautches were held. Several prisoners were released from the Subsidiary Jail.

ATMAKUR (KURNOOL).

The population of this town is 3,498; of whom 2,525 are Hindus, 887 Mussalmans, and 86 Native Christians. There are a Deputy Tahsildar's Office, and two Local Fund Vernacular Schools, one being Hindu, and the other Mohammedan. The town carries on a brisk trade in grain and timber.

Jubilee Committee.—Messrs. R. SUBBA RAO, *Chairman*; R. KONETI AIYAR, B.A., *Secretary*; HAJI KHAJA HUSSAIN SAHIB; M. SUBBARAYA MUDELLIAR; D. RAMA RAO; KISHEN SING; PITCHAYYA; NAGI REDDI; SARABHAYA; SANJIVI REDDI; MAHOMED MIRAM SAHIB; and MAHOMED KASIM SAHIB.

The whole of the streets were dressed with evergreens, and flags were displayed on which the words "Jubilee," "God save the Queen," &c., were conspicuous. Several triumphal arches had been erected in the chief thoroughfares. The Deputy Tahsildar's Cutcherry, the Police Station, the Sub-Registrar's Office, the Local Fund Hospital, and the Choultry were tastefully decorated. The Chairman of the Jubilee Committee sat at the Choultry in the forenoon of the 16th February, distributing food, cloths, and copper coins to the poor. *Abishekams* and *archanas* were performed in the Hindu temples, and prayers for Her Majesty were said in the mosques and churches. At 4 P.M. a Durbar of the leading inhabitants of the station was held in the open *maidan* opposite the Deputy Tahsildar's Cutcherry. About 1,500 people of all castes and creeds were present. Mr. R. Subba Rao, who was voted to the chair, addressed the assembly in Telugu on the advantages of British rule. Haji Khaja Hussain Sahib made a speech in Hindustani to the same effect. Mr. Ramasawmy Aiyangar sang some Telugu verses, which he had composed for the occasion. The boys of the Mohammedan School sang a Hindustani song, composed by Haji Khaja Hussain Sahib. The boys of both schools also recited several vernacular stanzas. Next followed wrestling matches, and acrobatic performances. There was a parade of the Police force of the station. Brahmin and Mohammedan priests invoked blessings on Her Majesty, and on the Royal family. The Presidential Address was adopted and signed. The National Anthem was sung in Telugu by the assembly, and the Durbar terminated with three hearty cheers for the Empress. The temple god, "Rama," was taken through the streets in procession, with music, &c. A "Choultry" is to be built at the town in commemoration of the Jubilee.

In several villages adjoining Atmakur, in the taluk of the same name, the event was celebrated with much enthusiasm.

ATUR (SALEM).

The population is 8,334, residing in 1,617 houses. There are 7,289 Hindus, 810 Mohammedans, and 235 Christians. The town has a Fort which was once of some importance, as it commands the pass from Salem to Sankaridrug. The chief trade of the place is in paddy, which is exported in large quantities to Salem. The town contains the offices of a Tahsildar, a Sub-Registrar, a Forest Ranger, a Local Fund Overseer, a Police Inspector, a Sub-Postmaster; and there is a Local Fund Dispensary, besides a Travellers' Bungalow, and a spacious Chuttram. Iron smelting is carried on to a small extent. There are two Indigo Factories. Cart-making also gives employment to many people. There is a London Mission School, a Grant-in-Aid School, two Pial Schools, one Girls' School, and one Mohammedan School.

Jubilee Committee.—KANAGA SABAPATHI MUDELLIAR, *Chairman*; D. DAWOOD KHAN SAHIB, *Secretary*; &c.

A Public Meeting, attended by about 700 people, was held in the afternoon of the 16th February, at Nabi Saib's Choultry. Invitations had been issued to the managers of all the schools in the towns to attend with their pupils; and the latter were arranged in front of the assemblage. Mr. Kanaga Sabapathi Mudelliar, Chairman of the Jubilee Committee, who presided, explained the object of the meeting. The Presidencial Address was adopted and signed. After several loyal speeches had been delivered, three hearty cheers were given for the Queen Empress, sweetmeats were distributed to the children, and flowers and *pan supari* to the adults. Cloths were distributed to the poor, and the gods were carried through the streets in procession. On the morning of the 17th, the scholars of the London Mission School were assembled in the Taluk Cutcherry compound for field sports, at the conclusion of which prizes and sweetmeats were distributed. A Thanksgiving Service was afterwards held in the Mission Church.

BALIGUDA (GANJAM).

Advantage was taken of the presence of Mr. J. C. Horsfall, C.S., the Government Agent, and three Police Officers (who had arrived on their Hill tour a few days previously) to make the celebration a success. Proceedings commenced at 7 A.M. on the 16th February with a parade of the Maliah Police Reserve. The Presidencial Address was read by Mr. Horsfall, and adopted, after which a *feu de joie* was fired. The rest of the day was given up to sports and festivities. Archery, tug-of-war, putting the shot, high and long jumps, and races followed one another in rapid succession. The Khonds were by no means slow to enter into the joyful spirit of the occasion, the chief difficulty being to confine the entries for each event within reasonable limits. A race in which nine elephants took part was an imposing spectacle. At sunset a huge bonfire of nearly 10,000 cubic feet of wood, blazed forth on the neighbouring hill of Morani, the name of which was changed to "Maharani" in honour of the day. At the same moment some hundreds of Khond "braves," who had been priming themselves since noon, at a feast provided for them by the Sub-Magistrate, burst into the Reserve lines, and commenced their national war-dance. The quadrangle covers some five acres of ground; on three sides are the lines of the Reserve, and on the fourth is a stockade. The whole was illuminated by innumerable oil lamps and Bengal lights. In the centre there was a fine bonfire, though a mere reflection, as it were, of the one on the hill. On one side there was an excited crowd with fireworks showering in their midst; on the other some two or three hundred dusky warriors clad in flowing robes, their heads adorned with bisons' horns and peacocks' plumes, brandishing battle-axes and bows, and gesticulating, shouting, and dancing to the strains of their own weird music. "Three cheers, and three cheers more" for the "Great Maharani," led off by the Agent, and taken up enthusiastically by the crowd, brought the day's rejoicings to a close. On the 17th rifle matches were held on the "Range," which is one of the most picturesque in the Presidency. The chief event was the "Queen's Prize" for picked shots of the Reserve. The prize was won by a Khond, one of the few hill-men in the Police Reserve, who shot remarkably well, making two-thirds of the "highest possible." There was again a large concourse of spectators who were considerably impressed, as few of them had ever seen what could be done with a "Snider" at long distances, their previous experience being limited to the "Brown Bess."

The Jubilee had a double significance in Khundistan, as it was in the year 1837 — the year of Her Majesty's Accession — that Captain Campbell arrived above the ghats for the purpose of suppressing the "Meriah," or human sacrifice, though it was not till some years later that a regular Agency was established for that purpose. The fifty years have, perhaps, made a greater change in the Maliahs than in any other part of Her Majesty's dominions. At the beginning of the period the whole tract of country was almost unknown to Europeans, and "Meriah" sacrifice prevailed. Now the country has been opened up by numerous roads, while carts can go as far as Baliguda itself. Schools have been started, and Police-stations established in many places. A Special Assistant Agent, three Magistrates and District Munsiffs, are stationed there for the administration of criminal and civil justice.

BANGANAPALLE (KURNOOL).

The State of Banganapalle in the Kurnool District has an area of 255 square miles, and a population of 30,745, of whom four-fifths are Hindus, and nearly one-fifth are Mohammedans. It contains sixty-four towns and villages, of which Banganapalle is the capital (population 2,[illegible]). The annual revenue amounts to about £22,500. The estate was granted in the seventeenth century by the Emperor Aurungzeb to Mohammed Beg Khan, the eldest son of his Vizier, in whose family it remained for three generations. The Chief died without male heir in 1747, and the Nizam of Hyderabad bestowed the estate upon the ancestor of the present Nawab. In 1800 the suzerainty was transferred by the Nizam to the British Government. In consequence of local disturbances the estate was administered by the Collector of Cuddapah from 1825 to 1848. In the latter year administrative powers were given to the Chief, upon whom the title of Nawab was conferred in 1876 on the occasion of the visit of H.R.H. the Prince of Wales to Madras.

The Jubilee was celebrated in this State with the greatest enthusiasm. All the buildings in the town of Banganapalle having been previously whitewashed, the festivities commenced by a banquet given on the 16th February, by the Nawab Syed Fatte Ali Khan Bahadur, C.S.I., to the Mohammedan population, which lasted until 2.30 P.M. At 3 P.M. the Nawab held a Durbar, which was attended by all the nobles of the Court, and the representatives of the agricultural community. At 5.30 a congratulatory address was read in English and Hindustani, and received with cordial cheers. This was followed by prayers in the Durbar Hall for the long life and prosperity of Her Majesty the Queen Empress. After this followed the release of eight prisoners from the State jail, and a reduction in the sentences of four others. This was succeeded by a salute of 31 guns from the ramparts of the Fort, and a distribution of attar and betel. From 6 P.M. till dawn of the following day, the Palace, public buildings, and the houses generally were illuminated with coloured and plain lights, whilst fireworks, music, and dancing continued during the night. On the morning of the 17th, a distribution of food was made to about 8,000 persons, including visitors to the festival from the outlying districts; and at night similar feasting took place, and there was another display of fireworks. During both of the celebration days prayers were offered in the temples and mosques for Her Majesty's long life and prosperity, and a distribution of alms was made among the poor. The Nawab defrayed all the charges.

BAPATLA (KISTNA).

The population of Bapatla is 6,086, composed of Hindus, Mohammedans, and 150 Christians. Bapatla was constituted a Union under the Local Boards' Act, and a Panchayet had been appointed. The Panchayet consists of two official and four non-official members. The town contains a Tahsildar's Office, a Post Office, a District Munsiff's Court, an Assistant Engineer's Office, and a Local Fund Dispensary. There are a First Grade Local Fund Middle School, three Vernacular Elementary Boys' Schools, an American Lutheran Mission Girls' School, an American Baptist Mission Girls School, a Mohammedan School, and a Boarding School.

Jubilee Committee.—Messrs. VARANASI SUBRAMANYAM PUNTALU, B.A., B.L., *Chairman*; MANCHALLA JAGANNADHAM, and ANNAVARAPU PUNDARIKOKSHUDU, *Joint Secretaries*; VANURI RAMANNA PUNTALU; RATNA SABAPATHI PILLAY, B.A., B.C.E.; MAHOMMAD FAZALLA SAIB; VELICENDI TIRUMALA ROW; VINJAMURI VENKATA LAKSHMI NARASIMHA ROW; Rev. E. BULLARD; and twenty-three others.

The celebration was of a most gratifying character. Spacious and handsome Pandals were erected in different parts of the town, and the street decorations, with appropriate mottoes in English and Telugu, were all that could be desired. At night on the 16th February the streets were illuminated with numerous lamps, and there was a grand display of fireworks, exceeding anything that had previously been seen in this town. Speeches were made in the evening in English, Telugu, Hindustani, and Sanscrit, and the Presidential Address was adopted and signed. The festivities were prolonged until midnight. It was resolved to pay over the balance of the subscriptions that remained after defraying the expenses of the local festivities to the District Committee at Masulipatam, for the proposed Industrial School and Museum at Bezwada.

There were Jubilee celebrations in almost every village of the taluk.

BELLARY (TOWN).

Bellary is the chief town of the Bellary District. It has a population of 53,460; of whom 34,636 are Hindus, 15,068 Mohammedans, 3,566 Christians, and 190 belong to other religions. It is the head-quarters of a Brigade of the Madras Army, and of the Collector and Judge of the District. It was ceded by the Nizam of Hyderabad to the British Government in the year 1800. Among the Hindus there are Lingayets, Brahmins, Vysies, Jains, and a few Kshatriyas. There is an extensive export trade in cotton, raw hides, areca nuts, jaggery, and dried cocoa-nut. The manufacture of rough cotton cloths, cotton carpets, woollen cumblies, and the tanning of leather, furnish employment to a large portion of the town population. There is a spinning mill, in which several hundreds of people are employed. There are two Schools teaching up to the Matriculation Standard.

Jubilee Committee.—Messrs. J. D. GOLDINGHAM, *Chairman*; P. ANANTHA CHARLU, *Secretary*; J. W. BUTTS; H. M. WINTERBOTHAM; COLONEL PARSONS; COLONEL J. M. C. GALLOWAY; A. SUBAPATHY MUDELLIAR, RAO BAHADUR; D. ABRAHAM; M. ABRAHAM; EBRAHIM SAIT BAHADUR; KAREEM SAHIB KHAN SAHIB; GADIGY EMAN SAHIB; and thirteen others.

At 6 A.M. on the 16th February there was a parade of the troops, when a *feu de joie* was fired, and cheers were given for Her Majesty. The ceremony of opening the "Victoria Jubilee Garden," one of the permanent memorials of the Jubilee in this town, was performed at 8 A.M. in the presence of a very numerous assemblage. The distribution of alms to the poor commenced at 9 A.M., at the Prince of Wales's Choultry. Over 1,200 people were presented with cumblies, cloths, and money. Between 3 and 6 P.M. sports, including wrestling, racing, and a steeple-chase, were held. In the evening the town was splendidly illuminated; prayers were offered in almost all the temples; and the deities were taken in procession through the principal streets. At 9.30 P.M. there was a display of fireworks on the esplanade between the Sessions Court house and the Dispensary building. The band of the 16th Regiment performed an excellent programme. Native music and dancing commenced at 11 P.M. in the Prince of Wales's Choultry, and continued till a late hour. A large portrait of Her Majesty was placed in the Hall of the Choultry. The Presidencial Address was adopted and signed. About 20,000 people took part in the celebration, and there was much enthusiasm. On the 17th a treat was given to the poor, and to orphan children.

BERHAMPORE (GANJAM).

This town is the head-quarters of the Ganjam District. It has a population of 23,599, occupying 4,973 houses. There are 21,692 Hindus, 1,401 Mohammedans, and 506 Christians. It possesses numerous public buildings. It carries on a large sugar trade; and silk cloth is manufactured here.

Jubilee Committee.—Messrs. J. G. Horsfall; C. L. B. Cumming; Colonel G. Murray; Mr. F. J. V. Minchin; Dr. J. L. Vangeyzel; Messrs. Fitzgerald; O. V. Ramayya Puntalu; B. Rajalingam Sastri; and thirty-four others.

In the morning of the 16th February prayers were offered in the Protestant and Roman Catholic churches, in the mosques, temples, and mutts. In the afternoon athletic sports were held for the College and Town schoolboys, and prizes were awarded. Sweetmeats were given to the boys and girls present. The Municipal Town Hall was gaily decorated, and there was a large meeting of people of all classes held there. Mr. Thompson, the District Judge, presided. The Presidencial Address was read in English, Telugu, Uriya, and Hindustani, and a volley was fired by the Town Police after each reading. It was then adopted with acclamation. In the evening gods were carried in procession through the town to the Esplanade, near the Municipal Office, accompanied by two nautch parties. There was also a grand display of fireworks. Attar, camphor, garlands, and lavender were distributed to the European and Eurasian ladies and gentlemen present. There was a large crowd. The town Police and Municipal establishment had a nautch party, and distributed *pan supari* and attar. The main street, in which the Post and Telegraph Offices are situated, was beautifully illuminated, and so also were many houses. On the evening of the 17th cooked rice, with dholl, vegetables, &c., was distributed to about 2,500 people.

BEZWADA (KISTNA).

Bezwada occupies the foremost place among the towns of the Kistna district. The population is 9,336, comprising 7,605 Hindus, 1,584 Mohammedans, and 145 Christians; others, 2. It contains ancient Buddhist temples and Hindu pagodas of much archæological interest. It lies on the left bank of the Kistna river, and is surrounded by hills. The Anicut constructed here across the sacred river is a source of manifold blessings. The telegraph wires from Madras to Calcutta are carried across the Kistna from hill to hill in a single span, the longest yet erected anywhere. Bezwada is the head-quarters of the Superintending Engineer, of the Executive Engineer, of the

Head-Assistant Collector, and the Tahsildar. It contains several public offices, and a Dispensary, a Library, a Reading-room, and the D.P.W. Workshops. The Taluk Board consists of twelve members, of whom four are officials, and five are non-officials. The Bezwada Union consists of nine members, of whom four are officials, and eight non-officials. The educational institutions are the Church Mission High School, and the Theistic Primary School. There are many Results grant Vernacular primary schools. There is also a Caste Girls' School maintained by the Church Missionary Society. The town is celebrated for its ancient monuments, inscriptions, temples, and caves. It is also a place of pilgrimage. In a few months it will become the terminus of the Nizam's Guaranteed Railway, and of the Bellary Kistna State Railway. In consequence of its rising importance, and the rapid increase of its population, measures have been taken to extend the limits of the town, and to form a new Pettah, to be called after the Duke of Buckingham and Chandos, Governor of Madras from 1875 to 1880.

Jubilee Committee.—Messrs. P. RAMACHANDRA ROW, *Chairman*; G. D. WYBROW; C. H. B. BURLTON; W. J. BENSON; the Rev. P. N. ALEXANDER, M.A.; the Rev. Mr. ATKINSON; Messrs. P. VEERASAWMY NAIDU, ROW SAHIB; MEER SHAMSUDDEEN SAHIB; M. ETHURAJULU PILLAY, ROW SAHIB; and twenty-four others.

The Jubilee was celebrated here with great enthusiasm by all classes. Early in the morning of the 16th February, Thanksgiving Services were held in all places of worship. At 8 A.M. a procession composed of the members of the Jubilee Committee and other gentlemen, headed by the Head-Assistant Collector, and preceded by musicians, left the Tahsildar's Cutcherry, and visited two of the important temples in the station. The procession, with Hindu music, passed a mosque at which Moslem service was just then being conducted. There was no desire expressed, or attempt made to stop the music, thus proving that all race and religious prejudice had been laid aside for the occasion of the loyal celebration. From 9.30 to 10 A.M. cloths were distributed at the Taluk Cutcherry to 50 men and women who had been selected for the purpose on the previous day. At noon 500 poor people were fed. Three prisoners were released. The streets were decorated with festoons of green leaves. The Tahsildar's Cutcherry, which had been selected for the public meeting, was specially decorated and fitted up for the ceremony. At the chief entrance was erected a grand arch, which bore in gold letters the mottoes "God save the Empress," and "Long live the Empress." On the record tower of the Cutcherry was hoisted a large Union Jack, and on each side there were rows of banners and bannerets. The interior of the Cutcherry was also prettily decorated with flowers. At the head of the hall a picture of Her Majesty and the Royal Family was placed on a throne wrought in purple and gold, surmounted by the Royal Coat of Arms. Evergreens were placed at the foot of the throne. Native music played throughout the day at the Cutcherry. The members of the Vignyanada Bezwada Sabha went in procession through the streets, distributing Telugu circulars, printed on yellow paper, having the ends dipped in saffron and attar, inviting the population to illuminate their houses.

The procession arrived at the Tahsildar's Cutcherry at 3 P.M., when the sports began. There were flat races, bucket races, sack races, egg and spoon races, and tugs-of-war. At the close of the sports the people repaired in large numbers to the Cutcherry. More than 4,000 people were present. At 5 P.M. the Presidencial Address was read in English by Mr. P. Ramachandra Row, Acting Head-Assistant Collector, the Chairman of the Jubilee Committee, and was enthusiastically adopted. Translations of it in Telugu and Hindustani were also read. A Sanscrit address, composed by the Vizayanada Sabha for the occasion, was read, and most favourably received. After a performance of Hindu music, "God save the Queen" was sung by the European ladies and gentlemen of the station present, to an harmonium accompaniment. A *feu de joie* was fired by the police. At nightfall the hall was illuminated with chandeliers and globes; and the compound with lamps, torches, and coloured lights. The arena in the compound was crowded with eager spectators who had assembled to witness a native dramatic performance. A display of fireworks followed, which lasted till about 10 P.M. Refreshments were provided for all who chose to partake of them. Beacons were lit on the hills. Some of the offices and a few private residences were illuminated. A nautch and native music party were held on the following day. In the unanimity and enthusiasm with which the Jubilee was celebrated; in the perfectly spontaneous character of the proceedings; and in the loyal ardour with which all classes demonstrated their attachment to their Sovereign, Bezwada did herself signal honour. The permanent memorial is to take the form of a "Technical Institute and Museum," in the new Buckingham and Chandos pettah.

BHADRACHALAM (GODAVERI).

The population of Bhadrachalam is 1,901, consisting of Brahmins, Banians, Sudras, and Mohammedans; the Sudras predominate. The jungle villages of the taluk are inhabited by Koyas and Reddies. Education is progressing. There are about fifteen Primary Vernacular Schools, both Government and Mission, in different parts of the taluk, besides a Government Second Grade Middle School.

Jubilee Committee.—Messrs. PATURY TIRUMALA RAO PUNTALU, *Chairman*; R. RAMASAWMY NAIDU, *Secretary*; KADURY SADASIVA RAO PUNTALU; YASAM RANGIAH NAIDU; and CHECCA MANIKYAM.

The town assumed a gala appearance on the morning of the 16th February. The streets and houses were prettily decorated. In the forenoon food and clothes were distributed among the poor and helpless, and the Koyas were treated in honour of the occasion. A beautifully decorated Pandal had been erected in front of the Government Middle School. A meeting was held here from 4 to 11 P.M. There were over 500 persons present, and addresses on the family, history, and good government of Her Majesty, were delivered in English and Telugu. The Presidencial Address was adopted and signed. Native music was played at intervals. Then followed a dance by a number of Koyas. At the termination of the public meeting there was a nautch, after which the whole assembly took part in the procession of Rama, the god of the town. The festivities wound up with a fine display of fireworks. A "Choultry" is to be erected as a permanent memorial of the Jubilee.

BHAVANI (COIMBATORE).

The population of this town is 5,930, of whom 5,672 are Hindus. There are four Results grant Schools in this town. Carpets and cloths of an excellent kind are manufactured here. The principal trade is in carpets, cloths, and grain.

On the morning of the 16th February the town presented a very bright appearance. A tastefully arranged Pandal had been erected in front of the Taluk Cutcherry. More than 550 poor people were fed, and a few of them were presented with cloths. Prayers were offered in all the temples and mosques for the long life of the Queen, and the prosperity of the British Empire. From 2 to 4 P.M. a Durbar was held in the Taluk Cutcherry building, where over 2,000 ryots and merchants had assembled to do honour to Her Majesty. A singing party was held, and sandal and betel-nut were distributed among all present. At the Durbar an address on the administration of the British Government was read by Mr. Dhondu Rao, and the Durbar terminated in the offering up, by the whole assembly, of a prayer for the prosperity and long life of the Queen Empress. The Presidencial Address was adopted and signed. At 4 P.M. a portrait of Her Majesty was taken in procession on an elephant, with great pomp, through the streets of the town, followed by a body of Police Constables in uniform. The procession returned at 6 P.M. The Hindu gods and goddesses were taken in procession at 8 P.M., followed by a large crowd of people, with music, fireworks, &c. The Mohammedans also went in procession from their mosque, which was prettily illuminated. On the morning of the 17th cloths were distributed to the poor, and at noon a Durbar was held. At 5 P.M. a distribution of sandal and *pan supari* took place. A prayer for the prosperity of Her Majesty was then offered. Addresses appropriate to the occasion were delivered. The permanent memorial of the Jubilee will take the form of a "Reading Room."

BHOWANAGHERRY (SOUTH ARCOT).

Early in the morning of the 16th February people of all classes met in the office of the Sub-Magistrate, in front of which a Pandal had been erected. An arch bearing the inscription, "God save the Queen Empress," had been placed at the entrance, and native music played. The assembly then went in procession through the streets, visiting the Local Fund School and the Mohammedan Girls' School for the purpose of treating the boys and girls to refreshments. At the former School there was a grand demonstration of joy. A brief account of the benefits of the British administration was read to the people amidst shouts of applause. Sandal and *pan supari*, sugar and flowers, were distributed to the boys, and to the people assembled. The Presidencial Address was adopted and signed. The streets were ornamented with festoons. Children of all classes were treated to sugar. In the temples of Vishnu, Siva, Pilliyar, and the village goddess, *abishekams* and *archanas* were performed, and in them and in the mosques prayers were offered for the prosperity and continuance of the Queen's reign. An *utsavam* was organised for Vishnu. The image was carried with great pomp to the banks of the Mullipallam tank. Here hundreds of poor were fed. In the evening there was again a gathering in front of the Sub-Magistrate's office, where sports were held. There was music and dancing. The streets, houses, and offices were splendidly illuminated. The image of Vishnu was carried in procession attended by a large crowd from the tank to the temple. A display of fireworks ensued, and the rejoicings were brought to a close by the people shouting "Victory to Her Majesty the Queen Empress."

BIMLIPATAM (VIZAGAPATAM).

This sea-port was ceded by the Dutch to the British Government in the year 1825. The population is 9,328, divided thus:—Hindus, 8,737; Mohammedans, 359; Christians, 232. There are two Municipal Schools—a Town School and a Middle School. There are eight Results grant Schools. Large quantities of gingelly, indigo, niger, rapeseed, turmeric, myrabolams, and jaggery are exported. Gunny cloths are manufactured. Various kinds of furniture, and gold and silver ornaments, copper and brassware are made here. Cloth-weaving and pottery-making are also carried on.

Jubilee Committee.—Messrs. V. Anantharow Puntalu, Rao Sahib, *Chairman*; J. A. D. McDougall; W. J. Evans; T. Kipping; W. P. A. Greenfield; Captain R. Minto; Messrs. Potta Veerakayya; C. P. Tummanah; and eighteen others.

More than 300 poor people were fed, and many of them clothed, on the 16th February. The illuminations of the temples, one of them situated on a conspicuous hill in the town, were very picturesque. The Jubilee meeting was convened at 3 P.M. in the Municipal Hall, which was crowded to excess. There were over 1,000 persons present. The Presidencial Address was read in English, before Her Majesty's portrait, and was received with cheers. It was also read in Telugu. It was then adopted. After the sprinkling of rose-water and the distribution of *pan supari*, the whole assembly went in procession, Her Majesty's photograph being carried in a howdah on an elephant. More than 2,000 persons accompanied the procession. The procession returned at 3 A.M. Just as darkness set in there was a grand display of fireworks. In honour of the Jubilee, Sri Rajah Vuppalapati Venkata Vizia Gopalrazoo Bahadur Garu, proprietor of the Gopalpore estate, promised to endow the Ripon Poor House, Bimlipatam, with land worth Rs. 5,000.

BOBBILI (VIZAGAPATAM).

Bobbili, the chief town of the ancient Zemindary of Bobbili, is the residence of the Rajah. The population is 14,946; of whom 14,545 are Hindus, 329 Mohammedans, 38 Christians, and 34 belong to other religions. The town has been made a Union under the Local Boards' Act. The chief offices located here are the Revenue Cutcherry, Sub-Magistrate's Court, Police Station, the Rajah's High School, Local Fund Dispensary, Sub-Registrar's Office, and Post Office. The American Baptist Mission has an establishment here. The weaving of cotton cloths and the manufacture of brass and bell-metal articles are carried on. The majority of the people live by cultivating rice, raggy, gingelly, and sugar-cane.

Jubilee Committee.—Messrs. K. NAGABHUSHANA RAO PUNTALU, *Chairman*; G. RAGHUNA-YAKULU PATRADU; C. SITARAMAYYA PUNTALU; S. SUBRAMANYA IYER, B.A.; C. L. SRINIVASA ROW CHETTY; P. VENKATAROW PUNTALU; and five others.

All the streets in the town, and the principal buildings belonging to the Rajah, were decorated with *thoranams*, festoons, &c. A triumphal arch, which bore the inscription, "God bless the Queen," adorned the large gate of the new fort. Guns were fired in quick succession, and the Rajah's sepoys paraded on the open ground in front of the new fort at 6 o'clock on the 16th February, and fired a *feu de joie*. The Rajah's band was in attendance. Between 9 and 11 A.M. fruits were distributed to the children of the Pial schools in the town. 190 poor and needy persons were fed with rice, dholl, and mutton, at noon; and again at night. Of that number 146 received cloths; the rest, who were the inmates of the Rajah's Poor House, had received cloths a month or two previously. In the Chuttram 100 Smarta Brahmins were fed, and 50 Vaishnavas were fed in the pagoda, in which prayers were offered, and *pujah* made in the name of the Queen Empress. The chief people of the town assembled in the Cutcherry Hall of the *Samasthanam* at 4 P.M., where essays were read, and speeches made describing the virtues of Her Majesty, and the benefits enjoyed by the country under the British rule. The Presidencial Address was adopted and signed. The meeting lasted till 6 P.M., when a grand procession, with Sri Venu Gopalswami, the god of the local pagoda, at its head, set out, and passed through the principal streets with great pomp. The Rajah was away at Waltair, whither he had gone to arrange for an entertainment to the European residents in honour of the Jubilee. He also arranged for decorating all the villages in the Zemindary with *thoranams*, &c.; and drums were beaten and trumpets sounded at intervals, throughout the day. The present market of Bobbili is in a bad state, and the construction of a new one in a convenient locality has been under contemplation for a long time. The Rajah took this opportunity to erect a suitable market, and named it "The Victoria Market." He also remitted arrears of revenue due from the ryots to the extent of a lakh and a half in honour of Her Majesty.

BODINAYAKANUR (MADURA).

The town of Bodinayakanur is five miles from the foot of the Travancore hills. It is the chief town of a Zemindary of ninety-eight square miles, containing twenty-one villages and hamlets. It has a population of 14,759, consisting of Chetties, Rowthers, Comalies, Elavaniars, and other caste people. There are 13,914 Hindus, 619 Mohammedans, and 226 Christians. The affairs of the town are looked after by a Panchayet Union. A good trade is carried on in tea, coffee, &c., produced on the Devikulam Hills.

Jubilee Committee.—Messrs. T. B. Kamaraja Pandian Naicker, *Chairman*; Vellayya Rowther and Kumaraswami Chettiar, *Joint Secretaries*; V. M. Joseph Nadar; Sahakaji Peerana Rowther; and Perumkeralavai Rowther.

A Royal salute was fired at daybreak on the 16th February, and the people who had been invited from the villages of the Bodinayakanur Zemindary by the Jubilee Committee assembled in front of the Zamindar's palace, which was beautifully decorated, and joined in offering prayer for Her Majesty. At about 8 A.M. the school children and boys mustered, and marched thence in procession to the school building, which had been gaily decorated. A large number of people were present, including the Zemindar. The children sang the *Kummi* song, and cheers were given for Her Majesty. That was followed by music and dancing. Native music was played at the Cutcherry all day at intervals. About 11 o'clock the ceremony of laying the foundation stone of the "Lamp Post," which is to be the local memorial of the Jubilee, in front of the palace, was performed by the Chairman of the Committee in the presence of a numerous assembly. A Jubilee proclamation was then read by Mr. Subba Iyer, and the people gave three cheers for Her Majesty. At about 3 P.M. the Zemindar of Periyur, in company with the Zemindar of the town and other gentlemen, went in procession to the school building, where a Tamil poet entertained the audience with an exhibition of *ashtavathanam* (an art by which a man meditates upon many subjects at the same time). A long speech on the Jubilee of Her Majesty, and on the blessings of British rule in India, was delivered by Mr. V. M. Joseph Nadar, Hospital Assistant, the Chairman of the Union. The Presidencial Address was adopted and signed. The people gave three cheers for Her Majesty. About 300 poor people were fed. A *fête* was given to about 500 school children and others. About 60 poor people were presented with new cloths. At 8 P.M.

there was a grand procession, in which the Zemindar of Periyur and the poet above referred to took part. During the procession betel-nuts and sandal were distributed to the people. The proclamation was again read as the procession passed along the decorated streets. The American Mission congregation, headed by their pastor, the Rev. E. Seymour, marched through the streets in procession. They had erected a triumphal arch, which bore the inscription, "Long Live Her Most Gracious Majesty the Queen," in large characters. From 10 to 12 at night there were several entertainments.

CALICUT (MALABAR).

This town is believed to have been founded by Cheraman Perumal. Vasco de Gama, discoverer of India, landed here on the 20th May, 1498. The Portuguese effected a settlement in 1501; the French succeeded them in 1722; the Danish followed in 1752; and the British in 1780. The town gave its name to "calico." The population is now 57,000, composed chiefly of Nairs, Tiers, and Moplahs. The staple exports are coffee, ginger, pepper, cardamoms, nux vomica, copprah, &c. The chief official residents are the Collector of Malabar, the District Judge, the Superintendent of Police, the District Surgeon, the Chaplain, the Port Officer, the Executive Engineer, the Local Fund Engineer, the Superintendent of Telegraphs, the Forest Officer, &c. For some years past a detachment of European troops has been stationed at the West Hill Barracks. Calicut is the head-quarters of the Malabar Volunteer Rifles. There is a Municipal Council, consisting of six nominated, and eighteen elected Councillors, supporting a Hospital and Dispensary, a Leper and Small-pox Hospital, as well as several schools.

At 6.30 A.M. on the morning of the 16th February there was a simultaneous parade of the Head-quarter Companies of the Malabar Volunteer Rifles, under the command of Major Logan (Collector of Malabar), on the *maidan* near the large tank of Calicut, and also of the detachment of the Royal Fusiliers stationed at West Hill Barracks, under the command of Captain Dease. The parade attracted a large crowd of people. A *feu de joie* and Royal salute were followed by three cheers for the Queen Empress, and the National Anthem was sung. The Volunteers and Regulars then marched to church, where a special service was held. From 9 A.M. to noon, the distribution of rice and food to the poor proceeded. At 3.30 P.M. between 7,000 and 8,000 people met to witness the sports. There were pony races, walking matches, sack races, obstacle races, high jumps, and long jumps. As the evening drew in, the Mananchera Tank and the Municipal Garden on its northern bank, were beautifully illuminated. On the four sides of both tank and garden is a wall of open stonework, along the whole length of which, as well as on the arches, lights were placed. The town generally was very prettily illuminated. The residence of the Collector was bright with lamps. That officer entertained Heads of Departments at dinner; while the District Judge, Mr. F. H. Wilkinson, was, in another quarter of the town, promoting brotherly feeling as President of the Kerala Masonic Lodge, at which Europeans, Eurasians, Nairs, Tiers, and Parsees sat down to a Jubilee dinner. For the multitude there were native theatricals and music at various Pandals on the tank *maidan*. On the 17th, at 3.30 P.M., there was a regatta, which was a source of much interest to large crowds of people who assembled on the beach near the pier. In the spacious compound of the German Mission House, and in that of the Government College, the juvenile portion of the Calicut community was entertained with sports and a treat. A banquet, in honour of the Jubilee, was given at the Malabar Club. The festivities were brought to a close by a display of fireworks from the beach and pier. The Presidential Address was adopted and signed.

CANNANORE (MALABAR).

Cannanore is a small seaport town in the north of Malabar. It was one of the earliest settlements of the Portuguese, and Vasco de Gama built a Fort here, which is still in existence, and made Cannanore the centre of the pepper trade. The town afterwards fell into the hands of the Dutch, and then, by purchase, became a possession, and the seat of Arakal Beeby, a Mohammedan female ruler of the Laccadives. Much trade was carried on with Arabia, Bengal, and the Laccadives. In 1774 Hyder Ali subjugated the place. In 1792, by the treaty of Seringapatam, it came under the British power, and was made a cantonment, and until the beginning of the current year it was the head-quarters of one of the Military Divisions of the Madras Presidency. The affairs of the town are administered by a Municipal Council, consisting of eighteen members, twelve of whom are elected by the people. The population is 26,386, namely, 10,656 Hindus, 11,617 Mohammedans, and 4,113 Christians and others. Education has made great progress among the Christian and Hindu population. There are several Primary Schools for boys under private management, receiving Results grants from the Municipality. There are also five Primary Schools for girls. The Basel Mission has three schools, of which one is a High School. The Municipality also has a High School.

Jubilee Committee.—DR. S. C. SARKIES, *Chairman*; W. P. SCHONTHAL, *Secretary*: Messrs. E. GADSDEN; W. G. B. BROWNE; A. ANNASAWMY IYER; B. D'ROZARIO; MANECKJEE DADABHOY; HAJEE ABDOOL RAHEEM; L. B. REID; W. P. GRIBBON; C. CHERIAN COOROOR; and seven others.

A spacious and beautiful Pandal had been erected in the centre of the *maidan*, and bore numerous appropriate inscriptions. Booths were built all round the plain, where a fair was held. The whole town was decorated with flags, inscriptions, and evergreens. Festoons were hung in every street. At 6.30 A.M. on the 16th February the European Detachment and the Native Regiment paraded in full dress on the *maidan*. They fired a *feu de joie*, gave three hearty cheers for the Queen Empress, and then marched past the saluting point. Special services of Thanksgiving were held at 7 A.M. in the Roman Catholic Trinity Church, and at 9 A.M. in the Basel German Mission Church, where prayers were offered on behalf of Her Majesty and the Royal

Family. At 10 o'clock rice was distributed simultaneously at two localities to nearly 3,900 poor people, including children. At 3 P.M. great numbers of people of all castes and creeds began to pour in from all parts of the town and the suburbs. All were in their gala dress. The Pandal afforded accommodation to about 500 persons, and between 12,000 and 14,000 persons were on the *maidan* to witness the sports. Before the sports commenced, at the request of the Jubilee Committee and on their behalf, Mr. T. Zecharias, Head Master of the B. M. High School, delivered an interesting address in Malayalam on the importance of the occasion, after which three hearty cheers were given for the Queen Empress. The National Anthem was then sung, both in Malayalam and in English by the children of the Hindu Girls' school. The Presidencial Address was* adopted and signed. The sports now commenced and lasted till 6.30 P.M. The Band of the 11th Regiment M. I. was in attendance. At 7 P.M. the illuminations commenced. The whole town as well as the Pandal was beautifully illuminated. During the night various entertainments were provided for the masses. A Malayalam drama, entitled Kathakali, was enacted. The proceedings terminated at midnight. At 3 P.M. on the following day the Pandal was again filled with people, and sports were held. At 6 o'clock the National Anthem was sung as before: and the town and Pandal were again illuminated. At 9 P.M. some 18,000 to 20,000 people assembled to witness the fireworks, which lasted nearly an hour. Another Malayalam play was enacted.

CHAGULMURRI (KURNOOL).

This is a small town situated at the southern extremity of the Sirvel Taluk near the Nallamala hills. It is the head-quarters of the Sirvel Taluk Cutcherry, Sub-Registrar's Office, Post Office, and Local Fund Dispensary. There are several Local Fund Schools. The population numbers 2,855, including 1,788 Hindus and 1,067 Muhammadans. Indigo is one of the principal articles of the trade. Weaving is carried on to a small extent.

Jubilee Committee.—Messrs. A. LUTCHMANA ROW, *Chairman*; D. SUBBA ROW, *Secretary*; B. VENKOBA ROW; VEERASAWMY NAIDU; M. VENKATANARASIMMAROW NAIDU; V. COOPOOSWAMY NAIDU; M. PATCHA SAHIB; MADALLAPALLI VENKATA SUBBANNAH; BISAM VENKATA CHETTY; and two others.

The procession of the Kasavaswami god, with music and a dancing party, was conducted through the principal streets of Chagulmurri by the principal inhabitants and merchants of the place. Prayers were offered in the temples and mosques for the welfare of Her Majesty. About 350 poor were fed, and sweets were distributed to about 70 children of the village, including those belonging to the Local Fund School. The Mohammedans went in procession with banners and music through the principal streets. The temples, mosques, and the principal streets were illuminated at night. Betel leaves and nuts were distributed among all those present in the temples after the prayers had been offered.

CHATRAPUR (GANJAM).

Chatrapur, the usual residence of the Collector of Ganjam has a population of 3,664 persons: of whom 3,463 are Hindus, 117 Mohammedans, and 84 Christians. It contains the Collector's Cutcherry, a Subsidiary Jail, and Police Hospital. The only educational establishment is the Onslow Institution, attended chiefly by Brahmins and Sudras.

The Jubilee was celebrated on the 16th February by a parade at sunrise in the compound of the Collector's office, at the conclusion of which a salute and *feu de joie* were fired. These were followed by Thanksgiving Services in the churches and in the Hindu temples. The distribution of rice and money to nearly 400 poor persons followed. When it grew dark there was a torchlight procession of the god Radhakantaswamy from 7 P.M. to midnight, accompanied by native music. A public meeting was held at 8 P.M. in the Collector's office, when the Presidential Address was adopted, with much enthusiasm. More than 500 persons were present. There was a display of fireworks immediately after the meeting.

CHICACOLE (GANJAM).

Chicacole is a Municipal Town under the management of sixteen Councillors. The population is, in round numbers, 19,000, composed chiefly of Brahmins, Komaties, Sudras, Mohammedans, and a few Native Christians. There are a High School, a Town School, a Girls' School, a Local Fund Normal School, and a Mohammedan School. The town has long been noted for its cotton manufactures, and especially for its muslins.

Jubilee Committee.—Messrs. B. RAJALINGAM SASTRI, *Chairman*; S. GUNNIAH PUNTALU, *Secretary*; P. SURIYANARAYANA ROW; V. GURAVIAH PUNTALU; SRI PHALAHARU MAHANTE HARINARAYANADASU BAVAJI; P. J. FOX; JAMMAL MAHOMED SAHIB; and eighteen others.

Very early in the morning of the 16th February a band of native musicians marched through the streets. About 7.30 A.M., a large number of people assembled at the school play-ground to witness the gymnastic performances of the schoolboys. Prizes were awarded to the successful competitors. A grand Durbar was then held in the High School hall, when there was a very large gathering of all classes of persons, including several Europeans. The building was tastefully decorated. Above the President's seat was suspended a large portrait of the Queen Empress, with a portrait of the Prince of Wales on the right, and of the Princess of Wales on the left of it; and below Her Majesty's portrait, which was adorned with garlands of flowers, there was a large picture of the whole of the Royal Family. The walls were surmounted with various inscriptions in large golden characters, the most prominent among them being "*Dei Gratia*," and "*Vivat Regina*." The proceedings opened with the singing of the National Anthem in Telugu, to an accompaniment of music. Mr. Evans, who occupied the chair, made an interesting speech, which was cordially received. Mr. Gunniah Puntalu, Secretary to the Jubilee Committee, read an address, in which he gave an excellent account of the life of the Queen Empress, and alluded to the many blessings of her reign. He then called for three cheers for Her Majesty. The call was enthusiastically responded to by all present. This was followed by the reading aloud Telugu and Sanscrit verses, composed in praise of Her Majesty by the School pundits. After this the Presidencial Address was read in English by Mr. G. Mukundarao Naidu, B.A., of the local High School, and translated into Telugu by Mr. B. Rajalinga Sastri, B.A., Head Master of the High School. The Address was adopted and signed. Songs were sung wishing health, prosperity, and happiness to Her Majesty. The Chairman made a few concluding remarks, after which three hearty cheers were given for Her Majesty. Votes of thanks were passed to the Jubilee Committee for their energetic exertions, and the Durbar terminated with a Royal salute fired by the Police. At noon the people of the Assistant Engineer's Office distributed alms at their office. From 1 to 4 P.M. Timmaraza Venkatarao Puntalu, a landed proprietor, fed 1,000 poor people, and a large number of other poor Hindus and Mohammedans were entertained at different places. Another meeting was held in the Durbar Hall, which was also very largely attended. A pundit addressed the meeting, and read some panegyrical verses in Sanscrit. Then a Mohammedan poet and teacher of the school recited Jubilee verses in Hindustani and Persian. A Native entertainment followed, and continued till 4 P.M. The people then moved to the front of the building where races and sports were held, until 6 in the evening, when the schoolboys and girls were treated with sweetmeats. The Police fired a *feu de joie*, and the people dispersed. At 8 P.M. there was a grand torchlight procession of the gods accompanied by music, nautch parties, and fireworks. More than 10,000 people were present. The procession passed through the main streets, and arriving at the High School building at 2 A.M. went round the large play-ground. Here a brilliant display of fireworks took place, winding up with the firing of a Royal salute. Almost all the streets in the town were gay with flags and festoons, and many private houses and premises were decorated with evergreens, garlands, and flags, the last-named bearing loyal inscriptions such as "God save the Queen," and "Long live the Empress." Some gentlemen had erected beautiful Pandals in front of their houses. At night the roads were lined with small lights on both sides. The Assistant Engineer's office, Telegraph office, Hindu temples, and Mohammedan mosques were illuminated, as also were several private residences.

CHIDAMBARAM (SOUTH ARCOT).

The town of Chidambaram (or more correctly Chithambalam, "the atmosphere of wisdom") is the head-quarters of a taluk of the same name, and contains subordinate Revenue, Judicial, and Police establishments. It attracts from 50,000 to 60,000 pilgrims and traders to its great fair held in the month of December. Its temples are held in the highest reverence throughout Southern India and Ceylon. The principal of these is the Sabhanaikar Kovil, or Kanaka Sabha ("golden shrine") sacred to Siva and his wife Parvati. This temple covers thirty-nine acres of ground, and contains 1,000 pillars, all monoliths, varying from 26 feet to 40 feet in height. The nearest quarry is forty miles distant. There are about seventy Chuttrums, or native rest-houses, in the town. The population is 19,837, consisting of Hindus, Mohammedans, Christians, and Jains. In Pacheappah's High School, the Municipal Middle School, the Arumuga Navalar's School, and Pacheappah's Feeder School, English and the Vernaculars are taught. Besides these there are the Government Girls' School, and six Pial Schools in which the Vernaculars are taught, and two Sanscrit Padasalas. Paddy is largely exported. The chief imports are grain, dholl, jaggery, and sugar. The weaving of silk and cotton cloths is carried on to a considerable extent.

Jubilee Committee.—Messrs. C. Varaha Iyengar, *Chairman*; P. N. Ramachendra Row, *Secretary*; V. Malhari Row; Syed Hussain Saheb; N. Devasikamany Mudaliyar; G. A. W. Fellows; K. Ramasami Aiyengar; V. Saminatha Jata Vallabhar; and twenty others.

The members of the Jubilee Committee, the Municipal Councillors, officers of the Judicial, Revenue, Magisterial, Police, Medical, Public Works, and Postal Departments, traders, merchants, artisans, cultivators, and landholders met at the Tahsildar's house at 7 A.M. on the 16th February, formed themselves into a procession, and went through the four streets round the temple, distributing sugar in honour of the Jubilee. The route was watered, ornamented with festoons, and lined by the Police. Every house was decorated. The procession was headed by a band, followed by dancing girls. A salute of 101 guns was fired from the temple yards, when the procession started. Europeans, Hindus, and Muhammedans vied with one another in demonstrations of joy and loyalty. The auspicious omen of the accidental flying of a Brahmini kite just as the procession started was viewed by the Hindu portion of the community as auguring well for the continuance of Her Majesty's happy reign. Passing through the western and northern main streets the procession halted at the Sanscrit Padasala in the eastern main street. Here Halasianatha Sastry, a student in the Padasala, read an address in Sanscrit in honour of Her Majesty. Mr V. Malhari Rao, the District Munsiff of the station, said he was sure nothing would be more gratifying to Her Imperial Majesty than to learn that Sanscrit, which had been neglected for many centuries, had of late made great progress, especially at this seat of religion, which was held in the highest reverence by all Hindus. After the distribution of refreshments to the students, the procession proceeded to the Padasala, where a student recited a Sanscrit poem in honour of Her Majesty. The procession next visited Pacheappah's High School, and marched to the Government Girls' School, where Pundit Sreenivasa Sastri expatiated on the virtues of the Queen Empress, and exhorted the girls to take Her Majesty for their example in life. Refreshments and flowers were distributed to the girls. The procession then visited the Siva Prakasa Vidyasala. At the Municipal School, where refreshments were distributed, Hazarat Syud Hoosain Sahib, a Police Inspector, addressed a few words of advice to the Mohammedan students, and exhorted them to avail themselves of the special privileges which Her Majesty's Government—deeply interested in the welfare of the Mohammedan community,—had afforded for their intellectual advancement. The branch of Pacheappah's School was next visited, and a distribution of sugar, sugar-candy, flowers, and *pan supari* was made amidst shouts of joy. This brought the procession to a conclusion. From 11 A.M. to 3 P.M. the members of the Feeding Committee were engaged in distributing food to the poor. In the evening the people, dressed in their holiday attire, assembled in the spacious hall of the Thousand-Pillared Mantapam in the temple. The Honorary Secretary of the Jubilee Committee read aloud the Presidencial Address, which was adopted with acclamation. Mr. V. S. Jattavallabarhar, of the local Pacheappah's School, then addressed the meeting in Tamil. He was followed by Pundit Sreenivasa Sastri, who gave a sketch in Sanscrit of Her Majesty's reign. Sanscrit verses, composed for the occasion, were read by that Pundit, and by Pundits Narayana Sastri, Dakshanamoorthi Sastri, and Vytheeswara Sastri of the local Sanscrit Padasalas. Hazarat Syud Hoosain Sahib, on behalf of the Mohammedan community, next addressed the audience in Persian. He was followed by Mr. K. P. Sabhapathy P. Pillay; each speaker terminating his address with a prayer for Her Majesty. The several speeches were received with cheers. The multitude then moved to the open ground in front of the hall, where fencing, athletics, jugglery, and climbing the greasy pole, brought the day to a close. All the gopurams, the streets, houses, offices, and mosques were profusely illuminated. A salute of guns announced the commencement of the programme for the night. Three famous singers entertained the audience with songs. The kolatam and kummi dances, in which numbers of dancing-girls joined, were performed. A grand display of fireworks, a distribution of sandal, flowers, and *pan supari*, and the sprinkling of rose-water, brought the festivities to a close at midnight, when a final salute was fired, and prayers were again offered for the long continuance of Her Majesty's reign. A building to be called the "Victoria Hall and Reading Room" will be erected as a permanent memorial of the Jubilee.

There were special celebrations in Mannargudi, Srimushanam, Bhavanagheri, and Porto Novo. In all the villages of this taluk the poor were fed, prayers were offered for Her Majesty, and there was general rejoicing.

CHINGLEPUT (TOWN).

Chingleput, after which the District is named, is a small town thirty-four miles to the south of the City of Madras. It is the seat of the District Judge, Sub-Collector, Zillah Surgeon, &c. It possesses an old fort, wherein several of the public offices are now located. The scenery around is picturesque. The town has a population of 9,000 persons: of whom 8,005 are Hindus, 763 Mahommedans, and 232 Christians. There are two High Schools for Boys, one under Mission management, and the other supported by native munificence. There are also three Girls' Schools in the town. Local Self-Government was introduced last year.

Jubilee Committee.—Messrs. V. Damodara Mudelliar, *Chairman*; M. Shaik Meeran Sahib, *Secretary*; M. Appadorai Mudelliar; C. Arunachala Mudelliar; S. Bashiagar Naidu; Darmakarta Veeraragava Chariar; and others.

At daybreak on the 16th February guns were fired in the temple, and at 7 o'clock the members of the Jubilee Committee assembled opposite the Railway Station gate, where a Pandal had been erected, and distributed cloths to a large number of poor persons. Mr. Kuppusami Naidu, one of the members of the Committee, had arranged for a grand festival at the temple, at 8 A.M., in honour of the occasion. This festival attracted crowds of all classes of people, who offered up prayers for the Queen Empress, and the new Gates of the temple were formally opened. A silver plate, bearing a suitable inscription in commemoration of the Jubilee, was fixed on the new Gate. The District Judge and several other gentlemen, European and native, witnessed the ceremony. A gold ornament was then presented to the Hindu god, Kothandaramaswami, in the name of Her Majesty. Sandal and *pan supari* were distributed, rose-water was sprinkled, and about 500 people were fed with holy *prasadams*. A large number of poor people were fed and clothed in the Sub-Collector's Office compound during the forenoon. In the afternoon a *fête* was given to the boys and girls of all the schools. A *Bhajanai* (singing of theological songs) was held in the temple, and prayers were offered to the god. A short Tamil poem, composed by himself, was sung by Pundit Jagannatha Pillay, at a large public meeting in the Hall of the Indian Press. The entrance to the Hall was tastefully decorated with bunting, &c., and over the doorway ran the inscriptions, "Long live our Empress," and "God save our Empress." The Hall was crowded. Tamil Jubilee odes were sung and explained. The Presidencial Address was adopted and signed. The District Munsiff, who presided, having made some appropriate remarks, the meeting dispersed after a distribution of sandal and *pan supari*, and the sprinkling of rose-water. At night the whole town was grandly illuminated.

CHIRALA (KISTNA).

This town belongs to the Bapatla Taluk. It is situated about four miles from the Kistna Canal, and is within the same distance from the sea. The population is 9,000, consisting of Hindus, Mohammedans, Native Christians, and one Eurasian family. There are several Pial Schools in which Telugu only, and one school where English is taught. A Local Fund Union has just been established. Dyeing and weaving are conducted on a large scale.

Jubilee Committee.—Messrs. R. D. Peake, *Chairman*; V. Venkatrow, *Secretary*; Ravula Subbaramulu; Ravula Venkatsoobiah; Munafully Ramiah; P. Venkatrutnum; D. Sadasiva Row; M. Ramabramham; Kasimedeen Saib; Dudu Lakshmiah; and six others.

The local Victoria Reading Club took an active part in celebrating the Jubilee. At 11 A.M. on the 16th February the Hindus congregated at their temples, and offered prayer for the Queen Empress. 150 poor persons were fed between 1 and 4 P.M. The Pandal erected for the occasion was elaborately decorated, and had the words "God save the Queen," in Telugu characters, over the entrance. After it was illuminated the people poured in, and were entertained with music of various kinds, and singing. A display of fireworks followed. From 9 P.M. to 4 A.M. there was a torchlight procession of the Hindu gods, accompanied by drums and dancing-girls.

CHITTOOR (NORTH ARCOT).

In front of a pretty little bungalow occupied by the local Native Association, a handsome Pandal had been erected, the entrance of which was adorned with the inscription, "May Victoria Reign Long" in golden letters, on a crimson background. In front of this Pandal there was a large circular piece of ground, which was fitted up as a gymnasium. A few yards to the east of this circle was the gateway, which was also adorned; and the road between the gateway and the Pandal was strewn with little flags. The Taluk Catcherry building was also tastefully fitted up. The Pandal in front of it was furnished with an arch bearing the inscription "God bless Queen Empress Victoria," with the Union Jack floating above it. The premises of the old Fort, now used as the Hospital, were adorned with arches, on which were inscribed in golden letters, "Long live the Queen Empress Victoria," and "God bless Her Majesty the Queen Empress of India." Early in the morning of the 16th February, the Hospital compound was thronged with all classes of the community. At 8 A.M. money and rice were distributed to poor Christians, and immediately afterwards the Mohammedan and Hindu poor received a dole. The members of the Local Theosophical Society fed a large number of Sudras at 4 P.M. The girls of the two Girls' Schools went in procession with music round the town, and reached the

Association Hall to take part in a treat provided for them by Mr. T. S. Narasinga Row. The European ladies and gentlemen of the town were present. The premises and the garden were thronged with people. The ceremony began by some of the girls singing songs. Then Mrs. Lancaster distributed slate pencils and black-lead pencils to the girls. Dr. Lancaster made a short speech. The girls then dispersed, and the rest of the party moved towards the Pandal in front to witness athletic sports by the students of the Government High School. The whole party, with a large portrait of Her Majesty in front, then marched in procession with music towards the Hospital, where Dr. Lancaster had arranged for the distribution of fruits and sweetmeats to the boys. After dusk there was a grand display of fireworks. The town, temples, and mosques were prettily illuminated. There were processions of the gods from the Vishnu and Siva temples at night, and they did not return till 2 A.M. The festivities continued throughout the following day. The Vaishnava sect of the community arranged for a picnic at Iruvaram, a village about two miles from Chittoor. In the afternoon there were further rejoicings. A meeting of the Collector's officials was held at Gramespett. The inscription "Hail Victoria" in letters of gold on crimson cloth, glittered over the entrance. The proceedings commenced with music, which continued for a short time, after which Mr. V. Krishnama Charlu made an excellent speech. Mr. Narasinga Row addressed the audience in Telugu, and the meeting terminated with a distribution of sandal, *pan supari*, flowers, fruit, and sugar-candy. The whole party drove to the Association Hall, where a treat was given to the boys of the several schools in the town. Ink-bottles, lead pencils, and slate pencils, supplied by the Collector's officials, sweetmeats supplied by Mr. C. V. Srinivasa Chariar, B.A., and fruits and sugar supplied by R. Subbaiya Chetty, were distributed among the schoolboys, who numbered over a thousand. Silk caps with gold embroidery were distributed among the boys of the Jamkhani Dramatic Company. The Mohammedan portion of the party then separated to conduct their procession round the town. Half an hour later the rest of the party, chiefly Hindus, went in procession in the opposite direction, and having met the Mohammedan procession at Bheema Row's Choultry, joined them. The united party then proceeded towards the Association Rooms, where the Mohammedans gave a cordial reception to the European gentlemen and ladies of the town, as well as to the Hindus. Some native music followed, after which the Europeans retired. The Hindu and Mohammedan gentlemen attended the Taluk Cutcherry, where the Tahsildar distributed *pan supari*, flowers, fruits, and betel leaves. After supper a nautch was held at the Association Hall, and continued until midnight. The Presidencial Address was adopted and signed.

COCHIN (MALABAR).

The population amounts to 15,698; comprising Christians, 8,360; Hindus, 4,383; Mohammedans, 2,942; and other religions, 13. The town contains 16 Boys' and 4 Girls' Schools; of the former, two are wholly maintained by the Municipality, the remainder being aided Schools. It is estimated that about 1,100 pupils attend these institutions. Local Self-Government was established here in 1866, and is working satisfactorily. The average income of the Municipality for the past five years has been Rs. 17,600 per annum, which is expended on Public Works, Education, Sanitation Medical Services, and other items. There is a large import and export trade. Rice and paddy, cotton goods, drugs, liquors, metals, seeds, &c., are imported. The annual value of the import trade is about Rs. 54,40,000. Cocoa-nut oil, coir yarn, coir fibre, coir rope, and copprah, coffee, pepper, and ginger are largely shipped to European and Indian ports. The total annual value of exports may be put down at Rs. 75,00,000. The manufactures consist chiefly of coir yarn, coir rope, and oil cake.

Jubilee Committee.—Messrs. GEORGE BRUNTON, *Chairman*; W. N. BLACK, *Secretary*; J. H. BOYER; G. BADENOCH; DHARSELY KHETSEY; HAJEE MOOSA HAJEE AHMED; ELIAS HAJEE VYDANA; W. KLEIN; A. KRISHNOSAWMY; KAKU DAKU; P. MAHOMED MAHIKAR; and two others.

This town was gaily decorated with flags, festoons, and other emblems of loyalty. At 6.30 A.M. on the 16th February the Volunteers held a parade, when a *feu de joie* was fired, and three hearty cheers were given for Her Majesty. There was special service in most of the churches. At 8 o'clock about 600 poor people were fed, and presented with money. At 2 o'clock a large procession arrived from Calvetty, consisting principally of members of the Mohammedan community, accompanied by native music, banners, and two elephants, the rear being brought up by acrobats. On their arrival on the *maidan* the sports began. They consisted of sword feats, sword dances, jumping through hoops, &c. They were witnessed by large crowds of people. Merry-go-rounds, swings, &c., had been erected on the *maidan* for the juvenile community. At dusk the town was very prettily illuminated. All along the principal roads and round the *maidan*, lamps, ten feet apart, had been erected. The Post and Telegraph Offices were prominent by their brilliancy, and many private residences were very tastefully lit up. Vypeen was also well lit up, and the church looked particularly brilliant. The backwater was illuminated, and a chain of boats connecting Cochin and Vypeen, all showing lights, had a striking effect. There were two native theatrical companies which attracted large crowds of people. The pieces performed were:—"The History of Charlemagne," by Native Christians, and "Aryamala Natakam," by Hindus. At 7 o'clock on the morning of the 17th the poor were again fed, and about 3,000 received alms. The chief attractions of this day were sports, which were held on the *maidan*. The ground was gaily decorated with flags, and tents were pitched for the accommodation of visitors. The sports commenced at 2.30 P.M., and there was no lack of competitors for the various events. On the programme being finished the prizes were distributed, after which three hearty cheers were given for Her Majesty. In the evening the town was again illuminated, and there were processions. The Presidencial Address was adopted.

COCONADA (GODAVERY).

At 8 A.M. on the 16th February the Presidencial Address was read in Hindustani and Telugu at the Jubilee Pandal (erected at the Rajah of Pittapur's College) by the Raji Sahib and the Chairman of the Municipality to a large number of people who had assembled. *Pan supari* was distributed, and nautches and native music followed. In all the Hindu temples and Mohammedan mosques special Services of Thanksgiving were held, and in the three Christian places of worship addresses appropriate to the occasion were delivered. In the Protestant Church the Bishop of Madras preached an excellent sermon on the Jubilee, in which he dwelt on the virtues of Her Majesty. The Godavery Volunteers had a Church Parade, and were marched to their respective places of worship headed by their band. A very large number of poor Hindus were fed at the Prince of Wales's Choultry, and about 500 Mohammedans in the principal mosque, at 3 P.M. A substantial dinner was provided for poor East Indians at the Victoria Hotel. Between 4 and 5 P.M. Hindu and Mohammedan school children assembled at the Rajah's College, and were treated to sweetmeats, fruits, cakes, &c. Meanwhile the children of St. Thomas, Timpany Memorial, and St. Joseph's Convent schools met at a house in Jugernaikpuram, and held sports, and had different amusements provided for them till 5 P.M., when, after singing the National Anthem, and giving three hearty cheers for the Queen Empress, they were supplied plentifully with cakes, fruit, and sweets. At 6.30 P.M. the A Company of the Godavery Volunteer Rifles, headed by their band, marched to the Jubilee Pandal, and served as a guard of honour, being drawn up in open order in rear of the Chairman's seat, under the command of their Adjutant, Captain Deane. The Pandal, which covered the whole of the College compound, was crowded. Among the European community were the Bishop of Madras and his Chaplain; and the native gathering was a most representative one. The Pandal was well lighted and arranged, and the College itself was beautifully illuminated; it had a transparency in front with the words "God save the Queen Empress." The chair was taken by Mr. Boyce. After a preliminary speech the Presidencial Address was handed by the Chairman to Major Baker, Commandant of the Volunteers, who read it aloud. The Address was then adopted with enthusiasm. The Volunteers presented arms, and the band played the National Anthem, after which three hearty cheers, led by Major Baker, were given. Nautches, native jugglers, and music occupied the time till 8 P.M., when a procession was formed, and wended its way, under illuminated arches and pandals, to the *maidan* between the Marine Villa and the Marine Lascars' lines, where a display of fireworks took place. The number of people present was computed at between 12,000 and 15,000; a more orderly crowd was never seen.

COIMBATORE (TOWN).

The population of this town is 38,967, the Hindus being in a large majority. The chief Hindu castes in the town are Brahmins, Kshatrias (warriors), Chetties (traders), Vellalers (agriculturists), Idayars (shepherds), Kammalars (artisans), Kanakkhans (writers), Kaikalars (weavers), Vanniyas (labourers and cultivators), Kushavar (potters), Shembadavan (fishermen and hunters), Shanars (toddy drawers), Ambattan (barbers), Vannan (washermen), Salini (mixed castes), and others. The town has a College which teaches up to the First-in-Arts Standard, and three High Schools teaching up to Matriculation. There are twenty-two Boys' and three Girls' Schools, two mixed Schools for Eurasians, and two Normal Schools, one for Boys, and the other for Girls. Coimbatore has been a Municipality since 1866, and is provided with fine roads. Its chief imports are silk, iron, and cotton goods; while its exports are cotton, jaggery, myrabolams, horse gram, and timber. There are extensive works where the coffee cultivated on the Nilgiris is prepared for the home market.

Jubilee Committee.—Messrs. G. D. LEMAN, *Chairman*; ANNASAMI RAO, RAO SAHIB, *Secretary*; PERIYASAMI MUDELLIAR; Rev. M. ROUDY; Colonel PICKANCE; Messrs. C. C. FLANAGAN; KASTURI RANGAIYANGAR; TIRUVENGADASAMI MUDELLIAR; RAMASAWMY CHETTY; SAIYED ABDUL RAZZAC; and six others.

Early in the morning of the 16th February there was a parade of the Volunteers of Coimbatore and Podanur with the Reserve Police and Jail Guard, under the command of Colonel Pickance. A large crowd witnessed the parade. The troops fired a *feu de joie*, and gave three enthusiastic cheers, led by the Colonel, for Her Majesty. After a few well-executed manœuvres the line advanced to the flagstaff, and gave the Royal salute. The Presidencial Address to Her Majesty was read in English by the Collector, in Tamil by Mr. N. Annasami Rao, Rao Sahib, and in Hindustani by Abdul Rahimon Sahib. It was adopted with acclamation. Householders in the town showed their interest in the occasion by decorating their houses, while *thoranams* overhung every street, and some very effective decorations with mottoes appropriate to the occasion were displayed, and illuminated at night. At noon the clemency of Her Most Gracious Majesty was made known to the prisoners in the Jail, and 200 male and 12 female convicts were released. The afternoon was taken up with athletic sports in which all classes joined, and which gave much amusement to crowds of people. During the sports a Fancy Bazaar was held in various tents that had been pitched on the ground. In the town 1,000 poor were fed, and Rs. 200 worth of cloths were distributed among them. In the evening the town was brilliantly illuminated, the effect at the Chavadamman and Kanniparameswari temples, and at the three native Banks, being exceptionally noticeable, while spacious and brilliantly lighted Pandals had been erected at various places. The Police Office, the Post Office, the Magistrates' offices, and public buildings were brilliantly illuminated, as also the private residences of several native gentlemen. On the 17th there was a continuance of the afternoon amusements of the previous day, and the festivities wound up with an entertainment arranged by Colonel Pickance, consisting of some very well-arranged tableaux, and some songs which were listened to with much appreciation by a large audience of all classes. The final tableau of Britannia was much applauded, and "God save the Queen" was sung with great fervour by the whole audience. This ended the Jubilee celebration, which was marked by the utmost loyalty and enthusiasm on the part of all classes of the population.

COIMBATORE (VILLAGES).

The event was also worthily observed in the villages, and reports of the celebration were received by the District authorities from forty-one places. A few of these reports were daubed with saffron paste to indicate the happy nature of the news they conveyed. They stated that feasts, decorations, illuminations, and prayers in the various temples, mosques, and churches were the order of the two celebration days, and that the Jubilee was observed with universal rejoicings and great enthusiasm. At Kalumam, Mr. Kaniyur Kristnaiyer, a wealthy landlord of the taluk, gave a splendid feast to the village Brahmin community, and held a grand service in the ancient temple of Siva, from whence the god was taken round the place in procession.

COONOOR (NILGIRIS HILLS).

The population of Coonoor is 4,778, divided thus:—Europeans, Eurasians, and Native Christians, 1,164; Hindus, 3,247; Mohammedans and other castes, 367.

Jubilee Committee.—Lieutenant-Colonel W. N. CAREY, *Chairman*; Mr. A. ALLAN; Rev. J. M. BRANDON, LL.D.; Rev. FR. J. DANIS; Rev. J. GILLINGS; Messrs. N. G. BENSON; G. N. GROVES; L. W. GREY; Colonel F. C. KEYSER, C.B.; Colonel F. TICKELL; Dr. G. L. WALKER; and others.

People of all castes and creeds took part in the celebration. At 9 P.M. on the 16th February prayers for the long life and prosperity of Her Majesty were offered in all churches, mosques, and temples. Sweetmeats were profusely distributed among the school children of Wellington and Coonoor, followed by the feeding and clothing of several hundreds of poor. At 2 P.M. a grand procession of Hindus and Mohammedans, with banners and different kinds of music, started from Coonoor, and proceeded to Wellington Race-course. Colonel Carey, Chairman of the Municipality, read the Presidencial Address, which was adopted amid enthusiastic cheering. This was followed by the reading of a Tamil translation of the Address by the Deputy Tahsildar. Tamil verses, composed in honour of the occasion, were sung to music, and an English translation of the same was read. The proceedings concluded with three enthusiastic cheers for the Queen. The assembly then adjourned to an adjoining open place, where sports were held under the management of Colonel F. C. Keyser, C.B. At about 7 P.M. a grand display of fireworks commenced, and large bonfires were burnt on the tops of several of the hills around. Almost all the bazaarmen and shopkeepers decorated their premises with bunting and ferns; and several triumphal arches had been erected at different places, which were prettily illuminated at night.

At Wellington, near Coonoor, there was a Thanksgiving Service in the Garrison and other churches at 9.30 A.M. At 11.30 a large concourse of the ladies and gentlemen of the neighbourhood arrived at the barracks to witness the trooping of the Queen's colours by the troops in garrison. The barracks, which had been tastefully decorated for the occasion, looked very pretty. They were decked in foliage, and here and there a Union Jack, a banner, or some scroll of parti-coloured paper with a suitable motto displayed, relieved the dark green of the background. At 11.35 Colonel Keyser, the officer commanding the station, rode on to the parade-ground, where the troops had been drawn up in line, under the command of Major Daly, of the Royal Fusiliers. Having inspected the men, Colonel Keyser gave the order to proceed with the trooping, which was very well performed by the various guards, after which the troops fired a *feu de joie*. Three hearty cheers for Her Majesty, led by the Colonel, were given. The parade was then dismissed, and the Officers entertained a party at tiffin. Then the Good Templars, Foresters, and other Societies marched in procession with the children of the place, and a negro troupe. A native procession of School Children and others arrived soon after, and these sang the National Anthem in the vernacular. Along the route triumphal arches had been erected. At the entrance to the Race-course a halt was made, and the President read the Presidencial Address to Her Majesty; the Tahsildar then read a Tamil translation of it, and copies of it, printed in the vernacular, were distributed. Sports then commenced, while the children and native poor were entertained with a feast. The band of the Royal Fusiliers performed a programme during the afternoon, whilst a negro troupe did much to enliven the proceedings. At dusk a capital display of fireworks took place, and on every peak a bonfire celebrated the joyous occasion. The barracks at Wellington were also illuminated, and a bonfire in the barrack square lighted up the surrounding hills, while the band played. The last event of the day was a Jubilee Ball given by the Warrant Officers and Sergeants of the Royal Fusiliers. About 9.30 the guests commenced to arrive, and dancing was soon in full swing, to the strains of the Regimental Band. The ball-room, which had been tastefully decorated, looked very pretty with the colours of the Regiment, guarded by two sentries at the upper end. A large number of people from Coonoor, Wellington, and Ootacamund were present. About 250 persons sat down to supper. The health of Her Majesty was drunk with the greatest enthusiasm, followed by three ringing cheers, and the National Anthem was sung with great spirit.

CUDDALORE (SOUTH ARCOT).

Cuddalore is the head-quarters of the District of South Arcot. It comprises within its limits the remains of Fort Saint David, a place of much importance in the last century. The factory of Cuddalore in the immediate vicinity of the Fort was founded by the East India Company in 1682, and was one of its earliest settlements on the Carnatic coast. It contains a population of 43,545; of whom 38,997 are Hindus, 2,968 Muhammadans, and 1,580 Christians. The Hindu population comprises large numbers of Brahmins, traders, weavers, and fishermen. The educational wants of the town are supplied by 47 establishments, in which 2,705 boys and girls are under instruction. In these establishments are included a College educating for the University F. A. Examination, two High Schools educating up to the Matriculation Examination, and five Middle Schools. The remainder are Primary Schools. The sanitation of the town is under the charge of a Council consisting of twenty Councillors, who elect their own Chairman. Of the Councillors one half are elected by the ratepayers, and the other half are appointed by Government. Only five of the Councillors are Officials. The principal articles of export are grouped nuts, refined sugar, and rum; the principal imports are coal and palmyra rafters. The most noticeable local manufacture is that of palampores.

Jubilee Committee.—Messrs. H. P. Gordon, *Chairman*; A. B. Fortune, and M. Arumuga Pillai, *Secretaries*; J. Hope; T. M. Hursfall; J. Lakshmikanta Row; Devanayaga Mudalliar; R. E. Norfor; Surgeon-Major A. H. Leapingwell; Hazarat Mahomed Muratt Markars; and four others.

From an early hour crowds of people were seen hastening to the spacious *maidan* at the New Town. At 6.15 A.M. on the 16th February a salute of 31 guns was fired. The day's programme included British and Indian sports, open to competitors of all classes of Her Majesty's subjects. There was much excitement during the flat races. Rations were distributed to poor Europeans and Eurasians. The best descriptions of mutton, beef, potatoes, and bread procurable were provided gratuitously. The native poor assembled at various parts of the town, and were served with rice, and presented with sufficient money to give them a good day's meal. At a special service in the Roman Catholic Church, after the *Te Deum* had been sung, a hundred voices composing the choir for the occasion sang the National Anthem; and at the Anglican Church, at the conclusion of the sermon, the National Anthem was sung by the entire congregation. At 7.30 P.M. all the buildings around the plain were lit up. A transparency showing the words "God bless our Gracious Queen, Long may She reign over her devoted Subjects," was very prominent. The Roman Catholic Church and College were excellently illuminated. At the Old Town, several private residences were prettily illuminated, and the transparencies "God bless our Queen," "God bless our Queen Empress," and "Long live our Queen Empress," were marked by much taste. At 9.30 P.M. there was a grand display of fireworks which lasted for an hour and a quarter, after which the great crowds of people cheered and dispersed. The Presidencial Address was adopted and signed.

CUDDAPAH (CUDDAPAH).

Cuddapah, the chief town of the District of the same name, is situated eight miles from the river Pennar, and is on the north-western line of the Madras Railway. It has a considerable trade in cotton, indigo, rice, ghee, turmeric, gram, &c. There is a Municipal Council consisting of sixteen members. The population is 18,985; of whom 12,216 are Hindus, 7,273 Mohammedans, and 496 Christians. It is the head-quarters of the District and Session Judge, the Collector, the Head Assistant Collector, the Police Superintendent, District Forest Officer, Executive Engineer, District Medical and Sanitary Officer, District Munsiff, and several other officials. The principal buildings are the Court House, the Collector's Cutcherry, the Post Office, the Jail, the Municipal Dispensary, and the Municipal High School. There are a High School, a Middle School, and two other Schools where the Vernacular is principally taught, a Normal School under the management of the Local Fund Board, and a School established by the London Mission for the education of caste girls in English. There are two Churches for Protestants, and one for Roman Catholics.

Jubilee Committee.—Messrs. L. MOORE, *Chairman*; M. W. ELLIOT, *Secretary*; A. W. B. HIGGINS; C. J. JOHNSTON; A. F. ELLIOT, District Munsiff; H. C. HARLY; Dr. M. IYASAWMY PILLAI; Messrs. K. SESHIAH CHETTY; ABDUL RAZAK MIAH SAHIB; K. SESHIAH CHETTY; and twelve others.

The morning of the 16th February was ushered in with a *feu de joie* fired by the Railway Volunteers. At 8 A.M. a Jubilee Service was conducted in Christ Church and in the London Mission Chapel. Thanksgivings were offered in all the mosques and temples. About 3,000 poor people were fed and clothed in Muthial Sastriar's Chuttram and in the Poor House attached to the Civil Dispensary. From noon to 3 P.M. there were numerous processions, the chief among them being that of the village officials with trumpets and drums. The grandest was the public procession at 4 P.M., from the Post Office. It numbered between 4,000 and 5,000 persons who marched with flags and banners, and a native band playing English airs. First went tom-tom beaters and trumpeters; next came a large assemblage of village officials; then a native band; and following the band were the leading officials, Municipal Councillors, and chief residents, headed by the Acting Collector, Mr. Gabriel Stokes. The procession slowly wended its way through two of the principal streets in the native quarter, and then entered the High School compound, where a spacious and gaily decorated Pandal had been erected, under the direction of Surgeon Iyasawmy Pillay. The procession was received at the entrance to the Pandal by a Police guard of a hundred men, under the command of Colonel Wilton, the Police Superintendent. When all were seated, Mr. Stokes, the Acting Collector, rose, and, after a short speech, read the Presidential Address in English. Telugu and Hindustani translations were afterwards read, and the Address was adopted with cheers. The National Anthem was next sung with a musical accompaniment, Mr. Tussaint, of the Forest Department, playing on the Church harmonium which was lent by the Trustees of Christ Church. Then followed the recitation of Sanscrit verses composed by Pundit Bhashacharla in honour of Her Majesty. After the recitation the Police fired a *feu de joie*. The Collector called for three cheers for the Queen Empress, and right loyally did all those present respond to the call. At about 6 P.M. there was a performance by some Mysore acrobats, which lasted till about 7 o'clock, when the nautch in the Pandal began. At 8 P.M. there was a grand display of fireworks in the plain opposite the High School, and at its termination, about 9 P.M. all returned to the Pandal, where *pan supari* was distributed, and garlands of flowers were placed round the necks of the ladies and gentlemen present. Dr. Iyasawmy Pillay proposed three cheers for Mr. Stokes; and Mr. Higgins called for three cheers for Dr. Iyasawmy. These cheers were given very heartily, and the festivities terminated at 10.30 by the band playing the National Anthem. The Municipal Council made a grant for a fountain in connection with the Cuddapah water project, which will be called the "Victoria Jubilee Fountain."

CUMBUM (KURNOOL).

Cumbum is an old town, with a population of 7,170; of whom 4,691 are Hindus, 2,471 Mohammedans, and 8 Christians. There is one Local Fund School here. The chief exports are indigo, jaggery, and carpets; the chief imports are salt, tobacco, cocoa-nuts, pepper, iron, and cloths of different kinds.

Jubilee Committee.—Messrs. K. Rustum Singh; D. Srinivasa Row; H. S. Addis; D. Jagganatha Row Puntalu; C. Krishnasawmy Aiyar; Hoossain Khan Sahib; and six others.

A large and beautifully decorated Pandal had been erected in the compound of the Deputy Collector's office, with a triumphal arch, covered with green foliage, having over the entrance the inscription "God save the Queen" in large characters. The Pandal and the compound around were crowded with about 4,000 people. All the leading Europeans and Natives of the station were present. During the day prayers for Her Majesty were offered in the churches, temples, and mosques in the town. About 2,000 poor people, including Hindus, Mohammedans, and Native Christians who had come in from the neighbouring villages, were fed; nautches were held; native music was played; and acrobats performed. At night there was a display of fireworks. The Pandal and the compound, as well as the road leading from the office to the town, a distance of about a mile, were prettily illuminated. The houses in the town were whitewashed and illuminated by their owners, and the day was observed as a high festival by all classes. Dancing and music were kept up till a late hour in the night. There were also sports and acrobatic performances on the 17th at 4 P.M., at the conclusion of which a *feu de joie* was fired. It was decided to erect a "Fountain" in memory of the Jubilee.

DACHEPALLE (KISTNA).

The celebration of the Jubilee in this town was a great success. A large and handsome Pandal was erected, where the people assembled in large numbers. A Royal salute of 31 guns was fired; several speeches were delivered extolling the virtues of Her Majesty; and odes composed for the occasion in honour of the Queen Empress were recited. The Presidencial Address was read and received with enthusiasm, and was signed by a few representatives. Prayers were offered in all the temples, mosques, and churches for the welfare of the Queen Empress, and the prosperity of the British Empire. Poor persons of all castes were fed, and cloths were presented to some of them. In the evening there were horse-races and other sports; and at nightfall the town was prettily lit up, the illuminations in some portions being particularly effective. The Hindu gods were carried round the main streets in procession, with music and nautch girls. The procession was headed by a portrait of Her Majesty placed in a richly decorated palanquin. Fireworks were let off at intervals. At the conclusion of the procession, which was very imposing, the people were entertained with dramatic performances, and there was a distribution of *pan supari*. The festivities concluded with the offering up of a universal prayer invoking Heaven's richest blessings on Her Majesty and the Royal Family.

DEKANIKOTA (SALEM)

Dekanikota is an agricultural town, with a population of 3,899. Of these 2,099 are Hindus, 848 are Mohammedans, and 52 belong to other castes. The town contains a Deputy Tahsildar's Office, a Sub-Registrar's Office, an aided Middle School educating up to the Lower Fourth, a Local Fund School, a Dispensary, a Forest Office, a Post Office, and a few Pial Schools. There are two large Hindu temples.

Jubilee Committee.—Messrs. P. BHAWANI SANKARA ROWJI, *Chairman*; K. SANKARA AIYAR, B.A., *Secretary*; B. VENKATARAMA CHETTIAR; P. AHMATHEER; M. TIRUMALA IYENGAR; T. GARUDIER; T. SESHAGIRI ROWJI; B. MARAT GOUNDER; D. VENKATARAVAPPA; D. CHOORAYGOWDE; RAMA CHETTY; and twenty-three others.

A capacious Pandal had been erected in front of the Deputy Tahsildar's Cutcherry, with an arch at its entrance bearing the inscription, "God bless Queen Victoria." The Pandal, the streets leading to it, and the open space around were crowded with spectators, who had begun to assemble from an early hour. Appropriate mottoes and monograms appeared in different parts of the town. People of all races, castes, and creeds joined in the festivities. The leading officials, merchants, pleaders, &c., were present. The Deputy Tahsildar, Mr. P. Bhawani Sankara Rowji, delivered an interesting speech extolling the Queen Empress, and dilating on the benefits of British rule in India. An Imperial salute of 101 guns was fired by the Police, followed by a *feu de joie*. The Presidencial Address was read, and adopted with much enthusiasm. About 1,000 children were treated to fruits and sugar; and alms and gifts were distributed to about 300 poor Hindus and Mohammedans. The Jubilee was observed in all *Devastanums* with appropriate solemnity. *Abishakoms* and *archanas* were performed, and special prayers were offered for Her Majesty in the temples, mosques, and other places of worship. There were grand processions through the main streets. As soon as it was dark the streets, offices, temples, mosques, and almost all the houses were prettily illuminated. The proceedings terminated with a distribution of sandal, flowers, and *pan supari*. Repairs to the Sri Betrayaswami and Sri Thevamjeswaraswami temples are to be executed in honour of the Jubilee; and a "Chuttram" is to be built, as a permanent memorial of the event.

DEVAH SHOLA (NILGIRIS).

The aboriginal Badaga villagers who work on the Cinchona plantations here are intelligent, and excellent workmen. But though all have heard of the Queen Empress, most of them have no conception, except from what they see at Devah Shola, of civilisation.

By the orders of Mr. J. W. B. Money all the Badaga workmen at the Cinchona Gardens had a day's pay, and a day's holiday in honour of the Jubilee. In the evening they were brought by their respective heads to a spot selected for the purpose, where from 8 to 9 P.M. they witnessed a display of fireworks. As most of them had never before seen fireworks, and as the collection of rockets, bombs, and golden rain, breaking into numerous many-coloured balls, was good, the expressions of wonder and delight by the spectators were pleasant to hear. It seemed to be inferred from the display that fire was an appropriate means of celebrating the Jubilee of the Great Ranee, for shortly afterwards the dry scrub on the adjoining hills suddenly burst into flame, and these fires were kept up in glowing lines all through the night. The Presidencial Address was adopted, and signed by the local Committee.

DHARAPURAM (COIMBATORE).

The population is 7,310; of whom 5,579 are Hindus, 1,525 Mussulmans, and 206 Christians. There is a Local Fund Middle School, which has been recently raised to the Standard of a High School. There are 12 Result Schools. There is a Union Panchayet formed under the Provisions of the New Local Boards' Act. The staple commodities are paddy, tobacco, and sugar-cane. Dyeing and weaving are carried on extensively.

Jubilee Committee.—Messrs. BILIGIRI RAO, *Chairman*; T. A. SHUNMUGA SUNDRAM PILLAI, *Secretary*; V. SUBBA RAO, B.A.; N. K. NELLIAPPA PILLAI, B.A.; E. BALAVENKATARAMA NAIDU; M. S. VENCATARAMANA IYENGAR; MICHAL PILLAI; RAMACHANDRA NAIDU; M. MUTHURGA SAHIB: and several others.

The bazaars, the streets, and lanes, were adorned with *thoranams*. A large Pandal had been erected in front of the Taluk Cutcherry, at the entrance to which was a triumphal arch, bearing, in gold characters, the words "Long Live the Empress of India," both in English and in Tamil. At sunrise two prisoners were released. Prayers and Thanksgivings were offered during the forenoon in all the Hindu temples and Mohammedan mosques. More than 2,000 paupers of all classes were fed. Alms were given to poor Brahmins. The members of the Jubilee Committee went in procession, headed by a small body of Police, to the spot where the memorial Well was to be dug. The first sod was turned by the Chairman. The procession then moved towards the Local Fund School, where the boys had already assembled. Sweetmeats and fruits were distributed to more than 1,000 schoolboys and girls. At about 3 P.M. a public meeting was held in the premises of the Taluk Cutcherry, which was specially decorated for the occasion. On a *dais* which was adorned with flowers and garlands, a photographic portrait of Her Imperial Majesty was placed, and an able essay on the great benefits of the British rule to the people of India was read by the Sub-Registrar, the purport of which was explained in the vernacular by the Taluk Sheristadar. Sanscrit verses in praise of the virtuous rule of the Empress, composed by a learned Pundit, were read before the assembly.

The portrait of Her Majesty was then placed in a beautiful palanquin, and carried in procession. Over 1,000 people followed it. The town was beautifully illuminated at night. The illumination of the Taluk Cutcherry compound was very attractive. The festivities concluded with a grand display of fireworks. The Presidential Address was read and adopted. The permanent memorial in commemoration of the Jubilee is to take the form of a Well, which is to be called "The Victoria Jubilee Well." A Tennis Club has also been started in honour of the occasion, under the designation of "The Victoria Lawn Tennis Club."

DHARMASTALA (SOUTH CANARA).

This is a small town, forty-six miles from Mangalore, containing a Temple, which is visited by pilgrims from different parts of India. This ancient place of worship, dedicated to Shiva, numbers its votaries by millions in southern India. To all who visit it provisions are supplied gratis, irrespective of caste, and whatever may be the length of time for which the supplies are required. There are no Government Offices here except a Police station.

The Jubilee was celebrated here on the 16th and 17th in grand style. Invitations had previously been issued throughout the taluk. There were not many Government officials present on the occasion, most of them having gone to Mangalore to take part in the Jubilee festivities of that town. In the morning of the 16th rice was distributed to a large number of poor people who had come in from the neighbouring villages. *Abishekams* were performed, and special prayers were offered for the long life of the Queen Empress. About 600 Brahmins were feasted in the temple. At night the temple premises were illuminated with thousands of lights, and there was a torchlight procession of the gods, followed by a display of fireworks. After the *puja* was over, sugar, dates, and *pan supari* were distributed among the people who had assembled there. The same ceremonies were repeated on the 17th, but the illuminations at night were on a grander scale. About 6,000 people took part in the festivities. The expenses were borne entirely by Mr. Manjaya Hegdey, the manager of the Dharmastala Manjunath temple.

DHARMAVARAM (ANANTAPUR).

The population of this town is 5,926, consisting chiefly of Hindus. There are a few Mohammedans, and native Christians, and one East Indian. The town has been made a Union under the Local Boards' Act. The chief manufactures are silk and cotton cloths, and rough blankets; country paper is also manufactured in some parts of the taluk. The town trades in silk and silk-cloth, chiefly with Madras and Salem.

Jubilee Committee—Messrs. H. Ragavendra Row, *Chairman*; P. Veerasawmy Naidu, *Secretary*; R. Gopalachariar: Hanumantha Row; J. S. Smith; T. Narasimha Charlu; T. Polliah; G. Venkataramiah; A. K. Jeevana Row; L. Dasappa Chetty; and some others.

On Jubilee Day the people gathered in large crowds from all parts of the taluk. *Abishekams* and *archanas* were performed in the Hindu temples, and prayers were offered in the Mohammedan mosques that Her Majesty might be blessed with long life and prosperity. The poor were fed. At 6 P.M. the town was decorated and illuminated as at the Kartekai festival. About 4,000 persons of all castes and creeds assembled in the Pandal that had been erected on an open *maidan*. The Presidencial Address was read and explained to the audience in Telugu; it was then enthusiastically adopted. A Pundit recited in Telugu verse the benefits of British rule. The people cheered repeatedly. This was followed by a musical entertainment, and a display of fireworks. At 9 P.M. the assembly dispersed, after the distribution of *pan supari* and fruits, with loud cheers for the Queen Empress. Sweetmeats were also distributed among the schoolboys. Later in the night there was a procession of the gods of the chief temple, followed by a large concourse of people. On the 17th the poor were again fed, and the most indigent of them were presented with cloths. There were sports in the evening, and prizes were distributed to the successful competitors. Sweetmeats were again distributed among the children. The permanent local memorial will be either a "Chuttram" or an "English School"—both much-felt wants.

DINDIGUL (MADURA).

Dindigul is the chief town in the northern part of the Madura District, and the head-quarters of a Sub-Collector. It is nearly 1,000 feet above sea-level. It is built to the east of a huge gneissic boulder rising abruptly on the south side to a height of 280 feet. At the summit is an abandoned Temple, the lower part of which is in some parts very finely carved. The top of the rock is strongly fortified, all the accessible parts being guarded by a huge stone wall of French construction. Hyder Ali's initials are inscribed over the principal gateway. Commanding the roads leading to the south, Dindigul was long considered an important military post. The garrison was withdrawn about twenty years ago. The population in 1881 was 14,182. There is an old-established Protestant Mission at work in the town, connected with which are a Hospital and a Dispensary, which are largely resorted to. There is a Normal School for the training of Christian Teachers. There are also four Middle Schools and one High School.

Jubilee Committee.—Messrs. C. H. MOUNSEY, *Chairman*; G. S. HICKEY, *Secretary*; J. E. EVANS; REV. DR. E. CHESTER, M.D.; Messrs. T. HEMPEL; W. YOUNG; ABDUL KARIM KHAN; MIR SULTAN MOHIDEEN; C. SHEARS; SUNDRAM IYER; RAGAVENDRA ROW; and others.

At daybreak an Imperial salute of 101 guns was fired, and immediately afterwards the church bells began a lively peal, and then the old Rock re-echoed the strains of a band. Soon a procession, headed by an elephant, went round the town, most of the leading native officials accompanying it. The procession came to a halt near the Rock, where a Durbar was held. At 9 A.M., the Sub-Collector,

Mr. C. H. Mounsey, took the chair, and opened the proceedings by reading, amidst loud acclamations, the Presidencial Address to the Queen Empress, which was adopted. A Tamil translation of the Address was read by Mr. Anantharayana Aiyar, and intoned by the students of the C.V.E.S. Normal School; the large audience listened attentively, and gave marked symptoms of their cardial appreciation of the tribute of loyalty to their Maharanee. Then a pupil of the Hindu High School stepped forward, and expressed, on behalf of all the schoolboys of Dindigul, their loyal devotion to so good and noble a Queen. The Schools of the town and surrounding villages were present, and sang "God save the Queen" in English and Tamil, with much heartiness. Sweetmeats were distributed among them. Garlands were placed round the necks of the chief persons present, and, after a few of them had signed the Address, the Durbar terminated. 1,700 poor persons were fed, and some of them received cloths. At 3 P.M. a very successful programme of sports was begun. Towards dusk the illuminations on the town-side of the Rock presented a very pretty sight. The Revd. Dr. Chester's Hospital, the Post Office, and the grounds of the C.V.E.S. Normal School were illuminated in a particularly attractive manner. The existence of this town is imperilled by lack of water, the nearest source of supply being four miles distant. The improvement of the supply is the first object to which the Jubilee Committee propose to apply the funds collected. If it be possible a "Town Hall" will also be erected, to commemorate the Jubilee, and will be named after the Queen Empress.

ELLORE (GODAVERY).

This favourite residence of military pensioners is one of the municipal towns in the Godavery District, and it is 90 miles from Masulipatam. Its population is 25,092. It is the head-quarters of the Head Assistant Collector, and contains a Subordinate Judge's Court, Munsiff's Court, Government Telegraph Office, Post Office, Tahsildar's Office, and Local Fund Engineer's Office. There are also a Church Mission Society's High School, three Hindu Caste Girls' Schools, two Mohammedan Girls' Schools, and one Christian Girls' School. The town is celebrated for its carpets.

Jubilee Committee.—Messrs. L. C. Miller, *Chairman*; E. Kachapeswarasastry Rao Saib, *Secretary*; Sri Rajah Venkatramiah Apparow Bahadur; Sri Rajah Venkatadri Apparow Bahadur; Sri Rajah Vellanki Venkata Krishnarow Bahadur; A. Sivaramakrishnama, B.A.; and twenty-three others.

At 8 o'clock A.M., Thanksgiving Services were held in all the churches, temples, and mosques of the town, after which the poor of all religions and castes were fed. At 3 P.M. a grand procession with elephants, horses, flags, banners, and music, started from the bungalow of the Head Assistant Collector, Mr. L. C. Miller. The procession was headed by that gentleman and the principal officials, and other residents, and was followed by the masters and boys of the C.M.S.

High School. After proceeding through the principal streets of the town, which were gaily decorated, the procession entered, at 5 P.M., the spacious grounds of the Fort. The Fort was beautifully decorated with flags, banners and arches, bearing suitable mottoes. In the centre of an enclosure, under the shadow of the flag of England, there was an ivory throne, and upon it was placed a portrait of the Queen Empress. Flowers were strewn upon the throne. The ceremony concluded with the reading of the Presidencial Address in English, Telugu, Hindustani, and Sanscrit. The Address was adopted amid the loud and prolonged cheering of the multitude of about 15,000 people who were present. The rest of the day was spent in various amusements, including the performances of acrobats and musicians; and the festivities terminated with a magnificent display of fireworks which lasted till midnight. At night the whole town was illuminated.

ERODE (COIMBATORE).

This rising town has a population of 9,864; of whom 8,338 are Hindus, 1,084 Mohammedans, and 439 Christians. It is the head-quarters of the Sub-Collector, and of the Assistant-Superintendent of Police, Coimbatore District. It contains a District Munsiff's Court, a Taluk Cutcherry, the Office of the D. P. W. Sub-Divisional Officer. A Taluk Board is established here. The educational institutions include a native High School, teaches up to the standard of the Matriculation Examination; a national Middle School teaches up to the standard of the Middle School Examination; a local Fund Normal School, training up for the Upper Primary Examinations; a Municipal Combined System School; a Municipal Girls' School; a London Mission School; a Mohammedan School; and many other Primary Schools under the Results system. Erode is one of the two junction stations of the Madras and South Indian Railways. It conducts a large trade in jaggery, cotton, turmeric, chillies, paddy, and other grains.

Jubilee Committee.—Messrs. V. A. BRODIE, *Chairman*; K. R. LAKSHMINARAYANA IYER, *Secretary*; I. DORASAWMY PILLAI; QUADIR ALLAVUDDIEN SAIB; P. KRISTNA RAO; T. L. NARASIMHA; and twenty-eight others.

A public meeting was held in Erode at 8.30 A.M., when about 5,000 people were present. A photograph of the Queen Empress decorated with garlands, flowers, and jewels, which is intended to adorn the walls of the Municipal Hall, was placed in front of the spacious Pandal that had been erected, and in which the meeting was held. The proceedings commenced with the singing of the National Anthem. The District Munsiff, Mr. Dorasawmy Pillai, was unanimously voted to the chair. Mr. M. Venkatarama Aiyar, B.A., the Head Master of the Native High School, Erode, addressed the meeting on the importance of the occasion. Other speeches followed. The people formed a procession and marched, headed by the band, through the main streets, and returned to the Pandal. Food and cloths were distributed to about 1,500 poor people. The pagodas presented a gay spectacle, all being splendidly decorated and illuminated. The gods were anointed with holy water, and *abishekams* were performed. A procession of the gods, tastefully decked out in rich cloths, with jewels and garlands, with silk hangings over the vehicles, then started, followed by the Brahmin priests, who sang hymns. The procession, which was headed by dancing girls, met, in the heart of the town, another which had set out from the Municipal premises. A native band played the National Anthem, and the rear of the procession was brought up by the officials, merchants, vakils, and mirasidars. Sweetmeats, fruit, flowers, sandal, rose-water, &c., were distributed to the boys of the various local schools. At evening lights were lit in all houses. There was a fine display of fireworks, and sandal, *pan supari*, &c., were distributed by the Deputy Munsiff. A musical entertainment was given, and a nautch was held. The proceedings terminated with three hearty cheers for Her Majesty. All classes of people cordially co-operated in making the celebration a success. The Presidencial Address was adopted.

GANJAM (DISTRICT).

In this District the Jubilee was most heartily observed by all classes of the people. The following description of the celebration in certain towns applies to every town and large village in the District. The Presidencial Address was adopted by the District Committee.

Biridi.—The festivities commenced with the holding of special services, and the offering of prayers to the gods and goddesses in all temples for Her Majesty. Food was given to Brahmins and the poor, and the latter were presented with new cloths. A Pandal had been erected for the occasion, and was decorated with festoons and plantain trees, and lighted up with lanterns and torches. A dramatic performance was given in this Pandal all night. The festivities wound up with a display of fireworks, the firing of a *feu de joie*, and the invocation of blessings on Her Majesty. The outlying villages in the Zemindary also observed the occasion in a very loyal manner.

Boddam.—The Jubilee was celebrated at Boddam, and at Parlakimedi, where the Proprietor resides. At the latter place a Pandal had been erected, and furnished with a canopy, under which was placed a portrait of the Queen Empress, set in a richly embroidered frame. The hall was well illuminated, and hung with boards on which were inscribed mottoes in English, Telugu, and Uriya, expressive of loyalty. A number of persons, including a few Europeans, assembled, and an address was read in English and Telugu, and three cheers given for the Queen Empress. This was followed by a recitation of Sanscrit verses composed for the occasion: a musical performance; and the singing of a Telugu version of "God save the Queen." The distribution of *pan supari*, &c. wound up the festivities. During the day special services were held in two temples for the health and prosperity of the Queen Empress, and the gods were carried through the streets in solemn procession followed by Brahmins chanting Vedic hymns. At Boddam the poor were fed, and at Parlakimedi presents were given to them.

BUDARASINGI.—The occasion was celebrated by special illuminations and offerings in all temples in the Zemindar's fort and the taluk. Food was distributed throughout the taluk.

CHINNA TOONGAM.—The day was observed as a holiday; and the blowing of conches and the beating of drums resounded from an early hour. Special services were held, and prayers were offered in the temples, which were illuminated during the whole of the ensuing night.

DANTA.—The day was kept as a high festival at the two proprietary villages of Danta and Siddhantam, and about 500 people were given a hearty meal. There were also illuminations, music, and a display of fireworks.

DEVABHOOMI-HUNDA.—The Jubilee was celebrated with great enthusiasm. Food was distributed to the poor and peasantry, numbering about 2,000. Special services were held, and prayers were offered for the Queen Empress in all the temples, which were well illuminated.

DHARAKOTE.—The Court of Wards having made a grant for the local celebration, the Brahmins of nine Agraharams were sumptuously fed, while rice and money were distributed to the poor, as well as to some distant connections of the Zemindar's family who are in indigent circumstances. The fort was illuminated, and there was a display of fireworks, &c. Prayers for Her Majesty were offered in the temples throughout the taluk, which were also illuminated. Everywhere there was general festivity.

GOPALPORE.—Rice and dholl, sufficient for two substantial meals, were distributed to about 200 men, women, and children, each adult being in addition paid one anna, and each child six pies. In the evening the pier was illuminated, and fireworks and coloured lights were shown. The children of the Hindu school were treated to sweetmeats, and those of the European and Eurasian school were entertained at tea.

ICHAPORE.—The Jubilee was celebrated in this town with great rejoicings. All the temples and mosques, and very many private residences, were illuminated. Special services were held, and prayers were offered for the Queen Empress. The Hindu gods were carried through the town in solemn procession, accompanied by nautch parties, and native bands. There was a display of fireworks. Uncooked rice, and money, were distributed to the poor and infirm both on the 16th and on the 17th. Offerings were given to the Hindu gods.

JARADA.—Brahmins and the poor were well fed, and the Jubilee was celebrated with a variety of demonstrations, among which were musical concerts and dramatic performances. The town was illuminated, and *attar* and rose-water were distributed. In the evening there was a grand display of fireworks.

MANDASA.—The Jubilee was celebrated in grand style in the town, and in the villages of the Zemindari, as well as in the Savara hamlets, and on Mahendragiri. The blind and lame were fed and clothed, and four "Free Scholarships" were instituted in the Rajah's School in honour of the occasion. Special prayers for Her Majesty were offered at services held in all temples, and the gods were carried through the town in procession. In the evening, after a Savara dance, the Rajah, accompanied by his family and retinue, went round the town, followed by a procession, with native music and nautch girls. The town was illuminated, and a grand display of fireworks brought the proceedings to a close.

PEDDA TOONGAM.—The god Venkateswaraswami was taken round the town in procession, accompanied by native music, dancing, and singing. The people of the village observed the day as a holiday, and illuminated their houses.

PRATAPAGIRI.—Some time previous to the festival notices had been circulated in the taluk of the intended celebration of the Jubilee, and the people were invited to participate in the festivities. About 4,000 people assembled at Pudamari on the 16th. Prayers, &c. were offered in the sixty-five temples and mutts, which were all illuminated. About 1,500 poor, including Uriya Brahmins, were fed, and to 1-0 cripples and orphans cloths were given. The town and the Zemindar's Fort were beautifully illuminated. A Pandal had been erected in the main street, where a large multitude assembled; and, after an appropriate speech in Uriya had been delivered by the manager of the estate, three cheers for the Queen Empress were called for, and enthusiastically responded to by the assembled crowd. A pyrotechnic display, which brought the proceedings to a close, followed.

RUSSELKONDAH.—Ablutions of the gods, offering in the Hindu temples, and a dinner to Brahmins formed part of the day's proceedings. Food was distributed to 500 poor persons. Four Pandals were erected in different parts of the town, under one of which, in the middle of the town, were assembled the native gentry, and an address was read explaining the chief features of Her Majesty's reign. The address elicited expressions of profound satisfaction. The whole town was illuminated and the Hindu god was taken around it in procession, accompanied by torches and blue lights, &c., the Khonds joining in. There was a display of fireworks. About 10,000 people assembled to witness the celebration. In the Mohammedan mosques the poor were fed. In all temples and mutts under the management of the Temple Committee prayers for Her Majesty were offered.

SANTA LUKSHMIPURAM.—The Jubilee was observed by feeding the poor and illuminating the villages, and by general festivity.

SERUGADA.—The Jubilee was celebrated by feeding the poor, by offering special prayers and rice offering, &c. to the gods, and by illuminating the Fort and the town. The outlying villages of the taluk also celebrated the Jubilee.

SOWDAM.—The festival was observed by feeding the poor, and by illuminations at night.

TALASAMUDRUM.—The town was adorned with festoons and illuminated; special services were held in the places of worship, and offerings were given to the god.

TECKALY.—The Jubilee was celebrated by illuminating the Fort and temples, where offerings were given in honour of the occasion, and food was distributed to the people.

GINGER (SOUTH ARCOT).

This town was once known as Bagayah, but it has been re-named Gingee, after the famous fortress in its vicinity. The Fortress was formed of three strongly fortified hills, connected by walls of circumvallation, enclosing an area of over seven miles in circumference. The fortifications are said to have been commenced in the year 1442 by a Governor of Tanjore. Gingee then became a stronghold of the Vijayanagar Kings. It was overthrown by the Mohammedan Kings of the Deccan in 1564. In 1677 Sivaji accomplished the capture of the fort. In 1690 the place was besieged by the armies of the Emperor of Delhi. The siege is said to have lasted eight years. In 1750 the French, under Bussy, captured Gingee. In 1761 it was seized by the British. In 1780 it was surrendered to Hyder Ali. The fortifications are now in ruins.

The local celebration consisted of illuminations; the offering of prayers for the Queen Empress in the temples, mosques, and churches; and the feeding of the poorer classes. The gods from the Vishnu and Siva temples were brought down to the river in procession, when *Mandagapadi* was performed. At night there was a grand torchlight procession, which was attended by large crowds. At about 7 A.M. on the 17th the gods were taken back to their respective temples. Thanksgiving Services were held in the Jain temples and in the Roman Catholic church, which was decorated and illuminated. In almost every house hymns were sung in praise of Her Majesty. *Fathia* was performed in the Moslem mosque, and many poor Mohammedans were fed. At 5 in the evening there was a great gathering of rich and poor people from all parts of the Division, when a sketch of the life of Her Majesty was read by C. S. Kristnasbma Aiyanger, and the people cheered enthusiastically. This was followed by a display of fireworks, which lasted for about an hour. Sandal and *pan supari* were distributed. The Presidencial Address was adopted.

GOOTY (ANANTAPUR).

The population is 5,373, and includes Hindus 3,749, Mohammedans 1,587, Christians 37. The town possesses a fortress of great strength, built in the early part of the sixteenth century, which was once a Mahratta stronghold. It subsequently fell into the hands of Hyder Ali, and passed to the English by a treaty with the Nizam, who had captured it after the fall of Tippu. There is a European cemetery in which for a time the body of Major General Sir Thomas Munro, K.C.B., Governor of Madras—who died here in 1827—rested before its removal to Fort St. George, Madras. There is a large Choultry, with a beautiful Well built in memory of Sir Thomas Munro, to mark public gratitude for his administration. Formerly travellers were fed in the Choultry. The endowment has been utilised in erecting the present Munro Dispensary building, and in partially supporting it. This is the head-quarters of the Gooty Division of the Anantapur District. The town contains a Deputy Collector's Office, a District Munsiff's Court, and a Tahsildar's Office, besides several other minor offices, a London Mission School, and a Sanscrit School. There are several Associations in the town engaged in promoting the political, social, and religious improvement of the people in the District.

Jubilee Committee.—Messrs. P. T. RAJAGOPALA CHARIAR, RAO BAHADUR, *Chairman*; P. KESAVA PILLAI, RAO SAHEB, *Secretary*; T. RAMACHENDRA ROW, B.A., B.L.; T. KRISHNAMOORTHY IYENGAR, B.A.; S. RAGHAVENDRA ROW; J. SRINIVASA ROW RAO SAHIB; A. OMER KHAN SAHIB BAHADUR; and twelve others.

The Jubilee was celebrated here with great enthusiasm and success. It was announced before sunrise by the firing of musketry on the Fort ramparts. The town put on a gala appearance. Her Majesty's photograph was carried through the chief streets with music. More than two thousand persons of all castes, creeds, and orders were entertained with sumptuous meals at the Munro Choultry. Prayers were said in all the temples, mosques, and churches. Sports were held in the evening, and prizes distributed. At 6 o'clock a mass meeting was held, at which Mr. P. T. Rajagopala Chariar presided. Mr. P. Kesava Pillai read the Presidencial Address, and said that under Her Majesty's beneficent reign the Indian people had derived many rights, and obtained various blessings. Mr. J. Srinivasa Row read a Telugu translation of the Address. The Address was then accepted in a very loyal manner. Mr. S. Vasudeva Rao, B.A., announced that it was proposed to establish a "Memorial Library" at the Sanscrit School in honour of the Jubilee and that efforts would be made to open this Library on the 20th June. Mr. P. Krishnama

Charry recited a Telugu ode composed for the Jubilee by himself. Mr. Ramachendrapah also recited some verses of the National Anthem, which was sung in Telugu by the Christian ladies and the London Mission School girls, the audience standing. Enthusiastic cheers were given for the Queen Empress; for the Marquis of Ripon, the late Viceroy of India; the Earl of Dufferin, the present Viceroy of India; Mr. Bourke, the Governor of Madras; Mr. Nicholson, the Collector of Anantapur: and for the Chairman. The proceedings ended with the firing of guns. The children were given sweetmeats. The gods were taken in procession round the town.

GUDALUR (NILGIRIS).

This chief town of the Nambalakod amshams contains 1,769 inhabitants. It is the centre of the coffee industry of South-east Wynaad. A Sub-Magistrate is stationed here. The place was transferred from Malabar to the Nilgiris in 1877.

At 8 A.M. the Roman Catholics attended Divine Service in their church. The Service commenced with a procession around the church, formed of the priest and congregation. The Litany of the Blessed Virgin Mary was chanted during the ceremony. On the procession entering the church, High Mass was celebrated. At the close of the celebration the officiating minister delivered an appropriate sermon in English. The *Te Deum* was then chanted. At 11 A.M. the native Protestant Christians assembled in their church for service. About 6.30 P.M. the Post Office, Roman Catholic Church, and the Hospital premises were illuminated. About the same time there was a display of fireworks at the Post Office. At 7 P.M. the Roman Catholics again assembled in their church, when the Benediction of the Blessed Sacrament was said. This was followed by the singing of "God save the Queen" in English. After this there was a display of fireworks in the grounds of the church and of the hospital.

GUDIVADA (KISTNA).

This is a place of great antiquity, and possesses interesting Buddhist remains. Its population numbers 4,041.

Jubilee Committee.—RAJAH KAMARAJA VENKATA NARASIMHARAO, *Chairman*; Messrs. DRONADULA SOBHANADRI NAIDU, and VATTEM VENKATASUBBAYYA SASTRI, *Joint Secretaries*; BHAVIRISETTI MANIKYAM; W. C. DE MORGAN; C. RAGHAVALAN PUNTALU; V. LAKSHMAN RAU PUNTALU; F. C. RODRIGUES, and others.

A large Pandal had been erected in front of the Anjenaya Temple, in the centre of the town. The chief street was decorated with elegant arches, over which the flags of different nations fluttered in the breeze. The pupils of the Local Fund Middle School marched in the early morning, accompanied by their teachers, to the temples, singing the National Anthem. After service the students were feasted. Some 300 poor people were fed. A grand mass meeting was held at the Pandal in the evening. A nautch then took place, and two plays were acted, after which the gods were carried through the chief streets of the town in procession. The festivities wound up with illuminations, and a display of fireworks. To permanently commemorate the Jubilee the Committee made a grant for the establishment of "Victoria Scholarships" in the Local Fund Middle School of the town. The Presidencial Address was adopted.

GUNTUR (KISTNA).

This town was ceded to the French by the Nizam in 1752. It came into the possession of the British in 1778. It is the head-quarters of the Sub-Collector, the Assistant Superintendent of Police, the Zillah Surgeon, the District Munsiff and Tahsildar. It has a Telegraph Office, a District Jail, a large Hospital, and a Branch of the Madras Bank. The trade is large and increasing, consisting of cotton, oil seeds, indigo, tobacco, chillies, and grain. There are two steam cotton presses, two large hand cotton presses, and four oil presses. The merchandise is taken either to Bezwada or Chirala on the Canal. The population is 19,646, including 14,706 Hindus, 4,619 Mohammedans, 314 Christians, and 7 others. The Town contains the following Schools:—2nd Class Mission College, Municipal High School, Local Fund Normal School, Hindu Anglo-Sanscrit School, Municipal Anglo-Hindustani School, three Night Charity Schools, several Results grant Schools, and two Girls' Schools. The Municipal body is formed of four official and twelve non-official Councillors.

Jubilee Committee.—Messrs. J. E. SHAW, *Chairman*; W. BHAVANACHARLU, *Secretary*; K. MRUTUNJAYARAZAN PUNTALU; C. M. MULLALY; R. F. GILL; W. SURYANARAYANA RAU PUNTALU; C. VENKATACHALAM PUNTALU; L. G. LINDSAY; G. VENKATAPPAYYA, C. G. HAY; D. CARLIKE, and twenty-eight others.

A magnificent Pandal had been erected in the compound of the Sub-Collector's house. The proceedings commenced with an official reception at the Pandal, at which all the officials, the Municipal Councillors, and most of the leading inhabitants of the town were present. Mr. C. M. Mullaly, the Sub-Collector, addressed the assembly, and proposed the adoption of the Presidencial Address. The Address was then read by Mr. Singaravellu Mudelliar, the Chairman of the Municipality, in English; after which Mr. B. Raghavacharlu, the Taluk Sheristadar, read a Telugu translation of it. The Address was then received with cheers, and signed. Mr. Ramachendrayya, B.A., a Native Christian, then read an address on behalf of the Native Christians. Addresses were read by Mr. Mustin Sheriff on behalf of the Mohammedans, and by the Rev. Mr. Unangst on behalf of the Lutheran Mission. After these were concluded the Joint Magistrate called up 61 prisoners, and released them. "God save the Queen" was played; and an Imperial salute and *feu de joie* were fired. Then the European community went to the Lutheran Mission Chapel, and engaged in a Thanksgiving Service. Similar services were held in all the temples and mosques. From 12 to 3 P.M. 1,375 poor were fed. The evening was devoted to the treating of school children. Sports were then held. One of the most interesting sights of the evening was the trooping of the children into the compound where the sports were held, with banners flying; and the prettiest sight of all was afforded by the girls of the Lutheran Mission School. All the schools had a treat of sweets and fruits, separate wings to the Pandal being set apart for the girls and boys. In addition to the sports there were acrobatic performances. The people dispersed at 7 P.M. The illuminations commenced as soon as it was dark. There was a dinner at the Club. The fireworks began at 9.30, and the evening concluded with a grand procession through the town. A fine painting of Her Majesty, in a richly decorated and illuminated frame, was carried in the centre of the procession. It was preceded by all the European officials and non-officials; while the leading native officials and non-officials, a Police guard, and musicians followed. The town was illuminated. The procession was a most enthusiastic and successful one; it was entirely native in its idea, and it continued up to 2 A.M. The festivities were continued on the following day. A theatrical performance was given by the Guntur Hindu Theatrical Company.

HARPANAHALLI (BELLARY).

The population of Harpanahalli Taluk is 70,620; of whom 66,806 are Hindus, 3.634 Mohammedans, 7 Christians, and 173 of other castes. The town of Harpanahalli was formerly the seat of a Poligar, who resided in the fort which is now falling into ruin. The population is 6,536, including a Jain colony. Canarese is the prevailing tongue. There is a Local Fund Middle School, where English, Telugu, and Canarese are taught. There are seven Pial Schools where Canarese is taught. There is also a Caste Girls' School, presided over by a Brahmin Head Mistress, where girls are taught Canarese as well as knitting and sewing. Cumblies are abundantly manufactured in almost all the villages of the taluk.

Jubilee Committee.—Messrs. COUKOOR GURU ROW, *Chairman*; V. KODANDARAMA AIYAR, *Secretary*; H. RAMA ROW; I. BHOMMANAH; BHEEMARANA ROW; M. MUKAPPAH; S. R. VONKAPPAH; ARASUPPAH; and H. VENKOBA ROW.

Almost all the houses in the town were whitewashed, and the streets were decorated with *thoranams*, or strings of flowers. Money was distributed to the priests of the Hindu temples and Mohammedan mosques, where prayers for the long life of the Queen Empress were offered at noon. From 7 A.M. to 10 P.M. cholam and rice were distributed to the poor of all classes, and cloths were given to the most needy. In the afternoon about 600 boys and girls of the different schools were treated to sweetmeats. Sports of various sorts were then held, and acrobats and rope-dancers performed. At about 5.30 P.M. the Presidencial Address was read by the Honorary Secretary in English, and explained by the Tahsildar in the vernacular to the collected audience; it was then adopted with acclamation, and signed by representatives of all classes. A grand procession was now formed, which, headed by a band of native musicians and nautch girls, and accompanied by the chief inhabitants of the town, and by a body of police constables, passed through the chief thoroughfares. It stopped opposite the Venkateswaraswami Temple, where the National Anthem was sung by the schoolboys, and prayers were offered by the people for the continuance of the reign of Her Majesty. The town was illuminated in the evening. From 7 to 9 P.M. there was a display of fireworks. From 9 to 12 P.M. there was a musical entertainment and nautch. The festivities closed at 1 A.M. with three hearty cheers for the Queen Empress, and thanks to the Chairman, the Secretary, and members of the Jubilee Committee for the admirable manner in which the festivities had been conducted. 3,000 people took part in the festivities, of whom 600 were fed, treated to sweetmeats, or presented with cloths.

HINDUPUR (ANANTAPUR).

A Durbar of the leading gentlemen of the town was held in the morning in Venkatamanaswamy's Temple, when it was resolved that "the Penukonda Newspaper Club be requested to convey its feelings of gratitude and loyalty to Her Most Gracious Majesty the Queen Empress of India." The Tahsildar, Mr. George Gopaul Rao Puntulu, delivered a short speech on the various benefits derived during Her Majesty's reign. Mr. Sundara Iyer also spoke on the same theme. This was followed by prayers and thanksgivings in the temples and mosques. Between 10 and 12 o'clock the poor were fed, and the generosity in this respect of Curnam Bhumanna and other merchants was conspicuous. At noon crowds began to collect in the plain near the market where there were sports and games, including gymnastic exercises, flat races, sack races, jumping, tug-of-war, wrestling, donkey races, three-legged race, and horse race. In the evening there was another Durbar, which was well attended. Telugu verses, composed by Mr. Anantaramachariar for the occasion, were recited amidst much applause. At 6 P.M. there was a procession of gods through the town, after which a great assembly met in the Flower Pandal that had been erected for the occasion by Mr. Appadorai Mudelliar, where a musical entertainment and nautch party were given. The Presidencial Address was adopted. A grand display of fireworks brought the festivities of the day to a close. The next morning the children of the schools in the town were given sweetmeats. Later on a sumptuous banquet was given to the officials and merchants, which was followed by a singing party, and nautch, which continued till sunset.

HOSPET (BELLARY).

This town is about forty miles from the town of Bellary. The population is 10,219, of whom 8,868 are Hindus, 1,231 are Mohammedans, 60 are Christians, and 60 are unclassified. A large proportion of the inhabitants are weavers. Hospet is the head-quarters of the Head Assistant Collector.

There was a large meeting in a Pandal on the 16th February, at which the leading inhabitants of Hospet and Chittavadigy were present. Mr. Campbell, the Head Assistant Collector, presided, and Mrs. Campbell laid the foundation stone of the "Victoria Dharmasala." The Presidencial Address was adopted. A nautch followed, with a procession from the temples. Gifts were made to Brahmins on the following day. A garden party was held, and prizes were given. Sweetmeats were distributed to schoolboys and girls. The National Anthem in Canarese, and several songs composed for the occasion were also sung. Then came sports and fireworks, concluding with hearty cheers for the Queen Empress.

HOSUR (SALEM).

Hosur is situated about 3,000 feet above the sea-level. The population numbers 5,869, viz. 5,170 Hindus, 655 Mohammedans, and 44 Christians. In addition to the Sub-Collector who has his head-quarters here, a Tahsildar, a Deputy Inspector of Schools, D.P.W. and Local Fund Supervisors, an Inspector of Police, a Civil Apothecary, and a Sub-Registrar usually reside here. There are Government and Mission Schools, both for boys and girls. The taluk produces country ponies and fine bulls. The Remount Depot of the Cavalry and Artillery in Madras is four miles from this town. The staple food of the people is raggi, which is very largely grown here. The Taluk Board was constituted last April, and the Union Panchayet last September.

Jubilee Committee.—Messrs. H. Subba Rao, *Chairman*; G. Venkataramana Chetti, B.A., *Secretary*; P. A. Ramasawmy Iyer; Kotha Rungappa Chetti; V. Ramachendra Chetti; Badami Subba Row; Khazi Rahiman Sahib; T. Srinivasa Row; Krishna Gounder; Ramalingiah; Nunjappiah; and five others.

At daybreak on the 16th February the cleanliness of the town, the festoons of fresh leaves and flowers placed at intervals on the roads, the houses decorated in the Oriental fashion, the triumphal arches exhibiting in glittering letters the words "God save the Queen Empress," "Long live our beloved Queen," "Happy Jubilee of Victoria;" and the activity of the leading inhabitants of the place, gave promise of a gala day. A large number of persons went to the temple of Rama, in the Fort, and, after the offering of poojahs, the deity was conveyed in procession with music to the site of the new temple. Two Pandals, exquisitely constructed and beautifully decorated, gave shelter to the great concourse of people who had assembled there.

Sunku, or the initiation ceremony for the new temple, which is to be one of the permanent local memorials of the Jubilee, was then performed, and hymns were chanted invoking the aid of the Divine Being in the erection of the building, and thus to perpetuate the name of the Queen Empress in the town. Mr. Subba Rao, the Chairman of the Jubilee Committee, explained the object of the festivities of the day. Divine service was held in all places of religious worship; and prayers were offered by Hindus, Mohammedans, and Christians for the health, prosperity, and long life of Her Majesty. At noon an Imperial salute of 101 guns was fired by a body of Police constables. Sweetmeats and other refreshments were distributed to the people freely. Three hearty cheers were given for Her Majesty amidst rapturous applause. In the evening all the churches, temples, mosques, schools, and many houses were beautifully illuminated. The Post and Telegraph Office exhibited the inscription "God save the Queen" in glittering letters. The festivities of the day culminated in a brilliant procession of the principal gods. The Presidential Address was adopted. On the 17th there were sports of various kinds lasting for a number of hours. At night there was a musical entertainment. In addition to the new "Temple" to be erected to Sri Kothundaramaswami in commemoration of the Jubilee, a Scholarship, to be called the "Jubilee Scholarship" is to be founded; and the Chudamathaswami Temple is to be renovated.

IDAIYANGUDI (TINNEVELLY).

The 16th February commenced with the firing of a Royal salute of 31 guns, after which the bells of Holy Trinity Church (S.P.G.) sounded forth a joyous peal, and a band that had been engaged for the occasion struck up lively airs, and attracted a large concourse of people to the Church Street. This crowd was soon joined by the clergy and the choir in their robes, and the members of the Church Council, and an imposing procession was formed, headed by the band, and the school children carrying gay-coloured banners. This procession passed through the principal streets of the village, and then entered the grand Gothic Church, which had been very prettily decorated. Here a solemn Thanksgiving Service was held, the officiating priests being the Rev. Messrs. S. Gnanamuttu, M.A., D. Pakyam, and P. Swamiadian. At the conclusion of the service the National Anthem was sung in an excellent manner. At noon another salute of 31 guns was fired, and at 1 P.M. a treat was given to the school children and the lace women, and one hundred poor people were fed. In the evening there were public games, races, athletic sports, fencing, &c., and the *Kolattam* performance.

At 6 P.M. the "Victoria Memorial Lamp" in the centre of the Church Street, which is to be the permanent memorial in this town of the Jubilee year of Her Majesty, was lighted amidst the general acclamation of the people, who had assembled in large crowds to witness the ceremony. At 6.30 P.M. there was a grand illumination of the streets, and the church. At 7 P.M. there was a procession of the clergy, the choir, and the people round the church. Evensong was then said by the Rev. D. Pakyam, and an appropriate sermon was preached by the Rev. S. Gnanamuttu, M.A., on the personal history of the Queen Empress; the brilliancy of her reign; the military, naval, and commercial power, glory and prosperity of the British Empire; and the many benefits conferred upon India by British rule. The National Anthem was again sung. At 8.30 P.M. an Imperial salute of 101 guns was fired, and the *Kolattam* was resumed by the young men of the village, who from time to time raised cheers for Her Majesty, the Prince and Princess of Wales, the Prime Minister, the Viceroy of India, the Governor of Madras, the Archbishop of Canterbury, the Metropolitan of India, the Bishop of Madras, Bishop Caldwell and his family, the District Magistrate, the District Judge, the Sub-Collector, and the Head Assistant Collector of Tinnevelly. This entertainment continued till the small hours of the morning, and the rejoicings were brought to a close by the Rev. S. Gnanamuttu calling for three cheers for the Queen Empress. The call was vociferously responded to by the large concourse of people. The Presidencial Address was adopted.

ISKAPALLI (NELLORE).

This seaport is situated about thirteen miles to the north of the Pennar river, and about twenty-two miles north-east of Nellore. It has a population of about 2,000; Hindus preponderate. The surrounding hamlets are chiefly occupied by boatmen and fishermen. The inhabitants are chiefly occupied in the manufacture of salt for supply to the interior of the District. The town is the head-quarters of two Officers of the Salt, and one Officer of the Public Works Department.

On the occasion of the Jubilee celebration the Salt and Public Works Department officers raised a subscription among themselves, fed their subordinate establishments, and arranged for sports, fireworks and illuminations, on the nights of the 16th and 17th February. On the morning of the 16th the Salt Contingent was drawn up on three sides of a square, and a short Address in Telugu, setting forth the purposes of the celebration, and the benefits the people had derived during the reign of Her Majesty, was read to the men, who then fired a *feu de joie*. At 4 P.M. the men of the Salt and Public Works Department establishments met on the ground prepared for the sports. The enclosure and entrance arch were gay with bunting, leaves, and flowers A tent, gracefully festooned with garlands of flowers, had been pitched for the accommodation of the ladies present. The sports were continued for two evenings, terminating with a display of fireworks, and three cheers for the Queen Empress. The road from the Salt Factory to the Salt Officers' quarters was illuminated on both nights. The Presidencial Address was adopted. Great enthusiasm prevailed.

JAGGAYAPETTA (KISTNA).

This prosperous town has a population of 10,072, divided as follows:—Hindus, 9,208, Mohammedans 851, and Christians 13. Twenty-five per cent. of the inhabitants are engaged in trade and weaving. Under the new Local Self-Government system, Jaggayapetta has become a Union. It contains the Deputy Tahsildar's Office, a Local Fund Dispensary, a Sub-Registrar's Office, a Sub-Post Office, a Police Inspector's Office, the C.M.S. Prayer House, the C.M.S. Boys' and Girls' Schools, the Local Fund Boys' and Girls' Schools, and twelve schools under the Result system. The town contains large quarries of marble. There are also ten Hindu Temples of great magnificence, and some Buddhist remains.

Jubilee Committee.—Messrs. T. VASUDEVAMOORTY PUNTALU, *Chairman*, DEVARAKONDA NARAYANAN, *Secretary*; SREERAM SREERAMULU; W. A. PASCAL; G. L. KELLY; REV. M. KALYANARAMIER; Mr. SREERAM APPANNA; and others.

From daybreak till midnight on the 16th February the whole town presented a very lively appearance, and the celebration was characterized by much enthusiasm and good fellowship. Prayers were offered for Her Majesty's prosperity and long life, and about 400 poor persons were fed. *Thoranams* overhung every street. Sports of various kinds were held in the afternoon. At night the streets were illuminated, and there was a good display of fireworks. At 10 o'clock there was a torchlight procession of the Hindu god of the town, in which some 7,000 people took part. The Presidencial Address was adopted.

JAMMALAMADUGU (CUDDAPAH).

The population is 4,848, including 3,600 Hindus, 1,241 Mohammedans, and 5 Christians. There is a Local Fund School in the town, besides three Pial Schools. The town forms part of the Proddatur Taluk, and the seat of the Union Panchayet. It is the centre of a large trade, the chief articles of commerce being indigo and cotton. It is 12½ miles from Muddhanur Railway Station, with which it is connected by a very good metalled road, constructed during the last famine. It exports to Sholapur the coarse cotton cloth that is manufactured to a considerable extent both in the town and the adjoining villages.

Jubilee Committee.—Messrs. PULLUR SUBBA RAU GARU, *Chairman*; P. RATNA MUDELLIAR, *Secretary*; PAVALALA PARTHASARATHY NAIDU; MAHOMED JAFFER HUSSAIN SAIB; RAMASWAMY IYAR; MARWADI NAAL CHUND; GAIBU SAIB; GANDICOTA NARAINA ROW; and SYED ABBAS.

Early in the morning of the 16th February the foundation stone of the "Jubilee Choultry" which bore a Telugu inscription, was paraded in procession through the principal streets preceded by native music, and followed by nautch parties. The procession was attended by the Chairman and members of the Jubilee Committee, by officials, merchants, and all the influential ryots of the town and adjoining villages. On reaching the temple dedicated to Siva, on the banks of the Pennar, the procession stopped. Then the Secretary made a short speech, and the ceremony of laying the foundation stone was performed by the President amidst cheering by the assembly. Three enthusiastic cheers were given for Her Majesty the Queen Empress, and the meeting terminated. The feeding of the poor then commenced and lasted till 1 P.M. The poor of every caste and creed, amounting in all to 800, were fed, and 100 of them were presented with cloths. At about 2 P.M. a treat was given to the boys of the Local Fund School, several of whom recited Telugu verses in honour of Her Majesty. At 2 P.M. there was a performance of legerdemain, which afforded great amusement to the assembly. Pundits recited Sanscrit verses composed by them in honour of the Queen Empress. A singing party was now given, which continued to amuse the assembly till 6 P.M. Then a meeting of the members of the Reading Room was convened, and it was announced that the name of the Reading Club had been changed to that of the "Jubilee Club" from that date. At 8 P.M. a nautch was held, and after that there were several dramatic performances. Prayers for Her Majesty were offered in all places of public worship throughout the day. The Presidencial Address was adopted. The town was illuminated as on the *Karthika* festival days. On the 17th, at about 8 P.M. a nautch party was given, and at 10 P.M. the people went in a procession to witness the fireworks which took place on the banks of the Pennar river. The assembly then returned to the Local Fund School Building, where three hearty cheers were given for the Queen Empress, and the proceedings terminated.

JAYANKONDA SHOLAPURAM (TRICHINOPOLY).

Jubilee Committee.—Messrs. A. SUBBOYA AIYAR, *Chairman*: MANIKAM PILLAY; BUDDU SINGH; SUBRAMANI CHETTI, and VEDVURASU RAU.

The Jubilee was celebrated with much *éclat*, and all classes cordially co-operated in doing honour to the occasion. The town presented an unusually bright appearance on the morning of the 16th February. The streets had been swept; the houses whitewashed; *thoranams* had been hung over the streets; and several Pandals and arches bearing mottoes expressive of the loyalty of the people had been erected at several places. Prayers were offered in both the temples on behalf of the Queen Empress, and blessings were invoked on Her Majesty and the Royal Family. The poor were fed in large numbers, and a few of the most needy were presented with money and cloths. Salutes were fired, and music played throughout the day. At night the gods were carried in procession with torches and music, through the illuminated streets. The festivities continued for two days. To permanently commemorate the happy event a "Well" has been sunk to meet a long-felt want. This was opened for public use on Jubilee day, and it was named the "Victoria Jubilee Well." The road leading to the well has been widened and repaired, planted on both sides with mango and jack trees, and named the "Victoria Jubilee Road." A drinking Water Tank, called the "Victoria Jubilee Fresh Water Tank," is being dug.

KADAPPERI (CHINGLEPUT).

At the north entrance of the large Siva Temple two large triumphal arches, covered with evergreens, had been erected on the 16th February, bearing appropriate mottoes, the chief among them being, "May God bless the Queen Empress of India." An *utsavam* was arranged for in the temple, and prayers were offered by the Brahmin priests for Her Majesty's long life, health, and prosperity. The poor were fed. At about 4 P.M. a grand procession started from the temple, with musicians and dancing girls, and proceeded to the Taluk Cutcherry, whence the procession organised for the whole of Madurantakam was to start. After passing through some of the principal streets, this procession came to the temple, which was brilliantly illuminated. In the Pandal that had been erected in front of the temple there was a *kolattam* performance, which lasted about half an hour. After witnessing this, the procession went through the other streets, all of which were bright with illuminations, then passed Madurantakam, and returned. The following day there was a *kolattam* performance at the temple, which was followed by a nautch. Sandal, *pan supari*, and flowers were distributed among the people.

KALAHASTRI (NORTH ARCOT).

Kalahastri is the capital of the Zemindari of 736 square miles of the same name. Its population is 9,933, of whom 8,607 are Hindus, 1,238 are Mohammedans, and 50 are Christians. It is situated on the right bank of the Suvarnamukhi at the extremity of the Nagari hills. It contains a Deputy Tahsildar's Cutcherry, a Sub-Registrar's Office, a Civil Dispensary, a Police Station, and a Sub-Post Office. It has a famous temple, large bazaars, and extensive suburbs. It is much resorted to by pilgrims. Good cloth is manufactured here.

Jubilee Committee.—THE RAJAH OF KALAHASTRI, *Chairman*; MR. M. TIRUVENKATA CHARLU, *Secretary*; THE FIRST PRINCE; MESSRS. DAMARA RAMA NAYANAM VAROO; PANAGANTY SESHACHELLAPATTY NAYANAM; MOONNERVENKATA SOUBA NAYANAM; V. RAMASAWMY IYER, B.A.; and five others.

On the 16th February about 500 Brahmins and 200 people of other castes were fed in the Agraharam close to the Palace of the Rajah, and cloths were distributed to nearly 1,000 poor people. Prayers were offered in all places of worship for the Queen Empress. At 3.30 P.M. His Highness held a Durbar in the Lutchmi Vilasam Hall of his Palace, which was attended by his brothers and other relatives, all the officers of the station, members of the Lutheran Mission, and other gentlemen. When His Highness took his seat a salute of 21 guns was fired. The Presidencial Address to the Queen Empress was read to the audience, first in English, then in Telugu; it was then adopted, and signed by His Highness and others. Three Pundits recited verses composed by them in honour of the occasion, extolling the virtues of Her Majesty. A performance on the *vina*, and a nautch followed. The Durbar closed with enthusiastic cheers for Her Majesty, and for His Highness; and by His Highness expressing a wish for the long life and prosperity of Her Majesty and the Royal Family. Another salute of 21 guns was fired. The Rajah then went in procession through the chief streets on his State elephant, attended by a large retinue, and followed by his brothers on elephants, and his friends in coaches. On his return to the Palace there was a grand display of fireworks. The churches, temples, and mosques, the palace, and other buildings were tastefully illuminated. The gods were taken through the streets in procession.

KALLAKURCHI (SOUTH ARCOT).

This head-quarters of a taluk of the same name has a population of 3,555, divided as follows:—Hindus 3,202, Mahammedans 344, and Christians 9.

Jubilee Committee.—Messrs. T. Bashyachellam Pillai, *Chairman*; C. Krishnaswami Aiyar, *Secretary*; P. Subba Row; Hazarath Hussain Ali Sahib; K. Dasikhachariar; C. Dorasawmy Mudelliar; T. Muthuswami Pillai; Vydhianadha Mudelliar; and others.

Before dawn on the 16th February guns were fired, and everybody rose early, and dressed in holiday attire. At 10 o'clock about 200 poor people of all castes and creeds were fed. These people then flocked to the south gate of the Taluk Cutcherry, which was very effectively decorated, and where a portrait of the Queen was exhibited, to receive new cloths. In the afternoon a Durbar was held in the Cutcherry, which was fitted up for the purpose, and a musical entertainment was given. Prayers were offered for the long life of Her Gracious Majesty, and *pan supari* and fruits were liberally distributed. *Abishakams* having been performed in the temples, Her Majesty's portrait and the gods were carried through the streets in procession. The streets were decorated with foliage, and overhung with *thoranams*; and several arches, bearing loyal inscriptions, were erected at several places. At night the whole town was illuminated. At 3 P.M. on the following day there was another large musical party at the Cutcherry, and another procession with Her Majesty's portrait.

KARKAL (SOUTH CANARA).

The population of Karkal is 3,392, consisting of 2,717 Hindus, 379 Mohammedans, 240 Christians, and 56 others. The Konkani Brahmins form the majority. The principal trade is in rice, cloths, and sandalwood oil. A colossal granite figure of Buddha, called Gommate Raya, about 50 feet in height, and a Jain temple called Chatis-Wunkita-Basti, are the chief objects of attraction. The town contains a District Munsiff's Court, a Deputy Tahsildar's Cutcherry, a Sub-Registrar's Office, a Police Station, a Civil Dispensary, a Local Fund Middle School, and an Elementary School.

Jubilee Committee.—Messrs. Ahmad Hyder Saib, *Chairman*; K. Rama Heggade, *Secretary*; A. Krishna Pillai; Sankappaya; Shunappaya; E. Krishnaya; M. Mangesh Rao; Imam Saib; and seven others.

The Jubilee day—the 16th February—was announced before sunrise by the firing of native guns. From 7 A.M. to noon rice and money were distributed among the poor of all classes; and cloths were given to the infirm. In the afternoon a treat was given to the boys and girls of the elementary schools in and about Karkal. Races and sports were held in the evening. The broad road in front of the Anantha Shayana temple was thronged with people, who joined enthusiastically in the festivities. At 6 P.M. the crowd marched in procession with music to the Travellers' Bungalow, which had been decorated for the purpose, and rose-water was sprinkled and *pan supari* distributed. The National Anthem was sung by the boys of the Local Fund Middle School. On the *maidan* in front of the Bungalow there was a beautiful display of fireworks, after which the procession passed by torchlight through the illuminated streets, and proceeded to the Temple Tank, where thanksgivings and *utsavams* were performed in the name of the Queen Empress. The town was decorated with festoons bearing mottoes such as "God Save the Queen" and "Long live Queen Victoria," in English and Canarese. The Presidential Address was adopted.

KARUR (COIMBATORE).

The present town of Karur bears no marks of great antiquity, but a town bearing the name, and situated near the present site, was known to the Romans in the second century, as the capital of the Chera or Kerala Kingdom, which extended to the western coast; and Roman coins have been found here at different periods. It was ceded to the British in 1799. It has a Taluk Cutcherry, a District Munsiff's Court, a Sub-Registrar's Office, and a Municipal Dispensary. The population is 9,205, distributed as follows:—Hindus 8,176, Muhammadans 733, and Christians 296. Trade is carried on in grain, ghee, oil, saffron, chillies, tobacco, saltpetre, &c. Cattle of good breed are to be had in the taluk. Municipal affairs are conducted by twelve Councillors. The Municipality maintains a High School, a Combined School, and a few Pial Schools. There is also a private School which teaches up to the Middle School Standard. Considerable progress is being made in female education. There are two Girls' Schools, one belonging to the Wesleyan Mission, and the other to the Municipality. The Wesleyan Mission has an Industrial School.

Jubilee Committee.—Messrs. A. David Pillay, *Chairman*; T. L. Subba Row, *Secretary*; Kasim Sahib; the Rev. Mr. Little; Messrs. Narasimah Chettyar; Kuppana Aiyengar; Muthu Veerana Chettyar; Putty Ramaiyar; Padmanabier; Chinnappa Mudelliar; Sambasiva Aiyar; and three others.

The streets of the town were swept, watered, and adorned with festoons on the 16th February. Four triumphal arches had been erected, bearing appropriate mottoes, at the corners of the chief thoroughfares. All the public offices, and many of the houses in the town were decorated. Guns were fired in rapid succession in the temples. A Thanksgiving Service was held in the Wesleyan Mission Chapel at 8.30 A.M., and prayers were offered in the temples and mosques. The schoolboys and girls, numbering about 700, were mustered in the Railway compound, and marched in procession to the Municipal High School. Each School carried its own banner, and a band marched at the head of the procession. The "Union Jack" was carried in front of the procession. On reaching the School compound, the children were marched into the spacious hall of the building, where the leading inhabitants of the town had assembled. Mr. David Pillay, the District Munsiff, took the chair. The Rev. Mr. Little, of the Wesleyan Mission, addressed the audience in English, and alluded to the chief incidents in the life of Her Majesty. His speech was translated into Tamil by Mr. Pathamanabier, the Chairman of the Municipality. Verses in Tamil and Sanscrit, composed in honour of the Queen Empress, were recited, and three cheers were given for Her Majesty. The schoolboys and girls were treated to sweetmeats, oranges, and bananas. About 2,000 poor persons were fed, and 300 cloths distributed among them. At 5.30 P.M. two corner-stones of a new Girls' School that is being built by the Wesleyan Mission were laid, one by Mrs. Little, and the other by Mrs. David Pillay. The boys and girls of the Orphanage, accompanied by the Rev. Mr. and Mrs. Little, Mr. and Mrs. David Pillay, and others, marched to the spot in procession from the Mission Bungalow, with banners and a band, headed by the Union Jack. On arrival at the scene a hymn was sung, and a prayer was offered by the Rev. Mr. Little. The ceremony of the laying of the stone was then gone through. The National Anthem was sung in Tamil; and after the benediction had been pronounced, three cheers were given for Her Majesty. At 9 P.M. a large portrait of the Queen Empress, decorated with flowers, was carried in procession through several streets, accompanied by a band of native musicians, and fireworks. This continued till about midnight, when the National Anthem was played, and the Police fired a *feu de joie.*

A nautch now commenced, which did not terminate until 2 o'clock next morning. The Presidential Address was adopted. On the 17th February, at 1 P.M., the people assembled again in the school-room and were entertained with music and singing. At 4 P.M. a large crowd of spectators repaired to the Fort glacis to witness the sports, which lasted for about three hours. The sports comprised flat races, hurdle races, sack race, tug-of-war, greasy pole, &c. They were followed by a grand display of fireworks, which lasted till about 11.30 P.M. The festivities terminated with a nautch, and a distribution of sandal, flowers, and *pan supari*. On the evening of the 18th the people assembled once more in the school-house at the request of the Mohammedans, when an address in Hindustani was read, together with a Tamil translation of it. Mr. David Pillay, who presided at the meeting, referred to the benefits conferred on the Mohammedan community by Her Majesty's Government, and thanked the Mohammedans for their large contributions towards the Jubilee celebration. The proceedings closed with a nautch, and three cheers for Her Majesty. About 10,000 people took part in the festivities at this town. The Committee intends to establish a "Reading Room and Library" as a permanent memorial of the Jubilee.

KASARGODE (SOUTH CANARA).

This seaport is about 30 miles to the south of Mangalore. It was the southernmost point of the ancient Tuluva Kingdom. Its population, numbering 5,000 souls, consists chiefly of Hindus and Moplas, and a few Roman Catholics. It has a Taluk Board, a Dispensary, a District Munsiff's Court, a Sub-Registrar's Office, a Local Fund Middle School, and a Primary School. The people live chiefly by trade and agriculture.

The morning of the 16th February was heralded by a salute of native guns. At 7 A.M. a tastefully decorated Pandal, erected to the west of the school-house, began to be crowded with officials, vakils, merchants, landholders, and other inhabitants. Sports commenced at 7.30 A.M., and lasted till 10 A.M. At 2 P.M. a salute of native guns announced that the entertainments for the afternoon were commenced. More than 800 persons, including a few ladies, assembled in the Pandal. The proceedings commenced by the reading of a sketch in Canarese of the life of Her Majesty, preceded and followed by the singing of a verse of the National Anthem in Canarese and English. Both during the reading of the sketch of Her Majesty, and after the singing of the Anthem, hearty cheers were given. A blind musician from Kumbla sang some Canarese, Marathi, Hindustani, and Konkani songs, and amused the assembly by his performance on the *Veena*, and his imitation of the voices of different animals. After further sports at 5 P.M. *pan supari* was distributed and rose-water sprinkled, and the children present received sugar-cane. The assembly then went in a body, with beat of tom-tom and singing, to the Bunder, which was tastefully decorated for the occasion, to witness a boat-race, and a display of fireworks. Amidst the booming of guns, the firing of rockets, the beating of tom-toms, and torchlight, the party returned in procession, headed by a banner bearing the portrait of Her Majesty, with the inscription "God save the Queen Empress of India," the Christians singing the National Anthem in Canarese and English, and the Mohammedans dancing and singing before the banner. When the Pandal was reached there was another display of fireworks. Three hearty cheers were then given for Her Majesty. The 17th was devoted to the distribution of rice to about 800 poor people. Three "Wells" will be sunk as permanent memorials of the Jubilee.

KODAVASSAL (TANJORE).

The population is 8,286. The people in this Union are generally well educated. The exports are chiefly paddy, cocoanuts, and turmeric; and weaving is carried on to a considerable extent.

Jubilee Committee.—Messrs. Kaliyana Ramier, *Chairman;* S. Saminatha Iyer, *Secretary;* Alagasingaraiengar; Devasigamani Mudeliar; Saminatha Iyer; T. Subba Iyer; Ponnusawmy Iyengar, &c.

Early in the morning of the 16th February *poojahs* were performed, and food was distributed to 350 people of all castes at the Siva and Vishnu temples. Special services were also held at the churches and in the mosque. *Thoranams* were stretched across the streets. At 4 P.M. there was a grand procession, which was headed by a "Union Jack" placed in a beautifully decorated palanquin, and attended by about 1,000 people. A body of Police formed a guard of honour to the ensign. The procession passed through the chief streets of the town, and as it went along sandal, flowers, sugar, sugar-candy, and *pan supari* were lavishly distributed. In one of these streets a rich Mirasidar prostrated himself before the palanquin, expressing his sense of loyalty and exclaiming, "God save the Queen; Long may Her benevolent Reign continue." In front of the Wesleyan Mission School the procession stopped for a few minutes at the request of the Catechist, who offered up a prayer for the long life and prosperity of Her Majesty. The procession halted at the Deputy Tahsildar's office, and 101 crackers were fired. The flag was then taken out of the palanquin by the Chairman, and suspended to a tree in front of his office, amidst the joyful shouts of the people. The assembly now sat down, and the Presidencial Address was read and explained by the Chairman, who dwelt upon the tranquillity, justice and freedom that India had experienced during the reign of the Queen Empress. An address in Sanscrit was delivered by a Pundit. He contrasted the present state of India with regard to education, sanitation, irrigation, registration, and local Self-Government with the state of things in days of old. Then there was a distribution of sandal and flowers, and music was played. The company dispersed amid shouts of applause. On the following night there was a grand nautch and musical performance. It is estimated that over 7,000 people took part in the festivities.

KOLLEGALL (COIMBATORE).

The chief town of a taluk of the same name. Its population is 8,462, of whom Hindus number 7,951, Mohammedans 493, and Christians 18.

The Jubilee was celebrated here with much enthusiasm on the 16th February. The Police held a parade, and fired a *feu de joie*. *Abishakams* were performed in the Vishnu and Siva temples, and prayers were offered in the mosques both on the 16th and 17th. The gods were carried round the town, which was gaily decorated and illuminated. There were grand displays of fireworks on both nights which attracted immense crowds from the town and the adjoining villages. The boys and girls of the Town Schools were treated to sweetmeats and fruits. About 400 poor people of all castes were fed and clothed on both days. Some trees were planted by M. Sashachellam Naidu, the Chairman of the Jubilee Committee, in the "Victoria Tope," which is to be opened in the north of the town as a permanent memorial of the happy event. The Presidencial Address was adopted.

KOTAGHERRY (NILGIRIS).

Kotagherry, the favourite residence of the Marquis of Dalhousie, Governor-General of India, is on the eastern side of the Nilgiri plateau. It is about 6,500 feet above the sea, and has a very salubrious climate. It was founded in the year 1830. The population is 3,691. It contains a Post Office, Police Station, Court House, a Munsiff's Court, and three Churches (one for all denominations, one Basel Mission, and one Roman Catholic). Most of the European residents are proprietors of tea estates in the neighbourhood. In the station is a large Kota village. The Kotas are a sturdy race, who live by working in iron. They do a little cultivation. The Badagas live by cultivation, and keep cattle. They are in a prosperous condition. On the slopes below Kotagherry are jungle tribes

Jubilee Committee.—Messrs. W. L. EdmINSTON, *Chairman*; T. BASTIAN, *Secretary*; F. R. GRIFFITH; GOOLAM HOOSAIN SAIB; and APPAJI IYER.

Two large and two small Pandals had been erected in the Bazaar Street on the 16th February, and arches had been constructed at the gateways of each of the large Pandals, bearing the inscriptions "Long live our Gracious Queen," and "God bless our Noble Empress." A large number of Europeans and Natives were present, including coffee planters, officials, and merchants. About 150 poor Hindus, Mohammedans, Native Christians and schoolboys, were fed at noon. Prayers were offered in all the churches, temples, and mosques, for the continuance of Her Majesty's reign. A Kota's band, the bandsmen being Badagas, was in attendance. Sports of all kinds were held at 3.30 P.M. There was a display of fireworks and a large bonfire at night. The Post and Overseer's Offices and the Police Station were handsomely decorated. A good many Todas, Badagas, Kotas, Eroolers, and Curumbers came from a long distance to take part in the festivities. The streets were crowded with spectators. Numerous buildings were illuminated after dusk, and the festivities continued till midnight. On the following day there were sports near the District Board Overseer's Office, and a display of fireworks at night. The permanent memorial will take the form of a "Town Clock."

KROSUR (KISTNA).

Krosur has a population of 1,912; of whom 1,588 are Hindus, 265 Mohammedans, and 59 Christians. It contains a Tahsildar and Taluk Magistrate's Offices, a Sheristadar Magistrate's Office, a Police Inspector's Office, a Sub-Registrar's Office, a Police Station, a Sub-Post Office, and a Local Fund Middle School. The principal trade is in cotton, oil seeds, indigo, cumbu, cholum, varigu, red gram, black gram, &c.

Jubilee Committee.—RAJAH VASIREDDI VENKATALAKSHMI NARASIMHA NAIDU BAHADUR, *Chairman*; CHIRUMAMILLA BUTCHIRAGHAVAYYA NAIDU, *Secretary*; Messrs. KOLLIPARA SRI RAMULU; VELAGAPUDI SUBRAMANIYAM; MAHOMED ABDUL KAREEM SAHIB; MAHOMED RAHUMTULLA SAHIB; and others.

The celebration on the 16th February passed off exceedingly well; all classes of the community showing the utmost loyalty. A *feu de joie* was fired at 6 A.M. From 7 to 10 A.M., all the temples in the station were open for worship. Thanksgiving Services were held at 11 A.M., and were attended by the local officials and others. From noon to 3 P.M., about 1,200 people of all castes were fed. Many of them had come in for the purpose from the surrounding villages. At 4 P.M., a grand procession started from the centre of the town, and passed along all the chief streets. At about 5 P.M., the procession arrived at the Pandal which had been erected for the occasion. *Thoranams* and flags were stretched over the Pandal and streets. Attar, rose-water, lavender, *pan supari*, cardamoms, cloves and mace, &c., were freely distributed. At 6 P.M., the Pandal was brilliantly illuminated, and at 9 P.M. there was a nautch. Shortly before midnight there was a grand display of fireworks. About 4,000 people took part in the celebration.

There were great rejoicings throughout the taluk. In every village and hamlet special services were held in the temples; *thoranams* were suspended in the streets; and the day was observed as one of great festivity.

KULITALAI AND MUSIRI (TRICHINOPOLY).

A procession of the Hindu gods went round the town on the 16th February. Bonfires were lighted on the Ramagheri and Thirusangy hills. The Pachamalai and Kollimalai Mountains, about fifty miles off, were splendidly illuminated, and could be seen for miles around, the jungle having been set on fire. In the bed of the river Cauvery large Pandals were erected for the purpose of the joint celebration by the two towns. More than 700 persons of all castes and creeds were fed, and about 150 were clothed. From 5 to 6 in the evening, pens, pencils, plantains, and sugar were distributed to the school children. Later on refreshments were served to the gentlemen of both towns. Music followed. The rejoicings continued till midnight, when the assembly dispersed amidst loud cheers for Her Majesty. The Presidencial Address was adopted.

KUMBHAKONAM (TANJORE).

Kumbhakonam is one of the most ancient and sacred towns in the Presidency, and is much resorted to by pilgrims. It was formerly the capital of the Chola Kingdom. It is now celebrated for its learning. It is a Municipal town, with 50,098 inhabitants; of whom 47,908 are Hindus, 1,228 are Mohammedans, 908 are Christians, and 54 are undefined. 80 per cent. of the Hindus are Brahmins. It is the seat of one of the most successful Colleges in the Madras Presidency. There are three High Schools.

Jubilee Committee.—Messrs. T. Ganapathi Iyer, *Chairman*; P. Thambuswami Mudelliar, *Secretary*; A. C. Narayanaswami Iyer; S. Seshayya; Krishnaswamy Naidu; Sundararama Iyer; Sivaswamy Odiar; &c.

The 16th February was a day of unprecedented enthusiasm. The prominent features of the Jubilee festivities were their spontaneity, and unofficial character. At daybreak a salute of 101 guns was fired. Between 8 and 10 A.M., over 500 poor people, male and female, were presented with cloths. Over 3,000 people of all classes of the population—Brahmin, Sudra, Musulman, Christian, and Pariah—were fed in the various places of public worship and in the choultries. In the evening a troupe of acrobats performed a series of exciting feats before a large and admiring crowd. The Post Office and other public buildings were tastefully decorated, and festoons were hung over all the streets. The illuminations at night were very striking. The Mahamakam and Pattamarsai Tanks presented a most picturesque appearance. Lights were placed upon the steps of the tanks, on the four sides, and the reflection upon the rippling water produced a magnificent effect. At about 8 P.M., a grand procession started from the Mahamakam Tank, and went through the main streets. A richly caparisoned elephant, with a howdah bearing Her Majesty's portrait, led the procession. There were the usual other features of an Oriental festival, as flags, dancing girls, band, music, &c. Sugar-candy and fruits were distributed. At the commencement of the procession, the Police presented arms in front of the portrait, and fired a *feu de joie*. The crowd that followed the procession numbered about 15,000 persons. All the resident Europeans were present. The procession having arrived at the Porter Town Hall, the Presidencial Address was read, and explained in Tamil by Mr. Krishnaswami Aiyar, and adopted with acclamation. There was then a grand pyrotechnic display, and the festivities ended with a salute of 101 guns. The permanent memorial will take the form of "Wells."

KUNDAPUR (SOUTH CANARA).

Kundapur is the most northern taluk in the West Coast Districts of the Madras Presidency. The Portuguese built a fort here in the 16th century. The town was occupied by the British in 1799. It has a population of 115,113; of whom 107,959 are Hindus, 4,332 are Mohammedans, 2,482 are Christians, and 340 are unclassified. The Hindus are mostly cultivators of land; and there are several wealthy merchants, who carry on trade with Bombay, Mysore, Bellary, and elsewhere. The town is the head-quarters of a Head Assistant Collector. It contains a Taluk Cutcherry, a District Munsiff's Court, a Taluk Board, a Local Fund School, and various places of worship.

Jubilee Committee.—Messrs. MAVIL RAMAIYA, *Chairman*; U. BABU ROW, *Secretary*; T. SADASHIVA ROW; NAGAPPA HOLLA; ANNAPPA SHETTI; SHAH HAZRAT; SHESHAGIRIAPPA; and fifteen others.

The Jubilee was celebrated in a splendid manner on the 16th February. Shortly after 1 P.M. the Taluk Cutcherry was crowded with about 5,000 people, dressed in their holiday attire, invitations having been sent throughout the entire taluk, and ferries having been made free by arrangement with the toll-farmers. The Tahsildar, the District Munsiff, the members of the Taluk Board, the Roman Catholic vicar, vakils, landholders, merchants, traders, artisans, &c., as well as all the schoolboys and schoolgirls of the place, were present, and were accommodated with seats. The Imperial Coat of Arms, beautifully executed, was brought into the Cutcherry with much ceremony, and placed in a prominent position. A band of native musicians was in attendance, and played English tunes at intervals. Then the Tahsildar read the Canarese translation of the Presidencial Address, the whole company standing. The Address was received with enthusiastic cheers, and was signed. The Mysore musicians played the National Anthem, and a salute of 32 guns was fired. All now resumed their seats, and two prisoners were brought forward, and released by the Tahsildar. Jubilee songs, both in English and the Konkani language, composed for the occasion, were sung by some schoolboys and schoolgirls, and were received with loud applause. The people were treated to sugar and fruit;

rose-water was sprinkled; and garlands and bouquets of beautiful and fragrant flowers were distributed. A nautch party followed. At 3.30 P.M., about 100 poor children were fed, and sweetmeats were distributed to about 200 schoolboys and schoolgirls of the Primary School and the Local Fund Middle School. A procession was formed under the spacious Pandal that had been erected in front of the Cutcherry, and, led by a band, marched slowly through the principal streets of the town. On arriving at the esplanade in front of the Local Middle School, the procession halted, and the people sat down. 900 poor people from the surrounding villages, who had been invited to be present, had assembled there. Each poor person received one seer (equivalent to two English pounds) of rice, and a quarter anna; while the blind, the lame, and the very needy received twice that amount. Races and sports of various kinds followed, including wire walking and rope dancing. The sports and the distribution of alms continued until 5.30 P.M., when another salute of 32 guns was fired, and the assembly broke up. The whole town was by this time illuminated with small open lamps, placed on bamboo poles. At 7 o'clock all the Government offices, temples, mosques, the Roman Catholic Church, and several private buildings and the principal streets of the town, were illuminated, and there was a display of fireworks. Special prayers were said, and evening service was held in all the places of worship; while from the two principal temples of the town public processions of gods went round the streets. An unique feature about the two Temple processions was, that although the gods started from temples belonging to different, and, at times, antagonistic castes of Hindus, yet, on the present occasion, the people forming the procession marched with torches and music in common, their religious differences being temporarily sunk in honour of the Jubilee. The processions returned to the temples about 10 P.M. Two native Dramatic Companies performed the same play in sight of each other in contiguous stages which had been erected in front of the Taluk Cutcherry. This "double play" was witnessed by upwards of 7,000 persons, and continued until sunrise the next day.

Similar arrangements had been made for illuminations, prayers, services, and processions in all the principal temples, &c., throughout the taluk, and the Committee received a report from each institution that everything had been properly carried out. In memory of Her Majesty's Jubilee the Kundapur Recreation and Debating Club will, in future, be known as the "Kundapur Victoria Jubilee Union." The permanent local memorial will take the shape either of a local "Victoria Jubilee Memorial Hall," or a scholarship to be called the "Victoria Jubilee Scholarship," available to those candidates of Kundapur Taluk who prosecute their studies in the Technical Institute at Madras.

KUNGUNDI KUPPUM (NORTH ARCOT).

Kungundi Kuppum, anciently called Koppum, includes the suburbs of Kothapetta, Koorabalapollea, and Robinson's and Stewart's Pettas. It has a population of 2,874 persons, divided thus: 2,543 Hindus, 321 Mohammedans, and 10 Christians. Jaggery and sugar are largely manufactured and exported. Tamarind, vendiom, coriander, gingelly and kanooga oil seeds are extensively cultivated. The public offices are the Deputy Tahsildar's Cutcherry, the Post Office, the Local Fund Middle School, Dispensary, Special Sub-Registrar's Office, Railway Station, Forest Ranges, &c., and a Police Station. There are two mosques and a temple.

Jubilee Committee.—Messrs. C. Narrayanasawmy Mudelliar, *Chairman;* Giddoo Kistnasundelian, *Secretary;* Esuff Allbekkan Sahib; Chinnasawmy Iyer; Govindarajooloo Naidu; N. Jagannadam Pillai; Soobramanyya Iyer; and Davasikamany Pillai.

More than 100 poor people were fed at the *Zemindar's* Chuttram on the 16th February. All the public officials of the place, together with a large number of merchants, tradesmen, artisans, and others started in procession from Kuppum, when 15 guns were fired. On its way the procession was joined by the boys and girls of the Local Fund School. It stopped at the Sub-Magistrate's Cutcherry Hall, when a salute of 27 guns was fired, and the schoolboys and girls were treated to sugar-candy and plantains, and were entertained with jugglery and other amusements. At night all the public offices and streets were illuminated, and the streets decorated. At the temples and mosques the day was observed as a festival, and special prayers were said in them for the Queen Empress. Cloths were distributed to the poor. In the Cutcherry Hall, there was a musical entertainment, followed by a nautch, which lasted till 11 P.M. The Presidencial Address was adopted. The festivities were continued on the 17th, and the proceedings terminated with hearty cheers for Her Majesty and the Royal Family.

KURNOOL (TOWN).

The chief town in the District of Kurnool. It stands on a spit of land at the junction of the Hindri and Tungabhadra rivers. It has a population of 20,329; of whom 9,995 are Hindus, 10,007 are Mohammedans, 320 are Christians, and 7 belong to other religions. It is the head-quarters of the Collector, the Judge, and District Courts. The old Fort was dismantled in 1865. Some members of the family of the late Nawab reside in the Palace.

On the 15th and 16th February, the chief street in the bazaar, a mile long, was gaily decorated, and more than twenty-one triumphal arches, bearing inscriptions expressive of loyalty and gratitude to Her Majesty, with wishes for her long reign and prosperity, were constructed by the townspeople at their own cost. Most of the shops and houses in the street were whitewashed, and adorned with flags, festoons, evergreens, and plantain trees. Garlands of leaves were suspended at short intervals, and ornamented the Municipal Office, the Hospital, and the Town Sub-Magistrate's Office. On the 16th at 11 A.M., prayers for Her Majesty's long life, and the continuance of her reign, were offered in the principal mosques and temples. Between 9 A.M. and 3 P.M., 1,250 of the poor people in the town, 466 of whom were Mohammedans, and the rest Hindus, Malas, and Madigas, were fed. The principal residents and merchants of the town met at 4 P.M., at the Municipal Office in the Kurnool Fort, where they formed themselves into a procession, and proceeded to the Town Sub-Magistrate's Office with music and dancing. The procession was joined by the Collector, the District Judge, the Superintendent of Police, the Executive Engineer, and other gentlemen of the place. More than 5,000 people of all classes of Her Majesty's subjects took part in the demonstration. At the Jumma Musjid a Mohammedan merchant of the town read an address of congratulation in Hindustani verse, and handed it to the Collector. A second address was read at the Cloth Merchants' Bazaar. The procession reached the Sub-Magistrate's Office, which was already crowded, at 5.30 P.M. The office was very effectively decorated. Mr. Kough, the Collector, was voted to the chair, and made an excellent speech. Mr. Somasundra Sastry, Deputy-Collector, then gave an account in Telugu of Her Majesty's life and the chief events of her reign. Mr. Sultan Mahomed Sahib gave eloquent expression in Hindustani to the loyal sentiments of the Mohammedan community. Mr. Subba Shastri, of Mannekunta, a Brahmin Pundit, sang a few Telugu verses composed by himself in honour of the occasion. Mr. A. Subba Rau, the Chairman of the Municipal Council, seconded by Mr. Vencoba Row, Municipal Councillor, and supported by Mr. Sultan Mahomed Sahib, moved that the Presidencial Address be adopted. The Address was now read in English, Telugu, and Hindostani, by the three gentlemen above named, while the audience stood. It was then adopted with acclamation. Three cheers for Her Imperial Majesty were given, and the police fired a *feu de joie.* The proceedings terminated with a distribution of *pan supari* and flowers, and the sprinkling of rose-water. At 7 P.M. the procession was re-formed, and proceeded through the bazaars, which were illuminated, to the Queen's Park, where after a display of fireworks and nautch, the crowd dispersed at 8.30 P.M. On the 17th there were sports, exhibitions of athletic skill by acrobats and wrestlers, donkey and bullock races, and dancing. These events came off on the *maidan* in front of the Collector's bungalow, between 3 and 6 P.M. Five large tents were pitched for the accommodation of the European and Eurasian community, and the native gentry of the town; while two rows of benches, each a hundred yards long, with a space of about eighty yards wide between, where the performances were exhibited, provided seats for a portion of the assembled spectators, whose numbers exceeded 2,000. The proceedings of the evening closed with a bonfire of tar-barrels kindled on the Esplanade. Before dispersing, the Collector thanked Mr. A. Subba Rau, the Chairman, and Mr. H. St. Rencontre, the Secretary of the Jubilee Committee, for the indefatigable zeal which they had displayed in the organisation of the celebration, and congratulated them on the success that had rewarded their efforts. Three hearty cheers were then given for the Queen Empress.

KUTTAPARAMBA (MALABAR).

Kuttaparamba has a population of 56,555 persons; of whom 44,862 are Hindus, 11,660 Mohammedans, and 33 are unclassified. Besides the Deputy Tahsildar's and Sub-Magistrate's Cutcherry, Kuttaparamba has a Sub-Registrar's Office, a small School maintained by the Basel Mission, a Post Office, and a Travellers' Bungalow. Education is progressing. Local Self-Government is carried on by the Taluk Board of Kottayam, of which Taluk Kuttaparamba forms a sub-division. About half of the population are engaged in the cultivation of the pepper vine. Of the other half, the Hindus are engaged in rice cultivation, and Mohammedans in trade.

Jubilee Committee.—Messrs. KUTTAL UPPI HAJEE, *Chairman*; M. OTHENA MENON, *Secretary*; T. GOVINDAN; RANDUPURAYIL KUNHI THUPPAR; KUTTAL MAYAN; KARUVANTEVALAPPIL MAYAN; NINGILERI KANHAMBU NAMBIAR; AKKARAVEETIL KRISHNAN NAIR; RANDUPURAYIL MAYAN; and two others.

Early in the morning of the 16th February a large number of Hindus assembled in the Siva temple, where *Mrityunjayam* (literally "victory over death," a Hindu religious ceremony for obtaining long life and happiness) was performed in honour of the Jubilee. The Mohammedans likewise assembled in large numbers at their chief mosque, and offered prayers for the health and long life of Her Majesty. Then a grand procession with elephants, tom-toms, music, and banners, left Kuttaparamba for Tellicherry (a distance of eight miles). It was headed by two large elephants, richly caparisoned, one of which carried on its head a crown, and the British Coat of Arms. A choir of Hindu singers marched in the procession, and sang a hymn composed for the occasion. Over 3,000 persons were present. 210 poor persons were fed. There were no sports, fireworks, or illuminations at Kuttaparamba, as the people were of opinion that it would be better for them, as far as those things were concerned, to join with the Tellicherry people. The festivities were marked with the greatest enthusiasm, and the Hindus and Moplahs of Kuttaparamba joined in the most cordial manner in doing honour to Her Majesty. The Presidential Address was adopted. As permanent memorials of the Jubilee it was resolved to establish a "Hospital" if funds were available; to erect a "Water Shed" on the *maidan* with a suitable inscription on stone; and to plant a long-lived "Tree," near a stone which will bear a memorial inscription.

MADAKASIRA (ANANTAPUR).

The population is about 4,500. Hindus predominate, but live in perfect harmony with the resident Mohammedans. The system of Local Self-Government was lately introduced, and is working well. Trade is flourishing.

In the forenoon of the 16th February, the poor of all classes were fed in large numbers. At 1 P.M. there was a public meeting, when about 1,000 people were present. An interesting lecture in Telugu on the origin and rise of the British Empire in India, was read by Mr. M. Vijiaraghavulu Naidu, Tahsildar. Another Address on the same subject was read by Mr. R. Gopala Rau. A short poem in Telugu, composed for the occasion by Mr. M. Narayan Row, Sub-Registrar, was read and explained to the audience. It was so interesting that the assembly insisted upon having it read twice over. The Presidencial Address was then read in English, Telugu, and Hindostani by Messrs. Vijiaraghavulu Naidu, Culur Sreenivasa Row, and Kalandar Sahib, respectively. Mr. Nunjunda Sastrulu, a Sanscrit scholar, then recited some Sanscrit odes. Music was played at intervals. The meeting terminated with three loud cheers for Her Majesty. At 6 P.M. the god Vencataramana was taken in procession, attended by about 2,000 people, with dancing, music, &c., through the streets, and on its return there was a display of fireworks. The streets through which the procession passed were illuminated, and were overhung by festoons at short intervals, and all the houses were decorated. On the following day, at 1 P.M. there was a musical entertainment, which lasted till 4 P.M. Over 2,000 people were present. Books, sweetmeats, and money were distributed among the schoolboys and girls. At 5 P.M. Her Majesty's photograph was taken in procession with music, dancing, &c., and was followed by over 4,000 persons. There were illuminations and fireworks as on the previous day. The permanent memorials include the "Queen's Jubilee English School," "Queen's Jubilee Girls' School," and "Reading Room." A "Temple" is to be erected to the goddess Lakshmi in Venkataramanaswamy's Temple by Mr. M. Vijiarghavulu Naidu, under the auspices of the Theosophical Society.

MADURA (TOWN).

The population of this important town is 73,807. About 87·8 per cent. of the population are Hindus, 9·1 per cent. are Mohammedans, and 3·1 per cent. are Christians. Among the Hindus the Brahmins number 5,921, and form about 8 per cent. of the entire population. There are over 70 Schools in the town, including one Government Second Grade College, one American Mission High School, and two Native High Schools teaching up to the Matriculation standard. More than 2,500 boys, and about 600 girls are under instruction. About 35·7 per cent. of the male population, and 2·5 per cent. of the female population are educated. The affairs of the town are managed by a Municipal Council, which consists of 24 Councillors, of whom 5 are official, and 19 non-official. The principal manufactures of the town are cloths, lace, jewellery, and brass vessels. Handsome turbans, fringed with gold lace, and dyed cloths of various kinds, are its specialities.

Jubilee Committee.—Mr. E. G. RICKETTS, *Chairman*; Dr. SMITH; Messrs. A. JOYCE; T. RENGA RAO; SREENIVASA NAYADU; G. SUBBARAYALU NAYADU; T. JAMBU CHETTIAR; QUADIR BACHA SAIB; KANNI EASWARAN CHETTIAR; R. VENKATESWARA AIYAR; SAYAD GULAM ALI SAIB; and thirteen others.

On the morning of the 16th February the sick poor in the Hospital were presented with cloths and sweetmeats, &c. by Mrs. Turner, wife of the Collector. 900 Brahmins, 5,100 Sudras, 2,000 weavers, 1,700 Mohammedans, and 372 Christians, amounting in all to over 10,000 persons, were fed. While the Brahmins were being fed, Sanscrit verses, composed for the occasion in honour of Her Majesty, were recited. 2,700 School Children of the town were entertained with sweetmeats. A procession of Native Christians marched through the principal streets attended with music. Towards evening Tirumal Nayak's Palace, the Post Office, the Municipal Office, the Collector's Office, and the Meenakshi pagoda with all its towers, were tastefully illuminated. Private houses, mosques, and churches were also illuminated. The illuminations in the Meenakshi temple were excellent; a floating car, beautifully illuminated, rendering the Golden Lily Tank especially attractive. The Meenakshi temple was crowded with thousands of worshippers, who joined in offering up prayers for Her Majesty. A large party of Europeans was entertained at dinner at the Club; the Queen's health was proposed by Mr. Weir, C.S., the Judge of Madura, President of the Club, and the National Anthem was sung with enthusiasm. About 8.30 P.M. there was a Hindu musical entertainment at Tirumal Nayak's Palace. Europeans and Natives of all classes attended. A song narrating in Tamil the blessings and glories of Her Majesty's reign, composed by Mr. T. M. Scott, was sung by the nautch girls. A large party then marched in procession with music, torchlights, banners, &c. as far as the temple. Sports and races took place on the following morning at 7 o'clock, at Dufferin Park, in the presence of an immense gathering of people. At about 3 P.M. the townspeople and the inhabitants of surrounding villages collected in thousands to witness the "*jallikat*" sports on the race-course. This was a most exciting event. Over 200 bulls were let loose with cloths round their necks, and were chased all over the course by people endeavouring to secure the cloths. At about 8 P.M. there was a feast for Brahmins in the "Perumal Kovil." On the 18th cloths were distributed to over 700 poor people, by Messrs. R. Ramasubbayar, Chairman of the Municipal Council, and A. L. A. R. Ramasami Chettiar. The number of persons who took part in the festivities was estimated at over 20,000. The permanent memorial is to be a "Museum and Library" to be named after Her Majesty.

MADURANTAKAM (CHINGLEPUT).

Madurantakam is the chief town of the taluk of that name in the District of Chingleput. It is the head-quarters of the Tahsildar of the taluk, and has a Sub-Registrar's Office, a Police Station, and a Local Fund Second Class Dispensary. The population of the town, together with the shrotriem of Kadapperi, is 4,511, consisting chiefly of Iyengar Brahmins. There are a few Mohammedans. The chief occupation of the inhabitants is agriculture. Madurantakam is the seat of the local Union, established under the District Boards Act. This institution is presided over by the Sheristadar, assisted by six non-official members called Panchayetdars. The town has three Schools; two of them (one for boys and the other for girls) are managed by the Wesleyan Mission; the third, called the Hindu High School, was founded by a few native gentlemen.

Jubilee Committee.—Messrs. S. Rukmini Pillai, *Chairman*; M. Sanjeevi Naidu, *Secretary*; Ramanada Iyer, B.A.; Annasawmy Iyer; Gnanasawmy Pillai, B.A.; and Umapathy Mudelliar.

At dawn on the 16th February an Imperial salute of 101 guns was fired, and from an early hour the whole town assumed a gala appearance. Every house was decorated with *thoranams*; numerous flags were placed along the streets, and near the public buildings; and several triumphal arches had been erected, bearing appropriate mottoes, such as "God bless the Empress of India," "Long live Her Majesty," &c. In the Siva and Vishnu Temples *abishekams* to the gods and goddesses were performed, and *archanas* were said in Her Majesty's name. At noon over 700 poor people of all denominations were fed, and presents of money were given to them. In the evening Her Majesty's portrait was carried in procession in a richly-gilt car decorated with the choicest flowers. The procession was formed as follows:—tom-toms first; then a body of police constables in two rows, under the orders of a head-constable; next the band of musicians with the dancing-girls attached to the Vishnu Temple; then the schoolboys, nearly a hundred in number, of the Mission and High Schools, with their respective masters; followed by the Taluk and other officials, zemindars, shrotriemdars, mirasidars, and the leading merchants of the town; the Siva Temple musicians came next, and immediately behind them was the car. About 2,000 people of all castes and creeds took part in the procession. The procession started from the Taluk Cutcherry, and passed through the chief streets of the town. At the Siva Temple the Durmakurtas received the whole assembly under a decorated Pandal, and entertained them with a performance of the *Kolattam* dance by the temple dancing-girls. It was nine o'clock when the procession returned to the Taluk Cutcherry. Cheers were given at short intervals during the procession for Her Majesty. A grand nautch followed. All present were then treated to a sumptuous repast, after which *pan supari*, garlands of flowers, and sandal were distributed, and rose-water was sprinkled. At night every house, hut, cottage, and bazaar was illuminated, as also were the towers of the Siva and Vishnu Temples. Her Majesty's portrait was eventually installed in the Court-house of the Taluk Cutcherry. The Presidencial Address was adopted. It was resolved to erect a "Choultry" in commemoration of the Jubilee.

MALAPURAM (MALABAR).

This town has a population of 6,501; of whom 3,863 are Mohammedans, 2,324 are Hindus, and 314 are Christians. It is 30 miles from Calicut. A Special Assistant Collector and a Detachment of British troops are stationed here.

As the sun shone out bright on the morning of the 16th February, it was seen that flags and bunting adorned every eminence in and around the cantonment. At 7 A.M. the Detachment of the 2nd Battalion Royal Fusiliers in garrison paraded. A *feu de joie* was fired; the troops presented arms; and three cheers for the Queen Empress rent the air. Crowds of natives witnessed this ceremony. The ringing of bells, the blowing of horns, and the clash of cymbals in consonance with the beat of tom-toms, testified to the loyal spirit in which all classes participated in the general rejoicing. In the afternoon sports were held. The evening's entertainment consisted of a concert in the Detachment Theatre. The concert was brought to a close by the singing of the "National Anthem." The audience then repaired to the scene of the illuminations. Here was already prepared for the torch an enormous pile of brush-wood, and the bonfire was soon in a blaze. The fireworks that followed concluded with the exhibition of a garland, enclosing the words "God bless Victoria." This elicited storms of cheers for Her Majesty, after which cheers were given for the officers and non-commissioned officers present. The Presidencial Address was adopted.

MANANTODDY (MALABAR).

This town has a population of about 5,000. It contains a Deputy-Collector's Cutcherry, the District Forest Office, the Tahsildar's Cutcherry, a Sub-Registrar's Office, a Hospital, and a small Public School; and, on the adjacent hills overlooking the town, are the bungalows of several Europeans, and the Club. Its elevation is 2,558 feet. It is the head-quarters of the Taluk of Wynaad, which has an area of 956 square miles, and a population of 88,091, consisting of Europeans, East Indians, Nairs, and Brahmins. The soil is generally of good quality, and almost the whole area is suited for cultivation. Magnificent virgin forests in the vicinity furnish a large quantity of cardamoms. There are also many coffee and cinchona estates here, and several pepper gardens. The cultivation of coffee was begun about 60 years ago, and the area now under cultivation is about 20,000 acres. Cinchona was introduced about 15 years since. On the eastern side there is a broad belt of excellent forest of the best quality of blackwood, teak, and other valuable trees, which yield a handsome revenue. Game is everywhere plentiful, and in great variety.

Jubilee Committee.—Mr. UNDERWOOD; Colonel WOOLDRIDGE; Mr. T. R. RICHMOND; Dr. HEWSTON; Messrs. WILKINS; C. PUDDICOMBE; A. CHATHU, Tahsildar; S. RAMACHENDRA. J. L. ROZARIO; &c.

The Jubilee was celebrated at this station on the 16th February in a brilliant manner, and the greatest enthusiasm was displayed by all sections of the community. Every house was decorated, many of them very prettily; and there was an Imperial salute of 101 discharges of dynamite. A considerable number of jemmis, ryots, and others had arrived from the surrounding country, and they continued to flock in during the morning till the little town was crowded with visitors, who paraded the streets, admiring the decorations. The morning was devoted to religious services and friendly intercourse. At noon three processions were formed on the three principal roads at the outskirts of the town, and these, headed by bands of music, with flags and banners inscribed with appropriate mottoes, marched to the place where a large and well decorated Pandal had been erected. Conspicuous among these was the procession of local School Children gaily dressed in white with red sashes, each bearing a small flag or device; they marched in excellent order to the music of their band, and displayed the "Union Jack" and other flags. They were loudly cheered on their arrival. The number of people assembled was about 2,000, consisting of no less than sixteen different castes. Mr. Chathu, the Tahsildar, addressed the people in Malayalim, and in an admirable speech, which elicited frequent applause, he explained the objects of the celebration, and said that it was incumbent upon all present to show on this occasion their loyalty and devotion to their beloved Sovereign, under whose rule the people of India had experienced many years of peace and prosperity. Mr. Wilkins spoke in Malayalim in praise of Her Majesty, and of the great advance that India has made during her reign. Colonel Wooldridge alluded to the virtuous life of Her Majesty, and the deep interest she had always taken in the welfare of her subjects. A move was now made to the site of the proposed "Memorial Fountain," where a deed of gift of the land to the town was executed by Mr. Wilkins, and Mrs. Wilkins performed the ceremony of turning the first sod, after which three cheers were given for the Queen Empress, and the National Anthem was sung by the whole assembly. The company then returned to the Pandal, where *pan supari* and *attar* were distributed, and money and cooked rice were given to about 200 poor people. In the meanwhile the native bands played, and various amusements were provided. At 3 P.M. the assembly marched in procession, with banners and bands playing, to the *maidan* to witness the sports, consisting of races, jumping and acrobatic feats, &c., which occupied the time till dark. At night a torchlight procession paraded the streets, and fireworks of various sorts were exhibited, and coloured lights burnt. The day's proceedings were brought to a close at 9 P.M., when about 3,000 persons again assembled at the Pandal, and, in a short address, Mr. Wilkins, on behalf of the Committee, thanked the people for their hearty co-operation, and the good-will and harmony they had displayed, after which three hearty cheers were given for the Queen Empress. The Presidencial Address was adopted. A "Jubilee Drinking Fountain" is to be the local permanent memorial of the happy event.

MANGALORE (SOUTH CANARA).

Mangalore is the chief town in the district of South Canara. It is also a military station, and a seaport with considerable trade. It became an English possession in 1799, under the Partition Treaty of Mysore between the English, the Nizam, and the Peishwa. It is picturesquely situated on the east side of a backwater, separated from the sea by a spit of sand, and formed by the confluence of two rivers, which empty themselves into the sea by a single outlet. Its population is 32,099, consisting of 18,590 Hindus, 5,896 Mohammedans, 7,568 Christians, and 45 Jains, Parsis, &c. The Christian population consists chiefly of converts from various Hindu castes, a few Europeans and Eurasians, the latter being chiefly the descendants of the early Portuguese. The Municipality is managed by a Council of twenty members, of whom three-fourths are elected.

Jubilee Committee.—Messrs. J. W. BEST, *Chairman*; W. ASHTON and N. SHIVA ROW, *Joint Secretaries*; REV. FR. J. CLARKE; Messrs. E. H. PALMER; T. M. RAMA ROW; V. M. FERNANDEZ; MANJESHWAR BARANNAYA; HAJEE ABDUBAKAR SAIB; BAIL ABDU BEARY; and thirty others.

Thousands of people were seen early on the 16th February hastening to the *maidan* which, with the splendid Jubilee Pandal that had been erected on the eastern side, with the Union Jack flying high over it, presented an imposing appearance. The Pandal was beautifully decorated with evergreens and bunting, &c. The inscription "God save the Queen Empress" was stretched across the centre arch in golden letters, and surmounted by a crown. The Pandal was crowded with officials and non-officials, both European and native, including representatives of the Judicial, Military, Revenue, Magisterial, Police, Educational, Medical, Marine, Public Works, Salt and Abkari, and Forest Departments; the Roman Catholic and Protestant clergy and laity; Municipal Councillors and Vakils, merchants, and landlords and the members of the Jubilee Committee. Several ladies were also present. The total number of people present exceeded 10,000. The proceedings commenced at 7 A.M. with a parade of the 31st Madras Light Infantry, when a *feu de joie* was fired, and three hearty cheers were given for Her Majesty. Mr. N. Shiva Row, one of the Joint Secretaries of the Jubilee Committee, then stepped forward, and read the Presidencial Address, which was adopted with acclamation. The Collector received it, and replied in a few appropriate words. The school children now sang "God save the Queen" in Canarese and English, after which three loud cheers were given for Her Majesty. A public meeting under the presidency of Mr. Best, the Chairman of the Jubilee Committee, was now held in the Pandal "to consider what steps should be taken to induce the people of this District to co-operate in the permanent commemoration of Her Imperial Majesty's Jubilee by the erection of the Victoria Technical Institute at Madras, and the Imperial Institute in England." It was resolved that subscriptions should be collected throughout the District for these Institutes, and for a "District Scholarship" in the Victoria Technical Institute, and that the District Munsiffs and Tahsildars should be requested to form Sub-Committees in the District to assist the Mangalore Jubilee Committee in raising funds for the above purpose. Liberal subscriptions were made on the spot. The meeting dissolved with a vote of thanks to the Chairman, and three cheers for the Queen Empress. At noon Thanksgiving Services were held in the Basel G. E. Mission in South Canara, and in the St. Paul's Church; as also in all the Roman Catholic churches and chapels in the Diocese. After service another *feu de joie* was fired by the troops, and an address was read to the Collector, describing the numerous benefits the Christians of Canara had received during the reign of Her Majesty. A large space in front of the Pandal had been fenced around with bamboos, striped white and blue, from the top of which there streamed white and red flags. The Pandal was flanked by tents, and three more were pitched on the other side of the enclosure. Of the latter, one was reserved for the accommodation of Christian ladies, one for Hindu caste ladies, and the third for Eurasian ladies. At about 1 P.M., people were seen coming in from all directions, and before 3 o'clock the space round the fence, the Pandal, and the tents were crowded, about 10,000 people being present. Sports of various sorts were held, at the close of which the prizes were distributed to the winners by Mrs. Best. Shortly after sunset there was a pyrotechnic display. The fireworks were very effective, the maroons especially eliciting repeated applause from the crowd. The whole *maidan* was lighted for nearly an hour with innumerable rockets, whirligigs, fountains of fire, Bengal lights, blue and crimson lights, &c. The outskirts of the *maidan* were illuminated with lamps placed on posts, and lights blazed from the top of St. Paul's tower. The Post Office, the Bank, the Basel Mission Book Depot garden and the Union building, were splendidly illuminated.

The Jubilee was celebrated right loyally by all the Catholics of Mangalore—a body of high-caste Natives of India, of Mahratta origin, whose ancestors were converted to Christianity in the 16th century by the first Portuguese Missionaries. Though owning Portuguese surnames, they are in all respects essentially natives of the soil, keeping up their native speech, and preserving their traditions and customs to a very great extent, and associating on the most familiar terms with their Brahmin fellow-countrymen. A grand evening service was given in St. Aloysius' College Chapel, in honour of the Queen Empress. Invitations had been issued to all Europeans of the Civil and Military Services as well as to the clergymen of the Basel Lutheran Mission, and the principal native residents, with the ladies of their families. Intimation had at the same time been given that all of whatever creed were welcome. The front of the building was beautifully illuminated at 8 P.M. and presented a magnificent spectacle. At 8.15, Mr. J. Sturrock, the Collector of the District, Mr. J. W. Best, the District Judge, Colonel Stevenson, the Officer commanding the troops, and the leading European and native gentlemen arrived. The Bishop of Mangalore, surrounded by the clergy and seminarists, knelt before the brilliantly illuminated altar, and intoned the hymn of St. Ambrose, which was caught up by the choir in the gallery above. The Benediction of the Blessed Sacrament was then sung. The choir also sang the National Anthem, after which crackers were fired, fireworks let off, and an Imperial salute of 101 guns was fired. After the service all the people witnessed a display of fireworks in front of the church. Three cheers for the Queen Empress were proposed, and a thousand voices most heartily responded to the call. Three more were given for the British Nation, as also for the ladies and gentlemen who represented it in Mangalore. The new Anglo-Vernacular School for Girls, erected by the Jesuit Mission in the Hindu quarter of the town, is to bear the name of Her Majesty. Mr. Emmanuel Lobo, the son of a gentleman who presented the site occupied by St. Aloysius' College, has made a donation of Rs. 500 to the Institution as the nucleus of a fund for a "Victoria Jubilee Scholarship." On the following morning 2,741 poor people were fed in the Pandal; the adults received two measures of rice and an anna each, while the children received half as much. The rice which remained after the distribution was divided by the Committee between the Basel Mission Poor-house at Balmatah and the Roman Catholic Poor-house at Jeppoo. In the afternoon sports were held at the Bunder, and were witnessed by about 30,000 persons. The programme included boat races, swimming races, and climbing the greasy pole. There were 58 entries for the swimming race which was splendidly contested. At the close of the sports an Imperial salute of 101 detonating shells was fired on the sea-shore. At about half-past [illegible] all the ladies and gentlemen and the people who had assembled at the [illegible] witness the sports started in procession from the Marine Office, with rows of lighted torches on each side, besides blue, red, and white lights, and passed through the bazaars and streets to the Mangalore Club, and the Union, which were decorated and splendidly illuminated for the reception of Europeans and Natives respectively. The streets were illuminated by small oil lamps in rows, and by globes hanging from the roofs, and wall-shades attached to the walls of the houses along the sides of the streets. There were also evergreen festoons and triumphal arches, while over the entrances to several houses and shops were appropriate inscriptions, such as "God save our Queen Empress," "Heaven rain blessings on our Queen Empress," "Long live Queen Victoria, Empress of India," in gold and illuminated letters both in Canarese and in English. As the procession passed, prayers were offered in the mosques and temples on the way. The ladies and gentlemen were invited to enter the temples to witness the ceremony of offering prayers. The temples and mosques were decorated and illuminated. About 25,000 people took part in the procession. A banquet was given in a Pandal that had been erected on the tennis-ground of the Club. The posts were covered with green leaves, and a chain was fastened from post to post, from which were suspended beautifully coloured and variously shaped Chinese lanterns and glass globes. Over the ceiling the flags of all nations gaily waved at every motion of the wind while "Union Jacks" were placed at the two ends. A number of Chinese lanterns were also suspended from the boughs of the trees on one side of the Pandal; while on the opposite side, in illuminated letters, was the inscription "Our Queen's Jubilee. Let us rejoice." At the banquet the toast of "The Queen Empress" was proposed and drunk with loud cheers, which were heartily taken up by the natives in the "Union" close by. During the dinner, the military band played at intervals. When the dinner was over, a deputation of the representatives of the native communities marched in procession, headed by the band, from the Union to the Club, and placed garlands round the necks of several ladies and gentlemen sprinkled rose-water, and offered attar and *pan supari*. Then four schoolgirls sang the Canarese translation of the Address to Her Majesty, to a musical accompaniment. Mr. Manguishaiya read several Sanscrit poems which he had composed in honour of the Jubilee. Pamphlets containing the poems, with English translations, were distributed to the ladies and gentlemen present. This was followed by the singing of a special hymn by the German Seminary Mission boys. "God save the Queen" was sung in Canarese, after which the Europeans present took it up in English. Three loud cheers were then given for Her Majesty, and the deputation retired.

Over the entrance to the "Union," the motto "God bless our Country and Empress," in gold letters on a crimson background, was placed under the arched signboards. Flags were planted on each side of the passage leading from the gate to the flight of steps at the western end of the building. Canarese and English mottoes, such as "God save the Queen," "Long live the Queen," were placed all over the walls. The tennis-ground was tastefully decorated with festoons, posts covered with fresh mango leaves, and sugar-canes. A chain was passed round the four principal posts in the corners, to which were hung, at equal distances, glass globes of various colours. Seats were provided for boys on benches assigned separately for the several schools, and arranged outside the tennis-ground. The place was beautifully illuminated with rows of lights, one above the other, and the front verandah showed lights in white and red tumblers. The people having assembled, four native girls sang a brief biography of Her Majesty in Canarese verse, composed for the occasion by Sajis Ramakrisknaya. Mr. U. Manguishaiya read a brief sketch in Sanscrit verse, composed by himself and by Mr. Putli Balappaya, of the Queen's life, and the benefits India had derived during her glorious reign. Printed copies of the poems were distributed. Then the assembly, numbering about 5,000 persons, loudly applauded the girls and the poet. This was followed by the firing of crackers by schoolboys who had been supplied with them for the purpose. *Pan supari* and attar were distributed to the whole assembly. The Europeans in the Club drank the health of the Queen Empress, and gave three loud cheers, which were responded to with great enthusiasm by the natives assembled in the Union. The latter then went in procession, headed by a band, to pay a visit to the local representatives of Her Majesty. On their return from the Club, the band played the National Anthem, and the assembly dispersed.

The most striking circumstance which marked the celebration of the Jubilee was the keen interest evinced in the event by the most ignorant of the district people. This was in great part due to the energy of the German Missionaries, Messrs. Hoch, Diez, and Christanuja, who had published an admirable biography of Her Majesty in a largely circulated Canarese magazine, the "*Chraista Sabha Patra.*" Mr. Diez had moreover given a Malayalim version of the essay in a Malayalim magazine, called the "*Keralopayari.*" Both translations were printed with a portrait of Her Majesty, together with two prayers at the end—one for Her Majesty, and another for the Royal Family. One thousand copies of the Canarese pamphlets were distributed gratis by Dr. Lee, the Civil Surgeon, among the school children. In this way all the people throughout the District were informed of the chief incidents of Her Majesty's life, and also of the benefits which they had derived during Her Majesty's reign. The Roman Catholic Clergy also rendered valuable aid in the same direction. A School for Girls, which had been started by the Roman Catholic Mission at the town, was opened, and named the "Victoria Girls' School," in commemoration of Her Majesty's Jubilee. Dr. D. Duncan, M.A., D.S.C., the Acting Director of Public Instruction, presided, and a large number of the residents of the town were present. The Municipal Town Council resolved to sink a "Well" in honour of the Jubilee. It was also resolved to establish "Scholarships" to enable students to proceed to Madras and prosecute their studies in the Victoria Technical Institute. At the concluding meeting of the General Committee a vote of thanks was unanimously offered on the proposition of Mr. J. Sturrock, Collector of the District, to Messrs. W. Arnot and N. Shiva Row "for the very valuable services rendered by them as Joint Secretaries, and for the great trouble taken by them in making all the arrangements which resulted in making the celebration of the Jubilee in Mangalore the great success that it undoubtedly was." The Committee appointed the leading men of the various castes and sects as Sub-Committees for the collection of funds for the Imperial and Technical Institutes, and it is hoped that Rs. 20,000 will be received by the 30th June.

MANJERI (MALABAR).

Manjeri is the chief town of the Ernad Taluk, the population of which is 296,143. It contains a Tahsildar's Cutcherry, District Munsiff's Court, a Sub-Registrar's Office, a Middle School, a Dispensary, and other offices.

Jubilee Committee.—The ELIA RAJAH OF NILAMBOOR, *Chairman*; Messrs. T. NARAYANAN NAIR, *Secretary*; C. RAMAKRISHNA PATTER; K. RAMUNNI; N. K. CHAMU MENON; M. AHMED GURUKAL; MANJERI KARANAMULPAD; TENAYANCHERI ELIAD; KUNHOLIN KUTTI; and K. E. KRISHNAN UNNI NAIR.

The celebration commenced at 8 A.M. on the 16th February, when the inhabitants collected at the School-house, which was well decorated. All the public offices, the Hospital, and the Bazaars were beautifully decorated with evergreens, palm leaves, &c. The police paraded in front of the School, and fired a *feu de joie*. Acrobats performed several interesting feats. The compound was soon thronged with Hindus, Mohammedans, and Christians. The local chiefs, Karanamulpad Avergal and Tenayancheri Eliad, arrived in palanquins, attended by their retinues. A procession was then formed. It was accompanied by elephants, musicians, and acrobats. It was met by another procession at the Hospital gate. Both processions then moved on together to the site of the proposed "Memorial Tank," and stopped at a spacious and beautifully decorated Pandal that had been erected on the *maidan*. Mr. N. K. Chamu Menon explained the object for which they had met there. The Presidential Address was then read in English and Malayalim, and adopted. The Karanamulpad, assisted by the Sub-Registrar, then cut the outline of the proposed Tank (which the Committee hope to open to the public on the 20th June), and after giving three ringing cheers for Her Majesty, the procession returned to the place where the poor were to be fed. The Hospital was prettily decorated. In the afternoon above 2,000 poor people, chiefly Chermars and Pulayas, were given a hearty meal. At night there was a native dramatic performance of *Kathakali*. On the 17th the schoolboys were treated to sweetmeats and tea, after which they gave three hearty cheers for Her Majesty. A "Portrait" of Her Majesty will be placed in the School-house.

MANNARGUDY (SOUTH ARCOT).

This chief town of a taluk of the same name has a population of 19,409; of whom 18,277 are Hindus, 643 are Mohammedans, 323 are Christians, and 166 are unclassified. It has a fine Pagoda, and is the seat of a Wesleyan Mission. A large trade is carried on in locally-made cloth and metal ware.

The streets and lanes were thoroughly swept, festoons were hung up, and at night the whole town was illuminated. All classes were fed, and the really destitute were clothed in honour of the occasion; special prayers for the Queen Empress were offered in all the Hindu temples, Mohammedan mosques, and Christian churches; processions went through the streets with a display of fire-works; a musical entertainment was given in the Vishnu Temple; and a brief sketch of Her Majesty's life in Tamil was read at a public meeting. It was resolved to give a prize to be styled "The Queen's Jubilee Prize," annually, to distinguished lads in one or more classes of the Local Fund School. Fruit, sandal, sugar, and *pan supari* were distributed.

MASULIPATAM (KISTNA).

The population of this seaport is 35,056; of whom 30,377 are Hindus, 4,288 are Mohammedans, and 391 are Christians. The town contains the Collector's Office, District Court, Office of the District Superintendent of Police, District Munsiff's Court, Port and Sea-Customs Office, Taluk Cutcherry, Magistrate's Office, Post Office, Telegraph Office, District Registrar's Office, Local Fund District Engineer's Office, a large Hospital, two Dispensaries, a Subsidiary Jail, &c. The Municipal Council consists of sixteen Councillors, of whom four are officials and twelve non-officials, seven of the latter being elected by the ratepayers. The Educational Institutions are: the Church Mission College, called the Noble College, which teaches up to the F. A. Standard; the Hindu High School; the Local Fund Training School; the Church Mission Society's Training School; the Municipal Middle School; the Jovarpet Middle School; two Results Schools on the combined system; thirty-nine Results Schools for Boys; eighteen Girls' Schools on the Results system, most of which are in charge of the London Mission; a Municipal Mohammedan School; and nine indigenous schools. The town exports rice, dholl, and oil-seeds. It is famous for its chintzes and carpets.

Jubilee Committee.—Messrs. C. A. BIRD, *Chairman;* AYYANKI VENKATA SUBBARAYUDU PUNTALU and RAJANALA NAGABHUSHANAM NAIDU, *Joint Secretaries;* R. SEWELL; PALAKURTI SRIRAMULU; KUVVAM NARASIMHA NAIDU; NAWAB HASSAN ALI; Colonel HALEMAN, Messrs. J. H. FLETCHER; and others.

It is impossible to overrate the loyalty and enthusiasm displayed by all sections of the community in the Kistna district. At Masulipatam, the capital, a signal-gun was fired at 6 o'clock on the morning of the 16th February, and was followed immediately by a salute of 31 guns at four different places in the town. At 7-30 A.M. a Thanksgiving Service was held in the English Church, which was handsomely decorated, and where was hung the Royal Standard, which had been worked in silk by the English ladies of the station. From noon to 3 P.M. 1,500 poor people were fed in several places, and the generosity in this respect of the Zemindarni of Davi was conspicuous. She also distributed cloths to 100 people amongst the most needy and infirm. At noon crowds began to collect in the principal square, and on the arrival at the decorated tent of the principal Zemindars and European and native residents, a Municipal address was read, followed by a recital of verses, composed for the occasion by the Chairman of the Municipal Council. The girls then sang a *mangalam*, and camphor was burnt before the portrait of the Queen Empress, which was decorated with strings of pearls, and garlands of flowers. A procession was now formed. After an advance guard of police came bands of musicians, and a large body of spearmen, with the Royal Standard carried on an elephant; a body of dancing girls and peons followed; then came Mr. R. Sewell, the Collector, and Mr. C. A. Bird, the District Judge, on a large elephant, richly caparisoned; followed by the chief inhabitants of the District on elephants, in carriages and palanquins, in the following order:—the Nawab of Masulipatam with his sons, the Zemindar of Mukhtyala, the Zemindar of Wuyur Pargana in Nuzvid, the Zemindar of Telaprolu Pargana in Nuzvid, the son of the Zemindar of Tsallapalli (Devarakota), Raja Durga Prasada Naidu Bahadur Garu, of Tsallapalli, Raja Venkata Ramalingaana Bahadur Garu, of Tsallapalli, the ex-Zemindar of Gurzala, several European gentlemen, members of the District Jubilee Committee, members of the District Board, members of the Taluk Board, members of the Municipal Council. Behind these came several camels, the riders of which carried standards, and next came a large body of policemen. The procession, which was accompanied by dense crowds, passed under several triumphal arches, conspicuous amongst which was one with four towers, that had been erected by the Municipality near the

Munsiff's Court-house. Numerous wreaths and *thoranams* were hung across the principal streets, which were gaily decorated with flags, and filled with crowds of spectators. After halting for a few minutes under a Pandal that had been erected by the Zemindarni of Davi, who caused flowers to be strewed over the Royal Standard, and camphor to be burnt before it, the procession arrived at the Munsiff's Court-house at about 3.30, where it passed between double lines of spearmen, a guard of honour of police being drawn up, who presented arms to the Royal Standard. The scene at this point was very effective. A State prisoner was brought forward, and the Collector announced that Government had been pleased to order his release. The procession then advanced up the hall, which was crowded. The Court-house had been handsomely decorated, and converted into a Durbar Hall for the occasion. Conspicuous over the *dais* was a Royal Crown, and a Star formed of bayonets. The procession was headed by a Jemadar, in full uniform, bearing the Royal Standard, all present standing, and the National Anthem being played. The Collector opened the proceedings with a speech, which was afterwards translated into Telugu. The Presidencial Address was then read, adopted, and signed, music being played at intervals. The Nawab of Masulipatam now presented an address on behalf of the Mohammedan community, which was read by his son, Nawab Suleman Ali Mirza Khan Bahadur. The addresses of the Zemindarni of Davi and the Municipality having been received, the Zemindar of Mukhtyala spoke a few words in Telugu. The Rajahs Rangayya Appa Rao Bahadur and Simhadri Appa Rao Bahadur of Nuzivid then announced that they wished to perpetuate Her Majesty's Jubilee by founding two "Jubilee Scholarships" for boys reading in the Hindu High School at Masulipatam. The Collector made a short speech. The National Anthem was sung by the boys of the Training Institution, and a Royal salute was fired by the police, followed by a *feu de joie*. On the *maidan* near the Court-house sports were engaged in until dark. At 7.30 P.M. the members of the Club entertained at dinner all the Europeans in the town. The large Club-room had been beautifully decorated by several ladies. At the conclusion of the dinner, Mr. Bird proposed Her Majesty's health. The toast was drunk with enthusiastic cheers. The whole town was in a state of festivity at night. The native houses were lit up as at the Dipavali festival. The chief streets were illuminated at the expense of the Municipality. The large houses, especially the residences of the Europeans, and the public buildings, were uniformly lit up along the roofs and verandahs by lanterns. The illuminations culminated at the Court-house, where the principal residents were received in a handsome Pandal erected, and tastefully decorated by Colonel Haleman. A very effective torchlight procession took place, consisting of all the elephants, horses, camels, spearmen, and other members of the Zemindars' retinues that had taken part in the procession in the middle of the day. The scene being brilliantly lit by coloured fires, made a beautiful spectacle, reflected as it was in the waters of a small lake in front of the Pandal. Then followed a display of fireworks, and the evening's entertainment concluded with the return of the procession in the same order as before. It is estimated that, including spectators from surrounding villages, nearly 50,000 people took part in the celebration at this town. The utmost loyalty and enthusiasm prevailed throughout. On the next day several entertainments were given. Three hundred native gentlemen of the higher castes assembled at the Maharajah's Choultry, breakfasted together, and were afterwards entertained by nautches. In the afternoon a very large crowd assembled to witness an exhibition of acrobatic feats and sports in Robertsonpett Square. In the evening the Europeans of the station were entertained at a grand banquet in the Durbar Hall, which was given by the same native gentlemen who had organised the breakfast to their countrymen in the morning. The hall was lit up by the light of numerous chandeliers, and the effect was heightened by the happy disposition of mirrors about the room. After the dinner a nautch was given, and Sanscrit verses were sung in honour of the Queen Empress. On the night of the 19th a banquet was given to the European community by Rajahs Rangayya Appa Rao Bahadur and Simhadri Appa Rao Bahadur of Nuzivid, after which the company went to the theatre of the Hindu Theatrical Company of Masulipatam to witness a performance of the *Sakuntala*. The local permanent memorial will take the shape of a "District Museum," with a "Technical School" attached to it.

MAYAVERAM.

Mayaveram is a picturesque town, with the river Cauvery running through its centre. Its population is 23,044; of whom 21,933 are Hindus, 484 are Muhammadans, and 627 are Christians. Its affairs are managed by a Municipal Corporation consisting of 18 Councillors, three-fourths of whom are elected, and one-fourth nominated by Government. Weaving is the chief local industry. The chief Educational Institution is the Municipal High School, with 500 pupils on its rolls. Two other Boys' Schools, and a Girls' School, are maintained by the Municipality. There are more than 20 Rural Schools, and the same number of other Schools in the town. The Municipality maintains a Hospital called the Webster Hospital.

Jubilee Committee.—Messrs. T. A. ALAGA PILLAI, *Chairman*; T. KRISHNA ROW; PATTAMUNGALAM NARAYANASAMI IYER; THIRUVENGADACHARIAR; K. LAKSHMANA IYER; T. KOTHUNDARAMA IYER; T. DURASAMI PILLAI; and eight others.

The celebration at this town on the 16th February was a complete success. In the early morning sports were held in the High School compound. Guns were fired in the precincts of various Hindu temples, as well as near churches, mosques, &c. The town was beautifully decorated with evergreens and festoons. *Abhishekams, pujahs*, and worship were performed for the welfare of Her Majesty. From 9 A.M. to 3 P.M. about 4,000 poor people were fed. Between 4 and 6 in the evening the "Victoria Lawn-Tennis Court" was opened. Thousands of people representing the various sections of the town community were present. The schoolboys were then given a treat. Late in the evening a grand procession started from the Tennis Court, and proceeded slowly to the High School building with torches, music, fireworks, nautch girls, &c. The procession halted in front of the High School premises, where the Presidencial Address was read and adopted amidst loud and repeated cheers, while the Police presented arms, and fired a salute. The pupils of the High School gave a series of performances; and congratulatory speeches were delivered in English, Sanscrit, and Tamil. The boys then acted the Court Scene from Shakespeare's *Merchant of Venice*. Then followed the distribution of fruits, sugar, flowers, and *pan supari*, and the sprinkling of rose-water. All public offices, the High School, the temples, churches, mosques, and many private houses were illuminated. Great enthusiasm prevailed.

MELUR (MADURA).

The population is 3,587. An American Mission has established an English Girls' School here, and the Local Fund Board gives grants-in-aid to some Primary Schools. Agriculture is the chief occupation of the people. Grain, dholl, and oil-seeds of good quality are largely produced.

Jubilee Committee.—Messrs. C. Kristnama Row, *Chairman*; Venkata Kristnamangar and Tirumalai Pillai, *Secretaries*; Rev. G. H. Gutterson; Messrs. A. Vythelingam Moodelliar; T. Venkataramier Vakil; Litchumana Perumal Pillai; Makathia Ravuttur; Sinnia Chettiar; and six others.

Early in the morning of the 16th February the town assumed a gay appearance. Houses had been whitewashed, festoons and evergreens had been placed on the road-sides and in front of the houses, and preparations for the illuminations were completed. In all the temples, mosques, and churches special Thanksgiving Services and prayers for Her Majesty were held. Meals were provided for upwards of 1,200 poor persons; cloths were given to about 80 of them; and a larger number received small presents of money and sugar. An open-air meeting was held at the Travellers' Bungalow compound, which was well illuminated, to which almost the whole of the people of the town, and a number of the people from the other villages of the taluk, proceeded with music, accompanied by schoolboys dressed in gay clothes. More than 1,000 people were present. The Tahsildar, Mr. C. Kristana Row, was voted to the chair, and explained to the assembly the object of the meeting. Other speeches followed, all of which dwelt on the virtues of Her

Majesty the Queen Empress. The schoolgirls then sang the *Kummi Pattu*, a poem composed in honour of the Jubilee by Mr. Scott, of Madura, and the American Mission Boarding School boys sang at intervals. Then followed a display of fireworks; and sandal, flowers, rose-water, and *pan supari* were freely distributed. The assembly then rose, and "God save the Queen" was sung. Three hearty cheers were then given, and the assembly returned to the town in procession with music and brilliant illuminations. The Presidencial Address was adopted.

METTAPALAIYAM (COIMBATORE).

The town of Mettapalaiyam is the Revenue head-quarters of a Deputy Tahsildar's Jurisdiction. Its population is 6,095, consisting of 5,145 Hindus, 667 Mohammedans, and 283 Christians. The chief occupation of the people is trade in Nilgiri coffee and tea. Agriculture is carried on to some extent. Being the terminus of the Madras Railway, and forming a rendezvous for visitors from all parts of India to the Nilgiri Sanitarium, the town is rapidly increasing in population. It possesses two Schools; one of which is the London Mission Middle School, and the other a Charity School for Infants under the grant-in-aid system.

Jubilee Committee.—Messrs. SYED RUSOOL SAHIB BAHADUR, *Chairman*; GHULAM AAN BURAQ KHAN, *Secretary*; D. B. GAMBLE; V. UNNAMALAIUDAIYAR; T. SUBBARAYULU NAIDU; V. UMAPATHY NAIDU; MALIK ABDUL RAHIM SAHIB; V. RANGASAWMY NAIDU; P. KRISHNAIYENGAR; C. S. RUNGIAH NAIDU; and others.

People of all classes met at the Pandal that had been erected on the plain. It was tastefully decorated with banners and bunting, with an arch at its entrance bearing the inscription "God bless our Empress." A band of native musicians was in attendance. The principal streets were ornamented with festoons. At 9 A.M. there was a special service at the London Mission Church, and in the evening prayers and thanksgivings were offered in the mosque and temple. At noon rice, cloths, and money were distributed to about 500 paupers, both male and female. At 3 P.M. a grand procession of Schoolboys, accompanied by the general public and by native music, and headed by the local police, marched through the principal streets. It arrived at the Jubilee Pandal at 4 P.M., when a *feu de joie* was fired by the Police. Sports were held, and continued till dusk. About 7 P.M. a grand display of fireworks took place, and the distribution of sandal, flowers, and *pan supari* and the sprinkling of rose-water brought the festivities to a close. The Presidencial Address was adopted. On the following morning a large assembly met at the Jubilee Pandal, when prizes were distributed, and a treat was given to the local school-children.

MULKI (SOUTH CANARA).

Mulki is a small town on the Western Coast, 24 miles to the north of Mangalore, and has a population of about 4,000. In it are located the Offices of a Sub-Registrar, a Sea-Customs

Superintendent, a Sub-Postmaster, and a Police Station; and it is the head-quarters of a Revenue Inspector.

Jubilee Committee.—Messrs. P. RAMAKRISHNAIYA, B.A., *Chairman*; MUNDKUR BHAVANI RAO, *Secretary*; MULKI SUBBAYA KUDWA; KARNAD SHRINIVAS RAO; MULKI MUKUNDA RAO; and the Rev. D. S. FERNANDES.

At 8 o'clock in the morning of the 16th February a procession, attended by a large number of people, including most of the leading men of the town, the Police, and the children of four schools, started from near the Police station, and marched in procession, headed by two native bands, to the Pandal that had been erected for the occasion near the Mission Town School. On its way the procession passed beneath a handsome triumphal arch, which bore a Mahratta inscription on each face of it, meaning "Success to Her Majesty the Queen Empress." Soon after the procession had entered the Pandal the Police force held a parade, and fired a *feu de joie*. After the parade the children of the Mission Orphan Girls' School sang the National Anthem in Canarese, the whole assembly standing. Three hearty cheers were then given for Her Majesty. At the request of the Jubilee Committee Mrs. Ott and Mrs. Ebb presented to the school-children, over 200 in number, a copy of a Canarese book, entitled "The Queen's Jubilee." Rice was distributed to about 250 poor persons. A special Thanksgiving Service was held in the Basel Mission Church, and prayers were offered in the temples for Her Majesty. The evening festivities commenced by about 3,000 people assembling near the Mission bungalow, and moving thence at sunset, in procession, preceded by two bands, towards the Pandal. As the procession went along, red and blue lights were burnt at intervals. The whole of the road from the Post Office to the Pandal, a distance of a furlong, was illuminated by small kerosine lamps fixed on poles placed on both sides. Three beautiful triumphal arches, bearing appropriate inscriptions, had been erected on that road. The decorated Pandal presented a charming appearance when it was lighted up. As soon as the procession reached the Pandal Mr. Mundkur Mangesh Rao made a speech in Canarese, and proposed three cheers for Her Majesty the Queen Empress. The cheers were enthusiastically given, and sugar and *pan supari* were distributed to all present. Rose-water was freely sprinkled, and sweetmeats were distributed among the school-children. A display of fireworks followed, after which there were gymnastic performances. At 9 o'clock the assembly returned in procession as far as the Post Office, and then dispersed. The Presidencial Address was adopted.

NAMAKAL (SALEM).

This town is held in much honour by Hindus as the traditional abode of Vishnu. The population is 5,147; of whom 4,540 are Hindus, 581 are Mohammedans, and 26 are Christians. The Local Taluk Board consists of four official and nine non-official members. The sanitation of the town is under the superintendence of the Union Panchayat, consisting of ten members. A first grade Middle School and Elementary Schools are under the management of the Taluk Board. The Government Girls' School is largely attended. The chief trade of the place is in paddy, cholam, and seeds. A superior sort of cloth is manufactured

Jubilee Committee.—Messrs. T. Nilakanta Subba Ramaiya Sastri, *Chairman*; T. Ramaswami Aiyangar, *Secretary*; P. Rajagopala Chariar, M.A., B.L.; P. Aiyavaiyar; Utankarai Srinivasa Iyer; Pichu Subramanya Iyer; N. Narasimha Pillay; S. T. Venkatapathi Iyer; and K. Sethu Rao.

Over 800 poor persons were fed and clothed between 8 A.M. and 6 P.M. on the 16th February. Prayers were offered in the temples and mosques. A procession of the Hindu gods started from the Narasimaswami temple, followed by a large concourse of people with Hindu music, and a Police escort. The procession halted at the Mantapam at 9 A.M. The children of the Girls' and the Elementary Boys' Schools were collected in the Literary Institute, whither the assembly halted for a few minutes. Here the Police mustered in force, and fired a *feu de joie*. The procession and the children then marched to the Middle School house, with Hindu music playing, headed by a body of police constables, who fired a volley occasionally during the march, and followed by a great number of all castes and creeds. As the party entered the school-house the boys shouted "God bless the Queen," "Cheers for the Queen Empress." There were recitations and dialogues by the boys of the Middle School, and the girls sang several appropriate songs. The children were afterwards treated to sugar and fruits. Three enthusiastic cheers were given for Her Majesty. The party returned to the Literary Institute, and then dispersed. In the afternoon there were *abishekams* and *archanas* in the temples for the prosperity and long life of the Queen Empress and the Royal Family. In the evening the party again met at the Literary Institute, whence they proceeded with music to the top of the Rock, where a sumptuous repast was provided for all. At the same time about 100 poor Brahmins, and an equal number of Sudras were served with food in the Runganadaswami temple by T. Ramaswami Aiyangar, the Secretary of the Jubilee Committee. After sunset, the rock, the town, and the temples were illuminated. At night the effigies of Runganadaswami and Narasimaswami were carried again in procession with music. That was followed by a pyrotechnic display. The Presidencial Address was adopted. In commemoration of the Jubilee a "Library," in connection with the Literary Institute was opened.

NANDALUR (CUDDAPAH).

All classes of Her Majesty's subjects took part in the festivities at this town. The principal inhabitants, including the Vakils, Court officials, railway officials, merchants, and ryots, assembled at 4 P.M. in the Pandal which had been erected for the occasion, in the compound of the Court House. The Pandal was tastefully decorated, and bore over its entrance the inscription, "God save the Queen Empress." The District Munsiff, Mr. Doddi Yogappah, who was unanimously voted to the chair, explained to the assembled crowd the benefits of the British rule. The Presidencial Address was read and explained in Telugu to the audience by Mr. C. Ananta Charlu, Secretary of the Jubilee Committee, after which it was unanimously adopted, and then signed by a few representatives. The meeting terminated with a distribution of flowers and *pan supari*, and with three hearty cheers for Her Majesty and the Royal Family. Rice and cloths were distributed to the poor. At night the whole town, including places of worship, was illuminated. The principal inhabitants went in procession to the great Hindu temple, and offered prayers for the long life and prosperity of Her Majesty and the Royal Family. Prayers were also offered in the Mohammedan mosques by the Mohammedan community. A money grant was made to the Nandalur Reading Room to enable it to start a Library, to be called the "Empress Jubilee Library."

NANDYAL (KURNOOL).

The population is 8,907; of whom 5,749 are Hindus, 3,112 are Mohammedans, and 46 are Christians. Nandyal is the head-quarters of the Head-Assistant Collector, Tahsildar, Munsiff, and Sub-Registrar. It contains a Local Fund School teaching up to the Middle School standard, a Normal School, several Elementary Schools, and nine Sivaite Pagodas. A Panchayet Union has been established here. A considerable trade is carried on in cotton and indigo. Jaggery is largely manufactured. Wheat is raised in the adjacent villages. The town is famous for lacquer work.

Jubilee Committee.—Messrs. C. VENKAYA JAGGA ROW, *Chairman*; K. SESHADRI AIYANGAR, *Secretary*; G. CHENGAL ROYA NAIDU; P. SAMBAYA; K. KRISTNA ROW; C. VIJAYA RAGAVACHARI; and others.

At sunrise on the 16th February tom-toms were beaten through the streets of the town, announcing that a distribution of food was to be made to the poor of all classes. The feeding continued from 8 o'clock till sunset, amid shouts of "Long live the Queen." About 2,000 persons in all were thus fed. At 11 A.M. prayers were offered in all places of worship for the long life and prosperity of the Queen Empress. All the houses, temples, and public buildings were decorated with festoons, *thoranams*, and flags. Several triumphal arches had been erected across the roads. The most prominent of these was one in front of the house of Mr. C. Venkata Jagga Row, C.S., Head-Assistant Collector and Chairman of the Jubilee Committee, bearing the inscription "God save the Queen" on one side, and "Aryavarta rejoices on Jubilee Day" on the other. At night there were illuminations. The streets were lighted with lamps, placed on poles planted on both sides. Shortly after dusk, the Hindu god, Mahanandiswara Swamy, was taken in torchlight procession along the public streets, from one end of the town to the other. The effigy was beautifully adorned with flowers and valuable ornaments. A dozen dancing-girls danced in front as the procession advanced, and music was played. All the officials and the leading inhabitants of the town were in attendance. There was a grand display of fireworks when the procession reached the western end of the town. The procession returned to the temple at half past one o'clock. Early on the following morning the pupils of the several schools assembled at the premises of the District Munsiff's Court, and were treated to sweetmeats. At 3 P.M. there were sports, consisting of hurdle races, chatty races, donkey races, tug-of-war, &c. The sports continued till sunset. At night a musical entertainment was given in a grand Pandal, which was splendidly lighted. Three sets of dancing-girls were in attendance. Several songs were sung in Telugu as well as in Hindustani, the girls dancing all the while. Slokas in Sanscrit and Hindustani, and a few stanzas in Tamil, were read by pundits, in praise of Her Majesty. *Pan supari* and sandal were distributed to all. More than 1,000 persons were present. The entertainment terminated with a grand display of fireworks. The Presidencial Address was adopted. A "Town Hall" is to be erected as a permanent memorial of the Jubilee. A "Portrait of Her Majesty" will adorn the building.

NARAYANAVARAM (NORTH ARCOT).

The population of the four important places of the division of Narayanavaram is as follows:— Karvatinagar, 5,874; Narayanavaram, 3,913; Nagari, 2,565; Puttoor, 2,491; total, 14,843. There is a Local Fund Primary School both at Narayanavaram and at Puttoor, and at Karvatinagar there is a school maintained by the Zemindar. At certain seasons of the year oranges are very plentiful, and are largely exported to other places. Narayanavaram is noted for the good cloths that its weavers, who form the main portion of the population, manufacture.

Jubilee Committee.—Raja Kavaraju Bahadur, *Chairman*; Messrs. C. S. Doraisami Pillai, *Secretary*; L. Saravana Pillai; V. Ramachendra Rao; C. Venkataramayya; K. M. Sundarasakacharriar, B.A.; Velu Chettyar; and others.

The Jubilee was celebrated here on the 16th February with great enthusiasm. At daybreak every house was decked with festoons, and there was not a house that remained unilluminated in the evening. Special service was held in the morning in Kalyana Venkatesa's temple, and prayers were offered for the continuance of Her Majesty's reign. The Mohammedans assembled at their mosque, and had morning worship with a similar prayer for the Queen Empress. About 2,000 poor Hindus and Mohammedans were fed, and cloths were distributed to the most indigent among them. There was an evening service in the temple in honour of Her Majesty. On the next day, special worship was again performed in the Kalyana Venkatasa temple, and a *Vyasa Puja* was made in honour of the Jubilee. On this occasion a Brahmin recited a Sanscrit ode, which he had composed in commemoration of the Jubilee. In the evening there was a grand procession of the god, which started about midnight, and returned about 5 o'clock in the morning. Fireworks were let off at intervals. When the procession came to an end, three cheers were given for Her Majesty. As permanent memorials of the Jubilee three "Lamp Posts" were erected, and a sum was deposited in the Post Office Savings Bank, the interest accruing from which will be utilised in distributing "Books" to the poor boys attending the schools in the Division.

NARSIPATAM (VIZAGAPATAM).

Narsipatam has a population of about 98,000. Education is in a somewhat backward condition, but every attempt has been made to encourage the Hill tribes to send their children to school. A Taluk Board has recently been introduced, and is working well.

Jubilee Committee.—Messrs. G. VIJAYA RAMAMURTY PUNTALU, *Chairman*; K. KURMIAH PUNTALU, *Secretary*; C. MANGAYA NAYUDU; and T. APPALANARASAYA CHETTY.

On the morning of the 16th February the town presented a beautiful appearance with festoons overhanging the streets, and mottoes expressive of loyalty. The "Union Jack" was hoisted in a central part of the town, amid shouts of applause from the assembled multitude. A large number of people assembled at the fine Pandal that had been erected on the Police Parade-ground. Here several loyal speeches were made, the speakers dwelling on the great benefits that the people of India had derived during the reign of Her Majesty, which had been pre-eminently characterised by even-handed justice. Cheers were repeatedly given for Her Majesty. The poor and needy were sumptuously fed and clothed. In the afternoon all the Native and European gentlemen of the place witnessed a nautch in the Pandal. This continued till 5 o'clock, when sweetmeats were distributed to the boys and girls of the various Schools in the town. The time between 5 and 7 P.M. was occupied by athletic sports on the Parade-ground. Prizes were awarded to the winners. At night a dramatic performance was given in the Pandal. It commenced at 9 o'clock in the night, and continued till daybreak. The Presidential Address was read and explained to the audience, and adopted amid hearty cheers. *Attar* and *pan supari* were then distributed to the Native and European gentlemen. The festivities wound up with a display of fireworks. It was resolved to establish a "Reading Room" in commemoration of the Jubilee, and to call it the "Queen's Reading Room."

NAZARETH (TINNEVELLY).

Nazareth is a small town of over 1,000 inhabitants, all of whom are Christians of the Church of England. It is the head-quarters of a Missionary of the S.P.G. It contains a Church, a Post Office, a Dispensary, a High School, Middle School, Primary Schools, Orphanages, and a Normal School for training School Mistresses. An Industrial Technical School prepares boys for the Government Examination in Drawing and Carpentry. Native cloths of good material are woven. Tailoring, blacksmith's work, rattan work, and lace-making are the chief industries. The bulk of the people are of the Shanar class. Many Christian graduates and clergymen in Southern India are natives of Nazareth.

The celebration began on the evening of the 15th February. At the special service, which commenced at 7 P.M., prayers were offered for the Queen Empress and the Royal Family, and a Native Missionary preached. He gave the congregation an account of the life of Her Majesty; pointed out a few lessons to be derived from Her Majesty's noble example; explained the nature of the present Government of India; contrasted it with preceding Governments in the country; and alluded to the privileges which India now enjoys under the peaceful Government of Great Britain. At the conclusion of the service native bands played, and an Imperial salute of 101 guns was fired. The festivities continued till 10 P.M., and were witnessed by a large crowd. Rice and mutton were distributed to the poor. On the morning of Jubilee Day, people poured in from several adjacent towns and villages. At 6.30 A.M. there was a celebration of the Communion, which was largely attended by Native Christians. At 10 A.M. a special form of prayer for the Queen's Jubilee was used, and an appropriate sermon was preached. At 11.30 A.M. a meeting of Mission agents and headmen of the congregations was held in the Boys' Orphanage. A Jubilee Fund, called "The Native Christian Provident Fund," for the benefit of Christians, was started. 119 prisoners were released from the Jail. The meeting closed with three hearty cheers for Her Majesty. From 4 to 5 P.M. the gymnastic instructor performed several wonderful tricks in jugglery. Vespers were sung at 7 P.M., and the church was well illuminated. From 8 to 12 P.M. there was a variety of performances which were witnessed by thousands of people. Some boys performed gymnastic and acrobatic feats. At intervals there were magic-lantern shows. At the end of every item in the performances tom-toms were beaten, and a harlequin made his appearance to enliven the people. From midnight to 2 A.M. there was a grand display of fireworks. The Presidencial Address was adopted. "Industrial Technical Schools" are in course of construction at this place, and they are to be finished at a cost of Rs. 10,000, during the Jubilee year.

NEGAPATAM (TANJORE).

Negapatam, one of the earliest European settlements on the Coromandel coast, is a busy seaport with a number of suburbs, the principal of which is Nagore. Its population is 53,776; of whom 36,326 are Hindus, 12,408 are Mohammedans, and 5,042 are Christians. There is a considerable export and import trade. The chief educational institutions are a Jesuit College, and a College maintained by the Wesleyan Mission. The state of female education is very satisfactory, owing chiefly to the labours of the Wesleyan Mission, there being nine Girls' Schools with upwards of 530 girls under instruction. The number of boys under instruction in Schools recognised by the Department of Education is upwards of 2,300. The town has had the benefit of Local Self-Government since 1865, with electoral privileges.

Jubilee Committee.—Messrs. C. E. Crighton, *Chairman*; P. Rethnasabapathy Pillai and T. K. Annasamy Iyer, *Joint Secretaries*; P. Oliver; P. Streesamoolu Naidu; M. Ganapathi Pillai; J. Twigg; Rev. W. H. Findlay, M.A.; Mr. G. S. Bruce; Rev. T. R. Darvall; and seventy-four others.

The morning of the 16th February dawned with the firing of guns in the various churches, mosques, and temples in the town, and with an Imperial salute of 101 guns both in the principal Hindu temple, and also at Nagore in a famous Mohammedan mosque at that suburb. Upwards of 3,000 poor people were fed in the course of the day, at the expense of Messrs. M. Ganapathi Pillai, M. T. Bavasa Ravuther, Atheenarayana Iyer, and R. M. S. Nagappa Chettiar. At 3 P.M. a grand procession started from the Railway Station, and marched to the site of the proposed memorial "Park," headed by the South Indian Railway Volunteer Corps with band. All corporate bodies in the town took part in the procession with appropriate devices and banners. The members of the Freemason Lodge, "Prudentia," marched in the procession with their insignia. A grand Pavilion had been erected on the Park *maidan*. The procession arrived at 4 P.M. Upwards of 400 Schoolgirls, who had been arranged in a gallery in the pavilion, greeted the party on its arrival by singing "God save the Queen." The memorial stone of the Park was laid, the ceremony being performed by the Freemasons, headed by Worshipful Brother W. J. Hooper, from Trichinopoly, who had been delegated by the Right Worshipful the District Grand Master of Madras for the purpose. After laying the stone, Mr. Hooper addressed the assembly, and dwelt upon the vast progress the country had made during Her Majesty's reign. Mr. Crighton, the Chairman of the Jubilee Committee, made an appropriate reply, thanking Mr. Hooper and his brother Masons for their kindness in coming to Negapatam, to officiate at the inaugural ceremony. At the conclusion of the ceremony the Volunteer Corps fired a *feu de joie*, and the band played the National Anthem. The Pagoda authorities then made over the ground of the Park to the Chairman of the Town Council, after which there was a distribution of *pan supari*, limes, and garlands. Three hearty cheers were given for Her Majesty. More than 20,000 people witnessed the ceremony, and the greatest enthusiasm prevailed. Before the meeting dispersed, Mr. Crighton, at the request of the Municipal Chairman, declared the "Victoria Industrial School" of the Municipality open. The meeting then broke up. The people again assembled at 9 P.M. to witness a grand display of fireworks. There was a most effective illumination of the Railway premises, the Post and Telegraph Offices, the European quarters, and the houses of several native gentlemen. The Presidencial Address was adopted. On the evening of the 17th upwards of 1,500 Schoolboys assembled in the pavilion, each school marching to its place with colours and band. Sports were then held, and prizes given, after which the boys were treated at the expense of Messrs. Frank Oliver, Annasami Iyer, Sreeramoolo Naidu, and Kupchan Lall. Late in the evening of the same day there was a grand procession of the god and goddess of the large Hindu temple.

NELLORE (TOWN).

Nellore is a town of considerable antiquity, situated 108 miles north of Madras, and 15 miles from the Bay of Bengal. Its population is 27,505; of these 22,128 are Hindus, 4,672 are Mohammedans, 700 are Christians, and 5 are unclassified. The town is the head-quarters of the District Collector, District Judge, Superintendent of Police, District Engineer, and Civil Surgeon. There are four Municipal Schools, a Normal School, a Hindu Matriculation School, a Matriculation School belonging to the Free Church of Scotland, a Roman Catholic School, and several Hindu and Mohammedan Private Schools. The American Baptist Mission has a Boys' School, a Girls' School, and an Industrial School for boys and girls. A considerable trade is carried on in rice, cotton, indigo, cholum, jaggery, ragi, and other grains. The town being on the delta of the Pennar, the chief product of the surrounding country is rice.

Jubilee Committee.—Messrs. L. A. Campbell, *Chairman*; Rev. D. Downie, D.D., *Secretary*; Messrs. A. Venkaya Puntalu; Syed Allikhan Bahadur; L. Sahabsalingam Naidu; W. G. Underwood; H. Moberly; H. M. Dhamtulla Sahib Bahadur, Captain C. B. Henderson, R.E.; and others.

The celebration of the Jubilee on the 16th February began with religious services in places of worship. From 10 A.M. till 1 P.M. there was a feeding of the poor in three parts of the town, at which 3,000 persons received a substantial meal. At 4 P.M. there was a mass meeting in the Cutcherry Square, where, for two hours, sports took place. Then followed the reading of the Proclamation of 1858 in English, Telugu, and Hindustani. The "Union Jack" was hoisted, and a salute fired. This part of the programme closed with the singing of "God save the Queen." A treat of sweets was given to the children of the town by Mr. A. Venkaya Garu. In the evening there was a display of fireworks, and an illumination of the town. The Nellore Club gave a dinner to the British residents at the house of Mr. C. A. Bull. The Presidencial Address was adopted. On the 17th, there was a Garden Party, given by Mrs. Lorne Campbell, the wife of the District and Sessions Judge, to the Europeans, Eurasians, and a large number of native gentlemen of the town. Tennis, badminton, and archery were engaged in until dark, after which the Rev. Dr. Downie gave a stereopticon exhibition of views of London and Windsor, and a number of the places on the route between England and India. At the close of the exhibition "God save the Queen" was sung. The illumination of Mrs. Campbell's garden and bungalow was very picturesque. The Committee decided to erect, as a permanent memorial, a "Victoria Hospital for Women," at a cost of about Rs. 15,000.

There were celebrations at Vencatagiri, Ongole, Chundi, Udayagiri, Kavili, Gudur, and other small towns of the Nellore District. The most notable of these was the celebration of the Rajah of Vencatagiri. This consisted of a feeding of the poor; a festival at each of the two temples; a procession in which a portrait of Her Majesty was carried on the howdah of an elephant gorgeously decorated for the occasion; a grand meeting at the Town Hall, at which the Rajah made a speech, in which he dwelt on the glories of Her Majesty's reign, and the great benefits that India had derived from it; a nautch; and a display of fireworks. As a permanent memorial the Rajah proposes to erect a "Jubilee House" at the Vencatagiri Railway Station, for the use of travellers.

OMALUR (SALEM).

Omalur is the name borne by a small group of villages ten miles to the north-west of Salem. These villages consist of 618 houses, with a population of about 3,000; of whom about 200 are Mohammedans, and the rest Hindus. It contains a Deputy Tahsildar's Cutcherry, a Travellers' Bungalow, a Post Office, and a Local Fund Middle School of the third grade.

Jubilee Committee.—Messrs. S. A. SUBRAMANYA AIYAR, *Chairman*; C. RAMASWAMY AIYAR *Secretary*; SANKARANARAYANA AIYAR; GOVINDA CHETTI; VENKATASUBBAIYAR; VENKATAPPA CHETTI; KRISHNA CHETTI; and twelve others.

The people of Omalur celebrated the Jubilee on the 16th February in a very loyal manner. *Abishekams* and *pujahs* were performed in all the temples, and prayers were offered for the continuance of Her Majesty's reign, and for the long life and happiness of all the members of the Royal Family. The Khazi and Mullah of the Mohammedan community offered prayers in the mosque. In the evening the villagers, including the school children, assembled in the Local Fund School House, where sandal, flowers, sugar, and *pan supari* were distributed. The Local Police Force, which paraded in front of the premises, fired a *feu de joie.*

The decorations were all that could be desired. The meeting opened with speeches delivered in Tamil, in which the blessings of peace and prosperity which had been enjoyed by the various nationalities in India under the benign rule of Her Majesty were alluded to. These speeches were received with great enthusiasm. After that, sugar, *pan supari*, &c., were distributed among the assembly, and the meeting terminated with three enthusiastic cheers for Her Majesty. Then a grand procession of the Hindu gods, attended by a large crowd of people, issued from the Siva and Vishnu temples, and it was past 10 P.M. when, after going through the principal streets, it returned to the temples. The Presidencial Address was adopted. The local permanent memorial will take the form of a "Water Pandal."

OOTACAMUND (NILGIRIS).

Ootacamund, the chief town of the Nilgiri District, is the summer head-quarters of the Madras Government, and the permanent head-quarters of the Madras Army. It is situate on the western slope of the Dodabetta Range, and its elevation varies from 7,190 feet above sea-level to 8,642 feet. The principal buildings are Government House, the Council Chamber, Secretariat Offices, the Courts and Offices of the Collector and Magistrate and of the Sub-Judge, St. Thomas's Church, St. Stephen's Church, the Post and Telegraph Offices, Breeks' Memorial School, Public Library, and Ootacamund Club. There is also a Botanical Garden. The town was constituted a Municipality in 1866. The population is 12,335, classified as follows:—Hindus 8,021, Mohammedans 1,364, Christians 2,950. The chief educational Institutions are the Lawrence Asylum, and the Breeks' Memorial High School. The former is intended for children of British Soldiers, and the latter is an efficient Middle Class School, and was founded in memory of the first Commissioner of the Neilgherry Hills. There are Elementary Schools of various classes maintained by the Local Fund and District Boards. The Murree Brewery Company has a branch here. The chief products are coffee, tea, and cinchona, introduced in 1844, 1851, and 1860 respectively.

Jubilee Committee.—Lieut.-General Sir HARRY PRENDERGAST, V.C., K.C.B., *Chairman*; Messrs. C. E. PLUNKETT, *Secretary*, L. R. BURROWS; General MORGAN; General WILSON; Colonel LIARDET; Messrs. M. A. LAWSON, M.A.; GOOL MAHOMED SAIT; EDULJEE; MARUTHACHELLA MUDELLIAR, and others.

Not only did the residents of the town unite in the festivities on the 16th February, but many people came in from the surrounding villages, including not a few representatives of the Hill tribes. The grand display of bunting and banners shown by the Murree Brewery Company attracted much attention. Two triumphal arches were erected on the Commercial Road. The first was between the Alexandra House gate and Bombay Hall. This at first glance appeared to be a sholah transplanted in its entirety from one of the adjacent hills. A triumphal arch was also erected over the Library gate. The proceedings commenced with an impressive Thanksgiving Service at St. Stephen's church. The members of the Freemason Lodge, "Faith, Hope, and Charity," attended in full costume. The National Anthem was heartily sung at the conclusion of the service. The special service at the Roman Catholic church was also a full choral one. At the mosque there was a special service at 9 A.M., at which the leading members of the Mohammedan community of the town were present. The Hindus met at their temple, and the other religious sects did honour to the occasion. A Review Parade of the Volunteers took place at the Hobart Park at noon. The head-quarters companies marched to the Park, headed by the band, playing the Jubilee march. On arrival there they were formed into line, and with ranks opened they received Lieutenant-General Sir Harry Prendergast, V.C., K.C.B., the reviewing General Officer, with the usual salute. After the General had inspected the men a *feu de joie* was fired, followed by a Royal salute and three cheers, led by Sir Harry Prendergast. The Volunteers then marched past in column of companies. After the march past, line was re-formed, and the General expressed the great happiness it afforded him to be present on such an auspicious occasion, and complimented the men on their soldier-like appearance. Several stanzas, composed by himself, were read in Tamil by Pandit Vencatarama Aiyangar. An Address on behalf of the Mohammedan community was presented by Munshi Syed Fackroodeen Sufi. At 12.30 money and clothing were distributed to 150 Hindu and 50 Mohammedan poor persons. At the Friend-in-Need Society's workshop, the European and Eurasian poor received small gifts. A procession of school children, of all classes and creeds, and numbering over 800, then took place. The Nazareth Convent Schools were remarkable for the various costumes of the pupils; there were the boarders in brown, the day scholars in costumes of their own, the native girls enveloped in white clothes, and the boys all neatly dressed. But for gaiety and variety of colours, the Hobart and Kandal Schools bore away the palm. The banner of the St. Stephen's Girls' School was prettily wrought, and besides the name of the school it had on it the words, "Victoria our Beloved Queen, Long may She reign." The Breeks' Memorial School, the Ootacamund Grammar School, the Baptist Mission, Wesleyan Mission, and Kaity Schools, were well represented, and with their many handsome banners, some made expressly for the occasion, they formed a very interesting feature in the proceedings of the day. At 5 o'clock the children were assembled to partake of refreshments. "God save the Queen" was then sung. The sports now commenced, each event being well contested. The crowd that assembled to witness these sports was unprecedented in Ootacamund. Besides the usual items of high jumps and long jumps, &c., there were a tug-of-war for Todas and Badagas; then followed two dances, one by the Todas, and the other by the Kotas, which appeared to be the most entertaining portion of the evening programme. A flat race for Badagas and Todas respectively were the next two events, and were well contested. A flat race between a Toda and a European resulted in the latter winning by several lengths, thereby gaining a purse, presented by General Faunce, Quartermaster-General. Sir Harry Prendergast assisted in directing the sports, and Mrs. Orr distributed the prizes. The display of fireworks at the Hobart Park, which commenced at the conclusion of the sports, occupied a short time, and was very good. There were four bonfires: one on the hill behind St. Stephen's; a second on Snowdon Hill; a third on Elk Hill; and the fourth—the largest—on Dodabetta peak. Lights were artistically arranged on Breeks' School, the Municipal Office, and the Post and Telegraph Office. The illuminations and decorations in the town were varied and numerous. The following firms illuminated their premises:—Messrs. Spencer and Co., Smith and Co., Oakes and Co., Marchant and Co., Aboo Mahommed and Co., and Esooph Sait. The Hindu and Mohammedan community held a musical *soirée* at Bombay Hall. The leading members of both communities were present. Pundit Venkatarama Aiyengar sang his stanzas, and received much applause. The proceedings of the day were brought to a close by a Ball at the Assembly Rooms. The Presidencial Address was adopted. It was resolved to obtain as a permanent local memorial of the Jubilee a full-sized "Portrait" in oils of Her Majesty.

ONGOLE (NELLORE).

The town of Ongole is the capital of the northern Taluk of the Nellore District, and is situated about 75 miles north of Nellore town. Its population is 9,200, composed as follows:—Hindus 7,556, Mohammedans 923, Christians 717; and others, 4. The town lies in the midst of the rich black cotton soil country; on the south and west of it are low rocky hills, which contain a large quantity of iron ore. It is connected with Madras by the Buckingham Canal. The town is noted for the size and beauty of its cattle. It contains a High School belonging to the American Baptist Mission, a Girls' School belonging to the same Mission, and a Municipal Middle School, besides numerous Primary and Pial Schools.

Jubilee Committee.—Messrs. W. J. TATE, *Chairman*; V. ANANDA ROW PUNTALU, *Secretary*; NALATURI VENCATARUNGACHARRY; N. NAMBIRAMALLA CHETTY; Rev. W. R. MANLEY; Messrs. TIRVENGADA PILLAI; and AHAMED HUSSAIN SAHIB BAHADUR.

The Jubilee was celebrated with much enthusiasm on the 16th February. Prayers were offered in all places of worship for Her Majesty. A handsome and elaborately decorated Pandal had been erected in a tope near a Hindu temple, outside the town, and thither the Queen's local representative (the Sub-Collector) was, on the afternoon of the 16th, conducted in procession. The "Union Jack" floated over the triumphal arch which adorned the entrance to the Pandal, on which was inscribed a suitable motto. As the procession entered the Pandal a *feu de joie* was fired, and the people cheered. Then cloths were distributed to the needy, who had already been fed in the morning. The Presidencial Address was read in English by Mr. V. Ananda Row, the Secretary to the Jubilee Committee, and in Telugu by Mr. N. Venkata Ronga Charlu. It was then adopted. Sanscrit and Telugu odes were recited. The company, which must have numbered over 3,000, then witnessed the sports, which lasted till sunset. A nautch followed in the now brilliantly lit Pandal. The people then marched in procession through the chief streets of the town, and eventually proceeded to the Sub-Collector's bungalow, where they gave three cheers for Her Majesty. Gymnastic feats, sports, nautches, and singing occupied the afternoon and evening of the 17th, and the proceedings wound up a little before midnight with a bonfire on the hill opposite the Pandal, with fireworks, and cheers for Her Majesty. The balance of the Jubilee subscriptions will be devoted to the "Improvement of the Water Supply" of the town.

PAKALA (NELLORE).

A *feu de joie* was fired at dawn on the 16th February by the Salt Contingent, and after prizes had been awarded to the best dressed peons, several sheep and a quantity of rice, provided by the Inspector, Mr. Mitchell, were served out to the Factory establishment and three Preventive parties. Rations were also distributed to the registered coolies, as well as to the poor of the place. In the afternoon, just before the sports began, another *feu de joie* was fired. There were hurdle, sack, three-legged, cheroot, pick-a-back, cooly, boys', girls', and women's races, as well as "bull in the ring," and other sports, with a tug of war, "Peons *versus* Coolies," which was won by the former. There was a torchlight dance by Brinjarie women; native music and dancing girls; and a display of fireworks, concluding with three cheers for the Queen Empress. In the village, and after the fireworks, there was a procession of gods from the Hindu temple. The Presidencial Address was adopted.

PALAMCOTTAH (TINNEVELLY).

This town is the head-quarters of the Collector of the District. The population is 17,964; of whom 15,098 are Hindus, 865 are Mohammedans, and 2,001 are Christians. It contains an Anglo-Vernacular School, a Boys' School of the C.M.S., a Boarding School for Christian boys and girls, and a Training School for Christian girls.

A crowd of nearly 10,000 persons assembled on the race-course to witness the sports. The sports-programme included pony and horse races. A *fête* was given to school-children in a tastefully decorated Pandal on the *maidan*. The principal residents of the district, including the Zemindars of Ettiapuram, Oothumalai, and Sevelpatti were present. The Presidencial Address was read, adopted, and presented to the District Magistrate. A good display of fireworks followed. The principal roads in Palamcottah and Tinnevelly, and the streets and houses in both the towns and neighbouring villages, were illuminated at night, as also the public buildings. At the principal places of worship special services were held. Gods were taken in procession in several Devastanams. On the 17th an address on the benefits of British rule in India was delivered at a large public meeting at which the District Judge presided. A nautch was held at night. Enthusiastic cheers were given for Her Majesty and the Royal Family.

PALANI (MADURA).

The population of this town is 13,515, and that of the whole taluk is 171,315. The place is noted for the temple of Thendayuthapani Swami, which is resorted to by pilgrims from all parts of India. The town was lately constituted into a Municipality. There is also a Local Board with three Unions. The chief occupations of the people are cultivation and trade. Weaving is the only manufacture. The American Mission has established a Girls' School. There is a Salary Results School in the town aided by the Municipality, and several Results System Schools in the taluk aided by Municipal or Local Funds.

Jubilee Committee.—Rev. H. C. HAZEN, *Chairman*; Messrs. T. GOVINDAN SAHIB, J. SAMUEL PILLAI, and C. RUNGA ROW, *Joint Secretaries*; SITHAMBARAM CHETTIAR; T. KRISTNA ROW; C. SUBBARAYER; and five others.

Early in the morning of the 16th February the town assumed a gay appearance. The houses had been whitewashed and adorned with flags and banners; and *thoranams* overhung the streets. The Navaranga Mantapam in front of the temple was tastefully decorated, and a beautiful Pandal had been erected there. A small Pandal had been put up at the entrance to the Municipal Office, with a triumphal arch bearing the inscription "Long live Her Majesty the Queen Empress of India." *Abishekams* and *pujahs* were performed in the Hindu temples of the town, and special services were held. Prayers were also offered in the churches and mosques. At noon about 3,000 poor of all classes were fed in different places, and about 150 of them were presented with cloths. In the afternoon sweetmeats were distributed to about 7,000 schoolboys and girls. In the evening there were magical performances and athletic sports. At night there was a grand illumination of all the houses, temples, mosques, churches, streets, and the Rock. The Post Office, Municipal Office, the Taluk Cutcherry, the Municipal Dispensary, and the Police Station House, as well as the Jubilee Mantapam, were beautifully illuminated. At 6.30 P.M. a large number of gentlemen and ladies assembled at the Navaranga Mantapam. A portrait of Her Majesty was placed in an elevated position, and was adorned with garlands. The Rev. H. C. Hazen who was voted to the chair, made an appropriate speech. Mr. Subbu Runga Naidu gave an account in Tamil of Her Majesty's life, and the chief events of her reign. Three hearty cheers were then given for the Empress, and sandal, flowers, *pan supari*, &c., were distributed to all. At about 8 P.M. the portrait was placed on a howdah mounted on an elephant, beautifully decorated for the occasion, and taken in procession through the four chief streets of the town, attended by about 5,000 people, including several European ladies and gentlemen. The dancing-girls who danced in front of the portrait sang the "*Kummipattu*," a poem composed in honour of Her Majesty by Mr. Scott, of Madura. There was then a grand display of fireworks which occupied more than an hour. On the return of the procession to the Jubilee Mantapam, at about 11 P.M. the party broke up. The Presidencial Address was adopted. On the evening of the 17th gymnastic sports and races were held and prizes distributed; and at night there were theatrical performances. A "Victoria Jubilee Lamp" has been erected in the town in commemoration of the Jubilee. It was lighted on the night of the 16th with much ceremony.

PALGHAUT (MALABAR).

Palghaut, the largest inland town in Malabar, is situated in the gap formed by the great depression of the Western Ghats, through which the railroad finds its way to the west coast across the Peninsula. The town was once the seat of a Rajah, but became subject to Hyder Ali of Mysore, for whom a fort was built here by French engineers. The fort was captured by the British in 1790. The population is 36,339; of whom 30,424 are Hindus, 4,854 are Mohammedans, and 1,061 are Christians. The majority of the people are traders and agriculturists. Paddy is cultivated on a large scale in the neighbourhood. The town is noted for its grass mats. It has a large inland trade. There is a Municipality of twenty Councillors, of whom fifteen are elected by the people, and five nominated by the Government.

Jubilee Committee.—Messrs. V. P. DE ROZARIO, *Chairman*; T. A. RAMAKRISHNA IYER and ONDEN RAMAN, *Joint Secretaries*; C. S. SWAMINADHA PUTTER KARIAKAR; K. P. ACHUTA MENON; T. C. ELSWORTHY; Rev. H. BACHMANN; V. RAMA SASTRI; and others.

People, not only from the town and the taluk, but also from distant places, had gathered together on the occasion. Several leading chieftains, including the Second Prince of the Zamorin family, the Elia Rajah of Nilambur, Kollangode Elia Nambidi, and others were present. At 6 A.M. on the 16th February an Imperial salute of 101 kathanas (a gun used in temples) was fired from the ramparts of the fort, and the Jubilee Parade of the Volunteers, which immediately afterwards took place, concluded with three enthusiastic cheers for Her Majesty, and the singing of the National Anthem. The European and East Indian community attended the Jubilee

Service in the Roman Catholic church. At 10 A.M. rice, cloths, and money were distributed to 2,000 poor. Beautifully caparisoned elephants, the largest of which carried a life-size portrait of Her Majesty, formed part of a procession which started at about 4 P.M. from the Jubilee Pandal that had been erected in the vicinity of the fort, where a large number of Europeans and natives had assembled, and passed by the English church, the Big Bazaar, and the Sultanpetta, returning to the Jubilee Pandal at about 7.30 P.M. About 20,000 people were on the *maidan* to witness the ceremony. The procession presented a brilliant spectacle, and red, blue, and green lights were burnt at intervals. When the portrait of Her Majesty was taken into the Pandal three hearty cheers were given for the Queen Empress, and the National Anthem was sung. A display of fireworks brought the festivities of the day to a close. The Presidencial Address was adopted. On the following afternoon a large number of European and native gentlemen assembled in the Jubilee Pandal, and the space around the Pandal was crowded with people who had met to witness some races. Shortly after dusk there was a grand display of fireworks. Three cheers and three *arpus* (the native way of cheering on the Malabar coast) for Her Majesty brought the loyal demonstration to an end.

PALLADAM (COIMBATORE).

Palladam is the head-quarters of one of the most important Taluks in the District of Coimbatore. The chief productions of the taluk are cotton, tobacco, and dry grains.

Jubilee Committee.—Messrs. C. SEETHA RAMAIYER, *Chairman*; SIBGATHULLAH CHIDA, *Secretary*; HANUMANTHA RAO; RAMANARAYAN DEVA; SUJAMBUL SAIT; KUPPAN CHETTIYAR; PALANI CHETTIYAR; GOVINDA RAO; MANIKKAPURAM KRISHNA RAO; DADA SAHIB; and MAKDOOM SAHIB.

The town was decorated in a variety of ways from early in the morning of the 16th February, and in the evening it was brilliant with illuminations. People of different castes were fed, and a money distribution was made to indigent Mohammedans. In the temples and mosques special thanksgivings were offered, and blessings were invoked for Her Majesty. In the afternoon a treat was given to the schoolboys. At 4 P.M. almost all the male population of the town and of the adjoining villages attended a public meeting that was held in a large Pandal in the Temple compound. The assemblage was immense for a town like Palladam, for no fewer than 1,000 people were present. The police paraded in front of the Pandal. Mr. C. Seetha Ramaiyer Tahsildar was voted to the chair. The proceedings opened with an address in Tamil by Mr. S. V. Seetharamaiyer, B.A., who explained the object of the meeting, described the blessings enjoyed by the

Indian people under the British rule, and alluded to the virtues of the sympathetic and benevolent Sovereign who adorns the British throne. The assembly then shouted "Long life and prosperity to the Queen and Royal Family." There was then a singing party, and when that was over, sandal, *pan supari*, plantains, and sugar were distributed to all present. The assemblage then went in procession, accompanied by music, to the Market compound, to witness a display of fireworks, which was preceded by a Royal salute by the police. The procession returned through the principal streets of the town to the original place of meeting, where, after hearty acclamations, the crowd dispersed. The Presidencial Address was adopted.

PALMANAIR (NORTH ARCOT).

The town of Palmanair stands about 2,500 feet above the sea-level. Before the opening of the railway to Mettupollium, it was much resorted to by European gentlemen of the neighbouring districts during the hot weather. The population is 3,679. Of these 2,875 are Hindus, 709 Mahomedans, and 95 Christians. It contains a Local Fund School. The American Mission has also established a School here. Besides this, there are three Pial Schools (purely Telugu). There is a splendid Local Fund Dispensary at this station. Palmanair was recently constituted a Union under the Local Boards Act. This town trades in sugar, jaggery and tamarind. It contains a Taluk Cutcherry, a Police Station, a Sub-Registrar's Office, a Forest Overseer's Office, a Distillery, and a District Munsiff's Court.

Jubilee Committee.—Messrs. K. Kristna Row, *Chairman*; E. Venkataramayya, *Secretary*; Viviani; G. S. Willicks; K. Rungayya Mudelliar; A. Balakrishna Row; C. Arunagiri Mudelliar; D. Kachapeswarayya; Gopalakristnappa Chetty; and others.

Religious processions, under strings of mango leaves, formed the staple of the demonstrations in the village on the 16th February. After drinking Her Majesty's health, Mr. J. H. Glenny, C.S., the Collector, and his guests received the Zemindar of Poonganoor, C.I.E., and his son, and the principal members of the local native society. Chinese lanterns hung about the trees, and *buttees* arranged along the paths, combined to produce a pretty effect in the starlight night. The school children were treated. The Presidencial Address was adopted.

PAMBAN (MADURA).

The population of this town is 5,000, most of whom are Hindus. A large number of pilgrims pass through the town to and from the celebrated temple at Rameswaram, eight miles distant. The S.P.G. Mission and the Jesuit Mission have established Schools here, as well as at other villages on the island; there are also a few Pial Schools. The inhabitants live for the most part by fishing. The import trade consists of food stuffs; and the exports are beche-de-mer, shark fins, cocoanuts, chanam, coral, and firewood.

Jubilee Committee.—J. James, *Chairman*; P. B. Gibbons, *Secretary*; V. Rajaruthnum Pillay; J. E. P. Steel; A. S. Penagapany Mudelliar; J. Venkatrayulu Naidu; A.

Vedakkan; A. Subramania Pillay; Abdul Rahiman Sahib; M. Muthu; and Mydeen Pitchai Maraikar.

Very early in the morning the chief street from the Cutcherry to the Cable House was decorated with bright-coloured bannerets and with flags, and many private houses were adorned with flags and garlands. At 9.30 A.M. the National Anthem was sung by the school children; and sweets and fruits were distributed to 400 children of all castes. Rice and curry were distributed to over 1,200 poor people. In the afternoon a Regatta took place in the north roads, consisting of a sailing race, canoe races, ship's boat race, and swimming matches, winding up with wrestling matches. Prizes were distributed by Miss James. In the evening the Post and Telegraph Offices and the houses of most of the officials were illuminated. The Presidencial Address was adopted. On the following day food was distributed to over 1,300 poor people, and in the afternoon land sports were held. The course, which had been gaily decorated, was situated at the back of the Cable House. The sports on this day consisted of an all-comers' race, veterans' race, pony race, tug-of-war, sack races for men and boys, chatty-race, boys' race, all-comers' tug-of-war, and a wheelbarrow race. About 4,000 people witnessed the sports, many having come in from the surrounding villages as well as from the main land. The sports lasted till dusk, when fireworks were let off, and a large bonfire was lit. The festivities terminated with the singing of the National Anthem, and three hearty cheers for the Queen Empress.

PANRUTI (SOUTH ARCOT).

Panruti is the commercial centre of the South Arcot District. The population of the town and its suburbs is 20,172; of whom 18,953 are Hindus, 1,135 Mahomedans, and 84 Christians. There are two Churches, one belonging to the Baptist Mission, and the other to the Lutheran Mission. A Girls' School is maintained by the Baptist Mission. There are, besides, a Government Girls' School, and a Local Fund Middle School for boys. The offices of the Deputy Tahsildar and Sub-Magistrate, Police Inspector, Sub-Registrar, Taluk Overseer, and Sub-Postmaster are located in the town. Ground nuts are largely exported.

Jubilee Committee.—Messrs. M. Parthasarady Raido, *Chairman*; M. Ramaswami Iyer, *Secretary*; A. Sivakolander Mudelliar, B.A.; P. Kuttusami Odayar; J. A. Kandava Pillai; A. Sreenivasa Chamberlain; and others.

At dawn on the 16th February salutes were fired in honour of Her Majesty. Early in the morning, service was performed in the Christian church, and *abishekams*, offerings, and *arjanai* were offered in Hindu temples. In the Mosque *fathiah* was grandly performed. At about 10 A.M. the feeding of the poor commenced. In the godown attached to the Choultry in the heart of the town, upwards of 1,000 poor people were served with food; and food was served to more than 1,000 mendicants in other centres. A number of gentlemen were entertained in the Choultry. The Public Offices were beautifully decorated with evergreens, festoons, the Union Jack, and banners, and with the inscription, "God save our Empress for another fifty years." At about 7 P.M. the illuminations were complete, and the town presented a brilliant appearance. The people thronged everywhere. Guns were fired at intervals, and there was a musical performance. At 8 P.M. the Arichandra Natakam gave a dramatic performance, the play selected being one which illustrated the principle of honesty as being characteristic of Her Majesty's reign. The play continued until daybreak. The Presidencial Address was adopted.

PARAMAKUDI (MADURA).

This is a town with a population of 8,822, consisting mostly of weavers. It has for many years been the seat of a District Munsiff, and latterly of a Sub-Registrar also. There are a number of Schools affording elementary education in English and Tamil, the highest of which is the English Middle School. There is also a Civil Dispensary maintained out of Local Funds. The weaving of cotton and silk cloths with lace borders is carried on to a considerable extent. A Union has been formed mainly for sanitary purposes, and is working satisfactorily.

Jubilee Committee.—Messrs. V. Coopooswami Aiyar, *Chairman*; Mohana Renga Naidu; Mahomed Hussain Malumiyar Saib; M. Nagalingam Pillai; G. T. Ananthanarayana Pillai; Ramaiengar; L. Nagaswamy Aiyar; Vedapuri Sastrial; and eight others.

Early in the morning of the 16th February gay flags were displayed in different parts of the town, and over all the public offices as well as from the tops of trees. *Thoranams* were hung across the streets, and parti-coloured paper lamps were suspended from the tops of long poles. Thanksgiving Services were held in honour of Her Majesty at Christian, Hindu, and Mohammedan places of worship. Temple guns were fired at short intervals throughout the day. About 500 school children of both sexes marched in procession to the place where the public meeting was held. A large crowd was present, and the proceedings were very enthusiastic. A Tamil address, explaining the importance of the occasion, was read, and different sorts of cakes were distributed among the children. Prizes were distributed to the pupils of the English Middle School. About 300 poor Brahmins were fed at the Chuttram and the Vishnu Pagoda, and about as many of other castes in a tope on the banks of the river Vaigai. About 100 were also clothed. At night the temples and mosques were illuminated. The higher classes took part in a public feast and a dramatic performance. The Presidencial Address was adopted.

PARAMATHI (SALEM).

This town has a population numbering 2,815. It is the head-quarters of the Deputy Tahsildar and Sub-Magistrate, of the Inspector of Police, and of the Special Sub-Registrar of Assurances.

English education is given in Local Fund Schools. The chief occupations of the people are agriculture, weaving, and money-lending. A good trade is carried on in cotton. Jaggery and saltpetre are manufactured. Paddy, plantains, and tobacco are largely exported.

Jubilee Committee.—Messrs. A. MUKTICHEDAMBARA, B.A., *Chairman*; T. RAMAKRISHNA AIYER, and C. RAMA ROW, *Joint Secretaries*; C. MANIKA MUDELLIAR; T. MAHOMED KASIM SAHIB; CHEDAMBARA REDDIYAR; GURUNADHA CHETTIYAR; VENKATA RAMA REDDIYAR; RAJA KAVUNDAR; and eight others.

The celebration was announced to the public by beat of tom-tom. The Dharmakarthas of the several temples were requested to offer prayers for the continuance of the beneficent reign of Her Majesty. A large Pandal had been erected on the site of the proposed "Victoria Lodge," which is to be the local permanent memorial of the Jubilee. It was elegantly decorated with foliage, garlands, banners, &c. In front of the Pandal was a triumphal arch, on which were inscribed, in bright colours, the words, "Long live our Gracious Queen Empress." Two other arches and a small Pandal were erected on the *maidan* close by. The streets were adorned with festoons. *Abishekams* were performed in all Hindu temples, and prayers were offered in the temples, mosques, and the Roman Catholic church. More than 300 poor people of all castes and creeds were fed. Two "Water Pandals" had been erected, one by the Jubilee Committee, and the other by the people of the town, in commemoration of the occasion, and water was served to all classes of persons. Sugar and fruit were distributed to schoolboys and children. In the afternoon athletic sports were held. Over 2,000 persons assembled to witness them. A public meeting was then held, at which Mr. P. Rajagopala Chariyar Avergal, M.A., B.L., Deputy Collector, presided. He opened the meeting with a speech, in which he gave a sketch of the life of Her Majesty, and of the advantages India had derived during her reign. Prayers for the continuance of the reign of Her Majesty were then offered, and the Chairman proceeded to lay the foundation stone of the "Victoria Lodge." A parchment roll had been prepared by Mr. A. Muktichedambara Mudelliar, the Chairman of the Jubilee Committee. It bore the following inscription:—

"16th February, 1887. Foundation stone of the 'Victoria Lodge,' at Paramathi, Namakal Taluk, Salem District, erected in commemoration of the celebration of the Jubilee of Her Majesty the Queen Victoria, laid by Mr. P. Raja Gopala Chariyar, M.A., B.L., in the presence of Messrs. A. Muktichedambara Mudelliar, B.A., Sub-Registrar, and Chairman Jubilee Committee; C. Manika Mudelliar, Deputy Tahsildar; T. Mahomed Kasim Sahib, Inspector of Police; Mr. C. W. W. Martin, District and Sessions Judge; and Mr. George MacWatters, Collector and District Magistrate."

This record was signed, wrapped round a newspaper, and placed inside a bottle, together with several of the Queen's coins and an ingot of gold. The bottle was placed in a cavity of the stone on which the foundation stone was placed. When the foundation stone was being lowered four sets of native pipers and other musicians played. A salute of 101 guns was fired, and the President declared the stone to be "well and truly laid." The Presidencial Address to Her Majesty was then read, and signatures taken thereto, amidst enthusiastic cheers. Nautches followed, and sandal, flowers, fruit, and *pan supari* were distributed. A good pyrotechnic display followed. Prayers were offered for the Queen Empress in the Vishnu temple, and the gods were taken round the town in procession, followed by a large crowd of people. The first day's festivities closed with the singing of the National Anthem by the nautch girls. On the following day sports of various kinds were held, after which there was a musical entertainment. Sandal, flowers, fruits, and *pan supari* were distributed, and repeated cheers were given for Her Majesty.

The Jubilee was celebrated in several of the surrounding villages with similar enthusiasm.

PARLAKIMIDI (GANJAM).

This is the chief town of the large and important Zemindary of the same name. It is picturesquely situated in one of the most beautiful valleys in India. The population is 20,812; of whom 10,621 are Hindus, 188 are Muhammadans, and 3 are Christians. Mats and baskets are made, but otherwise the articles of manufacture are few. The town is essentially agricultural, the surrounding valleys yielding an abundance of grain. The education of the town is well cared for by the Zemindar, who maintains a High School at his own expense, besides which Primary Education is promoted by the Municipality which was constituted last year.

The houses in the principal streets had been whitewashed, and arches and Pandals erected in several places with bright banners bearing mottoes expressing loyal wishes for the health, happiness, and long life of Her Majesty. The town presented an unusually animated appearance, brightened by the natural beauty of the surrounding scenery. In the forenoon of the 16th February a breakfast was given to all the poor in the town. Every one who asked for a meal received one. The lame, the blind, and the dumb were also presented with cloths. The *Zemindar* gave a cloth and a piece of money, varying in value from ¼ anna to 8 annas, to every poor person in the town. In the afternoon there were sports of all sorts, including foot races, chatty races, egg-on-spoon races, tug-of war, donkey races, and fencing. They were followed by a nautch and musical entertainment. There were special services in all the temples and muttums, and a procession of the Hindu gods, with the priests marching in front chanting prayers for Her Majesty. At night the principal streets and roads were illuminated, as well as the Palace, the Post Office, and several private residences. There were several displays of fireworks in different places, the best display being in front of the Palace. The town and the surrounding valley are overlooked by a hill about 600 feet above the plain, and on the top of this a large bonfire was lighted about 9 P.M. At the house of Mr. Jagannatha Row Puntalu an address was read by his son; and a Pundit sang to his own music a Telugu version of "God save the Queen." The Presidencial Address was adopted.

PATUKOTA (TANJORE).

The population is 4,677; of whom 4,274 are Hindus, 258 Mohammedans, and 145 Christians. Both education and trade are improving. It contains an ancient fort.

Jubilee Committee.—Messrs. Syed Khader Padshah Saheb Bahadur, *Chairman*; Venkatrama Chettiar, *Secretary*, Venkatrama Iyer; Ramasawmy Iyer; Muthanjee Iyer; Rama Chunder Row; Chinnia Iyer; Srinivasa Pillay; and others.

The chief buildings of the town were decorated, and about 300 poor persons were fed. Sweetmeats were distributed to the school children. There were grand processions from the temples and mosques both in the evening and at night. A mass meeting was held, speeches were made, the Presidencial Address was read and adopted, and *pan supari* was distributed. There was a display of fireworks.

PEAPULLY (KURNOOL).

The population of this town is 3,392, comprising Brahmins, Kumtiies, Kapus, Balijas, Jangams, Christians, and Mohammedans. There are two Schools, in which Telugu is taught. A considerable trade is carried on in grain, cloth, and leather.

Jubilee Committee.—Messrs. Syed Majaheras, *Chairman*; M. Panchanadam Pillay, *Secretary*; R. Lakshminarasimo Puntalu; N. Veeraraghaviah; D. Kotilingama Devara; Y. Krishtappa; Chinna Subbasastri, and others.

Almost all the inhabitants of the place assembled at Nagunnah Chuttram in the afternoon of the 16th February, and were treated to music. A Telugu translation of the Presidencial Address was read aloud, and adopted, and the signatures of a few representative gentlemen were taken to it. The people gave three hearty cheers for the Queen Empress. There was a liberal distribution of sugar and *pan supari*. About 125 poor people, the majority being Mohammedans, were given a substantial meal. The town presented a gay appearance; *thoranams* overhung every street, and during the night all the temples, mosques, and streets were decorated and illuminated. Prayers were offered for the long life and prosperity of Her Majesty. The Mohammedans carried a Jubilee banner in procession, and invoked blessings on Her Majesty. The Hindus assembled at the temples of Siva Veerabadra, and Kasiva Swamy, and thence carried their gods in procession with music through the streets. These processions commenced at 7 P.M. respectively, and continued till 2 A.M. A "Chuttram" is to be erected in commemoration of the Jubilee.

PENUKONDA (ANANTAPORE).

This town belongs to the civil district of Bellary, and to the revenue district of Anantapore. It was the capital of the ancient kingdom of the Bijapur Rajahs, whose territories extended to the bank of the Kistna River. It is full of ancient structures. There are beautiful vineyards, and guava and pomegranate gardens. The population is 5,331; of whom 4,149 are Hindus, 1,160 are Mohammedans, 17 are Christians, and 5 are unclassified. A Local Fund School teaches boys up to the Fourth Standard, while three Pial Schools are devoted to elementary education. There is a School for Mohammedan boys and one for caste girls. The Local Self-Government scheme was introduced last September. Taluk Boards and Panchayet Unions have been formed.

Jubilee Committee.—Messrs. H. Kristna Row Puntalu, *Chairman*; G. Narasinga Row, *Secretary*; P. Pasupati Row; T. Varadiah Naidu; V. Hanumantha Row; N. Bhima Row; K. R. Rangasawmy Iyengar; and twenty-five others.

The festivities commenced on the 16th February by a monster gathering in a large stone Mantapam called the "Jubilee Mahal" within Ramaswamy's temple. The Mantapam was beautifully decorated, and a handsome Pandal had been erected at its entrance. Long before 8 A.M., the time appointed for the meeting, over 1,000 people of all classes and creeds, and in all positions of life, had congregated to take part in the adoption of the Presidencial Address to the Queen Empress. Behind the public officers sat landowners, tradesmen, artisans, and other citizens. Boys from all the schools of the town were arranged on benches, while the girls of the Caste Girls' School sat on the carpeted floor between the two front rows. The bright costumes, and the glittering jewels of the girls, added to the holiday attire of the male sex, gave a highly picturesque appearance to the scene, which was further enhanced by the mellow light of the morning, and the artistic decorations of the Hall. The Head-Assistant Collector, Mr. Macleod, having been voted to the chair, proposed the adoption of the Presidencial Address. Mr. G. Narasinga Row, First Grade Pleader, seconded the proposition, which was carried with acclamation. The District Munsiff, Mr. H. Kristna Row, then read the Address in English to the assembly, after which one of the masters of the Local Fund School read a Telugu translation of it. The Address was then adopted amid acclamations. It was resolved that in honour of the Jubilee, the Penukonda Newspaper Club Girls' School be henceforth designated the "Penukonda Jubilee Girls' School." Sweets were distributed to the schoolboys and girls, after which the Chairman, and Mr. Lodge the Forest Officer, were presented with garlands and bouquets, and conducted home in procession, accompanied by music. From 11 A.M. to 3 P.M., nearly 400 paupers of all castes and creeds were fed. At 3.30 P.M. the District Munsiff, the Tahsildar, Vakils, and other officials, accompanied by over 1,000 people, marched with music, tom-toms, and nautch girls, to the bungalow of the Head-Assistant

Collector, and conducted that officer with his wife and children, and Mr. Lodge, in state, to the "Jubilee Mahal," where sports were held. A tennis tournament was then played. A tent had been pitched on the ground and chairs and tables placed for the European party, who were served with refreshments. The Native gentlemen and the people were also provided with refreshments. More than 3,000 persons assembled to witness the sports. As night set in the whole town was lighted with lamps. A procession was then formed at the "Jubilee Mahal," of officers in Her Majesty's service, tradesmen, artisans, labourers, school children, and others, numbering more than 2,000 persons, who, with gods, music, nautch girls, and fireworks, marched through the illuminated high street to the north gate of the town where a "Memorial Lamp" was to be fixed. Here Mr. and Mrs. Macleod and Mr. Lodge awaited the arrival of the procession, and when it arrived Mrs. Macleod laid the foundation stone of the Lamp Post. Three hearty cheers were given in honour of Her Majesty, and garlands and flowers were placed round the necks of the ladies and gentlemen present amidst shouts of applause. The procession then retraced its way, while the Europeans drove to the Tank bund where a banquet was provided for them. The Natives then had their supper and hurried to the "Jubilee Mahal" where a nautch was held. It was 10 o'clock when this performance began, and presently the European guests arrived, and took their seats on the *dais* reserved for them. Nearly a thousand people assembled to take part in the recreation. The scene presented was a very attractive one. The entertainment was brought to a close at midnight. On the following day at 4 P.M. crowds of people gathered at the Tennis Court, where a tennis tournament was played by the members of the Club. When darkness set in, there was a display of fireworks in front of the Tennis-court. At 9.30 P.M. there was a nautch, which did not conclude before 2 A.M. On the third day a similar programme, with a few slight alterations, was gone through. There were tennis matches, fireworks, and nautch parties. At nightfall there was another display of fireworks.

PERIAKOLAM (MADURA).

The population of this town is 16,446; of whom 14,564 are Hindus, 1,233 are Mohammedans, and 649 are Christians. There is also a High School in which Sanscrit is taught. There are thirteen Primary Schools, including one for Girls. There is also a Night School. The affairs of the town are looked after by a Taluk Board of twelve members. It has seven Unions and one Association under its management. The principal articles of export are paddy, raggy, cholum, gingelly oil seed, cotton, plantains, cardamoms and coffee, bamboos, dye barks, leather, and timber. The principal articles of import are salt, iron ware, piece goods, ground nut, castor and kerosene oils. The chief manufactures are country cloths, gunny bags, woollen cumblies, bamboo mats and baskets, country carts, saltpetre, brass vessels and earthen pots.

Jubilee Committee.—Messrs. K. N. NARAYANA AIYER, *Chairman*; C. F. P. SEBASTIAN PILLAI; P. RENGASAMI AIYER; SUNDRA ROW; E. J. STEPHENS; NARAYANA ROW; LUTCHMI NARAYANA AIYER; SRINIVASA AIYER; GANAPATHY AIYER; KRISHNA IYER; T. M. NAMASIWAYAM PILLAI; and nine others.

The streets of the town were decorated with flags, festoons, bunting; and ornamental arches were erected bearing loyal mottoes, such as, "*Vivat Regina,*" "Heaven bless our Gracious Empress," "May peace and plenty ever signalise our Queen Mother's Reign," in large characters, both in English and in Tamil. The centre of attraction was the spacious Local Fund Choultry, which was very artistically decorated with foliage. A Pandal had been erected in front of the Choultry. Here about 1,000 people of all castes and conditions assembled at 7 A.M. on the 16th February. A Brahmin pundit recited some Sanscrit verses, and entertained the people with readings from the Ramayana, appropriate to the occasion. These recitations and readings were translated into Tamil, which the spectators listened to with great attention. Sanscrit odes composed in honour of Her Majesty were sung, after which a Pleader delivered an eloquent address, in Tamil, on the many blessings that had resulted from Her Majesty's reign. From 8.30 to 10 A.M. there was a mnemonical entertainment, which the spectators witnessed with great wonderment. Between noon and 1 P.M. the old and infirm, the poor and the needy, of all classes were fed, and 70 very destitute persons of both sexes were provided with cloths. Then native music played, and at 4 P.M. there was a Police Parade. After the "review" the Police fired a *feu de joie*. At about 5 in the evening the crowd moved to the spacious compound of the Hindu High School, adjoining the Local Fund Choultry, where the pupils of the several Boys' and Girls' Schools entertained the assembly—the girls singing in Tamil the "Victoria *Kummy*," the song composed by Mr. Scott, of Madura; and the boys engaging in athletic feats, which lasted nearly an hour. The boys and the girls were then treated to a feast of cakes, sweetmeats, fruits, and flowers. After sundown the town was brilliantly illuminated with a large number of lights and lanterns arranged at short intervals along the public roads. Between 8 and 10 o'clock there was a grand torchlight procession of the Hindu gods and goddesses. It was preceded by a number of Brahmin priests, who chanted hymns and mantrams, and offered prayers for the long life and prosperity of the Queen Empress and the members of the Royal Family. There were also present a number of dancing girls who performed the *kolattam* dance. Throughout the day and night there were special services of thanksgiving in the Christian, Hindu, and Moslem places of worship. The Presidencial Address was adopted. An Institution to be named the "Victoria Reading Room" is to be established to commemorate the Jubilee.

PITTAPUR (GODAVERI).

This town is the head-quarters of the Pittapur Zemindary, which covers 200 square miles, and contains 68,161 inhabitants The population of the town numbers 11,593; of whom 10,512 are Hindus, and 1,081 are Mohammedans. It contains the Rajah's Palace, and various public offices.

At a preliminary meeting held at the Victoria Mahal in the Fort of Pittapur, on the 11th February, the Rajah of Pittapur, who presided, said :—

"LADIES AND GENTLEMEN,—I thank the members of the Jubilee Committee, and also our Collector Bahadur, for having deemed me worthy of filling the chair on such a momentous occasion. It gives me very great pleasure to have been afforded the rare opportunity of showing my deference and loyalty to Her Most Gracious Majesty Queen Victoria, whose beneficent rule stands matchless in the whole history of Bharata Varsha. Neither the ancient Hindu Kings nor the later Mohammedan Emperors could have any idea of the immense peace and prosperity brought home to us by the British rule. Railways, telegraphs, and steam navigation were not even dreamt of by the ancients. No Government in the history of India has dealt such impartial justice even to the poorest classes without the least distinction of caste, colour, or creed. Former Kings were one and all selfish, and cared for the welfare of their own race, and of certain classes only. But Her Majesty has treated the many coloured races of Her mighty Empire with no more difference than what a mother would observe among her manifold children. England and India are her twins. As it has pleased Providence to link together these two countries, I call upon all educated natives who owe their rise and livelihood to the British Government to forget all differences of religion (for the truths inculcated by the Vedas and the Bible are the same) and join with one voice to invoke the choicest blessings of the Almighty upon our glorious Empress and her illustrious dynasty, and may war and rebellion never disturb the peace and plenty of her golden rule! It only remains for me to ask you, Gentlemen, to prove yourselves worthy of the name of Hindus by observing the 16th February as the day of your greatest rejoicing, and by joining with a prompt and cordial mind in any demonstration which the Committee may decide upon in honour of the occasion. A word more to add that you, my Hindu brethren, should not in the least hesitate to entertain Europeans equally with our Hindu brethren, for our Sastras do not at all sanction such a difference of treatment, and unanimously proclaim that to whatever creed or race a guest belongs he should be treated kindly, and fed without prejudice as far as circumstances will allow, and thus the gap now existing between the European and native races may gradually disappear. In conclusion I propose that 'God bless Her Majesty, and long live our beloved Empress' be our watchword during the whole *fête*."

The following Jubilee Committee was then elected :—

THE RAJAH OF PITTAPUR, *Chairman*; MESSRS. A. VENKATA NARASIMHA ROW DEWAN, and T. JAGANNADHAM, *Joint Secretaries*; V. APPASAWMY NAYUDU, H. RAMA-ROW PUNTALU, M. B. JAGANNING, K. DHARMA RAZULU, and eight others.

The Jubilee was celebrated on the 16th February with an enthusiasm unprecedented in the history of this Zemindary. The population is composed chiefly of Hindus of various castes. 4,000 people took part in the rejoicings and festivities of the day. About 2,000 people of all classes were fed, and 200 poor persons were supplied with new cloths. At 5 P.M. a grand procession left the Victoria Mahal.

First came the leading officials and other residents of the town dressed in their holiday attire; than followed Her Majesty's portrait, which was placed in a howdah on a fine elephant, splendidly caparisoned. A hundred Mohammedan retainers of the Rajah, in uniform, led the van, each bearing a white standard in his hand. Then followed the insignia given to the Royal Family of Pittapur by the Emperors of Delhi and the Nizams of Hyderabad, with sabres, shields, coat of arms, truncheons, &c., and then a few elephants and horses followed. The procession, which was accompanied by musicians, passed through the chief streets of the town, all of which were adorned with festoons, and brilliantly illuminated at night. There were several triumphal arches, which bore loyal inscriptions, such as "God bless Her Majesty," "Long live our Empress Victoria," &c. There were four nautch parties in attendance. Bands of devotees from adjacent villages brought up the rear, singing songs and dancing with much enthusiasm. Bells pealed in all the temples, where the Brahmins offered prayers for the prosperity of the Empress, and the continuance of her rule. Fireworks illuminated the scene. The procession returned at 8 P.M. to the Victoria Mahal, where Her Majesty's portrait was installed in a prominent place with much ceremony. Several addresses were then read in English, Sanscrit, Telugu, and Hindustani. The Presidential Address was read, and unanimously adopted, amid shouts of applause. Several speeches followed, and nautches were held. The distribution of fruit, flowers, perfumes, and *pan supari* concluded the proceedings. A vote of thanks was passed to His Highness the Rajah for his munificence in celebrating the Jubilee at his own expense, and three cheers were given for Her Majesty. On the following evening there were horse-races, wrestling, and other sports. A treat was given to schoolboys, and at night there was another display of fireworks, followed by a musical entertainment and several nautch parties.

POLLACHI (COIMBATORE).

The population is 5,089; of whom 4,468 are Hindus, 548 are Mohammedans, and 66 are Christians. It is the head-quarters of the Head-Assistant Collector, of the Tahsildar, of the Police Inspector, and of the Sub-Registrar of Assurances. The Local Fund Dispensary is a fine building erected by public subscription. There are two Schools maintained by the Local Fund Board, one teaching up to the Middle School Standard, and the other is a Primary School. There are also two Mission Schools and several Pial Schools. A Reading Club has been lately started. The largest Fair in the Madras Presidency is held here every Thursday. Timber is the chief article of merchandise; and grains, ghee, oil, cotton, and chillies are also extensively exported.

Jubilee Committee.—Messrs. KRISTNIER, Tahsildar, *Chairman*; S. M. PONNOOSWAMY PILLAY, *Secretary*; P. NARAYANASWAMY NAIDU; VENCATASUBBIER; COOPER; RAMASAWMY IYER; VENCATARAMAN IYER; and ten others.

On both the 16th and 17th of February the caste people were treated to a sumptuous banquet, and about 500 poor people were fed. All the streets were adorned with festoons, and the houses were whitewashed and well illuminated. On the morning of the 16th prayers were offered in the several places of worship, and a grand entertainment was given in the evening at the local Police-station. A large number of officials, non-officials, and rich Mirasidars attended. The proceedings began with a Parade of the Police force, and a Royal salute was fired. At the termination of the proceedings *pan supari* and flowers were distributed. There was a display of fireworks at night, and the gods were taken round in procession, preceded by two richly caparisoned elephants, and attended with music. On the 17th a very large meeting was held at the Local Fund Chuttram, when the Presidencial Address was read and adopted. Some speeches were delivered, and verses in honour of Her Majesty's reign were recited. These were received with loud acclamations. After this there was a singing and dancing party. With three hearty cheers for Her Majesty, the meeting dispersed.

To commemorate the Jubilee permanently, a "Well"—a much-felt want—is to be sunk. A "Gong" has also been presented for the use of the public. The Zemindar of Ramapatnam has promised to open at his own expense a "Badminton Court."

POLOOR (NORTH ARCOT).

Poloor, the head-quarters of a taluk of the same name, has a population of 5,649, consisting of 4,320 Hindus, 1,227 Mohammedans, and 172 Christians. It has a Taluk Cutcherry, a Sub-Registrar's Office, a Post Office, a Local Fund Hospital, and a Local Fund Middle School. Rice, gram, dholl, &c., are largely exported. Lace and silk cloths are manufactured to some extent.

Jubilee Committee.—Messrs. PATEL HOOSMAUN SAHIB, *Chairman*; SUBBAROYER, *Secretary*; OOGOOR STEEENIVASA ROW; KAJA MEAN SAHEB; KRISHNIER; S. RAGHAVA CHARLU; B. VENKATAPATHY NAYADU; and V. MASELAMONEY MUDALYAR.

A prettily decorated Pandal had been erected in front of the large tank, where the inhabitants assembled in large numbers on the 16th February to do honour to Her Majesty. The Presidencial Address was read in English, Tamil, and Hindustani, and was adopted amid enthusiastic cheers. Fifty poor Mohammedans were fed, and cloths were distributed to the most indigent. Books and sweetmeats were distributed to the schoolboys. The town, the tank, the temples, the mosques, all the public buildings and several private houses were grandly illuminated. There was a distribution of attar and *pan supari* among the persons assembled in the Pandal and at night there was a display of fireworks.

PONANI (MALABAR).

Ponani is situated on the Malabar coast, about fifty miles south of Calicut, at the mouth of the Ponani River. The population is 12,421; of whom 9,916 are Mahommedans, 2,478 are Hindus, 26 are Christians, and 1 is unclassified. The High Priest of the Moplahs lives in the town, and young men from Malabar and South Canara resort to him for instruction in the Koran. The Christian population is composed of Syrian Christians, who trace their origin to the time of St. Thomas; their church at Palayur is said to be one of the seven founded by the Apostle on this coast. They are engaged in cultivation and trade. The German Missionaries have opened a station at Kotakal, where they have a small church. The Moplahs subsist by cultivation and trade, and a large proportion of them called Puthia Islam, or new Islams, obtain their livelihood by fishing. Large quantities of the produce of the cocoanut palm are exported. There is a private school in the town for Boys, and a Girls' School is shortly to be established.

Jubilee Committee.—Messrs. KIZHAPATT SANKARA MENON, *Chairman*; PULICAT JOSEPH ITTEYRAH, B.A., *Secretary*; MELEPROTH KOUTHI MENON; EACHERATTIL AMBU NAIR; MANANKKANDATH AVUTHRAMANKUTTY, KAKU SETTU; KOSHIKUTE VEETIL THACHEN MENON; PARTIKKAL TIKAMU MENON, &c.

The 16th February was ushered in by an Imperial salute of native guns. A Parade of the Police force was held at 9 o'clock in front of the Pandal, and a *feu de joie* was fired. The "Jubilee Pandal," which had been erected by the side of a tank, was an immense structure. It was decorated with silk and other cloths, ferns, palm leaves, bunches of cocoanuts, mangoes, areca, and other articles of local produce. In the centre was a *dais* with an artistically designed canopy. In front of the Pandal, about fifty yards removed from it, a triumphal arch had been erected, which was tastefully decorated with ferns, flags, silk hangings, and palm leaves, and which bore the name "Victoria" in large golden letters, and the words "Queen Empress, Mother, Friend," underneath it. A roadway was constructed from the arch to the Pandal, over which hung festoons of flowers and palm leaves. After the parade about 3,000 poor people began to assemble in a yard near the Pandal, and rice was distributed to them. At 2 P.M. about 5,000 people collected near the Pandal, among them being the Rajah of Terumalasherri Kotta and the Valia Jarathingal Thangal, who were accompanied by large retinues of musicians, athletes, sword-bearers, palanquins, horses, and elephants. These, with several other influential gentlemen, having taken their seats on the *dais*, Mr. Sankara Menon expressed the pleasure he felt at seeing such a large body of persons assembled to do honour to the Queen Empress. Mr. T. Vaidhyanadder delivered an address in Malayalim, in the course of which he described the benefits of the British rule. Mr. Krishnan gave a short sketch of the virtuous life of the Queen Empress. At its conclusion a deafening shout of applause for Her Majesty burst forth from the assembled multitude. The Rajah, the local Head of the Hindus, and the Thangal, the local head of the Mohammedans, sat side by side on the *dais*, and thus illustrated one of the beneficent effects of the British *régime*. There were also a few Frenchmen and Germans on the *dais*. Athletic sports were held in front of the Pandal, and were witnessed by about 8,000 people. The chief road was beautifully illuminated at nightfall with coloured lamps and Chinese lanterns. A procession of elephants, decked with front-pieces of gold and silver, and accompanied by music, started from the Pandal, and made a circuit of the town. At 7 P.M. there was a grand display of fireworks, consisting of rockets, red lights, blue lights, flower-pots, maroons, whirligigs, &c. The fireworks being completed, a native dramatic troupe gave a performance in the Pandal, which was witnessed by about 3,000 people, and continued till daybreak. On the 17th several prizes were awarded for boat races, swimming races, jumping, &c. At night there was a magical performance in the Pandal. The Presidential Address was adopted. In commemoration of the Jubilee an annual "Prize" will be given at the Girls' School.

POONAMALLEE (CHINGLEPUT).

The town of Poonamallee has a population of 7,670; of whom 6,162 are Hindus, 814 are Mohammedans, and 694 are Christians. What is termed the "New Town" has been turned into a Military Station, and affords a convenient retreat to pensioned Europeans and Eurasians. In the New Town are the Cantonment Magistrate's Office, the Staff Office, the Sub-Jail, the Deputy Tahsildar's Office, the Sub-Registrar's Office, the Post Office, and the Scotch Mission Middle School. In the Old Town are the District Munsiff's Court, the Local Fund Dispensary, the Normal School, and the Mission Girls' School, besides the two important temples of the town. There is a Convalescent Depot for British troops. It is said that the Old Town was once a flower garden, and that it was named after the goddess "Valli Thayar" who was found amidst the flower trees; for Poonamallee is the contracted form of Poovirunthavalli, that is, "Valli who existed amongst the flowers." Poonamallee is noted for the flowers which grow in luxuriance in and around the town. The chief industries of the town are cotton spinning and weaving, and the manufacture of indigo.

Jubilee Committee.—Messrs. CHELLAPA NAIKER, *Chairman*; KRISTNASAWMY IYER, B.A. *Secretary*; T. SUBRAMANIA IYER; C. DANDAYUTHAPANI IYER; S. NADAMUNI IYENGAR; AUROTE MUDALIAR; P. S. RAGUNATHA NAYANAR; SURIYA PRAKASA ROW MUDALIAR; SRINIVASA SWAMIAR; and four others.

On the 16th February the streets were decorated with *thoranams*, and with flags bearing inscriptions, such as "God bless the Empress Victoria," "Long live Empress Victoria," "May the British Empire prosper," "May the British Empire last long," and "God save the Empress." It having been announced on the preceding evening throughout the town and the surrounding villages, that people would be fed at the Vishnu temple and at the Panayatha Amman Kovil, vast crowds began to pour in from a very early hour. About 1,000 people, male and female, were fed with rice and curry at the Panayatha Amman Kovil. Besides this a large number of people were fed by the Cantonment authorities. About 300 Brahmans and other caste Hindus assembled at the Vishnu temple at noon, and joined in offering *pujah* to the gods for Her Majesty; they were also fed. The people of the town assembled, dressed in holiday attire, at about half-past 5 P.M. at the Siva temple, where the Presidencial Address was read by Mr. N. Kristnasawmy Iyer, and adopted, amidst deafening shouts of acclamation. Mr. V. Kristnama Charriar's *History of the Queen Empress* in Tamil, was then read aloud by Sawmy Govindu Naidu, the Head Master of the Girls' School, and several copies were distributed amongst the people. Sugar, fruit, sandal, betelnut, rose-water, and cakes were distributed, after which the whole assembly went round the chief streets of the town in procession, accompanied by music. The houses, temples, and streets were decorated and illuminated. The principal road was lined on each side with flags of many kinds bearing loyal inscriptions and mottoes, and festoons of lamps extended from pole to pole, so that when these were lit, the whole roadway was flooded with light. The Normal School and the Court House of the District Munsiff were particularly well decorated. An arch had been erected, bearing the inscriptions "God bless Empress Victoria," and "Long live Empress Victoria," at the entrance gate of the Panayatha Amman Kovil, where the poor were fed. Prayers were offered in all the temples for the long life and health of Her Majesty, and for the prosperity of the British Empire. The gods were also taken round the temples in procession, and the children were treated to sweetments.

PRODDATUR (CUDDAPAH)

Proddatur is a picturesque town on the river Pennar in the Cuddapah District. It contains a District Munsiff's Court, a Tahsildar's Cutcherry, Sub-Registrar's Office, a Civil Dispensary, a Post Office, a Police Station, and the offices of the Vice-President of the Taluk Board and the Union Panchayets. It is also the head-quarters of the Police Inspector, the Forester, the Local Fund Overseer, the Vaccinator, and the Revenue Inspector. There are 6,510 inhabitants, a large number of whom are profitably engaged in the indigo and cotton trades. There are 4,828 Hindus, 1,667 Mohammedans, and 15 Christians.

Jubilee Committee.—Messrs. B. Subba Row Puntalu, *Chairman*; M. V. Kamakshi Row, Pleader, *Secretary*; B. Tirumala Row Puntalu; H. Ramayya; S. Ramayya Chettiar; M. Dhurmalingam Pillai; Rajendram Pillai; C. P. Gurumurthi Shastriar; C. Sabbah; and four others.

In the morning of the 16th February 4,000 poor people of all castes were fed, and the most indigent of them were supplied with cloths. All public buildings and houses in the town were decorated by day, and illuminated at night. The Reading

Room was decorated with pictures and portraits, conspicuous among the latter being one of Her Majesty. Over the entrance the words, "God bless our Empress," and "Long live Victoria," were inscribed in large glittering characters. All the Hindu temples, mosques, &c., in the town were illuminated, and prayers were offered therein for the long life and prosperity of Her Majesty. There was a grand procession in the evening of the 17th, in which people of all castes and creeds took part. It passed through the thoroughfares attended by a band of musicians, and preceded by a portrait of Her Majesty. It reached the Reading Room at 6.30 P.M., where a nautch was held. Then Mr. M. V. Kamakshi Row explained the word Jubilee, gave a brief sketch of the life of the Queen Empress, and detailed the various advantages derived by the people of India during her Majesty's reign. The meeting concluded with a distribution of *pan supari* and sugar candy, &c. The Presidencial Address was adopted. Mr. Narayana Subbarayanigauri Subbayya Chetti, a merchant, presented the Committee with a large building, to establish a "Reading Room" in commemoration of the Jubilee.

PULIANGUDY (TINNEVELLY).

This town has a population of 6,401; of whom 5,602 are Hindus, 714 are Mohammedans, and 85 are Christians.

All classes of people assembled on the 16th February on the Nambyar Paramba *maidan*, where two spacious Pandals had been erected for the distribution of food to the poor, and there was a neatly decorated Pandal in the centre of the *maidan*. In the two former food was distributed to the poor until 1 o'clock. Rice was distributed to such of the poor as could not take their meals in the sheds. Sports, athletic feats, and jugglery followed. At 6 P.M. loud and prolonged cheers were given for Her Majesty. Theatricals were performed at the *maidan* on the night of the 16th, and in Trikandiyoor Choultry on the night of the 17th. Subscriptions were collected towards the erection of a "Hospital," which is to be the permanent Jubilee Memorial at this town.

PULLAMPETT (CUDDAPAH).

The population of this town is 2,341, most of whom are weavers. Cloths, noted for their fine texture, are manufactured to a considerable extent. There is a large trade in indigo and tobacco. There is one elementary Pial School here. The local affairs of the town are managed by the Taluk Board.

Jubilee Committee.—Messrs. Pingalay Dhondu Row, *Chairman*; Nimkum Venkojee Row, *Secretary*; Narayana Govinda Rajulu Naidu; B. Govinda Rajulu Naidu;

S. Kanagarayen Anna Pillay; Pundi Varadacharry; Govindasami Pillay; and several others.

The 16th and 17th February were days of great rejoicing at Pullampett. About 500 poor people were fed on the morning of the 16th. A tastefully decorated Pandal, in front of which was placed a beautiful arch, bearing the inscriptions "God save the Queen" and "Long live the Queen Empress," in English and the vernacular, had been erected opposite the Taluk Cutcherry. The town was adorned with *thoranams* in every street, and was illuminated after dusk. Sports of various kinds were held during the two days, such as horse and pony races, tug-of-war, high and low jumps, &c., and were witnessed by a very large number of people, many of whom had come in from different parts of the Taluk. The Chairman and members of the Committee marched in procession to the temples and mosques in the town, where thanksgivings and prayers were offered for the Queen Empress. Much enthusiasm was shown by the people. A display of fireworks took place during both nights. The Presidencial Address was adopted. In commemoration of the Jubilee a sum of money has been lodged in the Savings Bank, and the interest accruing therefrom is to be used in founding a "Prize" to be awarded to one of the successful candidates in the University Matriculation Examination from the Cuddapah High School.

RAIDROOG (BELLARY).

Raidroog is a town with 8,766 inhabitants, viz. 7,298 Hindus, 1,455 Mohammedans, 2 Christians, and 11 unclassified. It carries on a large trade in cholum, ragi, rice, wheat, gram, and other produce. It is 32 miles to the south of Bellary, and is the head-quarters of the taluk. The population of the taluk is 83,799. Silk and coarse cotton cloths are manufactured to a great extent. Raw hides and tanning bark are sent to Madras. There is also a saltpetre refinery and a tannery. The town has a Taluk Cutcherry, a Sub-Registrar's Office, a Civil Dispensary, and a Local Fund Middle School.

Jubilee Committee.—Messrs. P. Annajee Row, *Chairman*; O. Swami Row, *Secretary*; K. Venkoba Row; C. Rama Row; H. D'Rozario; Rajagopaul Mudelliar; and others.

The houses were whitewashed; the streets were decorated with *thoranams*, &c.; a large Pandal had been erected opposite the Dispensary; and several other small Pandals were erected by the merchants opposite their shops. At 6 A.M. on the 16th February ceremonies were performed, and prayers said in the temples in Her Majesty's name, and about 300 paupers were fed. In the evening sweetmeats were distributed to the children. At 6 P.M. all the houses in the main streets were illuminated. At 9 P.M. the Hindu gods were taken in procession through the decorated and illuminated streets. When the procession, in which more than 2,000 people took part, reached the Pandal there was a grand display of fire-works. On the following evening, sports, races, &c., were held, and 200 paupers were fed. Prayers for Her Majesty were offered in the places of worship. At night there was a nautch party. It has been resolved to construct a "Chuttram" as a permanent memorial of the Jubilee.

RAJAMUNDRY (GODAVERY).

This town, on the left bank of the Godavery, has a population of 24,555; of whom 22,480 are Hindus, 1,785 are Mohammedans, 285 are Christians, and 5 are unclassified. It contains the Courts of the District Judge, District Munsiff, and Magistrate, as well as numerous public offices and educational institutions.

The Jubilee was celebrated here with much spirit by all classes. On the morning of the 16th February signs of rejoicing were to be seen at almost every house. The best wishes of the people for the Queen Empress were expressed by inscriptions and mottoes, such as "Long live Victoria," and "Victoria is a Mother to us All!" Some bazaarmen put up the words "Love, Liberty, and Loyalty" in gilt letters over their shops. At about 4 P.M. the students of the College, and the pupils of the various schools, dressed in their holiday attire, and with flags and banners, marched, with music at their head, in procession along the chief road, from the College premises at one end of the town to the Museum at the other end. The procession was led by the Principal, Mr. Metcalfe, and the Professors of the College. Rajamundry is a favourite resort of Telugu and Sanscrit pundits, and many excellent verses and songs extolling the reign and character of Her Majesty, and expressing wishes for her happiness, were recited. The procession was met at different places on its way by parties of little girls belonging to various schools, and was entertained by them with songs. At about 6 o'clock in the evening the procession joined the crowds that had assembled opposite the Museum to witness the sports. All the European residents of the place were present. After the sports, several of the leading men of the place met at the Museum, where, in the presence of the Sub-Collector, Mr. Metcalfe and others, various songs composed in honour of the occasion were sung. At about 10 o'clock there was a display of fireworks. The Presidencial Address was adopted. It has been decided to connect the projected Town Hall with the Jubilee, by calling it the "Victoria Jubilee Hall," and to open the building by the 20th June.

RAMACHENDRAPUR (GODAVERY).

The population of this town is 2,092, of whom 2,284 are Hindus. There are a few Schools. A good trade is carried on in paddy and jaggery. There are no manufactures.

Jubilee Committee.—RAJAH KAKARLAPUDI RAMACHENDRARAZ BAHADUR, *Chairman*; Messrs. R. RAMALINGESWARAPPA, *Secretary*; S. NADHAMUNI MUDELLIAR; G. NARASINGA ROW PUNTALU, and G. AUDINARAYANASAMY.

At daybreak on the 16th February two convicts were released from the Sub-Jail. *Abishekams* and *archanas* were performed in the temples in the name of Her Majesty, and prayers were offered for the continuance of British rule. About 300 poor people of all castes were fed, and a few were presented with cloths. The streets, offices, and several private buildings were decorated, and at night they were illuminated. In the evening there was music, and just as the shades of evening fell crowds of people assembled at the large Pandal that had been erected in front of the Taluk Cutcherry. A dramatic performance was given. Fireworks were let off at intervals, and at the close of the performance cheers were given for Her Majesty, and the Police fired a *feu de joie*. On the 17th, at noon, sports were held, and in the evening there was a grand procession, headed by a portrait of Her Majesty. Nautch girls danced in front of and behind the portrait, while the priests who marched in front of the gods chanted Vedic hymns. The Presidential Address was adopted. A "Choultry" is to be erected as a permanent Memorial of the Jubilee.

RAMNAD (MADURA).

Ramnad is the seat of an ancient Zemindar, who enjoys the title of "Sethupathi," which means the guardian of the sacred "Sethu" or Rama's bridge. Crowds of Hindu pilgrims from all parts of India to the sacred shrine at Rameswaram continually pass through Ramnad. The Zemindary, one of the largest estates in the Presidency, is at present under Government management, the Zemindar being a minor under Government wardship, and receiving his education at Madras. The population is 10,519, made up of 8,532 Hindus, 1,693 Mohammedans, and 294 Christians. Ramnad is chiefly an agricultural town, with no trade or manufacture worth mentioning. It is the seat of a Taluk Board under the Local Boards Act, and is the head-quarters of a Head-Assistant Collector and an Assistant Superintendent of Police. It is also an important station in the S.P.G. Mission District, and has a High School, two Girls' Schools, an Orphanage, and an Industrial class maintained by the Society. A Native Middle School, and many other Schools are under the Results grant system.

Jubilee Committee.—Messrs. P. KOTAISAMI TEVER, *Chairman*; S. H. SHUTIE, *Secretary*; T. RAJARAM ROW; P. SIVARAMA IYER, B.A.; M. SAMAVIER; P. SIVAGNASAMI TEVER; P. PANDITHURAISAMI TEVER; M. KANTHIMATHINATHA PILLAI, and A. SELOOVAVAGAM PILLAI.

The 16th February opened with the firing of an Imperial salute of 21 guns. More than 2,000 persons of all castes and creeds were fed in the various choultries and muttams, after which they assembled in the S.P.G. High School compound, where cloths were distributed, and small presents of money were given. There was also a grand treat given to all the school children in the town. At evening the leading men in the place and a large crowd of people assembled under a large and tastefully decorated Pandal that had been erected in front of the Zemindar's Palace. Her Majesty's portrait, which was carried in a howdah on the State elephant, under a rich canopy of gold and silver tapestry, was brought into the Pandal. At 7.30 P.M. a grand procession, headed by the elephant, followed by all the insignia of the ancient Zemindary, and accompanied by the civil and other officers of Government, and of the Zemindary, started, amidst hearty cheers for Her Majesty. The procession passed through the chief thoroughfares, and arrived at the S.P.G. High School at 8 P.M. The portrait was taken by Mr. Kotaisawmi Daver, Sub-Division Zemindar of Ramnad, and Mr. Raja Ram Row, the Deputy Collector, and placed upon a grand pedestal, which had the Royal Coat of Arms painted on it, in a conspicuous position in the Hall, which was elegantly decorated with evergreens and flowers. The "Jubilee Version" of the National Anthem was sung. A letter from the Minor Zemindar (now at Madras) addressed to the Secretary of the Jubilee Committee expressing great interest in the proceedings, was read, and several addresses were delivered. Mr. S. A. Shutie, the Principal of the S.P.G. High School, made an excellent speech in English. He was followed by Mr. Pandithuraiswami Daver, one of the Sub-Division Zemindars of Ramnad, who read a Tamil address. Various poems were recited in Sanscrit and other languages, and the meeting terminated with a musical concert, and a grand display of fireworks. The principal streets and houses were brilliantly illuminated at night. The Presidencial Address was adopted.

RANIPETT (NORTH ARCOT).

Ranipett, with its three suburbs, has a population of 8,419; of whom 6,483 are Hindus, 1,567 are Mohammedans, and 369 are Christians. It is the head-quarters of the Head Assistant Collector of the District, of a large Distillery, and of the American Mission Society. It contains a Local Fund Dispensary, a Middle School, a Post Office, a Pension Staff Office, the D. P. W. Sub-Division Office, and the Office of Assistant Commissioner of Salt and Abkari Revenue.

Jubilee Committee.—MESSRS. R. H. SHIPLEY, *Chairman*; RUNGANADA ROW, *Secretary*; C. BALAKRISTNA MUDELLIAR; COLONEL W. KELLY; MESSRS. C. W. WEST; R. G. MORDUN; REV. J. CONKLIN, and others.

On the morning of the 16th February special services were held in all the churches, mosques, and temples, which were largely attended. The public buildings and houses were decorated with flags, and there were illuminations at night. About 300 poor of all classes were fed in the forenoon, in two parties; and in the evening a large concourse of people assembled to witness the ceremony of laying the foundation stone of the "Jubilee Victoria Reading Room" by

Mr. R. G. Morison. The National Anthem was sung by the American Mission boys, and speeches were made in English, Tamil, and Hindustani, by Messrs. R. R. Narayana Iyer and Ranoogopala Chettyar, who explained the object of the meeting, and stated how India was indebted to the great lady whose Jubilee was being celebrated. At night the people of Ranipett met the inhabitants of Wallajapet at a spot half way between the two towns, where a brilliant nautch and a splendid display of fireworks took place. The 17th was devoted to sports, which were attended by an immense crowd. At night there was a grand display of fireworks at the sports-arena, after which there was a nautch at the premises of Messrs. Morison and Sons. Next night there was a nautch in the house of Mr. Rajaratna Mudelliar, Chairman of the Ranipett Union, which was followed by another, on the night of the 19th, at the house of Mr. C. Balakrishna Mudelliar, Vice-President of the Taluk Board. The Presidencial Address was adopted. The permanent memorial is to take the form of a "Reading Room."

REPALLE (KISTNA).

The population of this town is 2,998; of whom 2,679 are Hindus, 239 are Mohammedans, and 80 are Christians. The inhabitants are chiefly agriculturists and weavers. The town contains the Taluk Tahsildar's Office, Sub-Registrar's Office, Local Fund Dispensary, and a Local Fund School.

Jubilee Committee.—Messrs. K. Ananda Row Puntalu, *Chairman*; P. Venkata Hanumanta Row Puntalu and V. Dakshinamurty, *Joint Secretaries*; M. Raghava Row Puntalu; K. Ramachendriah; Bhashyakarlu Naidu; M. C. L. Narasimhacharlu; Rajam Subarami Row, and others.

The celebration of the Jubilee passed off with great *éclat* on the 16th and 17th February. The streets were adorned with numerous *thoranams*. A "Union Jack" was hoisted on the northern corner of the rampart wall of the old fort. The chief street of the town, which faces the western gate of the fort, was particularly well decorated. The Banyans vied with one another in their endeavours to adorn their shops. The morning began with prayers in the Hindu temples and Muhammedan mosques for the continuance of the reign of the Queen Empress, and blessings were invoked on Her Majesty and on the Royal Family. At midday the feeding of 250 poor and infirm began; and 45 of them received new cloths. At 3 P.M. the Police paraded, and fired a *feu de joie*. A procession was formed at the Local Fund Dispensary Building in the western extremity of the village. This building was well decorated, and a large crowd had assembled there. The procession was headed by the ex-Zemindars (two Brothers) of Vullipaliem with their retinue, and everybody felt it his duty to show his feelings of loyalty by joining it. At 5 P.M. the procession entered the Durbar Hall of the Fort, which was elegantly decorated.

In the centre of the Hall sat the chief gentlemen of the town. Mr. Narayanan Iyer, B.C.E., read the Presidential Address, and spoke of the great benefits which the people of India had derived during Her Majesty's reign. The Address was then explained in Telugu by the Tahsildar to the masses, and it was adopted. Another salute was fired, and cheers were given for Her Majesty. A nautch was held, music played, and the school children were treated to sweetmeats. The National Anthem was sung both in English and Telugu, amidst the loud applause of all those assembled. At night the town was illuminated. At 9 o'clock there was a brilliant display of fireworks. On the morning of the 17th, a garden party was held and the people of the town were feasted. At 3 P.M. there was a procession of the gods of the temples, which passed through all the streets of the village. During the night the Kuchipudi Brahmins acted the well-known popular play "*Bhagavati*," and the proceedings, which were very enthusiastic throughout, then came to an end.

ROYACHOTI (CUDDAPAH).

The town of Royachoti is situated in a hilly tract of country. It has a population of 4,367. The chief feature of the town is a stream with beautiful cocoanut and mango topes on its banks. The town has a large Hindu temple, to which pilgrims resort during festival days. The public offices include the Taluk Office, Sub-Registrar's Office, Police Station, Sub-Post Office, and Local Fund Hospital.

Jubilee Committee.—Messrs. T. Srinivasa Row, *Chairman*; C. Mohiyaddeen Khan, *Secretary*; C. Subbarayalu Naidu; Chundupalle Nagi Reddi, and others.

On the 16th February the poor were fed, and prayers were offered in the mosques and temples. At about 2 P.M., people from all parts of the taluk began to assemble in the Civil Dispensary compound, where a Pandal had been erected. At about 5 P.M. Mr. W. H. Welsh, Sub-Collector, arrived, and was received with loud cheers, and the firing of a *feu de joie* by the Police. Garlands were presented by Mr. T. Srinivasa Row, Tahsildar. Sports were held, after which Mr. S. Michael Pillay read the Presidential Address to Her Majesty. The Address was interpreted in Telugu by Mr. A. Ramanuja Charlu, and was adopted with cheers. The Chairman made an appropriate speech in which he referred to the great services which had been rendered to India by Her Majesty's Government. The Sub-Registrar then thanked the Chairman. A nautch party followed, and at its close there was a distribution of *pan supari*, sugar-candy, &c. A display of fireworks brought the festivities to a close. In commemoration of the Jubilee a "Well" is to be sunk in the northern part of the town.

SAIDAPET (CHINGLEPUT).

The town of Saidapet contains a population of 4,917 inhabitants; of whom 4,655 are Hindus, 199 Mohammedans, and 63 Christians. It has a Government High School, a Local Fund Primary School, and a Girls' School maintained by the Wesleyan Mission. There is also the Madras Agricultural College, which is attended by students from all parts of India, this being the only institution of the kind in the country. The town has been constituted a Union under the Local Boards Act, and is the head-quarters of the Taluk and District Boards, and was once famous for its dyeing and weaving manufactures, but these have been supplanted to a large extent by the importation of cheaper fabrics from England than can be produced locally.

Jubilee Committee.—Messrs. E. C. Johnson, *Chairman*; V. Ragava Chariar, *Secretary*; Ramiengar; Vathilinga Mudelliar; Bujunga Rao; Varadarajulu Reddiar; and twenty-one others.

Early on the 16th February a band of native musicians marched through the principal streets of the town playing lively tunes, and it was announced that the poor of all classes would be fed at the large Choultry in the Bazaar Street. Accordingly more than 1,000 persons of all classes assembled at the spot. The feeding lasted from 11 A.M. to 5 P.M. In the evening the temples, mosques, and other large buildings of the town were illuminated, and prayers were offered in all places of worship for the long life and prosperity of the Queen Empress. The Presidencial Address was adopted. At noon on the 17th a grand musical entertainment was given, at which the whole of the people of the town and a few gentlemen from Saint Thomas's Mount were present. In addition to the bandsmen who had come the previous day, a set of pipers, who had been brought from Conjevetam, and a few dancing girls who played upon the *vina*, were in attendance. The entertainment lasted till about 6 P.M., when a grand procession was formed. A large coloured portrait of Her Majesty headed the procession, being conveyed in a Victoria Phaeton, which was beautifully decorated for the occasion, and drawn by a pair of handsome Pegu ponies. The procession, with music and dancing, marched slowly to the Vishnu temple, where there was a large crowd. The procession left the temple at 8 P.M., and returned to its destination at about 9.30 P.M. The streets through which the procession passed were crowded, and overhung with *thoranams*. It is proposed to found a Jubilee Memorial "Prize," to be awarded to the students of this District at the Technical Institute in Madras.

SALEM (TOWN).

This is a well-built town with 50,667 inhabitants; of whom 44,614 are Hindus, 4,669 are Mohammedans, and 1,384 are Christians. It is the chief town of the District of the same name, which has an area of 7,483 square miles, and a population exceeding two millions. There are the following Schools in the town: the Salem College, educating up to the First in Arts Standard, the London Mission High School, the Government and Mission Girls' Schools, and about twenty nine

Elementary Schools for Boys and Girls. A large trade is carried on in rice; and the principal imports are salt, tobacco, and saffron. Native cloths of very good quality, and Indian steel goods, are largely manufactured.

Jubilee Committee.—Messrs. C. PRITCHARD, *Chairman*; C. VIJIAYARAGHAVA CHARRIAR and T. NARASINGA ROW, *Honorary Secretaries*; V. KISTNASAWMY IYER; BERTHO; A. DIGNUM; MIDDLETON; MACKENZIE; S. MANNAPALIER; THAMANSING; and twenty-six others.

A special Thanksgiving Service was held at Christ Church early on the 16th February, and prayers were offered up in the principal mosques and temples for the long life of the Queen Empress and the prosperity of the British Empire. At 9 A.M. the feeding of the poor commenced. The Mohammedan poor were fed separately, and there was a liberal distribution of rice and curry to the Hindu poor at Aroonachellam's Choultry. Races and sports were held in the Judge's compound. At 2 P.M. the road from Salem to the rendezvous was so filled with people that riders and drivers found it difficult to wend their way to the sports ground. At 3.45 the compound was crammed with people. The sports continued till about half-past six. In the evening there was a special service in the temples, and a procession of the temple gods. The Presidencial Address was adopted. At 7 o'clock the next morning there was considerable excitement near the College, whither the boys and girls of the different schools had been summoned. At about 8 o'clock the children marched in procession with flags and banners, headed by the band, to the Jubilee Pandal near the Reading Room. A large number of spectators were present. The children sang a Jubilee song composed for the occasion in Sanscrit. Plantains, oranges, and sugar-candy were then distributed to the children; and sandal, rose-water, and *pan supari* to all. The Jubilee song was again sung by the pupils; and three enthusiastic cheers were given for the Queen Empress. Then followed the distribution of cloths to the poor. In the evening, at about 8.30, the Pandal presented a very gay appearance. It was beautifully illuminated. A large crowd had assembled there to witness the fireworks. At 8.45 there was a nautch. This was followed by singing, and a performance on the *sarubat*. A few English airs were played by Saradhamba of Salem. Performances on the violin and *veena* followed. The National Anthem was sung in chorus, the audience standing. At about 11 P.M. the fireworks began. On the archway over the gate leading into the compound in which the Pandal had been erected a transparency with the words "Long may She reign," was exhibited. At the conclusion of the fireworks the native band played, and three cheers were given for Her Majesty. The proceedings were characterised throughout by much enthusiasm and cordiality. The subscription list has not as yet been closed for the permanent memorial, which is to take the form of a "Market" with a Clock Tower.

SANKARANAINAR COVIL (TINNEVELLY).

The population is 8,212; of whom 7,679 are Hindus, 455 Mohammedans, and 78 Christians. There are two English Schools which train boys for the Middle School Examination, and several Pial Schools. The town is governed by a "Union Panchayet," the majority of whose members are non-officials. There is also a branch Mahajana Sabha, consisting of about 80 members. Rough cloths and bell-metal vessels of very good workmanship are manufactured. The town contains a celebrated temple, which is largely resorted to by pilgrims during the Audithapasu festival.

On the 16th February the streets, bazaars, Public Offices, Chuttrams, and Muttums, and many houses, were decorated with evergreens and festoons of flowers. At about 2 P.M. about 500 people of all classes and creeds were fed in the Local Fund Chuttram, and cloths were distributed to the very needy among them. Bananas were given to the school children. At about 6 P.M. the whole town was illuminated. The Sankaranarayana Swami temple was beautifully decorated both inside and outside, and was well illuminated at night. The Nagasonai Tank within the temple was prettily lighted up, and the reflection upon the water was very attractive. The temple tower was dotted over with small lamps, and stood out brightly in the darkness of the night. In front of the temple a large and decorated Pandal had been erected, at the entrance to which there was a handsome triumphal arch, bearing an appropriate inscription. The god and goddess within the temple were adorned with jewels and garlands. At about 8 P.M. a procession started from the Chuttram, accompanied by music, and followed by a large number of people, and proceeded to the temple. Special prayers were offered for the long life and prosperity of the Empress, and *archanas* were performed. The party then proceeded to the Pandal in front of the temple, where the Presidencial Address was read, first in English, then in Tamil. The Address was received with great cheers. Sandal, betel-nut, flowers and garlands were distributed to all present. Then the whole party moved in procession round the town, the Address being carried in front, with native musicians playing English airs. A nautch followed, and the festivities terminated at midnight with enthusiastic cheers for Her Majesty. The illuminations were repeated on the 17th, and there was a singing party at 7 P.M., which was attended by a very large gathering. It continued until 2 o'clock next morning.

SATYAMANGALAM (COIMBATORE).

This town has 5,842 inhabitants. It contains a Native High School, and the London Mission Middle School. There is a Local Board consisting of three official and nine non-official members.

Jubilee Committee.—Messrs. MEENAKSHI SUNDRAMANY, *Chairman*; P. S. RAMASAWMI AIYAR, *Secretary*; IBRA MULK SAHIB, *Vice-Chairman*; SAHIB KHAN SAHIB; RUNGIAH NAIDOU GARU; P. VENKATA SUBBIA; and a few others.

A Pandal was erected in honour of Her Majesty, and in this a large number of people assembled to take part in the festivities. More than 1,000 poor persons were fed both in the town and in Gopichettipolliem attached to the taluk. The proceedings included thanksgivings and prayers according to class and creed, a singing party, and distribution of *pan supari*. After that there was a procession attended with fireworks. A salute of 101 guns was fired. A nautch followed, and continued till a late hour. A Reading Room was opened bearing the name of the "Victoria Institute," in commemoration of the occasion. The Presidencial Address was adopted.

SHIVAGUNGA (MADURA).

Shivagunga, 27 miles to the east of Madura, is the capital of the Zemindary of the same name. In it are located the Ayin and Devastanam Head Offices, a District Munsiff's Court, a Criminal Court, the head-quarters of the Police Division, a Sub-Registrar's Office, a Post Office, and a Local Fund Dispensary. The population is 8,343, divided thus: Hindus 7,528, Muhammadans 719, and Christians 96. There are two High Schools, one maintained by the Zemindar, and the other by the Jesuit Mission. There is a Primary School, maintained by the American Mission, and there are several indigenous Primary Vernacular Schools. There is also a Girls' School, where elementary vernacular education and sewing are imparted; this is maintained by the Zemindar. There is a good trade in paddy, dry grains, and cotton. The smiths in Shivagunga are noted for their excellent workmanship in steel, brass, and silver. Weaving is carried on.

Jubilee Committee.—Messrs VENKATA RAMAIYA, B.A., B.L., *Chairman*; C. JANAKIRAM NAIDOO, *Secretary*; M. KRISHNA ROW; S. SANKARIER; M. ALAGIRISAWMY NAIDOO; K. PATTABIRAMIER; D. CARNERY PILLAI; SIVA ROW; T. SANKARALINGAM PILLAI; R. V. SREENIVASAIENGAR, Pleader; and four others.

Between 11.30 A.M. and 5 P.M. on the 16th February about 4,000 poor persons were fed. The new Hall of St. Joseph was beautifully decorated, and a picture of the Royal Family was placed in the most prominent part of it, on a raised *dais*. Here a large number of people assembled at 8.30 P.M. The Zemin Tahsildar, Mr. Sankaralingam Pillai, in an impressive speech in Tamil, reviewed the beneficent rule of Her Majesty. Mr. Venkata Ramaiya, the Chairman of the Jubilee Committee, read the Presidencial Address, which was adopted, and signed by a few representatives, amid great applause. A distribution of sandal and *pan supari* followed, and native music was played at intervals. Then there was a singing and dancing party, which ended with three cheers for Her Majesty. Fireworks commenced at 10 P.M., and lasted for an hour. The assembly then left the Hall, and marched in procession accompanied with music, through the main streets of the town. Prayers were offered in all places of worship for the long-continued prosperity of Her Majesty. About 300 poor persons were fed, and there was a procession of the goddess of the Siva temple, with much pomp. That was followed by a display of fireworks.

The people of all castes were very enthusiastic in their manifestations of loyalty to Her Majesty. On the following evening the crowds again assembled at the Hall of St. Joseph, and there was a singing party from 4 to 7 P.M. At the close of the meeting prayers were offered for Her Majesty. The temples were profusely illuminated, and Thanksgiving Services were held. In the Chuttrams of the Zemindar, and in those of Nattukottai Chetties more than 20,000 people were fed in honour of the Jubilee. The Zemindar has undertaken to commemorate the event locally by erecting a handsome "Lamp" in front of his palace. The Committee has resolved to put up another "Lamp" in the most convenient part of the town.

SHIYALI (TANJORE).

Shiyali contains a population of 5,190, and has a large Siva temple, and a Vishnu temple of some note.

Jubilee Committee.—Messrs. ADINARAYANA CHETTIAR, *Chairman*; K. SESHAIYAH, Tahsildar, and R. CHUKKRAPANI ROW, B.A., Sub-Registrar, *Secretaries*; SAMANAYAGA MUDELLIAR; KRISTNASAMI VATTAD; and others.

Large crowds of people of all castes and creeds were fed in the morning of the 16th February, in the Choultry at Kyenlangery, a suburb of Shiyali town. In the evening there was a grand procession, in which all the local officers, several rich Mirasidars and Vakeels, and about 2,000 other persons took part. Portraits of the Queen Empress, the Prince and Princess of Wales, the Duke and Duchess of Edinburgh, and the other Members of the Royal Family were placed in an ornamented palanquin at the head of the procession. On the way the procession halted at the "Victoria Badminton Court," which was formally opened. The party then assembled in the Native High School, where the Presidencial Address to Her Majesty was read, and explained in Tamil to the audience. It was then adopted. A Sanscrit Pundit now offered a prayer for Her Majesty in prose and verse. A musical entertainment followed, which terminated with a distribution of *pan supari*, sandal, rose-water, and flowers, &c. There was another music party on the afternoon of the 17th. Special Services of Thanksgiving were held in the local temples, churches, and mosques, both on the 16th and 17th.

SHOLINGHUR (NORTH ARCOT).

The proceedings on the 16th February commenced with the erection of a "Lamp Post" in front of the Vishnu temple. The foundation stone was laid by Mr. P. V. Rungacharriar, District Munsiff. The post bears the inscription: "Let justice be done. The Victoria Jubilee Lamp, fixed 16th February, 1887, by the people of

Sholinghur." This inscription is in English on one side, and in Telugu on the other side. *Abishakams* were offered in the temple, which was crowded. At 5 P.M. a procession left the temple with music, and a Brahmin lit the lamp on the Lamp Post amidst acclamations of joy, the air resounding with shouts of "Long live the Queen Empress." The procession of the god was accompanied by musicians. At night the whole town was prettily illuminated. At 10 A.M. the Mohammedans, accompanied by music, proceeded to their mosque, and offered up prayers for Her Majesty. The festivities terminated at midnight with enthusiastic cheers for Her Majesty, for the Viceroy, and for the Governor of Madras. On the 17th the day opened with the setting up of another Lamp Post in front of the Siva temple. *Abishakams* were performed at noon, and in the evening the lamp was lit with ceremony. There was a procession of the Siva god on the night of the 17th, and the town was again illuminated. The Presidencial Address was adopted. A "Reading Room" is to be erected here in commemoration of the Jubilee and it is intended to open it on the 20th June.

SIVAGIRI (TINNEVELLY).

Early on the 16th February every house had been whitewashed and decorated as on marriage occasions, the streets were neat and clean, and lantern posts had been fixed at intervals of ten yards in the chief streets. Before 8 A.M. a large number of the poor from many parts of the country poured into the garden where arrangements had been made for feeding them. Several thousands were fed, and many of them were presented with cloths. At about 4 P.M. a grand procession went round the town. The Zemindar was seated in a howdah, placed on a large elephant. On another elephant was seated an officer who carried the Sanscrit and the Tamil verses that had been composed in honour of the occasion, and which were to be read aloud to the assembly. The procession went round the chief streets, its destination being the house of the Zemindar on the northern side of the town. At the request of the Zemindar Mr. H. Ramayana Sastriar read aloud and explained the meaning of the Sanscrit verses. The Zemindar's Revenue Inspector read the Tamil verses, after which a Tamil address was read. Music was played at intervals. The schoolboys of the Primary Schools sang in praise of Her Majesty. Sugar and sugar-candy were distributed to them, and sandal and betel to all the inhabitants of the town. The procession then went to the principal temple, which was illuminated both inside and outside, and presented a very grand appearance. *Pujah* and *archana* were performed to the gods, and a large assembly prayed for the prosperity and long life of Her Majesty and the Royal

Family; and for the long continuance of British rule in India. The procession then passed through several streets, and returned to the place from whence it had started. The streets and several of the houses in the town were illuminated at night. After supper the inhabitants attended a music party at the Zemindar's house. The Presidencial Address was adopted. The Zemindar spared no pains to make the celebration a success, the entire cost being borne by him. He also made large contributions for the proposed Technical Institutes at Tinnevelly and Madras, and the Imperial Institute in England.

SRIPERAMBUDUR (CHINGLEPUT).

The population is 5,092, most of whom depend upon agriculture as a means of livelihood. Local Self-Government was introduced last year, and a Board of Panchayetdars superintend the sanitation of the town. The Free Church Mission has a School here, which teaches up to the Upper Primary Standard.

About 700 poor Hindus of all castes, and 300 Mohammedans, were fed at noon on the 16th February, and during the evening about 500 people of all castes and creeds went round the streets in procession with music, and then proceeded to their respective places of worship, and offered up prayers for the continuance of Her Majesty's beneficent reign, and for the welfare of Her Majesty and the Royal Family. During the night the temples, mosques, and several private residences were illuminated, and there was a musical entertainment which lasted till midnight. The Presidencial Address was adopted. It is proposed to erect a building in commemoration of the Jubilee, to be called the "Victoria Jubilee Hall."

SRIRANGAM (TRICHINOPOLY).

Srirangam is situated on the island between the sacred river Cauvery and its branch the Coleroon. The population is 19,773, consisting of 19,543 Hindus, 61 Mohammedans, 169 Native Christians, &c. A Girls' School, and six Combined System Schools, are maintained by the Municipality, and Results grants are paid to seven Private Schools. There is a Vishnu shrine in Srirangam, known by the name of Sri Runganadha Swamy Covil, to which pilgrimages are made from all parts of India. The Municipal Board consists of sixteen Councillors.

In the forenoon of the 16th February 1,600 poor of all classes were given a substantial meal, and 420 poor persons received cloths. The boys and girls of the poor schools were also given a treat, and sugar-candy was distributed among them. They were also presented with new cloths. The school children, headed by a native band, marched in procession from the Pagoda to the Hospital, accompanied by a large crowd of spectators. The temples and goporams in Srirangam and Jambookeswara were illuminated at night, and the gods and goddesses were decked with costly jewels as on festival occasions. Hundreds of people worshipped there and prayed for Her Majesty's long life. In addition to this the Chairman, Mr. Kristniengar, caused *poojahs* to be performed in the temples of Srirangam, Jamboukeswara, and the Rock Fort. Two Bhagavatas went round the four chief Chittrai Streets in Srirangam singing sacred songs to a musical accompaniment, followed by a large crowd. The Presidential Address was adopted. The Municipal Council has resolved to construct a "Flight of Steps" on the east of the Natuvakal Bridge as a permanent memorial of the Jubilee.

SRIVILLIPUTUR (TINNEVELLY).

The population of Srivilliputur is 18,256; of whom 17,422 are Hindus, 353 Mohammedans, and 481 Christians. There are two Schools in which English is taught, and a few Vernacular Pial Schools. The Union Panchayet system was lately introduced. The chief manufactures are weaving and working in bell-metal.

Jubilee Committee.—Messrs. SREE RUNGA CHARIAR, *Chairman*. SANKARA IYER, B.A., *Secretary*. S. VISVANATHA IYER, B.A.; M. SRINIVASAM PILLAY; R. ANANTHA RAMIER, B.A.; V. SINGAM IYENGAR; ANNANGAR TIRUMALAI IYENGAR; SAMEE KRISHNAIENGAR; SUNDRARAIER; and ten others.

Almost every part of the town was decorated on the 16th February with festoons, and with arches bearing mottoes which expressed, in the vernacular and in English, the loyalty of the people, such as "God save the Queen Empress," "Long live the Queen Empress," "The Matchless Lady," "Aundal's Blessing for Ever," "Peace and Prosperity," and "Honour to the Viceroy." Many houses were adorned with festoons and *kolams* (drawings on the floor in white powder). The first part of the festivities consisted of a splendid procession through the streets. About 400 School Children, with their teachers, marched at the head of the procession, followed by a large concourse of people, including all the officials of the place and rich Mirasidars. As the procession advanced, large crowds joined it. The girls who were all neatly dressed, sang several songs, composed for the occasion by a Tamil Pundit named Tirunamyan Iyengar, in praise of Her Majesty; while the boys, led by the Head Master of the Hindu School and Secretary of the Jubilee Committee, Mr. Sankara Iyer, B.A., and by Mr. Paul Peter Pillay, Head Master of the Local Mission School, shouted out at intervals joyful exclamations similar to the inscriptions on the arches. The procession started at 7 A.M. from the residence of the District Munsiff, and after passing through several streets it stopped in front of a temple, where all the people joined in a prayer invoking blessings on Her Majesty. Here the children were treated to sweetmeats and fruit. About 11 A.M. *poojahs* were performed in the temples. At 2 o'clock the beating of the large temple drums and the booming of guns announced the commencement of the public meeting at Kaliyana Mantapam. A salute of 101 guns was fired. Over 2,000 people, representatives of all classes, castes, and creeds, assembled there. The Chairman and Mr. R. Anantha Ramier made excellent speeches, and several Pundits recited Sanskrit slokas and Tamil verses composed by them in praise of Her Majesty. Some professional singers entertained the assembly with several songs, after which Messrs. Gopalswamy Theethachariyar and Paul Peter Pillay addressed the meeting, and impressed on the people the necessity of starting a local memorial of the day. They suggested the diversion of a stream from the neighbouring mountains to be called the "Queen Empress Jubilee River." The suggestion was unanimously agreed to, the feasibility of the project being reserved for future consideration. The Presidencial Address was adopted with loud cheering. Then the National Anthem was sung in English by four Christian gentlemen present, the whole audience standing. The meeting was brought to a close by the distribution of *pan supari*, the copious sprinkling of rose-water, and the playing of music. Three cheers were given for the Queen Empress. The party broke up at 6 o'clock. Half an hour later the people again assembled, and went round the town in procession, led by the high officials and followed by a numerous train. The pagoda elephant, which carried presents of cloth and other articles of worship for the goddess Aundal, also marched in the procession. In front there was a large body of athletes displaying their dexterity to the great amusement of all. A body of dancing-girls preceded the elephant, and as they went on they sang the glory of Her Majesty. Almost all the houses in the town were illuminated. The procession finally returned to the temple, where prayers were again offered. Divine services in Christian churches were conducted till late in the night. The mosques were illuminated. In front of the temple a native circus troupe gave a performance. Over 1,000 poor persons, men, women, and children, were fed.

ST. THOMAS' MOUNT (CHINGLEPUT).

St. Thomas' Mount is a cantonment nine miles from Fort St. George. There is a hill about 250 feet high, with a Portuguese church and signal station for mail steamers. There are extensive Barracks which used to be the head-quarters of the East India Company's Artillery, and are now usually occupied by Batteries of Royal Artillery. The station contains a commodious Church and a fine Mess House.

The P. and Q Batteries of Royal Artillery fired an Imperial salute of 101 guns at 6.45 A.M. on the 16th February. Special services were held at all churches. At 4 P.M. a treat was given in the South Barrack square to 185 European and Eurasian

School Children, with a substantial tea. The widows of 53 European and Eurasian pensioners were presented with Rs. 2 each. On the 17th, the Royal Artillery held Regimental sports on the General Parade-ground at 4 P.M., which lasted till dark, when there was a display of fireworks from the roof of the north barracks, which was witnessed by an enthusiastic crowd assembled on the Parade-ground. The Presidencial Address was adopted.

TADPATRI (ANANTAPUR).

Tadpatri is situated on the banks of the river Pennar, with a population of 8,585; of whom 5,972 are Hindus, 2,559 Mohammedans, and 54 Christians. It contains two large and beautiful Temples, and a large Mosque, a Local Fund Middle School, four Primary Schools for Hindus, and two for Mohammedans, a Hindu Girls' School, and a Mohammedan Girls' School. The sanitary arrangements of the place are directed by a Local Fund Union, and the medical wants of the people are supplied by a Local Fund Dispensary. Cotton, cholum, gram, dhol, liquor, and other articles are largely exported. There are two Cotton Presses and a large Distillery. Tadpatri is noted for the excellent cloth that it manufactures.

Jubilee Committee.—Messrs. T. WALLA, *Chairman*; M. GOPAUL ROW PUNTALU, *Secretary*; P. BASHNAM NAIDU; W. KRISTNA ROW; A. OOMMARKHAN SAHIB BAHADUR; N. CHENGUL ROW; Y. APPA ROW, and twenty others.

At 2 P.M. on the 16th February a procession of people of all castes, creeds, and ages, went through the bazaar from the Post Office to the Jubilee Pandal opposite the Travellers' Bungalow, where a large crowd awaited its arrival. The Pandal was decorated with flags and festoons of various descriptions, and the inscriptions displayed were expressive of the loyalty of the people. A portrait of Her Majesty was placed in the centre of the Pandal. Sweetmeats were distributed to pupils of the schools in the town. Sports of various kinds, such as tug-of-war, foot races, long jump, high jump, side jump, donkey race, three-legged race, sack race, chatty race, &c., were held. The Presidencial Address was read and explained in Telugu, and was unanimously adopted. A few Telugu stanzas, composed by a local Pundit in honour of the Jubilee, were sung by the school children in a very hearty manner, and cries of "Long live the Queen," "May She be Happy and Prosperous," were heard from all quarters. The ceremony terminated with three hearty cheers for Her Majesty. In the Hindu temples *abishekams* and *archanas* were offered. In the mosques *pathiah* and *moulooth* were grandly performed. After sunset the town was illuminated, and presented a brilliant appearance. Mr. Oommarkhan Sahib, the Tahsildar, fed the poor at his own cost, and there was a display of fireworks in front of the Taluk Cutcherry. On the following night prayers were again offered in all places of worship for the welfare of Her Majesty. The foundation stone of the local memorial, "The Victoria Jubilee Choultry," will be laid on the 20th of June.

TALIPARAMBA (MALABAR).

Taliparamba is about sixteen miles to the north of Cannanore. It has a population of 8,363; of whom 5,900 are Hindus, 2,434 Mohammedans, and 29 Christians. It contains a District Munsiff's Court, a Deputy Tahsildar and Second Class Magistrate's Cutcherry, a Sub-Registrar's Office, a Sub-Post Office, and three Elementary Vernacular Schools. Pepper, grown in the neighbourhood, is largely dealt in.

Jubilee Committee.—Messrs. J. F. PEREIRA, *Chairman*; P. W. CHACKO, *Secretary*; K. RAMAN; M. A. D'CRUZ; K. A. SHUNGOONY MENON; P. SHANKARA MENON; T. H. RAMA PUTHUVAL, and ten others.

The streets and houses had been cleaned and decorated by dawn on the 16th February, when a salute of 101 temple guns was fired in front of the Magistrate's Cutcherry. Spectators assembled dressed in holiday attire. The Magistrate now arrived, and the business of the day commenced with the release of a prisoner from the subsidiary jail. This was followed by the distribution of rice to 1,868 poor persons at three centres. A band of native musicians was in attendance, and played at intervals throughout the day. In the afternoon, there were sports consisting of flat, hurdle, chatty, and consolation races, which were competed for by both Hindus and Moplahs on the *maidan* adjoining the Munsiff's Court premises where a Pavilion had been erected, and decorated with festoons and bunting. A tug-of-war, followed by fencing, in which twelve Moplah athletes took part, brought the sports to a close at 5 P.M. Three sets of native violinists now appeared on the scene, and entertained the people with music till darkness set in, when there was a grand display of fireworks which continued for three hours. The remainder of the night was taken up by a theatrical performance, which was largely attended. Hindus, Christians, and Mohammedans held special services and invoked Divine blessings on the Empress. The Presidencial Address was adopted.

TANGACHERRY (MALABAR).

Tangacherry is a small British Settlement to the south-west of Quilon. It originally belonged to the Rajah of Quilon, and, after being held by the Portuguese and by the Dutch, it came into the possession of the British in the year 1795. It is not more than a square mile in extent. It contains a population of 1,665, of whom the greater number are Native Christians. There are also some descendants of the early Portuguese and Dutch settlers. The people live for the most part by the cultivation of cocoanuts. Their properties are freehold. Nothing is paid to Government by way of tax. This immunity has been enjoyed by the town since the time of the Portuguese. There is only one Government Institution, viz., the office of the Deputy Tahsildar. There are three Schools maintained by the Roman Catholic Mission, two for boys and one for girls.

Jubilee Committee.—The Rev. Fre John of the Cross, *Chairman*; Messrs. R. J. Mesquita, *Secretary*; Nanoo Menon; Brother Peter; J. P. Rodrigues; J. N. Martin; M. R. Gonsalves; J. Moreira; J. C. Surrao; F. Rodrigues, and seven others.

Before sunrise on the 16th February, large crowds assembled at the foot of the flagstaff in the old Fort, and while the flag of England was being hoisted, three enthusiastic cheers were given for Her Majesty. The cheers were followed by the firing of guns and the playing of "God save the Queen" by a native band of musicians. The people then marched to their places of worship, accompanied by music. High Masses were sung, and Thanksgiving Services were held in the two Roman Catholic churches. In the former, the Very Rev. C. J. M. Abreu, the Vicar-General of the Portuguese Mission, officiated; and in the latter, the Chairman of the Committee, Rev. Fre John of the Cross. In both the churches, sermons appropriate to the occasion were preached. After service rice was distributed to nearly 500 poor people, including paupers who had come in from the adjoining territory of the Maharajah of Travancore. In the afternoon there were sports, consisting of boat races, athletics, &c. The principal streets and several houses were decorated and illuminated. On the road leading to the fort two triumphal arches—one at the entrance to Tangacherry, and the other at the junction of the road leading to the Tahsildar's Cutcherry—had been erected, bearing suitable inscriptions. Festoons and flags overhung these roads. The spectacle which the town presented during the illumination was charming. There were fireworks at 8 o'clock, followed by a native dramatic entertainment. The day's festivities were brought to a close by the delivery of a public address by Mr. J. C. Surrao, one of the members of the Committee, on the blessings of Her Majesty's reign. The Presidencial Address was adopted.

TANJORE (TOWN).

Tanjore, the chief town of the District of the same name, contains a population of 55,445, classified as follows:—Hindus, 47,195; Mohammedans, 3,152; Christians, 4,874; and Jains, &c., 224. Its manufactures consist chiefly of silk, metal-ware, pith-work, and flower garlands. There are a first grade institution, St. Peter's College, maintained by the S. P. G., and many Elementary Native Schools.

Jubilee Committee.—Messrs. E. Gibson, *Chairman*; K. Govinda Row, *Secretary*; J. A. Davis; S. H. Wynne; T. A. Saminatha Ayar; C. E. Smith; Rev. Mr. Nicholson, and others.

On the morning of the 16th February an Imperial salute of 101 guns was fired in the great temple. Sports were held in the People's Park from 7 to 9.30 A.M., and were witnessed by a large crowd. These were followed by special Thanksgiving Services in the several churches, temples, and mosques, and by the feeding and clothing of nearly 10,000 of the poorer inhabitants of the town. 124 prisoners and two civil debtors were released from the Tanjore Jail. At 3 P.M. the sports were resumed, and continued for several hours to the great enjoyment of thousands of people. A grand procession was formed at 6.30 P.M. to take a portrait of the Queen Empress, placed in a howdah on an elephant, round the town, and into the Palace. All the houses and thoroughfares were brilliantly illuminated as the procession passed. At 10 o'clock a public meeting was held in the Durbar Hall of the Palace, when the adoption of the Presidencial Address to Her Majesty was proposed by Mr. T. Saminada Iyer, and carried with acclamation, the Palace band playing the National Anthem. The Address was signed by the Ranees and many others. The proceedings terminated with a nautch dance, fireworks, and the distribution of *pan supari* and flower garlands. Great enthusiasm was displayed by all classes of the inhabitants throughout the day. As a permanent memorial of the happy event it has been determined to erect a local "Technical Institute" or an "Agricultural College." Subscriptions have been promised from all parts of the district, amounting to Rs. 33,000.

TANUKU (GODAVERY).

The population of this place is 3,072, composed for the most part of Hindus, among whom education has made considerable progress. There are several Schools.

Jubilee Committee.—Messrs. L. C. Miller, *Chairman*; A. Ramachendra Rao, *Secretary*; R. Hanumantha Rao; V. Vijayaramiah; Hanumantha Rao; K. Venkatramiah; Abdul Khader Sahib.

The 16th and 17th of February were red-letter days with the people of this town. Large crowds poured in from the neighbouring places to take part in the rejoicings. At about 3 P.M. on the 16th, more than 200 poor people were fed, and several were presented with new cloths. Sports were held, and proved a great success. In the evening a nautch was held in the handsome Pandal that had been erected for the occasion in the centre of the village. At night there was a grand procession of the gods round the village with music, &c., and fireworks were let off at intervals. The Presidencial Address was adopted. As memorials of the Jubilee, it has been resolved to erect a "School House," and to make a grant to the "Poor Fund Association," lately started here with the object of distributing rice once a week, and cloths twice a year, to the poor who are rendered unable, by bodily infirmity, to earn their livelihood.

TELLICHERRY (MALABAR).

The population of Tellicherry is 26,410—comprising Hindus, 16,496; Mohammedans, 9,149; and Christians and others, 1,765. There are two High Schools, namely, the Brennen Zillah

School under Municipal management, and the German Basel Mission Parsee School under the management of German Missionaries; two Middle Schools, the Tiruvengad Middle School under Municipal management, and the Roman Catholic Boys' School in charge of the Roman Catholic Vicar; there are also about twenty Village Schools, two Night Schools for the use of the labourer and artisan class; and a second grade Normal School. There are three Girls' Schools. The Municipality was introduced in January, 1866, and in July, 1883, the elective system came into force. The present strength of the Council is eighteen. A large trade in coffee, pepper, rice, cardamoms, copra, timber, gingelly seed, ginger, and sandalwood is carried on. There are three coffee-curing yards belonging to European merchants, where coffee brought from the Wynaad and Coorg is cured for export to Europe. The principal articles of export are coffee, pepper, cardamoms, and ginger, sandalwood, timber, and gingelly seed. The chief articles of import are rice, grains, timber, tobacco, and piece goods.

Jubilee Committee.—Messrs. H. SEWELL, *Chairman*; A. F. LEMBELE, *Secretary*; E. SHERMAN; R. TATHAM; KALAI AMANATH; and several others.

Early in the morning of the 16th February High Mass was sung at the Roman Catholic church, and after the *Te Deum* a Royal salute was fired by the constabulary. After the service the Tellicherry Company of the Malabar Volunteers marched from the church to the *maidan*, where they paraded in review order at 7 A.M. The Boys of the several Schools in the town also marched in procession, with music and banners, bearing Jubilee mottoes on them, and took their stand on the western side of the *maidan*. The "Union Jack" planted in the centre of the *maidan* formed the saluting point. A *feu de joie* was fired, and the Volunteers "marched past." Three cheers for Her Imperial Majesty the Queen Empress were then called for, and were heartily given by the crowd. "God save the Queen" was sung by the Volunteers and the Boys of the assembled Schools. The Volunteers now marched back to the Fort. A native procession, with a Jubilee banner and native music, marched round the town, and the people gave expression to their loyal feelings by shouting and cheering as they marched along. Next came the boat-race, which caused much excitement. This was followed by the sports of the schoolboys, at which the boys of the German Mission and Parsee High Schools distinguished themselves; and then came a foot-race for Volunteers. Just as the sports were over the members of the Kuthuparamba Sub-Committee came up in procession, bearing the Royal Coat of Arms and banners on elephants, accompanied by music, sword-players, dancers, &c., and were cordially received at the Pandal that had been erected on the *maidan*, by the members of the Tellicherry Committee. Jubilee songs were then sung in Malayalim by some men of the Kuthuparamba party. Three triumphal arches, bearing appropriate mottoes, and numerous banners, spanned the road crossing the *maidan*, on which were erected booths, pandals, and tents for the accommodation of spectators. Native music was played throughout the day. A treat was given to the patients in the

Hospital. From 2 to 4 P.M. there was an entertainment of native music in the Brennen High School. A Sanscrit song composed for the occasion was sung by a distinguished Brahmin musician. At 2 P.M. the Moplahs assembled at the Odathil mosque for a Thanksgiving Service, after which they marched in procession round the town with elephants, music, &c., the Moplah merchants joining with the Kuthuparamba party. Several of the leading residents, Europeans and Hindus, accompanied it. Rose-water and flowers were sprinkled over them as they passed through the decorated streets. On the return of the procession to the *maidan* the Volunteers drew up in review order, and three cheers for Her Majesty were given by the whole assemblage. Then followed acrobatic feats, Moplah gymnastic exercises, rope dancing, wire dancing, trapeze, &c. The sports continued till dusk, when all the buildings round the *maidan*, and the *maidan* itself, were grandly illuminated. The Club, the Bank, Travellers' Bungalow, Taluk Cutcherry, the Mosque, and several private houses facing the *maidan* were tastefully lit up. On the sloping bank of the Bastion, which forms the western limit of the *maidan*, the word "Victoria" was written in letters of fire. The fireworks commenced at 9 o'clock, and were followed by two native dramatic performances, which lasted till 3 o'clock in the morning. Rice and money were distributed to 3,604 poor persons in the Fort on the 17th. Sports were again held, and the Regimental Band from Cannanore played at intervals. The *maidan* and the surrounding houses were illuminated at 6.30 P.M. in the same manner as on the previous day, and at 7 P.M. there was another display of fireworks, which closed the day's proceedings. At a rough estimate, about 15,000 persons took part in the festivities here. Everything went off with the greatest order and regularity, the crowd being exceedingly good-tempered, orderly, and enthusiastic. The Presidential Address was adopted. The local memorials will take the shape of a "New Market" and a "Clock Tower."

TINNEVELLY (TOWN).

The population of the adjoining towns Tinnevelly and Palamcottah is 41,185; of whom 85 per cent. are Hindus, 9 per cent. Mohammadans, and 6 per cent. Christians. The large proportion of Christians is due to the existence in the District for upwards of a century of numerous Mission agencies. The number of persons under instruction in the town is 2,260 males and 720 females. The progress in female education has been rapid. The Peckle School at Tinnevelly, the Osborne Memorial Home, and the Sarah Tucker Female Training School at Palamcottah are the principal institutions for girls in the District. Higher education is imparted in the Hindu College at Veeraraghavapuram, and the C.M.S. College at Tinnevelly. The number of Primary Schools in the two towns is thirty-one for boys and fourteen for girls. A Municipal Council has been constituted for each of the towns, consisting of sixteen and twelve Councillors respectively, three fourths of the members being elected. The principal exports are cotton, jaggery, rice, blankets, twist, coffee, and spices. The principal imports are piece goods, silk, gram, pepper, cocoanut, spices, sugar, paper, &c. The principal manufactures are cloths, blankets, mats, copper vessels, &c.

Jubilee Committee.—Messrs. J. LEE-WARNER, *Chairman*; RAMAKRISHNA AIYER, *Secretary*; J. C. HUGHESDON; RIGHT REV. BISHOP SARGENT; REV V. W. HARCOURT; REV. R. WALKER; DR. H. HYDE; Messrs. R. C. LOWRY; B. S. SREENIVASAM; KRISHNA RAO; KRISHNA AIYER, and others.

On the morning of the 16th February the road from Tinnevelly to Palamcottah presented a very lively appearance. Arches had been erected bearing appropriate mottoes and inscriptions; and numerous flags were displayed. Some benevolent persons put up temporary water Pandals for the use of wayfarers. At about noon great crowds were seen hastening to the race-course at Palamcottah, where a commodious T-shaped Pandal had been erected, the frontage of which presented a very attractive appearance. The whole course was liberally decorated with flags. Sports engaged public attention from 2 to 6 P.M. Mrs. Lee-Warner, wife of the Collector, then distributed the prizes to the winners, in the Pandal. About 2,000 Boys and 600 Girls belonging to the several schools and colleges marched in procession to the Pandal preceded by elephants and the Union Jack, and accompanied by music. Sweetmeats were provided for them, and a set of acrobats exhibited their skill. The Presidential Address was read to the assembly by the Honorary Secretary of the Committee, amid loud cheering, and was received by the Collector, who was seated on a *dais* surrounded by the principal District Officers, the Zemindars of Ettiapuram, Oottoomalai and Sevalpatti, and a great many non-official residents of the District. Then followed the recitation of Sanscrit verses composed for the occasion in honour of Her Majesty. There was also a distribution of flowers, sandal, rose-water, and *pan supari*. At nightfall, two huge bonfires were lighted on the top of hills near Palamcottah. The fireworks began at 7 P.M. The principal roads in the towns and the four-mile road from Tinnevelly to Palamcottah were illuminated. The gopurams of the temples, the kiosks of the mosques, and the steeples of the churches were traced in lines of light. The shopkeepers and the house-owners had also illuminated their buildings. During the day upwards of 3,000 poor people of all classes and creeds were fed. Special services were performed in the churches and in the several temples of Tinnevelly and Palamcottah. The Hindu gods were also taken in procession through the principal streets. It is calculated that altogether more than 10,000 people took part in the festivities. At the conclusion of the proceedings enthusiastic cheers were given for Her Majesty and the Royal Family. On the 17th, an address on the benefits of the British rule in India was delivered at a large public meeting, at which Mr. Hughesden, the District Judge, presided, and a nautch was held at night.

The Jubilee was also celebrated in the several stations in the District of Tinnevelly. The poor were fed, the streets and the temples illuminated, and special services were performed. The following are among the towns in which the celebration took place:—Srivilliputtur, Tenkasi, Srivaikuntham, Trichendur, Nanguneri, Shermadevi, Satur, Virudupati and Otapidaram, as well as in other towns whose proceedings are recorded elsewhere in this volume. The permanent District memorial of the Jubilee is to be the "Victoria Industrial Institution" in the town of Tinnevelly.

TIRUKOILUR (SOUTH ARCOT).

Tirukoilur has a population of 4,676 inhabitants; Hindus predominate. The town contains two Middle Schools, a Normal School, several Local Fund Schools, and numerous indigenous Schools. The affairs of the town are looked after by a Local Board and Union Panchayet. The people are generally engaged in agriculture. There are two sugar factories in the place.

Jubilee Committee.—Rev. A. Ixle, *Chairman*; Messrs. S. Chandrasekhara Mudelliar, *Secretary*; K. Subba Row Puntalu; V. Narayana Row; J. A. Majoribanks; S. Sesvaji Row; V. Srinivasa Row; and twenty-eight others.

At daybreak on the 16th February, a salute of 50 guns was fired. Sports and races were held at 7 o'clock and hundreds of poor persons were fed. In the evening a large number of people met at a Pandal that had been erected opposite the Court House where an entertainment was provided. Her Majesty's photograph was taken thence in procession through the main streets, which were decorated with festoons and triumphal arches. The streets were illuminated at night, as also were the public office buildings and several private houses. Prayers for the long life of Her Majesty were offered in all places of worship, by all classes of people. A musical entertainment was given, at the close of which sandal and *pan supari* were distributed. The Presidencial Address was adopted and signed. The festivities wound up with a display of fireworks, and three cheers for the Queen Empress. On the following day a nautch was held, and the people were entertained with music and singing. The Jubilee is to be commemorated by "Scholarships" for the two Middle Schools of Tirukoilur and Kallakurchi.

TIRUMANGALAM (MADURA).

The population of this town is 5,480, consisting of Mohammedans, Shanars, and other Hindus. It has a Taluk Cutcherry, Taluk Board Office, Union Office, Post Office, Railway Station, Native Middle School, an American Mission School, and a Local Fund Dispensary.

The 16th and 17th were days of great rejoicing. The whole town was prettily decorated, and at night was illuminated. Special services were held in the temples and mosques for Her Most Gracious Majesty. The poor of the town and of the adjacent villages were fed. In the American Mission compound the schoolboys and schoolgirls were given a splendid treat. A special service was conducted in the American Mission Church. The Presidencial Address was adopted. The permanent memorial will take the form of a "Lamp Post" which it is proposed to complete before the 20th June.

TIRUPATI (NORTH ARCOT).

Tirupati is a remarkable place of antiquity and sanctity, dedicated to the god Sreenivasaswamy. There are two Vishnu temples, one dedicated to Govindarajaswamy, and the other to Ramaswamy. The population is 13,232, composed of 12,645 Hindus, 544 Muhammadans, and 43 Christians. The town has been constituted a Municipality. The Hermannsburg Lutheran German Mission supports an English High School which is in a flourishing condition. There is another English High School maintained by the Mahunt from the Devastanam funds. There is a Dispensary under the supervision of the Municipality, but maintained by the Mahunt. There is also a District Munsiff's Court. A considerable trade is carried on in rice, indigo, jaggery, and raggi and cloths.

At Upper Tirupati, on the 16th February, Garuda *utchavam* was performed; and at Lower Tirupati the gods Govindarajaswami and Ramaswami, followed by a number of Alwars, were taken to Alwar Thirthum, a distance of two miles to the north at the foot of the hill, which is the place where there is a constant waterfall for the greater part of the year. On the Thirthum there are two temples named Alwar Kovil and Kapileswarar Kovil, connected by picturesque mantapams. It was there that the gods were placed for the day. At 3 P.M. men of all castes and creeds, about 2,000 in number, were fed, and sandal and *pan supari* distributed. The Sri Mahunt went to the place at about 4 o'clock in the afternoon, and made money presents to a great number of those present. At about 6.30 the gods were brought back to Tirupati in a grand torchlight procession, with the Mahunt seated on a stately elephant behind. The procession was attended with fireworks and went round the town. The gods were taken to their respective temples, and the Mahunt was escorted to his Muttum. The same festival, with a similar distribution of food and money, and with a similar procession, was repeated at Alumelumangammah's temple at Trichanoor on the following day. The Presidencial Address was adopted. The festivities on both days were performed by the Sri Mahunt at his own cost. One-sixth of the public Jubilee collections has been reserved for a permanent memorial.

TIRUPATUR (SALEM).

The population of the town of Tirupatur is 14,278; of whom 8,686 are Hindus, 5,488 are Mohammedans, and 104 are Christians. Tirupatur is a Municipal town, and the head-quarters of the Assistant Collector, and of the Assistant Superintendent of Police, Salem District. It has a Taluk Board established under the recent scheme of Local Self-Government. It contains a Municipal School which teaches up to the standard of the Middle School Examination; a Local Fund Normal School training up for the Upper Primary Examination; a Municipal Mohammedan Primary School; a Girls' School of the London Mission; and seven Primary Schools under the Results system. A large trade is carried on in jaggery, dholl, rice, and other grain.

Jubilee Committee.—Messrs. C. Annamalai Chettiar, *Chairman*, C. Runganada Mudelliar, and R. V. Karthekeya Pillay, *Joint Secretaries*; Ossoor Soobba Row; K. V. Karthekeya Pillay; C. Perumal Nadar; T. T. Ranga Chariar, B.A., B.L.; C. Kuppiah Garu; L. Balaji Row, and six others.

The celebration on the 16th February commenced with the offering of prayers for the Queen Empress in all places of worship. The Hindus marched in procession to their temples with music and the beating of drums, and performed *archanas* in the name of Her Majesty. At 10 A.M. about 2,000 poor Mohammedans and Hindus were fed. About 500 Brahmins were entertained by Mr. Perumal Nadar; Messrs. Chinnah Moodelly and Ademoola Moodelly undertook the feeding of the other Hindu poor; and Mr. Choteba Sahib also fed a portion of the Mohammedan poor at his own expense. At 2 P.M. over 600 schoolboys were treated to fruits and sugar-candy by Mr. Perumal Nadar. Between 3 and 6 P.M. sports were held for European, Eurasian, and Native children, and prizes were distributed. In the evening the European and Eurasian children were given a treat. The town was illuminated. The roads leading up to the Pandal in the Government Garden were lit with rows of lamps on either side, with flags of different colours intervening. At 7 P.M. a grand procession, attended with music and blue lights, marched from the Post Office to a beautifully decorated Pandal that had been erected for the Jubilee. A portrait of Her Majesty decorated with garlands was placed in a conspicuous place on the *dais*. The Presidencial Address was read in English, Tamil, Telugu, and Hindustani, and was adopted. Three hearty cheers were then given for Her Majesty; "God save the Queen" was sung; and the Guard of Honour in attendance presented arms. Flowers, *pan supari*, sandal, and rose-water were freely distributed, and a famous piper of Tanjore performed. The fireworks commenced at 9, and concluded by 11 P.M. On the afternoon of the 17th a music party was held in the Pandal and was largely attended. At 7 P.M. a magic lantern exhibition followed. It included portraits of Her Majesty and of the Prince of Wales, which were greeted with loud cheers. A nautch party in the Pandal engaged the attention of the meeting between 9 and 11.30 P.M. The proceedings then terminated with a small display of fireworks. Upwards of 8,000 people, including the spectators from adjacent villages, attended the celebration of the Jubilee. It was resolved to construct a "Reservoir" in the name of Her Majesty, and in commemoration of her Jubilee.

TIRUPATUR (MADURA).

The population of this town is 4,628. There are no European or Eurasian residents. The Mohammedans form about one-third, and the Native Christians a very small fraction of the whole population. The rest are Hindus, chiefly Brahmans. The chief ryots and merchants of the place are Mohammedans. There is an Anglo-Vernacular School, several Pial Schools, and one Hindustani School. This town with four other villages constitute a Union under the Local Boards Act. Paddy and cocoanuts are extensively produced and exported.

Jubilee Committee.—Messrs. K. GURUPADA MUDELLIAR, *Chairman*; NARAYANA AYER, *Secretary*; S. BALASUBRAMANIA PILLAI, B.A.; SABAPATHI THAMBERAN; RAMASAWMY AIYER; SESHA IYER; MOOTHOOVIRUO PILLAI; and PIR MAHOMED AMBALAM.

On the 16th February *abishakams* and *pujah* were performed in the temples, and prayers were offered in churches and mosques. The different sections of the community met in the early morning, at a place selected for the purpose, and marched in procession, with music, to their several places of worship, and offered prayers for the long life and continued prosperity of Her Majesty. They then returned in the same manner to the Zemindar's bungalow in the heart of the town, and after the playing of music for some time, and the distribution of sandal and *pan supari*, and the sprinkling of rose-water, they dispersed. Between noon and 2 P.M. about 500 poor people were fed. Between 2 and 5 P.M. there was *Manjivirattu*, the occasion being one of exceptional public rejoicings. Between 7 and 8 P.M. there was a splendid procession of the goddesses of the Siva temple, accompanied by about 1,000 people. Between 9 and 10.30 P.M. there was a singing and nautch party, at the conclusion of which flowers, sandal, and *pan supari* were distributed, and rose-water was sprinkled. From 11 until 12 P.M. a display of fireworks took place. Hindus, Mohammedans, and Christians took part in the celebration; and they were equally enthusiastic in showing their loyalty to Her Majesty. Never was so much union shown among the different classes of the people of this town as was witnessed on this memorable occasion.

TIRUSHULI (MADURA).

Tirushuli has a population of 2,780. Of these 2,579 are Hindus, 194 Mohammedans, and 7 Christians. It is the head-quarters of a Deputy Tahsildar, Police Inspector, Sub-Registrar, Zemindari Tahsildar, the Devastanam Ameen, the Local Fund Overseer, and an Inspecting School master. It contains a School aided by a grant from the Local Fund; a Sanitary Association; a Local Fund Dispensary; and a Post Office.

About 300 Hindus, rich and poor, young and old, were fêted at noon on the 16th February, at the Chuttram. At 4 P.M. a meeting was held in the Sub-Magistrate's office, which was attended by a large number of persons of all classes. It was opened by a Pundit, who dwelt on the blessings of the British administration of India under the reign of Her Majesty. The Presidencial Address was adopted. Music and singing followed, and the meeting terminated with the distribution of sugar and *pan supari*. At 7 P.M. *abishakams* were performed in the temple, which was profusely illuminated, and the streets were decorated with *thoranams* and lights. At about 9 P.M. the god and goddess were taken in procession in *Rishaba Vasanam*, as is done on sacred and pious occasions. The procession was attended by about 2,000 people, who had come in from the outlying villages. There was music and dancing, accompanied by a display of fireworks. The Jubilee was also loyally celebrated in the towns of Aruppukotta, Palampatti, and Palavantham.

TIRUVADAMARUDUR (TANJORE).

The population of the town is 10,809, including Brahmins, Sudras, Native Christians, and Mohammedans. There are two Anglo-Vernacular Pial Schools. A Union Punchayet has been established under the Local Boards Act. It consists of sixteen members. Weaving is carried on to a large extent. Paddy is extensively cultivated.

Jubilee Committee.—Messrs. CHELVANDIVSAMY PILLAI, *Chairman*; J. SREENEVASA IYENGAR, *Secretary*; GOVINDASAMI PILLAI; S. R. KRISHNAMACHARIAR; K. M. SREENIVASALOO NAIDU; NATESA IYER; SAMINAGAIYAR, and several others.

At daybreak on the morning of the 16th February an Imperial salute of 101 guns was fired. *Pujahs*, *abishakams*, &c., were performed in the Hindu temples, and special services were held in the Christian and Mussulman places of worship. Between 10 A.M. and 2 P.M. 600 people of different castes and creeds were fed, and 50 of them were clothed. The Presidencial Address was read and adopted amidst much cheering. At about 5 P.M. a procession started from the principal Hindu temple, accompanied by music, the British Standard being borne in front. After passing through the chief streets, which were prettily decorated, the procession reached the Committee Meeting Hall at 6 P.M. A musical entertainment was given here. The assembly dispersed after the distribution of *pan supari*, &c.

TIRUVANNAMALAI (SOUTH ARCOT).

This town is situated at the foot of a hill of the same name, rising to about 2,700 feet above the level of the sea. It contains a population of 9,572 inhabitants, distributed as follows:—

Hindus, 8,398; Mohammedans, 1,147; Christians, 31; and others, 16. The people are mostly agricultural. There is a Middle School teaching up to the Lower Fourth Class under the management of the Taluk Board.

Jubilee Committee.—Messrs. M. SREENIVASA CHARIAR, *Chairman*; S. VENKATACHELA PUNTALU and R. KRISHNA ROW, *Joint Secretaries*; K. R. MIDDLETON; KHADER HUSSAIN SAHIB; APPASAMI NAIDU; ARUNACHELLA MUDELLIAR; K. SUNDARA RAJAH; and sixteen others.

At daybreak on the 16th February a salute of 31 guns was fired. The town was beautifully decorated with arches and festoons. At 10 A.M. *abishekams*, *archanas*, &c., were performed at the shrines, and prayers were offered for the long life and prosperity of Her Majesty. At noon 500 poor Brahmins and 790 Mohammedans were treated to a sumptuous repast. The Presidential Address was adopted. In the evening the residents of the town beautifully lighted up their houses, and the pagoda and the four gopurams were illuminated. At about 7 P.M. there was a grand procession of the Arnachelleswara god, and there was a fine display of fireworks in front of the temple. The procession lasted till about 2 A.M. About 15,000 people from all parts of the Taluk took part in the celebration. On the 17th, about 1,500 poor persons of all classes were fed. It is proposed to commemorate the Jubilee by contributing a sum to the Middle School Poor Boys' School Fee Fund, which is in future to be designated the "Jubilee Fee Fund," for the encouragement of education of poor boys attending the School, and also by an "Annual Festival" on the 16th of February, to be known as the "Jubilee Vincharam."

TIRUVALUR (TANJORE).

Tiruvalur is a town with a population of 9,181 persons; of whom 7,897 are Hindus, 1,213 are Mohammedans, and 71 are Christians and others. It is noted for a Siva Temple, which is much resorted to by Hindu Pilgrims. It has a Munsiff's Court, a Sub-Magistrate's Office, a Police Station, a Post Office, a Local Fund Dispensary, a Local Fund High School, an Elementary School, and a Reading Room. It is the head-quarters of the Local Fund Union, of the Police Inspector, and of the Supervisor of the Local Fund Public Works Department.

Jubilee Committee.—Messrs. KRISHNASAMI MOODALI, *Chairman*; A. NARAYANASAMI IYER, *Secretary*; N. R. NARASIMHA AIYER, B.A.; NAGASIMHULU RAJA; and DORASAMI PILLAI.

On the 16th February prayers were said and offerings made in the Hindu temples, in the Mohammedan mosques, and in the Christian church; and food was distributed to the people on a liberal scale. The Siva temple was grandly decorated. *Abishekams* were performed to the village deities. At 2 P.M. the chief inhabitants assembled in the Munsiff's Court House, and at 2.30 they started in procession, accompanied by music and by dancing-women gaily attired. The procession went towards the temple, which is entered by the western gateway, and proceeded up to the Thousand-pillared Dome, which had been decorated for the occasion. The chief servants of the several religious institutions attended with *prasadams* from those institutions. The proceedings commenced by the District Munsiff delivering a short address in Tamil on the blessings of British rule. Sanscrit and Tamil verse, invoking the Almighty's blessings on the Queen Empress, and praying for her long life and prosperity, were recited. Then the audience were entertained with music on the *vina*, and two dancing-girls sang some songs. The police fired a *feu de joie*, and a Royal salute was fired during the proceedings from the temple *athirvedis*. The Presidencial Address was adopted amidst cheers, and it was signed by a few representatives. Sandal, betel, fruits, and sugar were distributed. At night the people were entertained with music and *nauram*. On the 17th the *gopuram* of the Siva temple was again illuminated. A grand musical entertainment was given at the School premises, when "Rule Britannia" was played on the violin, and the people shouted "God bless our Empress." Sanscrit verses, composed for the occasion, were recited, followed by loud cheers for Her Majesty. A procession went to the Vishnu temple at Madapuram. The company separated after refreshments and the distribution of *pan supari*. In commemoration of the Jubilee, a sum has been invested at 6 per cent. interest in good landed security for the purpose of awarding an annual prize in Sanscrit, called "The Victoria Jubilee Sanscrit Prize," to the student of the Local High School who, in passing the Matriculation Examination, obtains the highest number of marks in Sanscrit. A Library, called the "Empress Jubilee Library," in connection with the Reading Room will be established.

TITTAKUDI (SOUTH ARCOT).

The population of Tittakudi town is about 1,800, including Brahmins, Kschatriyas, Vysias, Sudras, Mohammedans, and Pariahs. There are about 300 weavers, who manufacture a coarse cloth.

Jubilee Committee.—Messrs. A. VENKATAKRISHNIAH, *Chairman*; T. SHUNMUGAM PILLAI, *Secretary*; SANTASI PILLAI; T. KUMARASAWMY PILLAI; NATARAJA PILLAI; VENKATASUBBA DIKSHITAR; KHADIR MEERA HUSSAIN ROWTHER, and five others.

The celebration passed off very satisfactorily. All the houses in the town were decorated, and at night illuminated; and prayers were offered in the temples, which were also illuminated. The gods were carried in procession through the chief streets. About 850 poor of all classes were fed on the 16th and 17th February. There were sports during the day, and nautches and dramatic performances at night. Bonfires were lighted on both the nights. The Presidencial Address was adopted. The gods in the several temples were anointed and adorned. The processions were conducted in an imposing manner, attended by music and dancing-girls. Many of the village heads and leading inhabitants of outlying villages made themselves conspicuous by their cordial co-operation. The proceedings were most enthusiastic.

TRANQUEBAR (TANJORE).

The population of this old Danish town is estimated at 5,000, about three-fourths of whom are Hindus, the rest are Mohammedans, Native Christians, &c. The town is the seat of a Second Grade College teaching up to the F. A. Standard; it also contains a High School, a Middle School, and several Primary Schools for boys and girls. The Leipzig Evangelical Lutheran Mission has opened an Industrial Institution where carpentry, blacksmith's work, weaving, and other handicrafts are taught. Fish curing, weaving, dyeing, and salt manufacture are the most important of the local industries. There are several wealthy merchants who trade with Mauritius, Seychelles, the Straits Settlements, and elsewhere. The town, with the suburban villages, has recently been constituted a Major Union, with a Panchayet of thirteen members to manage its affairs.

Jubilee Committee.—REV. K. PAMPERRIEN, *Chairman*; DR. E. A. MORRIS, *Secretary*; Messrs. N. W. SUBBARAYALU NAIDU; A. S. DANIEL PILLAI; C. APPASAWMI CHETTIAR; M. D. MANIKMONEY PILLAI; A. PAKYAM PILLAI, and several others.

At the eastern end of the *maidan*, opposite the old Court-house, a spacious Pandal had been erected. It was tastefully decorated with evergreens, festoons, lustres, globes, and fancy articles of various descriptions; and an excellent portrait of Her Majesty occupied the most prominent position. "Long live our Empress" was the motto placed over the entrance. Flags of divers colours were planted round the esplanade, and on both sides of the streets. The proceedings opened with the firing of an Imperial salute, upon which the "Union Jack" was hoisted on the flagstaff of the *maidan*. The band played the National Anthem, and the Police and Salt Contingent presented arms. The bells in the churches and temples rang merry peals. A band of Tanjore musicians was in attendance and played airs at intervals. After the firing of a *feu de joie* there was a parade of the Police and Salt Force on the *maidan*. The force marched along the chief streets with music. At 8 A.M. on the 16th February Services of Thanksgiving were held in all the Christian churches (three Protestant and one Roman Catholic), where appropriate sermons were preached; and prayers were offered in the Hindu temples and Mohammedan mosques for the continuance of the reign of Her Majesty. In the forenoon rice and money were distributed to upwards of 1,200 poor persons in "Danesburg Castle," opposite the *maidan*. Each person received a measure of rice and half an anna. At 2 P.M. about 600 children of the different schools in the town marched in procession to the Pandal with banners flying, and with music. They were treated to sweets of various kinds. Sports were then held, each event drawing many competitors. After dusk the western gate of the Fort, and the town, were illuminated. The Pandal was brilliantly lit up. At 7 P.M. a portrait of Her Majesty was placed on a handsome new carriage, and taken in torchlight procession accompanied by English and Native music, songs, and fireworks. The procession went through the main streets, and returned to the Pandal. A short account of the life of the Queen was then given in Tamil by Mr. Pakyam Pillai, and was listened to with great attention. The students of the Evangelical Lutheran Seminary sang the National Anthem in Tamil to a harmonium accompaniment. *Pan supari* was distributed among the people. A nautch party followed. Refreshments were supplied to all visitors. The festivities wound up with an excellent display of fireworks. At 10.30 P.M. the band played "God save the Queen," when three hearty cheers were given for Her Majesty and the crowd dispersed. The Presidencial Address was adopted. It was resolved to found a prize to be called the "Victoria Jubilee Prize," to be awarded annually to the boy who stands first in the Matriculation Examination in the Tranquebar and Porayar schools.

TRICHENGODE (SALEM).

Trichengode is the head-quarters of the Tahsildar, the Deputy Inspector of Schools, the Sub-Registrar, and the Police Inspector. There are two Siva Temples. A Union was recently established here under the Local Boards Act, and there is a Minor Hospital. There is a Local Fund Middle School teaching up to the third standard, a Mohammedan Primary School, a Government Girls' School, two Primary Schools under the Results system, and four other Private Schools. Trichengode is noted for its sandalwood balls, and a good trade in [illegible] and cotton is carried on. The population is 5,889; of whom 5,600 are Hindus, 273 Mohammedans, and 16 Christians.

Jubilee Committee—Messrs. M. R. [illegible], *Chairman*; C. S. CHOCKALINGAM PILLAY, *Secretary*; C. RAMALINGA IYER; M. CHENKAKESAVA IYENGAR; GUFFUR KHAN SAHIB BAHADUR; S. PARAMASIVA GOUNDEN; MAHALINGA IYER; [illegible] IYER, VENGAPATHY CHETTIAR, and five others.

The forty-pillared Mantapam (or pavilion) opposite to the Kylasanadhaswami's temple was tastefully decorated, and a Pandal had been erected in front of it. At the entrance to this Pandal a triumphal arch had been put up, bearing the inscription, "Long live our Empress." In the morning of the 16th February the members of the Committee attended the Mantapam in full dress. Some of the Zemindars of Pokkampalayam and Puthoor took part in the rejoicing. Money was given to the trustees of the temples to have *abhishekams* and *poojahs* performed, and prayers offered for the long life and prosperity of Her Majesty. The chief residents of the town took their seats on the beautifully matted and carpeted floor of the Mantapam, and large crowds of people collected around. There was also a very large gathering of mendicants. From 6.30 to 7 A.M. there was a parade of the Police Force in front of the Pandal. From 7 to 9 o'clock cloths were distributed to poor people. This was followed by the feeding of a large number of poor people. The members of the Committee, numerous Zemindars, officials, merchants and others, accompanied by a great concourse of people who had come in from the surrounding villages, went in procession with music to the place where the feeding took place. At 10 o'clock the people went home, and re-assembled at the Mantapam at 1 P.M. The proceedings began with a short musical entertainment and the beating of drums. The Honorary Secretary brought a portrait of the Queen Empress from the Reading Room Hall in grand procession to the Mantapam, and placed it on an elevated pedestal that had been prepared for it, while all the people stood up. Two Police Peons were posted on the right and left side of the portrait with drawn swords as a guard of honour. From 2 to 5 P.M. there was an entertainment of vocal and instrumental music by dancing-girls and vocalists. The portrait was taken back to the Reading Room at 5.30 P.M., with much ceremony. At night there was a grand illumination of the temples, mosques, and houses in all the streets. The Mantapam was also beautifully lit up. At 8 P.M. there was a nautch, which terminated with a liberal distribution of betel-nut, sandal, and the sprinkling of rose-water, and with three enthusiastic cheers for the Queen Empress. The party broke up at 1 A.M. The Presidencial Address was adopted. From 6 to 7 P.M. on the following day sugar and plantains were distributed to schoolboys and girls. The Zemindar has promised to give a house for a "Chuttram" in commemoration of the Jubilee.

TRICHINOPOLY (TOWN).

Trichinoply, the head-quarters of the District of the same name, is situated on the southern bank of the Cauvery, at a distance of about 56 miles from the sea at its nearest point. The most important feature in the town is the Rock in the centre of the Fort, rising abruptly out of the plain to a height of 273 feet above the level of the street at its foot. Upon it is a Siva Temple, and at the top is a small Temple dedicated to Ganesa. The population is 84,449. Hindus number 71,996, Mohammedans 11,993, and Christians and others 460. There is a fair sprinkling of Europeans. The town possesses two First Grade Colleges—the S.P.G. and the St. Joseph's—a National High School, under purely native management, forty-five Middle and Primary Schools with a strength of 2,413 pupils, and eleven Girls' Schools. Trichinopoly is the seat of a Municipality, a District Board, and a Taluk Board. The chief manufacture in the town is that of cigars. There is also a considerable trade in gold and silver jewellery.

Jubilee Committee.—Messrs. G. D. IRVINE, *Chairman*; W. F. AUSTIN; COLONEL J. H. M. BARNETT; MAJOR A. C. SMITH; THE REV. F. PENNY; Messrs. T. M. SWAMINATHA IYER; W. S. BETTS; MAJOR D. HEMMING; THE REV. H. A. WILLIAMS; THE REV. FATHER SEWELL; THE REV. R. S. BOULTER, and others.

At 6 A.M. on the 16th February the Volunteers and a detachment of the 4th Madras Pioneers were paraded. The troops fired a *feu de joie*, the band played "God save the Queen" and the troops marched past. At 7.30 there was a Thanksgiving

Service at St. John's church, which was well attended, and to which the Volunteers were marched. At the conclusion of the service the congregation, led by the choir, sang the National Anthem with much heartiness. The day was taken up with feeding and clothing the poor; and a number of prisoners were released. There were rejoicings and festivities among the Native Christian boys and girls in the S.P.G. Boarding Schools, and cloths were distributed to poor children. In the afternoon a Gymkhana meeting was held on the race-course, and the Sepoys of the 4th Madras Pioneers had two hours of sports and foot-racing. The Rock was beautifully lighted up after dark, and looked like a fairy picture printed in soft mellow light, upon the dark moonless sky. The Teppacolum at the foot of the Rock was also illuminated, and coloured lights were burnt in the Mantapam in the centre of the tank. The reflection of the lights on the water added greatly to the beauty of the scene. Fireworks were let off from the roof of the small temple of Ganesa on the summit of the Rock. A Pandal had been erected on the wall of the gateway. Here were assembled several of the chief native gentlemen of the neighbourhood. Mr. Irvine, the District Judge, read the Presidencial Address, which was adopted, and the audience gave three enthusiastic cheers for Her Majesty. Then came the presentation of the usual garlands, and the sprinkling of rose-water. On the following afternoon Mr. Austin, the Collector, drove to Wariore to assist in the ceremony of laying the foundation stone of a "Branch Dispensary," which is to be the local permanent memorial of the Jubilee. An address was read by Mr. V. Muthuswami Iyer. The Collector then laid the stone, first placing beneath it a bottle containing coins of the realm, a number of the current *Fort St. George Gazette*, a pearl, and some precious stones. Mortar was daubed over the stone, and three Masonic taps given with the handle of a silver trowel made for the occasion. At the conclusion of the ceremony there was some native music. The celebration terminated with a dance at the Public Rooms.

TUTICORIN (TINNEVELLY).

Tuticorin is the southern terminus of the South Indian Railway, and has a population numbering 16,281. It is provided with a First Grade College—the Caldwell College—the students of which are for the most part Christians, who receive secular and religious training to fit them for Mission work. There is also a Second Grade Normal School attached to the College, besides two Branch Schools. In addition to these there are Schools connected with the French and Chinese Missions, and a small Hindu School. Two hundred girls are being educated by the S.P.G., and a Normal School for training Schoolmistresses is soon to be opened. The Roman Catholic Missions also teach a number of girls. Cotton and palmyra sugar are largely exported.

A salute of 31 guns was fired at sunrise on the 16th February, and the town and shipping assumed a gay appearance, the latter being dressed in bunting. The College students hoisted a red ensign, gave three cheers for the Queen Empress, and sang the National Anthem. Thanksgiving Services were held in the English church by the Rev. J. A. Sharrock, of the S.P.G., and in the Tamil church by the Rev. D. Samuel, B.D. High Mass was said in the two Roman Catholic churches. After the early services, about 1,300 Children from all the Schools, went in procession round the town, headed by a band, and carrying banners. Sweetmeats and fruits were subsequently distributed among them. Some 1,303 poor people were served with rice. The Volunteers paraded, and fired a *feu de joie*. A public meeting took place in the afternoon in the College Hall, which was beautifully decorated with flags and flowers, and was crowded with visitors. All classes were well represented. The Chairman explained what steps had been decided on by the Executive Committee, and then the Secretary read the Presidencial Address to Her Majesty. This was received with acclamation. The Right Rev. Bishop Caldwell delivered an excellent speech, and was followed by Mr. Iyemperumal Pillai, and the Rev. D. Samuel, B.D., who spoke in Tamil. Glees were sung by the College choir, and native instrumental music was performed. Mr. Lazarus' Tamil translation of "God save the Queen" was then sung with great heartiness. Three cheers were given for Her Majesty; and the meeting terminated with the distribution of betel, &c. There were gymnastics, sports, and a display of fireworks at night. The permanent memorial is to take the shape of a "Storage Tank" to keep the town supplied with water throughout the year; and a tablet bearing an appropriate inscription is to be put up in a prominent position near the tank to commemorate its origin.

UDAMALPET (COIMBATORE).

The population of this town is 8,627, of whom a third are engaged in commerce, another third in agriculture, and the remainder in handicrafts. There are a Local Fund High School, a Primary School, and Girls' School, besides several smaller Pial Schools. There is a Civil Dispensary which, with the High School, has now come under the management of the Taluk Board.

Jubilee Committee.—Messrs. T. Ramasawmier, *Chairman*; N. Kandasawmy Mudelliar, B.A., *Secretary*; R. Ramachendrier; A. Venkatasubbiar; C. Devarajolu Naidoo; M. C. Ramasawmy Iyer, and sixteen others.

Invitations by beat of tom-tom had been made to the inhabitants to have their houses whitewashed, and the streets cleaned, to erect triumphal arches and Pandals at intervals, to decorate the town profusely with *thoranams*, and to illuminate it at night. At daybreak on the 16th February an Imperial salute of 101 guns was fired. The members of the Jubilee Committee and the leading inhabitants proceeded to the High School premises, where the boys and girls were assembled in holiday attire with their teachers. A treat to children formed the first of the festivities of the day. A large concourse of people had assembled to witness the distribution of sugar-candy, plantains, and sugar to the children, who, on receiving the good things, shouted, "Long live our Empress," at frequent intervals. The gentlemen present now formed a procession, headed by the peons and dalayets of the public offices, and marched towards the Local Fund Choultry where meals were being prepared for distribution to the poor. It was about 10 A.M. by this time. The party passed beneath beautifully decorated arches and *thoranams* to the temples of Siva and Mari-Amman, and there offered their prayers, with appropriate ceremonies, for the long life and prosperity of Her Majesty and the Royal Family. *Abishekams* and *archanas* were performed in the name of the Queen Empress. Special Thanksgiving Services were also held in the churches and mosques of the town. The procession retraced its steps to the School Hall, paying visits to the mosque and Bajanai Matam, on its way, and the people returned to their homes at about 11 A.M. The Tahsildar gave a feast at his house to nearly 400 Brahmins; about 200 Naidus were entertained by the Inspector of Police; about 150 Sivites had a repast provided for them at the house of Mr. Muniappa Pillai, pleader; and about 500 Chetties were treated by Mr. N. Ramalinga Chettiar. As many as 1,335 poor people of all castes were fed. The people afterwards re-assembled in the spacious School Hall, where a band of musicians was in attendance throughout the day. The Hall was prettily decorated. A triumphal arch with flowing pennons had been erected at the entrance, on which was traced in golden characters, the inscription "Long live our Empress Victoria." In the middle of the hall was placed a *Chithira Vimanum* (a representation of a vehicle in which the gods are carried in procession). It was adorned profusely with flowers, and inside it were placed portraits of Her Majesty, and of the Royal Family. The Hall was crowded. Sandal, *pan supari*, flowers, and rose-water were distributed, and Hindu songs were sung. The Police Force presented arms in front of the portraits, and went through a series of manœuvres, after which they fired a *feu de joie*. At 7.30 P.M. the Hall was brilliantly illuminated by lights of every description, and was again crowded. The Chairman of the Jubilee Committee having taken his seat amid loud cheers, the Police again stepped forward, and presented arms. A paper, setting forth the principal events in Her Majesty's life, and alluding especially to her motherly and womanly virtues, and her solicitude for the well-being of the millions of her subjects, was read in Tamil, by Mr. T. N. Subbiar, of the Local Fund High School. This was followed by an English address on the same subject by Mr. Rajagopala Chari, B.A. Mr. Syed Makhdoom Sahib read a short essay in Persian on the blessings that had been derived by India during Her Majesty's reign. Two Tamil verses, composed by Mr. Muniappa Pillai, a Tamil Pundit, were recited. The Head Master of the School, Mr. Ramasawmier, then read aloud the Presidencial Address, and a Tamil translation thereof, and explained how it was proposed to be placed at the foot of the Throne. The signatures of the Chairman and three other non-official gentlemen of the taluk were taken with the unanimous consent of the assembly, who cheered loudly, and cried, "Long live our Queen Empress." The portraits of Her Majesty and of the Royal Family were then placed in a beautifully decorated palanquin, and carried in procession through the principal streets of the town which were now illuminated. The crowd was immense, many persons having come in from the surrounding villages. The procession started at 10 P.M., and blue lights were burnt, and fireworks let off at intervals. The "Victoria Jubilee Lamp," which had been erected by the Inspector of Police in front of his house in commemoration of the event, was greeted with acclamation. The procession returned at 3.30 A.M. to the School. A beautiful display of fireworks then took place on the open space in front of the School. *Pan supari* was distributed; and the people having given three enthusiastic cheers for Her Majesty, dispersed about 5 A.M. They re-assembled in the School Hall at 4.30 P.M. on the 17th, to witness the distribution of prizes to the deserving girls of the school. In the course of the proceedings the Taluk Sheristadar, speaking in Tamil, extolled the British Government for the benevolent character of its institutions, and explained, by a Sanscrit *slokam*, the divine right of Kings to the homage of the people. Some music followed, after which *pan supari* and flowers were distributed, and the festivities terminated with cheers for Her Majesty. The permanent memorial will take the form of "Prizes" in the Girls' School, which in future will be known as "The Victoria Jubilee Girls' School."

UDIPI (SOUTH CANARA).

Udipi is a town of some importance, 36 miles from Mangalore. It contains a Tahsildar's Cutcherry, a District Munsiff's Court, a Registrar's Office, a Post Office, a Dispensary, and a Middle School. The Basel Mission has a Seminary and Orphanage here. The principal traffic carried on is in rice, oil, cocoanuts, &c.

Jubilee Committee.—Messrs. DODDI YOGAPPAH, *Chairman;* C. ANANTHA CHARLU, *Secretary;* ANANTHANAM KRISTNIAH; P. GOPAUL KRISTNIAH; JANGA VENKATASUBBIAH; C. CHALLA PILLAI CHARLU; and SREENIVASA CHARLU.

Early in the morning of the 16th February a salute of native guns was fired, and at 7 o'clock a service was held in the Mission Church which was numerously attended, and the Canarese version of the National Anthem was sung. *Abishekams* and *utsavams* were performed in the name of the Queen Empress in the temples, and later on a service was held in the Roman Catholic chapel. Food was distributed by the

Temple authorities to the poor of the town. In the evening the European residents met at the house of the Rev. W. Stokes, and after tea, there was a display of fireworks, and a bonfire was kindled. The Presidential Address was adopted. Three hearty cheers were given for Her Majesty, and the proceedings terminated with the singing of the National Anthem. As a permanent memorial of the event a new building which is in course of construction to accommodate an Association, which has been set on foot for the physical and intellectual improvement of the people of this taluk, is to be named the "Victoria Jubilee Club."

USALAMPATTI (MADURA).

This is a small town with 1,700 inhabitants. The people are mostly Kallars, with a sprinkling of Nadars and Vellalars. There are only ten Mohammedan houses in the place.

At noon on the 16th February the feeding of the poor commenced, and 500 people of all castes and creeds were given a hearty meal. At 5 o'clock, the infirm and very needy people, both males and females, were presented with cloths and small pieces of money. At 6 P.M. the town was illuminated. Meanwhile the Zemindar of Cothappanaikanur and other gentlemen from the out-stations, besides the inhabitants of the town, had assembled in front of the Tahsildar's house, from whence they went in procession, with music and fireworks, to the Deputy Tahsildar's Office. A very large crowd had already collected there. The Chairman addressed the assembly, and explained what they had assembled to celebrate. Mr. Anduperumal Pillai gave a short account of the Royal Family, and the benefits that India had derived from the glorious reign of the Queen Empress, who had ever been solicitous for the welfare and prosperity of her Indian subjects. When the assembly was about to disperse, a Mohammedan lad, aged about fifteen, rose, and, holding a paper in his hand, begged the audience to listen to him. He stated that Her Majesty possessed all the attributes of a Sovereign which demanded the loyalty of all her subjects, and proposed a vote of thanks to the members of the Jubilee Committee for their exertions in carrying out the celebration. He then offered a short prayer that the Queen Empress and her Royal Family might be blessed with long life and happiness. The prayer was joined in by all those assembled. The meeting dispersed at 7 P.M., and the procession returned to the Deputy Tahsildar's house. About 70 Brahmins were given a sumptuous meal in honour of the occasion, and 150 poor people of all castes and creeds were fed. At 10 P.M. there was a musical entertainment, which continued till about 1 A.M. The Tamil stanzas which had been composed in honour of the occasion by Mr. T. M. Scott, of Madura, and printed and circulated to all Unions in this district, were sung, and cheers were given for Her Majesty. The Presidencial Address was adopted.

UTTARAMALLUR (CHINGLEPUT).

Uttaramallur is a rich agricultural town with a population of 7,305. Of these 6,893 are Hindus, 105 Muhammadans, and 307 Christians. The Wesleyan Mission has an Anglo-Vernacular School for boys, and there are more than half-a-dozen Pial Schools (Tamil and Telugu), receiving grants from the Local Fund. A few months ago Uttaramallur was constituted a Union under the Local Boards Act. Weaving is carried on to some extent.

Jubilee Committee.—Messrs. T. ALWAR PILLAY, *Chairman*; T. THULASINGAM MUDELLIAR, *Secretary*; A. S. KRISHNASAWMY REDDIYAR; S. PONNUSAWMY PILLAY; A. KANNAIYA NAIDU; C. ISURAPPA MUDELLIAR; A. RANGAIYAR; ACHA TIRUMALAI AIYANGAR; W. AIYADURAI NAIDU, and eleven others.

Poor people of all castes and creeds began to pour into the town from an early hour on the morning of the 16th February, and collected in three places. The manager of the Vishnu temple had the hundred-pillared mantapam cleared out, and a throne for the reception of the god in the evening, was erected on the platform. The Jubilee Committee had a large Pandal erected on the eastern bund of the Utaka Mahadevi Tank. The weavers of Uttaramallur constructed a handsome Pandal in the form of a mantapam on a *maidan* opposite to the Sub-Registrar's office. At about 8 A.M. the gods left their respective temples, and proceeded in procession, with umbrellas, music, and tom-tom, to the Pandals provided for them. There *abishekams* and *prasadams* were performed, and prayers were offered for the long life and prosperity of Her Majesty. The people were then made to sit in rows, and sandal, *pan supari*, rice, ghee, dholl, broth, vegetables, and cakes were distributed. Over 1,300 people were fed. Temple guns were fired from 3 P.M. at intervals of five minutes. At 7 P.M. the gods and goddesses were taken in procession, large crowds following them. The temples were beautifully illuminated. The festivities wound up with a grand display of fireworks. The Presidencial Address was adopted. In honour of the day a Chuttram, now under construction, has been called "The Empress Victoria Chuttram." A granite slab bearing an appropriate inscription in two languages will be placed in a conspicuous part of it.

UTTENKERE (SALEM).

Uttenkere being an adjacent taluk, and a part of the Head-Assistant Collector's division, a small sum allotted for local celebration from the Tirupatur Jubilee Fund was contributed towards the feeding of the poor, and a treat for school children at the town of the same name. About 1,000 poor were fed in the Local Fund

Choultry. Meetings were held on the evenings of the 16th and 17th February, all the officials, and nearly all the inhabitants of the town being present. Speeches were made in English and Tamil, and the National Anthem was sung. The Presidencial Address was adopted. The local Police paraded, and fired a *feu de joie.* Oranges, sweetmeats, and bananas were distributed to the schoolboys, and cloths to the poor. Sandal and *pan supari* were served to the audience. A procession went round the town with flags and music.

VALLAM (TANJORE).

The festivities on the 16th February included the distribution of food and cloths to 500 poor people of all nationalities; a musical entertainment; fireworks; and Thanksgiving Services in the mosques, temples, and other religious institutions. The feeding of the poor occupied a considerable portion of the forenoon, and after that was over, the Deputy Tahsildar, accompanied by all the members of the "Union," went to the Collector's bungalow, and conducted the Collector, Mr. E. Gibson, in procession to the handsome Pandal where a musical entertainment was to be given. There were more than 1,000 spectators; the Pandal was crowded, and many persons had to stand outside. When darkness set in there was a display of fireworks, at the close of which the Deputy Tahsildar placed handsome garlands of flowers round the necks of the Collector, the chief local representative of the Queen Empress, and the other European gentlemen present. A free distribution of sandal, flowers, *pan supari*, and the sprinkling of rose-water concluded the proceedings. The Presdencial Address was adopted.

VANIYAMBADI (SALEM).

The population of this town is 20,468. Besides ten or eleven Results System Primary Schools, there is the London Mission School, teaching up to the Middle School standard. The sanitation of the town is looked after by a Municipal Council of twelve members, of whom three are officials.

Jubilee Committee.—Messrs. C. Soorappa Chariar, *Chairman*; Narasinga Lala and Syed Adam Sahib Bahadur, *Joint Secretaries*; Middakara Zinul-Abideen Sahib Bahadur; J. M. Suviseshamuttu Pillai; Naivasal Jaffer Sahib Bahadur, and others.

Early in the morning of the 16th February rice was distributed to 1,000 poor people of all castes and creeds, in a spacious Pandal that had been erected for the occasion. Each adult received half a measure of rice, and half an anna in cash, while each child received half as much. In the afternoon the children belonging to the Results System Schools assembled in the London Mission School. At a o'clock the boys marched out in procession. Each School carried a banner, which had words of congratulation to the Queen Empress inscribed in golden letters upon it. The procession was headed by a band of native musicians, and accompanied by hundreds of spectators. On the arrival of the procession at the Pandal each boy received a small packet of sweetmeats. The boys were then drilled, and at 3 o'clock sports were held, and Mr. Sootappa Chariar, and Mr. Narasinga Lala Mittadar distributed prizes to the winners. A very large number of spectators were present. Mr. Savishamuttu Pillai read the Presidencial Address in English. A Hindustani translation of it was then read by Mr. Syed Adam Sahib; and Mr. Narasinga Lala read a Tamil translation. The Address was adopted, and signed amidst enthusiastic cheering. Betel nut, sandal, and bananas were then distributed to all present, and rose-water was sprinkled. There was then a display of fireworks. At 9.30 P.M. there was a gymnastic performance.

VAYITRI (MALABAR).

Vayitri is the most important town, next to Manantoddy, in the Wynaad. It is the centre of the coffee industry, and has a population of 5,779, consisting of Hindus, Mohammedans and Christians. It has a Deputy Tahsildar's Office, a District Munsiff's Court, a Sub-Registrar's Office, and a combined Post and Telegraph Office. There is a Club for European planters at Pukote on the banks of a lake.

Jubilee Committee.—W. E. UNDERWOOD, *Chairman*; S. ANANTA PATTER and V. BAPPU, District Munsiff, *Joint Secretaries*; P. THIAGARAJA MUDELIYAR; W. P. DAMODARAM; B. BAPPU; THANU CHETTY; SHAMU PATTER; HUSSAN RAVUTHAN; AHMED KHAN, and eight others.

The celebration commenced in the morning of the 16th February with acrobatic performances, and a match at the Rifle Range for a silver cup and money prizes presented by the officers of the Wynaad detachment of the Mercara Volunteer Rifles. At noon there was a Jubilee Thanksgiving Service, conducted by the Chaplain of Calicut. At 3 P.M. the Volunteers "fell in," fired a *feu de joie*, marched past, &c. The parade was followed by athletic sports which lasted nearly till dusk, when the prizes were presented by Mr. Underwood. The town was well illuminated at night; the poor were fed; and cloths were distributed. The Presidencial Address was adopted.

VEDARNIAM (TANJORE).

Vedarniam is a small town on the sea-coast, about thirty miles south of Negapatam. The population is about 2,000. There is a small school which teaches up to the Fourth Standard. The affairs of the town are managed by a Union Panchayet. Vedarniam carries on a rather extensive trade in salt and tobacco.

The bells at the temple chimed at 5 A.M. on the 16th February to call the worshippers to offer their prayers for the long life of their Sovereign. When the prayers and *pujahs* were over, an Imperial salute of 101 guns was fired from the temple swivels, followed by a *feu de joie* fired by the local Salt and Police Contingent. The assembly then moved to the handsome Pandal that had been erected for the occasion, where speeches were made by several official and non-official native gentlemen, all of whom gratefully acknowledged the benefits the country had enjoyed under Her Majesty's rule. The speeches were received with great applause. A singing entertainment followed, and Jubilee odes composed for the occasion were sung to a musical accompaniment. Money and cloths were distributed to 300 poor people. The meeting broke up at noon, after the distribution of sandal and *pan supari* and the sprinkling of rose-water. In the evening at about 5 P.M., the Mohammedans of an adjacent village, Thoputhorai, entertained the public with single-stick, double-stick, fencing, and other athletic feats. At 8 P.M. there was a torchlight procession round the town, preceded by musicians and dancing-girls. The procession halted at several places, and gave frequent cheers for Her Majesty as they moved along the illuminated and decorated streets. The procession returned at 10 P.M. to the Jubilee Pandal, and a grand display of fireworks followed, which lasted till 11 P.M. The Presidencial Address was adopted. At 5 P.M. on the 17th, there were sports, and at 9 P.M. there was a nautch party, which continued till close upon midnight. Great enthusiasm prevailed throughout the proceedings.

VELLORE (NORTH ARCOT).

The population of Vellore is 37,491; of whom 27,509 are Hindus, 8,296 are Mohammedans, and 1,686 are Europeans, Eurasians, and Native Christians. The Schools are numerous. They include several Mission Schools, the Hindu Union High School, the Native High School, six Municipal Schools for all creeds, and one for Mohammedans especially, the Government Girls' School, and several small Schools which receive grants from the Municipality. The town carries on a very large trade in rice and other grains, jaggery, and indigo. The principal industry in Vellore is the making of brass utensils. Woollen-pile carpets and cotton durries are manufactured in the Central Jail; the former are in great demand not only in India, but also in Europe.

Jubilee Committee.—Messrs. G. W. FAWCETT, *Chairman*; R. PEMBERTON, *Secretary*; C. E. SAUNDERS; SUBRAMANIA SASTRIAR, B.A., B.L.; V. DESIKACHARLU; C. NARASIMHACHARIA KOTIAH; SUBADAR MAJOR SHAIK BABOON SAHIB; SUBADAR AHMED KHAN, and thirty-one others.

The festivities commenced on the 16th February by a Parade, in the Fort, of the Sepoys attached to the depots of the 15th and 17th Madras Infantry Regiments, and the details of other Regiments in the station. A *feu de joie* was fired, and three hearty cheers were given for the Queen Empress. At the conclusion of the parade, a Thanksgiving Service was held in St. John's church. Between 9 A.M. and 3 P.M. about 4,000 poor people were fed; the Mohammedans in the Huzerath Mahkahn, the Hindus in Kandaraja Choultry, and other castes in Messrs. V. Doorasawmy and Co.'s compound in the Officers' lines. From 3.30 to 6.30 P.M. there were sports on the parade-ground, and at the close of the meeting Mrs. Fawcett presented the prizes to the successful competitors. After dusk the temples and mosques, the parade-ground, the fort, the hill, and all public and private buildings were brightly illuminated, and at 9.30 there was a grand display of fireworks. The Family Guards of the 3rd, 5th, and 16th Regiments, each consisting of one Native Officer, one Havildar, and 12 privates, fed the poor in their lines. The depots of the 17th and 15th Regiments had a feast in their lines, to which they invited the Guards of the other Regiments. There was another display of fireworks on the night of the 17th. The Presidencial Address was adopted. Two of the Hindu members of the community—Messrs. Nathamuni Moodely and Veerasawmy Moodely—placed Rs. 500 at the disposal of the Committee to erect a "Water Pandal" to be named the "Jubilee Pandal." The foundation stone was laid by the two donors on the 16th with some ceremony. Subscriptions are now being raised to erect a "Town Hall."

VENUKONDA (KISTNA).

The population of the town of Venukonda is 5,638; of whom 977 are Mohammedans, 3 are Christians, and the remainder are Hindus. The town contains the General Deputy Collector's Office, Taluk Cutcherry, Sub-Registrar's Office, Post Office, Railway Sub-Division Office, Railway Telegraph Office, a Local Fund Dispensary, and a Subsidiary Jail. The educational institutions are :—The Local Fund Middle School; five Results Schools for Boys; a Girls' School; and two Indigenous Schools. The town is famous for its carpets.

The Jubilee was celebrated here on the 16th February with great enthusiasm. Prayers were offered in the temples, mosques, and churches. 1,000 poor people were fed, and cloths were distributed. At night the houses were lit up as at the Dipavali festival. The principal squares, streets, and the Venukonda hill were illuminated. The General Deputy Collector's office compound, and the Taluk Cutcherry were decorated in the daytime, and effectively illuminated at night. There was a display of fireworks. Shikaries fired a *feu de joie* and performed native military manœuvres. A native drama was played by the Ellore Theatrical Company to a large concourse of people, including several European gentlemen, in a Pandal specially erected, and decorated for the purpose. The Presidencial Address was adopted. On the night of the 17th there was a second display of fireworks, and the native community of the town and of the surrounding villages, met again in the Pandal to witness a dramatic performance. A "Jubilee Choultry" is to be erected in the new Soorisrow Pettah, to permanently memorialise the event.

VIZAGAPATAM (TOWN).

Vizagapatam, the head-quarters of the District of the same name, contains a population of 30,291 souls. These are divided thus: 26,264 Hindus, 2,606 Mohammedans, 1,389 Christians, and 32 others. The education of the town is amply provided for by the Hindu College, the London Mission High School, St. Aloysius School, St. John's School, several Primary Schools, a Normal School, four Girls' Schools, a Mohammedan Boys' School, and a Girls' School. The Municipality enjoys the right to elect its own Chairman, and three-fourths of its members. The town has a first-class Civil Dispensary, a Roman Catholic Orphanage, a Protestant Orphanage, and a native Poor House. Jaggery, gingelly seeds, myrabolams, hides, skins, grey cotton piece-goods, horns and turmeric are largely exported. The chief articles of import are apparel, cotton twist, piece-goods, corals, metals, spices. The town is celebrated for its gold and silver jewellery, and for its manufactures in ivory, horn, and porcupine quills.

Jubilee Committee.—RAJAH GAJAPATI ROW, *Chairman*; Messrs. TUMMALAPALLI RAMAMURTI PUNTALU and VEPA KRISHNAMARTI PUNTALU, M.A., *Joint Secretaries*; H. J. TURNER; NADIPILLI CHINA NARASIMHULU CHETTY; K. RAMALINGA SASTRI; P. PURNAIYA PUNTALU; A. SAMBAMURTI IYER, and four others.

The programme included a Volunteer parade, a feast to the poor, a Durbar, fireworks, a nautch, &c. The Durbar was held at 4 P.M. on the 16th February, the chair being taken by the District Judge, who delivered an appropriate speech. The Presidencial Address was read in English, Telugu, and Urdu, and received with cheers. Music, both Indian and European, followed, after which *pan supari*, betel, and rose-water were distributed. At 7.45 P.M. Rajah Gujapatee Rao entertained the Europeans at a banquet. Mr. Turner, the Collector of the District, placed his house at the disposal of the Rajah for the purpose. Covers were laid for forty guests. The speech by the Collector, who proposed Her Majesty's health, was received with the greatest enthusiasm, the band playing the National Anthem. The Queen's health having been drunk, Mr. Kelsall, the District Judge, proposed the health of Rajah Gujapatee Rao, to which the latter responded in eloquent terms. Mr. Turner then proposed the health of the Rajah of Bobbily and other distinguished visitors of the evening. After some other toasts the loving cup was passed round. Many of the guests now attended a nautch which had been provided by the Jubilee Committee in Vizagapatam. The festivities wound up with fireworks, a nautch, and a Hindu dramatic representation of the earthly career of Kristna. On the 17th a feast was given to children. At the Durbar it was announced that Mr. A. V. Narsinga Rao had founded a Scholarship in connection with the High School, to be called the "Autkethum Jubilee Endowment Scholarship." The Mohammedan community opened a "Reading Room" in honour of the Jubilee for the benefit of its own members. The form which the permanent memorial will take has not yet been decided. The "Water Supply" of the town will be improved, or a "Chuttram" will be built.

VIZIANAGRAM (VIZAGAPATAM).

The population of the town and cantonment of Vizianagram is 30,000, consisting of Hindus, Mohammedans and Christians. The town contains one First Grade College, one Boarding Girls' School, and one Native Girls' School, besides three Municipal Schools, the Ripon Hindu School, and an Industrial School. There are also two Schools in the cantonment. There is an English weekly newspaper in the town, and there are two Political Associations. The new scheme of Local Self-Government has been successfully introduced. The town is rising in commercial importance. Rice, gingelly seeds, indigo, jaggery, myrabolums, hides, horns, lac, jute, and other articles are largely exported. There is an extensive market, erected by the late Maharajah of Vizianagram in memory of the visit to India of H.R.H. the Prince of Wales. There are three native Banks. Articles made of ivory and horns, embroidery, carpets, furniture, lace, caps, porcelain, native musical instruments, &c., are manufactured.

Jubilee Committee.—Messrs. Rai Bahadur Sri P. Jagannadha Raju Sahib, *Chairman*; A. Venkatarow Puntalu, *Secretary*; K. Ramanuja Chariar, M.A., B.L.; V. Madhava Row, M.A.; K. Narayanaswami Naidu; P. Sattiah; Aga Syed Mahomed Sahib; V. Venkata Krishnamaraju, and eleven others.

Early in the morning of the 16th February the festivities began with a salute of 101 guns from the bastions of the Maharajah's fort. Between 7 and 9 A.M. Divine Service was held in all the temples and mosques for the prosperity of the Queen Empress and the Royal Family. 1,500 schoolboys and girls of the town and cantonment were treated to Benares sweetmeats. Country sweetmeats and sugar were distributed to about 3,000 children of the town and cantonment. Under the orders of Her Highness the Maharani Sahib 5,000 people, of whom 3,000 were Rajputs, 500 Brahmins, and 1,500 other castes, were fed, and cloths were distributed to the most necessitous. A grand Durbar was held under a spacious Shamiana that had been erected on the *maidan* in front of the Fort. A very large gathering of people assembled there. The Dewan, Rai Bahadur Sri P. Jagannadha Raju Sahib, took the chair. Appropriate speeches were delivered by Mr. C. Subbiah Sastri, District Munsiff, Mr. K. Venkanniah Puntalu, and others. A short sketch of Her Majesty's life was read, both in English and Telugu. Verses in English, Sanscrit, and Telugu were recited. Mr. V. Jagannadha Rao Puntalu, the Divisional Officer, then read the Presidential Address, which was adopted amid enthusiastic cheers. Verses were sung in praise of Her Majesty, and Native music was played at intervals. A nautch then followed, at the close of which *pan supari*, attar, garlands, &c., were distributed. In the evening there was a grand procession of the Maharajah's State elephants, camels, horses, carriages, troopers, infantry, and band. A very large concourse of people attended. There were fireworks and other illuminations at intervals. A State elephant, with a golden howdah upon it, bearing the portrait of the Queen Empress, headed the procession, followed by the European and Native officers of the Regiment on elephants and in carriages. Other gentlemen followed in carriages. The Police and Sepoys lined the road on both sides. The procession was a mile long. It started from the Shamiana at 5 P.M. and went towards the Fort gate by the Industrial School to the cantonment, passing through which it entered the town near a triumphal arch on the main road, near the Maharajah's Dispensary. Thence it proceeded through the main road of Swetapettah, and after stopping a short time at the Clock Tower, it moved on to the open space near the Big Tank, where there was a grand display of fireworks at half-past 8 o'clock P.M. The fireworks were followed by a Native musical entertainment in the Durbar tent, which continued till midnight. On the afternoon of the 17th from 2 to 6 P.M. there were athletic sports, racing, wrestling, long jump, &c. A large number of people witnessed the sports, at the conclusion of which they gave three cheers for the Queen Empress, the Viceroy, the Governor, the Maharajah, and the Maharani Sahib, the mother of His Highness. At night four dramatic performances were given in various parts of the town and cantonment to crowded audiences. There was a brilliant gathering in the Durbar tent, which was splendidly decorated and illuminated. In commemoration of Her Majesty's Jubilee the tops of almost all the principal temples and mosques are to be plated with brass sheets, and to receive certain improvements at a cost to the Maharajah of Rs. 10,000. His Highness also made a munificent donation, in his mother's name, to the Imperial and the Madras Institutes; devoted a large sum towards the maintenance of temples, and the support of poor families; and remitted nearly four lakhs of revenue due by his ryots. Rai Bahadur Sri P. Jagannadha Raju Sahib, Dewan to His Highness, presented land valued at Rs. 12,000, and yielding an annual income of Rs. 600, for the benefit of 25 families, viz. : 6 Brahmins, 12 Kschatrias, 6 Valams, and one Baniyan.

VRIDHACHALAM (SOUTH ARCOT).

Vridhachalam is 38 miles south-west of Cuddalore. The population is 7,347, composed for the most part of Hindus. The town includes a large suburb, called Pudupet, on the east bank of the river, and was with two small adjacent villages, viz., Munaluor and Pocathorum, constituted a Union last year. The trade is chiefly in grain and ground nuts which are largely exported to Cuddalore, Panruti, and Pondicherry. Vridhachalam is the head-quarters of the Head-Assistant Collector of the Taluk Board; of the D.P.W. Sub-division, &c. It contains a Tahsildar's Cutcherry, Sub-Jail,

District Munsiff's Court, Local Fund Hospital, Sub-Registrar's Office, Middle School for Boys, Girls' School, Post Office, Lutheran Native Mission Chapel, a small Mosque, and two large Chuttrams.

Jubilee Committee.—Messrs. R. FRANKLIN, *Chairman*; C. MURUGESA PILLAY; C. RAMANJULU NAIDU; J. R. KASI ROW; V. MUTHUKUMARA PILLAY; DORAISAWMY IYER, and others.

At an early hour on the 16th February large crowds congregated to take part in the festivities. Prayers were offered in the five Hindu temples for the welfare and long life of Her Majesty, and the gods were taken round the town in procession. The poor of all classes were fed, and some of them were presented with cloths and money. Sports of various kinds were held in the forenoon, and prizes were awarded. There were other processions in the evening, and at night the streets and temples were brilliantly illuminated. As darkness set in there was a display of fireworks, and several bonfires were lit, after which there were nautches and dramatic performances, which lasted till past midnight. The poor were again fed on the following day. The Presidencial Address was adopted.

WALAJAPET (NORTH ARCOT).

Walajapet has a population of 10,387; of whom 9,566 are Hindus, 803 Mohammedans, and 18 Christians. It has a Municipal Council, and is the head-quarters of the Tahsildar and Police Inspector. A Dispensary and a High School are under the management of the Municipality. Silk-weaving, carpet making, and dyeing are carried on to a considerable extent. Silk cloths manufactured here are much valued for their durability.

Jubilee Committee.—Messrs. V. BASHIAKA CHARLU, *Chairman*, S. SWAMINATHA AIYAR, *Secretary*; T. SRINIVASA ROW; A. RAJARUTHNA MUDELLIAR; RANGANATHA ROW; SUNDERA ROW, and ten others.

Almost every house was more or less decorated, the most attractive being the Post Office, which was particularly well embellished. In the morning of the 16th February 500 poor were fed, and to about 100 of them cloths were distributed. At 4 P.M. the leading men of the place met at the High School house, and witnessed a gymnastic competition among the boys. Two odes, in Tamil and Telugu, composed in honour of the occasion, describing the principal features of Her Majesty's reign, were sung by boys, and cheers were called for, which were responded to very heartily. The boys were then given sweetmeats, sugar-candy, toys, &c. A procession was formed with tom-toms and music, which passed through the principal streets of the place. It eventually reached the Jubilee Pandal which had been erected outside the town, where several European gentlemen from Ranipet joined it. In the centre of the Pandal was placed a portrait of Her Majesty. A nautch was held, and then the whole assembly adjourned to the adjacent open space where a good display of fireworks took place. The Presidencial Address was adopted. The permanent memorial of the Jubilee will take the form of a "Public Hall" with a "Reading Room" attached to it.

WALVANAD (MALABAR).

Angadipuram is the chief town of the Walvanad taluk. The population of the amshoms of Angadipuram and Perintalmanna, on the borders of which Her Majesty's Jubilee was celebrated, is 12,860; of whom 7,401 are Hindus, 5,439 Mohammedans (most of whom are Moplahs), and 20 Christians. Angadipuram contains a Tahsildar's Cutcherry, a District Munsiff's Court, a Sub-Registrar's Office, a Local Fund Middle School, a Local Fund Supervisor's Office, a Local Fund Overseer's Office and a Post Office. Besides the Middle School there are six Elementary Schools for boys, aided by the Local Fund. The town trades chiefly in paddy, pepper, ginger, and timber.

Jubilee Committee.—Messrs. KUNHUNNI RAJAH, *Chairman*; KRISHNA VADIER KASI IYER and PADINJARACALATHIL GOVINDAN NAIR, *Joint Secretaries*; KANNAMBATH VADAKAIL CHAPPUN NAIR; VUDUNATHA PUTTER; NARAYANA PUTTER; THAZHE KOONJAMBOO; VENGALIL RAMAN MENON, and ten others.

Pujahs were performed in three temples for the prolongation of the happy life and reign of Her Majesty. A service was held by the Native Christians, and a *mouluth* was offered by the Mohammedans to the same effect. Rice, cloths, and money were distributed to the poor from 7 to 11 A.M. on the 16th February. A treat was given to the schoolboys, and to the prisoners in the Sub-Jail. Theatricals, gymnastics, and fireworks followed. The Presidencial Address was adopted. The town was well decorated and illuminated.

WANDIWASH (NORTH ARCOT).

Wandiwash is a historic town in the district of North Arcot, with 4,130 inhabitants; of whom 3,339 are Hindus, 709 Mohammedans, 32 Christians, and 50 Jains. Nearly one-fourth of the inhabitants are merchants. The local products are ground-nut seeds, indigo, cholum and rice. The chief manufactures are mats, and coarse kinds of cotton cloth. There are two or three tanneries. The town forms a minor Union, with one Chairman and five Panchayetdars, nominated by the Government. It contains a Local Fund Middle School, where boys and girls are under instruction.

At 3 P.M. on the 16th February about 500 of the inhabitants assembled in the School playground, Mr. V. Subramaniah Sastriar was voted to the chair. In opening the proceedings, he spoke at length about the advantages of British rule, and the duty of showing gratitude to Her Majesty. Then the life of the Queen Empress in Tamil was read. The Presidencial Address was read by Mr. K. Gopalachariar, Taluk Sheristadar, and was received with much cheering. Several speeches were made in Tamil and English, after which sandal, sugar, and *pan supari* were distributed, and the party went in procession to the Temple. At 9 o'clock there was a good display of fireworks, and a procession of gods. The festivities continued until midnight. The assembly dispersed with cheers for her Majesty.

VERCAUD (SALEM).

The population of the Shevaroy Hills is 10,513, chiefly composed of Malayalies or Hill men whose sole occupation is cultivation. The Hills produce coffee, wheat, samai, varagu, apples, pears, loquats, peaches, and oranges. Vercaud is the Sanitarium of the District, and the Head-quarters Station of the Planters. It has a population of 1,338; of whom 635 are Hindus, 23 Mohammedans, and 680 Christians. It contains a Protestant Church, a London Mission Chapel, Lutheran Evangelical Mission Chapel, and a Roman Catholic Chapel; a Library, Cutcherry, a Local Fund Dispensary, a Travellers' Bungalow, and Chuttram; a School for the children of Europeans and Eurasians; and three Schools for Native children.

Jubilee Committee.—Deputy Surgeon General J. SHORTT, *Chairman*; Messrs. E. A. SMITH, *Secretary*, C. O. LECHLER; F. D. SHORTT; K. CHERRY; B. DALY, and others.

On the 16th February Thanksgiving Services were held at Trinity church, the Roman Catholic chapel, the Lutheran Mission chapel, and the London Mission chapel. The Volunteers marched in two sections, one to Trinity church under the command of Lieutenant Shortt, and the other to the Roman Catholic chapel, under the command of Lieutenant MacMahon. On the arrival of the Protestant section of the Volunteers at Trinity church, the Hymn "Onward, Christian Soldiers" was sung. The service concluded with the National Anthem. A large Pavilion had been erected by Lieutenant MacMahon, and had been tastefully decorated by Mrs. MacMahon. About 1 P.M., 3,000 people, mostly Malayalies, Coolies, and other Natives assembled opposite the lake, in the vicinity of the Pavilion, some bearing banners with appropriate devices. The Pavilion contained refreshments, which were kindly provided by the ladies of Vercaud. The sports commenced at 1.30, and were well contested. After the sports there were Malayalee dances and acrobatic performances. The Volunteers paraded at 4 P.M., and fired a *feu de joie*, and three hearty cheers were given for the Queen Empress. About 100 children, chiefly of the London Mission School, and a large number of natives, were treated to sweets, &c. At night there was a brilliant display of fireworks, at the termination of which the National Anthem was sung, and three hearty cheers were given for the Queen Empress. The Presidencial Address was adopted.

THE CELEBRATION IN NATIVE STATES.

THE STATE OF TRAVANCORE.

Travancore, the most important Native State subject to the authority of the Government of Madras, is situated at the south-western corner of the Indian peninsula. It possesses an area of 6,722 square miles, occupied by a population of nearly 2½ millions. More than 20 per cent. of the inhabitants are Christians. Succession to the Raj goes by the female line. The turning point in the history of the State was contemporaneous with the assumption of the direct Government of India by Her Majesty the Queen. Since then, the beneficent moral influence of the Paramount Power has been increasingly brought to bear on the executive, and a vast improvement has taken place in the administration of affairs. Oppressive monopolies have been abandoned; numerous petty and vexatious taxes have been swept away; English and Vernacular schools have been founded throughout the country, with a Central College at the capital; hospitals have been established; a sound system of Police has been established; Public Works have been promoted; the salaries of public servants have been increased; the tone and efficiency of the public service have been raised; the administration of Civil and Criminal Justice has been improved; the reciprocal execution of decrees between the Travancore and British Courts has been arranged; irrigation has been extended; land assessment has been equitably readjusted; trade has expanded; and the finances have attained a condition of much prosperity. The total income of the State twenty years ago was 41 lakhs, against an expenditure of 40½ lakhs; in 1884-85 the revenue was 66¾ lakhs, and the expenditure was 65 lakhs. Taking the revenue derived from all sources—land, customs, excise, abkari, opium, salt, and stamps,—and it is found that the incidence of taxation in Travancore is Rs. 2, against Rs. 2-5-6 in the Madras Presidency. Taking land revenue only, it is Rs. 0-10-1, against Rs. 1-8-8 in Madras.

TRIVANDRUM.

This town is the Capital of Travancore, with a population of 41,173. It is the usual place of residence of the Maharajah, and the head-quarters of the British Resident at His Highness's Court and the principal officers of the State. It is the head-quarters also of the Nayar Brigade, officered from the British Military Service, which consists of two Battalions of Infantry, numbering 1,420 men; Artillery 4 guns and 30 men; Body Guard 60 horses. There are several Palaces in the Fort occupied by the Princes, Ranees, and other members of the Royal Family. The principal buildings are the great Pudmanabaswmy Pagoda, within the Fort, the Public Offices, the Maharajah's College, the Zillah and Moonsiff's Courts, the General and Lying-in Hospitals, the Lunatic Asylum, the Napier Museum, the Observatory, the Protestant and Roman Catholic Churches, the Residency, the Central Jail at Poojapura, and the Engineer's Office. The Educational Institutions are the College, the High School, and the Preparatory School, the Fort and Town High Schools, the Central Vernacular School, the Vernacular Normal School, the Roman Catholic Boys' School, two Hindustani Schools, several Vernacular Grant-in-Aid Schools, including Schools of the London Mission, the Government English School for Girls, the Convent School, three Zenana Mission Schools, and two Government Vernacular Girls' Schools.

Jubilee Committee.—Messrs. T. RAMA ROW, Dewan, *Chairman*; R. RAMANATHA ROW, and Mr. LA BOUCHARDIERE, M.A., *Secretaries*; T. L. GOMEZ; K. KRISHNASAWMY ROW; The VALIA COIL THUMBURAN; Dr. R. HARVEY, M.A.; Messrs. F. WATTS; J. R. NARAYANA PILLAY, and sixteen others.

As soon as it was known that the Viceroy had fixed the 16th February for the celebration of the Jubilee His Highness the Maharajah countermanded the arrangements then in progress for a tour to Madras and Bombay, and commanded his new Dewan M. R. Ry. T. Rama Row Avergal to make preparations for commemorating the day in a manner befitting the occasion. The Dewan issued a programme which embraced the observance of the 16th and 17th as public holidays throughout the State, and invitations were issued to the European and principal Native officers at Trivandrum and the out-stations, to the Bishops and Clergy of the Protestant, Roman Catholic, the Syrian Churches, and to the leading merchants, planters, and land-holders to take part in the festivities at the Capital. European ladies were included in the invitation. At sunrise on the 16th the Artillery of the Nayar Brigade fired a salute of 101 guns. At 6 A.M. the Cavalry and Infantry with the Band of the Nayar Brigade took up a position in line on the Brigade Parade-ground, under the command of Lieutenant-Colonel W. D. B. Ketchen, Madras Cavalry, commanding the Brigade. On the arrival of the Maharajah the artillery fired a salute of 21 guns, and the Brigade gave a Royal salute. Mr. Hannyngton, M.C.S., the British Resident, was also received with the usual salute from the troops. The Cavalry and Infantry then formed up for marching, the Cavalry in column of troops, the Infantry in quarter column on the right company, and moved off to the saluting base, the Cavalry by troops, and marched past by squadron, the Infantry by fours in quarter column, advancing in column and saluting as they passed the flagstaff near to which His Highness had taken up his position. The Cavalry then moved on to the Parade line while the Infantry changed ranks, and marched past in quarter column, first in quick time and then in double time, wheeling at the end of the saluting base, and on arriving at the fourth point resumed their original position in line. The Cavalry then trotted past, and having wheeled about by troops, galloped past in squadrons. The Infantry were then put through the manual, firing, and sword-bayonet exercise, after which the Cavalry performed the sword exercise and pursuing practice at a walk and in quick time. They then resumed their original position upon the right of the line. The whole Brigade then advanced in review order and gave a Royal salute upon halting before the flagstaff. The Cavalry formed column of troops on the right of the Infantry, who had formed quarter column upon one of the centre companies, officers and colours taking post in review order. The Maharajah then addressed Colonel Ketchen, expressing the greatest satisfaction with the appearance of the troops, and the manner in which they had gone through the several evolutions. At the conclusion of His Highness's address a Royal salute was given, and the troops marched to their barracks. Before leaving the Parade ground the troops gave three hearty cheers for Her Majesty and His Highness. The review was witnessed by the Elliah Rajah, the First Prince, the Dewan, General Hodding (who had come to inspect the Resident's Escort), by many ladies and gentlemen, and a large assemblage of spectators. At 11 A.M. a public breakfast was given at the Dewan's residence to about 300 Hindu officers of the State and other native gentlemen. At 4 P.M. the Maharajah held a Durbar in the Hall of the new Public Offices, for the purpose of receiving from the British Resident a *Kareeta* addressed to His Highness by the Viceroy and Governor-General of India. One battalion of Infantry, one troop of Cavalry, and a detachment of the Artillery (4 guns) again paraded, and were drawn up in the enclosure facing the Durbar Hall. The Resident's Escort took up a position on the left. The State elephants, fully caparisoned, were also on the ground in rear of the troops. The Maharajah, escorted by the Body Guard, and preceded by their Highnesses the Elliah Rajah and the First Prince, arrived shortly before the hour appointed, and was received with a Royal salute from the Artillery and troops. The British Resident came in one of His Highness's carriages, and under an escort of His Highness's Body Guard, the Artillery and troops saluting him. On alighting from the carriage, he was received by the Dewan, and was met at the entrance to the Durbar Hall by the Elliah Rajah, who conducted him to the centre of the Hall, where the Maharajah, after an interchange of greetings, offered his arm, and led him to his seat on the right of the Throne. The company being seated, the *Kareeta* was delivered on a silver salver to His Highness, who opened it, and gave it to the Dewan to be read aloud. It ran as follows :—

"HIS HIGHNESS SRI PADMANABHA DASA VANJI BALA RAMA VARMA KULA-SHEKHERA KIRITA PATHI MANY SULTAN MAHARAJAH RAJ RAMA RAJA BAHADUR SHAMSHER JANG, TRAVANCORE.

"MY HONOURED AND VALUED FRIEND,—It is with sincere pleasure that I have heard of the preparations which Your Highness has made in order to commemorate, in a manner befitting the occasion, the fiftieth year of the reign of Her Most Gracious Majesty the Queen, Empress of India. I shall not fail to inform Her Majesty of this spontaneous expression of loyalty and affection on your part. Queen Victoria's long and tranquil rule has been marked throughout her wide dominions by the ever increasing prosperity and happiness of the millions entrusted to her charge. In India it has established an uninterrupted and unbroken peace; and under its protecting shelter, the ruling Chiefs of this country, undisturbed by the fear of invasion from without, or of revolution from within, have been able to devote their time and attention to the welfare of their subjects and to the moral and material advancement of their States. I am happy to learn that Your Highness has so readily taken the opportunity afforded by this auspicious occasion to show your just appreciation of the great benefits you have experienced under the benign and beneficent rule of Her Majesty the Queen. I can assure you that it is our Gracious Sovereign's desire to extend to you, on all occasions, her warm sympathy and hearty assistance, to support your authority, enhance your personal consideration, and to maintain unbroken the cordial relations which have at all times subsisted between Her Majesty's Government and Your Highness. I desire to express the high consideration which I entertain for Your Highness, and to subscribe myself

"Your Highness's sincere friend,
(Signed) "DUFFERIN,
"Viceroy and Governor General of India.

"Fort William, the 3rd February, 1887."

After the *Kareeta* had been read, the Viceroy's salute of 31 guns was fired with a *feu de joie* after each instalment of the guns, the National Anthem being played; and three cheers were given for Her Majesty the Queen Empress. His Highness the Maharajah then, through the Dewan, addressed the assembly as follows:—

"MR. HANNYNGTON, LADIES AND GENTLEMEN,—I need hardly say how grateful I am for the kindly assurances of good will contained in the letter which I have just had the honour of receiving from His Excellency the Viceroy, and for his appreciation of my humble efforts to celebrate this day in a manner befitting the occasion. I request his Representative, my friend here, to convey to His Excellency my warmest acknowledgments. It has pleased the Almighty to extend to half a century a reign at once beneficent and glorious, and while we unite in thanksgiving for this great mercy, we likewise pray that He may vouchsafe to prolong it to the longest span. We are justly proud of our liege Lady—sitting enthroned on the four quarters of the globe, and on islands in every ocean—sending forth her ships to collect and distribute the material blessings of the earth, and her agents to carry everywhere the still higher blessings which humanize and elevate mankind—herself endowed with every virtue which can adorn a Sovereign, or grace a woman. Her armies have marched to victory over forces mightier than her own, but never for vain-glory—her flag, wherever it flies, is the symbol of protection to the good, and a sign in the air warning the wicked from his evil course. My House has been fortunate enough to ally itself to the great British power in India from the earliest times, and to that alliance I owe the Musnud on which I sit; for it saved the country at a critical time, and has maintained it in peace ever since. To the influence of Her Majesty's supremacy is due also whatever of prosperity and enlightenment Travancore has attained to; for her Representatives have guided our footsteps in the path of progress, and her countrymen have contributed largely to raise our people and develop our resources. It is not, then, surprising, Gentlemen, that bound by these ties of gratitude, I should avail myself of this opportunity to call you together to honour the Lady who commands our highest admiration and respect. To impress the occasion on the minds of all my subjects, I have this day remitted certain arrears of revenue. Nor have the rising generation, nor the poor been forgotten, while a few convicts go free to bless the day. All India rings to-day with a long-drawn shout of '*Vive la Reine*' which the Himalayas will catch up and echo to the countries beyond, till all the world hears it, and hearing, will know that Princes and people are united in one strong bond of loyalty and affection to their beloved Queen. We join in the cheer.

"Christian and Hindu and Moslem are we,
Yet all of us one, in our cheering for thee,
"Victoria.

"Long live Victoria, Queen of England, Empress of India."

At the conclusion of this address, twelve convicts, one of whom was a woman were released, and the following Proclamations were read in Malayalim to the people assembled outside the Hall:—

"PROCLAMATION BY HIS HIGHNESS SRI PATMANABHA DASA VANCHI BALA RAMA VARMA KULASEKHARA KIRITAPATI MANNEY SULTAN MAHARAJA RAJA BAHADUR SHAMSHER JANG, MAHARAJA OF TRAVANCORE, issued under date the 4th Kumbhom 1062.

"Whereas by the Proclamation issued on the 5th Karkadagom 1059 the levying of a fee of 2 per cent. on certain transfers of Pandara Pattom lands was relinquished by the State with effect from the 1st Chingom 1060, and whereas We are given to understand that the fees and penalties on transfers anterior to that date are still being levied, thus causing hardship and trouble to Our ryots, We are pleased, with a view to relieving Our subjects wholly from this impost, to command the relinquishment of the said transfer fee altogether.

SIGN MANUAL."

"PROCLAMATION BY HIS HIGHNESS SRI PATMANABHA DASA VANCHI BALA RAMA VARMA KULASEKHARA KIRITAPATI MANNEY SULTAN MAHARAJA RAJA RAMARAJA BAHADUR SHAMSHER JANG, MAHARAJA OF TRAVANCORE, issued under date the 4th Kumbhom 1062.

"Whereas instruments engrossed on unstamped cadjans are subject to a penalty of 3 per cent. of the consideration recited in the deed, and whereas owing to the enactment of the Registration Regulation of 1043 and the Stamp Regulation of 1059 the practice of engrossing documents on cadjans has ceased; and whereas We have already exempted from the payment of this penalty instruments produced in connection with investigations conducted in the course of the Revenue Settlement now in progress, We are now pleased to relieve Our subjects henceforth from the payment of the above penalty on all documents executed on unstamped cadjans wherever such documents may have to be produced in evidence.

SIGN MANUAL."

Attar and pan were then presented to the Resident, and Mrs. Hannyngton, and to the Commandant of the Nayar Brigade, and Mrs. Ketchen, by His Highness the Maharajah; and to other Europeans by their Highnesses the Elliah Rajah and First Prince. His Highness and the Resident then left the Hall under the usual salutes from the Artillery and troops, and the Durbar broke up.

The same evening, at 8 P.M., the Maharajah gave a State Dinner in the suite of apartments adjoining the Durbar Hall, at which the Elliah Rajah, the First Prince, the Resident and Mrs. Hannyngton, and nearly all the European ladies and gentlemen who had attended the Durbar, were present. The dining saloon was very tastefully decorated. The Durbar Hall itself, which was fitted up as a drawing-room, was brilliantly lighted. The roads in the town, which were gaily decorated during the day, almost at every gate, with plantain trees, evergreens, bannerets and mottoes expressing good wishes for the Queen Empress, were illuminated in the evening for several miles, extending from the landing place beyond the Fort to the Residency, and from Puttum to Tiruvellum. The Palaces, the Residency, the entrance to the Barracks, the residence of the Commandant of the Nayar Brigade, the College, the Police Office and Stores, the Dewan's residence, the Telegraph and Post Offices, and the Public Offices where the dinner was held, were ablaze with light, the latter being hung with festoons of Chinese lanterns along its long verandahs. Private residents vied with the State in demonstrations in this direction, and crowds of people paraded the streets to a late hour of the night. A guard of honour was drawn up in the grounds of the Public Offices, and the Band of the Nayar Brigade played during the dinner. Her Majesty's health was the only toast given during the dinner. It was proposed by His Highness the Maharajah in these words:—

"LADIES AND GENTLEMEN,—I rise to propose the toast of the evening, and I have no doubt as to the manner in which it will be responded to. We celebrate to-day the fiftieth year of a reign which has brought happiness and prosperity to the millions who are fortunate enough to come under the rule of Her Most Gracious Majesty. That rule is synonymous with justice and benevolence, with liberty and toleration, with the suppression of vice, and the elevation of virtue. Hers is a name which can make the tyrant tremble on his throne of misrule, yet send a warm glow into the heart of the lowly cottager, from her sympathy with the poor and the suffering. When we wish and pray for her long reign and happiness, we wish and pray for the continuance of peace and prosperity to a large portion of the human race. Let us then drink to the health of our liege Lady whom we all respect and admire; let us drink to the health of Victoria, Queen of England, Empress of India. Long live the Queen Empress."

The toast was received with hearty cheers, the Band playing the British National Anthem. After the Dinner there was a splendid display of fireworks, which was witnessed by several thousands of spectators. At 4.30 P.M., on the 17th, there were rope dancing and acrobatic performances in the Public Garden, witnessed by a large assemblage composed of all classes. At 7 P.M. Mr. and Mrs. Hannyngton had a dinner party at the Residency to which the European society of Trivandrum and the visitors from out-stations were invited. The Resident proposed Her Majesty's health, which was responded to with hearty cheers, the company singing "God save the Queen." Mr. Hannyngton next proposed His Highness's health:—

"MAHARAJAH, PRINCES, LADIES AND GENTLEMEN,—We have joined in wishing to Her Majesty the Queen Empress of India continuance of life and happiness. We have in our midst this evening, in the person of His Highness the Maharajah of Travancore, one of Her Majesty's most loyal allies. Under Her Majesty's protection, favoured with her friendship and aided by her advice, Travancore holds no mean position among the States of India. The occasion of Her Majesty's Jubilee has afforded to the people of Travancore an opportunity of expressing their loyalty and affection for their friend, counsellor and protector, and this opportunity they have not been slow to grasp. The demonstrations which are being made, not in the Capital alone, but throughout the State, testify to the cordial feeling with which our Queen is regarded by the people of Travancore. As the humble representative of Her Majesty the Empress in this State, I desire to express to His Highness the Maharajah personally, and to the people of Travancore in the person of their

Maharajah, my grateful appreciation of the loyal demonstrations of confidence and affection which have been tendered throughout the State to my Mistress and Queen, and I desire, gentlemen, that you join me in giving three cheers for His Highness the Maharajah of Travancore, and in drinking to his health and prosperity, and to the prosperity and happiness of his people."

The company received the toast with cheers, and His Highness acknowledged the compliment in appropriate words.

At 9.30 P.M. the Public Garden and the Museum were brilliantly illuminated under the direction of Colonel Ketchen, the Honorary Secretary. The whole of the western façade of the Museum, and both the northern and southern ends of the building were lit up, several devices and monograms being conspicuous. All the roads had lights on both sides, and each terrace was illuminated. Along one, in large letters from end to end, were "V.R.I. 1887. Jubilee. 1887. V.R.I." The lower gardens and the upper and lower lakes were lit up. The Chinese Pagoda in the middle of the latter was illuminated from its base to summit. Chinese lanterns were suspended from numerous trees throughout the gardens. Thousands of people visited the gardens. A dancing platform was erected near the Band stand, and dancing was enjoyed by many from 10 P.M. to 2 A.M. Refreshments were laid out in a Pandal. The Maharajah, Mr. and Mrs. Hannyngton, and the party at the Residency visited the garden on their return from the dinner. The same evening, His Highness the Maharajah gave a dinner to the Mohammedan community in a pavilion erected at Chingam Thope. It was presided over by Mr. Syed Abdul Khader, the Stables' Karbari. The troops received a bonus of two days' pay, and the Band three days' pay.

On the morning of the 16th February the poor were fed at the expense of the State at four different places at the Capital, and in the towns of Cottayam, Alleppey, Quilon, and Pulpanabapuram, under the supervision of Government officers. Funds were provided for a treat to the boys and girls attending the public and private schools at Trivandrum, Nagercoil, including Kotar, Parachalay, Neyoor, Quilon, Cottayam, and Tiruvellah.

On the 12th, three of the Schools in the suburbs of Trivandrum connected with the London Mission, assembled at the Mission House, and received a couple of cloths each, after which fruits, cakes, and sweets were distributed, songs were sung, and the Public Gardens visited under the care of the teachers. On the afternoon of the 14th, five other schools, comprising nearly 200 children, were assembled and had various games. "God save the Queen" was sung in Malayalim by the Boarding School children. Prizes of picture books, dolls, &c. were distributed; and cakes, fruits, and sweets were given to all. Each of the girls attending the Zenana Mission schools received a present of money, as it was found difficult to arrange a treat for the different classes attending those schools. The students of His Highness's College, the High School and Preparatory School, as also the pupils of the Government Girls' School in the Cantonment, and of the Roman Catholic Convent School, assembled each on its own grounds on the afternoon of the 19th instant. They had games and races and other sports, up to a late hour in the evening, when refreshments were served, and cheers were given for Her Majesty the Queen Empress, and for His Highness the Maharajah —"God save the Queen" being sung by all. At the College there was vocal and instrumental music, and Dr. Harvey delivered an address appropriate to the occasion. At the Convent School there were magical performances, and an exhibition of the magic-lantern. His Highness the Maharajah and other members of the Royal Family, the British Resident and Mrs. Hannyngton, and several ladies and gentlemen were present at the sports in the College. Treats were also given at Trivandrum to the Roman Catholic Parochial Boys' School in the Cantonment, to the Mohammedan School, to the Grant-in-aid English Schools, and the 2,669 boys and girls of the Vernacular Schools.

At the out-stations, the Protestant, Roman Catholic, and Syrian Christians, Hindus, and Mohammedan boys and girls, numbering about 10,000, were entertained. Funds were remitted to the London Mission Hospital at Neyoor, to the Archbishop's Hospital at Verapoly, to the Women's Workshop, and to the Society of St. Vincent de Paul, Trivandrum, and it was suggested to the Managers to provide a treat and a supply of clothing to the poor of those institutions, but they were left at liberty to utilise the funds in any other way they considered best. The Maharajah contributed Rs. 10,000 to the Imperial Institute in London, and Rs. 2,000 to the Victoria Technical Institute proposed for Madras. Rs. 50,000 are set apart for a local State Memorial, which will probably take the form of a School for the training of Hindu females as midwives and sick-nurses. A contribution was made to the funds being collected for a Reading Room at Neyoor, to be called the "Victoria Reading Room." A contribution was also promised to the funds being raised by public subscription at Alleppey to build a Charity Hospital in commemoration of the Jubilee.

The people of Trivandrum decorated their gates on the Jubilee day, and illuminated them at night. A public meeting, called by Mr. T. Rama Row, the Dewan, was held at the College on the 12th, to concert measures for forwarding a respectful Address of Congratulation to Her Majesty, to reach her on the 20th June, and to take other measures for commemorating the 50th anniversary of her reign. The meeting was largely attended, and was presided over by Mr. J. C. Hannyngton, the British Resident.

During the evening of the 16th a meeting of Hindu Ladies was held at the Palace of Her Highness the Junior Rani, at her invitation. Her Highness, on taking the chair, addressed the audience on the subject of Her Majesty's life, and explained the importance of the occasion. Her Highness's address closed with a prayer to Sri Padmanabha to bless Her Majesty with long life and prosperity. A letter from Panappillai Lekshmy Kallyani Pillai (Lady of His Highness the late Rama Varma Maharajah, G.C.S.I., C.I.E.) of sympathy, &c. was then read. It was unanimously resolved:—"That an Address (in Malayalim with English translation) be prepared expressing the feelings of the deep love and loyalty which the female section of the Native community entertain towards Her Imperial Majesty and be forwarded so as to be presented to Her Majesty on the 20th June ensuing." And:—"That as the institution of a permanent local memorial to perpetuate the remembrance of Her Majesty's name amidst our community is considered highly desirable, funds be raised for founding a Model Girls' School in Trivandrum." Her Highness the Junior Rani, Mrs. C. Krishna Pillai, Mrs. A. Govinda Pillai, and Mrs. Chinnama of Kilakkeimaddem, were empowered to carry out the resolutions of the meeting. Mrs. T. Kunhiraman Nair and Lekshmy Pillai then addressed the meeting, extolling the greatness of Her Majesty and the appropriateness of a homage of the kind proposed being paid to Her Majesty. Sandal, rose-water and *pan supari* were distributed. The meeting dispersed after thanking Her Highness for convening the meeting, and presiding at it.—(From the *Travancore Government Gazette Extraordinary*.)

ALLEPPEY (TRAVANCORE).

Alleppey is the principal sea-port town in Travancore, and has a population of 25,754. There is a lighthouse 115 feet high, lighted by a revolving light, and an iron screw pile pier. A European gentleman occupies the position at this port of Commercial Agent to the Travancore Government. The town contains a Palace, Zillah and Munsiff's Courts, a Jail, Civil and Charity Hospitals, a District High School (English), a District Vernacular School, Schools of the Church Missionary Society, a Convent School, a Roman Catholic Boys' School, a Theological Seminary, a Protestant, a Syrian, and two Roman Catholic churches, and several mosques and pagodas. The European and American merchants settled here have large warehouses and coir-manufactories. There are also several wealthy Mohammedan and Hindu merchants.

At 6 A.M. on the 16th February the Union Jack and the Travancore Ensign were hoisted, and the flagstaff was decorated. An Imperial salute of 101 guns was fired from the beach. Prayers for the Queen Empress and the Royal Family were offered up in all the temples and mosques. In obedience to a circular issued by the Archbishop of Verapolay, a High Mass was performed at the local Roman Catholic church, and the *Te Deum* was sung. Divine Service was held in the English church. All private houses, buildings, and public offices were decorated. In the afternoon about 4,000 of the poor of the town and its suburbs were fed. A congratulatory telegram was sent by the local Jubilee Committee to the British Resident for transmission to Her Majesty. The public were entertained with various *fêtes* and athletic sports. At night the town was brilliantly illuminated. There were dramatic and musical performances, and a good display of fireworks at the beach. A large Pandal, erected for the occasion in front of the Commercial Office, was tastefully decorated and illuminated. A large portrait of Her Majesty was placed above the entrance to the Pandal. People returning from the beach, after the sports, were entertained with music in this Pandal, and presented with attar, flowers, sandal, and *pan supari*. The orphans in the Convent were provided with food and clothing at the expense of Mr. James Darragh. On the afternoon of the 17th the poor were again fed at the cost of the Government. At 4 P.M. there was a boat race in Pullathurathy river, after which all the boats with music proceeded to the beach end of the canal where the boatmen, together with the crowd assembled on the pier, gave three hearty cheers for Her Majesty, and three more for the Maharajah. On the 22nd, the children of the Convent and Parochial schools, and of the District and aided schools, were given a treat at the expense of His Highness.

CHENGANUR (TRAVANCORE).

The District of Chenganur lies in the heart of Travancore. It contains half-a-dozen ancient Syrian churches, and four great Hindu temples, with a number of smaller ones. Chenganur, the chief town, is situated on the Pampar river, and is a place of considerable antiquity, and archæological importance. The beautiful Syrian church, St. Mary's, built about 650 years ago, and the older Hindu temples, are entirely built of granite. Chenganur has a population of about 10,000, the majority being Syrians.

At daybreak on the 16th February a salute of *kathinas* was fired in the Church compound. The boys of the Sahodara Vidya Sala were fed at the expense of the Sadachara Sangham. At 6 P.M. the Most Reverend Mar Dionysius, Syrian Metropolitan of Malabar, held a Thanksgiving Service, assisted by seven Katthanars. After service he proceeded to the District Cutcherry, which was the chief centre of attraction. On his way he passed through the principal Syrian Street, which was tastefully decorated by day with *thoranams* and palm-leaf arches, and splendidly illuminated at night with torches, lamps and blue lights. Fireworks of various descriptions were displayed all along the way. The Metropolitan, attended by a large number of clergy and laity of the Syrian community, was received in the Cutcherry, which also was well decorated and illuminated by a large concourse of people. In a short speech he explained the term Jubilee and its application to the occasion. Then followed a musical entertainment, in which three Brahmin Bhagavathas took the leading part. At the conclusion of the entertainment flowers and *pan supari* were distributed.

COTTAYAM (TRAVANCORE).

This is the head-quarters of the Dewan Peishcar of the Northern Division, and of the Church Missionary Society in Travancore. It is also the seat of the Anglican Bishop of Travancore and Cochin, and of the Syrian Metropolitan. The public institutions are the Division and Taluk Cutcherries, a Munsiff's Court, a Civil Hospital, the Church Mission College, the Cambridge Nicholson Institution, a Printing Office, a Reading Room, and several Schools for boys and girls established by the Church Missionary Society; the Syrian Metropolitan's Theological Seminary, Government and aided Schools. Of ecclesiastical buildings there are the Pro-Cathedral, other Protestant churches, a Syrian church, and a Roman Catholic church. There is also a celebrated Pagoda. An Experimental Farm has been started by private enterprise, aided by Government. There is also an Agricultural Association which holds an annual exhibition of cattle and market produce. The population is 11,203.

The streets, roads, public buildings, and private dwellings were decorated on the 16th February, the Church Mission College, the Syrian Seminary, and the Reading Room being especially remarkable for their tasteful appearance. Prayers and Thanksgiving Services were held in all places of worship. The poor were fed in large numbers at Government expense. At noon an Imperial salute of 101 guns was fired from the *maidan* opposite the new Public Office buildings, and the public were entertained with sports and acrobatic performances, music being provided by a Syrian band. At the close of the sports the Elephants belonging to the Government pagodas in the suburbs were paraded in procession, and presented an imposing appearance with their gold and silver trappings. At night all the churches, pagodas, chapels, bazaars, houses, and public buildings were brilliantly illuminated. There was a display of fireworks in front of the Division Cutcherry, in the presence of His Highness the Second Prince of Travancore. On the 17th the College boys had races and sports at which His Highness the Second Prince was present, and gave away the prizes. The girls of the Hindu Girls' School were given money prizes. Feasts were given to the girls of Mrs. and Miss Baker's Schools, and to the children of the Schools under the management of Archdeacon Koshi. The Syrian Christians held Thanksgiving Services, and offered special prayers for Her Majesty. In some churches the poor were fed at the expense of the well-to-do Syrians. In the Seminary the celebration extended to the 17th and 18th. There were processions with music and banners, and the firing of guns, and a grand service in the church. At the end of the service cheers were given for Her Majesty in the Syrian form. The children of the Syrian schools were feasted, and their teachers received presents of cloths. At night the Rev. C. A. Neve exhibited a magic lantern at the Division Cutcherry; the entertainment was very largely attended. Archdeacon Koshi then delivered an address extolling the virtues of the Queen Empress, and dwelling on the peace, enlightenment, and glory of the British Empire under her rule. The meeting dispersed after giving three hearty cheers for Her Majesty and another three for His Highness the Maharajah.

ERNEEL AND NEYOOR (TRAVANCORE).

Neyoor is a town in the Erneel district in South Travancore, and is one of the districts of the London Mission Society in South Travancore. A Chapel, a Hospital, and several Schools have been established by the Mission in the town and its suburbs. About two miles from Neyoor is the populous town of Erneel, which is the head-quarters of the Tahsildar of the district, and where a large market is held.

At sunrise on the 16th February the firing in front of the Taluk Cutcherry at Erneel of 50 guns, being one gun for each year of the reign of Her Majesty, and 21 guns as a salute for His Highness the Maharajah, announced that the Jubilee Day had dawned. Erneel and Neyoor form one town, the first-named being the cusbah village of the taluk of the same name, while Neyoor is a large and flourishing Christian village of the London Mission Society, being the head-quarters station of what is known as the Neyoor Mission District. The streets were decorated with strings of leaves woven into pretty designs, which were hung across at short intervals. At the entrance to the compound of the London Mission was a triumphal arch, on which were inscribed the words "Victoria Jubilee," while on the site of the proposed "Erneel Jubilee Reading Room" was erected a spacious ornamental Pandal, in the front of which, from tall flagstaffs, floated the Union Jack and the Standard of Travancore. At 8 A.M. the Sircar officials paid a visit of ceremony to the Europeans of the station. At 11 A.M. a Thanksgiving Service was held in the Mission Church. The reading-desk was draped with the flags of England and Travancore. At noon 68 guns, corresponding to the age of Her Majesty, were fired in front of the Taluk Cutcherry, and 21 guns were fired in honour of His Highness the Maharajah. Food was then distributed to a large number of poor people. At 4 o'clock in the afternoon, the laying of the corner stone of the "Victoria Jubilee Reading Room" took place. Two brass bands were in attendance. All being assembled under and around the Pandal, the Rev. J. H. Hacker explained the purpose for which they had assembled. Mr. Chatterton then addressed the meeting. In the course of his remarks, he mentioned that in Travancore there had been but one Sovereign who had reigned over 50 years, viz., Chara Odea Manthanda Vurma Kulasekhara Perumal Rajah, who began his long reign of sixty-two years in A.D. 1382. An Imperial salute of 101 guns was fired, the brass bands played a lively tune, and the ceremony of laying the corner stone of the Reading Room was performed by Mr. Chatterton. A bottle containing coins in circulation in British India and Travancore, a copy of the last issue of the *Travancore Times*, and a paper containing an account of the circumstances under which the building was erected, signed by the European and Native gentlemen present, was placed in a cavity underneath the corner stone, which, on being placed in position, was declared to be "well and truly laid." The National Anthem was then sung by the School Children in English, Dr. Fry, Medical Missionary, accompanying on the harmonium. Mr. N. Pulpanaba Pillai now addressed the meeting. A salute of 21 guns was fired in honour of the Maharajah, the bands at the same time playing. The School Children then sang "God bless the Maharajah" in Tamil, with harmonium accompaniment, and Mr. S. Narayana Pillai made a suitable speech. The following telegram, having been approved by the meeting, was despatched to His Highness: "Corner Stone Erneel Reading Room just laid. The inhabitants of Erneel Taluk and school children of Neyoor Mission District tender their loyal good wishes to His Highness the Maharajah, and grateful thanks for the kindness shown by His Highness to them on this joyful occasion." A prayer was then offered, and the Benediction was pronounced by the Rev. J. H. Hacker. Acrobats now came forward and performed some feats. The Rev. Mr. Hacker distributed hundreds of copies of a specially prepared Jubilee Tamil Tract, which were eagerly received by the people. At dark the town and market were illuminated. At 9 P.M. a display of fireworks took place in front of the Taluk Cutcherry, which was witnessed by a large crowd. A Native Dramatic Company then gave a performance.

At sunrise on the following day the church bell summoned all to prayers, after which the children of the Neyoor Boarding School were formed up, and, headed by a brass band, escorted the colours of England and Travancore to the place appointed for the assembling of all the School Children of the Mission District, a second brass band bringing up the rear. The place appointed for the meeting was to the north of the populous village of Teruvancodu. At half-past seven o'clock a procession was formed. Forty-seven schools had assembled, numbering over 2,000 children, with several hundred Native Christians, the whole forming a line of more than one mile in length. The procession passed through the town of Teruvancodu, and returned by the road to the north-east of Erneel town. Here large crowds were assembled. It was just at this point, the only one all along the route, that the whole line of the procession could be seen at one time. The bright colours of the children's clothes, and the ninety-four banners and bannerets, including the Union Jack and the Standard of Travancore, formed an imposing spectacle. The procession passed through Erneel, and reached the Taluk Cutcherry, where a large band of native drummers joined the procession, taking their places in front of the Union Jack. Skirting the Market the procession passed along the main road, and entered the Mission compound under the triumphal arch. The flags of England and Travancore were placed in the centre, and the banners and bannerets grouped round in order. Acrobats performed some wonderful feats; and sports for the children, with prizes for the winners, brought the festivities to a close. The expense of the entertainment to the school children was borne by His Highness the Maharajah. About 5,000 people of all classes took part with the utmost goodwill in the festivities.

NAGERCOIL (TRAVANCORE).

The population of the town is 16,534. It is the head-quarters of the London Mission Society in South Travancore. The Institutions include the Zillah and the Munsiff's Courts, the Civil Hospital, High School, London Mission Seminary, Printing Office, District Vernacular School, and several other Schools mostly belonging to the London Mission Society, aided by the Government. It is the seat of the lace manufacture in Travancore, the workers being Native Christian women.

The morning of the 16th February dawned with the ringing of church bells, and the beating of the drums. At 6 o'clock a procession was formed by the Seminary and Town Boys, who paraded through the principal streets, clad in their gayest attire, and with banners and music. They were met by similar processions from other Schools. They returned to the Mission grounds, and were feasted there to the number of 1,000. The pupils of the Sirkar and Roman Catholic Schools also formed in procession, and partook of the treat prepared for them. Thanksgiving Services were held in all places of worship. The town was gaily decorated during the day, and illuminated at night. There was also a grand display of fireworks. All the public offices and buildings were decorated, and private individuals vied with one another in evincing their loyalty by decorating and illuminating their premises. The poor were fed in large numbers.

PULLAM (TRAVANCORE).

The Bishop of Travancore and Cochin held a Thanksgiving Service in his Cathedral at this town on the 16th February, and provided a treat for the school children and the poor. On the 17th he gave another treat to the children chiefly belonging to the Pulayer caste, in the out-station schools.

QUILANDY (TRAVANCORE).

The Jubilee festivities passed off very satisfactorily. At 8 A.M. on the 16th February a salute of 101 guns was fired. Between 9 A.M. and noon rice was distributed to the poor. In the afternoon the undermentioned nobles, accompanied by a large retinue with music, and caparisoned elephants, were received at the decorated Pandal by the Eledath Ramar Nair, viz.: Puthalath Aval, Punathal Avail, Kuttali Nair, Kolpither Nair, Toodipunattil Nair, Vydiaragath Kuttasanji Arangatt, and Rumunna Kidavu. There were acrobatic feats, native music, and plays at 5 P.M. The National Anthem was sung by the German Mission boys and girls. Subsequently there was a native procession through the town. It returned at 7 P.M. by torchlight. There was a display of fireworks until 10 P.M., and native theatricals until dawn.

QUILON (TRAVANCORE).

The town is the head-quarters of the Dewan Peishcar of the Division. The British Subsidiary Force is stationed here. There are a Palace, a Residency, Zillah and Munsiff's Courts, District Jail, Civil Hospital, English and Vernacular District Schools, Schools belonging to the London Mission, a Convent School, several Vernacular aided Schools, a Protestant and three Roman Catholic Churches, and a Cotton-Spinning Mill. The population is 13,588.

Thanksgiving Services were held in all places of worship. The public buildings, private dwellings, and streets were gaily decorated, and illuminated at night. The poor were fed at convenient localities, and the children of all the schools had a treat given them.

SHENCOTTAH (TRAVANCORE).

This town contains a Tahsildar's Cutcherry, a Munsiff's Court, a Civil Hospital, and English and Vernacular Schools. The principal trade is in timber and grain. The population is 7,882.

Jubilee Committee.—Messrs. A. PERANPERUMAL PILLAY, B.A., *Chairman*; VISWANATHA IYER, *Secretary*; K. KUNJUNNI MENON, B.A., B.L.; RUNGANADHA PILLAY; HARRIHARA IYER; N. SUNDRAM IYER; SOOBRAMANIA IYER; SUNDRALINGAM PILLAY, and NALCHADALINGAM PILLAY.

Special *pujahs* were performed in the temples on the morning of the 16th February, and prayers were offered for Her Majesty. The principal officers and inhabitants met at the school, and addresses extolling Her Majesty's reign were delivered, after which an Imperial salute of 101 guns was fired. The poor were fed. All the streets and houses were decorated and illuminated. The village deity was taken in procession through the principal streets with much pomp. After the procession there was a nautch, followed by a display of fireworks, native music, acrobatic performances, and a distribution of *pan supari*, flowers, and sugar.

OTHER STATIONS (TRAVANCORE).

The Jubilee was celebrated on the 16th February at these out-stations: Paravoor, Shertally, Moovathupulay, Meenachel, Shodupulay, Shovalay, Augusteeswarem, Calculan, Velavencode, Nayattunkary, Parachalay, Sherangil, Neduvengaud, Kottarakary, Pathanapuram, Cunnatoor, Karunagapally, Kartigapally, Tiruvella, Chenganoor, Meavelitrary, Ambalapoolai, Vycome, Ettumanoor, Changanacherry, Moovattoopulay, Counathunanid, Alengaud, &c. In all these places the poor were fed; sports and other entertainments were provided during the day; and there were illuminations and fireworks at night. The Zillah Judge, the Munsiff, and the Acting Tahsildar at Paravoor, instituted a medal called the "Jubilee Medal" in one of the local schools.

THE STATE OF COCHIN.

The protected State of Cochin lies between British Malabar on the north and Travancore on the south. It has an area of 1,361 square miles, more than two-thirds of which are under cultivation. It contains a population of 600,278 souls; of whom 429,324 are Hindus, 136,361 are Christians, 33,344 are Mohammedans, and 1,249 are Jews. The Christians form 23 per cent. of the whole population. In the neighbouring State of Travancore the proportion is, as has been already remarked, upwards of 20 per cent., but in the Madras Presidency generally, it is only 1·5 per cent. The Rajah claims to hold his territory in right of descent from Chereman Perumal, who governed the whole country of Kerulam about the beginning of the ninth century of the Christian era. The Marumakkatayam law, *i.e.* the right of inheritance through the female line, governs the succession to the Throne. During Her Majesty's reign the Courts of Justice have been constituted, and Procedure Codes, based on the lines of the British Indian Codes, have been introduced. State Education has been introduced and fostered. A Police Force has been organized on the system obtaining in the Madras Presidency; the Registration of Assurances has been brought into practice; the Department of Public Works has opened several hundred miles of roads, constructed many bridges, and commenced the execution of a large scheme of irrigation; obnoxious taxes on articles of commerce, and the monopoly on tobacco have been abandoned; free trade has been introduced; the soil-serfs have been emancipated, the ancient system of exacting forced labour for State purposes has been abolished; the emoluments of public servants have been liberally increased; hospitals and dispensaries have been established on a scientific basis; and vaccination has been greatly extended. The revenue of the State for the year 1837 was about 6¼ lakhs, with an expenditure of about 6¼ lakhs; while the revenue in 1885-86 amounted to 16½ lakhs, against an expenditure of 15½ lakhs.

ERNACOLLUM (COCHIN).

The festivities commenced at this, the capital of the State of Cochin, with the firing of a salute of 101 guns at sunrise on the 16th February. This was followed by a salvo from numerous small cannons. His Highness the Rajah, the Elliah Rajah, and many of the junior Princes, came in from Tripoonatorah, their ordinary residence, to Ernacollum to take part in the rejoicings. From the Government landing-place to the Durbar Hall, and in many other directions, the roads were decorated with festoons of leaves, flowers, and banners. The magnificent lagoon, or back-water that intersects the country and divides Native from British Cochin, presented a very interesting spectacle. Native rowing boats, cabin boats, canoes, &c., arrived in large numbers to compete for the races which commenced at 8 A.M. and continued during the greater part of the forenoon. The sight was witnessed by a vast concourse of enthusiastic spectators. On the termination of the sports Captain Howlett, Assistant Resident, as well as the European gentlemen present, were entertained at breakfast at the High School. At noon food was distributed to about 4,000 poor persons, and at 7 in the evening a sumptuous treat was given to Brahmins and Sudras. Foot-races, rope-dancing, gymnastics and other athletic sports were performed in the open green in front of the Durbar Hall from 2 to 6 P.M. The chief event of the day was the Durbar held by His Highness the Rajah at 4 P.M., to receive from the Assistant Resident the following *Kareeta* from His Excellency the Viceroy and Governor General of India :—

HIS HIGHNESS SRI RAMA VARMA, K.C.S.I. ; RAJAH OF COCHIN.

"MY ESTEEMED FRIEND,—It is with sincere pleasure that I have heard of the preparations which Your Highness has made in order to commemorate, in a manner befitting the occasion, the fiftieth year of the reign of Her Most Gracious Majesty the Queen, Empress of India. I shall not fail to inform Her Majesty of this spontaneous expression of loyalty and affection on your part. Queen Victoria's long and tranquil rule has been marked throughout her wide dominions by the ever increasing prosperity and happiness of the millions entrusted to her charge. In India it has established an uninterrupted and unbroken peace, and under its protecting shelter the ruling chiefs of this country, undisturbed by the fear of invasion from without, or of revolution from within, have been able to devote their time and attention to the welfare of their subjects, and to the moral and material advancement of their States. I am happy to learn that Your Highness has so readily taken the opportunity afforded by this auspicious occasion to show your just appreciation of the great benefits you have experienced under the benign and beneficent rule of Her Majesty the Queen. I can assure you that it is our Gracious Sovereign's desire to extend to you, on all occasions, her warm sympathy and hearty assistance, to support your authority, enhance your personal consideration, and to maintain unbroken the cordial relations which have at all times subsisted between Her Majesty's Government and Your Highness. I remain, with much consideration,

"Your sincere friend,

(Signed) "DUFFERIN,

"Viceroy and Governor General of India.

"Fort William, the 3rd February, 1887."

The *Kareeta* having been presented and read with the usual honours, His Highness the Elliah Rajah, or heir-apparent, rose and addressed the company on behalf of his Royal brother, the Rajah. His Highness gave eloquent expression to the universal joy that prevailed throughout Her Majesty's Indian dominions on the memorable occasion of the Jubilee, and gratefully acknowledged the many inestimable blessings and benefits which the Cochin State had derived under her benign rule and protection. His Highness also took occasion to pay a graceful tribute to Her Majesty's domestic virtues, the purity of her life, and the beneficence and justice of her reign, and concluded with a request that the sentiments of unswerving devotion and attachment to Her Majesty's august Person and Throne, which have always animated the ancient House of Cochin and all its members, might be conveyed to His Excellency the Viceroy. The Durbar ended with the distribution of attar and garlands. His Highness the Rajah telegraphed to the Viceroy and Governor General:—"Please accept my warm and sincere congratulations on the Jubilee of Her Most Gracious Majesty's happy and beneficent reign. All my people rejoice with me." Illuminations of unexampled splendour followed. The lagoon banks of Cochin, Ernacollum, Benthoorthy, Ramanthoorthy, and Balghautty were brilliantly lighted up. The island of Balghautty, on which the Residency is situated, was illuminated again on the 17th February. A brilliant pyrotechnic display took place in front of the High School at 10 P.M., to witness which the Resident, the Elliah Rajah, several of the junior Princes and many European and native gentlemen had assembled. As a permanent memorial of the Jubilee a School has been established at Ernacollum by the Rajah, under the designation of the "Victoria Girls' School," and the Park at Trichoor has been designated the "Victoria Jubilee Park." Grants were made for giving treats to the children of the State schools, as well as of the private and aided schools. Besides providing for the celebration within the State itself, His Highness made a donation to the Imperial Institute in London, and to the Technical Institute in Madras.

TRICHOOR (COCHIN).

The population of Trichoor is 104,695, comprising Hindus, Muhammadans, and Christians. The town contains, in addition to two Sirkar Institutions for boys and girls, three others worked by Mission agency. It is also the seat of a great Sanscrit Vedic School for Namboodri Brahmins. Cultivation is the chief occupation of the people. Trichoor carries on a large trade in paddy, timber, bamboos, &c.

Jubilee Committee.—Messrs. C. TIRUVENKATA CHARRIAR, B.A., B.L., *Chairman*; K. NARAYANA MENON, Tahsildar, *Secretary*; A. SANKARIAH, B.A.; J. C. KOHLHOFF; T. R. RAMA PISHARODY; F. R. BENNET; J. CHANDY; A. P. SUBRAMANYIAR, B.A.; GOVINDA MENON and four others.

The Gardens, in the centre of which stands the Hannyngton Mantapam, was the centre of attraction on the 16th February. The grounds were prettily laid out, and the Mantapam was very artistically decorated. A spacious and well-decorated Pandal had been erected in front of the Mantapam. Over the entrance to the Pandal the word "Jubilee" was conspicuous. A magnificent arch had been placed at the Western Gate bearing the inscription "God save the Queen Empress" on the one side, and the word "Jubilee" on the other. At 6 A.M. the small detachment of the British troops stationed here paraded in review order in the Residency grounds, and fired a *feu de joie*. The troops then gave three cheers for Her Majesty, and the cheering was taken up enthusiastically by the crowds that had assembled. The troops returned to their barracks, and the crowd moved on to the Promenade. At 6.30 A.M. the Gardens and the public roads on the three sides were crowded with spectators. The detachment of the Nair Brigade belonging to the station was drawn up on one side. Mr. A. Sankariah, the Dewan Peishkar then, in the presence of the whole assembly, unveiled a portrait of Her Majesty, and in doing so made a speech, in which he enumerated the chief incidents of Her Majesty's reign. His remarks were explained in the vernacular to the masses. The Brigade presented arms, and fired a *feu de joie*, after which an Imperial salute of 101 guns was fired. Her Majesty's portrait was now formally installed in the centre of the Mantapam. The Dewan Peishkar then read a proclamation of the Maharajah abolishing the duty on pepper, and set at liberty two prisoners to whom he gave small sums of money to enable them to reach their homes. The public reassembled at the Mantapam at 2 P.M., when a musical entertainment was given. *Pan supari*, sandal, and rose-water were distributed. At the close of the entertainment the Chairman, Mr. C. Tiruvencata Charriar, B.A., B.L., recited a Sanscrit song which he had composed in honour of the occasion. Five elephants handsomely caparisoned, were brought on the scene, and the people formed themselves into a procession with Her Majesty's portrait in front. The procession started at 4 P.M., with the usual musical accompaniment, from the main gate; it marched past the Public Offices, and arrived at 6 P.M. in front of the Pasmacav Temple, whence it moved on with torches and blue lights. The Promenade Mantapam was reached at 8 P.M., and Her Majesty's photograph was then taken back to the Mantapam. A display of fireworks followed. The illuminations consisted of lights artistically arranged along the four roads of the Promenade, and on the walls of the several public buildings which surround it. The large temple in the town as well as several private buildings were also illuminated. The platform in the centre, and the various walks in the Gardens, and the façades of the Public Offices in front of the Gardens, presented a very attractive appearance with the blue and red lights that adorned them. The display of fireworks which followed was a complete success. The National Anthem was then sung, and the people dispersed to meet again the next day. On the 17th, at 2 P.M. sports were held. The grounds looked very pretty. On the 18th rather more than 1,000 poor persons were fed, and the festivities were brought to a close by the singing of the National Anthem. A proposal to open a Memorial Park at Viyoor, to be called the "Victoria Jubilee Park," received the sanction of His Highness's Government.

VERAPOLAY (COCHIN).

Verapolay is the seat of the Roman Catholic Archbishop of the Diocese, who has established a Hospital here. It is one of the principal timber depots of the Government. In and about Verapolay are several Roman Catholic churches, and Convents.

In accordance with the wish expressed in a Pastoral Letter issued by the Most Reverend the Archbishop of Verapolay to all the churches and chapels under his jurisdiction, Her Majesty's Jubilee was celebrated by special Thanksgiving Services. Imperial salutes were fired; the poor were fed and clothed; school children were feasted; entertainments were given; and roads and buildings were decorated and illuminated.

THE STATE OF PUDUKOTA.

PUDUKOTA (TRICHINOPOLY).

Pudukota, the "Tondaman's Country," has an area of 1,101 square miles, surrounded by the Districts of Madura, Trichinopoly, and Tanjore. The population is 302,127, of whom 281,809 are Hindus. The town of Pudukota has a population of 15,384. The Rajah exercises independent jurisdiction, subject to the advice of the Madras Government. He maintains a military force of 81 cavalry, 126 infantry, and 3,260 militia, besides armed servants.

As the Pudukota State was in mourning on account of the late Rajah's death, no local rejoicings had been arranged for the 16th February, but the Dewan-Regent postponed the celebration to the 20th of June, by which date the period of mourning would be over. He arranged, however, for the offering up of prayers on the 16th February for the long life and prosperity of Her Majesty in all the temples and mosques in the State (about 100 in number), and he subscribed for 1,000 copies of Mr. Krishnama Chariyar's *History of the Empress* for distribution among the people in all the villages in the Pudukota territory. He further subscribed Rs. 3,000 on account of the State, and Rs. 500 on his own account, for the Institutes in Madras and London, and for the celebration of the Jubilee at Trichinopoly. The Presidencial Address was adopted.

THE STATE OF SANDUR.

SANDUR (TOWN).

This is the capital of the Sandur State, which has an area of 164 square miles, and consists of two ranges of hills with an intervening valley. The tract lies within the British District of Bellary. The town is situated thirty miles to the west of Bellary. On one of the highest hills, Ramandrug, a Sanitarium has been formed for European troops serving at Bellary. The mean elevation of the valley above the sea is 1,900 feet, and of the hill-ranges, 3,000 feet. In fiscal matters the State enjoys considerable independence. The chief exports from Sandur are cholam, tobacco, betel, jaggery, pulse, oil-seed, timber, and firewood.

Jubilee Committee.—Messrs. H. H. Ramachendra Vitthal Row Ghorpade, *Rajah of Sandur, Chairman;* J. G. Firth, Dewan, *Secretary;* Abdul Rahim; and Vencata Row.

A dome-shaped Pavilion, neatly covered with cloth, and ornamented with paper of various colours stamped with patterns in gold, and surmounted by a golden umbrella, had been constructed in the Palace-yard, and alongside of it, on a tall flagstaff, floated the Union Jack. In the centre of the Pavilion was placed a chair covered with brocaded velvet, to represent the Sinhásan, or Throne of Her Most Gracious Majesty the Queen Empress. A little before 5 P.M. on the 16th February the poor of the town, who had received an invitation to attend, began to arrive; and after they had been arranged in rows, the Rajah, dressed in purple and maroon, distributed alms to 101 adults, and 86 children, in the presence of a large number of people, dressed in holiday attire. After a short interval the chandelier and coloured globes in the Pavilion, and the rows of lamps on posts at short intervals, which extended from the Palace down into the chief bazaar, were lighted, and, every one standing up, the Rajah read the following address in Marathi (his native tongue):—

"This day, the 16th February, has been appointed by the Governor General of India for the celebration of the Jubilee of Her Most Gracious Majesty, Queen Victoria, Empress of India, this being the fiftieth year of her reign. During the fifty years that Her Majesty has occupied the throne of Great Britain, India has enjoyed the innumerable benefits which have been conferred by her just and benign rule; and the various tribes and peoples of this great country have lived together in peace and amity. And since she has taken India under her own control and management, now nearly thirty years, our country has made great strides in education, and commerce has been largely developed by the railroads, which are spread all over the land. Her Majesty has also taken under her special protection the independent States of India, and has assured their rulers that she will maintain their independence, and acknowledge their right of adoption as soon as long as they continue loyal to the Paramount Power, under whose generous protection and guidance those States are now in a more prosperous and flourishing condition than they ever attained to before. It is, therefore, right and proper that we, the inhabitants of the Sandur State, should, on this day, gratefully acknowledge the benefits conferred upon us by our Most Gracious Empress, Queen Victoria, and earnestly pray that the great Creator may prolong Her Majesty's life for many years, and bestow peace, happiness and prosperity upon all her dominions, and every needed blessing upon her Royal self and her Family."

The English version of the address was read by Mr. J. G. Firth, the Dewan; and the Canarese version by Mr. Abdul Rahim, the Head Munshi. Then the Dewan with his wife and three children sang "God save the Queen." The trumpets, drums, and clarionets now sounded, and shouts pealed forth of "*Maharani Victoria-avara jaya! Victoria Maharani-yavara jaya!* (Victory to the Empress Victoria!) Two prisoners were then released, and attar and betel-nut having been distributed, and rose-water sprinkled, the Rajah and his brother, Bala Sahib, who was in his police uniform, followed by the people in crowds, proceeded to an open space outside the town, where a good display of fireworks commenced at about 7.30 P.M. and lasted till 9 P.M.

On the 18th, the Rajah wrote to the British Political Agent:—

"In acknowledging your letter, dated 15th February, 1887, I find myself unable to express my feeling of deep gratitude for the honour done me in associating me with the expression of joyfulness felt throughout the British dominions on the auspicious occasion of the celebration of the Jubilee of Her Majesty the Queen Empress of India, to whose gracious rule I and all the other independent States in India are under obligations so great as to firmly establish in our hearts the principles of loyalty to her throne, and love to her person. May I therefore beg to be permitted to join with the other Princes of India in presenting my humble congratulations to Her Most Gracious Majesty Queen Victoria, Empress of India, and to assure Her Majesty that no prayers more fervent or earnest than mine have been, or will be, offered up to the Almighty Creator for the long life, happiness, and prosperity of Her Gracious Majesty and the Royal Family."

SUPPLEMENTARY.

AMBASAMUDRAM (TINNEVELLY).

A musical entertainment was given on the 20th June in the upstair hall of the Tahsildar's house. *Pan supari* was distributed to the assembly, and loud cheers were given for Her Majesty. The whole assembly then went, with music, in procession to the site of the "Jubilee Reading Room," and there the Singampathy Zemindar, who had generously promised to provide a building for the Reading Room, and a Recreation Ground, laid the foundation stone of the former, and *pan supari* was distributed. The streets were illuminated. At about 8 P.M. a procession of the temple god took place with music and fireworks, a large number of persons taking part in it. The festivities terminated about 11 P.M.

ANANTAPUR (ANANTAPUR).

The Anantapur Theosophical Society celebrated the conclusion of the Queen's Jubilee year on the evening of the 20th June, when rice and money were distributed to poor people of all castes. A Theosophical *conversazione* was held in the house of Mr. B. P. Narasimmiah, Vice-President, to which a large number of people were invited. The social gathering was brought to a close with the distribution of sugar-candy, almonds, sandal, flowers, and *pan supari.*

ANGADIPURAM (MALABAR).

A grand religious ceremony took place in the Siva temple on the morning of the 20th June, many Brahmins and Sudras being present. The District Munsiff with the Vakils of his Court attended. Prayers were offered that the reign of Her Majesty might be long continued. *Abishekams* were performed to the Hindu god, and a Shastri, well versed in Sanscrit, read the Bhagavat and explained it in the vernacular to the assembled people. The ceremony was brought to a conclusion by the offering of incense, and the invocation of Divine blessings upon Her Majesty and the Royal Family. The bells of the temple then rang merry peals.

BELLARY (BELLARY).

The 20th June was observed as a holiday in this town, and memorial trees were planted by General Way in the Victoria Jubilee Gardens. That officer remarked, in the course of his speech, that "Bellary is not a very extensive place, but its loyalty is, I am sure, not inferior to that of other cities, as is evident from the enthusiastic manner in which all classes have taken part in the Jubilee rejoicings. It therefore gives me great pleasure to assist in planting these trees, and I hope that they will grow to afford shelter to this and future generations, and become the nucleus of flourishing recreation grounds for the benefit of the loyal citizens in Bellary." Sports were held at 5 P.M. in the Protestant Orphanage, which was decorated. After the sports were finished, an address was delivered by a native gentleman, followed by the distribution of prizes. There were fireworks in the evening, at the close of which the National Anthem was played by the band. The children were then conducted to the hall, where they partook of dainties provided for them.

BEZWADA (KISTNA).

The principal feature of the celebration of the termination of Jubilee year, on June 20th, in this place, was the laying of the foundation stone of the "Victoria Museum and Technical Institute," under the auspices of Mr. Robert Sewell, the Collector. In the morning a Thanksgiving Service was held in the L.M.S. Mission School by the Rev. Mr. Stone. At 4 P.M. a procession of decorated boats, towed by the steam launch *Alexandra*, started from the head of the Masulipatam Canal, conveying the company about a mile to a landing-place close to the site where the Museum is to be built. Most of the European inhabitants of the district were present, together with some of the principal Zemindars, many of the native officials, and a large number of other gentlemen. From the landing-place the company proceeded to the site of the Museum, where they were accommodated in a spacious shamiana. Mr. Sewell opened the proceedings with a speech. A Sanscrit ode composed in honour of the occasion was then sung by a Hindu student. Mr. P. Ramachendra Row, Head Assistant Collector, requested Mrs. Haleman to lay the foundation stone of the Institute. He said: "My countrymen desire to mark not only their gratitude and loyalty to the Throne, but also their affection to the noble English Lady who is ruling over them from the far West, by asking an English woman to take the principal part in this evening's ceremonial." He dwelt briefly on the benefits to be conferred by the foundation of the Institute, not only on the Kistna district alone, but to some extent on the whole Presidency and the adjacent dominions of His Highness the Nizam. He said that "the name of Mr. Robert Sewell, already a household word along the banks of the holy mother Krishna, will hereafter for ever be associated with this Institution." Colonel Haleman then returned thanks for the honour done to Mrs. Haleman in asking her to perform the ceremony of laying the foundation stone. A silver trowel made for the occasion was handed to Mrs. Haleman, who, under the guidance of Mr. C. Scott, C.E., spread the mortar on which the stone was to be laid. The stone was then lowered into position and was declared by Mrs. Haleman to be "well and truly laid." The greatest enthusiasm prevailed amongst those assembled in the shamiana and the crowd outside. Thanks were returned to Mrs. Haleman by Mr. C. H. B. Burlton for the graceful performance of the task asked of her. Mr. Sewell offered a few concluding words, and the Presidency telegram to Her Majesty the Queen Empress was unanimously adopted. The proceedings terminated with the singing of the National Anthem, a *feu de joie* being fired between the verses. At 9.30 P.M., the procession of boats, illuminated with small lamps, returned to the starting place. The banks of the main canal, the principal street of Bezwada, and the adjacent hill were brilliant with myriads of lamps. A large company then assembled in a brightly decorated pandal to witness a nautch, and a fine display of fireworks brought the proceedings to a close.

CHITTOOR (NORTH ARCOT).

The 20th June was a gala day with the people of Chittoor. The townspeople were invited by beat of tom-tom to observe the day as a national festival, and the rejoicings were marked by the greatest enthusiasm. The streets were overhung with festoons, and the Taluk Cutcherry, which was the centre of attraction, was gaily decorated. At 7 o'clock in the morning a Thanksgiving Service was held in the English Church, *pujahs* were offered in the Hindu temples, and prayers were said in the Mohammedan mosques for Her Majesty's health and happiness. Alms were given to a large number of the poor, and sweetmeats and fruits were liberally distributed among all the school children of the place. In the evening a public meeting was held at the Taluk Cutcherry, Mr. Jeyram Row, the District Munsiff, presiding. Several speeches were made; the proposed congratulatory telegram from the Presidency to Her Majesty was read; and the people cheered. At the conclusion of the meeting *pan supari* was distributed, and there was an excellent display of fireworks. The temples and mosques were brilliantly illuminated at nightfall, the illumination of the Jumma Musjid being especially noteworthy.

COIMBATORE (COIMBATORE).

In the morning of the 20th June there was a parade of the troops, consisting of the Coimbatore Volunteer Corps, the Jail Police, and the Police Reserve, commanded by Colonel W. J. Pickance. The parade over, the troops, headed by the Volunteer band, marched to a pandal that had been erected in front of the College building, and there formed up on three sides of a square.

Mr. J. Grose, M.A., the Collector, was conducted in procession, with native music, from his residence to the pandal, accompanied by a deputation which had waited upon him. The procession marched through rows of about 2,000 school children, each school exhibiting a beautifully prepared banner with some motto or device on it. The banners of the Government Female Normal School bore the words "We cheer thy Reign and its Glory," under the letters "V. I. R.," surmounted by a crown worked in gold. When the procession reached the pandal the troops presented arms. On the Collector taking his seat, the congratulatory telegram to the Queen, as adopted by the Madras Committee, was read in six different languages representing the various sections of the community. The speakers were Mr. Periyasami Mudalyar, the Municipal Chairman, in English, Mr. S. P. Narasimmalu Naidu in Tamil; Mr. K. Subbroyadu Puntalu in Telugu; Mr. H. Rama Rao in Canarese; Mr. Syed Abdul Razac Sahib in Hindustani; and Mr. J. P. Lewis in Malayalim. The telegram was then handed to Mr. Grose, who accepted it, and made a speech, which was loudly applauded. The troops fired a *feu de joie*, which was followed by three hearty cheers for the Queen Empress. The troops marched past the Collectors to the strains of the C. V. C. band. Special Thanksgiving Services were held in the Roman Catholic Cathedral, and in All Souls' Church. The day concluded with an evening entertainment in the College Hall, to which admission was free. The entertainment consisted of songs and native music, in which Europeans and Natives took part.

On the 21st June there was a large gathering in Mr. Robert Stanes's Schoolroom for the purpose of sending from the Hindu ladies in the town a congratulatory Jubilee Address to the Queen. The meeting was due to the efforts of the Misses Dawson, and the majority of the audience was formed of Zenana pupils, and their relatives and friends. Mrs. Grose, the wife of the Collector, presided, and was supported by the Misses Dawson, Mrs. Boddy, Mrs. Porter, Mrs Monk Jones, Mrs. Gordon, Mrs. Long, Miss Menke, and Miss Claridge. The proceedings commenced with a brief speech from Mrs. Grose, whose remarks were interpreted by Miss E. V. Dawson. Mrs. Grose observed that she was glad to be present at a gathering of women desirous of taking part in the Jubilee, and congratulated those present on the courage they had shown in appearing in this semi-public way. Our Ruler, she continued, is a woman, and hence it is peculiarly fitting that women should take part in these rejoicings, and the Queen, for her part, would derive great pleasure from the good wishes expressed by her female subjects in this country. Urging her hearers to emulate Her Majesty's goodness, and expressing the hope of meeting them some day at her house, Mrs. Grose concluded her remarks, which had been received with much cordiality. Miss E. V. Dawson then explained why the meeting had been convened. Hindu ladies being unable to attend public meetings with their husbands and brothers, had been called together to express for themselves their hearty congratulations, and to show their loyalty to the Queen Empress, who, like themselves, a woman, is peculiarly interested in what concerns women, and is anxious to alleviate their burdens and sufferings. The speaker added that the customs which formerly bound the women of India had not to be endured by those present, and it was sincerely to be hoped that the amount of freedom and learning which the men of India enjoyed might soon be the happy portion of India's women also. Mrs. S. P. Ethiraja Ammal, a Zenana student, and wife of Mr. S. P. Narasimmalu Naidu, Editor of the *Crescent*, then read in Tamil the Address to Her Majesty, which it was proposed to send. The Address was heartily adopted. The graver portion of the proceedings having been concluded, those present were favoured by a piano solo by Mrs. Boddy, a song from Mrs. Long, a duet from Mrs. Monk Jones and Miss E. V Dawson, and a second piano solo by Mrs. Boddy. Half an hour's conversation followed, and meanwhile preparations were made for a magic lantern exhibition. The portrait of Her Majesty fitly formed the first and the last picture on the sheet. During an interval in the programme, the National Anthem was sung in Tamil.

CUDDALORE (SOUTH ARCOT).

Grand demonstrations were made at Cuddalore on the 20th June, in honour of Her Majesty. Early in the morning the European residents in the town met at the Meeting Room, and held a special Thanksgiving Service, at the close of which they proceeded to the *maidan*, and played a cricket match. Her Majesty's health was drunk with enthusiasm, and hearty cheers were given. The Royal Standard was kept flying at the flagstaff all day, and the ships in the roads were dressed in flags. In the evening there was a brilliant display of fireworks from the s.s. *Principia*. A large number of people assembled on the beach to witness it.

DENKANIKOTA (SALEM).

A large and tastefully decorated Pandal had been erected in front of the Deputy Tahsildar's Cutcherry, on the roadway leading to which several triumphal arches, bearing appropriate mottoes, were placed. A portrait of Her Majesty, in a well-decorated frame, was placed on an elevated seat, specially constructed for it, in the pandal. About 4,000 people met here on the morning of the 20th June. The Deputy Tahsildar and Sub-Magistrate, Mr. Bhawani Sunkar Row, read the proposed congratulatory telegram to Her Majesty, and the people cheered. Several speeches were then made, at the close of which an Imperial salute of 101 guns was fired by the Police. The portrait was then placed in a decorated palanquin, and taken in procession through the decorated streets of the town, accompanied by music and dancing parties. The procession halted at several places, and garlands were placed round the portrait. The procession returned at 1 P.M., when a treat was given to the boys of the Middle and Hindustani Schools. Between noon and 4 P.M. about 700 poor people were fed. About 7 P.M. the god of the Stri Datraya Swami temple was taken in procession.

DHARAPURAM (SALEM).

More than 1,000 poor people were fed during the 20th June at the Local Fund market. The Mohammedan fakeers were fed separately. The streets of the town were decorated with festoons, and prayers were offered in the temples and mosques for the long life and prosperity of the Queen. In the evening there was a social entertainment at the Taluk Cutcherry, and at night there was a procession of the gods, attended by native music. The procession halted at the "Victoria Jubilee Well," where a nautch was held. The festivities terminated at midnight with a display of fireworks.

GOOTY (BELLARY).

A public meeting was held at 7 P.M. on the 20th June, in the Sanscrit School, which was decorated for the occasion with evergreens and flags, and was also beautifully lighted. Mr. P. T. Rajagopalachariar, Deputy Collector, presided. The Chairman opened the "Victoria Jubilee Library," and requested Mr. A. L. Narasimham, B.A., B.L., District Munsiff, to read the rules framed for its maintenance and management. Mr. Narasimham complied. Mr. Ramachendra Rao, B.A., B.L., spoke a few words on the utility of a library. A vote of thanks to the Chairman terminated the proceedings. All present then passed to the adjoining rooms, where they were provided with refreshments by Mr. Y. Choulappah.

JAMMALAMADUGU (CUDDAPAH).

At 6 A.M. on the 20th June there was a large gathering of people, official and non-official, in the Local Fund School premises, which was decorated, and the congratulatory telegram to Her Majesty was cordially adopted. The people then went in procession through the principal streets of the town, all of which were decorated, attended by nautch and bhajana parties. At 2 P.M. rice and money were liberally distributed among the poor. At night several houses and the temples and mosques were illuminated.

JAYANKONDA SHOLAPURAM (TRICHINOPOLY).

From an early hour on the 20th June crowds from the neighbouring villages began to pour in to witness the concluding Jubilee festivities. At 7 A.M. prayers were offered for the Queen and the Royal Family in the Siva and Vishnu temples. Then the poor of all castes and creeds, numbering about 1,000, were fed by the village Munsiff, Manikkam Pillai, and Rengasami Aiyengar, late Manager, Udaiyarpolian Estate. At 4 P.M. the local gods were carried in procession to a grand pandal that had been erected for the occasion near the bund of the "Victoria Jubilee Fresh-water Tank," which is to be the permanent memorial of the Jubilee in this place. In the absence of the Collector of the District, the ceremony of opening the tank was performed by Mr. H. Subbaraya Aiyar, the Deputy Collector, who eulogised the labours of the Committee. The procession then passed through the streets of the town with music and dancing, being headed by the Deputy Collector. The streets were decorated, and several triumphal arches bearing appropriate inscriptions had been erected. At 10 A.M. a public meeting was held under the auspices of the members of the Young Men's Reading Room, at which the Deputy Collector presided. After a report had been read by the Honorary Secretary, the Chairman offered a few words of advice to the members, a subscription list was opened, and a proposal was set on foot to erect a permanent building for the Reading Room. The Chairman and other influential visitors subscribed liberally for the purpose. When the new building has been constructed the name of the Society will be changed to "The Victoria Reading Room, Jayankonda Sholapuram." Flowers and *pan supari* were distributed at the close of the meeting.

KODAIKANAL (MADURA).

A special Service of Thanksgiving was held in the new Church at Kodaikanal, Pulney Hills, on the morning of the 20th June, when a large congregation was present. The Right Rev. Bishop Caldwell of Tinnevelly, who officiated, preached the sermon. After explaining the origin of jubilees, the Bishop said:—

"Soon after our Queen came to the throne, in 1840, when she was twenty-one years of age, she was happily married to Prince Albert, afterwards called the Prince Consort, who did more to promote the honour, usefulness, and happiness of the Queen, and not of the Queen only but of the whole country, than any other person could have done. He was the founder of the Great Exhibition of 1851, of which all the Exhibitions that have since taken place in all parts of the world have been the outcome. But he rendered eminent service to the country and the world in every department of life. The refinement and culture which now prevail were to a great extent owing to his influence. I consider that he occupied the very first place among all the monarchs and princes England has ever seen. Even King Alfred I think comes second. One great characteristic of Queen Victoria's reign has been her loyalty to the Constitution. She has never set her own opinion of things and her own judgment above those of her Ministers and Parliament. She has been strictly a Constitutional Sovereign, and in this respect she has excelled her immediate predecessors, especially George the Third, whose obstinacy lost America to England—if indeed that can be called a loss which proved eventually so great a gain to the world. Another characteristic of her reign has been the purity of her personal character, reflected in the purity of her Court, as compared with the courts of former sovereigns, and the purity of her great officers of State, not one of whom during her long reign has ever been accused of bribery or corruption. Her consistent profession of religion has also done much to promote religious life and Christian virtues throughout the country, even amongst those whose religious creed differed from her own; and with the profession of religion a higher tone of morals has also prevailed wherever her influence extended. The Queen's chief personal characteristic has been the sympathy for the suffering she has always displayed. She takes, we know, a warm interest in everything in which her people are interested, and makes herself acquainted with everything that passes. But what I chiefly refer to, and chiefly admire, is the ready and hearty sympathy of the telegrams of condolence she sends to every part of the world, as soon as she hears of any disaster. This has greatly endeared her not only to the English people but to all people of every race and creed throughout the world. I need not say anything of the unparalleled progress made during the Queen's reign in education, in everything that tends to promote the comfort and welfare of the people, in all the sciences, and in all the fine arts, as they are called, in which the Queen has proved herself no mean proficient. The Victorian Era will be known in future ages as the era of progress. An Imperial Institute is about to be established in England for the perpetual exhibition and promotion of all the industries in the world, and this will, I hope, prove to be a worthy commemoration of the Jubilee we are celebrating this day. In this church, specially erected for the better performance of the worship of the Church of England, I cannot but call to mind the wonderful revival of faith, Church life, and Christian zeal which has taken place during the Queen's reign, especially in the Church of England. In every great movement there is sure to be a proportion of persons who bring discredit on a good cause by their extremes, or even by wandering off in a wrong direction, and so it has been in this case; but making all due allowance for human errors, it must be admitted that the movement which has led during the last fifty years to the erection of such a multitude of beautiful churches, to the founding of so many excellent institutions, to the improvement in such a degree of the externals of Church worship, and to the formation of so many episcopal sees and episcopal missions throughout the world, must be a movement for which we should be thankful to God, and for which the reign of Queen Victoria will always be remembered. I trust that these good works and all the other good works, social, moral, and religious, which have distinguished this reign, will not diminish or languish as time goes on, but will go on from year to year, from century to century, continually increasing in number and improving in excellence and fruitfulness, till the time arrives when it shall be apparent in all its fulness of meaning that 'the earth is the Lord's and the fulness thereof,' and when the Jubilee of the Universe shall be celebrated with universal rejoicings."

MALAPURAM (MALABAR).

Early in the morning of the 20th June a salute of fifty guns was fired, [illegible] by a distribution of rice to the poor, which was personally supervised by [illegible] Wedderburn, the Special Assistant Collector. Over 1,000 poor people [illegible]. The Queen's portrait was unveiled, and carried in procession on an elephant with music, singing, &c., to the Special Assistant Collector's office. The ceremony of unveiling the portrait was performed by Mr. Wedderburn in the presence of a numerous assemblage, including all the officers of the detachment. Mr. K. U. Narayana Menon having addressed the meeting, the people proceeded to the *maidan* in front to witness sports and acrobatic performances. At 8 P.M. there was a fine display of fireworks.

MANAPARAI (TRICHINOPOLY).

The Jubilee was celebrated here with much *éclat* on the 20th June under the auspices of the members of the local Reading Room. About 500 poor people were fed, and the Mohammedan Deputy Tahsildar entertained the Mohammedan poor of the town. The Tahsildar of Kulitalai distributed cloths to the most deserving among the poor. About 250 people of all castes were feasted in the afternoon. At nightfall the town was illuminated. About 8 o'clock a meeting was held in the Roman Catholic School Hall, which was tastefully decorated with evergreens, and was well illuminated. The schoolboys enacted a few dramatic scenes, and prizes were distributed to them. Speeches were made in English by A. Rajahbahadur Mudalliar, Sub-Registrar, and in Tamil by his Head Clerk, V. Periaswamy Aiyer. The speakers expatiated on the private virtues of the Queen Empress, and on the merits of her administration. The usual distribution of sandal, flowers, *pan supari*, and rose-water followed. After music and singing, the meeting broke up with three cheers for Her Majesty.

MANJERI (MALABAR).

The rejoicings on the 20th June commenced at 8 o'clock in the morning, when a public meeting, which was very largely attended, was held at the Cutcherry Hall. Mr. Manjeri Karanamulpad was unanimously voted to the chair. After various speeches the Chairman, followed by those around him, moved out of the Hall into the Cutcherry compound, and planted a jack tree as a Jubilee Memorial. Others did the same, and fifty such trees were planted. At the conclusion of the ceremony cheers were given for Her Majesty. Special prayers for Her Majesty were offered in all places of worship in the town, and a large portrait of the Queen Empress was unveiled by Mr. Wedderburn, the Special Assistant Collector. The portrait was the carried in procession to Mallapuram and Tiroor, and on the 21st it was brought back to Manjeri in procession, with tom-toms and music, and installed in the School hall.

METTAPALAIYAM (COIMBATORE).

On the morning of the 20th June special services were held in the London Mission Church and other places of worship for the long life and prosperity of the Queen Empress, and at 4 P.M. a large procession of schoolboys and the general public passed along the main road. A portrait of Her Majesty was carried in front of the procession, and bands of native musicians and Erula dancers were in attendance. The procession reached the Jubilee Pandal, which was decorated with different inscriptions and mottoes. At 5 o'clock the Police fired a *feu de joie*. Races, sports, &c., followed, and continued till dark. A display of fireworks then took place, and the people were entertained in a refreshment booth, and *pan supari* and flowers were distributed. On the following morning a treat was given to the school children, and money was distributed to about 400 poor people.

MULKI (SOUTH CANARA).

The fiftieth anniversary of the Accession of Her Majesty the Queen Empress of India was celebrated here with great *éclat*. Special services were held in honour of the day in all Hindu, Christian, and Mohammedan places of public worship. A public meeting was held at 2 P.M. in the Hall of the Town School, which had been tastefully decorated for the occasion. The proceedings of the meeting commenced by the Chairman explaining the event which they had met to celebrate. Mr. M. Mukunda Rao made a speech in Canarese, after which the Rev. Mr. Ehle, of the Basel Mission, offered a prayer in Canarese at the request of the meeting. The *pujaries* of the Hindu temples distributed sweetmeats, &c. (*prasad*), in token of the services held in their temples, and recited Sanscrit verses, invoking the richest blessings of the Almighty on Her Majesty. Two Canarese songs prepared for the occasion by a poet of the station were sung. One of the songs consisted of a prayer for the Queen Empress, while the other was a brief description of the celebration of the Jubilee of Her Majesty in India. After the singing there were performances of various kinds, and a Mussalman musician entertained the audience with some music on the *sarang*. Sugar, *pan supari*, and sweetmeats were distributed among those assembled, and rose-water was sprinkled. Fragrant sticks were burnt in the hall all the time. A native band was in attendance. The meeting dispersed with three hearty cheers for Her Majesty, and a vote of thanks to the Mission Agents for the use of the hall.

NANDYAL (KURNOOL).

This town was decorated on the 20th June with festoons, palms, &c. Prayers in the several temples and mosques for the long life and reign of Her Majesty were offered in the morning, and in the evening the sacred buildings were beautifully illuminated. A nautch was held in the premises of the Local Fund Normal School Hall at night, at which the chief inhabitants of the town were present. The Hall, which was brilliantly lighted, was crowded. Three sets of nautch girls danced, and several Hindustani and Sanscrit songs were sung by amateurs. An English dance followed, and cheers resounded from all parts of the building. The telegram to the Queen Empress adopted by the Committee at Madras was read and explained to the audience in Tamil, Telugu, Malayalim, Canarese, Mahratti, and Hindustani. The telegram was approved. The Chairman, Mr. Vencatajagga Row, then made a speech, in which he pointed out the marked advance Kurnool had made of late years. Sandal, flowers, *pan supari*, and rose-water were distributed, and three cheers were given for Her Majesty.

NEGAPATAM (TANJORE).

The fiftieth anniversary of Her Majesty's accession to the Throne was observed on the 20th June in a most befitting manner. Mr. Pedro, of the local Bank, made arrangements to hold a Jubilee meeting in his Hall. There was a very large gathering of people of all classes. The chair was taken by Mr. R. Morris, the Head Assistant Collector. At the close of the meeting the National Anthem was sung, the whole audience joining heartily in it.

ONGOLE (NELLORE).

Sports of various kinds were held on the 20th June, in which the boys and girls of the school took part. After the sports prizes were distributed, and the school children sat down to an excellent treat provided for them. At night a Pandal erected opposite the Municipal School was illuminated, and here, at 9 o'clock, a meeting was held, with Mr. Moberly, C.S., in the chair. There was a large gathering of people present. The Chairman made a speech, and read the proposed Madras congratulatory telegram to the Queen Empress. The telegram was adopted with acclamation, and the National Anthem was sung. Three hearty cheers were given for Her Majesty, a *feu de joie* was fired by the Police, and a display of fireworks followed. The proceedings terminated with a nautch, and the distribution of *pan supari*.

OUCHTERLONY VALLEY (NILGIRIS).

The 20th June was observed in a very loyal manner by the planters of South-East Wynaad. The chief event of the day was a Jubilee service held at Lauriston Store by the Rev. A. W. L. Smith, Chaplain of the District. Most of the planters and their families from Neddivuttum, Gudalur, and the Valley attended this service, in which they joined most heartily. The offertory, which was a very handsome one, was for the completion of the Church at Gudalur. The National Anthem brought the service to a close.

PALGHAUT (MALABAR).

On the 20th June the bazaars were decorated, and strings of leaves were suspended at intervals across the roads. In the evening there was an illumination. A special service, conducted by the Rev. W. Dilger, of the Basel Mission, was held in Trinity Church. The attendance was good. The musical portion of the service was most creditable to Mrs. Dilger, who presided at the harmonium, and to those who volunteered their services as choristers. The church was profusely decorated with crotons, palm-leaves, ferns, and flowers. After the service, three trees to commemorate the Jubilee were planted by three ladies in the church compound. The Rev. W. Dilger (who had already preached an eloquent sermon suitable to the occasion) made an appropriate address after the planting of the trees. The company separated after having sung the National Anthem, and given three cheers for the Queen Empress.

PARAMATHI (SALEM).

The fiftieth anniversary of Her Majesty's accession to the throne was celebrated at this town on June 20th with great *éclat*. A large and enthusiastic meeting was held in the "Jubilee Hall" in front of the "Victoria Lodge," which was rapidly approaching completion. Native music played all day, and prayers for Her Majesty's long life were offered in all the temples. A treat was given to the school children, and over 200 poor persons, including the labourers employed in the construction of the "Victoria Lodge," were sumptuously fed. At night the public offices were brilliantly illuminated. *Pan supari* was distributed. Great enthusiasm prevailed.

PENUKONDA (ANANTAPUR).

At daybreak on the 20th June a salute of 31 guns was fired, and at 7 o'clock a meeting was held in Ramaswamy's temple for the purpose of opening a Choultry which a citizen of Penukonda, Mr. Etigowny Hanumiah, has established as a permanent memorial of Her Majesty's Jubilee. The Choultry is situated within the precincts of the temple, which was beautifully decorated. A large gathering of people witnessed the ceremony, which was performed by Mr. B. Macleod, the Head Assistant Collector, who made an excellent speech. Mr. H. Krishna Rao, the District Munsiff, also addressed the meeting. Other speeches were made in the vernacular, and the village priest performed the Hindu ceremonial of worshipping the god

Ganaisa, and breaking a cocoanut. The Chairman having declared the "Jubilee Choultry" open, sweetmeats and mangoes were distributed among the school children present. The assembly then marched in procession, headed by music, to the plot of ground adjoining the Fort ditch, near the northern entrance to the town (measuring about two acres), which Mr. H. Krishna Rao had resolved to present to the town for a Fruit Garden. Mr. Macleod performed the ceremony of planting the first tree—a grafted mangoe—in the "Jubilee Park." Cheers were given for Her Majesty at frequent intervals. A procession then marched to the house of the Head Assistant Collector, where the school children were feasted. The poor were fed during the day. Sports were held in the afternoon, and at 7 P.M. there was a grand procession of the temple gods, with native music. The procession halted at the northern gate of the temple, where the Memorial Lamp was lighted by Mrs. Macleod, and the people cheered.

RAMNAD (MADURA).

Early in the morning of the 20th June the Minor Zemindar held a State Durbar, when the usual presentations were made. At 10 A.M. about 700 Brahmins were fed at three different places erected for the Smarthas, Vaishnavas, and Madhvas respectively. The poor of the town were liberally fed in the Estate Choultry. Later on services were held in the Protestant and Roman Catholic churches, and prayers were offered in all the mosques and temples throughout the Zemindary, the Minor Zemindar attending the service in the great temple in the Palace. At 3 P.M. a procession left the Palace under an Imperial salute of 31 guns. Her Majesty's portrait, decked with flowers, was placed in the State howdah on the State elephant, which was beautifully caparisoned. The elephant was preceded by all the ancient insignia of this State. On the right rode the Minor Zemindar in full uniform, bearing the Royal Sword; and on the left rode his brother, also in full uniform, bearing the Royal Standard, hoisted on a lance. The Palace band and elephants preceded the procession, and the high officials of the State brought up the rear. When the procession reached the gate of the Magistrate's office a halt was made, and a "Jubilee Lamp," erected by Mr. Henry, the Head Assistant Collector, was formally declared open. The company reached Lakshmipuram at 5 P.M. The portrait was taken out of the howdah, and was carried by the Minor Zemindar and Mr. T. Rajah Ram Rao to the Chattram gate, and placed on a lace carpet under a canopy, supported by four silver posts. The Palace Dalayats, with swords drawn, took up positions in front of the picture, forming a guard of honour. Sports were next held, and prizes distributed to the winners. The sports included horse races, tent pegging, elephant race, donkey race, flat race, sack race, three-legged race, chatty race, wrestling, single-stick, and fencing. The sports being over, the whole place was illuminated. The illumination of the tank was especially excellent. The hundreds of lamps around it and the illumined boats produced a charming effect. Music was played on an ariston. The Minor Zemindar rose, amid much applause, and addressed the large assembly. Mr. Kotaisawmy Thaver, the Sub-Division Zemindar, next delivered an eloquent address in Tamil, and the Head Assistant Collector made a speech. Sweetmeats were next distributed to the school children, and attar and *pan supari* to the audience. Everybody present then stood up, and the National Anthem was sung by the Church Choir, the Zemindar and others joining heartily in the hymn. A banquet was laid out in tents for the European guests, and at 9.30 P.M. a grand display of fireworks took place on the bund of the tanks. The proceedings closed with three hearty cheers for the Queen-Empress, in which the multitude of people present joined.

RANIPET (NORTH ARCOT).

At 8 A.M. on the 20th June the inhabitants turned out in large numbers to witness the ceremony of opening the new Reading Room, the foundation stone of which was laid on the 16th February. The Rev. Mr. Conklin presided on the occasion, and performed the ceremony of declaring the Room open. Cheers were given for Her Majesty, for the Collector of the District, for the Assistant Collector, and for the Chairman. A liberal distribution of garlands, *pan supari*, &c., and the sprinkling of rose-water followed. The meeting terminated with the singing of the National Anthem.

SHOLINGHUR (NORTH ARCOT).

During the 20th June *abishekams* were performed in the Hindu temple on the hill, in the name of Her Majesty, and there were great rejoicings in the town. The poor were fed, and at night the gods of the Vishnu and Siva temples were carried round the town in procession, accompanied by Hindu music and dancing girls. At the conclusion of the procession, the District Munsiff made a speech appropriate to the occasion. The proceedings terminated with three hearty cheers for the Queen Empress.

TADPATRI (ANANTAPUR).

Early on the 20th June prayers for the long life and prosperity of Her Majesty were offered in all Hindu and Mohammedan places of worship. About 500 poor people were fed between 9 A.M. and 1 P.M. The streets were decorated with festoons.

A meeting was held in the Taluk Cutcherry at 2 P.M., and was largely attended, Mr. J. Balls, the President of the Jubilee Committee, taking the chair. The portrait of the Queen Empress was placed in a prominent position. The proceedings began with native music and singing. Then Mr. Vijiaraghavalu Naidu, on behalf of the President, addressed the meeting in Telugu on the blessings of Her Majesty's administration, and was followed by Messrs. Chengal Rao, and the Rev. Mr. Williams. The Sub-Postmaster, Mr. Jaffer Hussain Sahib, addressed the meeting in Hindustani. The Madras congratulatory telegram to the Queen Empress was read in three different languages, and was unanimously adopted. Garlands and *pan supari* were distributed, and three hearty cheers were given for Her Majesty. The portrait was carried in procession at 6 P.M. through the town, accompanied by music and dancing. The procession returned to the Taluk Cutcherry at 9 P.M.

TANJORE (TANJORE).

On the 20th June a public meeting was held at the Reading Room, Tanjore, at which Mr. S. A. Saminatha Iyer presided. The Chairman spoke of the manifold blessings showered upon India during the reign of the Queen Empress. A Jubilee Memorial Library, for the use of the public, was inaugurated in connection with the Reading Room. The meeting terminated with three cheers for Her Majesty. The Volunteers held a rifle meeting at the range. A large tent was pitched on the ground, where light refreshments were served. Firing commenced at 6 A.M., and ceased at noon. Several small money prizes were competed for, after the distribution of which three hearty cheers were given for the Queen Empress, and the National Anthem was sung.

TIRIPATUR (SALEM DISTRICT).

A public meeting of the inhabitants of the town was held at 5.30 P.M. on the 20th June, and was very largely attended. Dr. C. W. W. Martin, the District Judge, presided. After the meeting was over, a procession, in which the leading men in the town took part, and attended with music, marched from the Post Office to a tent pitched near Boopathiroyans tank. On arriving at the latter place, Dr. Martin laid, with the usual ceremonial, the foundation stone for the improvement and extension of the tank as a permanent memorial of the Jubilee. The guard of honour presented arms, and the assembly cheered. An Imperial salute was then fired. The Chairman having resumed his seat, a Jubilee portrait of the Queen Empress was taken round, and shown to the people, who saluted it. Flowers, *pan supari* and rose-water, &c., were distributed. A vote of thanks having been passed to the

Chairman, three cheers were given for him, and the proceedings terminated with three hearty cheers for Her Majesty and the Royal Family.

TRICHINOPOLY (TRICHINOPOLY).

By permission of Lieutenant-Colonel J. H. M. Barnett, Commandant of the 4th Pioneers, Subadar Major Mahomed Baig Bahadur of that corps made arrangements with the rest of the native officers, all non-commissioned officers, men and public followers who heartily and unanimously co-operated with him, to celebrate the Queen's Jubilee on the 20th June. The buildings occupied by the Regimental Girls' Schools and Reading Club were set apart for this purpose, and decorated with flags, festoons, &c. A magnificent Pandal was erected in front of these buildings. The whole place was illuminated at night. The Queen's "Jubilee Portrait" was set up in the Centre Room. There were present the Collector of Trichinopoly and almost all the European gentlemen and ladies residing in this town, the regimental officers, both European and native, and some pensioned native officers. The officers and regimental guests took their seats in the Pandal, after visiting the rooms, at 10 P.M. There they heard the benefits of Her Majesty's reign described in English by the Regimental Schoolmaster. The translations of his remarks were also read in Hindustani, Tamil, and Telugu. 160 rank and file, who paraded in review order under a native officer, now fired a *feu de joie* and gave three cheers, after which a few men were put through the bayonet exercise. The officers and guests drank the health of the Queen Empress, garlands of flowers were distributed, and rose-water sprinkled. The girls attending the Regimental School sang a song praying for Her Majesty's long life and prosperity. They were accompanied by native music. The regimental band was in attendance. Some of the drummers disguised themselves as negroes, and played a farce. Then there appeared two men and a boy in Burmese disguise, and amused the assembly a great deal. The assembly then witnessed some gymnastic performances. A brilliant display of fireworks followed, which lasted till midnight, when the band played "God save the Queen," and the assembly dispersed.

VELLORE (NORTH ARCOT).

The 20th day of June was a day of universal rejoicing with the people of Vellore. Festoons and evergreens graced the principal buildings of the city, while private residences were decorated in humbler ways. At daybreak a thanksgiving service was held in the Fort Church, a large congregation being present. The Hindu gods of the place were collected on the Esplanade, whither they were taken in procession, with music, through the streets. At sunset there were illuminations and bonfires, and some of the principal buildings of the place were magnificently lit up. *Abishakams* and *Archanas* were performed in the Hindu temples, and prayers for Her Majesty were said in the Mohammedan mosques. The European portion of the inhabitants met at the house of Mr. Andrew, the Sub-Collector, and drank to the health and long life of the Queen Empress. A procession of the people of Vellore marched to the house of Mr. Andrew, to offer their congratulations to their "Sovereign Mother" on the happy event of the Jubilee. Then followed a nautch by the dancing-girls attached to the temple establishment. The National Anthem was sung enthusiastically. Garlands of flowers were placed round the necks of Mr. Andrew, Colonel J. B. Taylor, and Colonel Stevenson, and rose-water was sprinkled. The deputation then withdrew, and marched back to the Esplanade, where there was a good display of fireworks, at the close of which sugar and *pan supari* were lavishly distributed. The gods were then carried back to their respective temples, in procession, escorted by the local dignitaries.

VIZIANAGRAM (VIZAGAPATAM).

As the Maharajah was absent in Madras at the official celebration of Her Majesty's Jubilee on the 16th February last, he determined to have another celebration on the anniversary day itself. He therefore gave a grand ball at the Mothi-Mahal Palace within the Fort. About fifty of the local and neighbouring officials, officers, and other gentlemen, were able to avail themselves of His Highness's invitation. The ball commenced about 10 P.M., and was kept up, with an interval for supper at midnight, with much spirit until nearly 3 A.M. The Palace was illuminated, a large transparency of the Royal Coat-of-Arms being displayed over the entrance gate to the Fort, and a portrait of Her Majesty over the Palace itself. Small lights were exhibited on the ramparts and the neighbouring houses. A portrait of Her Majesty occupied a prominent position in the supper room, surmounted by a large crown and a silver star, with "50 Years" inscribed in the centre, and "God save our Empress" in gold letters on a crimson scroll, and supported by the Royal Standard and the Union Jack. The Maharajah attended by his staff received the guests as they arrived. The troops paraded in front of the Palace. The entertainment concluded with a magnificent display of fireworks. At the supper His Highness proposed Her Majesty's health in appropriate terms, and Mr. Turner, the Collector and Agent of the Governor, replied in a few well-chosen words, and proposed the health of the popular, loyal, and hospitable Maharajah. The toasts were drunk with enthusiasm. The houses of the Maharajah's staff were prettily illuminated. On the 22nd instant, Colonel Puckle and the officers of the 28th Regiment M.I. entertained all the gentlemen of the station at dinner, at which the Maharajah was present. There was also a special Jubilee gymkhana meeting on the 20th and 22nd, when several races were well contested. On Thursday, the 23rd, a dance was given by the ladies in the station, and went off exceedingly well.

WALLAJAPET (NORTH ARCOT).

At 10 o'clock on the morning of the 20th June, a large number of the inhabitants of the town assembled in the Taluk Cutcherry to witness the ceremony of laying the foundation stone of the new "Jubilee Hall" to be erected in front of the Cutcherry. The Rev. Dr. Hokhuis of the American Mission, Ranipett, presided, and performed the ceremony. Several speeches were made, the National Anthem was sung in chorus, and prayers for the long life of the Queen Empress were offered. At the close of the meeting garlands and *pan supari* were distributed. Special Thanksgiving Services were held in all places of public worship in the evening, and at night the town was illuminated, and there was a procession of the temple gods through the streets. Fireworks were let off at intervals. Over 300 people were fed, and sweetmeats were distributed.

TRICHOOR (NATIVE COCHIN).

The 20th June broke cloudy and threatening; but it eventually turned out a splendid day. In the grey of the morning the Maharajah's troops fired a Royal salute in front of the Cutcherry; this was followed by the usual march past. At 8 o'clock the *élite* of the place assembled some three miles out of the town to witness the opening of the "Victoria Jubilee Park" to the public. The Dewan Peishcar, Mr. A. Sankariah, B.A., said a few appropriate words, and then the new iron gates were opened, and all passed through in procession, headed by ten large elephants, with a fine portrait of Her Majesty in a prominent position. The Park covers a large area, and is a most charming spot on a hill; in the centre is a handsome Mantapam erected in honour of Sir Mountstuart Grant Duff. The proceedings terminated with three hearty cheers for the Queen Empress. At 2 o'clock a large gathering assembled in the Promenade Gardens to witness the formal opening of a Mantapam in honour of Mr. J. C. Hannyngton, the British Resident. It is a handsome building in the Tanjore style of architecture. A fine Pandal had been erected at the back of the Mantapam, where music was played at frequent intervals. The building was adorned with a few excellent photographs, taken by Mr. Hannyngton. Mr. Sankariah expressed the pleasure it afforded him to declare the building open, and to commemorate the occasion still further, suggested that three cocoa-nut trees be planted, one for the Queen Empress, one for the Maharajah, and the third for Mr. Hannyngton. This being pre-eminently the land of the cocoa-nut, it was thought no more suitable tree could be chosen. Accordingly Mr. J. S. Sealy was requested to plant a young cocoa-nut tree in honour of the Queen Empress, which he did, at the same time expressing his appreciation of the honour done him, and the great pleasure it gave him. Mr. Teruvenkata Charriar, the Judge, did the same on behalf of the Maharajah; and the Dewan Peishcar himself planted the third nut in the name of Mr. Hannyngton. This ceremony being concluded sports were held. During the afternoon a *feu de joie* was fired by His Highness's troops. Nair girls sang some native songs. Badminton and lawn tennis were played with great zest by a few, and afforded amusement to many, till the shades of evening put a stop to the games. The thirsty ones then refreshed themselves with tea. A little later a concert of native music was held in the Hannyngton Muntapam, and amongst others Mr. Teruvenkata Charriar, Judge of Trichoor, sang several songs with great taste, including a Jubilee ode in Tamil, which he had composed. The Muntapam and Gardens were prettily illuminated.

SANDUR (SANDUR).

On the 20th June the Palace and all the public buildings, together with some private dwellings were decorated, and garlands of leaves were hung in festoons over the main streets. By 5 P.M. 213 poor adults and 297 children who had assembled at the Palace gates, received a money dole. A procession then set out from the Palace, consisting of the Rajah, his brother and his son-in-law, the Dewan, Mr. J. G. Firth and family, the officials, and a large number of townspeople, preceded by music. Passing the Hospital, the Post Office, and the Police Station, the procession turned to the right by the road leading past the Vithoba temple, and in about half an hour reached the new building intended for the use of the Anglo-Vernacular and Sanscrit School. This building, though not quite finished, is in a forward state of preparation, part of the roof being already put on. It was decorated with festoons of foliage, and lighted with pretty Chinese lanterns. The hall was soon filled, and so were the two verandahs. An address in Canarese was read by the Munshi, Mr. K. Abdul Rahim, setting forth briefly the many benefits that have accrued to India during Her Majesty's reign, and declaring the Rajah's desire to commemorate the present joyful celebration by naming the building the "Victoria Jubilee School-room." After acclamations a speech was made by Mr. Raghavendra Achary, the master of the School, followed by recitation of a Sanscrit poem by the Sanscrit teacher, Mr. Komar Bhatt, composed in honour of Her Majesty's Jubilee. The National Anthem was now sung by the Dewan, his wife, and four children, accompanied by the harmonium, which was played by the Dewan. The people again clapped their hands, and shouted in Canarese "Victory to Queen Victoria!" Some native singing and music followed, and after the distribution of *pan supari*, the crowd dispersed. Afterwards the Rajah had a nautch at the Palace, which a large number of people attended.

ALLUSIONS IN THE NARRATIVES

Explained by the late Mr. Vembaukum Ramiengar, C.S.I., &c.

Abishekam is not a part of the daily ritual in pagodas, but is performed on extraordinary occasions. It is the act of anointing the god ceremonially, with the view of removing any pollution, or defilement. Oil, milk, turmeric powder mixed with water, water taken from tender cocoanuts, and aromatic substances are all used in washing the image, and the ceremony is accompanied by the recital of appropriate hymns from the Vedas. The image is then draped and decorated. Offerings of food, flowers, and fruit are then made, and the god is worshipped.

Archanai is that part of the Hindu worship which consists in praise. The priest takes a quantity of *tulasi* (Ocymum Sanctum) and flowers in a salver; recites what is called *Sahasranamam* (literally "thousand names") which recounts the attributes, and lauds the exploits of the deity during his several incarnations on earth; and offers the *tulasi* and flowers at the feet of the image. This ceremony is supposed to free the person in whose name, or for whose benefit it is performed, from ills from which he may be suffering, or to which he is liable, and to confer upon him the blessing of the god.

Ashtavathanam is a performance in which eight different things are done, or attended to by the same person at the same time. For instance, he plays at chess with one person; he answers questions put to him by another; he composes and recites a poem of a given metre, and on a given subject; and so on.

Bhagavatam is the one of three well-known epic poems in Sanscrit, which describes the life, and details the exploits of Vishnu in his incarnation as Krishna. It is read in order to invoke the blessings of Krishna on any person, or family on whose behalf it is read.

Chithira Vimanam.—This is the same as Vimanam, but decorated and ornamented.

Distribution of sandal, flowers, attar, &c.—This is customary on festive occasions.

Distribution of sugar.—This is not a necessary part of every rejoicing, but forms a feature of the ceremonial at births.

Kathinas (a word used on the western coast), and *Athirvadies* (a word used on the eastern coast) mean the same thing. An iron tube is attached to a block of wood. The tube is charged with gunpowder, with clay over it, well rammed in. This is taken about during a procession, or festival, and at short intervals the gunpowder is set fire to by the man in charge, and goes off with a loud report.

Mantapapadi.—When a god is taken in procession, *mantapapadi* is a halt made by the god in what are called *mantapams*, or open stone structures, resting on stone pillars, or in booths erected for the occasion. It is considered very meritorious on the part of a person to get the god to rest at his *mantapam*, or booth. During the stay, which is generally brief, offerings are made to the god, and food, fruits, and flowers are distributed to the assembled crowd.

Mrityunjayam.—The word literally means conquest of death. It is the house-name of the Zemindar of Sangamvalsa in the Vizagapatam District. His capital is called Mrityanjaya Nagaram, or the city of Mrityanjaya.

Pan supari.—*Pan* is the betel leaf, and *supari* is the areca nut. The natives of India chew this with lime. It may be said to be a part of their daily food. No labourer can do his work well without it. When one friend goes to see another, it is etiquette to give *pan supari* to the visitor before he leaves the house. There is no rejoicing of any kind in India at which the distribution of *pan supari* does not form a necessary accompaniment.

Prasadam.—This is the food distributed to people after it has been offered to the gods in the pagodas.

Puja means worship in the prescribed manner by reciting hymns and prayers, offering flowers, fruits, food, &c. *Pujaris* are those who perform puja in pagodas.

Rose-water sprinkling is an accompaniment of festivity. What in a cold climate would be considered somewhat disagreeable, is grateful and refreshing in the tropics.

Rudrabishekam.—This consists of two words, *Rudra* and *Abishekam*. *Rudra* means Shiva the Destroyer, of the trinity of the Vedas. *Abishekam* has already been explained. The word taken as a whole means the anointing, or the purification of Rudra.

Thoranams are rows, chiefly of mango leaves, artistically arranged, and fastened to strings stretched across entrances to private dwellings on occasions of private rejoicings; or, in case of public processions or rejoicings, across roads or streets, attached on either side to the branches of avenue trees, or to posts specially provided.

Utsavam.—This means literally rejoicing, but it generally refers to the festival which takes place in a pagoda.

Vimanam.—This is a self-directed and self-moving chariot which is supposed to carry the gods through the skies. It also means the roofing (often plated with gold) which covers the innermost and holiest part of the temple.

THE ACKNOWLEDGMENTS

OF

HER MAJESTY THE QUEEN EMPRESS.

The following is the text of a telegram from the Right Honourable the Viscount Cross, G.C.B., Secretary of State for India, to His Excellency the Right Honourable the Earl of Dufferin, G.M.S.I., &c., Viceroy and Governor General of India, dated London, 22nd February, 1887:—

"I am commanded by Her Imperial Majesty the Queen Empress to inform your Excellency that she has been much touched by the manifestation of Loyalty to her Throne and Person which has been evinced by all classes of her subjects in her Indian Empire in the celebration of this fiftieth year of her reign, and by the numerous messages of congratulation which have been communicated to Her Imperial Majesty. The Queen Empress desires you to assure her Civil and Military Officers, and the Princes, Chiefs and People of India, of the deep interest and affection with which she regards them, and of her heartfelt wishes for their prosperity and happiness."

JUBILEE HONOURS CONFERRED IN MADRAS.

The following appointments were announced in the *Gazette of India* on the 16th February, 1887:—

THE STAR OF INDIA.

His Excellency the Grand Master of the Most Exalted Order of the Star of India is pleased to announce that Her Majesty the Queen and Empress of India has been graciously pleased to make the following appointments to the said Order:—

TO BE COMPANION.

The Honourable Charles Gilbert Master, Madras Civil Service, Member of the Council of His Excellency the Governor of Fort St. George.

M. R. Ry. K. Sheshadri Iyer, B.A., B.L., Dewan to His Highness the Maharajah of Mysore.

THE INDIAN EMPIRE.

Her Majesty the Queen and Empress of India has been graciously pleased to make the following appointments to the Most Eminent Order of the Indian Empire:—

TO BE KNIGHT COMMANDER.

His Highness the Honourable Pusapati Ananda Gajapati Raz, Maharajah of Vizianagram, and Member of the Legislative Council of His Excellency the Governor of Fort St. George.

TO BE COMPANION.

M. R. Ry. Palle Chentsal Row Pantalu Garu, Superintendent of Stamps and Stationery, Madras.

PERSONAL DISTINCTIONS.

TO BE KNIGHT BACHELOR.

Her Majesty the Queen and Empress of India has been pleased to confer the honour of Knighthood on the undermentioned gentleman:—

M. R. Ry. P. S. Ramaswami Mudelliar, C.I.E., Sheriff of Madras.

TO BE MAHAMAHOPADHYAYA.

His Excellency the Viceroy and Governor-General is pleased to confer the title of Mahamahopadhyaya upon the following gentlemen as a personal distinction:—

M. R. Ry. M. Raja Sástriyár.

M. R. Ry. T. Srikrishna Tátáchâriyar.

M. R. Ry. S. Srimán Perámra Alaghasengam Bhuttar.

M. R. Ry. T. Venkata Rangachâriyar.

TO BE SHAMS-UL-ULAMA.

His Excellency the Viceroy and Governor-General is pleased to confer the title of Shams-ul-Ulama upon the following gentlemen as a personal distinction:—

Haji Maulvi Bakr-ud-din Sayyid Muhhammad Khaderi.

Hafiz Muhammad Lutfulla.

Maulavi Tamaiah Khan Bahadur.

H H b

TO BE RAJAH.

His Excellency the Viceroy and Governor-General is pleased to confer upon the undermentioned gentleman the title of Rajah as a personal distinction:—

The Honourable T. Rama Row, Member of the Legislative Council of His Excellency the Governor of Fort St. George, and Vakil of the High Court, Madras.

TO BE DEWAN BAHADUR.

His Excellency the Viceroy and Governor-General is pleased to confer upon the undermentioned gentlemen the title of Dewan Bahadur as a personal distinction:—

M. R. Ry. T. Venkaswami Row, First Assistant Revenue Secretariat, Madras.

M. R. Ry. J. Lakshmikanta Row Pantalu, Deputy Director of Revenue Settlement, Madras.

M. R. Ry. P. Srinivasa Row Garu, Judge of the Court of Small Causes, Madras.

TO BE KHAN BAHADUR.

His Excellency the Viceroy and Governor-General is pleased to confer upon the undermentioned gentlemen the title of Khan Bahadur as a personal distinction:—

Mahomed Ishak, Saiub Bahadur, Assistant Paymaster of Carnatic Stipends.

Ghulam Mahammed Haidar Sahib, Inspector of Police, Madras.

Haji Mahomed Abdulla Badsha Sahib, Merchant, Madras.

TO BE RAI BAHADUR.

His Excellency the Viceroy and Governor-General is pleased to confer upon the undermentioned gentlemen the title of Rai Bahadur as a personal distinction:—

The Honourable S. Subrahmanya Aiyar, B.L., Member of the Legislative Council of His Excellency the Governor of Fort St. George, and Vakil of the High Court, Madras.

M. R. Ry. Runganadha Mudelliar, M.A., Professor of Mathematics, Presidency College, Madras.

M. R. Ry. P. Ramaswami Chettiar, Vice-President of the Madras Municipality.

M. R. Ry. P. Rajaratnam Mudelliar, Sheristadar of the Board of Revenue, Madras.

M. R. Ry. P. Ananda Charlu, B.L., Vakil of the High Court, Madras.

M. R. Ry. Kodi Narayanaswami Naidu, Inspector of Police, Madras.

M. R. Ry. Nallari Jagganatha Row Pantalu, Deputy Collector, Madras.

M. R. Ry. V. Bashyam Iyengar, Vakil of the High Court, Madras.

M. R. Ry. Arcot Dhanakoti Mudelliar, Madras.

M. R. Ry. K. Kunjan Menon, Subordinate Judge of Tellicherry.

M. R. Ry. Adaki Sadananda Row, Deputy Collector, Madras.

M. R. Ry. T. Subramanya Pillai, Assistant Engineer, P.W.D., Madras.

M. R. Ry. S. Ayyaswami Shastri, Tahsildar of Kumbaconum.

The following notification was published in the *London Gazette* of the 13th May, 1887:—

THE PEERAGE.

TO BE BARON OF THE UNITED KINGDOM.

Whitehall, May 10, 1887.—The Queen has been pleased to direct Letters Patent to be passed under the Great Seal of the United Kingdom of Great Britain and Ireland, granting the dignity of a Baron of the said United Kingdom unto the Right Honourable Robert Bourke, Governor of the Presidency of Madras, and the heirs male of his body lawfully begotten, by the name, style, and title of Baron Connemara, of Connemara, in the County of Galway.

The following notification was published in the *London Gazette* of the 21st June, 1887:—

THE INDIAN EMPIRE.

The Queen has been pleased to make on the occasion of the celebration of the completion of the fiftieth year of Her Majesty's reign, the following appointment to the Most Eminent Order of the Indian Empire, viz.:—

TO BE KNIGHT GRAND COMMANDER.

The Right Honourable Robert, Lord Connemara, Governor of the Presidency of Madras.

The following notification was published in the *London Gazette* of the 8th July, 1887:—

KNIGHTHOOD.

TO BE KNIGHT BACHELOR.

Windsor Castle, June 30, 1887.—The Queen was this day pleased to confer the honour of Knighthood on Charles Allen Lawson, Esq., of London, in the County of Middlesex, England, and of Madras, in the East Indies.

THE RELEASE OF PRISONERS.

The Viceroy and Governor-General in Council has been pleased to issue orders as follows for the release, as an act of clemency and grace, of a certain number of prisoners (Criminal and Civil) and the remission of a portion of the sentences of other prisoners in all the Jails throughout British India, and in the Penal Settlement of Port Blair and the Nicobars, on the day appointed for public rejoicing to celebrate the fiftieth year of the reign of Her Most Gracious Majesty the Queen Empress of India. Local Governments and Administrations have been desired on this day to release 10 per cent. of all the convicts under sentence, provided that their conduct during imprisonment has been good, and that their release is not likely to give rise to a revival of blood feuds or professional crime. With a view also of extending clemency and grace to criminals whose cases would not be covered by the above concession, but who are appropriate objects of clemency on this occasion, His Excellency in Council has directed the release of all female convicts whose offences were not of a serious nature, and of all convicts, male and female, the term of whose sentences expires on or before the 20th June, 1887, the fiftieth anniversary of Her Majesty's accession. His Excellency in Council has also been pleased to extend a measure of grace and clemency to those who in the interest of society cannot now be released, by directing that remissions of sentences be made which shall be graduated according to the character of the sentence in each case, and which may extend to a month's remission for each year of imprisonment passed in jail. As regards the convicts in the Andamans, the Governor General in Council has directed the absolute release this day of 37[illegible] convicts, and has instituted enquiries with a view to the release, if possible, of 50 more, under sentence for dacoity. His Excellency in Council has further sanctioned, in the case of other convicts in the Settlement, certain concessions which, while lessening the severity of the sentences on those who have by their good conduct merited consideration, will not diminish the punitive or deterrent character of the sentences of convicts who have made no progress towards reformation. As regards civil prisoners, the Governor General in Council has been pleased to order the release of all persons confined in prison in execution of decrees of the Civil Courts whose debts do not exceed the sum of Rs. 100, provided they are poor, and not fraudulent; and the payment by Government of the debt or debts for which they are detained. The number of prisoners who will be released this day in accordance with these orders is as follows:—

From Jails in British India — —	21,240 Males.	1,437 Females.	22,677 Total.
From the Andamans — — — —	400 "	30 "	430 "
Civil Prisoners — — — — —	198 "	— "	198 "
Grand Total — — —	21,838 Males.	1,467 Females.	23,305 Total.

Gazette of India, 16th February, 1887.

THE QUEEN EMPRESS'S JUBILEE FUND.

Principal Subscriptions Received by the Madras Central Committee.

	Rs.
Accountant-General's Office	[illegible]
Adam, M.A., Mr. John	[illegible]
Allison, Sergeant-Major Hamlet	30
Anonymous	25
Arbuthnot, Mr. George Gough	1,000
Arbuthnot, Mr. Reginald J. H.	250
Arbuthnot & Co.'s Office	[illegible]
Arcot, H.H. the Prince of	700
Army Clothing Office	58
Arnee, the Jagheerdar of	150
Arsenal, Madras, Employés	25
Azeem-un-Nissa Begum Sahibah	100
Babu Rao, Mr. M.	50
Batchelor, Captain W. L. C.	45
Banganapalle, the Nawab of	[illegible]
Barclay and Morgan, Messrs.	250
[illegible], the Hon'ble R. W.	[illegible]
Barrow, Mr. Cecil M.	100
Bartlett, Mr. W. H.	50
[illegible], Colonel Frank	50
Benson, Mr. C.	50
Best and Co., Messrs.	[illegible]
Bhashyam Iyengar, Mr. V.	100
Bill, Mr. Frederick	50
Black, the Rev. John	50
[illegible], Mr. T. C.	25
[illegible], Colonel Edward O.	50
Bobbili, H.H. The Rajah of	2,000
Bond, Mr. H. M.	50
Bosworth, the Rev. E. F.	30
Bourke, the Right Hon'ble R.	1,000
Boyson, the Hon'ble J. A.	1,000
Bradley, Mr. Herbert	75
Brandt, the Hon'ble Mr. Justice	500
Branfoot, Dr. A. M.	75
Branson, Mr. J. C. L.	50
Branson and Branson, Messrs.	100
Browne, The Ven. Archdeacon J. F.	25
Buckingham Mill Employés	35
Burnett, The Rev. E. P.	50
Burton, Mr. E. F.	25
Cable Telegraph Office	80
Calder, Mr. Donald	25
Campbell, Mr. J.	50
Carnatic Mill's Employés	100
Chambers, Mr. George L.	150
Champion, Mr. A.	100
Chapman, Mr. R. C.	50
Chengalroy Chetty, Mr.	25
Chentsal Rao, Mr. P.	25
Chester, Mr. E. H.	30
Chief Secretariat Office	24
Chingleput Collector's Office	25
Christian College Students	40
Christian College Teachers	80
Chingleput Court Officials	30
[illegible], Mr. Herbert F. P.	100
Cochin, G.C.S.I., The Rajah of	1,500
Colgan, The Most Rev. Archbishop	100
Collins, The Hon'ble Sir Arthur	500
Commercial and L. Mortgage Bank	317
Commissary General's Office	32
Comptroller's Office Establishment	67
[illegible], Dr. C. O.	50
Coorg Military Acc'ts Office	25
Cooling, The Rev. J.	50
Cooper, The Rev. Charles	50
Coopooswamy Naidu, Mr. G.	35
Coppen Chetty, Mr.	100
Cox, Lieutenant-Colonel H. W. H.	50
Cutler, Palmer & Co., Messrs.	100
D'Angelis, Mr. G.	100
[illegible] & Co., Messrs. D. W.	100
De [illegible], Mr. Albert	100
[illegible] & Co., Messrs.	40
[illegible], Mr. W.	50
Drake-Brockman, Surg.-Maj. H. E.	25
D'Rozario, Mr. J. J.	20
Duncan, Dr. David	150
Dymes & Co., Messrs.	300
[illegible] & Co., Messrs.	500
Eliot, Mr. E. H.	24
[illegible], Major Charles A.	30
Engineering College and Staff	75
[illegible] Dayaram Bahadur	100
Examiner P. W. Acct. Office	40
Examiner Transport Acc'ts Office	67
Examiner Commissariat Acc'ts Office	34
Exam: Transport Off: Bangalore	62
Family Payment Office	27
Farrer, Mr. H.	50
Fawcett, Mr. G. W.	50
[illegible], Mr. James P.	50
Fisher, Lieutenant-Colonel, F. C.	60
Fowler, Mr. J. Townshend	100
Galton, Mr. Charles A.	100
Gajapathi Rao, Rajah G. N.	3,000
[illegible], Mr. G. S.	100
Gantz, Cassels & [illegible]	50
Gantz, Cassels & Co.'s Office	32
Garstin, C.S.I., Mr. John Henry	[illegible]
General Hospital Nursing Depot	62
General Post Office Establishment	138
Gill, Mr. Francis N. C.	100
G. L.	100
[illegible], Mr. William Henry	75
[illegible], The Rev. J. B.	100
Gordon, Woodroffe & Co., Messrs.	500
Gould, Mr. Michael	75
Government Press Employés	77
Grant and Laing, Messrs.	100
[illegible], Mr. James	250
Gov. Body Guard N. C. Offrs. & Men	107
Graves, Mr. Frank	50
[illegible], Colonel J. C.	100
Gunpowder Factory Employés	73
Guthrie, Colonel Thomas Key	100
Hackett, Surgeon-Major A. L.	91
[illegible], Mr. G.	50
Hadjee Abdoolah & Abooboker	250
Hadjee Mahomed Badsha Saib & Co.	1,000
Hadjee Mahomed [illegible] & Co., Messrs.	250
Hadjee [illegible] & Co., Messrs.	250
Hadjee [illegible] J. Mahomed & Co.	250
Hadjee John Mahomed & Co., Messrs.	250
Hall, Mr. H. A.	25
Hall, Mr. C.	50
[illegible], Mr. Murray	60
Hamnett, C.S.I., Mr. George	175
Handley, Mr. J. W.	100
Harrington, Mr. J. C.	250
Harbour Works Office	[illegible]
Hari Row, Mr. S.	40
Hasted, Colonel J. O.	100
Hawkins, Colonel H. P.	125
Higginbotham & Co., Messrs.	100
Higginbotham & Co.'s Office	32
Hill, Mr. Rowland	25
Hindu, Proprietors of the	50
[illegible], Mr. A.	40
Homayoon Jah Bahadur, C.I.E., Hon.	100
[illegible], Lieut.-Colonel W. H.	50
Howell, Mr. H. L.	40
Howlett, Captain A.	40
Hunt, Brigade-Surgeon S. B.	25
Hunt, Lieut.-Colonel E. Leigh	30
[illegible], Mr. Charles L.	25
Hutchins, The Hon'ble P. P.	750
[illegible] P. W. D. Office	21
Irish Press, Proprietor of the	100
Irvine, Mr. George Duncan	50
Johnson, C.B., Major Gen. A. C.	77
Johnston, Surgeon-Major W. E.	40
Jones, Mr. J. Alfred	40
Jones, Mr. O. H.	25

	Rs.
Kalahastry, The Rajah of . . .	1,500
Kangundi Estate, The Guardian of	75
Kearney, Hon. Surgeon William	20
Karvetnagar, The Rajah of . . .	50
Keith, Colonel George S.	100
Kernan, The Hon'ble Mr. Justice	500
Kodandarama Iyer, Mr. S. . .	65
Krishna Murti, Mr. T.	50
Krishnama Charry, Mr. V. . . .	500
Laing, Surgeon-Major J. A. . . .	200
Lawrence Asylum Press Employés	97
Lowry, Mr. Basil	35
Lunatic Asylum Employés . . .	78
Lys, Lieutenant-Colonel A. M. .	50
Madava Row, C.S.I., Rajah Sir T.	400
Madras Government, The . . .	10,000
Madras (Rt. Rev. F. Gell) Bp. of	200
Madras Mail, Proprietors of the	500
Madras Mail Office	100
Madras Ry. Chief Engineer's Office	20
Madras Ry. Traffic Department	75
Madras Ry. Audit Department .	691
Madras Salt Trading Co.'s Office	29
Mahomed Mahomed Khan Bahdr.	75
Mahadeva Chetty, Mr. Gopaldas	1,500
Mahomed Oomer Sait, Mr. . . .	200
Manicavelu Moodelliar, V. J. Mr.	100
Marjoribanks, Mr.	20
Marshall, Mr. T. E.	25
Martin, Mr. H. A.	50
Maskell, Mr. J. M.	25
Master, C.S.I., The Hon'ble C. G.	750
Mayne, Mr. F. G.	25
McCarthy, Mr. Samuel Trant .	100
McDowell & Co., Messrs. . . .	500
McMaster, Colonel John . . .	75
Medical College Employés . . .	28
Medical Subordinates, Vellore .	28
Meyer, Mr. W. S.	50
Mitchell, Mr. R. R.	125
Military Hospital, Medical Depart.	90
Miller, C.I.E., The Rev. Dr. W.	500
Millett, Mr. E. L.	50
Minchall, Mr. J. M.	24
Mohideen Sheriff Khan Bahdr., Dr.	50
Moore, Lieut.-Colonel G. M. J.	100
Morley, The Rev. Samuel . . .	25
Moses & Co., Messrs.	50
Moss, Mr. Louis S.	50
Municipal Office Establishment .	451
Murugesa Moodelliar, Mr. M. .	25
Murree Brewery, Unaccounted .	500
Muthusawmy Iyer, C.I.E., Hon. T.	500
Narasimmalu Chetty, Mr . . .	1000
Nangavaram Estate	40
Norton & Co., Messrs.	50
Norton, Mr. Eardley	50
Oakes & Co., Messrs.	500
Oakshott, Mr. E. F.	250
Ogilvie, Mr. James M.	20
Oppert, Dr. Gustave	60
Ordnance Office Employés . . .	12
Orme, Mr. H.	50
Orr and Sons, Messrs. Peter . .	600
O'Shaughnessy, Mr. J. E. . . .	20
O'Sullivan, The Hon'ble P. . .	250
Paper Currency Office	57
Parker, The Hon'ble G. A. . . .	500
Parry & Co., Messrs.	1,000
Parsons, Mr. R.	20

	Rs.
Pemberton, Surgeon Robert . .	50
Pennycuick, Lieut.-Colonel J.	100
Perambur Estate	100
Phipps, Mr. C. E.	10
Pogson, C.I.E. Mr. Norman R. .	50
Pogson, Miss E. Isis	25
Pogson, Mr. W. N.	25
Police Inspector General's Office	70
Police Officers and Constables .	640
Porter, Brigade-Surgeon Alexander	55
Post Office Establishment . .	95
Positive Insurance Co., the Agent	50
Prendergast, Colonel Hew L. .	34
Price, Mr. Frederick	100
Prince R. C. Arcot ... Madras	100
Press St. Thomé Mission . .	121
Puddicombe, Mr. C. J. . . .	21
Pittapur, The Rajah of . . .	1,500
Pudukota, Prince Regent of .	1,000
Public Works Secretariat Office	22
Public Works Workshops Estab.	135
Quinn, Surgeon Thomas . . .	20
Rae, The Rev. G. Milne . . .	50
Rajaratnam Chetty, V. and ...	500
Rajaratna Moodelliar, Mr. P. .	35
Ramachandra Iyer, Mr. C. . .	50
Ramaswamy Mudaliar, C.I.E., Sir P. S.	10,000
Rama Row, Dewan Bahadur Mr. P.	200
Ramanjulu Naidu and Sons, P.	500
Ramanathan Vasan, J. Tharaven	100
Ramiengar, C.S.I., Mr. V. . .	500
Ranganatham, Mr. P.	105
Ranganadham Mudr., Mr. P. .	50
Registrar's Office, High Court	54
Revenue Settlement Employés .	95
Revenue Board Office	473
Rice, The Rev. Henry	25
Ross, Dep. Surgeon General, S. B.	100
Rowlands, Mr. C. M.	50
Rowlandson, Mr. Frederick . .	50
Rule, Mr. S. R.	50
Runglah Lall & Co., Messrs. . .	50
Sabapathy Chettiar, Mr. Padmam	50
Salisbury, Mr. J. Walker . . .	20
Salmon, Mr. G.	25
Salt and Abkarry Revenue Office	55
Sandur, The Rajah of	150
Schmidt, Mr. W. M.	100
Sewell, Mr. W.	20
Sell, The Rev. E.	20
Short, Mr. James	25
Sibthorpe, Brigade-Surgeon Chas.	50
Sim, Mr. H. A.	75
Simpson and Co., Messrs. . .	250
Simpson and Co.'s Office . .	150
Simpson, Mr. C. S.	20
Skinner, Mr. J. M.	50
Skinner, The Rev. William . .	50
Smalley, Lieutenant-Colonel F.	50
Small Cause Court Employés .	115
Smith and Co., Messrs. W. E.	15
Smith, Colonel Charles John .	200
Smith, Mr. C. Michie	60
Smyth, Mr. J. A. P.	50
Somasundaram Chetty, Mr. J. .	60
Sreenivasa Chetty, P. & Brothers	600
S. P. C. K. Press and Depôt .	33
Spencer & Co., Messrs. . . .	500
Spencer & Co.'s Office, Madras .	50
Spencer & Co.'s Office, Ootacamund	30
St. Leger, Mr. W. Douglas . .	40
Stokes, Mr. Henry John . . .	50
Stokes, The Hon'ble H. E. . .	200

	Rs.
Stone, Mr. J. M.	25
Stuart, Mr. G. H.	50
Subba Row, Mr. B.	50
Subba Row, Mr. A. C.	100
Subramania Iyer, The Hon'ble S.	500
Subbiah Chetty, Mr. T.	200
Sullivan, Mr. W. J. A.	75
Sunderam Sastri, Mr. C. V. . .	20
Surgeon-General's Office . . .	105
Survey Office Central, Employés	28
Taylor, Captain J. H.	50
Taylor, Mr. G. W.	20
Taylor, The Rev. Alfred C. . .	50
Thomas, Mr. Henry Sullivan .	100
Thompson, Colonel Ross . . .	50
Thorogood, Mr. F. N.	60
Tirupati, The Mahant of . . .	150
Tirupati, The Peishkar of . .	500
Tirupati Dist. Munsiff & Pleaders	28
Travancore, The Maharajah of	10,000
Underwood, Mr. A. J.	20
Vans Agnew, Mr. Charles E. P.	150
Venkatagiri, The Rajah of . .	10,000
Venkataswamy Row, Mr. T. . .	20
Vuyyur, The Zemindar of . . .	500
Vizianagram, The Maharajah of	[illegible]
Walker, Lieut.-Col. J. Campbell	100
Walker, Mr. James Liddell . .	50
Walton, Mr. William	100
Walajah Lalljee, Mr	250
Wedderburn, Mr. H. G.	57
West, Mr. H. C.	25
Wheeler, the Hon'ble W. S. . .	200
Wilson, Major-General C. M. .	100
Wilson and Co., Messrs. . . .	750
Wilson and Co.'s Office . . .	50
Wilson, Mr. J. J.	50
Winckler, Mr. E.	25
Winter, Mr. G. K.	50
Yethirajulu Naidu, Mr. C. . .	50

JUBILEE COMMITTEES.

Adirampatnam .	Tanjore .	5
Alamur	Godavery .	40
Amalapuram . . .	Godavery	50
Anjengo	Malabar .	15
Arcot	N. Arcot .	44
Attur	Salem . .	100
Bellary	Bellary . .	1000
Bellary	[illegible] .	400
Bhadrachellam . . .	Godavery	200
Cannanore	Malabar .	250
Chandragiri	N. Arcot .	38
Chidambaram . . .	S. Arcot .	125
Chingleput	Chingleput	100
Chingleput	District . .	1,430
Chirala	Kistna . .	50
Cochin	Malabar .	100
Cocanada	Godavery .	200
Cuddapah	Cuddapah	100
Cuddalore	S. Arcot .	225
Cumbum	Kurnool .	75
Denkanikota	Salem . .	200
Dharmapuri	Salem . .	200
Dindigul	Madura .	200
Ellore	Godavery	697
Gingee	S. Arcot	25
Guntur	Kistna . .	30
Gudiyatam	N. Arcot	67

Place	District	Rs.
Jammalamadugu	Cuddapah	25
Jeypore	Vizagapatam	70
Kodachar	Bellary	25
Karur	Coimbatore	150
Kistna	District	1,000
Kotagherry	Nilgiris	80
Kottapatam	Vizagapatam	19
Kurumbranad	Malabar	200
Kurnool	Kurnool	300
Madura	Madura	400
Narasaraopett	Nellore	150
Mangalore	S. Canara	100
Manjeri	Malabar	125
Mettupalaiyam	Coimbatore	25
Namakal	Salem	100
Nandyal	Kurnool	300
Narayanavanam	N. Arcot	60
Negapatam	Tanjore	310
Nellore	Nellore	640
Nilgiri	District	824
North Arcot	District	151
Ongole	Nellore	30
Palghat	Malabar	150
Palmaner	N. Arcot	100
Pamban	Madura	75
Panruti	S. Arcot	125
Paramakudi	Madura	28
Paramathi	Salem	50
Pattikonda	Kurnool	680
Peddapuram	Godavery	80
Periakulam	Madura	50
Pithapur	Godavery	400
Poonamallee	Chingleput	438
Ponnani	Malabar	105
Ramachandrapur	Godavery	100
Rajahmundry	Godavery	90
Salem	District	700
Sholinghur	N. Arcot	25
Sivaganga	Madura	50
South Arcot	District	728
Taliparamba	Malabar	80
Tellicherry	Malabar	100
Tindivanam	S. Arcot	25
Tinnevelly	Tinnevelly	4,950
Tirukoilur	S. Arcot	601
Tirupati	N. Arcot	250
Tiruppattur	Salem	100
Tiruvannamalai	S. Arcot	270
Tiruvadi	S. Arcot	60
Tranquebar	Tanjore	298
Trichinopoly	District	3,836
Trichur	Cochin	125
Uttramalur	Chingleput	100
Vaitry	Malabar	50
Vaniyambady	Salem	150
Vedaranyam	Tanjore	100
Vellore	N. Arcot	275
Vriddhachalam	S. Arcot	40
Yercaud	Salem	45

ABSTRACT OF RECEIPTS AND EXPENDITURE.

COLLECTIONS.

Subscriptions received		Rs. 1,45,836

APPROPRIATIONS.

To the Imperial Institute, London—		
By the Government of Madras	Rs. 10,000	
„ H. H. the Rajah of Cochin	4,310	
„ H. H. the Rajah of Kalahasty	2,000	
„ H. H. the Rajah of Pudukota	7,366	
„ H. H. the Maharajah of Travancore	10,000	
„ H. H. the Rajah of Venkatagiry	5,000	
„ H. H. the Maharajah of Vizianagram	18,879	
„ Other Donations	[illegible]	
		Rs. 60,[illegible]
„ Victoria Technical Institute, Madras		36,8[illegible]
„ Victoria People's Hall		7,00[illegible]
„ Local Celebration, Madras, Feb. 16th		13,270
Do. do. June 20th		3,000
Balance to meet the cost of the Two Caskets, the Memorial Volume, Photographs, Engrossing the Address, Stationery, Postage, and Sundries		32,000
		Rs. 1,45,836

N.B.—The Account had not been closed when this Book was printed.

APPENDIX.

THE MADRAS PRESIDENCY.

THE Madras Presidency extends from Cape Comorin in lat. 8° 4′ N., to the northern extremity of Ganjam in lat. 20° 18′, and from E. long. 74° 9′ to 85° 15′. Bombay, the Nizam's Dominions, and Bengal bound it on the north, and its eastern, southern, and western sides are formed by an almost unbroken line of sea-coast nearly 2,000 miles in length. Its greatest length is about 950 miles, and its greatest breadth about half that distance. It has an area of 141,000 square miles. The climate is hot; hotter (on the whole) than any other part of India. More rain falls on the west coast than on the east. Some districts, as Coimbatore, share in the rain brought by both monsoons, while those which are far removed and separated from the sea by ranges of mountains, as Bellary, get the least rain of all. On the Malabar coast, where the atmosphere is moist, the mean temperature is 78° F., being seldom lower than 68° F. or higher than 85° F; on the Coromandel coast the average temperature is 84° F., rising occasionally during the hot season to more than 100° F. Along the coast the sea breezes, which set in shortly after noon almost throughout the year, do much to moderate the temperature.

Iron ore occurs in several places, but in abundance in South Arcot and Malabar; copper ore in Nellore and the Eastern Ghats; magnesia in Salem; and salt is obtained from the sea by evaporation. Rice is grown throughout the Presidency, but especially in the alluvial grounds of Godavery, Kristna, Tanjore, Malabar, and Canara. Maize, millet, and ragi are also everywhere cultivated; so also are oil-seeds, tobacco, and sugar-cane. Along the coast and in other sandy tracts cocoanut and other palms are extensively grown. Cotton is grown mostly in Cuddapah, Kurnool, Bellary, and Tinnevelly; indigo in Cuddapah and Nellore; coffee on the Palnais, Shevaroys, and Nilgiris; tea and cinchona on the Nilgiris; and pepper and cardamoms on the western coast. Most of the hills are covered with forests producing drugs, dyes, and gums, and some very fine kinds of timber, such as teak, sisu, black-wood and sandal-wood; while oranges, limes, mangoes, plantains, pineapples, and other Indian fruits are produced almost everywhere. Elephants, tigers, cheetahs, bears, and bison frequent the forests; deer are met with in all parts; monkeys and jackals are numerous in the cultivated country and in towns; lizards, snakes and other reptiles are found in all places: as are crows, kites, and other birds, and mosquitoes and other insects. Fish is plentiful in the rivers and along the coast; oxen are numerous, and are kept for draught purposes; buffaloes, sheep, goats and poultry are everywhere common.

The population exceeds 31,000,000. The great bulk of the people profess the Hindu religion. Brahmins are numerous, especially in the district of Tanjore. Brahmin temples may be seen in every town in Southern India, but those of Tanjore, Srirangam, and Madura are especially renowned. Mohammedans, 1,900,000 in number, are fewer in proportion to the population than in the north of India. All Europeans and their descendants, and many natives, especially in Tinnevelly, are Christians. The principal languages are Tamil, Telugu, Malayalim, and Canarese. These languages are all very closely allied, and are classed as "Dravidian," from Dravira, the ancient name of a tract of country nearly conterminous with that now occupied by the Tamil race. Education is rapidly extending. Madras has a University, and there are Colleges of the highest class at Madras, Kumbhakonam, Rajahmundry, and Trichinopoly. There are several second grade Colleges also, and many thousands of schools under Government inspection. Two-thirds of the population are engaged in agriculture. The only important manufactures are cotton cloths, sugar, indigo, brass vessels, and pottery. Coarse earthen vessels are made in almost every town and village, and weaving and dyeing are carried on to a trifling extent in almost every town. In some places, as Trichinopoly, small trades, such as the manufacture of jewellery and other articles of taste, are carried on.

The rivers of this Presidency being almost unnavigable, communication is held by means of roads, canals, and railways. Good roads connect all the large towns. Many of the roads are kept in excellent order, and lined on both sides with avenues of trees. Rest-houses are erected, either by the Government or the bounty of individuals, at intervals of every ten or twelve miles; bridges are constructed over deep streams, and except from occasional accident caused by the heavy periodical rains, communication between most parts of the Presidency is easy and uninterrupted. The canals of the Presidency were constructed chiefly in connection with the systems of irrigation in the Godavery, the Kistna, and the Cauvery deltas. In each of these localities there is a perfect network of irrigating canals, the larger channels serving also as lines of navigation. Along the eastern coast, a continuous series of salt-water canals runs through the districts of South Arcot, Chingleput, Madras, and Nellore. Great traffic is carried on in these in fish, firewood, chillies, salt, and shells for lime. On the western coast the shallow parts of the Cochin "backwater" have been deepened, and an excellent channel of communication exists for nearly 200 miles, along which the rich produce of Travancore and Malabar are transported.

The Madras Railway runs south-west by Salem and Coimbatore to Beypore on the Malabar coast, a distance of 406 miles. At Coimbatore a short line branches off to Mettupalaiyam near the foot of the Nilgiris; at Jalarpet, 132 miles from Madras, another line diverges to Bangalore, a distance of 84 miles; and at Arkonam, 42 miles from Madras, another line branches north-west by Cuddapah and Gooty to the town of Raichur, in the fertile valley of the Raichur Doab, where it joins the line from Bombay. The South Indian Railway extends from Madras through Tanjore and Trichinopoly to Tuticorin and Tinnevelly; and from Negapatam to Erode Junction on the Madras line. A light line of railway running from Chingleput to Conjeveram, and thence to Arkonam, serves to connect the Madras and the South Indian Railway systems.

The chief imports are cotton, woollen and hardware goods, manufactured metals, books, wines, spirits, timber, and horses. The exports include cotton, sugar, coffee, indigo, rice, hides, jaggery, cocoanut-oil, oil-seeds, cardamoms, ginger, and pepper. The greater part of the trade is with the United Kingdom; the rest with Bombay, Calcutta, and other Indian ports, Ceylon, Singapore, France, Mauritius, and Australia.

The ports, though numerous, are by no means well adapted for commerce, for harbours are few. The chief ports are Bimlipatam, Vizagapatam, Cocanada, Masulipatam, Madras, Pondicherry, Negapatam, Tuticorin, Cochin, Calicut, Tellicherry, Cannanore, and Mangalore.

The Presidency is divided into twenty-two Districts, viz., Ganjam, Vizagapatam, Godavery, Kistna, Nellore, Madras, Chingleput, North Arcot, South Arcot, Trichinopoly, Tanjore, Madura, Tinnevelly, Cuddapah, Kurnool, Bellary, Anantapur, Salem, Coimbatore, the Nilgiris, Malabar, and South Canara. The twenty-two Districts are subject to the direct control of "The Governor of Madras in Council;" Jeypur is under the superintendence of the Governor's Agent at Vizagapatam; Travancore, Cochin, and Pudukota, are ruled by their respective Rajahs, subject to the interference of the British Government. The revenue is derived from land, salt, customs, stamps, excise, forests, fisheries, and other sources. It amounts annually to rather more than seven crores of rupees.

The masses of the people are, in common with those of other parts of India, very poor; but considering their simple habits and the nature of the climate, they are far from being in the uncomfortable state in which the people of colder countries would be on the same poor incomes.—Extracted by permission from George Duncan's *Geography of India*.

MADRAS JUBILEE RETROSPECTS.

THE MADRAS ARMY.

THE Army of the Presidency of Fort St. George, formerly called the Coast Army, and more commonly known as the Madras Army, has seen many vicissitudes, though but little active service, during the fifty years that Her Majesty has reigned. The Honourable East India Company's Forces on the Madras Establishment comprised in 1837 a Brigade of Horse Artillery, four Battalions of Foot Artillery, and two Battalions of Infantry, all Europeans; eight Regiments of Cavalry, a troop of Horse Artillery, and a Battalion of Foot Artillery (Golandauze); and fifty-two Regiments of Native Infantry, organised in single battalions. There was besides a corps of British Engineer officers, who manned the Department of Public Works, and filled the Military Engineering posts under Government, besides officering the native corps of Sappers and Miners. The whole strength of the Army was over 50,000 sabres and bayonets, and it was officered by nearly 2,000 British officers. These officers had passed through the East India Company's Military College at Addiscombe for the Engineers and Artillery, or had been appointed direct to the Cavalry or Infantry by the nomination of an East India Director. All promotion was by pure seniority, and even exchanges from one regiment to another were not allowed; but promotion was so slow that purses were made up in corps and regiments to buy out senior officers—a system of private purchase that was allowed by the Court of Directors. Of the large body of officers not one half were serving with the troops; the rest were absorbed in the multifarious staff, civil, and political appointments which are necessarily recruited in India from among the regimental officers, for there is nobody else to fill them. When the regiment was ordered on field service, all the officers rejoined it; but the great blot of the system was that when an officer was promoted to Lieutenant-Colonel, he perforce obtained the command of a Regiment. Thus many men who had been all their lives in the Commissariat, the Pay Department, or in Civil employ, were thrust into the commands of Regiments when elderly men, to the great detriment of the Army; but the claims of seniority were looked on as so sacred that an officer was hardly ever shelved, or passed over, even when manifestly unfit for his post. Officers could only obtain leave to visit England once during their whole service, when they could get three years' furlough, one year almost of which would be spent in the voyage round the Cape, for the Overland Route was as yet undreamt of.

The pay was the same in 1837 as it is now, but there were no extra allowances for serving with native troops. Things generally were much cheaper; officers lived far less expensively than they do at present, and very few of them were married. Yet debt was much more common than it is nowadays, and the majority of officers were heavily involved, chiefly owing to the large sums which they had to subscribe towards purchasing out their seniors. Drinking and duelling were common, and General Courts-Martial, mostly arising out of these two causes, were ordinary events. The discipline of the European troops was good, though they were not so smart generally as Queen's Regiments. They were dressed and equipped just the same as the latter, only wearing white suits and white cap-covers in the hot weather. The sepoys were dressed in the same way, only in inferior material, and with the exception of their head and foot-gear; for the former they wore a black-varnished top-heavy cap, and for the latter the Foot Artillery, Sappers, and Infantry wore sandals. The Europeans were lodged in barracks on the ground floor which would nowadays not be thought good enough for stables; and the sepoys lived in thatched huts which were often burnt down during the hot weather. All the Police work of the Presidency was performed by the troops. The military main guards answered the purpose of police thannahs; while detachments of sepoys guarded the jails, escorted the chain-gangs, and conveyed treasure in country carts from place to place. The troops were armed with flint-lock, smooth-bore muskets. Seven regiments of Native Infantry had, however, Rifle Companies, the Light Company of the regiment being dressed in green, and armed with two-grooved Brunswick rifles with belted ball. There were no rifles among the European troops. There were Veteran Corps both for Europeans and natives, into which the superannuated men were drafted to do garrison duty in the large towns. The great object of Government in those days was to keep down the non-effective lists, and one-fourth of the total number of officers and sepoys kept on the rolls were only fit for the pension list. A sepoy could only obtain his pension after putting in forty years' service, and then had to be declared unfit by a Medical Board.

When Her Majesty ascended the Throne a tedious warfare was being waged by Madras troops against the Hill tribes of Goomsoor and Orissa—a warfare that has been twice repeated during her reign under almost exactly similar circumstances, namely, once in 1847, and once again in the little war of 1879-80, known as the Rampa rebellion. Soon afterwards, however, Madras troops were called upon to take part in the first Chinese, or Opium War, and six regiments of Madras Infantry—the 2nd, 6th, 14th, 36th, 37th, and 41st—were embarked for China. The ship in which one wing of the 37th Regiment embarked was never heard of again, and was supposed to have foundered in a typhoon. This Regiment was made a Grenadier Regiment on account of the gallant stand made by one of its Companies which, when out foraging near Canton, was surrounded by the whole Chinese host. Heavy rain had wetted the priming-pans of the muskets, and the sepoys had to keep the Chinese pikemen off with their bayonets, until they were rescued by a battalion of Marines from Canton, armed with percussion muskets. Captain, now Colonel Hadfield, Honorary Aide-de-Camp to the Viceroy, commanded the Company. The 14th Regiment also was granted the motto "*Tayyar-o-Wafadar*," or "Ready and True," for its alacrity in volunteering for foreign service on this occasion, at a time when native troops were still possessed of a strong prejudice against crossing the "*Kala Pani*" (black water) in the "*Jita Janaza*" (living coffin), or ship. The Madras troops took a prominent part in all the operations in China, including the storming of Chinkiangfoo; and the Regiments which served in the war, including two Companies of Sappers, were permitted to wear the Chinese Dragon as a badge, with the word "China" on their colours. At the same time another Company of Madras Sappers took part in the conquest of Scinde, and served under Sir Charles Napier at the battles of Meeanee and Hyderabad.

The Nawab of Kurnool being suspected of meditating rebellion against the Company, a Field Force from Secunderabad invested and captured Kurnool in 1839, and dispersed the Arabs and Rohillas whom the Nawab had assembled there. Kurnool was annexed to the British dominions, and the Nawab ended his days as a State prisoner at Bellary. In 1844 a rebellion took place amongst the Southern Mahratta chieftains, which was quelled by a Field Force of combined Madras and Bombay troops. The hill-forts of Punalla, Powanghur, and Buddurghur were stormed, not without heavy loss, and Babajee Ircha, one of the chief fomentors of the rebellion, was shot dead by a sepoy of the Palamcottah Light Infantry as he tried to cut his way out through the fort gateway of Punalla. The Madras Army was not again employed in hostilities until 1852, when the 1st Madras Fusiliers and a number of Native Infantry Regiments were despatched to Rangoon, Bassein, and Martaban to commence the Second Burmese War. The Madras Army bore the chief brunt of the operations, resulting in the conquest and annexation of Pegu; and, for several years after the peace, from fifty to twenty battalions of Madras Infantry remained to garrison the conquered province. Madras troops were also constantly called on from time to time to garrison Penang, Singapore, Labuan, and even Hongkong, as the British garrisons of those places were withdrawn owing to the stress of operations elsewhere. A Madras Infantry Regiment formed part of the garrison of Aden on its first occupation in the reign of Her Majesty, but was relieved in 1856 by a native Regiment from Bombay.

During the Crimean War many officers of the Madras Army served in the Turkish Contingent, or as Volunteers with the Turks against the Russians. The heroic Sir William Neill, of the Madras Fusiliers, was a staff officer in the Contingent; and Arnold of the 3rd Madras (Palamcottah) Light Infantry, with several comrades, was killed while leading the Turks on against the Russians in the indecisive conflict at Guirgevo. A Company of Sappers and the 1st Madras Fusiliers formed part of the Field Force sent, under Sir James Outram, to Bushire, in 1856, to coerce the Persian Shah into the abandonment of Herat; and the Fusiliers had no sooner returned to Madras than they were hurried off to Calcutta on the first news of the outbreak of the Mutiny of the Bengal Sepoy Army. Under Neill the "Blue caps" took the chief part in the battles which recovered Cawnpore, and relieved Lucknow, where their brave commander, whose statue now stands in the chief thoroughfare of the City of Madras, fell in the moment of victory. Many of the Madras Native troops were also sent, some to Bengal, where they served against Koer Singh and the Dinapore mutineers; others to Central India under General Whitlock, where they drove the Bengal mutineers from their position at Banda at the point of the bayonet. A third Madras European Regiment had been raised for the Company shortly before, and this new Regiment now went through its "baptism of fire" at Banda. Immediately afterwards took place the capture of Kirwee by Whitlock's column, consisting almost entirely of Madras troops. The booty taken from the Rajah of Kirwee's treasury, and divided among the troops, surpassed any capture of prize on record. The Madras troops everywhere displayed the most excellent spirit during the Mutiny, nor was there a single instance of disloyalty amongst them, nor of misconduct, with one unfortunate exception. The 8th Regiment of Cavalry, when ordered for service, refused to march unless the old rates of field batta, which had been in force previous to 1836, were restored. Misled by some designing men, they hoped to make capital out of the necessities of the crisis. But they were at once dismounted and disarmed, and the regiment was soon afterwards disbanded.

Madras Sappers served with Sir Hope Grant's Army at the capture of Pekin in 1860, and in 1867, under Sir Robert Napier, at the storming and burning of King Theodore's straw-thatched stronghold on the Mount of Magdala. Many Madras troops served in 1878 and 1879, in Afghanistan, in the two campaigns which preceded and followed the murder of Sir Louis Cavagnari; and several Madras Infantry Regiments were despatched in 1882 to Egypt to take part in the operations against Arabi Pasha. The Sappers took part in the action at Tel-el-Kebir; and a company of Sappers also fought well at the battle at Tofrek, where two of their officers were killed, and the third wounded, and Madras Infantry Regiments were afterwards employed to garrison Suakin. In the war in Burmah in 1886, Madras troops composed the chief portion of the forces which effected the downfall of King Theebaw, and the annexation of his dominions, and the whole task of garrisoning the new accession to Her Majesty's possessions will probably devolve eventually upon the Madras Army.

An unfortunate chapter in the history of the Madras Army is now reached. After the Mutiny, the European portion of that Army, who had done so much towards gaining its laurels, was drafted into the British Army. Most of the officers went over with them to the British service

The Madras Army was then transferred from the rule of the Company to that of the Crown. As a large reduction in the force of the native soldiery was demanded by the situation, three more regiments of Madras Cavalry and twelve of Infantry were disbanded between 1860 and 1864, while in Bengal new levies raised during the Mutiny were embodied as regiments. The surplus officers and non-commissioned officers of the disbanded Madras regiments were drafted into the remaining regiments with the effect of putting a stop to all promotion owing to the number of supernumeraries to be absorbed; and the Army is only now recovering from the effects of this stagnation of promotion. Moreover, in 1882, just as it had recovered, a fresh reduction of eight more Infantry regiments was made, reducing the total number to four regiments of Cavalry and thirty-two of Infantry, or to little more than half the former strength of the Army. Besides these reductions, the Madras Army, though no fault was to be found with its former organisation, was re-organised on the pattern of the new Bengal Army, and the British officers, removed from the cadres of their regiments, were formed into a separate Staff Corps. This measure has tended to destroy the mutual knowledge and sympathy between the British officer and the sepoys which formed the chief hold of the former on the affections of the latter. As the number of the English officers is now reduced to a few hundreds, the regiments are always under-officered, and it is rare to find an English officer who has been more than two or three years in the same regiment.

The Native Artillery was disbanded by degrees after the amalgamation, the men being pensioned, or transferred to the Infantry. The Veteran battalions were also broken up; a few of the European Veterans, however, still survive, and are formed now into a single Company. Before 1850 the flintlock musket had been entirely replaced by that fired by means of the percussion cap; and at the same time a shoulder-belt and waist-belt were substituted for the cross-belts hitherto worn. After the Mutiny a lighter smooth-bore musket was substituted for the "Brown Bess;" and in 1870 the Enfield rifle was issued to the Madras Native Army; and, five years later, was replaced by the Snider breech loader. On the issue of the rifles to the Army, the old Rifle Companies were abolished, with their distinctive dress and appointments. The establishment of an armed Police force after the Mutiny relieved the Army of the petty and harassing police duties which it formerly had to perform; and the extension of railway communication made the movement of troops from point to point so much more rapid and easy that the reduced Army continued to garrison the same extended area that it had done before.

Meanwhile a great change had come over the life of the officers. On the establishment of the Staff Corps Regimental officers were allowed to break up the messes and bands, and to divide the property; the old regimental life was destroyed, and comrades of a lifetime were scattered all over the Army; hence most of the officers took to matrimony, to make new homes for themselves. For a long time it was difficult to find an unmarried officer in the Madras Staff Corps. New furlough regulations, introduced in 1854, gave the officers more facilities for visiting Europe, and these facilities were extended by fresh furlough rules issued in 1868, 1875, and 1886.

Many distinguished officers have held the post of Commander-in-Chief of the Madras Army during Her Majesty's reign. At the time of her accession the command was held by Sir Robert O'Callaghan. Sir Peregrine Maitland was afterwards Commander-in-Chief, and he was succeeded by Sir Hugh Gough, afterwards Viscount Gough, of Sutlej renown. At the time of the Mutiny, the chief command was held by a Bengal officer, the present Field Marshal Sir Patrick Grant, who was succeeded by Sir Hope Grant. Lately it has been held by three distinguished officers in succession, Sir Neville Chamberlain, Sir Frederick Roberts, and the late Sir Herbert Macpherson. The present incumbent is Sir Charles Arbuthnot. During Sir Frederick Roberts's tenure of office many reforms were introduced into the Madras Army. The dress was altered from the European pattern to the native style of dress worn by the new Bengal Army, to the great increase of the comfort, and the great improvement of the appearance of the men; a system of messing was introduced; and efforts were made to diminish the number of the families residing in the lines, always a great drawback to the efficiency of the Madras sepoy. The pay and pension of the sepoy have been much improved within the past fifty years; but the improvement has not kept pace with the increase of wealth and comfort among the civil population, and there is more difficulty experienced in procuring suitable recruits to keep up the Army to a strength of 25,000 to-day than there was in keeping it at 50,000 fifty years ago.

In conclusion, it may be said that the Madras Army, in its early days, materially contributed to the building up of the Indian Empire. Its Telinga sepoys were the only native troops who fought under Clive at Plassey, and under Wellington at Assaye. In later times, when guarding territories compassed only by the inviolate sea, it has, perforce, been contented to rest upon its laurels. But it is ever ready to renew its youthful fame, and to meet Her Majesty's enemies anywhere, on the banks of the Helmund, on the sands of Suakin, or on the confines of China. The unswerving loyalty of the Madras sepoy is the same now as it was in the time when he was vainly tempted by the emissaries of Tippoo, or in the dark days of the Mutiny of the Bengal Army.

THE VOLUNTEER MOVEMENT.

In the month of June of the year 1857, when Southern India was startled by the news of the Mutiny of the Bengal Army, the citizens of Madras offered to take up arms in support of the Government, and in *self-defence*. Lord Harris, the Governor, called a meeting in the Banqueting Hall, which was largely attended by Europeans, East Indians, and Natives, and resulted in the immediate formation of a Volunteer Brigade, consisting of cavalry and infantry, of which Colonel Carthew was appointed the Colonel Commandant. Within a week of enrolment, there assembled on the Island, to receive arms, ammunition, and accoutrements, 536 men for the Infantry, and 95 men for the Cavalry Volunteers. The Governor, his staff, and a large number of the inhabitants of Madras were present. The Cavalry was formed chiefly of Judges of the Sudr Adalut, Secretaries to Government, merchants, and barristers. The Infantry, with the exception of the gentlemen selected for commissions, consisted mainly of the working classes of the city. Captain G. B. Roberts, of the 7th Light Cavalry, was appointed Commandant of the Volunteer Cavalry Guards, with the rank of Major; with Veterinary Surgeon T. Pritchard of the Governor's Body Guard as his Adjutant. Major A. C. Silver, of the 4th Regiment N.I., who afterwards became Military Secretary to Government, was appointed Commandant of the Infantry Volunteer Guards, with the rank of Lieutenant-Colonel, with Captain Drury, of the 20th N.I., and Lieutenant H. P. Hawkes, of the 44th N.I. (now Commissary-General in India), as his Adjutants. Lord Harris accepted the position as Commander in Chief. Colonel Silver proved a most efficient commanding officer of the Infantry. To use his own words, he stayed with the Regiment long enough to see it muster double the number of the Calcutta Volunteers, who were afterwards raised; then to see it number as many rifles as the whole of the other Volunteers in India put together; and lastly to see it the only Volunteer Regiment in existence in India. In fact, when he left the Regiment it had developed into a highly disciplined body. Both Cavalry and Infantry constantly took part with the regulars in Brigade exercises and sham fights which were very frequent in those stirring times; and during the Moharrum, the Cavalry Guards furnished night patrols, while the city bristled with piquets formed of the Infantry Guards in various localities, where their presence was calculated to establish confidence. The Infantry Regiment was presented with colours on the 10th of March, 1858. This ceremony was carried out with great *éclat* in the presence of the Governor and his staff, and the whole of the troops composing the garrison. The Chaplain of Vepery consecrated the colours, and Lady Rawlinson (wife of Sir Christopher Rawlinson, the Chief Justice) presented them to the Regiment.

The Volunteers met in the Banqueting Hall on the 30th of March, 1859, to present Lord Harris with a farewell address. Sir Charles Trevelyan, the new Governor, who was present, alluded to the fact that the body consisted mainly of East Indians, "a class," he said, "which, uniting many of the characteristics of the European and the native, form our interpreter, agent, and help-mate in working out the wonderful resources of this great country." Like his immediate predecessor, the new Governor evinced a very lively interest in the Volunteers. Major Robertson was succeeded in the command of the Cavalry Corps by Major Raikes, of the Governor's Body Guard, the beau ideal of a Cavalry officer. But the Volunteers and Madras society in general suffered a terrible shock by the death of this officer. While riding along a public road his horse fell with him, and in the fall Major Raikes sustained a severe fracture which proved fatal. Partly owing to the loss of their commanding officer, and partly to the decline of enthusiasm as affairs began to settle down in the north, the Cavalry Volunteers slackened in their attendance at drill until they mustered only 24 on parade. Sir Charles Trevelyan took a rather severe view of this, and in June 1859, an order was passed disembodying the Cavalry, but permitting the members to retain their arms with the privilege of appearing in uniform on public occasions. Several members of the Cavalry thereupon passed into the ranks of the Infantry.

About this time the Infantry was placed on a firm basis in respect to organisation and funds. The complement of the regiment consisted of 700 rank and file, divided into ten companies, with one Colonel in Chief, a Lieutenant-Colonel Commandant, two Majors, ten Captains, twenty Lieutenants, ten Ensigns, one Adjutant, and one Quartermaster; and for the up-keep of the Regiment an annual grant of Rs. 24,000 was assigned. The movement found warm supporters in Sir William Denison, Lord Napier, Lord Hobart, and the Duke of Buckingham and Chandos. Colonels Drury and Rutherford proved most efficient successors to Colonel Silver in the command of the Regiment, and it was also fortunate in having a zealous Adjutant. Four Volunteer officers deserve special mention for money, time, and labour devoted by them to the cause. The first was the late Colonel J. G. Coleman, who was connected with the movement from the very first. In July 1878 he resigned his connection with the Madras Volunteer Guard, after a service of twenty-one years with the Corps. During that period, besides being zealous in the performance of his duties, he materially helped the funds of the Regiment. He responded to the call of the Duke of Buckingham and Chandos, and by his personal influence raised a Battery of Artillery (composed of 70 stalwart East Indians), of which he became the Major Commandant, the newly-formed corps being named "The Duke's Own Volunteer Artillery." The next officer who deserves mention is Colonel W. M. Schadneb, now Acting Chief Presidency Magistrate. He enlisted in the Cavalry as a Volunteer in 1857, passed as a Corporal from the Cavalry into the Infantry, on the disembodiment of the former in 1859, and received his commission as Ensign in 1860. In recognition of this officer's long and faithful service the Madras Government last year conferred upon him the honorary rank of Colonel. The next officer who deserves special mention is Major F. J. James. He joined the Cavalry in 1857, and passed over as a corporal to the Infantry in 1859. He received his commission as Ensign in 1861. The honorary rank of Major was recently conferred upon him. The other officer who remains to be mentioned is Major Spring Branson, now Acting Advocate-General of Madras. Many years ago he retired from the Volunteer Guards; but when Colonel Coleman raised the Artillery, Major Branson joined him as Captain, and succeeded to the position of Major Commandant on Colonel Coleman's lamented death.

From 1857 to 1868 the Madras Volunteer Guards represented the whole Volunteer organisation in Southern India, during which period some 200 officers acquired a military training, while from 3,000 to 4,000 men passed through its ranks. The Bangalore Volunteers came into existence in 1868; the Nilgiri Volunteers in October 1878; the Duke's Own Volunteer Artillery at Madras, in 1879; and the South India Railway Volunteer Rifle Corps in August 1884. In the Spring of 1885 when the Russians were at Penjdeh, and a declaration of war by England was considered a certainty, the Government of India called for Reserve Volunteers, and committees were nominated to act at the principal centres, while Collectors of Districts were urged to do what they could. In the City of Madras alone 400 men—mostly old Volunteers, and men who had served in one service or another—sent in their names, and a mounted company of 40 to 50 gentlemen was attached to the Volunteer Guards. In the provinces various Volunteer corps were formed. The Godavery Rifle Volunteers was constituted in June 1885; the Bellary Volunteer Rifles in July 1885; the Coimbatore Volunteer Corps, the Malabar Volunteer Rifles, and the Madras Railway Volunteers in August 1885; the Vizagapatam Rifle Volunteers in October 1885; and the Yercaud Rifle Volunteers in February 1886. The Madras Corps has now 500 men in its ranks.

THE MEDICAL DEPARTMENT.

The Madras Medical Department was organized on a regular system in 1786. It consisted at first of an establishment of Surgeons, and Hospital and Regimental Mates—equivalent to Assistant Surgeons—and was administered by a Board, consisting of a Physician General, and a Chief, and Head Surgeon with a Secretary. The designations of the two last named members of the Board were subsequently changed to those of Surgeon-General and Inspector of Hospitals, and the Senior Surgeons of the establishment also performed administrative duties. The first Physician General was Dr. James Anderson, a distinguished botanist, as well as medical man, and who did much to develop the industrial resources of the Presidency. His memory is kept green by a portrait in the Library of the Madras Medical College, and by a fine marble statue by Chantrey in the chief entrance to St. George's Cathedral. As illustrations of the liberality of the East India Company to its officials it may be mentioned that the pay of the Physician General was £2,500 per annum, and that of the two other members of the Board £2,000 and £1,900 respectively. Considering the difference in the value of money then and now, and that the salaries were not subject to the freaks of exchange, it is obvious that the administrative officers of 1786 were much better paid than the corresponding officers are at the present time. Neither must it be lost sight of that one officer, viz., the Surgeon General, is now required to perform the duties which a century ago, when they were infinitely less onerous, were considered sufficient to engage the time and attention of a Board of three members.

In 1857 the Medical Board was abolished, and the Administration was vested in a Director-General, an Inspector-General, and ten Superintending Surgeons. Subsequently, from time to time numerous changes, always in the direction of reduction, were made in the members of administrative officers, and their titles have also been frequently changed. Prior to 1880 there were two distinct Departments conducting the medical duties connected with the Army, viz. the British Medical Service in connection with the European troops, and the Indian Medical Department, which, in addition to its Civil duties, attended on the native soldiers. On the 1st April, 1880 the administration of the whole of the medical duties connected with troops European and Native, was vested in an officer, styled Surgeon-General of Her Majesty's Forces, who may belong to either the British or Indian Medical Service, although hitherto the selection has been confined to officers of the former Department. This fusion does not, however, extend beyond administration, as native troops are still attended to by executive officers of the Indian Medical Department; and even in the administrative grade the Indian Service is fully represented, as four of the six Deputy Surgeons-General belong to it.

For a long time after the organization of 1786 the duties of the Department were mostly confined to medical attendance on the Company's employés, military and civil, although there are proofs that the Court of Directors was from an early period desirous to extend the benefits of European medical science to the general population of the country. Gradually, under the auspices of enthusiastic medical men, the nucleus of Mofussil Hospitals and Dispensaries was originated. In 1842 there were six Civil Dispensaries working at some of the larger up-country stations, and some time prior to this the chief Hospital in Madras City was opened. During 1842 the number treated in Civil Hospitals, inclusive of those in Presidency institutions, was 13,252. In 1852 the number of Dispensaries was 25, and the total sick treated 119,619. In 1862 the numbers were respectively 57 and 272,502; and during the succeeding years a great impetus was given to the development of Hospitals by the Local Funds and Towns Improvement Acts, 1871. In 1872 there were 93 Dispensaries with 416,116 out-patients; in 1882 there were 275 Dispensaries and 1,538,570 out-patients; and in 1885 there were 307 Dispensaries and 1,895,936 out-patients. The money for the maintenance of these institutions is provided partly by Municipalities and partly by Local Boards, and one gratifying feature of the organisation is that the people are eager to increase the number of Hospitals whenever funds will permit.

With such an enormous increase in numbers the difficulties of administration have of course been very greatly enhanced. Scattered as these hospitals are all over the Presidency, and often located at remote and inaccessible places, it would of course be impossible for the Surgeon-General to visit them all in person, and the inspection of the minor institutions has therefore to be entrusted to the Civil Surgeons, on whom thus depends to a large extent their successful working. It will thus be seen that what with medical, and what with sanitary work the duties of the District Medical officers have of late become very onerous and important, in fact much more so than those of most Presidency appointments. To get on well with the local authority much tact and judgment are required; while to govern his subordinates well and inspire confidence, the District Medical Officer must have strong administrative qualities, and be at the same time a good-all-round man.

But although the rise in number and importance of civil Hospitals has been so great and rapid they only as yet make provision for a mere fraction of the sick poor, and it will be the duty of the Medical Department to promote their multiplication and consolidate their administration. For the accommodation of in-patients there were in 1885 a total of 3,371 beds, of which 2,039 were for males, and 1,332 for females. In the same year the number of Hospitals in any one District ranged from 5 in Trichinopoly to 37 in Tanjore. Of the 307 institutions opened, 221 were provided with buildings specially erected for them, and 86 with ordinary houses rented for the purpose; a fact very creditable to local authorities, as bricks and mortar are expensive investments. The mean cost of treating each patient in Mofussil Dispensaries in 1885 was only Rs. 0-5-3.

THE SANITARY DEPARTMENT.

During the earlier years of the British occupation of Southern India very little attention was paid to sanitation, and the sites of military encampments were chiefly determined by the necessities of war. For a long period the heavy sickness and mortality which affected troops did not attract much notice, as they were believed to be due to the inevitable hardships of service, and to an exhausting climate; but the exigencies of the great wars of 1856 to 1858 awoke attention to the heavy losses, exclusive of those in battle, which were taking place in the Army. The result of this was the appointment in 1859 of a Royal Commission to enquire into everything connected with the health of European and Native troops in India, and to submit recommendations for the prevention of disease. One outcome of this investigation was the appointment, in 1864, in each Presidency of a Sanitary Commission which embraced Civil, Medical, Military, and Engineer Officers. The duties of this body were partly consultative and partly administrative and were broadly defined as follows:—viz. "to give advice and assistance in all matters relating to the public health, such as the selection of new stations, and the sanitary improvements of existing stations and bazaars; to examine new places for barracks and hospitals; to advise on the laying out of stations and bazaars; the sanitary improvement of native towns; the prevention and mitigation of epidemic diseases, and, generally, to exercise a constant oversight on the sanitary condition of the population, European and Native, and to report on the prevalence, cause, and means of preventing sickness and disease."

The Sanitary Commission in its original form lasted till 1866, when it was abolished, and its duties were entrusted to an officer of the Civil Service, aided by a Medical Officer as Secretary. Up to 1869 the cost of the Staff was included in the Military budget, but as by that time the civil duties had become very extensive, the charges connected with the Department were then transferred to the Civil budget. In the same year, on the death of the Medical Secretary, it was deemed advisable to appoint a Medical Officer to be Sanitary Commissioner in lieu of a Civilian, and this arrangement still exists. The existing sanitary laws embrace the following objects;—Registration of births and deaths; vaccination; supply of drinking water and its protection; cleansing of towns and villages and disposal of refuse; provision of drains and sewers; provision of public latrines; provision and regulation of slaughter-houses; regulation and provision of markets; prevention of nuisances and control of offensive and dangerous trades and unwholesome buildings or lands; regulation of burning and burial grounds; improvement of village sites; and prevention of infectious diseases.

Although the duties of Sanitary Commissioner are mainly civil, he is still the constituted sanitary adviser of the Government in its Military Department, and can inspect all stations within or without the Presidency wherever Madras troops may be garrisoned. At the present day the Sanitary Department consists of the Sanitary Commissioner in direct communication with Government, assisted by a Deputy Sanitary Commissioner, District Sanitary officers (the Civil Surgeons) and subordinate establishments. The Sanitary Commissioner possesses no executive powers, but is the recognised adviser of Government, Municipalities and Local Boards on all sanitary matters. He also controls, inspects, and reports on Municipalities, Jails, Lunatic Asylums, Dispensaries, Schools, and Colleges. The smaller towns and villages are inspected by the Deputy Sanitary Commissioner and District officers, and the former officer has in addition the charge of vaccination.

As regards practical sanitation the cardinal requirements and chief aims have been the cleansing of premises and streets, the removal and disposal of house sewage, and the careful guarding of drinking water from contamination. In the smaller towns it is probable that, at least for the present, the most efficient arrangements regarding drainage will be to level and improve the surfaces of public streets, lanes, and house compounds; to provide ready escape for rain and surface water by well-made, impervious surface drains, properly graded to the out-fall, so that all water may flow rapidly away and nowhere form surface pools; to combine with this an efficient conservancy system, to keep as much of the house sewage as possible out of the surface drains; to shut up bad wells, and to improve and protect existing wells from subsoil pollution. Other necessary steps in sanitation have been receiving attention. Special attention has also been paid to the inspection of food supplies in markets, and to the sanitation of Schools and Colleges. The mode of birth and death registration differs in towns and country. Among the rural population the District Municipalities Town Act makes the registration of births and deaths compulsory in the areas affected by the Act, and special Registrars are appointed to collect and register the events. In the Districts among the rural population, the voluntary system still obtains, and registration is effected without any special law. In the absence of any abnormal causes giving rise to undue mortality, it is believed that, under ordinary circumstances, the registration of births and deaths is defective when the results in the case of births fall below 2·5 per cent. of the population, and of deaths below 2 per cent. The English birth-rate is understood to be about 3·5, and the French 2·6 per cent., the corresponding death-rates being 2·2 and 2·3 per cent. respectively. The great want in Madras at the present day is that of a Sanitary Engineer to formulate, and put into practical shape the suggestions of the Sanitary Commissioner, and to see that all such works are executed at a reasonable and possible cost. Until this is provided, nothing beyond the simplest improvements can safely be attempted.

REVENUE ADMINISTRATION.

The Revenue Administration of the Madras Presidency during the past half century has undergone several material changes. In 1837 the Revenue Survey did not exist. Land assessments were then, and were for twenty-five years later, based on the old village revenue accounts, the field areas in which were obtained from measurements, very roughly taken with rods or ropes, by ignorant, untrained, and often interested men, who were not under efficient control. The results obtained in this manner were naturally but approximations to truth. The records on which the Revenue Administration was dependent for its facts, consisted for the most part of bundles of palmyra leaf strips, which were sealed volumes to the European district officers, and usually had to be interpreted by the village accountant, who could make them support any case he wished to espouse. In 1852 Captain Priestley commenced an experimental Survey; and a few years afterwards a general Survey of the Presidency was sanctioned by Government. Now, in 1887, about 100,000 square miles have been covered; fifteen of the twenty-one Districts in the Presidency have been completely surveyed; and considerable progress has been made in four of the remaining Districts. The results aimed at and obtained are:—For each village, a map on a sufficiently large scale ($\frac{1}{5000}$) to show the boundary of every property; an area list, giving the correct area in acres, and cents of every field; and a register, numbered to correspond with map and area list, and giving all information regarding the name of owner, the nature of tenure and cultivation, and other particulars for every field. Small scale maps (one inch to a mile) are compiled from the village maps and published by taluks, which vary from 200 to 800 square miles in extent. Combined sheets of the country are also compiled, and eventually incorporated in the Revised Atlas Sheets of India.

The system, and the results obtained, have been eulogised by Her Majesty's Secretary of State in the following terms:—"The scientific accuracy and precision with which the village maps have been constructed reflect great credit on Colonel Priestley and his staff, and furnish conclusive proof of the efficiency of the Madras Revenue Survey; the work indeed is quite on a par with anything that has been executed in Europe." Many important advantages have accrued both to the Administration and to the people from this Survey. Numbers of serious boundary disputes of long standing have now once for all been settled—disputes which for generations past had been fertile sources of litigation, feud, and even bloodshed. And light has been thrown in dark places where it was much needed; many cases of great hardship and injustice have been disclosed, where rich and influential landholders had been too lightly assessed, often at the expense of their poorer neighbours. Now, the village maps and register place the poor cultivator beyond the power of the unscrupulous petty officer, and every European District authority has at hand the means of ascertaining for himself the merits of every land case that may come before him. Considerable progress has also been made in the compilation of combined topographical maps of the country. Until recently the only general maps of India available were the quarter-inch Ordnance sheets, which were reduced from surveys made in the period 1800 to 1830. These surveys were carried out rapidly and roughly in the face of many difficulties; and vast alterations have taken place since those days. Sheets revised to date from the material provided by the Madras Survey are now being incorporated with the General Atlas of India under preparation in Calcutta.

Briefly, the object secured by the Survey and Settlement measures is the accurate ascertainment of the areas under Ryotwar Settlement, and the imposition of a moderate assessment on the half net principle; that is, that the State's demand shall be limited to half the net produce after deducting the cost of cultivation. Almost simultaneously with the new settlement were introduced liberal principles in administrative detail. Under these, the ryot is free to raise any crop he likes, and is allowed the full benefit of his own industry and improvements. The exemption from enhanced demand of cultivation under private wells, first limited to those sunk in dry fields beyond a defined distance from a Government source of irrigation, was extended in 1884, under certain restrictions, to wells dug in wet fields, and the reservation in regard to proximity to a Government work was removed. A revision of the land revenue instalments, having for its object accommodation to the ryot in respect to the disposal of his produce, has been for some time under consideration, and its final introduction awaits the information which has been called for in regard to local conditions.

The two other important branches of the Land Revenue Administration are the Departments of Agriculture and Forest Conservancy. The former, as a distinct Department under the direction of the Director of Revenue Settlement, was only created in 1882; but a great deal has been done by both State and private enterprise in previous years towards developing the resources of the country. The coffee plant was first introduced into the Wynaad by Major Bevan in 1834, but it was not until 1840, when a regular plantation was opened out by Mr. Glasson, that the experiment proved so far a success as to lead to the opening of estates over an extended area. Tea was first introduced on the Nilgiris in 1844; but it became an active enterprise only about the year 1870. The introduction of the Cinchona plant in 1861 on the Nilgiris, where it is now an established industry, was a Government enterprise, which has proved most successful. The Government Cinchona Plantations, with the Botanical Gardens on the Nilgiris, opened in 1844, are under the charge of an officer now styled the Director of the Government Cinchona Plantations, Botanical Gardens, and Parks. The measure next adopted was the establishment of the Government Experimental Farm in 1865, followed by the Agricultural College in 1876, at Saidapet. In the meantime, periodical Agricultural Exhibitions, first started in 1855, were followed by ploughing matches and travelling shows of implements, in which modern improvements were adapted to indigenous requirements.

Among the duties pertaining to the Agricultural Department, is the preservation and improved breeding of cattle. The first step taken in this direction was a legislative enactment passed in 1866 to prevent the spread of contagious diseases among cattle; a Veterinary Hospital was opened in 1879; and a class for the instruction of students in Veterinary science was established in 1882, in connection with the Agricultural College. At the same time, a system of cattle disease inspection under competent direction throughout the country was organised. Two other subjects which have recently engaged the attention of this Department are pony-breeding and experiments in ensilage, in view to providing an abundance of preserved green fodder for agricultural stock. Forest Conservancy was first initiated in 1856, when its direction was entrusted to Dr Cleghorn. In 1883 this Department was placed on an efficient and expansive footing by adequate protective legislation and executive organisation, and it seems sufficient to say that the forests of Madras, from their beneficial influence on the climate, and on economic conditions, have a hopeful future.

Under the rules recently framed, loans on easy terms may be obtained from the Government Treasury for the improvement of land as well as to meet agrarian necessities. For the construction of wells, which are of great importance as serving to mitigate the effects of drought, they may be obtained on specially liberal terms. The Madras Famine Code gives minute instructions as to the measures to be taken for the prevention, as well as relief of distress. During the famine of 1876-78, the total State outlay was:—On relief works, 386½ lakhs; and on gratuitous relief, 170½ lakhs; total, 557 lakhs. During the height of the famine, the number employed daily on relief works rose to as many as 1,070,000; and the number admitted to gratuitous relief to 1,600,000. An important measure carried out in connection with the administration of land revenue is the settlement of Inams (tenures held wholly or partially free from the payment of revenue), whereby security of property and validity of title have been assured.

Whilst, as above shown, the interests of the agricultural classes in direct relation to the State have received every possible attention, those of the tenantry of Zemindars, Inamdars, and other private landlords have not been neglected. The early legislation to regulate the relation of landlord and tenant not having been found to be satisfactory, it was revised in 1865, and further improvements, which experience showed to be necessary, are embodied in a bill now about to be laid before the Government. Since the discovery of gold reefs in the Wynaad in 1865, the development of the mineral resources of the Presidency has received considerable attention. Licenses to prospect and mine in Government land are granted on liberal terms, and all uncertainty as to the proprietary rights of the ryot to mineral products in their holdings has been removed by the declaration that those products belong to the landholder, subject only to the payment of a special assessment when mines are worked. A mineralogist has recently been appointed to inspect and report on all localities which show indications of the existence of mineral wealth. The system of Government Fish-Curing Depots recently introduced, under which salt used for curing fish is exempted from the payment of duty, has proved highly successful. During the year 1885-86 no less than 27,000 tons of well-cured, wholesome fish were added to the food supply of the country. The Pearl Fishery on the Tinnevelly Coast, which for some time has been in an unsatisfactory condition, has recently formed the subject of investigation. Further measures for the more complete revival of the industry are under consideration.

During the past half century several important measures have been carried out in view to improving the efficiency of the revenue administration. Among these may be mentioned the alteration of the limits of Districts; the reconstitution of the Board of Revenue; and the improvement of the district, taluk, and village establishments so as to enable them to cope with the increasing work of the Administration. The first—in which a beginning was made by the creation of the new District of Anantapur in 1882—is expected to be completed shortly, and the second very recently came into force. As regards the third, a revision of the village establishments has been proceeding concurrently with the new land revenue settlement, and remains to be introduced in only a few Districts. The improvement of the superior establishments has been deferred from want of funds to meet the increased cost involved.

Notwithstanding that progress was, at intervals, arrested by the calamitous visitations of drought and famine, the revenue statistics furnish abundant proof that in the fifty years of Her Majesty's reign the Madras Presidency has attained to a state of prosperity hitherto unknown. Taking the dates for which statistics are available, it appears that the population increased from about 22⅓ millions in 1851-2 to about 31 millions in 1881. The area occupied for agriculture under direct settlement with Government increased between 1853-4 and 1884-5 from about 12 to 18½ millions of acres; and the number of holdings under such settlement from about 1⅓ million to over 2¼ millions. The total land revenue collections increased from about 334 lakhs of rupees in 1853-4 to 470 lakhs in 1885-6. It is, however, the other sources of revenue, viz., salt, abkari, and stamps, which furnish a surer index to the material progress of the country. The revenue from these three sources has, during about the same period, improved as follows:—Salt, from 45 to 144½ lakhs; Abkari, from 22 to 80½ lakhs; and Stamps, from 5½ to 99 lakhs. At the same time, the interests of trade have been advanced by the abandonment of the monopolies of tobacco, pepper, betel, &c., and of the moturpha taxes on trades and professions, as also by arrangements made with Travancore and Cochin to secure free trade between those States and British territory.

SALT.

Fifty years ago Salt was a Government monopoly in Madras, upon which a duty of 14 annas per maund was raised, and which yielded a revenue of 36 lakhs of rupees. The administration was in the hands of Collectors in subordination to the Board of Revenue. For nearly twenty years Collectors and their Head Assistants were allowed a commission of 1 per cent. and ½ per cent. respectively, on the revenue collected. For upwards of fifteen years there were no changes in the administration, but the duty was raised to Rs. 1-8 in 1844, and reduced in 1845 to Re. 1 per maund, remaining unchanged till 1851. In 1852 the Court of Directors suggested the appointment of a separate officer for the charge of Abkari and Salt, but the Board of Revenue held, and the Government of Madras agreed, that it would be better to improve the status of the subordinate establishment, and to appoint a separate Uncovenanted Assistant to aid each Collector in salt administration. This suggestion was not immediately carried out except at Madras, where a special Uncovenanted Assistant was assigned to the Collector. In other Districts the Head Assistant Collector transacted most of the salt administration until 1860. In that year the Board of Revenue began to see that some such measure as that proposed by the Court of Directors, in 1852, was necessary, and suggested the appointment of an Inspector General. This proposal, however, was never carried out, but a special Deputy Collector for Salt was placed under the orders of every Collector except those of Godavery and Malabar. A Salt Deputy Collector was subsequently sanctioned for Godavery, and in 1875 a Deputy Collector for Salt and Sea-Customs was appointed to Malabar. The insufficiency of the subordinate establishments was first pointed out by the Commissioner in charge of the Northern Districts in 1854, and in 1860 a general revision of establishments was undertaken by Mr. Pelly, a member of the Board of Revenue, which was brought into effect in 1863, and remained in force until the organization of the Salt Department between the years 1878 and 1885. During these changes the rate of duty was gradually raised to Rs. 1-5 in 1861, Rs. 1-8 in 1866, Rs. 1-11 in 1869, Rs. 2-8 in 1878, and again reduced to Rs. 2 in 1882.

In 1876 the Madras Salt Commission held its inquiry. After going very fully into every question connected with the administration, visiting factories in most parts of the Presidency,—with the assistance of a special analyst, Dr. Hadett, and the reports of Dr. Ratton, who had been engaged for nearly five years, examining every factory in the Presidency,—its conclusions and recommendations were generally approved by the Local and Supreme Governments, and the Secretary of State. The most important suggestions made by it were the constitution of a Salt Department, under a separate head; the abolition of the earth salt works in the inland districts; the establishment of a preventive force; and the introduction of the excise system. The first of these suggestions was carried out in February 1878 by the appointment of Mr. H. W. Bliss, C.S., to be Commissioner of Salt Revenue for the Presidency. From the 1st of July of that year the Collectors of districts ceased to have any concern with the salt revenue. The present Salt Department was then gradually organized by the Commissioner, special attention being paid to the subdivision into circles of the Districts, each of which had previously been under Deputy Collectors. An officer entitled an Inspector was placed in charge of each circle, his rank being practically the same as that of a Deputy Collector. The organization of the Department as far as the Madras Presidency is concerned was practically completed in 1885; but the salt revenue of the province of Orissa has since been placed under the Commissioner, and the additional subordinate establishment required is not yet completely organized. The superior establishment for inspecting purposes consists of 3 Deputy Commissioners and 10 Assistant Commissioners. Under them are employed 58 Inspectors, 79 Assistant Inspectors, 223 Sub-Inspectors, 244 clerks and shroffs, and over 6,000 menials.

In dealing with a Department of this kind, which is employed in levying a tax upon a necessary of life, one of the most important questions that have to be considered is the effect upon the consumer of the changes which have been introduced during the last fifty years. One important change was the great reduction in the number of salt factories in the Presidency. In 1855 there were no less than 122 "stations;" in 1876 these had been reduced to 81; and at the present date there are not more than 48 factories. The first impression from these figures would naturally be that the facilities for obtaining licit salt had been greatly diminished; but this is not the case. The improvements in communications consequent on the extension of railroads, canals, and roads have really placed salt factories within much easier reach of the population generally than they ever were before. The factories which have been closed were chiefly those south of the Kistna District, the alterations in the Northern Circars being comparatively few. Numerous small factories have been closed in Nellore and the Districts south of Chingleput; but the Buckingham Canal in the former, and the South Indian Railway in the latter, have made intercourse comparatively cheap and easy. On the West Coast the abolition of the local factories has closed a source of the supply of very inferior salt, which has been replaced by Bombay salt, which can be imported all along the coast. The principles upon which the selection of factories for abolition was made, provided sufficiently for local supply; the petty factories which scarcely paid their way, those difficult of access, and those which produced notoriously bad salt were abolished, while manufacture has been concentrated in the neighbourhood of means of communication. Previously to the organisation of the present Salt Department, the factories were placed in the charge of ill-paid subordinates, who could be but indifferently supervised by the Salt Deputy Collectors; and the Collectors themselves having little time to attend to this branch of their duties, there was a general tendency to look upon the Department merely as a means of producing revenue, little consideration being paid to its working as affecting the people generally, or to broader questions, such as that of the distribution of salt, from which danger to the revenue might be apprehended. This has been entirely altered; the status of officers in charge of factories has been greatly improved; and a careful review of the operations of the Department in its broader aspects is made by the Commissioner, and embodied in his annual reports.

The preventive force which has been organised for the protection of the revenue has been most successful in its operations from the point of view of the authorities. It is supposed that there is a tendency to work the law harshly, and that the people are harassed. Of course the poorer classes were more free before there was any preventive force, or before the introduction of the amended law forbidding the possession and use of salt earth. The law which prevents a poor labourer or fisherman from helping himself from the stores of spontaneous salt which he finds outside his door is consequently animadverted upon. But to those who are cognisant of the sanitary condition of the surroundings of an ordinary native house, it is a matter for consideration whether a law preventing the use of what is collected there is not a highly salutary one. Few of those who speak of the harshness of the laws are aware that except in swamps and places where sea-water collects and evaporates, spontaneous salt is rarely found in a form fit for human consumption, and that stores of salt are not available outside every native house along the coast of the Presidency. If it were so the salt law would be unnecessary, and a preventive force useless; the poor peasant would eat his rice in his back yard, and supply himself with salt from the surface. Effloresced salt earth rarely contains more than 6 or 7 per cent. of salt. Illicit salt has to be collected and prepared by a long process of lixiviation and boiling, so that a man cannot commit an offence against the salt laws owing to a sudden temptation caused by a natural craving for a necessary of life. Every such offence is premeditated, and carried out with more or less careful preparation.

The fundamental principle of the preventive force is that no person shall be arrested under the salt laws without being brought before an Inspector. Inspectors are men of good education and position, drawing salaries ranging from Rs. 250 to Rs. 400 per mensem, and are supposed to be the equals in position of Deputy Collectors. Inspectors, and no others, are empowered to release the persons arrested after an enquiry, when such persons are infirm or children, or when they are first offenders, with respect to a quantity of salt not exceeding one seer, or when they have committed an offence through ignorance or inadvertence, or when there is not sufficient evidence against them. It is found that about 85 per cent. of the releases fall under the second head; and although at first releases under the fourth head were common, the law is now generally understood by the subordinates, and only about 2 per cent. of the releases fall under it. As soon as a person is arrested it is the duty of the officer making the arrest to send a report to his immediate superior, and to take the person to the Inspector, if he be within ten miles, or, if not, to the nearest Police Station. The officer in charge of the station can release the offender on bail, or forward him in custody to the Inspector. The report sent by the officer making the arrest is in a printed form, and it is carefully compared with the counterfoil, so that it is impossible for a peon to hush up a case after it has once been reported. Every care is taken by the Government to enable the salt laws to be worked with as little harshness as is compatible with the safety of the revenue.

The excise system was first introduced into the factories of South Canara in the season of 1878-79. In 1882-83 it was introduced into the Tuticorin factories, and has since been extended, with the exception of six factories, to the whole of the Presidency. Under the monopoly system the manufacturers were required simply to manufacture salt which they delivered to Government at fixed rates, the salt being stored, and sold at 3 annas per maund by Government. Under the excise system the manufacturers are bound to keep up all the works in each factory, which are connected with the manufacture, storage, and protection of the salt, the Government merely supervising storage and sales, and guarding the salt, while the manufacturers make their own terms in disposing of it. It was hoped that the new system would benefit the manufacturers, who would get better prices for the salt, and also the public, who through competition among manufacturers would obtain a better quality of salt at a cheaper price. So far from this being the case, the quality of the excise salt has shown no improvement, while prices have risen almost everywhere, in some places to as much as 12 and 14 annas per maund. The manufacturers as a body have not sufficient capital to enable them to execute the necessary works before manufacture is commenced, and to wait for their remuneration until their salt is stored and sold. They have therefore been compelled to place themselves in the hands of capitalists who give them advances, and who have really taken the place of Government under the monopoly system. These men having found it easier to combine than to compete, and having been assisted by a succession of bad seasons for manufacture, have been able to force the price of salt up to an unprecedented figure. The excise system has had hardly a fair trial up to the present time, and there is very little doubt that the present prices must fall; but it is scarcely probable that they will ever go down generally to the price under the monopoly system. The quality has also been found, if anything, to have deteriorated. This is simply the result of the manufacturers studying the market. Salt is sold to the dealers by weight, and retailed by them by measurement. It is therefore their object to get the lightest salt they can, and light salt is, as a rule, bad salt. Weighment was introduced in 1828; measurement was substituted for it in 1846; and weighment was re-established gradually between 1857 and 1866. A Committee is now discussing the possibility of insisting upon a standard quality of salt.

One of the most satisfactory of the operations of the Salt Department is the extension of the fish-curing industry. Ten years ago most of the cured fish consumed in the Presidency was partly sun-dried, and partly salted with salt earth frequently containing not more than from 5 to 7 per cent. of salt. Upwards of 130 yards have now been opened along the coast, and salt is sold within them for use in fish-curing at a price just sufficient to cover its cost, and the cost of conveying it to the yard. In the official year 1885-86 nearly 750,000 maunds of fish were cured at these yards.

Financially the Salt Department has justified its existence in the last fifty years. In 1837 the total amount realised was 36 lakhs of rupees; in 1886 it was 144 lakhs. The increase in the consumption of salt since the reorganisation of 1878 has been 17 lakhs of maunds, and the increased consumption within the Presidency is about 4 lbs. per head of the population. If this has replaced an equal quantity of the unwholesome illicit salt that was formerly used, the reorganised Department has done good work.

EMIGRATION.

The present well-regulated system of emigration in the Presidency of Madras has come into existence during the reign of the Queen Empress. In 1834 slavery was abolished throughout the British Colonies, and inducements began to be held out to labourers to emigrate from British India. It was not until 1839, however, that a legal enactment was passed to afford checks against Her Majesty's Indian subjects being decoyed away under false pretences, and also to ensure them a comfortable voyage, and protection after arrival. Further enactments, designed to improve the condition of emigrants, were passed from time to time. Mauritius was the first British Colony to attract Indian labour, and it is still the favourite with Indian emigrants. Natal now attracts a large number of emigrants from Madras; emigration has taken place also to British Guiana (Demerara), Jamaica, and Trinidad. In 1860 and 1861 the first conventions were signed with France, and Indian emigrants proceeded under it to Réunion (Bourbon), Guadaloupe, Martinique, and French Guiana. It must have been a strong inducement that first led the agricultural classes of the Presidency to cross the ocean, *per se*, but the stories of wealth to be acquired in foreign lands were doubtless made alluring. Proximity to Ceylon, moreover, to which place the Tamulians of Southern India had for a long period previously been accustomed to cross, doubtless led to longer voyages being undertaken. In times of widespread agricultural distress there is sometimes a rush to emigrate, when families—sometimes whole hamlets—go abroad; but such occasions are happily rare, and at times—in spite of the considerable inducements offered—emigrants come in slowly, and it is often difficult to complete contingents. Emigration is always an outlet for the criminal who has made his first slip, and feels the eye of the Police upon him. Many such emigrate and prosper, instead of becoming habitual offenders, and peopling the jails, or emigrating involuntarily to the Andamans. So does many a woman under a cloud at home, begin a new life in a new country. Family squabbles, expulsion from caste—the latter especially—add their quota to emigration.

Emigrants to British Colonies are embarked by the Protector of Emigrants at Madras; and those for French Colonies by the British Consular Agent at Pondicherry. The system for the British Colonies is as follows. The Emigration Agent applies to the Protector for licenses for recruiters—the number asked for being regulated according to the requisitions for labour from the Government of the Colony which he represents,—specifying in what districts of the Presidency he intends them to work. On being licensed the recruiters spread themselves over the selected localities, and endeavour to make recruits. The wages offered vary from Rs. 5 or Rs. 6 a month, increasing every year by 8 annas monthly—with liberal rations, free medical attendance, &c. A free passage back after ten years is promised by some colonies, and liberty to return after five years is allowed by all. In British Guiana the wages offered were lately as high as 8 annas a day, out of which, however, a small sum was deducted on account of rations. The conditions are all printed in the vernacular of the district and in English, on each license. When recruited the intending emigrant is taken before the District Magistrate, or one of the Divisional Officers of the District, for to remove a man without doing this is punishable as kidnapping. Here the terms of the contract are clearly explained to each cooly, and if, as sometimes happens, he declines to ratify the contract, he is free to return to his village, otherwise an agreement is signed by him, and attested by the Magistrate. (In the city of Madras all emigrants recruited are brought direct to the Protector to be passed.) After this the recruiter is free to take his batch of intending emigrants to the port of Madras, where they are lodged in the "depots" at Cassimode, which are spacious enclosures containing barracks, and a hospital. Here food and all necessaries of good quality are abundantly supplied to the emigrants.

The depots are periodically inspected by the Protector, the Medical Inspector, and the Depot Surgeon, the two former being Government officers of high position. The emigrants are examined by the Medical Inspector as to their fitness to undertake the voyage, and by the Depot Surgeon as to their ability to labour, and rejections by these officers, against which there is no appeal, are frequent. All the emigrants who are passed have to appear personally before the Protector, by whom the terms of their agreements are again minutely explained to them, and their willingness to embark is ascertained.

Sailing ships are nearly always used for the conveyance of emigrants from Madras, though steamers have been occasionally employed, and are much preferred by the bulk of emigrants. When a ship has been chartered she is carefully examined as to her sea-worthiness and fittings by an officer of the Marine Department, and then by the Protector and the Medical Inspector as to her ventilation and fittings, hospital accommodation, &c. Alterations and additions that are thought necessary for the comfort of the emigrants are frequently ordered, and have to be made. Each ship carries a duly qualified surgeon approved by the Medical Inspector. Provisions of all sorts and "medical comforts" are provided according to a fixed scale, regulating the dietary on board. All stores, &c., when ready for shipment are carefully weighed, counted, and examined, and their quality as compared with the samples previously approved is carefully verified by the Protector and Medical Inspector, the Surgeon Superintendent being also present. The water is scrupulously analysed, and the Master has to certify that the requisite quantity of it is on board. After being surveyed the provisions are shipped from the Emigration Yard, and the signature of the Chief Officer, certifying to their receipt, is taken. In fact the same measures are adopted as when a regiment of Her Majesty's troops is shipped, and the very low average of deaths on the voyage—there are often none—shows that these elaborate precautions are not in vain. When all is ready, the Protector sends in a certificate to Government that the provisions of the Emigration Act have been complied with. A license for the ship to sail is then granted. The emigrants are now marched from the depot to the Emigration sheds; here they are drawn up in rows, inspected one by one—man, woman, and child—by the Medical Inspector to see that they show no signs of epidemic disease, and by the Protector to see that each has a copy of his agreement, and that he or she is willing to embark. In case of unwillingness to embark even though expressed at the last moment, the emigrant is not allowed to be put on board, though it is open to the Emigration Agent to prosecute him or her for breach of contract. But such refusals are not frequent, and prosecutions are still more rare. An amicable arrangement is either come to with the Agent at the depot by those who change their mind, the latter paying the expenses; or, if they are paupers, they abscond prior to the date of embarkation. When all the emigrants have been inspected, leave to embark is given, and the sea between the beach and the ship is soon dotted with the masulah boats into which the emigrants are put—sixteen to a boat. As soon as all are on board, the Protector signs the nominal rolls, the ship obtains her port clearance, and sails for her destination.

The great majority of the emigrants eventually elect to remain in the land of their adoption. Of those who do return, many bring with them large savings, and a very considerable percentage of them after a short stay in their native land go back to the Colonies. This speaks well for the way in which they are treated in the Colonies, and for the efficiency of the arrangements made by the Indian and Colonial Governments, by Conventions, Labour Ordinances, &c., to protect Her Majesty's Indian subjects in their distant homes.

REGISTRATION.

In the year 1834 the Court of Directors of the East India Company proposed the enactment of a law making registration of deeds relating to immovable property compulsory, under such penalties and safeguards as might be deemed requisite. Legislative proposals were accordingly made, and the subject was referred from time to time to various Committees, until, in 1864, a Bill, containing the main substance of the present law on the subject, was passed by the Government of India. This Act underwent several modifications in 1865, 1866, 1868, and 1871.

The Acts provide the machinery necessary for registration; lay down the duties and powers of the different classes of officers; declare what are the registrable documents and the effects of registration and non-registration; and prescribe the mode, time, and place of presentation and registration. The main feature of the Registration law is the distinction of registrable documents into those which must be registered in order to obtain validity, or what are called compulsory documents, and those which it is in the option of the parties to register or not, as they think fit. Documents under the first head lose all validity if not registered. In the case of documents under the second head, it is provided that a registered document of the same class shall take priority over a non-registered one. To remove a technical doubt, it is also provided that all registered documents, whether compulsory or not, shall take priority over non-registered documents. Optional registration has gradually expanded since 1877, and now represents more than half of the total registration of the Presidency of Madras.

With certain limitations the following documents are compulsorily registrable:—Instruments of gift of immovable property; other non-testamentary instruments which purport, or operate to create, declare, assign, limit, or extinguish, whether in present or in future, any right, title, or interest, whether vested or contingent, of the value of Rs. 100 upwards, to or in immovable property; non-testamentary instruments which acknowledge the receipt or payment of any consideration on account of the creation, declaration, assignment, limitation, or extinction of any such right, title, or interest; leases of immovable property from year to year, or for any term exceeding one year, or reserving a yearly rent; and authorities to adopt and not conferred by a will. The following documents are optionally registrable:—Instruments (other than instruments of gift and wills) which purport, or operate to create, declare, assign, limit, or extinguish, whether in present or in future, any right, title, or interest, whether vested or contingent, of a value less than Rs. 100, to or in immovable property; instruments acknowledging the receipt, or payment of any consideration on account of the creation, declaration, assignment, limitation, or extinction of any such right, title, or interest; leases of immovable property for any term not exceeding one year; instruments (other than wills) which purport, or operate to create, declare, assign, limit, or extinguish any right, title, or interest, to or in movable property; wills; all other documents not required to be registered.

For registration purposes the Madras Presidency—which contains an area of 138,985 square miles, and a population of 30,832,448—is divided into 22 districts, and 332 sub-districts, the districts being conterminous with the limits of the Revenue Collectorate. The sub-districts are also, as a rule, co-extensive with the taluks and the divisions of Deputy Tahsildars and Sub-Magistrates. The Department is administered by 22 Registrars, 332 special and official Sub-Registrars, and 20 Probationary Sub-Registrars, under the control of an officer, designated Inspector-General of Registration. The Registrars are located at the head-quarters of the District, and are paid by fixed salaries, varying from Rs. 100 to Rs. 500, and by a commission of 20 per cent. on the amount of fees collected and remitted by them during the month, the maximum being fixed at Rs. 50 for all Registrars, except the Registrar of Madras, who is allowed Rs. 100 a month. The special and official Sub-Registrars, of whom there are 316 and 16 respectively, are located at the Taluk and Sub-Division stations. The special Sub-Registrars are distributed into seven classes, or grades, and are remunerated partly by a fixed salary, and partly by commission, the former ranging from Rs. 30 to 75, and the latter being at the same rate (Rs. 50) as that allowed to Registrars generally. The Probationary Sub-Registrars, who are University graduates, are paid Rs. 20, and those who are undergraduates and matriculates Rs. 15 a month. The establishments of Special Registrars and Sub-Registrars are paid partly by salary, and partly by a commission of 19 per cent. on the gross collections remitted into the treasury. The official Sub-Registrars receive a commission of 20 per cent. as personal remuneration on the fees they remit, and 24 per cent. for their establishments. The special registering officers are required to obtain a practical knowledge of their work in the office of the District Registrar before entering upon their duties.

The annexed abstract statement shows the results of the working of the Department in Madras since the Act was introduced :—

	1864-65. 6 months.	1873-74.	1883-84.	1885-86.
Number of Offices	34	305	318	334
Instruments relating to immoveable property ...	8,393	193,790	444,560	542,786
Do. do. to moveable do. ...	4,223	12,783	32,774	41,098
Total number of documents	12,623	206,573	477,334	583,884
Receipts	Rs. 5,489	Rs. 331,180	Rs. 624,613	Rs. 839,080
Expenditure	„ 42,089	„ 256,649	„ 593,505	„ 659,849
Average fee per document	„ 0-11-0	„ 1-9-0	„ 1-5-7	„ [illegible]

The surplus of receipts over expenditure was Rs. 75,531 in 1873-74; Rs. 31,108 in 1883-84; and Rs. 179,239 in 1885-86. The aggregate value of the transactions was 6¾ crores in 1873-74, 11$\frac{7}{10}$ crores in 1883-84, and 13$\frac{1}{10}$ crores in 1885-86.

It was remarked by the late Governor of Madras, that by means of registration "the comfort of the people is very greatly increased; a sense of secure possession, which some highly enlightened countries might well envy, is being engendered; while the income of the community is greatly benefited, and is likely to be more and more benefited for years to come." Any disfavour with which the Registration law might have been viewed upon its first introduction in India, in consequence of the stringent provisions which it contained enforcing a somewhat minute description in instruments relating to immoveable property, disappeared upon its attaining its two great objects, viz. discouraging forgery and false evidence, and creating a trustworthy record of title to immoveable property. Registration offices have been, and are being, established in centres convenient to the inhabitants of the country to facilitate resort to registration; notices have been, and are being, freely circulated among them, pointing out the advantages of registered over non-registered documents; and the special registration officers, who devote their whole time and attention to expanding the business of the Department, strive to make registration everywhere popular, by preventing unnecessary delays and obstructions, and by rendering the procedure as simple as possible. The instruments that are now most commonly registered are wills, gifts, deeds of adoption, authorities to adopt, settlements, partition and maintenance deeds, sales, mortgages, perpetual leases, agricultural and non-agricultural leases, awards of arbitration, agreements, bonds, &c.

The Supreme Government, in its review of the Administration Reports of Registration of the several provinces for the year 1880-81, remarked :—"The steady progress which takes place in the development of registration in the Madras Presidency appears to the Government of India to be decidedly satisfactory, and the Governor-General in Council concurs with the Madras Government in the view that every such extension is a matter for congratulation, as implying greater security of title and diminished litigation, accompanied by reduced State expenditure on law and justice." Again, on the Reports for 1884-85, the Supreme Government said :—"To begin with the Madras Presidency, the progress which has been so marked during the past few years has been fully maintained. The financial results are also very satisfactory, the income of the year having risen to nearly 7½ lakhs, showing an increase of 19 per cent. above the highest revenue obtained in any year since the organisation of the Department."

POST OFFICE.

"It is hereby enacted that the exclusive right of conveying letters by post from place to place within the territories of the East India Company shall be in the Governor-General of India in Council." So ran the provisions of the Act of 1837; and, to quote the words of a well-known authority on the administration of the Post Office, "Until 1837 it was a positive privilege to be allowed to send private letters by the Government Dak." Three schedules were annexed to this Act showing the rates of inland postage, and it was enacted "that the full postage shall be paid either on receipt, or on delivery, at the option of the sender, and that, if the thing conveyed be transferred from a Post Office in one Presidency to a Post Office in another Presidency, no additional charge shall be made on account of such transfer." Postage was collected in cash, and the fee was regulated according to the distance to which the article had to be carried. The lowest fee was one anna; and this was charged for carrying a letter not exceeding one tola in weight, or a newspaper not exceeding three and a half tolas in weight, a distance not exceeding 20 miles. For carrying the same letter 500 miles the charge was nine annas, and for 1,000 miles one rupee. The highest charge on a newspaper not exceeding three and a half tolas in weight was three annas, and this was imposed when the distance exceeded 400 miles.

Thus, while that schedule of rates was in force, the postage duty on a letter sent from the City of Madras to the head-quarters of the Ganjam District, a distance of over 700 miles, was no less than eleven annas, and that too although the letter might not weigh more than half a tola; and on a letter from Madras to Tinnevelly, a distance of over 400 miles, the charge would be eight annas. Subscribers to a Madras newspaper residing in Calicut would be required to pay three annas postage on each copy they received, and six annas if it exceeded three and a half tolas in weight. In the case of letters, when the weight exceeded one tola, but did not exceed two tolas, the charge was doubled; and for each additional tola, or fraction of a tola, single postage was added. The postage fees on parcels were proportionately heavy, and the schedule to this Act makes no reference at all to parcels exceeding 600 tolas, or 15lbs. in weight. The duty on a parcel of that weight if carried 500 miles was Rs. 20¼, and if carried 1,000 miles Rs. 31½. Postal communications even under these conditions were not very widely extended, as only main lines connecting places of importance in the interior with the seat of Government were kept open. Post Offices in the interior of the Presidency of Madras were with a few exceptions under the charge of the Collectors of Districts; and the management of the whole was in the hands of a local Postmaster-General who acted under the control of the Local Government.

In the year 1850 a Postal Commission was appointed in India, and its report, which was published in the following year, led to the passing of the Act of 1854, whereby the Act of 1837 was repealed. Provision was for the first time made for the use of postage stamps; rates of postage were fixed without reference to the distance to which an article was to be carried, except in the case of parcels, and the whole of the postal arrangements in India were placed under the control of a Director-General. The rates of letter postage then introduced were, roughly speaking, double those now in force; and the postage on newspapers was peculiarly high, the charge being two annas for three and a half tolas, four annas for six tolas, and when the weight exceeded six tolas, two annas for every additional three tolas. The duty on the *Madras Mail* in its present form according to the table then in force would be six annas. The charge on newspapers was rapidly reduced, a rate of one anna for ten tolas having been introduced in 1866, which was further reduced to only half an anna in the years 1871-72. Letter postage was reduced to the rate of half an anna for half a tola from April 1869; and in the meantime the additional charge of postage whenever an article was redirected, had been abolished. The Act of 1854 authorised the imposition of this additional charge.

The duty on parcels was not fixed at a uniform rate irrespective of distance until the year 1870-71. After several modifications had been made from time to time, the rates now in force were finally adopted in 1880. According to the table in the Act of 1854 the charge for conveying a parcel weighing two hundred tolas a distance of 500 miles was three Rupees. The same parcel can now be sent any distance within British India, or from any place in British India to any place in British Burmah, for a fee of only two Annas. On the introduction of official postage stamps, the rates of postage for official correspondence were at first the same as for ordinary correspondence; but remarkable reductions have since been made, and at the present time a weight not exceeding ten tolas can be sent by post for one anna, and only one anna extra is charged for every additional ten tolas up to forty tolas.

Since the year 1854 the development of the Post Office in the Madras Presidency has proceeded with great rapidity. In the year 1856-57 the mails were being carried over a distance of 7,878¼ miles; in the year 1885-86, the distance over which they were carried by the several modes of conveyance was 10,239 miles. In the former year they were carried only 65 miles by rail, while in the latter year they travelled over 2,154 miles by that means; and from this it may be understood how much the time in transit must have been reduced throughout the greater part of the Presidency.

In the year 1854 only 130 Post Offices had been established in the Presidency; in 1860 the number had risen to 163; at the close of 1871-72 there were 360; at the close of 1880-81 there were 717; and on the 1st April, 1886, no less than 1,065 offices were open. In spite of this rapid increase, however, it is still only in towns and very large villages that offices have been established; but, in order to provide greater facilities elsewhere, 614 letter boxes had been placed in outlying villages before the close of 1885-86, and 476 village postmen had been appointed whose duty it is to clear these letter boxes and deliver articles in rural tracts. Since the 1st April, 1886, there has been a further increase in the number of Post Offices in the Presidency; and there is now an office for every 121 square miles of country, and for every 26,728 of population.

By converting square miles into square kilometres, the postal system of the Presidency in respect to area and population may be compared with those of countries in the western world. Roughly speaking then there is found to be one office to every 300 square kilometres. In Great Britain there is one office to every 18 square kilometres, and every 2,161 of population; in Germany one office to every 30 square kilometres and every 2,684 of population; and in Sweden one office to every 213 square kilometres, and every 2,311 of population. The country where the development of the Post Office most closely resembles that which has been reached in Madras is Greece, which has one office to every 295 square kilometres, and every 9,205 of population. In Egypt there are 3,522 square kilometres, and 42,807 of population for each office.

The number of officers, clerks, and others employed in the Department in the Presidency has not increased in the same ratio as the number of offices; and, as will presently appear, the increase in this respect is insignificant in comparison with the vast expansion in the work of the Post Office that has taken place. The number employed on the 31st March, 1870 was 5,134; on the 31st March, 1881, it had risen to 5,289; and on the corresponding date in 1886 it was 6,495. The number of articles, including letters, newspapers, parcels, and book and pattern packets given out for delivery in 1856-57 was 5,828,220; in 1871-72 it was 13,922,227; in 1880-81 it was 26,451,680; and in 1885-86 the number had increased to 38,603,264. During this period the number of letters rose from 5,000,000 to 33,000,000, and of newspapers from 601,000 to nearly 3,000,000.

The use of Inland and Foreign Post Cards was introduced in July, 1874; and it may be interesting to mention that the numbers given out for delivery during 1885-86 was no less than 8,523,219. These are included in the 33,000,000 of letters.

In the rules for the management of the Post Office which were first issued in 1854 it was directed that "in order to protect as far as possible the public mails from the chance of robbery, officers in charge of Post Offices shall not knowingly receive coin, bullion, precious stones, or jewels for despatch either by letter or banghy," but from the 1st January, 1878, the insurance of registered letters or parcels, the contents of which were valuable, was introduced. The insurance fee was at first 8 annas per cent., but it was subsequently reduced to 4 annas only. In the year 1884-85 there were 24,169 registered letters received in the Madras Presidency, the insured value of which was Rs. 6,103,623; and 23,072 parcels, the insured value of which was Rs. 5,879,531. The insurance fees realised amounted to Rs. 31,427, and thus, although the fee is so small, a considerable revenue has been derived from this business. What is most satisfactory of all in connection with the working of this system is to find that, in spite of the temptation that it may seem to offer, it has led to so few frauds on the part of postal *employés*. Judging, however, from what is stated in paragraph 57 of the Director-General's report on the operations of the Post Office for the year 1885-86, there would appear to be some danger of the system being occasionally abused by senders of insured articles who desire to cheat the addressees, and hold the Post Office responsible. This they can at least endeavour to do by enclosing contents other than those which they declare.

The value payable business was introduced from December 1st, 1877, and has, like the other principal branches of Post Office work, passed through a rapid development. During the year 1878-79 there were 101 articles received in the Presidency for despatch, the declared value of which was Rs. 2,995. In 1881-82 the number of articles had risen to 14,198, the value of which was Rs. 146,508; and in 1884-85 there were 40,281 articles sent, the amount specified for recovery by the Post Office being Rs. 430,983.

On the 1st January, 1880, the Money Order Department was transferred to the Post Office, and has since shown remarkable powers of expansion. In 1880-81 the number of money orders issued in the Presidency was 218,597, and their value Rs. 5,542,507. The orders issued in 1882-83 were 363,361 in number, and their value Rs. 84,34,427; while in 1885-86 the number had risen to 511,824, and the value to Rs. 11,165,396. The number and value of paid orders increased at the same rate, the figures for 1885-86 being 533,052 orders, and the amount paid on them Rs. 11,630,947. This rapid growth is no doubt due to the greater facilities which the Post Office affords in comparison with the Treasury Department, with which the management formerly rested. Post Offices are much more numerous than Treasuries, and much more easy of access, and arrangements have been made whereby the Post Office transmits the money order from the office of issue to the office of payment, delivers the amount through a postman to the payee, and obtains an acknowledgment of payment from the latter for the satisfaction of the remitter. The practice of delivering the amount of the order to the payee at his residence has not yet been widely introduced in outlying villages; but the number received for payment in such places is not considerable.

The Post Office Savings Bank was established from the 1st April, 1882: and at the close of the year 1882-83 there were 4,416 accounts open with a balance to the credit of depositors of Rs. 2,60,741. On the 1st April, 1885, there were 16,119 accounts open, the balance of deposits being Rs. 13,46,871; and on the 1st April, 1886, the accounts had increased in number to 20,609, and the balance at credit of the depositors to Rs. 19,23,018. Since the date last mentioned all accounts in the District Savings Bank have been transferred to the Post Office, and the number of accounts and the balance of deposits have in consequence increased enormously. In Rule 318 of the *Indian Postal Guide* it is intimated that "the object of Government in establishing Post Office Savings Banks is to provide a ready means for the deposit of savings, and so to encourage thrift;" and from the foregoing particulars it would appear that a considerable degree of success has been attained towards the fulfilment of this object.

In the year 1856-57 the total receipts of the Post Office in the Madras Presidency were Rs. 6,70,072, and the disbursements Rs. 6,33,201, leaving a profit of Rs. 36,871; in the year 1871-72 the receipts were Rs. 12,28,263, the disbursements Rs. 7,28,980, and the profit Rs. 4,99,283; while in 1885-86 the receipts had risen to Rs. 17,69,594, and, as the disbursements were only Rs. 10,06,548, there was a profit of Rs. 7,63,046. The expenses in connection with the operations of the Railway Mail Service in the Presidency are excluded from these disbursements.

In October, 1883, the system of Combined Post and Telegraph Offices was introduced, and on the 31st March, 1886, there were 66 offices of that description open. As 37 telegraph offices remained under the direct management of the Government Telegraph Department, there were in all 103 offices for the receipt and despatch of messages on the above date. Previous to the introduction of this system there were only 61 Government Telegraph Offices at work; and it is thus manifest that the measure has been attended with greatly increased facilities in regard to telegraphic communication. The total charge to the Telegraph Department for working these combined offices during 1885-86 was Rs. 25,592, and the revenue realised was Rs. 54,385. There was thus a substantial profit, and this is due to the fact that the management is marked by that economy which is so carefully observed in all the branches of business now under the conduct and control of the Post Office.

TELEGRAPHS.

In August, 1853, the Telegraph stores lying in the Madras Arsenal were inspected, and, with the aid of the various Collectors and Engineers of the districts between Madras and Hoompanagur, on the Bombay frontier, they were distributed, and arrangements were made for the erection of flying lines. By the end of July, 1854, 28 miles of local lines were erected in the vicinity of Madras, with a double wire from Madras to St. Thomas's Mount. Offices at Black Town, Madras, at Fort Saint George, Guindy, St. Thomas's Mount, and Poonamallee were opened to the public. 401 miles of line from Poonamallee to Bellary were erected, with offices at Vellore, Bangalore, Tumkur, and Bellary. By the end of 1854, 91 miles of line from Bellary to Hoompanagur were completed, with offices at Hurrihur, Hoompanagur, and Dharwar. Preparations were made for the erection of a flying line from Bangalore to Mysore, a distance of 84 miles of line, which was completed in March, 1855, and an office was opened at the latter station. This line was extended from Mysore to Ootacamund, a distance of 82 miles, and an office at Ootacamund was opened on the 26th April, 1855. In September, 1856, 203 miles of flying line from Mysore to Calicut were completed, and offices were opened at Mercara, Cannanore, and Calicut. In January, 1857, arrangements were made to construct a flying line from St. Thomas's Mount to Ceylon, through the French Settlements of Pondicherry and Karikal; but the work was greatly delayed by the detention of the wire expected from England. In August, 1857, 99 miles of line from Madras to Pondicherry through St. Thomas's Mount had been completed, and an office at Pondicherry was opened. On the 24th November, 1857, 271 miles of line from Madras to Bezwada, *via* Nellore and Ongole, were completed, and an office at Nellore was opened, and another at Bezwada. By August of the following year, 280 miles of line south of Madras, from Pondicherry to Chetty Chuttrum were completed up to Negapatam, and to Ramaisweram in October following. A submarine cable, consisting of a 7-strand copper wire protected by an outer coating of tarred yarn and large iron wire, was successfully laid across the Gulf of Manaar from Thonicodi Point and Tullamanaar.

In May, 1858, orders were received to construct a line from Calicut to Cochin, a distance of 103 miles, and upon its completion an office at Cochin was opened on the 18th December following.

Preliminary operations were commenced to extend the line from Cochin to Ramnad *via* Alleppey, Quilon, Trivandrum, and Tuticorin, and from Cannanore to Ukarwar, traversing Mangalore and Honore, but proceedings were postponed. In 1862-63, some portions of the following sections, from Madras to Bangalore, Bangalore to Bellary, Bangalore to Mysore, Mercara to Calicut, and Calicut to Cochin, were reconstructed, and the alignments of the above sections were slightly modified to avoid several large river-crossings, paddy fields, &c. The Government again sanctioned the extension of the line from Bombay to Tuticorin, *via* Cannanore, Cochin, and Palamcottah on the Western Coast. That portion of the route within the limits of the circle was surveyed, and estimates and indents were submitted. An office at Tellicherry and three temporary ones on the banks of the Vypeen and Beypore rivers, and in Seerah were opened respectively. The estimates, &c., referred to having been sanctioned, the construction of the line was commenced in 1863-64 from Tuticorin, *via* Tinnevelly, Trivandrum, Quilon, Alleppey, and Cochin, and from Mercara to Mangalore and Coondapore. The direction of the line formerly contemplated to run on from Cannanore to Bombay was changed in view to avoid the numerous water-crossings to the north of Cannanore on the Western Coast. Offices at Cuddalore and Beypore were opened. In 1864-65, the lines from Tuticorin to Cochin, and from Mercara to Mangalore and Coondapore towards Bombay, measuring 365½ miles were completed, and offices at Palamcottah, Alleppey, Nagercoil, Trivandrum, and Mangalore were opened, as also an Office of Observation at Kotapermuba.

Various extensions were made in subsequent years, and the extent of the line advanced from 892 miles in 1867-68 to 2,108 miles (with 13 Departmental, 46 Combined, 19 Mysore State Railway, 11 Canal, and 35 Private Line offices), on 31st December, 1886. The Departmental Offices of the Madras Division—which forms about one-third of the whole Presidency—are situated at Madras, Fort St. George, Negapatam, Vellore, Pondicherry, Trichinopoly, Madura, Tuticorin, Pamban, Bangalore, Wellington, Ootacamund, and Lovedale. Combined offices have been established at Adoni, Arcot, Chittoor, Coimbatore, Coonoor, Cuddalore, Cuddapah, Dindigul, Erode, Gudiyattam, Hosur, Karikal, Karur, Kotagiri, Kumbakonam, Kurnool, Mount Road, Mannargudi, Mylapore, Mysore, Nagore, Nungumbaukum, Palghat, Paramakudi, Poonamallee, Pudukotah, Ramnad, Salem, Saidapet, Sowcarpett, St. Thomas's Mount, Tanjore, Tirupati, Tranquebar, Trichinopoly Fort, Triplicane, Vaniyambadi, Vepery, Viruthupati, Walajanagar, and Woriur. The number of messages of all classes transmitted from the different offices in the Madras Division advanced from 23,394 in the year 1858-59 to 287,929 in the year 1885-86, and the value from Rs. 46,465 in the former to Rs. 6,20,151 in the latter year.

When the telegraph was first introduced into India the signals were composed and read off by the right and left deflections of a magnet placed within several convolutions of copper wire. Shortly before 1857 the Morse system was introduced, and reading by sound from the taps of an electro magnet is now universal in India. Formerly there was but one system of working, that is by the ordinary open current; now in the Central Telegraph office at Madras circuits are worked by ordinary open circuit, by through circuit, by closed circuit, by double current single working, by double current duplex working, and by quadruplex working. Formerly all interruptions were repaired by line runners. A fault occurred between two stations, say 100 miles apart, and a man was started from each end, and had to examine every inch of the line until the fault was reached. The two men having met, repaired the fault, and returned to their respective stations. Now all the lines are tested twice a month to see that they are in good electrical order, and whenever a fault occurs it is easily localised within a few yards of the place; a runner is ordered out to the spot, and the accident is usually repaired in a few hours. All the signallers have to pass an entrance examination in general elementary education, and, after nine months to a year of technical education, they have to pass a final examination.

PUBLIC WORKS.

In the year 1837 the state of Public Works in the Presidency of Madras was thus described by Captain (now Sir Arthur) Cotton, of the Madras Engineers :—

"That the nature and importance of the subjects of the Irrigation and Communications has been hitherto altogether misapprehended, leading to a loss of Revenue and a retardation of the progress of improvement in the state of the community which is quite beyond calculation.

"That, as respects Communications, no country whatever can prosper if they are not made the very first objects of attention, and that in respect to Irrigation it is in this country owing to the peculiar character of the climate, undoubtedly the very first subject to be attended to; inasmuch as we cannot naturally expect that there will not be famine and want of every kind, just in proportion as the cultivation is more or less dependent upon local rains, without the help of artificial works.

"But the expenditure upon the Irrigation has certainly not exceeded one-third of what, upon the strictest principles of economy, it ought to have been; and that from the little consideration that the subject of Communications has been thought worthy of, there has been in most cases nothing at all expended, and in others the most expensive and unaccountable expenditure, totally disproportioned to the advantages to be obtained, and to the real necessities of the case.

"Though the country cannot advance without good Judicial and Revenue management, yet it is indisputably certain that nothing will avail unless the Irrigation and Communications are attended to. While the population are mainly dependent upon the local rains of so precarious a climate for their cultivation, that four-fifths of them must be employed in merely raising food, every five or six years we must witness the deaths of tens of thousands by famine, and the great body of the people must be without clothing or anything but a bare subsistence, even in fruitful seasons. And without Communications, nine-tenths of the natural resources of the country must continue to be useless. Above all the want of Communications is almost a total bar to the progress of knowledge, and improvement generally."

The system under which this lamentable condition of affairs continued had been gradually evolved from that by which, in the early days of British rule, every Collector was his own Engineer, and, in addition to collecting the revenue, expended annually, without professional assistance, considerable sums on the up-keep and improvement of the works from which the revenue was derived. Though logically it must be admitted that the Collectors who were responsible for the revenue should also have much to say to the works upon which the revenue depended, yet, as no amount of zeal will make up for want of professional training, it followed that the waste of money attracted attention, and from time to time efforts were made to aid the Collectors by appointing "Superintendents of Tank Repairs." But for many years the number of the latter officers was too limited to be of any practical benefit; and it was not until 1825 that the whole Presidency was divided into three divisions, each under the charge of a "Civil Engineer," with a suitable establishment, and the whole placed under the control of an Engineer officer at the Presidency town, styled the "Inspector General of Civil Estimates." In 1836 it was decided that the Board of Revenue should have the benefit of the experience of the Inspector-General, and that officer was given a seat at the Board, under the title of Chief Engineer, an Engineer Secretary to the Board being at the same time appointed, upon whom devolved the administrative duties previously performed by the Inspector-General.

Such, then, in the first year of the reign of Her Majesty was the "Maramut" or "Repairs" Department, which had the control of all irrigation works and navigable canals, and all roads and bridges not situated in Military cantonments. Side by side with the "Maramut" Department was the Engineering Department of the Military Board, an institution dating so far back as 1785, and which was responsible for the superintendence of the fortifications generally; of the roads, bridges, and public buildings, both Civil and Military, at the Presidency town; together with all Military (and Civil up to 1838) buildings in the provinces; and roads and bridges in cantonments. The engineering works under the Board were distributed in ten divisions, corresponding with the divisions of the Army. Five of these divisions were controlled by Superintending Engineers, with executive officers, a suitable establishment of overseer Serjeants, &c.; and in the remaining five, the execution of works was undertaken by the Commanding, or Staff Officer. Thus it will be seen that fifty years ago the conduct of Public Works in the Presidency of Madras was divided between a Military Works Branch and the Public Works proper. This arrangement did not work well; and in 1838 the importance of the "Maramat" Department to the revenue of the country, and the necessity of strengthening it so as to enable it to cope effectually with the vast amount of work devolving upon it, became more apparent.

It was therefore resolved that the whole Presidency should be rearranged to form eight "Maramat" divisions, each under a "Civil Engineer," to whom were, at the same time, transferred the construction and repair of all Civil buildings in the provinces, formerly under the Military Board; while the other works, under the control of that body, were placed in charge of the Staff Officers at Stations, and at Division Head-quarters, under the Quarter-Master General of the Division Staff. By this reorganization, whatever efficiency the Engineering Branch of the Military Board had possessed, was gradually destroyed, but it was not until twenty years later that the Board was abolished. In 1850, the importance of the systematic management and execution of Public Works throughout the Presidency engaged the attention of the Court of Directors in England, and a Public Works Commission was appointed in the following year. In 1852 the Commission issued a very full account of the existing system of Public Works Administration, and reviewed at length the working of the "Maramut" Department, the Trunk Road Department, and the Engineer Department of the Military Board. It pointed out the generally neglected state of public works of the country, except in a few favoured districts; it dwelt on the insufficiency of the annual grants allotted for public works, and on the inadequate establishments appointed to look after them; and it brought to notice the benefits to be derived by the State from the systematic and judicious expenditure of public money in the promotion of public works. The Commission also recommended the establishment of one Department for the management of all Public Works, Civil or Military. At this date the entire cost of the Public Works Establishment was 5⅞ lakhs per annum, and the expenditure on works 24¼ lakhs. The proposals of the Commission involved an annual charge of nearly 14⅝ lakhs for establishment, and an annual expenditure of 48 lakhs. After much discussion, the new establishment was sanctioned for the year 1858, and thus, for the first time in its history the Department, as a whole became an executive Department. In consequence of the Mutiny in Bengal, the expenditure on Public Works was much restricted, and a considerable part of the Public Works establishment sanctioned in 1858 was discharged in the year 1859. In 1860 doubts arose as to whether the organization was not too elaborate, and in 1863 the question was referred to a Committee upon whose recommendations some radical changes in the executive were made. In 1870, in consequence of the difficulty of maintaining the minor irrigation works, a Commission was assembled to consider the expediency of further reorganization, but it was not until 1872 that practical effect was given to its recommendations. The principal changes were the appointment of twenty-one District Engineers in direct communication with the Chief Engineer. The cost of the new establishment was set down at 21¾ lakhs. This organization was succeeded in 1878 by the Superintending Engineer system; the Presidency being divided into five circles, each under a Superintending Engineer, and 39 Executive divisions. In 1879 considerable reductions were made in the Executive Staff, in consequence of financial pressure caused by the famine; and the number of executive divisions was reduced to 29. It being found that with the increased areas thus given to each division, the staff of the Department was no longer equal to the work expected from it, the greater part of the Public Works in the Local Fund Circles were handed over to the Local Fund Boards for execution by their own agency. The consequent reduction in the contribution of the Local Funds to the cost of the Public Works establishment, amounting to about 5¾ lakhs, together with the financial pressure then existing, involved a still further reduction in 1880-81 when 15 officers of the Engineer Establishment, and 79 upper subordinates were retired. But in the year 1881 brighter times dawned upon the Department, which admitted of a large increase in the establishment, and the Presidency was re-arranged into six Superintending Engineers' circles, subdivided into 30 executive divisions; which, with the exception of alterations made from time to time in the number of divisions, is the organization now in force.

Having thus outlined the rise and formation of the Public Works Department, and briefly sketched its organization, it only remains to mention a few types of its work. The most important of the Public Works of the Madras Presidency—other than those of Irrigation—may be divided into three classes, viz.: Communications, Harbours, and Buildings. With a few exceptions no works of the first class remain under the Department, and the exceptions referred to will, as soon as they are completed, be handed over to the Local Fund Boards concerned. Up to a very recent date all the bridges in the Presidency town were maintained by the Department; but they have now been handed over to the Municipality; and in future years it is not probable that any roads or bridges will be constructed by the Department, except in cases where the Local Fund Boards are unable on account of the expense to undertake the work. With regard to Harbours, the works at Madras are described on another page. The pier at Gopalpore is also alluded to, and it is merely necessary to add that it will be completed during the present year. The improvement of the Cocanada harbour by means of lengthening the groynes at the mouth of the Cocanada river, has lately engaged the attention of the Department, but it is probable that the idea of extending them will be abandoned in favour of dredging on the bar. The works at the Paumben Pass have, since 1879, been carried on by the Marine Department, but prior to that date they were under the Department, and consisted chiefly of blasting and dredging to make a passage for coasting vessels. The harbours of Mangalore and Negapatam have also been considered, but they present exceedingly difficult problems, and their improvement is not likely to be attempted for some time. The Cruz Milagre dam at Cochin gave rise to some uneasiness two years ago, but the remedial measures taken had the desired effect.

To turn now to the class of "Buildings," it must be admitted that in proportion to its size and importance the Madras Presidency has few modern buildings of architectural importance, but within the last ten years much has been done at the Presidency town and at Ootacamund to improve matters. Among the largest and most important Military buildings constructed by the Department may be mentioned the Military Convalescent Depot at Wellington costing 17½ lakhs; the Lawrence Asylum at Ootacamund, 8¼ lakhs; Family quarters in Fort St. George and Cannanore; Barracks at Fort St. George, Cannanore, St. Thomas's Mount, Bangalore, and Bellary, and many other Military buildings of various descriptions. It may be added that most of the buildings named above were completed with little deviation in cost from the estimated amount. Among the Civil buildings, the most important that have been constructed of late years are Government House, Ootacamund, the Postal and Telegraph Offices, Madras, the Senate House of the Madras University, the Presidency College, the Lying-in Hospital, and the Ophthalmic Hospital. With these, and many other buildings, the name of Mr. R. F. Chisholm, late Consulting Architect to the Government of Madras, will be honourably handed down to posterity.

From this brief sketch of the Department, it will be seen that since 1837, when the reproachful words of Sir Arthur Cotton were written, much has been done to ensure the public works of the Presidency being carried on in a systematic manner. The result has been most satisfactory. The main lines of road, and thousands of miles of cross roads have been metalled and bridged, and (since 1879) handed over to the Local Fund Boards, who year by year are improving the "Communications" by making new roads and repairing existing ones; thus leaving the Public Works Department free to devote more attention to the subject of "irrigation." The difficulty, however, of the up-keep of the minor irrigation works still continues, and in 1883 it was found necessary to entrust the work of obtaining hydraulic information and preparing estimates for these works to a separate branch of the Department known as the "Tank Maintenance" scheme. Unfortunately, owing to financial pressure, nearly the whole of the establishment for this work had to be abolished at the commencement of this year, and for some time it was feared that the scheme would have to be held in abeyance for an indefinite period. It is now, however, contemplated to recommence operations upon a modified scale, for there can be no question of the great importance of carrying out the repairs to these minor works (which include 31,648 tanks) in a systematic manner and upon scientific principles. This retrospect should not be closed without mention of the Corps of Madras Engineers, the officers of which have from the earliest days taken a prominent part in the public works of the Presidency; so much so that a Civil history of the corps (the Military history has already been written) would be almost a complete history of the Public Works Department.

RAILWAYS.

Although some progress had been made with the construction of Railways in England at the time of Her Majesty's accession, it was not until several years after that event that practical steps were taken for their introduction into India. Some of the earliest Indian Railway Companies were formed in London in 1845, but the projectors found it impossible to raise the necessary funds without the assistance of Government. This led to the adoption of what is known as the "guarantee" system, under which lines are made through the instrumentality of Companies who receive from Government a guarantee of a certain rate of interest upon the capital expended, the rate being at first 5 per cent., with half the surplus profits beyond that figure. The direct pecuniary interest which, under this arrangement, the Government has in the success of railways, involved the necessity for some supervision and control, which is provided for in the contracts, and is exercised in England through a Government Director, and in India through the Consulting Engineers for Railways.

The Madras Railway Company was originally formed on the 8th July, 1845, its object being the construction of a line from Madras to Arcot. The Company was dissolved in the following year, and it was not until the East Indian and Great Indian Peninsula Railway Companies had obtained a guarantee of interest that the subject of a railway in the Madras Presidency was revived. In 1849 the Madras Company endeavoured to obtain terms similar to those in other Presidencies, but was unsuccessful. A report on railways was then made by Major (now Sir Thomas) Pears, of the Madras Engineers, who recommended that a trunk line should run from Madras to the Malabar Coast, *viâ* Vaniambady, Salem, and Palghat; and that another should diverge from it, at about seventy miles from Madras, and climbing the Eastern Ghauts near *Palmaner*, be carried *viâ* Bangalore to Bellary, and thence to Poona and Bombay. In the selection of his lines Major Pears seems to have been guided entirely by facilities of construction, and subsequent economy in working. The Supreme Government did not approve of the line *viâ* Bangalore to Bellary, but decided upon a main line from Madras to the West Coast, with a branch from Vaniambady to Bangalore, and another from Coimbatore towards the Nilgiris; and a line also from Madras to Cuddapah and Bellary.

The present Madras Railway Company was formed in 1852, and its first contract was for the construction of an experimental line from Madras towards the West Coast. The question of the general system of lines was still unsettled, but the arrival of an Agent in January 1853 rendering a commencement necessary, the Government of India shortly afterwards directed that a line from Madras as far as Mussal be at once constructed, as the best line for an extension of the railway in any direction that further surveys might show to be desirable. The first sod was turned on the 9th June, but before much progress had been made it was agreed that the line should be extended to the West Coast. A contract for this purpose was executed in 1855. A further contract for the construction of the North-West Line was entered into in August, 1858. The first section, from Madras to Arcot, was opened for traffic on the 1st July, 1896, and the South-West Line, from Madras to Beypore, was opened throughout on the 12th May, 1862. The Bangalore branch was opened on the 1st August, 1864, and that to Mettupalaiyam on the 31st August, 1873. On the North-West Line commencing at Arkonam, the first section to Nagari was opened on the 4th March, 1861, and the line was completed to Raichur on the 15th March, 1872, the Bellary branch being also opened in the same month. The doubling of the line from Madras to Perambore was completed on the 7th February, 1874, and from thence to Arkonam on the 28th August, 1877. The short branch to Bangalore city, which was originally undertaken as a portion of the Mysore Railway, was handed over to the Madras Railway for construction as a broad gauge line, and opened for traffic on the 1st July, 1882. These lines are all on the 5′ 6″, or Indian gauge, selected by Lord Dalhousie, and their total length is 861 miles; but on the 1st February, 1887, the Bellary Branch, 30 miles in length, was transferred to the Southern Mahratta Company, so that the total length of the Madras Railway is at present 831 miles. Calicut is now being substituted for Beypore as the western terminus, and this extension, 9 miles in length, will be opened towards the end of this year. A branch, 2½ miles long, from Palghat Station to the town is also under construction.

The South Indian Railway, which is also "guaranteed," consists of a main line from Madras to Tuticorin with branches from Chingleput to Arkonam, from Villuperam to Gingee river, where it joins the Pondicherry Railway, from Tanjore to Negapatam, from Trichinopoly to Erode, and from Maniyáchi to Tinnevelly. The first portion of the undertaking was on the 5′ 6″ gauge from Negapatam to Erode, but when the extensions to Madras and Tuticorin were sanctioned, it was determined that the entire system should be on the metre gauge. The line from Negapatam to Erode was commenced in May, 1859, by the Great Southern of India Railway Company, and completed in December, 1861. The line from Arkonam to Conjeeveram was commenced in March, 1864, by the Indian Tramway Company, and was completed on the 5′ 6″ gauge in May, 1865. The Carnatic Railway Company took over the latter, and entered into a contract in 1870 for its extension to Cuddalore; but in July, 1874, the two undertakings were amalgamated, under the title of the South Indian Railway, and the whole system is now on the metre gauge, the conversion of the Negapatam to Erode section having been completed in December, 1879, and that of the Arkonam to Conjeeveram section in July, 1878. The line from Trichinopoly to Tuticorin was completed in January, 1876, and that from Tanjore to Madras in July, 1879. The Pondicherry branch was opened in December, 1879, and the Chingleput to Conjeeveram section on the 1st January, 1883.

These being until quite recently the only open lines in the Madras Presidency a few remarks may now be made as to their financial results. Unlike most of the guaranteed lines in other parts of India, the Madras and South Indian Railways, though comparatively cheaply constructed, have never paid the guaranteed interest, a result due to the comparatively small traffic which they command. The chief causes assigned for this are:—The geographical character of the country served, lying as it does within the narrowest part of the peninsula; the absence of leading staples of traffic, and of any great trade centre on which they might concentrate from a long distance; and the poverty and simple habits of the southern people. The same will probably be true of any future extensions.

The capital of the Madras Railway is 10⅓ millions sterling, of which 3⅜ millions bear interest at 5 per cent. The line has cost £12,250 per mile. The capital of the South Indian Railway is 4½ millions, and the line has cost £6,800 per mile. Up to the end of 1885 the guaranteed interest of the Madras Railway amounted to 12⅜ millions, while the net profits reached only 5⅜ millions, leaving a balance of 6⅞ millions to be met from the revenues of India, in addition to the expenditure on land which was given free.

The interest and profits of the South Indian Railway are 3⅓ millions and 1⅜ millions respectively, leaving a balance of 1⅓ millions against the State. Much has been urged against the fact of the Madras

M M

Railway passing at a distance from the large towns of Arcot, Vellore, Salem, and Palghat, but the short-distance traffic thus lost could have no appreciable effect on the general results, and it is questionable if 1,300 miles of railway could have been laid in the Madras Presidency which would have yielded traffic exceeding in any degree that earned by the existing lines. The Madras Railway now pays nearly 3 per cent., and the South Indian, excluding abnormal outlay which is now being incurred, may be expected to pay 4 per cent.

The work done by these lines has increased largely of late years. In 1885 the Madras Railway carried 5½ millions of passengers an average distance of 45 miles, and 646,000 tons of goods a distance of 153 miles; and the South Indian Railway carried 6¼ millions of passengers an average distance of 36 miles, and 524,000 tons of goods a distance of 72 miles. The gross earnings of the two lines during the same years were 76¼ lakhs and 45½ lakhs respectively, and the net profits amounted to 32¾ lakhs, and 15¾ lakhs. About 99 per cent. of the passengers travel third class. Rates have been greatly reduced, and the lines are performing their proper function in developing the resources of the Presidency. Although the Government has every year to make up a large deficit (in 1885 this was £275,000) there can be no doubt that the advantages in improved and cheapened administration, and in the development of the country, far outweigh the charges thus incurred. A notable instance of the use of railways was furnished during the famine of 1876-78, when, as stated by the Viceroy, the railways saved Southern India.

As to other lines in the Madras Presidency, it may be mentioned that the only open length is a portion of the Southern Mahratta Railway from Bellary to Hospet, 40 miles. As already stated this Company now owns the branch of the Madras line, which will be converted to the metre gauge to afford connection with the railway under construction by the State from Guntakal to Bezvada. The latter has a length of 259 miles, and is designed to convey the surplus produce of the Kistna Delta to the unproductive portions of Bellary, Anantapur, and Cuddapah. A similar line, 86 miles long, on the metre gauge, is being made from Tirupati to Nellore to connect the above-named districts with the Pennair Delta. This line and a portion of the former, known as the Bellary-Kistna, will be opened during the present year. In order that they may fulfil their object extensions are required from Guntakal to Hindupur and Bangalore, and from Tirupati to Dharmavaram. A line is also projected from Villupuram to Pakali (near Damalcheruvu) crossing the Madras Railway at Vellore, to convey the produce of the Tanjore Delta, and, together with the extensions described above, to connect the metre gauge systems of the South Indian and Southern Mahratta Railways. A line on the broad gauge, 21½ miles long, is now under construction from Bezvada to the Hyderabad Frontier, to join that being made by the Nizam's State Railway Company to the Singareni coal fields. The coal is of good quality and inexhaustible in quantity; and its use on the railways of Southern India will lead to considerable economy in working. At present the Madras Railway works one-fourth of its trains with patent fuel, and three-fourths with wood; the South Indian Railway uses coal almost entirely. Several surveys for minor lines have been carried out from provincial revenues.

THE MADRAS HARBOUR.

The construction of a Harbour at Madras has been the greatest engineering work of the kind undertaken in India during the reign of Her Majesty, and, perhaps, as a purely marine work, in no way connected with quays, locks, or canals, it is one of the largest works ever attempted out of Europe. To Lord Hobart is chiefly due the origin of the Harbour, for to him, in 1873, Mr. William Parkes submitted his plan, of which the Governor highly approved, and which he warmly recommended for the sanction of the Secretary of State. The idea was not to form a Harbour of Refuge, but to overcome the drawbacks of the surf, and by this means to make such a saving on boat hire as would pay 5 per cent. interest on the capital to be laid out in constructing the Harbour, the estimated cost of which was Rs. 56,45,165. In March, 1875, the scheme was sanctioned by the

Secretary of State, and preparations were immediately made for commencing work at Madras. Engines, cranes, and machinery, with cement, and various stores, were sent out from England; while, in Madras, arrangements were made by Mr. James May, the Superintendent, for quarrying stone and laterite in the neighbourhood of Madras for the work, and organising establishments. Very little progress, however, was made in 1875, as the commencement of forming the north pier, or surf bank, was a mistake, and the work had afterwards to be relinquished. In December 1875, it was resolved to connect the name of the Prince of Wales (who was then in India) with the undertaking. Accordingly, on the 20th of that month, with all due ceremony, and in the presence of a very large number of the inhabitants of Madras, His Royal Highness laid a Memorial Stone in commemoration of the commencement of the undertaking.

In January 1876 work was begun in earnest, Mr. May being ably assisted by Mr. Beardmore, who had arrived in the previous November from England. The north surf bank was pushed out rapidly into the surf. In May, Mr. May died in the fifty-eighth year of his age. This threw the responsibility of a great amount of work upon Mr. Beardmore, who did excellent service. In the following August, Mr. F. N. Thorowgood arrived, and took command of the works, which had by this time been brought into a good state of efficiency for a proper start at construction. But the advance of sand to seaward with the progress of the piers caused much apprehension, and the Government telegraphed to Mr. Parkes to visit Madras to report what was going on. This he did in October 1876, when he allayed many of the fears in the public mind by showing that the sand accumulation was only temporary. From December 1876 until April 1877 the progress at the north pier was regular, but in April the stone foundation was found to be buried with sand in one night. This hindered progress to such an extent that, from March 1877 to January 1878, an advance of only 58 feet was made. This slow rate of progress excited so much alarm, and the need for economy in public expenditure was so pressing, that had it not been for the Duke of Buckingham and Chandos, who was then Governor, the works would probably have been discontinued by the Government of India. Soon afterwards, however, the work at both piers went on briskly, and in 1880 a rate of advance was attained which is not known to have been equalled before in any deep sea work in the world. In the working months of that year a length of 1,235 feet of the north pier, and 1,420 feet of the south pier was built. In October 1881 the Harbour was nearly an accomplished fact. The water that it enclosed was smooth; and sailing ships of large size, and numbers of smaller native craft anchored inside with comfort. All seemed well. The pier heads were reached, and were half completed. Moorings on a comprehensive scale were being put down, and were paid for out of the savings gained in the construction of the Harbour, so cheaply had it been built. Mr. (now Sir Mountstuart) Grant Duff, the new Governor, inspected the works on November 7th, and was led to hope that one of his first acts in Madras would be to open the cheapest harbour that ever was made. But five days after this inspection the two piers of the Harbour, which had taken nearly six years of hard work to build, and had cost the health and the lives of many men, were destroyed during a storm, from the curved work of each arm outwards, thus leaving the space between the two piers nearly open to the sea.

This caused a complete stoppage to the works, which had, up to this date, cost Rs. 58,06,414, and had swallowed up in construction 13,304 concrete blocks of about 27 tons each, besides 1,201,486 tons of rubble stone. From this date almost up to April 1885, or for nearly three and a half years, no real action was taken to restore the dilapidated harbour, but the time was chiefly employed in discussing how a proper harbour ought to be built. Mr. Parkes did not admit that there was any fault in his section of wall, but he proposed to add another row of blocks, and so make the work wider. In 1884 this proposal was sanctioned by the Madras Government, and many blocks were made for this new design. But it was decided by the Secretary of State that the whole matter should be thoroughly re-investigated; and consequently Sir John Hawkshaw, Sir John Coode, and

Professor Stokes were appointed to consider the best means of reconstructing the harbour. In January 1883 these experts published their report. Briefly, they recommended a different style of building with concrete blocks, but retained Mr. Parkes's width. The side of each pier was to be protected by a "wave-breaker" composed of random blocks of 30 tons weight each, piled up against the wall; and finally, each pier was to receive a solid capping of concrete about six feet deep. The entrance also was to be reduced to 450 feet, instead of 550 feet as in the original design. But this design did not meet with approval at Madras, where a strong desire was expressed for an entrance at the north-east corner instead of opposite the centre of the harbour area. A Committee was formed in Madras, of which Captain Taylor, R.N.R., Master Attendant, Colonel Sankey, C.B., Secretary to Government Public Works Department, Mr. Thorowgood, Captain Marshall, Assistant Master Attendant, and Mr. Beardmore were members; and they drew up a scheme for closing the eastern entrance, and forming one to the north-east. The matter was again referred to London, but the Home Committee declined to alter its opinion. While this volume was passing through the press, Captain Taylor was engaged in London in endeavouring to induce that Committee to modify its views in deference to Madras opinion.

In August 1884 the new design was submitted to Mr. Parkes for approval, and he prepared a detailed estimate for it amounting to Rs. 45,90,051. This estimate came into operation on January 1st, 1885, since which date the expenditure has been about 19 lakhs of rupees. The work of restoration is now going on with fair rapidity, considering the amount of material that has to be used up for every yard of advance, as not only has the regular pier to be built, but each season's work has afterwards to be protected by a screen of 30-ton blocks in the wave-breaker. At this date there have been about 300 feet of the new south pier built, and 464 feet of the north pier. A storm of considerable violence in November 1886 did no damage to the works, so it may be hoped that the present design will prove sufficiently strong to resist a first-class cyclone. On June 1st, 1886, the works were transferred to the control of the Harbour Trust Board, which has just been constituted.

The Harbour covers an area of about 210 acres, of which 170 acres contain a depth of water from three to eight fathoms, and 40 acres of a less depth than three fathoms. Silting up had been prophesied from before the commencement as a sure thing, but periodical surveys, carried out with great accuracy of detail, distinctly show that no alarm need be felt on this head. The depth at the eastern entrance is the same as it was at that spot eleven years ago. But sand has entered the Harbour to some extent at the south-west corner, although here the depths are variable; as, for instance, shallower in 1886 than in 1882, but deeper than in 1879, as in this last-named year sand was driven in from the wide eastern gap, and was afterwards washed out again. The periodical surveys show beyond question that no serious silting has occurred in the Harbour as a whole. To the south the sand has steadily advanced; but corresponding almost exactly in area to the land gained to the south there has been an encroachment to the north, showing that the Harbour, viewed as one huge groyne, has brought about the results always observable with groynes where sand travels parallel to the line of coast. The total expenditure on the work, including the first construction, the pause between destruction and reconstruction, and the reconstruction to date, has been Rs. 84,93,117, and to complete the design as now contemplated will take about Rs. 26,51,000 more, so that nearly one million sterling will have been spent before all is completed.

The construction of the Harbour has been an arduous undertaking, calling for much physical endurance, and since the first block was set in December 1876, of the whole of the executive staff, including locomotive engine drivers, the principal contractors, foremen, and others in responsible posts, there only remains one—namely, the present Superintendent, Mr. Thorowgood, who was present at the setting of the first block. The rest have either died, or left the work on account of ill-health.

IRRIGATION.

The net result during the last fifty years of the work of the Public Works Department in the matter of ordinary irrigation works, that is, old native works, such as tanks and channels, may be summarised as follows. A great number of works have been kept in good repair, and others greatly improved; but the condition of the bulk of them is in the year 1887 much what it was in 1837. On the other hand, much valuable information has been collected at the cost of much time and trouble, and is recorded in a convenient shape, and matters have generally been put in train for the steady and continuous repair and up-keep of this important class of works on scientific principles. It may reasonably be hoped therefore that the reviewer of fifty years hence will be able to record great and uniform progress. If, in the matter of ordinary irrigation works, the progress may not be considered altogether satisfactory, in the conception and execution of works that are great in an Engineering point of view, and successful beyond measure as pecuniary investments, and as a source of wealth and prosperity to the country, the fifty years since the Accession of Her Majesty have been most fruitful.

Among the most successful and important may be mentioned the Coleroon, Godavery, and Kistna Anicuts, which, constructed across the rivers of the same names, ensure the irrigation of the three great deltas of the Presidency; the Nellore, Streevaikuntham, Palar, and Pelandorai Anicuts, built respectively across the Pennair in Nellore District, the Tambraparni in Tinnevelly, and the Palar and Vellaur in the North and South Arcot Districts. The channels taking off from these latter anicuts feed series of tanks, all old native works, the supply to which, now fairly certain and sufficient, was in days previous to the anicuts most precarious and variable. These works therefore may be considered productive, that is they give in some cases a very large, and in every case some percentage of return on the outlay incurred. Among later works the Sangam and Barur Projects may be mentioned. Neither of them is yet fully completed. The former consists of an anicut across the Pennair river in Nellore District, below the existing Nellore Anicut, and is intended to render certain the irrigation under existing tanks, and also to greatly extend it; while the latter is a scheme for the improvement of the supply of water to a number of existing tanks by constructing an anicut across the Pennair river, in Salem District. The Sangam Project, which should be completed in 1889-90, is calculated to give a return of 5 per cent. on the total capital outlay; while the Barur, which is now nearly complete, will, it is expected, pay 6 per cent.

Of the works mentioned, the most famous are the great delta works of Tanjore, Godavery, and Kistna, and some description of these may not be out of place. The Cauvery delta system is virtually of native origin. The delta differs in one most important and essential particular from the deltas of the Godavery and Kistna. While in the two latter the irrigation and drainage channels have to a great extent to be artificially constructed, in the Cauvery delta, on the contrary, the numerous deltaic branches of the river form in themselves the natural sources of irrigation and drainage. This essential difference may explain why even under the native *régime* the delta of the Cauvery was a thriving district, while the districts of the Godavery and Kistna were miserably poor.

Tanjore came into the possession of the English about the year 1800, and at that time the irrigation was carried on by cuts in the banks of the various rivers of the delta. This system, defective in itself, was rendered still more so by the precarious nature of the supply available. The fall of the Coleroon, which branches from the Cauvery, is far greater than that of the latter river, and consequently there was always a tendency for the Coleroon to draw off too much water, and for the Cauvery to silt up at its head. The prevention of this was a source of constant trouble and anxiety to the officers of the district. It was not till 1836, when, at the instigation of Captain (now Sir Arthur) Cotton, the Upper Coleroon Anicut was built, that all fears on this head were set at rest. Since that time improvements in the shape of regulating works, sluices, and embankments have been steadily carried out; and quite lately the construction of the Cauvery and Vennar regulators may be said to have practically ensured the safety of the delta against future floods. These regulators built across the Cauvery, and its main branch the Vennar, in connection with the Grand Anicut,—an old native surplus work, which has been much improved,—allow of the supply during floods being so distributed between the Coleroon, the Cauvery, and its several branches, that the delta need never receive more water than it can with safety dispose of, a danger to which it had always been exposed since the construction of the anicut, which, while it effectually prevented the possibility of a too scanty supply created the opposite evil of a too excessive one. Some idea of the success of the Cauvery delta as a financial investment may be gathered from the returns of 1885-86, which give the total outlay on new works and improvements at Rs. 16,59,254, the area irrigated as 905,884 acres, and the percentage of net revenue on outlay as 38·98.

Next in order of age came the Godavery Delta Works, which were commenced early in 1847. The desirability of throwing an anicut across the river had first been brought to the notice of Government towards the close of the last century by Mr. Topping, a Civil Engineer, but no steps were taken in the matter till 1844, when the rapidly decreasing revenue of the district, and the poverty of the ryots, led to the project being again taken up. In this year Sir Arthur Cotton submitted a general report, followed in 1845 by a more complete one, together with detailed estimates for the anicut, and approximate estimates for the system of channels in connection with it. The project received the approval of the Court of Directors, and the construction of the work was commenced early in 1847. The total outlay incurred to the end of 1885-86 was Rs 1,21,67,097, the area irrigated 553,908 acres, and the percentage of net revenue on outlay was 10·29; the project will, it is expected, be fully completed in 1889-90 at a cost of Rs. 1,30,32,653, when the area under irrigation will be 612,000 acres, and the percentage of net revenue on outlay 12·7.

The Kistna Delta Works, which come next in order to the Godavery, were commenced in 1852, when the construction of the anicut was put in hand. The outlay incurred to the end of 1885-86 was Rs. 75,55,996, the area irrigated 380,139 acres, and the percentage of net revenue on outlay 11·01. On the completion of this project, which it is hoped will take place in 1901-2, the figures are expected to stand as follows: total expenditure Rs. 1,45,00,944, area irrigated 475,000 acres, and percentage of net revenue 8·22. The decrease in this last figure is due to the fact that a considerable expenditure has to be incurred in increasing the efficiency of existing works, without extending irrigation, and on this expenditure there will be no return.

How greatly these works have benefited the country may be gathered from the fact that in the famine of 1877-78, when every unirrigated district was importing grain in enormous quantities, the grain exported from the Godavery was valued at £1,740,000; and yet, in the year 1844, the district was described as being in a poverty-stricken state, with a steadily declining revenue. Similarly with the Kistna. This district, now one of the richest and most thriving, was, previous to the construction of the anicut, one of the very poorest in the Presidency, and suffered very severely in the famine of 1833-34. A noticeable feature of the works described is their construction solely at the cost of Government. This system, with its concomitant evils of grants varying in accordance with the state of the Exchequer, explains why many of the works were so long in hand, and why the actual outlay in many cases was much in excess of the original estimated cost. It appears to justify the view that a more liberal policy on the part of Government in encouraging their execution by private enterprise would have given better results. The Kurnool Canal, however, the one solitary example in this Presidency of a large irrigation work carried out by a Company under Government guarantee, by no means supports this idea. The Company, known as the Madras Irrigation and Canal Company, for the execution of the Tungabudra Project, as the scheme was then called, was incorporated in 1858, and the regular contract deed was signed in 1863. In 1866 the Company was already involved in monetary troubles, and from that period to 1882, the year of the transfer of the Canal to the Secretary of State for India, its history was one long record of financial difficulties ending in eventual failure. Since its transfer, the work has been a losing speculation to the Government, and when the large capital already sunk is considered it is to be doubted whether the works can ever be remunerative.

The works above alluded to may be generally classed as productive; that is, works the outlay on which was in the first instance justified by the more or less large percentage of returns expected. The occurrence of the famine of 1876-78 first compelled the acceptance of the necessity of protective works, that is, works which, though not sufficiently remunerative to justify their being classed as productive, are still calculated to be a preventive of famine, and to guard against a future heavy expenditure in relief to the people. Of this class of work, only one, the Rushikulya Project in the Ganjam District, has as yet been commenced. Sanctioned in 1883, the preliminaries for commencing work were undertaken towards the end of 1883-84, and it is expected that the year 1894-95 will see it completed. The scheme is to utilize the waters of the Mahanuddy and Rushikulya rivers for the purposes of irrigation and navigation. The net revenue anticipated on the completion of the works is 5 per cent. on the total capital outlay. Among the schemes not yet put in hand may be instanced the Peryar Project, which has received the sanction of the Secretary of State; it is a scheme for diverting, by the construction of a dam across the Peryar, the waters of that river into the Madura District, a district which at present receives but a scanty supply from either monsoon, and in the last famine was among the localities which suffered most severely. The Project is to take six years to complete, and on completion is calculated to pay 7·8 per cent. net revenue on total outlay. It may therefore be fairly classed as productive; but in addition to this, its importance as a protective work cannot be over-estimated, as its successful execution would convert the barren district of Madura into a veritable garden. The Tungabhadra Project is a scheme for giving the cantonment of Bellary a good supply of water, and at the same time extending irrigation in the district. The Marandahally Project is designed to improve the supply to certain tanks in the Salem District. The last two Projects, though fully worked out as regards investigation, have not yet been sanctioned. Other important Projects have been suggested and investigated, but the want of funds has indefinitely postponed their execution.

Turning from irrigation works proper, some mention should be made of the lines of water communication in the Presidency. In the two northern deltas the main lines of Canal are utilized both for navigation and irrigation, but until the last few years, these deltas, though connected with each other, had no connection with the south of the Presidency, and it was not till the Famine of 1876-78 that the importance of water communication between the north and south was fully realised, and that an attempt was made to improve and extend the East Coast Canal, to meet the fresh-water high-level Canals of the Kistna Delta. The East Coast Canal, or, as it is now called, the Buckingham Canal, in honour of the Duke of Buckingham and Chandos, Governor of Madras, 1875 to 1880, is a salt-water Canal, and to some extent tidal. It was begun so long ago as 1801, but up to the years 1876-78, the total expenditure upon it was only about 5½ lakhs of rupees. In the years mentioned, the Canal was taken up at the instance of the Duke as a famine relief work, and an expenditure of 29 lakhs was incurred. Since that date improvements have been carried out steadily and continuously, and at the present time there is very fair through communication between Madras and Pedda Ganjam in the Kistna District. At this point the Buckingham Canal meets the Kistna high-level fresh-water Canals, and is, through them, connected with the Godavery system, thus opening up traffic with the sea-port of Cocanada. The completion estimates lately sanctioned amount to nearly 100 lakhs, and it is expected that the works will be completed in 1893-94. Until this is the case, and the Canal has been fully protected from river floods, it cannot be considered an altogether safe means of communication. Its value, as a cheap means of transport, is already recognised; its prospects in the future are very favourable; and by connecting the City of Madras, or the head-quarters of the trade and railway system of the Presidency, with the deltas of the Godavery, Kistna, and Nellore, it will be simply invaluable in times of famine.

On the West Coast also the subject of water communication is receiving much attention. The benefits to be derived from expenditure on a large scale are, however, not so obvious as in the case of the Buckingham Canal; for already Cochin has very good water communication with Trichoor, a town situated twenty miles from the Madras Railway station of Shoranoor. From Tirur, another station on the same line, there is also a continuous line of canal to Cochin. Portions, however, are not excavated to full depth, and in consequence the traffic is diverted to Trichoor. Estimates for improving this latter line have been prepared, and the work will no doubt be put in hand when funds can be spared. From the above brief sketch, it will readily be admitted that whatever may be the shortcomings in regard to ordinary irrigation works, the fifty years since Her Majesty's accession have been marked by progress that has materially improved the condition of a very large number of Her Majesty's subjects in Madras.

COMMERCE.

The growth of trade during the past fifty years would, having regard to the vast natural wealth of the Presidency of Madras at the commencement of that period, and to the fact that such wealth had been but very partially developed, necessarily have been considerable; but a retrospective glance discloses a rate of progress far greater than these considerations alone would suggest. This remarkable progress may be attributed to a stable and good Government, under which that confidence, so necessary to the employment of capital and the encouragement of enterprise, has been preserved; to the opening up of the country by railways, roads, and canals, by means of which districts, even the most remote, have found an outlet for their products, the demand for which was previously limited by local requirements; to more extensive and more rapid means of communication by telegraph and post, whereby the inland trader obtains information in a few hours which previously occupied as many days, or weeks, in transmission; to the introduction of, and improvements in machinery, the effect of which on production has been the more marked, seeing that what little was previously in use was cumbrous and defective; to the stimulus given to coffee and tea planting by European enterprise; and to such stimulating influences as cheap freights, brisk competition, marine telegraphing, &c.

The export trade of the Presidency fifty years ago was valued at two crores of rupees (two millions sterling), and the import trade at one crore and thirteen lakhs of rupees; now, the figures are eleven and seven crores respectively, thus showing that the import trade is about six times, and the export trade five and a half times as much as it was. It is patent that this great expansion of trade means a corresponding increase in the wealth of the country, in the material prosperity of its inhabitants, in the field for the employment of the labour, and in the ability of the producer to employ it. Not only has there been a remarkable increase in the productions of the Presidency, and consequently of its power to import foreign commodities, but new industries have come into existence, and trade has been more distributed throughout the interior. Thus, whereas, fifty years ago, the great centres of commerce were confined to sea-ports, where almost exclusively the European merchants were established, now the agents, and sometimes the chief offices of those merchants, are to be found scattered over the Presidency, including remote country districts, which, if previously heard of at all, were only known by report. The natural results of this have been the clearing away of the many obstacles to trade involved in slow and uncertain correspondence, and the employment in other fields of industry of numerous middle-men who formerly stood between the producer and the consumer, or exporter. This development of commercial enterprise, has stimulated the spread of Banking, the introduction of foreign capital, and the multiplication of European traders and producers. Another feature of the age is the substitution for the manual labour that was solely available fifty years ago, of machinery which is now largely employed in spinning, weaving, the preparation and packing of raw cotton, the cleaning of coffee, &c. In the same connection may be mentioned the complete revolution of the shipping trade.

The traffic by sea of the Presidency, which was carried in 1840 by sailing ships, aggregating about 40,000 tons burden, is now almost entirely conveyed by steamers, annually aggregating 2,700,000 tons, since vessels carrying 500 or 1000 tons cargo, and occupying four months or more in the passage to or from England, have been replaced by steamers carrying from 2,000 to 3,000 tons, covering the same distance in five weeks. Taking some of the leading products of the Presidency as illustrating the growth of trade during the half century, it is found that the export of raw cotton has increased from 12,000 tons, valued at Rs. 40,00,000, to 25,000 tons, valued at Rs. 1,00,00,000. The cultivation of coffee is comparatively a modern industry, the opening up of the important districts of the Wynaad, Neilgherries, Coorg, Mysore, Travancore, &c., having been accomplished during the fifty years. The present production is about 17,000 tons, of the value of Rs. 1,25,00,000, whilst the export in 1840 was only 150 tons of the value of Rs. 70,000. Cinchona was unknown commercially as an article of production twenty years ago, and may even now be said to be in its infancy. But the export already reaches the value of Rs. 12,00,000. The manufacture of indigo remains now, as hitherto, exclusively in the hands of natives, but it has increased from 400 tons, valued at Rs. 17,00,000, to over 2,000 tons, valued at Rs. 1,00,00,000. The foreign trade in rice shows no gain, the increased production being necessary for the increase in population. Madras has always taken the lead in India in the tanning industry, and the trade throughout the past fifty years has steadily grown, the skins prepared being much sought after, on account of their excellence, not only in England and on the Continent of Europe, but also in America. The value exported in the earlier years of the period under review amounted to only a little over Rs. 2,00,000, whilst the export last year was valued at about Rs. 1,85,00,000, equal to about 12 millions sterling. The export of oil seeds has been comparatively of modern growth, the annual value of castor and gingelly seeds being each about Rs. 20,00,000. The value of sugar, and other saccharine matters produced, has increased fifty-fold, viz. from Rs. 1,00,000 to Rs. 50,00,000. Tea planting was commenced within the last twenty years, but as yet the total value produced has not exceeded Rs. 3,50,000.

Turning to imports, it is remarkable that notwithstanding the development of the mill industry, the quantity of manufactured cotton annually brought into the Presidency from Europe is maintained, whilst the total import of 1837 is insignificant compared with that of modern years; thus the buying power of the population must have increased, a fact which testifies to their prosperity. The value of yarn now imported is from Rs. 80,00,000 to Rs. 90,00,000 against about Rs. 9,00,000 in 1841. But it is curious to find that at that time the importation of what are known as Manchester goods, such as cotton cloths, &c., amounted to only Rs. 5,00,000; whereas now the value reaches from Rs. 1,50,00,000 to Rs. 2,00,00,000. In bygone years the annual value of machinery imported did not exceed Rs. 2,000 or Rs. 3,000 a year against Rs. 5,00,000 to Rs. 20,00,000. The use of wrought iron has increased from Rs. 2,00,000 to Rs. 10,00,000. The establishment of large manufacturing industries, which form so important a feature in the progress of the Presidency, comprises coffee works, cotton presses, cotton and woollen mills, sugar factories, and iron foundries. There are in the Presidency, at the present time, upwards of twenty large coffee works employing about 7,000 hands; thirty large steam factories for pressing and ginning cotton, employing about 3,000 hands; and ten spinning and weaving mills employing about 4,000 hands, besides others projected, or in course of construction. The local manufacturing industries here enumerated are only the largest concerns, and to them must be added an enormous number of native establishments, including tanneries, oil mills, rice mills, &c., which have come into existence during the half century;

these give employment to many thousands of hands, and largely contribute to the volume of trade, the increase of which is so marked a characteristic of the age.

The interests of Madras trade have been sedulously guarded and promoted by the Chamber of Commerce,—an association of merchants at the Presidency capital, which was incorporated on the 29th September, 1836, and celebrated the completion of its Jubilee year, by a banquet on the 18th December last, which was honoured by the presence of the Governor, the Commander-in-Chief, the Members of Council, the Bishop, the Secretaries to Government, Heads of Departments, and other public functionaries. The vitality of the Chamber was in abeyance from the year 1841, when its first Secretary left for Europe, until 1855, when his successor was appointed, but it made up during the latter moiety of the period under review for any want of activity that may have characterised it in the first decade of the half century. Its practical experience of matters intimately connected with the conservation and development of the material resources of the country has been largely utilised by the Government of Madras, and its opinion has been frequently invited by the Government of India. Imperial legislation connected with such subjects as Customs, Stamps, Contracts, Bankruptcy, Partnership, Administration of Estates, Probate Jurisdiction, Regulation of Factory Labour, Coolie Emigration, Merchant Shipping, Master and Servant, Municipal Taxation, Currency, Government Securities, Presidency Banks, Adulteration of Raw Products, &c., has received material assistance from the Chamber, which has also bestowed much attention on such technical subjects as boat notes, tonnage schedules, port rules, port clearances, fees to port officers, Marine Courts, landing charges, railway freights, train service, negotiable instruments, weights and measures, trade marks, value payable parcels, bills of lading, general average, rates of interest, notarial fees, usance of bills, commercial statistics, detention of mails, telegraph codes, &c.

Shortly after its formation, the Chamber evinced much interest in the establishment of steam communication with Europe; and, in 1846, it contributed £100 to the London fund for presenting a testimonial to *Lieutenant* Waghorn, the pioneer of the Overland Mail Route. It was keenly alive to the importance of opening steam communication between Indian ports. The improvement of the navigation of rivers, and the extension of irrigation also engaged its attention from time to time. The Chamber has interested itself greatly in the improvements of the port of Madras. On the 17th September, 1859, its Chairman assisted the Governor and the Commander-in-Chief in screwing down the first pile of the Screw Pile Pier. Between 1869 and 1872 projects for mitigating the natural disadvantages of the port by means of a breakwater, or of a boat harbour, were exhaustively discussed by the Chamber; and in 1873 the Chamber gave its general support to the scheme of Mr. W. Parkes, C.E., for the construction of the harbour (referred to elsewhere) at an estimated cost of a little more than half a million sterling.

The development of the railway system in Southern India was watched by the Chamber with much sympathy, and the importance of encouraging traffic by low charges and reasonable conveniences was on many occasions advocated. The improvement of anchorages was a subject that the Chamber considered from time to time, as well as the desirability of reducing port charges to the lowest practicable scale. The Chamber has always advocated judicious thrift in the expenditure of the Government, and advised more free recourse by the State to the labour markets of India and England; but it has not sympathised with the policy that would illiberally remunerate good work in India. It disapproved of the relinquishment of the import duties on Manchester goods on the grounds that India was not in a position to make the sacrifice of revenue, and that as revenue must be had, the duties afford not only Her Majesty's subjects in India, but also the subjects of Native States that are protected by Her Majesty, the opportunity of contributing insensibly to the cost of the administration. It has been opposed to the interference of the Government with the ordinary operations of trade; and, as soon as that industry had largely engaged private enterprise, it deprecated the continuance of the connection of the State with cinchona cultivation.

The Chamber has steadily maintained that, in a country densely populated by relatively poor people, the Postal and Telegraph charges should be low in comparison with the charges obtaining in the United Kingdom, and it has had the satisfaction of seeing this principle recognised in regard to Postal rates. The Chamber identified itself with the Madras Exhibition of 1854, and took an active interest in the scheme for Provincial Exhibitions, as well as in the success of periodical Exhibitions in Europe. It acted in 1863 as the recipient for public subscriptions for the Lancashire Cotton Weavers' Relief Fund, and collected Rs. 75,900; in 1870 it similarly collected Rs. 12,775 for the Sick and Wounded in War Fund; and in 1873 it received Rs. 12,473 for the relief of sailors shipwrecked, and of families bereaved by the Madras cyclone.

The Chamber had the honour, in 1859, of communicating its loyal congratulations to Her Majesty on her assumption of the direct sovereignty of India. It informed Her Majesty that it hailed "this auspicious event as the promise to this country of an era of enlightenment and prosperity," and it prayed that her Government of her "Indian Empire may be distinguished by the blessings of peace, and by the advance of civilisation." The Chamber submitted an Address to the Earl of Mayo, the Viceroy Designate, on his arrival in Madras in 1869; to the Marquis of Ripon, Viceroy of India, on his arrival in 1884; and to the Earl of Dufferin, Viceroy of India, on his arrival in 1886. It offered its respectful condolence to the Countess of Mayo, on the assassination of Lord Mayo in 1872; and to Lady Hobart on the death of Lord Hobart in 1865. The Chamber has had the honour of being represented in the Legislative Council of Madras since 1862.

MARINE.

The sea-board of this Presidency extends about 1,500 miles, from the district of Ganjam, on the East Coast, round Cape Comorin to the district of South Canara, on the West Coast. At the beginning of Her Majesty's reign the Marine Department was presided over by a Marine Board, composed of a Member of Council as Chairman, and the Commissary-General, Quarter-Master-General, and the Master Attendant, Madras, as members, with a Secretary. This body was maintained till the year 1858, when it was abolished, and an officer, called the Superintendent of Marine, was appointed to perform its duties. This designation was changed in 1868, when the offices of Superintendent of Marine and Master Attendant were amalgamated, and placed under one head, called the Master Attendant. This title was further altered in 1886 to Port Officer, but the administrative duties and control over all the ports of the Presidency has remained all along vested in the same officer.

With regard to the outports, there were in 1837 nine ports in charge of Masters Attendant, viz., Calingapatam, Vizagapatam, Coringa, Masulipatam, Tuticorin, Quilon, Cochin, Calicut, and Tellicherry, which formed the principal outlets of commerce. The sea-borne trade in those days belonged to a class of sailing ships called Indiamen, and the coasting trade was conducted by country craft, but later on the advent of steamers caused a complete revolution in the means of sea transport. Steam liners have been established between India and Europe extending to China, Japan, Australia and New Zealand; and coasting steamers have been started between ports in India, and Ceylon, Burmah, the Straits of Singapore, and Malacca, thus taking away the occupation of the old Indiamen, and diverting a large share of the former employment of coasting craft. With the facilities afforded by steamers, the construction of trunk roads, and the opening of railway communication with the large districts supplying produce for export were carried out. Additional outlets for trade thus came into existence, and largely increased the number of ports. There are now twenty-one principal ports, viz., Gopalpore, Calingapatam, Bimlipatam, Vizagapatam, Cocanada and Coringa, Masulipatam, Madras, Porto Novo, Cuddalore, Tranquebar, Negapatam and Nagore, Paumben, Tuticorin, Cochin, Calicut and Beypore, Tellicherry, Cannanore, and

Mangalore. There are also one hundred and forty-eight minor ports. Of the former, twelve are in charge of Port Officers, and seven in charge of Sub-Conservators; while the latter are in charge of Superintendents, or Assistant Superintendents of Sea Customs, or heads of villages acting in the capacity of Port Conservators.

There were only three lights in 1837—one at Madras, which was an ordinary light exhibited on the top of a house in Fort St. George; the second at Coringa, or Hope Island, which was an ordinary country lantern; and the third at Tellicherry. The one at Madras was substituted, in January 1844, for a first-class revolving catadioptric light, exhibited on a fine granite column, 125 feet high, erected on the Esplanade near the beach, north of the Fort. The light is visible for twenty miles. The Coringa or Hope Island light has been improved to a 4th order dioptric fixed white light, visible fourteen miles; and at Tellicherry there is now a 6th order dioptric fixed white light, visible eight miles, exhibited on a small tower on the Fort wall, instead of from the flagstaff as formerly. Besides these improvements, seventeen additional lights have been established, so that both the East and West Coasts are now lighted throughout. In 1839 a light was established at Cochin, the lighthouse being built on the bastion of the old Fort to the south of the harbour. It was improved in 1858 to a 4th order white fixed catadioptric light, visible for fifteen miles. In 1842 a lighthouse was built at Mangalore, on a hill above the town; and in 1870 this light was changed to a 4th order dioptric white fixed light, visible for fourteen miles. In 1843 a light was exhibited at Cannanore from the flagstaff, and in 1850 it was improved to a 6th order dioptric fixed red light, and transferred to a small column erected on the Fort rampart, visible for from six to eight miles. In 1845 the lighthouse at Tuticorin was built, and in 1874 a 4th dioptric fixed white light, visible for fourteen miles, was exhibited. In 1846 a light was exhibited at Negapatam, and in 1870 it was improved to a 4th order dioptric white fixed light, visible for fourteen miles. In the same year (1846) a lighthouse was built at Paumben on a sand-hill about one mile east of the northern channel, and the light was changed to a catadioptric, with fixed light of the 4th order, in 1860; it is visible for fourteen miles. In the year 1847 a light was exhibited at Calicut, which was converted in 1870 to a 4th order dioptric fixed white light, visible for fourteen miles. In 1849 a light was exhibited on the top of a house built on Santopilly Hill, three quarters of a mile inland, to warn vessels off the dangerous reef known as the Santopilly Rocks. The light was changed to a 4th order dioptric fixed white light in 1871, visible for fourteen miles, and it was substituted in 1886 by a 2nd order dioptric fixed white light. In the year 1857 a light was erected at Point Divy, two miles north-west of the Point, and it was improved in 1870 to a 4th order dioptric fixed white light. In 1853 a lighthouse was constructed at Mausapallem, in the Nellore district, to warn vessels off the Armeghon Shoal. The light was changed to a 4th order dioptric white fixed light in 1870, visible for fourteen miles. It was again converted to a flashing light in 1881. In the year 1859 a red light was exhibited at Pulicat. The lighthouse is built near the beach, the column having white and black bands. The light is intended to warn vessels off the Pulicat Shoal. It was improved in 1870 to a 4th order dioptric fixed light, and in 1880 the colour of the light was changed from red to white. In 1871 a 3rd class light, visible ten miles, was exhibited at Gopaulpore from the white flagstaff, as a guide to vessels making the anchorage at night. In the year 1875 a light was temporarily exhibited at Muttum to warn vessels off the Crocodile Rock, and in 1883 a 1st class dioptric fixed white light was exhibited on a dark grey granite column, visible for twenty miles. In the year 1875 a 3rd class white fixed light was exhibited on the obelisk at Calingapatam, to warn vessels off a small reef which projects from the Point. A lighthouse is now being built on a rock at the Seven Pagodas to warn vessels off the Tripalour Reef. It is to be a red light visible for about ten miles.

Other improvements have also been carried out, such as the erection of jetties, wharves, quays, and piers at Gopaulpore, Cocanada, Masulipatam, Porto Novo, Negapatam, Tuticorin, Cochin, Calicut, Cannanore, Barkur, Kumbla, Kasaragod, and Mangalore. Madras, in addition to a screw pile pier, is being provided with an artificial harbour at a cost exceeding one million sterling. Buoys have been laid down at Cocoanada, Madras, Paumben, Cochin, and Calicut. A semaphore has been erected at Madras for notifying the time to the shipping by an electric current from the Observatory. Tide gauges have been established at Cocoanada, Madras, Negapatam, and Cochin. Arrangements have been made for recording meteorological observations at the ports of Gopaulpore, Cocoanada, and Calicut, in connection with the Meteorological Department of the Government of India. Pilots have been appointed at Madras, Paumben, Keelakarai, and Cochin. Steamers have been subsidised for running between ports on the Coromandel Coast and Rangoon. A cyclone code has been established, and also a system of telegraphing bad weather warnings to the different outports for the information of shipping. Cocoanada and Negapatam have been supplied with Priestman and Bruce dredgers. Legislative enactments have been passed relating to Indian Merchant Shipping, for the registration of vessels, for the protection of native passengers by sea, for the management of boats and catamarans, for the conservancy of ports and collection of port dues, for enforcing quarantine, &c. In short, every year has witnessed some improvement in the direction of affording facilities for the advancement of trade and navigation in the Presidency.

FORESTRY.

Fifty years ago "Forestry" was unknown in the Madras Presidency, nor was it until twenty years later that a recognised "Forest Department" was instituted. It is true that, in 1807 Government made an attempt at conservancy by establishing a royalty over teak, and other timber in the Districts of Malabar and Canara, but this speedily developed into a monopoly throughout the Coast Districts, failed in its object, and led to such hardship that it was abolished by Sir Thomas Munro in 1822. For the next thirty years or so the forests were left entirely in the hands of Collectors, without any systematic control. In Coimbatore District things were latterly somewhat different; for, in 1847, Captain F. C. Cotton (now Major-General, C.S.I.), the Executive Engineer of Malabar, in an interesting account of a journey into Cochin territory through the Anamalai forests, brought their value to the notice of Government, and Lieutenant J. Michael (now Colonel, C.S.I.), was appointed to explore, conserve, and work them in connection with the Public Works Department,—an arrangement which lasted seven years. An extensive teak tract was leased from the Zemindar of Colengody, a forest establishment was organised, roads and timber slips were opened out, and a system of strict conservancy was initiated. On the whole, however, it was usual in those days to regard a forest as an enemy to be extirpated; and, considering the prevalence of fever, and of dangerous animals, it is scarcely surprising that a Collector who encouraged cultivation to its utmost limits was esteemed a public benefactor. In the words of the late Governor of Madras "we did not step in to conserve the Indian Forests an hour too soon, and large parts of the country would, if we had not done so, have soon become uninhabitable deserts."

Meanwhile, the importance of tropical forests began to attract attention at home. It was known that large and valuable forests in India were being cleared, regardless of ultimate consequences; and, as the results of this wholesale denudation became more apparent, the necessity for organizing a Forest administration, which would enable the authorities to economise public property for the public good asserted itself with increasing force. The subject came before the British Association for the Advancement of Science at Edinburgh in 1850, and a Committee was appointed to consider the question, consisting of Dr. Forbes Royle, King's College, London; Colonels R. Baird Smith and R. Strachey of the Bengal Engineers; and Dr. Hugh Cleghorn. The results of the Committee's deliberations were laid before the Association at the Ipswich meeting in 1851, whence it appeared that neither Government, nor the community at large was deriving from the Indian Forests those advantages which they were well calculated to afford. Apart from the wasteful destruction of useful material, numerous products, valuable to science, and otherwise profitable, lay neglected in the forests. These and other representations were not without effect, and, as regards Madras, were instrumental in preparing the way for the Forest Department, which was organized in 1856—under the Governorship of Lord Harris—with Dr. Cleghorn, one of the Committee above mentioned, as Conservator.

To Dr. Cleghorn must, in all fairness, be conceded the title of *Pioneer of Forestry in Madras*, but it is due to Mr. Conolly, C.S., Collector of Malabar, whose efforts preceded his by many years, to allude to the magnificent teak plantations at Nilambur. They are probably not approached, and are certainly unsurpassed by anything of their kind in India, and, as a unique, interesting, and valuable State property, they form an enduring memorial to their author's sagacity. The plantations were first suggested by Mr. Conolly, in 1840, their object being, in his own words, "to replace those forests which have vanished from private carelessness, and rapacity, a work too new, too extensive, and too barren of early return to be ever undertaken by the native proprietor." It happened at the time that one of the many religious bodies holding lands in the Nilambur valley was in want of funds, and owned some of the best sites for planting that could have been selected had the whole area been available to choose from; and in this accident, probably, originated the idea of Mr. Conolly's enterprise. For the first year or two, there was much difficulty in getting seed to germinate, and various experiments were tried; but in 1843 Dr. Roxburgh discovered the true method, which with some slight modification is still followed; and, in 1844, Mr. Conolly having raised 90,000 healthy plants, was able to report that his experiments were successfully concluded, and to add 61 acres to the 31 which had been planted up to date. It is melancholy to have to add that Mr. Conolly was assassinated at Calicut by Moplah fanatics in 1855, a few days after he had received intimation of his well-deserved promotion to the Council of Fort St. George.

In 1862 the Nilambur Plantations, by this time covering an area of 1,623 acres, valued at 20 lakhs, were transferred to the regular Forest Department, and, in the five-and-twenty years which have since elapsed, have been enlarged by about 2,000 acres, and may now be set down in round numbers at 3,600 acres. They have cost from first to last (*i.e.*, up to the beginning of the official year 1886-7) including outlay in acquiring fresh sites, about Rs. 7,28,190, and have yielded a revenue of Rs. 7,31,222 derived from saplings thinned out, and from the better classes of timber felled for clearance. Assuming that regular felling operations may begin in 1904, when the first planting will be about sixty years old, it has been calculated, after allowing compound interest at 4 per cent. for unproductive periods, that a clear profit of Rs. 4,23,11,820 will eventually be realised.

Returning to the Forest Department at the opening of its career in 1856, we find it began with the forests of Anamalai in the Coimbatore District; with Sigur and Mudumalai in Malabar; and with those of Salem and North and South Canara. By 1862 it had taken in hand the Wynaad and Chenat Nair forests in Malabar, the Madura, North Arcot and Cuddapah forests, and included the Australian Plantations and Cinchona experiments on the Nilgiris, as well as the Teak Plantations at Nilambur. In the following year the forests of North Canara were transferred to Bombay; whilst those of Kolampatti, Bhavani and Collegal in the Coimbatore District; Gumsur and Surada in Ganjam, and the Kurnool forests were under conservancy. At Dr. Cleghorn's retirement in 1867, the forests of South Arcot and Tinnevelly had been added to the list; and the Golcondah Hill tracts, which had been for a short time under the Department, were handed over to the Collector. When reviewing Dr. Cleghorn's administration of the Department during its first eleven years of existence the Government, in October 1867, particularly noticed "the attention paid to the vastly important subject of fuel reserves with reference to the present and prospective needs of the Railways, to the propagation of the more valuable kinds of timber, as teak, red sanders, and sal, in suitable localities, and the assistance rendered to District officers towards the most advantageous employment of the local planting funds." Of the financial position the Government remarked that "the ultimate gain to the

State by the labours of the Department amounts to Rs. 18,38,038, while a most valuable public property has been brought under conservancy; the vast timber resources of the country have been carefully developed; and the future interests of the Government and of the public have been protected from risks which are daily assuming greater magnitude, but which, until comparatively recent years, had scarcely attracted attention." Referring to the inroads of cattle and hardships complained of in several Districts, the Government observed that "the subject is one that will be duly weighed in connection with the proposed introduction of the Forest Law, which is under consideration;" defined the primary object of conservancy as "the development of the sources of supply, and the careful protection of those sources from waste;" and remarked that "a large revenue, although it may be, and doubtless often is, a satisfactory indication of the advantages of economical administration is a comparatively secondary consideration." Having regard to all that has since transpired words such as these are very significant.

Colonel, then Captain, Beddome, succeeded Dr. Cleghorn as Conservator, and held that appointment until 1872, when a "re-organization" took place, by which Forest administration was committed to the Board of Revenue, and Collectors were invested with the responsibilities and authority of District Conservators. Local Forest officers thus became the Collector's Assistants, while the Conservator became "Inspector of Forests," and was constituted a general adviser on Forest affairs to Government, the Board, and Collectors. When this occurred forest operations had everywhere developed, and divisional charges had to be rearranged. Plantations and fuel reserves had progressed, and the Department was strengthened by the addition of several new officers. In 1876 control was once more placed in the hands of the Conservator as head of the Department; officers were put in charge of Trichinopoly and the Upper Godavery, whilst others submitted special reports on the Bellary, Kistna, and Nellore jungles. A Deputy Conservator was also detailed on special duty for the selection of reserved forests, and by this means preliminary proposals were framed for the Coimbatore, Tinnevelly, and Madura Districts, and a beginning was effected in Salem. Efforts meanwhile continued to be directed towards the development of revenue, and a more efficient control generally, but the absence of a forest law, the paucity of officers, and other difficulties proved serious impediments. Colonel Beddome retired in December, 1881, after a Departmental service of twenty-four years, thirteen of which were passed as chief. During his tenure of office the forests of the Presidency were thoroughly explored and reported on, and valuable contributions were made to the public knowledge of their economic value and botanical interest. He was the author of the well-known *Flora Sylvatica*, as well as of a standard work on the ferns of Southern India, besides being a naturalist of no mean reputation. The financial results of his term of office amounted to a net profit in favour of Government of 9¼ lakhs, which was less by 8¾ lakhs than that which distinguished the administration of Dr. Cleghorn. This is easily explained. The Department at first confined itself to the chief timber yielding forests of the Presidency, and in those days the receipts from North Canara and the Anamalais were very considerable. The extension of operations to less remunerative tracts; the heavy outlay on plantations, and fuel reserves, amounting to nearly 6¾ lakhs; the transfer of North Canara to Bombay; and the abolition of the Indian Navy, which had been a large purchaser of Anamalai timber, all conspired to reduce the annual surplus. The price of labour had also risen, whilst the necessity for capital outlay producing no direct or immediate return grew with the development of the Department.

Lieutenant-Colonel Campbell Walker now became Conservator, and the year which followed his assumption of charge was remarkable for a series of events which heralded the approach of a new era in the history of the Department. It witnessed the advent of Sir Mountstuart Grant Duff, a Governor keenly interested in the progress of Forestry, and the arrival of Sir D. Brandis, Inspector-General of Forests to the Government of India, who was directed to discuss and arrange the introduction of long-needed reforms. After several months occupied by the Inspector-General in visiting some of the more important Forest Districts, Committees were appointed to discuss legal, and other measures of reform. A draft Act, with a comprehensive report on Forest legislation in the Madras Presidency, was submitted in May; and another report as to the future relations of Civil and Forest Officers was submitted in June. In September the Inspector General laid his proposals for reorganisation before Government, together with a financial forecast for the next five years; and before the end of the year the Act had become law, and the reorganisation an accomplished fact.

At the beginning of the official year just concluded, 1,648 square miles of "Reserved Forests" had been constituted under the Act, which with those already "reserved" under previous orders gives a total of 2,737 square miles. "Reserved lands" had also been notified under the Act to the extent of 7,060 square miles, while leased and other forests covered 1,311 square miles. The total area placed under the legal control of the Department was thus 11,108 square miles, which Government appears to consider about as much as the requirements of the country are likely to demand. Much of course remains to be done in the way of transfers from reserved lands to reserved forests, but in both circles and in most Districts this is being steadily accomplished. Demarcation naturally follows reservation, and this too has annually progressed, the length of boundaries laid down during 1886 being upwards of 1,400 miles. The subject of forest surveys has not been overlooked, though, as yet, most of the work done in this direction has been performed by the Madras Survey Department, but proposals are now under consideration for the formation of a Special Forest Survey Party. As regards the all-important work of fire protection, it appears that at the end of the fire season of 1886, an area of 1,483 square miles had been attempted, and 1,445 square miles successfully maintained. In this connection, however, Government justly remarked, that until reserved forests are settled, demarcated, and finally set apart, progress must necessarily be comparatively limited. Grazing should be capable of producing considerable revenue without oppressive taxation, but it is at present something of a vexed question, the solution of which, as the Board of Revenue says, "lies at the bottom of all forest conservancy in this Presidency."

Under the head of "Police" the percentage of convictions obtained seems to warrant the belief that complaints are not generally laid except on good grounds. Roads are being extended in all directions; tramways laid down; and numerous buildings for the accommodation of all ranks erected, a work without which no adequate supervision is possible. As regards natural reproduction the effect of protection on the forests has been most favourably apparent; and under the head of artificial reproduction it may be noted that no less than 18,657 acres are classed as plantations, 30,760 acres as topes, and 1,043 acres as cultural operations, which means the re-stocking of blank areas in forests as distinguished from regular plantations. Financial results have more than justified the forecast framed in 1882. Receipts have risen from about 9 lakhs in 1882-83 to nearly 12 lakhs in 1885-86, the annual surplus averaging about 3½ lakhs. Expenditure for the same period has been at the rate of about 8 lakhs per annum.

Much, too, has been done of late years in the way of experiments with various exotics. The most marked success has occurred in the case of the mahogany tree, which is doing well in both circles, and particularly at Nelambur, where the ceara rubber tree has also been thoroughly established, and where the ipecacuanha plant and giant bamboo are also thriving. *Eucalyptus citriodora* is said to be fairly satisfactory at moderate heights, but no variety has yet been discovered suitable for growth on the plains. Conifers and maples from Northern India are coming up on the Nilgiris, and manilla hemp and the edible date (*Phoenix dactylifera*) both promise well in the Southern Circle. Amongst other duties Forest Officers have found time to assist at ensilage experiments, and in making the representative collections which have enabled the Department to compete with honour at the various Exhibitions held on the Continent, in the Colonies, and at

Calcutta, Edinburgh and London. Much useful information has also been contributed on such subjects as apiculture and sericulture, and a complete collection is about to be undertaken for the Central Museum at Madras illustrating the sericulture of the Presidency by specimens of eggs, cocoons, larvæ and the leaves on which the insect feeds. A Departmental Museum has been started in Madras, which already contains an interesting and valuable collection of timber specimens and samples of forest produce—such as gums, resins, seeds, oils, and fibres, as well as a herbarium. If forestry since its initiation in 1856 has not advanced "by leaps and bounds," if for years subsequently its progress was fitful and fluctuating, the fault—if fault there be—does not all, or nearly all, rest with the Department. Recalling the promising beginning indicated by the review of operations up to the date of Dr. Cleghorn's retirement in 1867, already quoted, when Government and the Conservator were apparently in perfect accord as to the essential lines and chief objects of a forest policy, it may well be asked why, for the next fifteen years, the Department was left to strive in vain for legislation, urging its paramount importance, and the futility of expecting permanent results without it, and still more, why it is that Madras, practically first in the field of forestry, was the last to pass its own Forest Law. Happily the measures adopted in 1882 are now proved to have been the forerunners of a substantial success.

CINCHONA.

Dr. Royle, who for many years was Botanist to the Government of India, was the first who gave serious attention to the introduction of the cinchona plant from its native country, South America, into India. In June, 1852, in a report on the subject, he wrote:—"Among the vast variety of medical drugs produced in various parts of the world, there is not one, with probably the single exception of opium, which is more valuable to man than the quinine-yielding cinchona. Its utility and employment have been greatly increased since its active principle has been separated in the form of quinine. So greatly indeed has the consumption increased, and so little care has been bestowed upon the preservation of the natural forests, that great fears have been entertained that the supply might altogether cease, or be obtainable only at a price which would place it beyond the reach of the mass of the community." And in the same report he said:—"The probability of entire success in the cultivation of the cinchona tree in India seems to admit of hardly any doubt, if ordinary care is adopted in the selection of suitable localities. I myself recommended this measure, many years ago, when treating of the family of plants to which the cinchona belongs. I inferred from a comparison of soil and climate, with the geographical distribution of cinchonaceous plants, that the quinine-yielding cinchona might be cultivated on the slopes of the Neilgherries and of the Southern Himalayas, in the same way that I had inferred that Chinese tea-plants might be cultivated on the Northern Himalayas."

Dr. Royle's recommendations, although approved of, remained in abeyance until 1859, when the increasing demand for the cinchona drugs, combined with their constantly increasing price, forced the subject again upon public attention. Indeed, things had come to such a pass, that it seemed almost certain that in the course of a very few years the wholesale destruction of trees which was going on in America would reduce the supply of bark to almost nothing.

Under these circumstances it was determined by the Government that steps should be immediately taken to obtain plants and seed of different species of cinchona for transmission to India. Fortunately, the Government was able to secure the active sympathy of a gentleman to whom the cinchona-growing countries were well known, for he had passed much time in travelling through them, studying the language and habits of the natives, and, although not a trained botanist, he had nevertheless made himself acquainted with several of the species in their living state. This gentleman was Mr. Clements Markham, a sailor, a scholar, and archæologist, who, in December, 1859, having been entrusted to carry out the undertaking, proceeded to South America for the purpose of organizing an expedition into the interior. With him were associated the following persons, whose names deserve to be held in much regard by all who have benefited by the cheapening of the fever-allaying alkaloids: Mr. John Weir, Dr. Richards Spruce—truly described by Mr. Markham as an eminent botanist, and most intrepid explorer—Mr. Robert Cross, Mr. Pritchett, and Mr. Ledger. These gentlemen, with the exception of Mr. Ledger, had received instructions to act under the orders which should be given to them by Mr. Markham, and that gentleman, in grateful testimony of the value of the assistance which he had received from them, wrote as follows:—"The early success of the enterprise mainly depended upon the selection of qualified agents, and in this respect I was most fortunate. No one engaged in important work ever had more able, loyal, and disinterested labourers to assist him." After a series of adventures, often attended with much danger and great discomfort, the first consignment of plants, consisting of *Cinchona Succirubra* was despatched from Guayaquil on the 2nd January, 1861, under the superintendence of Mr. Cross, to England, and from thence they were transported, by the Red Sea, to Madras. Here 463 of them arrived in good condition. These were taken to the Nilgiris Hills, the beautiful district previously selected by Dr. Royle, as most probably that in which the different varieties would thrive best in India. For the hardier kinds, Mr. Markham selected a site near the top of Dodabetta, the highest rounded knob of which is about 8,700 feet above the level of the sea; while, for the more tender descriptions, he selected a tract of country about Naduvatam—a small Toda village on the edge of the hills facing the west, at an elevation of from 5,500 to 6,000 feet. The plants, on their arrival, were delivered to Mr. W. G. McIvor, who for some time previously had held the appointment of Superintendent of the Government Gardens at Ootacamund; and it was to his care that the rapid and enormous increase of the plants was chiefly due. Easy as it is now found to propagate and raise the different kinds of cinchona, it ought never to be forgotten that this is the result of the intelligence which Mr. McIvor brought to bear upon their cultivation, at a time when nothing about the tree was known, and everything had to be discovered by experiments.

Shortly after the introduction of these plants into India, plants and seed of other kinds of cinchona were forwarded by those of the collectors who remained behind in America for farther exploration, and their labours have resulted in furnishing India with the following species, and an innumerable number of varieties:—*Cinchona Officinalis*, *C. Succirubra*, *C. Calisaya*, *C. Ledgeriana*, *C. Javanica*, *C. Santa Fe*, *C. Morada*, *C. Verde*, *C. Zamba Moranda*, *C. Carthagena*, *C. Pahudiana*, *C. Humboldtiana*, *C. Pitayensis*, and *C. Micrantha*. Of these the kind which are largely grown in Southern India are *C. Officinalis* and *C. Succirubra*, and a large number of varieties, which are believed to be hybrids between these two species and *C. Ledgeriana*. The other kinds are kept only as botanical curiosities, for they are either worthless as quinine-yielders, or their properties as such are not yet demonstrated.

So soon as the cultivation of cinchona was proved likely to be successful on the Nilgiris, several private gentlemen opened out estates of their own, notably Mr. J. W. B. Money, who is proprietor of estates at Devashola and Welbeck, besides owning others at Kartairy, and the great Oakington estate. These estates have proved eminently advantageous to those who hold them. Many others have since been opened out, not only on the Nilgiri plateau, but also on the Wynaad and other hill tracts. An idea of the extent to which the production of cinchona bark has been increased during the past quarter of a century may be gathered from the following statement of prices realised for Renewed Crown bark:—1877, 13*s.* 5*d.*; 1878, 10*s.* 11*d.*; 1879, 10*s.*; 1880, 10*s.* 3*d.*; 1881, 5*s.* 11*d.*; and 1882, 5*s.* 7*d.* In the year 1883, the price of all kinds of bark fell rapidly, till at the present time, 2*s.* 6*d.* per pound may be taken as a good price. This rapid decline was largely due to the enormous area of land which had been planted with cinchona in Ceylon during the previous decade. Large plantations of coffee had been destroyed by leaf disease, but, with characteristic energy, the islanders, profiting by experience gained in Madras, replaced coffee with cinchona and tea.

THE MADRAS AGRI-HORTICULTURAL SOCIETY.

Almost coeval with the reign of Her Most Gracious Majesty, and fostered and encouraged by the peace which has shared her throne in the Carnatic, has been the prosperous career of the Madras Agri-Horticultural Society. To the enthusiasm of Dr. Robert Wight,—the eminent botanist, and author of *Icones Plantarum Indiæ Orientalis*, which is to this day the standard work of the kind, and a monument that will endure while libraries exist,—the Society to a great extent owes its being. On the 15th of July, 1835, at a well-attended meeting of Native and European gentlemen held at the College Hall, it was inaugurated. Two days later the first Committee of twelve met, and it was announced that Sir Frederick Adam, the Governor, had accepted the invitation of the Society to become its first patron, the Honourable Mr. John Sullivan, the Junior Member of Council, being its first President, and Mr. Baynes its first Secretary. A little later the Nabob of the Carnatic and Sir R. Palmer, the Chief Justice, were invited to become Vice-Patrons. In 1836 the Society was in occupation of the land which now forms the larger portion of the Ornamental Garden on the Mount Road, Madras. "This was then," we read in Dr. Bidie's Report, "the only spot available; it was very ill-suited for horticultural experiments, and the Society was long embarrassed by expenses connected with its improvement" The Society has once or twice since been embarrassed, notably ten years ago, when the shed in which the Office and Committee business was conducted was turned into what it is now,—a house filled with beautiful and luxuriant ferns; the Office was transferred to what was till then the Superintendent's house; a comfortable house was built for the Superintendent in the Experimental Garden on the other side of the Cathedral Road; and the Red Hills water was carried through the Gardens to the native huts beyond. All pecuniary difficulties were, however, from time to time tided over by a small extra grant from Government; by the liberality of the Society's bankers; or by the zeal of the Secretary for the time being enabling the Society to save the pay of a professional Superintendent, and to let his house at a monthly rent. The finances of the Society are now in a fairly flourishing condition.

In 1837, at the time of Her Majesty's Accession, the work of the Society was in full swing, and very successful efforts were being made to improve by the distribution of better seed the class of cotton grown in the various districts of the Presidency,—efforts which ripened their fruit when the American War closed the ports of the Southern States to the buyers at Liverpool, Manchester, and elsewhere. In the same year some tea plants received from China were forwarded by the Society to Mysore and the Neilgherry Hills, and it is believed that some of these very plants still survive in the neighbourhood of Coonoor, so that Neilgherry tea, one of the most important products of Southern India of the present day, is now also celebrating its Jubilee. The following year a supply of Mauritius sugar-cane was obtained through the Board of Revenue, propagated, and subsequently distributed. Prior to and during the year 1840, when Mr. Glasson opened the first coffee plantation in Wynaad, the Society struggled to grow coffee profitably in Madras, and freely distributed it in plants and seeds to more favourably situated places. During the next few years records are found of the introduction of European and West Indian fruit trees, some of which doubtless still thrive, or have been displaced by their descendants, or by superior varieties. More than one species of mulberry was introduced to feed and improve the silkworms, and wonderful strides were made in the cultivation of indigenous and foreign culinary vegetables now classed generally, and consumed even by the poor, as "country vegetables." In 1844 an attempt was made to introduce the use of guano as manure, and a valuable collection of Australian seeds reached the Society. In 1845 Major Sir Walter Scott, of H.M.'s 15th Hussars (the eldest son of the "Wizard of the North"), then stationed at Bangalore, was elected a member of the Society. In 1850 the Society successfully sent a case of grafted mango plants to Sir William Hooker at Kew; and seeds of the valuable hurrialee grass, the staple food of Madras horses, was transmitted to Australia and the Cape of Good Hope. In 1853 the Society was largely engaged in raising and distributing vast numbers of the Casuarina for planting on the sand dunes on the coast north and south of Madras, now the source of almost the whole fuel supply of the town—the power which moves the railway engine and the spinning mill, cooks the rich man's banquet, and the poor man's rice.

It is possibly invidious to select a few items of good work such as those mentioned above, but it is necessary, as to do more than mention the Society's experiments with cinchona and spices, fruits and flowers, drugs and tanning materials, fibre plants and dye stuffs, cereals and forage plants, would fill many pages. The Society's nurseries now contain thousands of such plants for distribution. The work of the Society is borne in upon the senses from every garden and hedgerow in the area as large as Paris which goes by the name of Madras Town; and many of the commonest plants of the roadside are foreigners that were distributed, if not originally introduced by the Society, within the last fifty years. A stroll round the Society's Gardens, limited in extent though they are, is one of unceasing interest. On every side are hundreds of species of the most useful and beautiful of tropical flora; creepers, and herbaceous plants in such rampant growth and luxuriance of leaf and flower as are seen only amidst the warmth of the tropics. Indigenous plants, which though doubtless abundant fifty years ago in the immediate neighbourhood, are now, owing to the needs of the wood-cutter, to the scarcity of fuel, to the enormous increase of population, and to the voracity of goats, rarely to be seen within many a mile of the town, are carefully preserved, and propagated. Every step in the Ornamental Garden will unfold some new beauty to the tree-lover. The noble mahogany, from the West Indies; the lichee and the diospyros from China; the Moreton Bay chestnut; the elegant araucaria from Australia; the giant talipot from Ceylon; the graceful date from Arabia; the stately cabbage palm from Brazil; the huge baobab, and endless others are to be seen. Shrubs too are not forgotten, such as the handsome South Sea Islands croton, with its quaint forms and variegations; the butter-cup-like ochna, once common but now rare in the jungles round Madras; jasmines and begonias of many sorts; and the sweet-scented gardenias and carissas. But space forbids further details.

Of the illustrious names that have been connected with the Society much might be said. Since the Society was founded each successive Governor has accepted the position of Patron, and in later years of Patron and President; Commanders-in-Chief, Chief Justices, and Members of Council have often borne office; high officers of State have served on its Committees; and distinguished botanists have worked as its Secretaries. Wallich, Royle, Wight, Roxburgh, Lindley, Thwaites, the Hookers, Trimen, Schomburgk, Von Müller, Cleghorn, and many others have been its contributors. Nor should the services of the professional gardeners, who from time to time have been in charge of the Gardens, be forgotten. In 1853 Mr. Jaffrey was sent out to the Society from the Caledonian Horticultural Garden, Edinburgh, and did good work for four years, until he obtained a better engagement at Bangalore, after he had contributed to the science of gardening his well-known booklet, *Hints to Amateur Gardeners in Madras.* He was succeeded by Mr. Robert H. Brown, the author of the useful *Handbook of the Trees, Shrubs, and Herbaceous Plants growing in the Society's Gardens and the Neighbourhood of Madras.* Mr. Denham, Mr. Henry, Mr. Storey, and some others came out from England in their turn, and after doing faithful work left the service for better paid appointments. The Society has for the last four years had the benefit of the assistance of Mr. J. M. Gleeson, who was sent out by the Secretary of State in 1869 to work at the Government cotton experiments in Central India, and who, besides the regular duties which he has loyally discharged, has compiled and published an admirable *Catalogue of*

Plants in the Agri-Horticultural Society's Gardens, Madras, and is now engaged on other useful literary work.

NILGIRI HORTICULTURE.

The horticultural establishment in Ootacamund, known as the Government Botanical Garden, was first set on foot in the year 1847, during the Governorship of the Marquis of Tweeddale; and the first gardener—appointed on the recommendation of Sir William Hooker, and Dr. Royle—was Mr. W. G. McIvor, who received his early training at the Royal Gardens, Kew, and eventually obtained much celebrity as Superintendent of the Government Cinchona Plantations on the Nilgiris. Mr. McIvor first opened out the upper part of the present Garden, and planted the space with many indigenous ornamental shrubs and trees, as well as with exotics obtained from China, Australia, the Cape, &c. He also made several ponds and terraces. At the same time he gave a great deal of attention to the introduction and cultivation of apples, pears, figs, grapes, oranges, lemons, plums, citrons, &c. He also cultivated European vegetables, the seed of which appears to have been freely distributed amongst the natives of the surrounding districts; and from this liberality on the part of Government has arisen the present plentiful supply of excellent vegetables with which Ootacamund and its neighbourhood are supplied. The climate and soil of the Nilgiris are so well adapted for the cultivation of the more common European herbs, that were it not for the cost of transporting all produce to the nearest railway station, towns and villages in the low country might have their markets constantly filled with fresh cauliflowers, cabbages, potatoes, celery, artichokes, carrots, turnips, &c. The late Sir Charles Trevelyan, Governor of Madras, visited the Garden for the first time in February, 1860, and recorded in a Minute that "It is both a beautiful pleasure ground, and a valuable public institution for the improvement of indigenous, and the naturalisation of foreign plants; it has been formed by Mr. McIvor with great industry and artistic skill, out of a rude ravine; and he deserves great credit for the manner in which he has laid it out."

In 1866, Mr. A. Jamieson, the present Curator, arrived at Ootacamund from Kew, to assist Mr. McIvor; and in 1871, as the latter gentleman's time was fully occupied in fostering the new Cinchona Plantation, Mr. Jamieson was made Superintendent of the Garden in Mr. McIvor's place. To him the present beautiful state of the Garden is chiefly due. The whole of the lower Garden has been laid out in a very tasteful manner, and has been planted with many rare trees and shrubs. The upper part of the Garden also, which adjoins the new Government House, has been transformed from an unsightly scrub into what will be, in a few years more, when the recently planted trees have grown up, a beautiful park. Many plants of medicinal and economic value have been introduced since the establishment of the Garden, such as ipecacuanha, jalap, digitalis, rhubarb, cinchona, mahogany, various kinds of pines, box, cocoa, mangosteen, litchi, various kinds of trees yielding india rubber, &c. Most of these have been distributed to different parts of the country, and many of them may be now regarded as quite naturalised in India.

Besides the present Garden at Ootacamund there are branch Experimental Gardens at Coonoor, Burliar, and Kulhatti. The one at Coonoor (Sim's Park) rivals in beauty the Garden at Ootacamund; it is situated in a ravine which lies between the upper part of Coonoor and the Wellington Race Course. It is well pathed and roaded, and consists of one portion which is laid out as an ornamental garden, and contains many beautiful trees, especially pines and eucalypti; and of another portion, which consists of sholah trees, that have been left in their natural condition. Nurseries also, for the propagation of the indigenous trees of the neighbourhood, have been recently made. The Park is named after Mr. J. D. Sim, C.S.I., the member of the Council of Fort St. George, at whose instigation it was founded in 1873. The Garden at Burliar is situated almost at the bottom of the Coonoor ghaut, at an elevation of about 1,800 feet above sea level. The temperature is very high. The soil is rich, and the average rainfall considerable, so that many plants can be grown there, which will not thrive in the higher situations of Ootacamund and Coonoor. It is there that the cocoa, mangosteen, and litchi fruit grows freely; but unfortunately, the climate is most unhealthy, and the inhabitants of the place suffer much from fever of a most virulent description. This Garden was acquired by Government in 1870; but long before that time it had been stocked by Mr. E. B. Thomas, the Collector of Coimbatore, with many rare and exotic trees of ornamental or economic interest. The only other Garden in possession of Government on the Nilgiri Hills is the one at Kalhatti, and this it is proposed to abandon, as the conditions of soil and climate do not differ sufficiently from those which exist at Coonoor to make its retention advisable; but it is intended to open out instead a new garden near Gudalur in South-East Wynaad. All these Gardens have been placed, since the year 1883, under the management of Mr. M. A. Lawson, M.A., late Professor of Botany at the University of Oxford, who is now both Government Botanist and Director of the Government Cinchona Plantations.

In addition to the work carried on by Government, many private individuals have done much to advance horticulture on the Nilgiris. Amongst these may be mentioned General Morgan, who has paid much attention to arboriculture; Mr. Griffith, of Kotagiri, who has introduced many ornamental plants from Europe; and Mr. Misquith whose pears and other fruits are well known to the residents and visitors in Ootacamund. Last year a Society was formed at Ootacamund for the study of the Natural History of the Nilgiris and adjoining districts. The meetings of this Society are held once every fortnight, and excursions are occasionally made by the members in the neighbourhood of Ootacamund. A Museum is also being created, which is intended to contain specimens of Natural History, and of objects of economic interest.

FISH CURING.

The waters of the tropical seas around the peninsula of Southern India are even more prolific of fish life than the seas of colder climes. Consequently there has always been a large fishing population, and the curing of the surplus "takes" that could not be disposed of fresh has always been an industry. But the stricter administration of the Government salt monopoly proved inimical to this industry. The fishermen could not pay in advance before obtaining the salt for salting their fish. And even if they did, the tax so raised the price of salt that it enhanced the price of salt fish to an extent which drove it out of the market. The fish-curing industry continued to struggle on, however, wherever salt could in any form be surreptitiously obtained free of tax. In the neighbourhood of spontaneous salt swamps that were not sufficiently guarded, or where the ebb and flow of tidal estuaries left on the margin a sun-evaporated line of salt that could be scraped off, or where earth salt could be got, fish-curing still lingered. But such surreptitiously obtained salt was not confined to fish-curing uses, and the maintenance of the salt monopoly made it imperative that salt-smuggling generally should be prevented.

While this struggle between the salt smuggler and the salt tax continued, the quality as well as the quantity of salt-fish naturally deteriorated, the salt being economised to the utmost by merely smearing the fish with a little salt mud, and by the drying powers of a mid-day tropical sun being mainly trusted to in place of salt. Fish thus sun-dried, and but partially cured, would not keep long, could be taken but short distances, and was very offensive in carriage. Nevertheless the demand for it continued great, especially among the poorer classes, with whom it was almost the only animal food they could ever afford to purchase. Where fish curing thus maintained its struggle with the salt monopoly there the fishing classes prospered, where it failed, they were impoverished, and in 1873 Dr. Day, the Inspector-General of Fisheries in India, wrote: "Salt has been subjected to so heavy a duty, that it is virtually unobtainable by the fish-curers at a price which would permit salt-fish being sold to the general public. Ruin to the fish curers' trade has reacted on other fishermen, due to curtailing their market, and so cutting off the stimulus for labour. It appears evident that to render the sea fisheries useful for providing wholesome salt fish inland, nothing is necessary but cheap salt to the fish-curers." But how to give cheap salt to the fish-curers without imperilling the salt monopoly was the difficulty. To sacrifice the salt monopoly was out of the question, for though it is a tax on a necessary of life, it is in effect an infinitesimal and indirect poll-tax, and as such it contributed in the Presidency of Madras alone 132 lakhs of rupees of revenue in the year 1885-86.

A way out of the dilemma was, however, found in the following compromise. It was suggested that enclosures might be constructed within which monopoly salt might be sold to fish-curers at its actual cost price to Government, and free of the Government monopoly tax, on the one condition that it should be used by them within the enclosure. This proposal was sanctioned in July, 1874, and these enclosures became curing-yards into which Government salt passed under police guard, but out of which no salt passed again except in the form of salted fish. These proposals were sanctioned. In 1876, the year in which the fish-curing yards were first opened, only 324 tons of fish were cured in the whole Presidency, whereas in the twelve months ending with September, 1886, 28,353 tons of fish were cured. Thus already no mean quantity of wholesome animal food is thrown into the market at a rate so cheap as to be within the purchasing power of the poorest. But the rate at which the advance has been made is a matter still more full of hope for the future, the results of each year having nearly doubled the results of the previous year, till, in the last six months of 1886, as compared with the similar season of the previous year, there was an advance of 957 tons of fish cured. And not in quantity alone, but in quality also, is there marked improvement. There is every prospect, therefore, of this industry growing rapidly to dimensions such as to make it worthy of taking high rank among the useful advances that have been made in the Presidency of Madras during Her Majesty's reign. Concurrently with the growth of this industry, the fishing classes are prospering, and their prosperity is calculated to tell again on the harvest of the seas gathered by their increasing capital, improved appliances, and stimulated energies. Great has been the benefit of the increase to the fish-food supply of the millions, of whom over 90 per cent. eat animal food—when they can get it.

PEARL FISHERIES.

Near the southern extremity of the Presidency lies Tuticorin, on the Gulf of Manaar, in which is a Pearl Fishery, worked on the southern shores of the Gulf by the Government of Ceylon, and on the northern shores by the Government of Madras. It enriched the Kings of Ceylon in the days of Marco Polo, who has recorded many quaint legends on the subject. But considerable scientific progress has been made since Marco Polo's time in exact knowledge of the habits of the oyster. The earlier researches of 1857 were made at the instance of the Ceylon Government; and those of 1884 were conducted under the orders of the Madras Government. The nature of these researches is of a scientific character that comes hardly within the scope of these notes. It is enough that they have been welcomed as an advance by leading scientists in England, and that the practical result is that from an improved knowledge of the habits of the fish, it may be hoped that the fishery will be improved. Already is there promise of a most extensive fishery in 1888 or 1889, for the pearl oysters in a healthy state cover an area of coral reef five miles long, and one-and-a-half or two miles wide, and so thick are they that they are clustered together in some places one over another, knee deep, and show, by experiments made, from 600 to 700 oysters a square yard.

Apart from studying the fish, attention has also been given to the mode of fishing. Hitherto pearl oysters have been brought up from the bottom of the sea in exactly the same way as they were in the days of Marco Polo. Descending with the aid of a large stone hitched to one toe, and without any diving dress, it is natural that in 8 or 9 fathoms of water the stay of the diver at the bottom is usually less than a minute; and a few pearl oysters hurriedly picked up are thrown into a small net attached to him. Less hurried and more thorough picking is to be expected of men who in European diving dress can stay down for hours together; and experiments in this direction are being made, in view to ascertaining the best means of meeting most economically the many practical difficulties with which the position is surrounded, such as the prevention of the theft of pearls, the maintenance of order amongst the large numbers assembled at a fishery, the giving to each diver an individual stimulus to exertion by a system of payment by shares, and the provision of suitable boats and gear in sufficient numbers to complete the fishery within the short time in which the weather allows of its being conducted.

The two last fisheries conducted by the Madras Government yielded in 1860 Rs. 2,50,276, and in 1861 Rs. 1,29,003; while the Ceylon fishery from 1860 to 1884 yielded an aggregate of Rs. 20,75,211. Madras in times past has thus been far behind Ceylon in the profitableness of her Pearl Fisheries. The primary reason for this lies, however, in the natural advantages of the Ceylon position, the pearl oysters preferring the southern side of the Gulf of Manaar on account of the lee side of the Island of Ceylon being sheltered from the strong current which, sweeping down the Bay of Bengal, turns westwards round the south of Ceylon, and then northwards into the Gulf of Manaar, impinging directly on the Madras side of that Gulf, while the Ceylon side is sheltered. But any deficiencies of Madras in pearl fishery revenue have been in a large measure recouped by her uniting with her pearl fisheries a fishery for the holy shell, called the Chank. It is the *Turbinella pyrum* of naturalists. This fishery is not followed in Ceylon though the shell fish are very abundant there, but on the Madras side it has been developed from almost nothing to about Rs. 25,000 a year, and under present management is calculated to yield a steady annual revenue of about the same amount, as well as to be the training ground of the divers on whom the working of the Pearl Fisheries is dependent.

JUSTICE.

In 1837 the scheme of judicial administration in Madras was substantially that which had been founded in 1800 by the Statute 39 and 40 George III, cap. 79. This Statute, besides authorising the establishment of a Supreme Court of Judicature, and a Court of Commissioners for the recovery of Small Debts in Madras, empowered the Governor and Council at Fort St. George to frame regulations for the establishment of Courts in the Mofussil. The Court-making Regulations were passed chiefly in 1802 and 1816; and by 1837, the judicial machinery for the whole Presidency was in regular working order. Each village had then, as now, its Civil and its Criminal Court. The headman was, by virtue of his office, at once the Munsiff and the Magistrate. As Munsiff, he had power to hear and determine, of his own authority and without appeal, suits of money (except for damages) or other personal property, not exceeding Rs. 10 in value. As Magistrate, he had power to try cases of a trivial nature, such as abusive language and petty assaults, and to confine offenders in the village choultry for a time not exceeding 12 hours. He was not liable to be called on to answer for his conduct as Munsiff except on a charge of corruption, or of exceeding his powers, and then only before the Zillah Judge.

Between the Village and the Zillah Courts came those of the District Munsiffs, of whom there were, in 1837, more than 100, each exercising Civil jurisdiction over one or more revenue taluqs. They were empowered to dispose of all kinds of suits against natives, their pecuniary jurisdiction being limited, in the case of suits for land exempt from paying rent to Government, to those of Rs. 100 or less in value, and to those not exceeding Rs. 1,000 in value, in the case of other land or money suits. In petty suits of not over Rs. 20 in value, their decisions were final; and the Munsiffs themselves were graded in three classes, paid Rs. 140, 115, and 100 per mensem respectively. It did not follow, however, that if the subject-matter of a suit exceeded the ordinary jurisdiction of the Village Munsiff, the parties were bound to journey to the District Munsiff's Court. The Regulations authorised Village Munsiffs as arbitrators to determine suits up to Rs. 100 in value, and to summon Village Panchayets for the disposal, with the consent of the parties, of all suits referred to them, without limitation as to value, and without appeal. Similar principles governed the decision of suits by District Panchayets, summonable, where both parties elected that form of trial, by the District Munsiff. To these Village and District Panchayets, which consisted of not less than five nor more than eleven respectable inhabitants, Collectors also had power to refer for decision of suits between proprietors and their ryots respecting the occupying or irrigating of land, or in cases of disputed boundary, or land-marks. The Assistants to Collectors were Magistrates within their territorial charges, and the Collector himself was the Zillah (or District) Magistrate.

Of the Civil Zillah Courts, there were, in 1837, 22 in number. The powers of the Zillah Judges extended to all suits not exceeding Rs. 5,000 in value, arising within their territorial jurisdiction, subject to a right of appeal in every case to the Provincial Court. In those days codes were not; and where no specific rules existed for their guidance, Zillah Judges were directed to act "according to justice, equity, and good conscience." All manner of assistance was given them, even in 1837, to relieve the overburdened files of their Courts. One Regulation empowered them to refer suits, not exceeding Rs. 200 in value, to their Registrars, or "Registers" as they were then termed. Another Regulation authorised the appointment of Assistant Judges with separate jurisdiction over parts of Zillahs, but with the same powers as the Zillah Courts themselves, including the powers to hear appeals from District Munsiffs. Another Regulation empowered the Zillah Judges to refer suits not exceeding Rs. 2,500 in value to their native law officers, the Sudder Amins, whose decisions in appeal from District Munsiffs were final in many cases. Yet another Regulation authorised the establishment of Native Courts under Principal Sudder Amins with the same powers as Assistant Judges, except that they were barred from hearing appeals from the decrees of their own Sudder Amins, or of any European officer of Government. The Principal Sudder Amins, Assistant Judges, and Zillah Judges, were also Criminal Judges within their Civil jurisdictions. Over all this collection of Zillah Courts and their auxiliaries were placed four Provincial Courts, each manned by three Judges. On the Original Side they disposed of suits exceeding Rs. 5,000, but not exceeding Rs. 10,000 in value, or of any suits transmitted to them by the Sudder Court; and on the Appellate Side their powers extended to special Appeals from the Appellate Decrees of Assistant and Zillah Judges, as well as to regular appeals from the original decisions of those Courts. In Criminal matters the Provincial Courts were constituted Courts of Circuit for the disposal of Sessions cases, but the Senior Judge had always to remain at head-quarters, and was competent, under certain restrictions, to exercise all the powers of the full Court. Above the Provincial Courts was placed the Sudder Court, known on its Civil Side as the Sudder, and on its Criminal Side as the Foujdari Adawlut, and consisting of a Chief and three Puisne Judges selected from the Civil Service. Their original business comprised suits of Rs. 10,000 in value and upwards without limit, and they exercised regular and special appellate powers in respect of the original and appellate decrees, respectively, of the Provincial Courts. The Foujdari Adawlut alone had the power of passing capital sentences, and of revising and annulling the sentences of all Lower Criminal Courts.

Such, in outline, from the Village up to the Sudder Court was the scheme of Mofussil justice in 1837. In the Presidency town, the Court of the Commissioners for the Recovery of Small Debts had jurisdiction in money suits up to the value of 120 pagodas; and crowning the whole judicial edifice, both Mofussil and Madras, was the Supreme Court of Judicature, consisting of a Chief Justice and two Barrister Judges with full powers in Civil, Criminal, Admiralty, and Ecclesiastical jurisdiction, subject only to the limitation that in cases where the value exceeded Rs. 10,000 an appeal lay to the Queen in Council.

In the fifty years of Her Majesty's reign the tendency of judicial changes has been towards

P P

simplification, and the reduction of the numerous varieties of intermediate Courts which characterised the scheme of 1837, while the expansion of litigation under the beneficent influence of evenly-administered justice had necessitated a constantly increasing extension of the powers of surviving Courts. In 1843 the Provincial Courts were abolished, and the Civil and Sessions Judge replaced both the Zillah and the Provincial Courts. By 1845 the exigencies of the wilder tracts of the Northern Circars had called into existence the Special Agency Court. In 1850 the Madras Court of Small Causes was established, and in 1860 similar Courts existed in various Mofussil towns only to disappear again in 1879. By 1857 the Police Magistrates' Courts in the Presidency town had been established. In 1862 the Sudder Amin disappeared, and the present High Court of Judicature replaced both the Sudder and the Supreme Courts. In 1873 the principal Sudder Amin developed into the modern Subordinate Judge; and the Courts of District Munsiffs, Subordinate, and District Judges, were placed pretty nearly on their present footing.

The series of Civil and Criminal Procedure Codes which began in 1857 greatly simplified the disposal of business. The existing scheme of judicial administration comprises a chain of Courts scientifically arranged, and highly appreciated, as a whole, by the law-going public. At the base of the pyramid, so to speak, there still continue the Village Munsiffs' Courts, but with powers extended, in their ordinary jurisdiction, to suits of Rs. 20, and, as arbitrators, to suits of Rs. 200 in value. The Village and District Panchayets still exist, though not much used. The District Munsiffs number 106, classed in four grades, ranging from Rs. 400 to Rs. 200 per mensem. Their jurisdiction extends to suits of Rs. 2,500 in value, and while all of them have the power of Small Cause Courts in money suits up to Rs. 50 in value, some have been entrusted with such powers up to Rs. 100, and others up to Rs. 200 in value. The status of the Subordinate Judges, like that of the District Munsiffs, has been raised, and they now number fourteen, graded in three classes, paid Rs. 800, 600, and 500 per mensem. Their jurisdiction in original suits, like that of the District Judges, is unlimited as to value; and they are empowered to decide such appeals against the decrees of District Munsiffs as may be referred to them by the District Judge. An appeal from the original decrees of Subordinate Judges lies in every case, in suits of Rs. 5,000 and upwards, direct to the High Court, and in other suits to the District Judge. All the Subordinate Judges and some of the District Judges have been invested with the powers of Small Cause Courts in suits not exceeding Rs. 500 in value. All Collectors and their Assistants constitute Revenue Courts for the trial of rent suits between landlords and tenants, and their decrees are appealable to the District Court. In Ganjam, Vizagapatam and Godavery, Special Agency Courts exist for the wilder tracts side by side with the regular Courts, with a similar system of appeal. Two separate Small Cause Courts survive at St. Thomas' Mount and Cannanore to meet cantonment exigencies. The District Courts, of which there are twenty in the provinces, have unlimited original jurisdiction, subject to regular appeal to the High Court, where also the right of second appeal against the appellate decrees of both District and Subordinate Judges now lies, and is freely exercised. In the town of Madras, the Presidency Court of Small Causes, consisting of a chief and two Judges, has jurisdiction in money suits up to Rs. 2,000 in value.

Turning to the Criminal side, the Village Magistrates continue on the same footing as in 1837. All other Magistrates are classed throughout the Presidency as first, second, or third class Magistrates according to the powers conferred on such classes by the Code of Criminal Procedure. The District and Joint Magistrates have also the right of hearing appeals from the Subordinate Magistrates' decisions, and their own decisions are, in turn, appealable to the Sessions Court. These latter Courts have full criminal powers, subject only, in the case of capital sentences, to confirmation by the High Court, and subject to appeal to the same tribunal. In Madras, the Presidency Magistrates take the place of first class Magistrates in the Mufussil, and the High Court, in its criminal jurisdiction, takes that of the Sessions Court. The High Court, which thus constitutes the apex of the existing judicial system, at present consists of a Chief Justice and four Puisne Judges, of whom two are Barristers, two Civil Servants, and one a Native Judge. It exercises all the powers of the Supreme Court of fifty years ago, Civil, Criminal, Admiralty, Ecclesiastical, and Insolvency; and it is only in cases of the value of Rs. 10,000 and upwards that an appeal is allowed to the Privy Council.

Some idea of the extent to which use is made of the judicial machinery here sketched may be gathered from the fact that in 1885 the Village Munsiffs in the Madras Presidency disposed of 84,500 suits; the Revenue Courts of 4,350; the Agency Courts of 550; the District Munsiffs of 66,500 ordinary suits, and 70,500 small causes; the Subordinate Judges of 740 suits, 13,750 small causes, and 2,500 appeals; the District Courts of 320 suits, and 4,750 appeals; the Presidency Small Cause Court of 27,750 suits; and the High Court of 370 suits, 186 insolvency cases, 140 regular appeals, and 1,090 second appeals, to say nothing of an immense amount of revisional and miscellaneous business. The work of all classes of Courts increases year by year, and it is notorious that no department of the State commands such public confidence among the natives of Southern India as the administration of Justice.

POLICE.

When Her Majesty ascended the throne the only organised Police in Madras was the Presidency town Police, which was then under the able management of Mr. Edward Elliot. This gentleman was also in his time Chief Magistrate, Chief Judge of the Court of Requests (subsequently Court of Small Causes), and Chairman of the Bench of Justices, as well as Superintendent of Police. He came into office on the 14th February, 1834, and held the post till the 15th April, 1856, a term of twenty-two years. His force retained the old names of Jamadar, Darogah, Duffadar, and Peon; and there are many persons still alive who speak with the highest respect and admiration of the good services rendered in those days by the Police under their able chief. In the rural districts Police duties were dependent on such fitful attention as they could receive from the Revenue officers, who were also "Heads of Police." The peons and other subordinates were employed indiscriminately on both revenue and police duties.

In the three Presidency towns the Police, the Justices of the Peace, and the Judges of the Superior Courts were governed by the English practice and procedure in criminal matters. The Police of three towns was administered chiefly by "Regulations." In 1856 an Act was passed for "regulating the Police of the towns of Calcutta, Madras, and Bombay, and the several stations of the Settlement of Prince of Wales' Island, Singapore, and Malacca." This Act consolidated all the Police law; constituted the Police Force on a footing with the Metropolitan Police in England and Ireland; and altered the designation of the Chief of the Police from "Superintendent" to "Commissioner." The City Police of the three Presidency towns were thus placed on the same footing, and governed by the same law. From 1854 the Madras Government had been urging the necessity for a thorough re-organisation of the Provincial (District) Police, and on the 9th June, 1857, the Honourable Court of Directors granted sanction for this reform. Some time was occupied in the preliminary steps that were necessary; and in 1859 an Act was passed "For the better regulation of police within the territories subject to the Presidency of Fort St. George." The duty of reorganising the District Police was entrusted to the able hands of Mr. (afterwards Sir William) Robinson, a member of the Madras Civil Service, who, besides a natural talent for Police administration, had thoroughly studied, when on furlough, Police details in Europe. In 1860 the campaign was opened in the North Arcot District, and at the close of 1862 the Government was advised that the new machinery was in full working order throughout the Presidency. About 13,500 troops were set free from harassing escort and other petty duties not strictly military. Large reductions were thus possible in the military branch of the service, and a considerable saving of expenditure was effected. Regiments, instead of being scattered in detachments over the Presidency, are now concentrated at the principal stations. The Madras police, as organised in 1859, became the model for all India, and on that model was based the General Police Act of 1861, which is applicable by notification of the Governor-General in Council to any presidency, province, or town.

In 1866 the Madras Government decided to incorporate the City Police with the general (District) Police, and for that purpose an Act was passed in the following year. By this Act the police of the town of Madras became part of the general police force of the Madras Presidency, but the Commissioner and his deputies continue to hold office as before, subject to the authority of the Inspector-General of Police. The Madras Police has done excellent work since its birth. The progress made has been steady. Crime will always exist in some shape, but the character of crime in the Madras Presidency has been sensibly affected. The Government in reviewing the last Administration Report of the Madras police, which deals with the twenty-five years' existence of the force as at present organised, states that, "with three exceptions, all disturbances of the public peace have been effectively dealt with by the police without extraneous assistance; dacoities have decreased by 82 per cent.; torchlight dacoity has been nearly stamped out, the yearly average number of robberies has fallen from 977 to 246; and there has also been a considerable decline in the number of cases of house-breaking and burglary. The figures under other heads of crime are said to be equally satisfactory. The great improvement that has taken place is undoubtedly due in a large measure to efficient police administration, and reflects great credit upon the officers and men of the force."

The sovereign power is to the ordinary ryot, living far from camps and military cantonments, represented by the police. It is to the police he looks for protection against lawlessness, and for the continued enjoyment of the tranquillity with which the Empire of India is blessed. The high-handed oppression of former times is now but a tradition, and if the police of the present day is not much noticed it is for reasons creditable to them. They carry on their duties unremittingly, and without ostentation. If occasionally there be hostile criticism actuated by personal interest, or disappointment, the police know that the same critics will, when they are in trouble, largely solicit aid from the guardians of the public peace, and, what is more satisfactory, will feel assured that it will be cheerfully accorded. In the rural districts recruits are, as a rule, obtained without much difficulty, although it is not easy to keep up the necessary strength of the force in some of the more unhealthy parts of the country, where many a humble and faithful servant of the people has died, or become permanently crippled. There is still a dislike on the part of the better educated classes to accept service in the subordinate grades of the force—a prejudice against the strict regulation as to wearing uniform being, it is believed, the principal objection. The pay of the constables is still very low, viz., for the rural force Rs. 6½, 7, and 8, and for the city constables Rs. 7, 8, and 9 per mensem, which compares unfavourably with the present pay of a sepoy who may be quite illiterate. A sepoy also gets an assured increase to his pay according to his service, besides compensation when the market rate of his food exceeds a fixed and liberal standard. Further, the sepoy is not like the constable, on duty every day, and he is spared the harassing escort work of the police officer. Greater difficulty is experienced in obtaining men for the City Police of the stamp required, the duties of the City constable being more severe than those of his rural brother, and the cost of living in the Presidency town being much greater than in the districts. The night duty is specially distasteful to a native. The City officer is also under constant and unremitting supervision, even the citizens constituting themselves into a volunteer supervising staff, and showing a praiseworthy and beneficial interest in the civic force.

The police are subject to the ordinary pension rules of the Uncovenanted Civil Service. Formerly the lower grades of both the City and the Mofussil Police contributed a certain proportion of their pay to superannuation funds. These funds were in a very flourishing condition in 1869, when Sir Richard Temple proposed, and the Government of India sanctioned, their abolition, the assets being taken over by Government, and the State assuming the responsibility of providing pensions and superannuation allowances. A police officer cannot now claim his pension until he has completed thirty years' service, at which time, and frequently much before, the hard work he has undergone has worn him out. During the late Jubilee celebrations the police alone were on duty, while the holiday-makers enjoyed themselves. But at all times and in all weathers the policeman must be afoot. While others sleep or feast, the constable labours. At each station where the Jubilee was kept the police cheerfully gave the material assistance without which it would not have been possible to carry out the programmes. In the City of Madras, which was *en fête* for two days in February, 15,000 poor people were fed in four different parts of the town, at some places the feeding being continued from 6 A.M. to dusk. 25,000 people attended at the Park at Government House to witness the public presentation to H.E. the Governor of the Presidential Address to be submitted to Her Most Gracious Majesty. There were illuminations throughout the City, and a display of fireworks on the large place known as "the Island" at night. Besides the crowds of foot passengers, all kinds of vehicles thronged the roads and streets. Yet neither in the City nor throughout the whole Presidency was an accident or an offence reported as having occurred on that, in every sense, auspicious occasion. This was a most gratifying testimony, not only to the discipline and organisation of the Police, but also to the good temper and docility of the multitudes who went forth to do honour to their Sovereign Lady the Empress of India.

JAILS.

The first practical measures of Prison Reform in India may be said to have been initiated with the Queen's accession. Consequent on a minute written shortly after his arrival in the country by Mr. (afterwards Lord) Macaulay, as a Member of the Law Commission, a Committee was appointed, and its Report was submitted in 1838. The state of Prison discipline that then prevailed may be judged from the fact that Lord Macaulay said of the prisoners in the Alipore Jail, near Calcutta:— "It is only a few months since they murdered the Superintending Magistrate. At present no visitor can enter the gates without danger." Such being the state of affairs at the seat of the Supreme Government, the condition of Mofussil Jails may be imagined. The next important step was the appointment of an Inspector General of Jails in each Province. In 1855 an Inspector General of Prisons was appointed in Madras, to whom was entrusted the introduction of regulations for the better management and discipline of Jails, and the general administration of the Department. At that time, Jails were in the immediate charge of the Judges of the District Courts, who had frequently not only to pass a sentence of death upon a fellow-creature, but to see it carried out. The executive charge of the Jail was, as might be expected, not felt to be a pleasant duty. In many instances the real administration was left to the jailers, a class wholly unfitted for the responsibilities thrust on them, and the discipline of the Jails was of the lowest order. In 1864 Sir John Lawrence, the then Viceroy—who as an old Bengal Civil Servant was thoroughly acquainted with the subject—pointed out that the full measure of improvement contemplated by the Report of the Committee of 1838 had never been carried out, and that whilst but little progress had been made in the improvement of the prisoners, or prevention of crime, the loss of life amongst prisoners continued year by year to be very great. A Committee was then appointed by his Government to report anew, and its recommendations generally endorsed those of the Committee of 1838.

In the Madras Presidency the difficulties of Jail administration were probably at their highest during the years 1860 to 1865. The introduction at this period of the Penal Code, simultaneously with the introduction of the new Police on an organised system, so disturbed the criminal classes, that the Jails were filled to overflowing, and the inadequacy of the existing accommodation became apparent. There were at that time 6,800 prisoners in Jails that were capable of accommodating only 4,490 at the prescribed standard of space; and for years the annual mortality was seldom less, and was often more, than 10 per cent. of the average strength of prisoners, or ten times the mortality in jails in the United Kingdom. This, in effect, meant that imprisonment in India entailed on offenders risks to life which the law never contemplated. The high rate of mortality was attributed to over-crowding, bad ventilation, the want of sanitary arrangements, deficiency of personal cleanliness, imperfectly cooked food, and defective dietaries. In February, 1865, Mr. Rohde, C.S., the first Inspector General of Prisons, and Mr. R. S. Ellis, C.B., C.S., the first President of the recently appointed Sanitary Commission, were directed to consider and report what additional prison accommodation was required, and what measures ought to be taken to improve existing Jails, and the system of Prison management generally. In April, 1865, they submitted their Report, together with a set of Rules for the better superintendence and management of Jails. Their proposals were generally approved. The necessity of Central Jails for prisoners sentenced to a term exceeding one year had already been recognised, and a proposition to build five Central Jails was adopted. Jails of this class had indeed been commenced at Coimbatore and Rajahmundry. These Jails were originally intended to accommodate 600 and 675 convicts respectively; but, owing to the want of Prison accommodation, it was determined to extend them so as to afford room for 1,000 convicts each. The erection of Central Jails at Vellore, Trichinopoly, and Cannanore was also determined upon, and it was arranged that some of the existing District Jails should be improved, and that others should be rebuilt on better principles and more healthy sites, as means became available.

The Sessions Judges were now relieved of the executive charge of District Jails, which were placed under the Civil Surgeons, and special officers were appointed to the charge of the Central Jails. The Penitentiary at Madras, which was under the exclusive management of the Commissioner of Police, was placed under the general supervision of the Inspector General. In July 1872 it was made a Central Jail, and a special officer was appointed to superintend it. In 1866 the new Jail Rules were introduced. Convicts had up to this time been granted a fixed quantity of grain, while as regards their other articles of food and firing they were allowed a small sum daily to provide themselves therewith. The result of this system was that so long as the value of money remained what it was fifty or sixty years previously, the sum allowed sufficed; but afterwards, as the value of money changed, this fixed allowance was barely sufficient to purchase salt, condiments, and wood, and left nothing for vegetable or animal food. Fixed diet scales, drawn up by Dr. Cornish, the then Sanitary Commissioner, were adopted when the new Rules were introduced, and with slight alterations these scales have been in force up to the present time. The chief change effected by the new dietaries was the substitution of cholum and ragi for the more luxurious, but less nutritious, rice hitherto issued, and the fixing of the amount of animal food, vegetables, and condiments. The concurrent measures thus adopted for the improvement of Jail accommodation, the enforcement of cleanliness and sanitary arrangements, combined with the radical change in the system of feeding the convicts, had a material effect upon the sickness in Jails, and the mortality which had in 1865 been 12·70 per cent. of average strength, fell in 1871, or in six years, to 1·84 per cent.

In 1869 an Act for the Regulation of Jails in the Madras Presidency and the Enforcement of Discipline therein was passed. This Act and the Rules based thereon still control the management and discipline of Jails. The next important step for the improvement of Jails in India was the convening of a Prison Conference at Calcutta in 1877. The Conference was almost exclusively composed of experts, as its principal object was to evoke specific recommendations based on actual experience of the working of Jails in each province. It submitted a comprehensive Report with suggestions and recommendations dealing with buildings, inspection and supervision, employment of prisoners, treatment, and marks. Many of the suggestions of this Conference were acted upon by the Government of India.

In 1868 a system of remission was sanctioned for Central Jails in the Madras Presidency, whereby well-behaved and industrious convicts were enabled to diminish the length of their sentences by periods not exceeding a certain fixed limit. Two years ago the system heretofore in force in the Presidency was modified in accordance with Revised Rules on the subject issued by the Government of India for all Jails in India. The new scheme differs in detail, and in the periods of remission obtainable, from that which was before in force in this Presidency, but the objects aimed at are the same. In 1883 a Revised set of Rules for the management and superintendence of Jails in the Madras Presidency were prescribed by His Excellency the Governor in Council. These Rules constitute a carefully prepared Code, in which are embodied all the regulations relating to Jails and Jail management that have from time to time been passed. They are partly based on the recommendations of the Jail Conference. Up to the end of 1871 it was the practice to put all convicts in the Madras Presidency in irons, with the exception of convict servants. It was then determined that convicts employed intra-murally in Central Jails should be relieved from fetters three months after admission, provided they conducted themselves well for that period. Fetters were, by the Jail Code of 1883, discontinued in the case of all convicts in Central Jails sentenced either to rigorous or simple imprisonment, their use being reserved for cases where a prisoner is violent, or where there is reason to believe that he contemplates escape.

With the completion of Central Jails manufactures were introduced, and labour became intramural. The whole of the clothing for the convicts themselves is made in the jails, while other public departments also receive large supplies from jails. Carpentary and blacksmith's work, carpet weaving, tent making, and other industries are carried on, a systematic method of working being followed, and tasks rigidly exacted, definite industries being prescribed for given jails. In 1865 the cash receipts on account of manufactures amounted to Rs. 44,706, whereas in 1878 the earnings or profits paid into the Treasury, after adjustment of advances, amounted to Rs. 1,72,225. For the last few years there has been a diminution of receipts, chiefly owing to the restriction placed on manufactures, but this restriction has been withdrawn, and the convict now contributes considerably towards the cost of his keep and custody. The establishment of jails, until a recent date, consisted of the warders, or disciplinary officers, while the safe custody of the convicts was entrusted to the Police. In 1885 the Police were relieved of the duty of guarding certain jails, which duty was undertaken by a warder guard. Last year, a comprehensive scheme for the guarding of all jails was submitted by the Inspector General, in accordance with which the guarding of all jails is performed by warder guards. An important feature connected with the discipline and guarding of Central Jails is the employment of convicts who perform all the duties of free warders, and take their turn of sentry duty by night. Prisoners are thus gradually prepared for liberation, taught self-respect and the value of continuous good conduct. Many other matters in connection with jail administration, such as questions of the system of confinement, employment, punishment, education, and reformation of the convict, have received attention. It may be well to mention that the cellular system has been added to some of the Madras Central Jails, and that convicts are required to pass certain fixed periods in cells before being passed into association, a salutary improvement both on disciplinary and sanitary grounds. In connection with the subject of jail administration is that of reclaiming the juvenile criminal. A Reformatory School has been recently sanctioned by the Madras Government. This School will be shortly opened, and it is hoped that the same beneficial effects which have been found to result from the system in England and France may be experienced in India, so that the juvenile criminal may be rescued before he develops into an irreclaimable "jail bird."

There are now in the Madras Presidency 7 Central and 18 District Jails under the control of the Inspector General of Jails, who also exercises supervision over Subsidiary Jails. Central Jails are in charge of special officers, as also are the District Jails of Tanjore and Tinnevelly, which were built a few years ago on the cellular system. All other District Jails are in charge of Civil Surgeons. In

Central Jails are confined prisoners sentenced to rigorous imprisonment for periods exceeding one year; in District Jails those whose sentences do not exceed one year; in Subsidiary Jails those whose sentences do not exceed thirty days. At the close of the year 1885 there were 7,336 prisoners in the Central, District, and Subsidiary Jails of the Presidency.

Her Majesty's clemency was extended to the convicts on the occasion of the celebration of her Jubilee by the release in the Madras Presidency, on the 16th February, of 2,505 males and 175 females, who were thus able to join in the rejoicings of the period. Of those who still remained in Madras Jails 2,167 males and 52 females received partial remission of their sentences in honour of the event.

EDUCATION.

No retrospect of the progress of Madras should fail to record the great achievements in the field of education during Her Majesty's reign. Eleven years before the commencement of that reign Sir Thomas Munro caused an inquiry to be made into the state of education in Southern India, and recorded his views in a minute which gave the first impulse to education in the Presidency. Under his auspices, fourteen Collectorate and eighty-one Taluk Schools were opened in 1826, with a school at Madras for training Teachers. But these schools had to be abolished in 1836, for proved inefficiency. The Madras School for training teachers was converted into the High School, which afterwards developed into the Presidency College. A few Missionary bodies were meanwhile striving against serious difficulties to impart elementary knowledge, chiefly through the medium of the vernacular languages. The only other educational agency in 1837 was the indigenous *Pial* school and *patasala*, in which no attempt was made to train the intellect, but all that was aimed at was to load the memory with a string of words, of which the teacher knew the meaning little better than the pupil.

Between 1837 and 1854, the year of the first great educational despatch, little progress was made. The General Assembly's Institution, started in 1837, gave birth to the present Free Church Institution and Madras Christian College, the Church of Scotland Institution, which only this year has been made a College, and the Free Church Mission Schools at Conjeveram, Nellore, and Chingleput. The Church Missionary Society and the Society for the Propagation of the Gospel commenced those labours which have since provided the Districts of Tanjore, Trichinopoly, Madura, and Tinnevelly, with many excellent Schools and Colleges. The London and the Wesleyan Mission Societies and a few Roman Catholic bodies were doing their share of the good work. Pachaiyappah's Central Institution at Madras was opened in 1842, and the branch schools at Conjeveram and Chidambaram in 1846 and 1850 respectively. The first Director of Public Instruction, Mr. (now Sir Alexander), Arbuthnot, remarked that "at the commencement of the year 1854-55, with the exception of trifling sums expended in the Districts of Chingleput, North Arcot, Nellore, and Tanjore, and on the maintenance of a few elementary schools in the hill tracts of Ganjam, the operations of Government were confined to the Collegiate institution at Madras, and to the two Provincial Schools at Rajahmundry and Cuddalore." The total number of pupils under instruction in 1854 was less than 25,000. The indigenous schools left to shift for themselves diminished in numbers, and, if possible, deteriorated in quality.

The despatch of the Court of Directors of the East India Company of 1854, which is often referred to as the educational charter of India, laid stress, among other things, on the maintenance of the existing Government Colleges and Schools, and, if necessary, the increase of their number; on the establishment of new Middle Schools; on increased attention to Vernacular Schools for elementary education; and on the introduction of a system of grants-in-aid to be administered on the principle of a strict religious neutrality. The first Grant-in-aid Code was issued in 1855. The provisions of this Code being found to be unworkable, a revised Code was issued in 1858, in which the conditions as regards salary grants were definitely prescribed. As no salary grant according to this Code was to exceed one-third of the salary, and as the allotment for expenditure on grants-in-aid was much too small, the aided system received but little impulse. A fresh Code came into force in 1865, and gave a powerful impetus to the development of aided education mainly by its liberal provisions in regard to salary grants, and by the introduction of the system of payment by results. The amount of salary grants rose from Rs. 1,21,272 in 1866-67 to Rs. 2,47,587 in 1870-71, and the total expenditure on grants-in-aid from Rs. 1,21,272 to Rs. 3,64,491. The results system was, however, only partially successful, as the standards prescribed were unduly high, and failure, even in a single subject, was held to disqualify for a grant. A new scheme for results grants was issued in 1868, and the fact that the rules of 1868 were better suited to the needs of the country than the rules of 1865, is proved by the increase in the amount of results grants from Rs. 24,499 in 1868-69 to Rs. 78,176 in 1870-71. The subjoined table shows the progress in general education during the period under review :—

Year.	Government.		Non-Government.		Fee Income.		Gross Expenditure.	
	Schools.	Pupils.	Schools.	Pupils.	Government.	Non-Government.	Government.	Non-Government.
1858-59 ...	222	6,488	327	10,490	Rs. 10,831	Rs. 17,316	Rs. 1,68,348	Rs. 1,85,123
1870-71 ...	129	9,166	2,560	113,650	,, 73,169	,, 2,92,569	,, 2,65,139	,, 10,29,030

The number of Government Colleges rose from 1 to 5, and the number of private Colleges opened during the period was 7. There were nearly eight times as many schools in 1870-71 as in 1858-59; the fee income in 1870-71 was twelve times as much as in 1858-59; and the gross expenditure on education increased almost sixfold. The number of Girls' Schools rose from 39 in 1858-59 to 138 in 1870-71, with an increase in the pupils from 1,885 to 10,185. These schools were entirely under agencies aided by Government, and all that Government directly did to encourage female education was to open a Female Normal School at Madras in 1870. The most noteworthy features in the history of this period are the cordial co-operation of managers of aided institutions with Government in promoting the growth of education of all grades; the marked rise in the fee income, which is an unerring index of a wide and sound appreciation of the value of education; and the efforts made by private bodies to promote female education, which as yet was in its infancy.

The legislative measures bearing on education during the decade 1870-71 to 1880-81, were the Madras Local Funds Act and the Towns' Improvement Act, which were passed in 1871. The former Act provided for the maintenance of elementary schools, either wholly, or by means of grants-in-aid, for the inspection of schools, for the repair of school-houses, and for the training of teachers. A special tax, known as the House Tax, was levied in the "unions" into which the rural parts of the Presidency were divided, and educational expenditure was the first charge on the proceeds of this tax. The Towns' Improvement Act contained similar provisions in regard to towns, with the essential difference of the absence of a special tax, and the existence only of a permission to apply Municipal funds for educational purposes. The house-tax had to be abandoned at the end of the year 1872-73, as it met with considerable opposition; and the expenditure on education was made a first charge on the one-third land-cess also levied under this Act. It was contemplated by this change to secure for educational purposes about eight lakhs and a half of Local Fund revenue. But different Local Boards manifested different degrees of interest in education, and there were instances in which funds, belonging of right to education, were diverted to other important purposes, such as the maintenance of hospitals. The main feature of this Act, as has been well pointed out, is that "it recognises the all-important principle of working through the people in small areas or districts, and that it constitutes in each a Local Board, composed of official and non-official residents, similar in character to those contemplated in the English Education Act 1870, with somewhat similar powers and responsibilities."

In 1873, Government announced its intention to employ for purposes of elementary education some portion of the funds hitherto devoted to higher education, and called upon the Director of Public Instruction to suggest ways and means. That officer proposed that salary grants should be reduced all round. Revised rules for results grants were issued in 1877, which raised the standards and reduced the grants. The salary grant rules now in force were sanctioned towards the close of 1879-80, but came fully into operation only in 1883. The general tendency of these rules was to make the conditions of grant more stringent than formerly. During the decade under review, the amount spent on salary grants was as much as Rs. 2,34,930 in 1873-74, while in 1880-81 it was only Rs. 1,53,705. But, as a set-off against this reduction, the amount of results grants rose from Rs. 92,207 in 1871-72 to Rs. 2,59,366 in 1880-81. The following table indicates the progress made by the several sections of the community during these ten years :—

	1871-72.	1881-82.
Number of Schools	5,[illegible]	[illegible]
Europeans and Eurasians	5,177	5,730
Native Christians	13,048	29,680
Hindus	111,984	268,159
Muhammadans	5,338	22,073
Others	18	2,58[illegible]

The number of schools rose during the ten years by over 150 per cent., and the number of scholars by 142 per cent. The Native Christian and Hindu pupils were more than twice as many at the end of the period as at the beginning of it, and the Muhammadan element had quadrupled. The number of Colleges rose in the period from 12 to 24, and the number of Girls' Schools for primary education from 119 to 500. During these ten years, Government expenditure on its own Colleges rose from Rs. 64,000 to Rs. 1,29,000, and on aided Colleges from Rs. 8,700 to Rs. 13,300. Government expenditure on its own secondary schools rose from Rs. 90,000 to Rs. 1,09,000, while that on aided secondary schools fell from Rs. 1,90,000 to Rs. 92,000. Government primary schools cost Rs. 76,000 in the last year, against Rs. 36,000 in the first, while Government expenditure on aided primary schools rose from Rs. 1,00,000 to Rs. 1,07,000. During the same ten years, the expenditure from Local and Municipal Funds on aided primary schools rose from Rs. 88,000 to Rs. 2,13,000, so that the aid given from "public funds" to primary education amounted in 1880-81 to Rs. 3,20,000. The gross expenditure on education showed a marked increase, rising from Rs. 19,06,000 in 1870-71 to Rs. 31,06,000 in 1880-81. The income from fees in all institutions rose from Rs. 3,83,000 to Rs. 8,23,000. In private institutions the fee receipts rose from Rs. 2,83,000 to Rs. 6,40,000, while the total grants-in-aid from all sources rose from Rs. 3,40,000 to Rs. 4,40,700. Thus the percentage of what is paid from "public funds" to what the pupils themselves pay fell from 120 to nearly 69. This development of self-help deserves attention as affording scope for the further extension of educational operations.

At the end of 1884-85 there were 8 Arts Colleges of the first grade, and 22 of the second grade, or a total of 30 as against 24 in 1880-81. There were besides three Professional Colleges for Law, Engineering, and Medicine respectively. Of the Arts Colleges, 10 were Government institutions, 18 were aided, and 2 unaided institutions. The number of pupils in the Government institutions was 895, as against 1,620 in the aided and unaided institutions. The total expenditure on Government Colleges was Rs. 1,76,326, as against Rs. 1,93,906 on the non-Government Colleges. Government contributed Rs. 1,25,430 to its own Colleges, and Rs. 39,774 to aided Colleges. The fee income in Government Colleges was about 28 per cent. of the gross expenditure on them, while in non-Government Colleges it was 32 per cent. The total number of secondary schools for boys was 596 with 28,724 pupils, and that for girls 166 with 2,648 pupils. The number of primary schools for boys was 14,139 with 565,681 pupils, and that for girls 379 with 30,293 pupils. There were 48 Normal Schools for Masters, 12 for Mistresses, and 14 special and Technical schools, containing 1,155, 366, and 810 students respectively. Of the 15,587 institutions above referred to, 141 were under Departmental management, 1,318 were under Local Boards or Committees, 9,172 were aided institutions, and 4,956 were unaided institutions.

Comparing the total number of pupils with the total population of a school-going age, it appears that 16·6 per cent. of the boys and 2·2 per cent. of the girls were under instruction, or in other words one boy out of every six, and one girl out of every forty-five received instruction. This result can be properly gauged only when it is remembered that the population of a school-going age in the Presidency consists of 2,391,735 boys, and 2,338,541 girls. Taking the statistics in regard to the several leading sections of the community, of the boys and girls of a school-going age, among Native Christians 51 and 52 per cent. respectively were under instruction; among Mahomedans 20 and 1·3 per cent. respectively; among Brahmins 74 and 9 per cent. respectively; among Vaisyas and Sudras 17 and 2 per cent. respectively. The total amount of school fees was Rs. 12,83,000 in 1884-85, *i.e.* about 31 per cent. of the gross expenditure, as against Rs. 8,23,000 in 1880-81. The grants-in-aid from provincial funds rose from Rs. 2,33,000 in 1880-81 to Rs. 3,66,000 in 1884-85, and the total amount of grants from "public funds" from Rs. 4,40,700 to Rs. 7,44,000. The whole amount expended on education was about Rs. 42,01,000. Of this about 10 per cent. was devoted to collegiate education, 66 per cent. to secondary and primary education, 7 per cent. to training and technical schools, and 17 per cent. to direction, inspection, University, buildings, and other charges. Out of the amount spent on education from Provincial funds, 16 per cent. was applied to collegiate education; 39 per cent. to secondary and primary education; 12 per cent. to training and technical schools; 23 per cent. to direction and inspection; and the remaining 10 per cent. was spent on buildings, scholarships, and special grants. Local Fund expenditure on secondary and primary education was 7 and 62 per cent. respectively of the total Local Fund expenditure on public instruction, and 31 and 53 per cent. of Municipal expenditure. These facts show that the bulk of the expenditure on education from Local Funds goes to support primary education, and that Municipalities in towns encourage both secondary and primary education.

It appears from the foregoing summary that the whole educational machinery now at work in the Presidency of Madras came into existence during Her Majesty's reign. At the beginning of this period, there was no School or College in the whole Presidency for imparting sound instruction. At present there are 30 Colleges and 743 Secondary Schools. The Pial schools are making room for Anglo-Vernacular and Vernacular Primary Schools, of which 14,299 exist. The agency required for promoting the spread of education is secured by means of the Training College established recently, and the Normal Schools for Masters and Mistresses in various parts of the country. There has been, year after year, a steady progress in the number of candidates presenting themselves for the several University Examinations. Of the graduates in Arts of the Madras University, over 1,500 are living at the present day, and a good many of these are undoubtedly exercising a beneficial influence on all around them. The steady increase in the number of pupils, and in the revenue from school fees; the interest and ardour evinced by Municipal and Local Boards in taking up the management of secondary and primary schools, and in encouraging the growth of education by means of grants-in-aid; the spirit of self-help and self-reliance which has led to the establishment of Colleges and High Schools in all parts of the country by local bodies and by enterprising individuals; the efforts made by Missionary bodies to combine the most efficient secular instruction possible with the religious instruction which it is their avowed object to impart; the attitude of religious neutrality maintained by Government, and the declared policy of Government to encourage the diffusion and development of education of all grades, are sure pledges of an educational future brighter even than the past.

This sketch cannot be better concluded than by bringing together testimony of high authority in regard to the value of the education given in the Colleges and Schools of the Presidency. Colonel Macdonald, Director of Public Instruction, wrote in 1873:—"Even hostile criticism can hardly deny that, in this Presidency at least, educated Hindus are filling important offices around us in an honourable and creditable manner; that a higher tone is being diffused by them through the public service; that, in integrity and truthfulness, they stand immeasurably above the men of the past generation; that many of them are striving with success to diffuse the blessings of education among their countrymen; and that the number of educated Hindus who can be pointed to as having brought dishonour on the training which they have received is singularly small."

In an address delivered at the Convocation of the Madras University, Mr. Porter, former Principal of the Kumbakonam College, observed that "the earlier pupils of our schools have reached or passed the prime of life, and many of them now hold high posts in all the departments of public life. Among these are men whose names are widely known among their countrymen, and who are honoured where they are known." Of the later pupils he said:—"I believe it is generally admitted that, especially in method and regularity, and I believe also in the tone of morality, the public service has vastly improved."

Sir Charles Turner, late Chief Justice of Madras, summed up the results of the higher education in these words:—"Modern India has proved by examples that are known to, and honoured by, all in this assembly, that her sons can qualify themselves to hold their own with the best of European talent in the Council Chamber, on the bench, at the bar, and in the mart."

His Highness the late Maharajah Rama Varma of Travancore, a highly competent and disinterested judge, stated it as his profound conviction, that "the native portion of the Government service and of the bar has immensely improved during the past forty years." There is no lack of other evidence to the same effect, but this will suffice.

No account of the great and good work done in the field of education in the Presidency of Madras can be complete which omits to pay a tribute of admiration and gratitude to Eyre B. Powell and John Anderson, to Edmund Thompson and Gopala Rao, to William A. Porter and William Miller. The labours of these educationists and others have enabled Madras to stand second to no other part of the Empire of India in general intelligence, in the efficiency and integrity of its public servants, and in a loyal appreciation of, and heart-felt gratitude for, the benefits of British rule.

Mention should also be made of the important assistance rendered to the cause of education by many benevolent ladies who have occupied positions of influence in the Presidency since the educational policy of the Government was formulated. The names of Lady Trevelyan, Lady Denison, Lady Napier, Lady Grant, Lady Hobart, Lady Robinson, Lady Chamberlain, Lady Mary Grenville, Lady Grant Duff, Lady Turner, Lady Connemara, Mrs. Frere, Mrs. Dalrymple, Mrs. Sim, Mrs. Powell, Mrs. Rideout, Mrs. Cornish, Mrs. Carmichael, Miss Gell, Mrs. Firth, Mrs. Donald, and others, are held in high honour in Madras, for they are intimately associated with the development of institutions for the promotion of the moral, intellectual, and physical welfare of the women and children of India.

THE MADRAS UNIVERSITY.

The Madras University dates back only to September 1857; but though not yet thirty years old, it has reached a stage of growth which in many of the older Universities was not reached till they had attained a much greater age. It was preceded by what was called the "University Board" in connection with the Government High School which developed into the Presidency College. The institution of this Board was part of a comprehensive scheme proposed by Lord Elphinstone for the development of education—a scheme which involved the formation of a University of Madras. In fact, the Presidency College, or rather the "High School," was often known as the Madras University, and the old "proficients" of that school still rank as graduates. The University was established, according to the preamble of the Act of Incorporation, "for the better encouragement of Her Majesty's subjects of all classes and denominations within the Presidency of Fort St. George, and other parts of India, in the pursuit of a regular and liberal course of education." This better encouragement was to be given by "ascertaining, by means of examinations, the persons who have acquired proficiency in different branches of Literature, Science, and Art, and of rewarding them by Academical degrees as evidence of their respective attainments, and marks of honour proportioned thereunto." Thus the University was instituted simply as an examining body of the type of the London University, but it differs from the type in one essential feature. The London University concerns itself only with the question "Can the candidates pass this examination?" and asks no questions as to previous education. In Madras, on the other hand, the University demands from all candidates for degrees proof that they have received their education at affiliated institutions. This is a point of great importance, for it not only gives the University a real control of the collegiate education throughout the Presidency, but it also insures that the candidates for degrees are men who have had an opportunity of learning something more than can be picked up from books. Student life has not yet reached a high state of development in India, and perhaps it will be well if some of the sides of student life with which the English student is familiar are never developed; but in the larger colleges there is springing up a feeling of comradeship, and a desire for united action, which is always a hopeful sign.

The first Matriculation Examination was held in September 1857, and the first Degree Examination in the following February. At that time there was no examination between the Matriculation and the B.A. Examination, the First Arts Examination not having been instituted till 1863-64. For some years after its institution the candidates were sent in for the F.A. Examination one year after they had matriculated, and for the B.A. Examination three years after passing the F.A. Examination, but this was soon found to be an unsatisfactory arrangement, and the F.A. Examination was then made to divide the College course into two equal parts as at present.

At the first examination, in 1858, only two candidates received the B.A. degree, both of them from the American Mission Seminary in Jaffna. In the following year the number increased to eight, of whom seven were from the Presidency College, and the other was a private student. In 1860 a Doveton College student made his appearance on the list, and in the following year Kumbakonam College obtained two passes. For a good many years the Presidency and Kumbakonam Colleges sent up almost the whole of the candidates. It was only in 1869 that graduates began to appear in the lists from the Free Church Mission Institution, which now, as the Madras Christian College, takes a prominent place every year. In that year there were 40 graduates, a great increase on previous years. In 1876 the graduates of the University were 11 Masters of Arts, 428 Bachelors of Arts, 3 Masters of Law, 91 Bachelors of Law, 2 Doctors of Medicine, 4 Bachelors of Medicine and Masters in Surgery, 1 Licentiate of Medicine and Surgery, and 12 Bachelors of Civil Engineering. Ten years later, in 1886, the numbers were as follows:—

Degree.	Passed Examinations for Degree.	Graduated.	Graduates Deceased.	Graduates at present on Rolls.
Bachelor of Arts ...	[illegible]	[illegible]	90	[illegible]
Master of Arts ...	40	[illegible]	4	[illegible]
Bachelor of Laws ...	[illegible]	[illegible]	30	[illegible]
Master of Laws ...	[illegible]	9	1	8
Licentiate of Medicine and Surgery ...	[illegible]	[illegible]	1	24
Bachelor of Medicine and Master in Surgery ...	[illegible]	9	1	8
Doctor of Medicine ...	5	5	1	4
Bachelor of Civil Engineering ...	41	36	...	36

The rapid spread of University education through the country is well illustrated by comparing the statistics given in the Syndicate's report for 1874-75 with those for 1885-86. In the former year the number of candidates presenting themselves for the Matriculation, First in Arts, and Bachelor of Arts Examinations were 1,947, 352, and 88 respectively; in the latter year they were 5,892, 1,380, and 485 respectively.

The Senate House, which forms one of the chief architectural ornaments of Madras, was begun in 1874 and completed in 1879, at a cost of Rs. 2,89,729. The Chancellorship of the University is always held by the Governor *ex officio*. The Vice-Chancellor is usually a Judge of the High Court, but there is no absolute rule on this subject. The list of Fellows of the University contains the names of a number of distinguished men who have helped to make the history of Madras during the last thirty years. Of the Fellows named in the Act of Incorporation only one, Mr. J. T. Fowler, is now in Madras; of the others some are dead, while others are enjoying a well-earned rest after a life of earnest work.

The financial condition of the University has greatly improved of late years, for in 1874-75 Government had to pay more than Rs. 11,000 towards the expenses, in addition to the amount received from fees, &c., while in 1885-86 the University was not only self-supporting, but had a balance of over Rs. 19,000 on the year's transactions. Though by no means rich in endowments, the University has at present Rs. 57,300 funded capital for providing prizes and scholarships, and some additions are made almost every year by persons interested in education, so that there is good reason to hope that in this respect, too, the University will soon be able to make a good appearance. With ever-increasing educational facilities, and dealing with an ever-widening range of subjects, the University of Madras should year by year exercise a more powerful influence for good in the Presidency.

TECHNICAL EDUCATION.

Three years prior to Her Majesty's accession, a Government Survey School was established at Fort St. George, with the object of training men for service in the Revenue Department. A quarter of a century later the growing needs of the Public Works Department rendered special training for its subordinates indispensable, and Captain Winscom, of the Madras Engineers, was charged with the task of converting the Survey School into a School of Civil Engineering, the buildings which formed the old Palace of the Carnatic being placed at his disposal for that purpose. In 1859 the students under training as Overseers numbered about fifty. In 1861 a special class was formed to train Draftsmen and Surveyors for the Public Works Department; and in 1862 classes for Engineers were established, which were open to commissioned officers of the Army, as well as to native and other civilians of liberal education. The institution was now known as the Civil Engineering College, and it began to send up candidates for the Examination for the University degree of Bachelor of Civil Engineering as early as 1865. The College, however, conferred its own diplomas and certificates as Assistant-Engineer, Supervisor, Overseer, Draftsman, and Surveyor, on the results of the final Examinations which were held by unpaid independent Examiners. Under the successive administrations of Colonel Carpendale, Major Edgcome, Colonel Rogers, and Captain Love, all of the Royal Engineers, steady progress was made, the number of pupils under instruction usually averaging 150, while a gradual rise in the standard of education was effected. During the last twenty years, the institution has consisted of a Collegiate Branch, educating undergraduates of the Madras, or other Indian Universities, to the standard required for an Assistant-Engineer in the Public Works Department, the course being adapted also to meet the demands of the degree of Bachelor of Civil Engineering conferred by the local University; and a School Branch, training students of all classes for the various grades of the Subordinate Establishment of the Public Works Department. The latter comprises an Overseers' class for the education of European non-commissioned officers and soldiers, and civilians of all races, to the standard required for upper subordinates; a Draftsmen's class; and a Surveyors' class. The courses of study, which extended for each class over a period of two years, were made as practical as possible, and included a considerable amount of work in the field.

In 1880 it was realised that the time had arrived when the Civil Engineering College at Madras should do more than subserve the purposes of a single Government Department, important as that Department undoubtedly is. A Committee was appointed to consider how the institution might be made more generally useful; and it submitted reports in 1881 and 1883, recommending the formation of a class of Mechanical Engineers, and the introduction of a practical training, both in workshops and on works, for students of the Engineers' and Subordinates' classes. It advised also that the period of theoretical study should be increased; that several new subjects should be introduced; and that all examinations should be conducted by a Board of paid Examiners. It was not, however, until 1885 that orders were finally issued reconstituting the College of Engineering on the basis recommended by the Committee. At the present date the remodelling has been only partial. Additional buildings, however, are in progress, and sanction is expected shortly to a substantial increase in the Staff. One appointment to the Engineer establishment of the Public Works Department is now guaranteed annually by Government to the most distinguished student of the Engineer class; and the whole of the subordinate establishment is recruited from the College. The remaining passed men generally find employment as Overseers, Draftsmen, or Surveyors in other Government Departments, in the Railways, and under Local Fund Boards, and Municipalities.

With the view of encouraging advanced instruction in Science and Art in this Presidency, arrangements were made by the Madras Government in 1886 to hold examinations in a great variety of technical subjects. Such of them as are connected with Engineering and with Drawing and Painting may be to some extent taken up by students of the College of Engineering, and of the School of Arts; but, in the absence of a Technical Institute, where instruction can be conveyed, it is unreasonable to expect that the examinations in subjects relating to scientific industries will be largely attended. This want it is now in contemplation to supply by the inauguration in the town of Madras, for the benefit of the whole Presidency, of a Victoria Technical Institute, in commemoration of Her Majesty's Jubilee. Towards this object the public has liberally subscribed.

THE MADRAS OBSERVATORY.

The Madras Observatory, started in 1792, besides being the oldest colonial establishment of the kind, is to this day the only Government astronomical observatory in India. At the commencement of Her Majesty's reign, it was under the charge of Mr. Thomas Glanville Taylor, who had then been engaged for nearly seven years with the necessary observations for a catalogue of 11,015 fixed stars, which was completed in the year 1847. Until very recently this great work remained unsurpassed, as the most extensive of its kind yet accomplished. The observations were taken by native assistants, with a transit instrument and a mural circle, both by Dollond, and the Astronomer's whole time and attention being given to personal superintendence of both observations and calculations, the results, including also numerous positions of the sun, moon, and old planets, were published by Mr. Taylor in seven quarto volumes. A reprint of his *General Catalogue of Fixed Stars* is now called for, as soon as other more pressing duties will permit of its being undertaken.

From 1849 to 1859 the Observatory was under the care of Captain W. S. Jacob, of the Bombay Engineers, who, not contented with mere supervision of ordinary routine work, and finding no instrument in the place adequate for the higher class of research he desired to carry out, privately purchased an excellent 6¼-inch equatorial telescope from Messrs. Lerebours and Secretan of Paris. The numerous measurements of double stars and of the satellites of Saturn made with this instrument would alone have raised Captain Jacob's name to the first rank amongst practical astronomers; but besides making all the observations himself, he subsequently used them for elaborate theoretical investigations, published in the *Memoirs of the Royal Astronomical Society*, after his departure from India. Observations with the old meridian instruments were still carried on by the native assistants, but with less important results than in Mr. Taylor's time, when the Astronomer had little else to attend to. The active superintendence of Major W. K. Worster, Madras Artillery, on repeated occasions between 1853 and 1861, when the permanent Astronomer was absent on leave, or between successive appointments, always gave a fresh impulse to the meridian work, and observations for a catalogue of about 2,200 stars, for the epoch 1855, chiefly due to that able officer, remain on hand, awaiting final reduction and publication. The Observatory was under the direction of Major J. F. Tennant, R.E., during a very troublesome period of instrumental transition, in portions of 1859 and 1860. Hourly magnetical and meteorological observations were recorded at Madras from March 1841 to March 1861; the results of ten years of the former and fifteen years of the latter having been printed, in five quarto volumes, and three more await publication.

The present Astronomer, Mr. N. R. Pogson, took charge in 1861, and speedily initiated a new order of pursuits, till then not attempted at any public Observatory, in England, or any of her colonies. Within three months of his arrival, a minor planet, the 67th of the group revolving in orbits between those of Mars and Jupiter, was found by Mr. Pogson, and being the first discovery of the kind made in this quarter of the globe, was named "Asia." Another planet, found in February 1864, and announced as "Sappho," proved, on calculation of its orbit, to be a re-discovery of "Freia," which had been completely lost, owing to insufficient observations on the occasion of its discovery at Copenhagen in 1862. Another planetary candidate for the name of "Sappho" was provided by Mr. Pogson in May 1864; followed by "Sylvia," in May 1866; "Camilla," in November 1868; and "Vera" in February 1885. A comet, in December 1872, and several new variable or changing stars are also on record as Madras discoveries.

The new line of discovery, commenced in 1861, was not permitted to interfere in any way with the steady routine of stellar observations, ever the first duty at a public Observatory. An excellent meridian circle by Messrs. Troughton and Simms, of London, was supplied early in 1858, but owing to frequent changes of Astronomers it was still unmounted in 1861, and could not be got into efficient working order until May 1862. A carefully selected catalogue of over 5,000 stars was under observation by the native assistants with this instrument up to the end of 1885; the results of which, based upon 52,074 complete observations, are now being published in a series of nine volumes, the first of which is just ready for issue.

A fine new equatorial, with an 8-inch object-glass, was sent out by the same makers at the end of 1865, and was mounted and in use by June of the following year. This, and the smaller equatorial, previously mentioned as procured by Captain W. S. Jacob in 1850, have been in constant use throughout for a variety of pursuits. The planet Mars was under observation for about a month at each of eight oppositions between 1862 and 1879, for investigation of the constant of solar parallax, or, in other words, the determination of the true mean distance of the sun from the earth. Celestial distances are measured by astronomers on two scales. The smaller standard is the earth's equatorial diameter; the larger one, the earth's mean distance from the sun. The labours of the various geodetical surveys furnish the value of the smaller standard in miles, but the relation between the two natural standards is only obtainable by the most refined processes of the astronomer; by means of transits of Venus, which recur in pairs more than a century apart; by Mars in opposition, which can be repeated at intervals of twenty-five months, but to the best advantage at only three oppositions in each successive period of seventeen years; and by other methods of less accuracy.

Telegraphic determinations of the difference of longitude or time between the Madras Observatory and selected stations at Pondicherry, Singapore, Avanashi in Coimbatore, Jaffna and Columbo in Ceylon, Karachi, Muddapur in Bengal, and Roorkee, were made between the years 1869 and 1875, the results of which were published in 1885. Observations of the changes of light of several variable stars and a set of nearly 200 maps of these interesting objects, with approximate catalogues containing upwards of 60,000 star positions reduced to the year 1900, have also been in hand with the equatorials, and are far advanced towards completion. Casual phenomena, such as eclipses of the sun and moon; occultations of planets and fixed stars; Jupiter's satellites; positions of comets and minor planets not observable in Europe; and a few southern double stars, have also received attention. It may be of interest to mention that the Banqueting Hall, Madras, at which their Royal Highnesses, the Duke of Edinburgh and subsequently the Prince of Wales, were entertained, on the occasions of their visits to Madras, was built at the beginning of the century under the superintendence of Mr. J. D. Goldingham, the first Madras Astronomer, who was also Civil Architect to the Honourable East India Company.

FAMINES.

[The following sketch of the history of Famines in the Madras Presidency is taken from the *Madras Manual of the Administration*, compiled under the directions of the Government, by Mr. C. D. Maclean, C.S., Mus.D., 1885.]

Regarding the famines that occurred before British occupation not enough is known to furnish even a correct list of the years of their occurrence. Some of them were due to war rather than to drought; and in all probability some have been altogether forgotten, the object of Indian historians being only to record the fortunes of a dynasty. Even regarding those famines which took place at the end of the last century in territories administered by British officers, the information is too scanty to enable the area or the degree of the calamity to be now defined. In Madras 1781 and 1782 were years of severe scarcity, caused mainly by the devastations of the war with Hyder Aly, but partly also by drought. In 1791 a severe drought afflicted the northern districts of the same Presidency as well as Hyderabad and the southern districts of Bombay, and in 1792 the famine there was intense. It was on this occasion that relief-works were first opened by the Madras Government for the support of those affected by the famine.

In 1802 there was a failure of rain, severe in the Bombay Presidency and in Hyderabad, partial in the northern districts of Madras; this was followed next year by famine in the former case and by scarcity in the latter. In 1806 there was a widespread failure of rain in the Madras Presidency, especially in the Carnatic, and in the parts around Madras, though the northern or Deccan districts were less heavily visited; and during the winter of 1806 and the early part of 1807 the distress caused by this drought became very severe. This was the first occasion on which there is distinct evidence of a fact which, as shown by later and more accurate observation, has characterised all subsequent famines in India. Large crowds of emaciated people, that is to say, flocked into the town of Madras, attracted thither by the existence of a charitable association, and in the expectation of obtaining gratuitous help without any limit. There was much discussion as to the proper measures to be taken by the Government on the occasion of this famine, some advocating the opening of works to give employment to the people close to their homes, others advocating the importation of grain by Government into the interior; the former was done to a certain extent, but the mortality among the cattle prevented the latter course. The Government at first declared against any interference with private trade, but in the end they conceived it necessary to purchase, guaranteeing a minimum price to importers; when the famine came to an end in 1807, large stocks were left on hand under the guarantee and had to be disposed of at a loss. The principle of non-interference with trade previously declared by Madras was followed by the Government of Bombay in 1812-13, when another drought occurred, entailing famine in Guzerat and the adjoining countries. In a subsequent scarcity of 1824-25, which, though not very acute, extended over nearly the whole of Bombay and the north part of the Madras Presidency, the same question arose again. In Madras the Government proclaimed their intention of not interfering directly with trade, but offered a bounty on grain imported from a distance to the distressed locality. On this occasion the drought visited Madras in 1823, Bombay in 1824, and the North-Western Provinces in 1825.

The Madras Presidency was the seat of the next great famine, that of 1833. On this occasion the northern districts suffered most, and especially the Goontoor district, in which the mortality was so terrible that the famine was known as the Goontoor famine. The total population severely affected was about five millions, and the area about 38,000 square miles. On this occasion the Government were taken by surprise, and the severity of the calamity was not recognised till too late. Very little was done to relieve distress except by the distribution of gratuitous food in the towns to which the sufferers from starvation flocked. It was estimated that 200,000 persons died in Goontoor out of a population of 500,000, and it was many years before the falling off of the land revenue was effaced. The adjacent parts of Bombay (that is, the Southern Mahratta country), of Mysore and Hyderabad, also shared in the calamity, though to a less degree. The drought of 1832 in the South was followed by drought in Upper India in 1833, which produced scarcity but not famine in the North-Western Provinces.

In 1854 a famine, severe, though limited in area, visited the northern part of the Madras Presidency; but its intensity was confined to the Bellary district, and the south part of Hyderabad, an area of about 30,000 square miles, with a population of about three millions. The rainfall of 1852 had been light, and that of 1853 was extremely deficient. The harvest was reckoned at only half an average crop. Relief was administered only by means of public works; but abundant employment was thus given; so much so that crowds of applicants flocked in from the Nizam's dominions, and for about nine months more than 50,000 people obtained relief on the works. The supervision was at first exercised by civil officers and was very lax; but by degrees it was brought under the charge of an engineer, with special officers under him, and the discipline and outturn of work improved, while the wage, which had been fixed too high, was cut down to a minimum rate. The total expenditure on these works was about Rs. 12,28,000. When the famine was brought to a close by a plentiful rainfall in the autumn of 1854, followed by a fair harvest, a valuation was made of the work done, and it was found to be worth about 38 per cent. of the money expended on it. The loss of land revenue and other income amounted to 42 lakhs of rupees, including the decrease in the receipts during the next two years, which was due chiefly to the loss of cattle and the consequent inability of the people to plough the land. It was estimated that in the worst part of Bellary four-fifths of the village cattle had died. Nothing definite is known as to the mortality among the inhabitants; but a census taken in 1856-57, in the imperfect form in use at the time, seemed to show that the usual rate of the growth of the population had received a serious check.

The drought of 1865 was felt along the whole eastern coast of India from Madras upwards; and it extended to some distance inland, visiting Mysore, the districts of Madras above the Eastern Ghauts, Hyderabad, the hill country in the south-west of Bengal, and Behar; but it was most intense along the coast in the districts of Ganjam and Orissa. The area severely affected in Madras was about 43,000 square miles, with a population of about six millions. The Government had now become familiar with the warnings of famine and the steps necessary to meet it, and were prepared to initiate the usual machinery of relief-works, relief-houses, and public subscriptions. But the distress was not very pronounced, and in all probability would have passed off with little notice had not the rainfall of the following year also, 1866, been so late as to cause general alarm, and so insufficient as to produce a very inferior crop. It was not till June or July that the need of relief became pressing, and works were then opened in considerable numbers, under civil officers. Prices rose to an extraordinary height, 10 and 12 lb. per rupee for rice being not uncommon, while coarse millets sold at 12 to 15 lb. per rupee; and the sufferings of the people of Ganjam and Bellary were severe. Still, in spite of unusually high wages and the absence of task-work, the numbers employed on relief-works were never large and averaged only 12,000 daily for fifteen months. Gratuitous relief was given to 31,000 persons daily for sixteen months, mainly in the form of cooked food and in relief-houses, managed to a large extent on the system introduced by Sir John Strachey and made known by Colonel Baird Smith's report. In Ganjam alone was there evinced any extreme dislike to this form of relief, and there only by the ryots and more respectable classes, to whom uncooked food was accordingly given. The prolongation of distress, due to the second failure of rain, caused the relief operations to last on till the next monsoon set in, in June 1867; the entire expenditure amounting to about 12 lakhs of rupees, of which two were contributed by the public and the rest fell on the Government. Not much is known as to the mortality; but the prolonged duration of high prices must have told severely on the population; and there are indications that the number of deaths in the last six months of 1866 increased by about 450,000, or was double the usual average.

The great famine in Southern India, of 1876-78, was in respect of the area and population affected, and the duration and intensity of the distress, the most important calamity of its kind experienced in British India since the beginning of the century. The failure of the summer rains of 1876 extended over about half of the Madras Presidency, the distress being most intense in the same tract, or that lying above the Eastern Ghauts, which suffered in 1833 and in 1854. The scarcity was felt with great severity over the whole of Mysore (except the hilly tracts that lie along the Western Ghauts), the southern half of the Hyderabad State, and all the Deccan districts of the Bombay Presidency. The area thus affected was about 200,000 square miles containing a population of 36,000,000. Like most widespread famines, this famine was caused by drought, but not by the drought of a single season or of a single year. The harvests of 1875 had been indifferent, especially in the Ceded Districts. In 1876, the south-west monsoon, or summer rains, on which the northern districts are largely dependent, proved very deficient; and the north-east monsoon or autumn rains, on which the southern and eastern districts almost entirely rely for their cultivation, failed still more completely. Except in the deltas of the Godavery and Kistna, the total rainfall of that year scarcely anywhere exceeded ten inches, as compared with an average of about thirty. When the monsoon failed in October, 1876, it was recognised that a twelve-months' famine was at hand, and inevitable. In 1877, the south-west monsoon failed a second time, and the distress was gradually intensified throughout that year. Relief was not obtained until November, 1877, when the north-east monsoon at last gave a sufficient rain-supply, and the crops of the coming season were assured. The area in Madras seriously affected by famine was estimated at 74,000 square miles, and a population of 16,000,000 persons. No districts entirely escaped between the Kistna river and Cape Comorin; but the distress was most severe in the tract immediately south of the Toongabudra, including the districts of Bellary, Kurnool, Cuddapah, and Nellore, and farther south in North Arcot and Salem. Mysore also suffered exceptionally.

It was found after a while that no adequate stores of food remained in the country, and but for the efforts of Government, and the vast imports of food brought into the country by the European mercantile houses from Bengal, Burmah, and the East, a much greater proportion of the population would have perished than actually occurred. During the eighteen months ending January 1878, the total amount of grain imported into Madras by sea was nearly 700,000 tons. The difficulty remained however of bringing these stores of food to the people, and this was with much labour and some delay effected by means of the railways, especially the Madras Railway,

The total amount of grain distributed in the interior by these lines between August 1876 and November 1877 was 724,339 tons, yielding a freight of Rs. 55,36,950. It will never be possible to obtain a complete record of the loss of life caused directly and indirectly by this great calamity, but probably nearly four millions of persons perished in that manner. In some large tracts of country half the population temporarily disappeared. In the famine area 21·8 per mille of population were entered in the recent census as having died under the general heading of "other causes," while in the non-famine area only 8·5 per mille were so entered. The following detailed statistics, though imperfect, will give a general conception of the character of the calamity, and the means adopted to alleviate it. In Bellary district one-third of the inhabitants were in receipt of relief, and one-half of the land fell temporarily out of cultivation. In one week of September 1877, a grand total of 2,341,692 persons received Government relief, of whom 708,055 were employed on works, and the rest were relieved gratuitously. The mortality in Madras City during the year 1877 was at the rate of 116·7 per thousand. At one relief camp in Salem district, during May 1877, 746 persons died out of an average strength of 7,000. The expenditure in Madras Presidency on account of famine during the two years ending March 1878 is officially estimated at about 624½ lakhs, to which must be added loss of revenue, about 191 lakhs, the total expenditure thus being about 815½ lakhs. The amount subscribed by private charity, chiefly at the London Mansion House, for the whole famine area reached a total of £820,000, the greater portion of which reached Madras. This sum was distributed through the agency of local committees, principally in providing seed grain, plough cattle, and other permanent necessaries of living, and in supporting those who for various reasons lay beyond the reach of Government relief. The fund was managed by a central committee at Madras. Favourable rains in September 1877 led to a rapid decline in the number of persons dependent on State relief, and this diminution steadily continued during the next three months. In January 1878 however prices began again to rise, and towards the beginning of March fresh works had to be started in Bellary and North Arcot. Relief operations may be said to have been finally brought to a close in October 1878.

THE ANGLICAN CHURCH.

A review dealing with the work and progress of the Anglican Branch of the Catholic Church in the Madras Presidency during the past fifty years divides itself under two heads:—the Church, in its ministrations to the European population; and the Church in its Missionary character towards the people of the land. It was within the limits of the future diocese of Madras that the East India Company first established itself in 1620; but for sixty years there was no visible token that the British settlers had any religion at all; and it was not until 1680 that the first building in India for Divine worship, according to the rites of the Anglo-Catholic Church, was opened in Fort St. George. In one of the earliest charters of the "English Company trading to the East Indies," bearing date the 5th September 1698, this provision was made:—"And we do hereby will and appoint, that the said Company hereby establish, and their successors shall constantly maintain, a minister and schoolmaster in every garrison and superior factory, which the same Company or their successors shall have in the East Indies, or other parts within the limits aforesaid; and shall also in such garrisons and factories respectively provide, or set apart, a decent and convenient place for Divine service only." Nor was the old Company altogether unmindful of the religious welfare of its native servants, as the charter goes on to say:—"And we do further will and appoint that all such Ministers as shall be sent to reside in India, as aforesaid, shall be obliged to learn, within one year after their arrival, the Portuguese language, and shall apply themselves to learn the native language of the country where they shall reside, the better to enable them to instruct the Gentoos that shall be the servants or slaves of the same Company, or of their agents, in the Protestant religion." The supply of Ministers, or Chaplains, in the early days, seems to have been proportioned to the wants of the several garrisons or factories, and the Chaplains so appointed were placed on a footing with the Military Officers of the Company's service. In 1836 the number of Chaplains sanctioned was 23. In 1854, 35 regular Chaplains were allowed, and a provision was made for supernumeraries if required, while four years later the number was increased to 40, which number remains unaltered to the present date.

The history of the last fifty years is almost the history of the Episcopate in the Diocese of Madras. It was but two years before the accession of the Queen Empress that the Anglican establishment in India was strengthened by the division of the vast Diocese of Calcutta. That diocese then included Ceylon, all British subjects within the limits of the East India Company, and in islands north of the equator, and all places between the Cape of Good Hope and Magellan's Straits, New South Wales, and its dependencies—an area which since then has been subdivided into thirty Bishoprics. In 1835 the Presidency of Madras, with the Island of Ceylon, was constituted a Bishop's See; and, on June 14th, the Venerable Daniel Corrie, then Archdeacon of Calcutta, was consecrated first Bishop of Madras. His Episcopate was but a short one; for he landed in Madras on the 24th of October, 1835, and died on the 5th of February 1837. The friend of Henry Martyn, Thomason, Brown, and Buchanan, himself eminent among the Chaplains of the East India Company for his missionary zeal, his career if short, was useful, and the beautiful marble statue by Weekes to his memory in St. George's Cathedral, Madras, as well as the Grammar School in Black Town, Madras, which bears his name, are testimonies to the affectionate regard in which he was held by all classes. On the 20th of June, 1837, the See of Madras was vacant, but in the records of the Archdeaconry, there is the acknowledgment of a loyal Address from the Archdeacon and clergy of Madras on the occasion of Her Majesty's Accession to the Throne, which Address was very graciously received by Her Majesty. Bishop Corrie's successor was the Right Rev. J. G. T. Spencer, D.D., consecrated 19th of November, 1837, but apparently not installed until the 4th of November, 1838. Soon after his arrival he made a visitation tour on the Malabar coast, including also Travancore and Tinnevelly. This was the first regular visit the Missions there had ever received from a Bishop. In his charge, delivered at Palamcottah on January 13th, 1841, to the Missionary Clergy of the Church of England, he remarked, "The country is not yet ready for a native Ministry, the hope and object of every Christian friend of India." (At the present date there are 142 native clergymen in the Diocese of Madras.) He resigned in 1849, and was succeeded by the Right Rev. Thomas Dealtry, D.D., who was consecrated at Lambeth 2nd December, 1849, installed at Madras 2nd February, 1850, and died at Madras on the 6th March, 1861. He was followed by the Right Rev. Frederick Gell, D.D., consecrated 29th June, 1861, and installed at Madras 27th November, 1861. Bishop Gell is the present occupant of the See of Madras, and his Bishopric covers more than half the period under review.

The founding of the Bishopric of Madras not only stirred up interest in Church work, but was instrumental in starting new agencies and institutions. In 1848 two Societies were founded, which have done, and continue to do, good work in the Diocese. About the year 1845 a Society was set on foot by the Chaplain of St. Matthias' Vepery, on the basis of the Pastoral Aid Society in England, to meet the spiritual wants of the Europeans and English-speaking people throughout the Presidency, not provided for by the Establishment. At this time the Chaplains were few, and their work was confined to the Government centres, whilst the Missionaries were almost exclusively engaged in evangelising the native population. To meet these spiritual wants the Madras Additional Clergy Society and the Madras Diocesan Church Building Society were called into existence. To the latter may be attributed some of the best specimens of ecclesiastical architecture in the Diocese, and an impetus that was given to Church building in general. There are few stations at the present date which do not possess either new or restored churches in some measure worthy of their purpose.

In 1837 there were only six churches belonging to the Anglican Church, in the town of Madras; they now number thirteen. Of the new churches built within the last fifty years in the Presidency it may be sufficient to mention, Bolarum, Trimulgherry, Chudderghat, Waltair, Rajahmundry, Dowlaishweram, Cocanada, Berhampore, Nellore, Kurnool, Cuddapah, Chittoor, Mysore, Madura, three in Bangalore, Coimbatore, Salem, Yercaud, Coonoor, two at Ootacamund, Kotagherry, besides the seven already mentioned in the City of Madras, the last of all being a new church at Wellington.

The work of the Additional Clergy Society has been to supplement the work of the Government Establishment. Closely connected with this work has been that of the Colonial and Continental Church Society. In communication with the Vepery Pastoral Aid Society, and with the cordial support of the Bishop and clergy, the Society commenced work in 1850 by sending a lay agent to help the Chaplain of Vepery, and a clergyman to meet the wants of the large District around Chintadripetta and Mount Road. Christ Church was built in 1852 under the Committee's auspices, and was opened on the 1st of January, 1853. The presentation was secured to the Colonial and Continental Church Society. In 1861 the Madras Additional Clergy Society and the Colonial and Continental Society were amalgamated, and until 1867 the following stations were aided with clerical or lay help:—Christ Church, Madras, John Periera's, St. Matthias' Vepery, Fort St. George, Pulicat under St. George's Cathedral, Bangalore Fort, Cochin, Shevaroy Hills, Cannanore, Wynaad, Nellore, and Kurnool. Since then the Committee has been gradually relieved of its responsibility, and at the present time the only stations worked in connection with it are Madras and Cochin, the Home Society contributing an annual grant of Rs. 4,000, and providing outfits and passage for the clergy sent to supply those places. The Additional Clergy Society was resuscitated in 1873, and has at the present time a clergyman in the Wynaad, and at Madura, and hopes shortly to place one at Nellore. The liberality of the shareholders of the Madras Railway Company enables the Bishop to employ three Chaplains whose duty it is to travel over the principal lines, and devote the whole of their time to the spiritual wants of the employés of the Company. Besides these Chaplains, either on the regular establishment, or provided by Local or Home Funds, Government grants-in-aid provide for clergymen at the following stations, who, in addition to their own regular duties, give English services to those who require them:—St. Thome Madras, Tranquebar, Negapatam, Tanjore, St. Thomas' Ootacamund (for six months in the year), Fort Church, Bangalore, and Tuticorin. The clergy ministering to European congregations have more than doubled in number in the fifty years. Well-fitted Churches are now found in numbers of stations where there were none in 1837, as well as Asylums, Orphanages, Schools, Temperance Societies, Guilds, and Associations. Church machinery which had no existence in 1837 is now actively at work, and shows that the progress, which is the most distinguishing mark of the reign of Her Majesty, has extended to Church work in the Diocese of Madras.

THE GOSPEL PROPAGATION SOCIETY.

In the year 1826 the Missions in the Madras Presidency previously connected with the Society for Promoting Christian Knowledge were transferred to the care of the Society for the Propagation of the Gospel, though the former Society did not cease to contribute to their support. In 1836 there were seven stations occupied by the latter Society in Madras Presidency, viz., Vepery and its vicinity, Cuddalore, Negapatam, Tanjore, Trichinopoly, Tinnevelly, and Bangalore. The number of persons belonging to the congregations was 11,743, and the number of children in the schools was 3,258. In the same year the Presidency was constituted a separate diocese, and from that period a progressive improvement commenced. Greater vigour was thrown into the operations of the Society, the Missionary Districts were subdivided and more effectual superintendence was effected. In 1842, the revision of the Tamil Prayer Book was commenced; and it was completed in about four years. In 1844 there were 50 stations occupied, exclusive of Tinnevelly, comprising 180 villages, and 18 Missionaries; but in 1851 several places were given up by the Society leaving the following places on their list:—Vepery, with its Missionary Institution and its Grammar School; St. Thomé; Vulliveram; Cuddalore; Bangalore; Secunderabad; Tanjore; Budalur; Canendagudy; Aneycada; Vediarpuram, with its Seminary; Combaconum; Erungalore; Trichinopoly; and Madura.

The Missions of the Society are now arranged into three Divisions:—*First Division*:—Tinnevelly and Ramnad. *Second Division*:—Trichinopoly, Erungalore, Ariyalur, Salem, Tanjore, Vediarpuram, Combaconum, Canendagudy, Aneicada, Negapatam, Nangoor and Tranquebar. *Third Division*: Mutyalpad, Kalsapad, Kurnool and Nandial; Secunderabad; Bangalore and Oossoor; Madras comprising Vepery, Egmore and St. Thomé, and Cuddalore. The First Division will be treated of in another page. In the Second Division there are now fifteen Native clergy, and 5,367 Christians, of whom 2,709 are communicants. In the Third Division there are five Native clergy, and 7,904 Christians, of whom 3,000 are communicants, besides 2,428 catechumens. Besides this geographical distribution of Missions into three divisions, they may also be financially classified as follows:—Missions which have no appropriate funds of their own are wholly dependent on the general fund, and upon local or other contributions; Missions, Seminaries and Schools which, while they have some income of their own, require to be supplemented from the general fund, upon which they are partially dependent; and Missions which are supported entirely by their own funds. The Native Church is learning to become more self-supporting, and is promising in time to become entirely independent of help from England. The Erungalore Mission, which was commenced in 1830, and was formed into a distinct mission in 1843, is an offshoot of the old Mission established in that town by the venerable Dr. Swartz in 1766.

For fourteen years the Rev. Dr. H. Bower was returned in the Society's reports as "unattached," his services having been transferred to the Madras Auxiliary Bible Society for the revision of the Tamil Bible. This work occupied his whole time and attention for thirteen years. The work which was commenced in March 1858 was completed in April 1871; and Dr. Bower's services were then engaged for the revision of the Tamil Prayer Book. He was afterwards appointed to the Trichinopoly Mission, where a good deal of his time was spent in editing the Prayer Book. After leaving Trichinopoly he took up work first in Tinnevelly, and afterwards in Madras, and died in 1885. At Trichinopoly and Erungalore the Society has Boys' and Girls' Boarding Schools, besides numerous other schools. The Tanjore Mission, which at one time was in a very flourishing condition, having four European clergy, five Native clergy, and one European layman working in different districts at the same time, unfortunately became gradually weaker. Of late, however, the Mission has been placed on a much more satisfactory footing, and there are now five Native clergy, including one at Nangoor. The Vediarpuram Seminary was closed in 1875, and the scholarships and grants attached to it were transferred a few years later to a Training Institution at Tanjore. The Cuddalore Mission dates far back, the oldest tombstone in Old Town being dated 1683. The Mission has had much property bequeathed to it. The Bangalore Mission is mainly a Native Pastorate with an out-station at Oossoor. Salem is also a Native Pastorate.

The Telugu Missions of the Society commenced about thirty-three years ago. The pioneers of the Mission gave all their time to preaching and conversing with enquirers, to teaching the congregations, to building schoolrooms and prayer houses. A Boarding School was soon started at Mutyalpad, in which young men are trained to be Teachers and Schoolmasters. The Badvel valley is now occupied by the Kalsapad Mission. This valley is separated from the plain in which Mutyalpad lies by extensive ranges of lofty hills, and by jungle some thirty miles broad, abounding in tiger and cheeta. The work has been very successful in this valley, and specially in the Cumbum

Taluk. Where in 1861 there were but four congregations and about 300 recent converts, there are now 49 congregations and 3,066 converts, of whom 1,572 are baptised, and the rest catechumens. It has its Boarding School for training Native Teachers. At Nandial the S.P.G. have just opened a Training Institution for Native Teachers, of whom it is hoped some will in time enter the Ministry.

St. Thomas' Mission at Secunderabad was first opened by the S.P.G. in 1842. There are four principal stations, viz., Secunderabad, Chudderghaut, Bolarum, and Trimulgherry, Secunderabad being the head station of the Mission. The difficulties of the work in this Mission are much greater than elsewhere owing to the different languages spoken by the people. It is quite a common thing to find boys in one school speaking Hindustani, Telugu, Tamil and a little English.

In the town of Madras there are now three Districts:—St. Paul's, Vepery; St John's, Egmore; and St. Thomé. The Vepery Mission is partly supported by the Gericke Fund, being the interest upon a sum of Rs. 77,500 left by the Rev. Mr. Gericke for the benefit of the Vepery Mission, and the Negapatam Mission. A Boarding School, bearing the name of the Gericke's Hostel, is occupied by thirty boys, most of whom are students at the Vepery High School; and every year several applications have to be refused for want of accommodation. The Vepery Mission Auxiliary Association, of which one object is to meet the spiritual and temporal wants of the mission and congregation, has been in existence for thirty-eight years, and has greatly helped in the working of the mission. The educational institutions of the S.P.G. are the Tanjore College, the Trichinopoly College, the Vepery High School, and the Nandial Training Institution. The Vepery High School was commenced on the 25th January 1864. In June 1880 the Tanjore High School was raised to the position of a first class College, and a B.A. class was opened the following month. The Trichinopoly High School was founded in 1863, and raised to a second grade College 1865. For twenty years it continued to be the only Institution in Trichinopoly affording instruction to this standard under European management. The College was raised to the first grade in 1883. All three Institutions have been working very successfully, one of them at a very small cost to the Society, and one has been self-supporting.

The Bishop of Madras is the President of the Madras Diocesan Committee, and the Archdeacon and Bishop Caldwell are the Vice-Presidents. The Secretaries to the Committee during the last fifty years have been the Rev. A. R. Symonds, the Rev. H. Jermyn, the Rev. J. M. Strachan (now Bishop of Rangoon), the Rev. G. Billing, now Secretary in Calcutta, and the Rev. W. Relton, the present holder of the office. Several Acting Secretaries have held office during different vacancies.

THE CHURCH MISSIONARY SOCIETY.

The progress of the Society's work in Southern India has been great during the last fifty years. One entire new Mission—that to the Telugus—has been formed, and in all the older Missions the work has gradually extended, while within the last few years a much sounder system of organisation has been introduced, giving power to, and placing responsibility on the more advanced Christian congregations. Indeed the chief feature of the Mission in Madras (which dates from 1814) is the fact that, with the exception of the Mohammedan Mission, the work is now wholly carried on by Native Christians. The Madras C.M.S. Native Church Council, of which the Rev. W. T. Satthianadhan, B.D., is the Chairman, administers the affairs of the Tamil Mission in Madras, St. Thomas' Mount, Palaveram, Pulicat, and Poonamallee. The grant-in-aid received from the Society is annually reduced, and the Council is thus on the way to become entirely independent of foreign aid. It consequently forms the nearest approach yet made in any Missions connected with the Anglican Church in South India, to a National Native Church of India. In the year 1856, the Harris School was opened by the Mission, in Madras, and, though for many years it had to struggle against prejudice, it is now a popular School amongst Mohammedans. Fifty years ago there were no

Native Clergymen in this Mission; the Agents numbered 16; the Native Christians 200; the Schools 16, and the Scholars 892. Now there are 5 Native Clergymen; 88 Agents; 1,748 Native Christians; 37 Schools; and 1,452 Scholars. Mrs. Satthianadham, and the wives of the other Pastors occupy their time in Zenana visiting, and in this way thousands of girls and women are taught in schools, and in their houses.

The work of the Society in Travancore commenced in 1816. The object of the Mission was to benefit the Syrian Church, not by interfering with its liberty to ordain rites and ceremonies, but to enable it to reform abuses, and to abolish superstitious practices. Colonel Munro, the British Resident at Trevandrum, took a great interest in this movement, and the present College at Cottayam largely owes its endowment to his influence. For a time the plan proposed worked well, but in 1837, the year of Her Majesty's Accession, it was found necessary to change the policy hitherto pursued, and from that time the Mission has acted independently of the Syrian Church. No attempt is made to withdraw Syrians from their own ancient Church, but if any prefer to join the Anglican communion they are received. Some thousands of Syrians have thus joined the Mission, and a considerable number have been ordained by Anglican Bishops. This has happened without any weakening of friendly feeling between the Syrians and the Missionaries. In fact, there is more cordiality now that each body works independently than when there was an attempt at co-operation. One effect of the work of the Mission has been to encourage a small reforming party in the Syrian Church itself, but of late years this party has lost rather than gained ground.

The principal station of the Travancore Mission is Cottayam, a place in a beautiful situation, where there are a College, a Divinity School, a Mission Press, and Girls' Schools. Alleppie is the oldest Mission Station, and the latest addition to the work carried on there is a Mission to the Lepers. It is proposed to erect a Hospital for them in connection with it. The Maharajah of Travancore has made a large donation to it. The late Rev. Henry Baker, a son of one of three Missionaries who arrived about sixty years ago, met with great success amongst the Aryans, a tribe living on the slopes of the western ghauts. The lower classes had been, from time immemorial, much oppressed in Travancore. Their condition is now much ameliorated. This is partly due to the influence of the Mission. In the adjoining State of Cochin, Trichur and Kunankulam are the chief Mission Stations. From the commencement of the Mission the Bishop of Madras exercised episcopal jurisdiction over the Mission in the two States of Travancore and Cochin; but in 1879 the Rev. J. M. Speechly was consecrated the first Bishop of the Anglican Church in Travancore and Cochin. In 1885, the Rev K. Koshi and the Rev. J. Caley were appointed Archdeacons of the new Diocese. Fifty years ago there were in this Mission 6 European Missionaries, no Native Clergymen; 63 Native Agents; no Converts; 54 Schools; and 1,836 Scholars. Now there are 8 European Missionaries; 19 Native Clergymen; 148 Agents; 19,744 Christians and Catechumens; 131 Schools; 3,837 Scholars. There, as in other parts of the Society's Missions in South India, the system of Church Councils has been introduced, and the congregations are being trained to see the obligation they are under to support their own native pastors.

The Telugu Mission of the Society was commenced in 1841. It was the ardent wish of Dr. Corrie, first Bishop of Madras, to see some mission work amongst the Telugus, but he died in 1836 before anything could be done. Others, however, took up the cause, and a sum of £2,000 was raised by Civil and Military officers for the purpose of founding a Mission School in Masulipatam. In 1841, the Rev. T. T. Noble, of Cambridge, and the Rev. H. W. Fox, of Oxford, arrived. The former at once opened the school now well known as the Noble College, the other devoted himself to evangelistic work amongst the people. Mr. Fox remained in the Mission only three or four years, and, returning home, died in 1848. He was a Rugby boy, and the present Bishop of Madras, also a Rugbean, started the Rugby-Fox Memorial Fund, subscribers to which are present and old Rugby boys. This Fund supports a Vice-Principal, called the Rugby-Fox Master. A Missionary sermon in connection with it is preached annually in Rugby School Chapel, and Rugby boys contribute to the funds of the games and sports club in the Noble College. A considerable number of Brahmins have, through the instruction received in the Noble College, become Christians, and several of them are now ordained Missionaries. The late Rev. M. Ratnam was one of the most prominent of these. He was baptised in 1852, ordained in 1864, and died in 1886, after a most useful and exemplary life. Before he became a convert, he invited a lady, Mrs. Darling, to teach his wife. This was the first attempt at Zenana work in the locality, and for years after nothing more could be done. Now there is a large number of Caste Girls' Schools in Masulipatam, and the difficulty is not to get pupils but teachers. Masulipatam is a principal station of the Church of England Zenana Mission, and last year some 2,900 Hindu ladies and girls received instruction there. There are also a Training Institution for Agents and Schoolmasters, and an excellent Boarding School for Girls—the Sharkey Memorial School—which owes its present high position to the labours of Mrs. Padfield. A convert from Islam, the Rev. Jani Ali, after a successful career at Cambridge, is now engaged in a Mission to Mohammedans in Calcutta. The Principals of the Noble College have been the Revs. R. T. Noble, J. Sharp, E. N. Hodges, and C. W. A. Clarke, the present incumbent. Of the Rugby-Fox Masters, the Rev. A. W. Poole was afterwards consecrated a Bishop in Japan. The Rev. W. G. Peel is the present Master.

The Telugu Mission has hitherto been confined to the Kistna and Godavery Collectorates, though within the last year or two some stations in the Nizam's Dominions have been formed. Arrangements are being made to occupy Kummamett as the centre of a new Mission District. In 1857, the Rev. W. F. N. Alexander, Trinity College, Dublin, arrived. His work has been in Ellore, a station opened in 1854. He still remains at his post, as vigorous as ever. In that District alone there are now 1,457 Christians, and 638 catechumens. The Bishop of Madras in his recent tour confirmed 290 persons in this district alone. Two large churches, and numerous school buildings, bear witness to Mr. Alexander's practical skill and foresight. The Mission in Bezwada was commenced in 1858. There is a good High School there, from which several Brahmin converts have been made. Connected with this Mission is that of the Raghavapuram district, formed in 1871. Progress here has been rapid. There are now 1,448 converts; and when the present catechumens have, after due instruction, been baptised, there will be more than 2,000. The Rev. J. Stone was the Missionary here for many years. He erected a large and handsome stone church in the village of Raghavapuram, capable of holding six or seven hundred people. The Dummagudem Mission was commenced in 1861. Sir Arthur Cotton, when engaged on the Godavery irrigation works, urged the Society to do something for the Kois, a branch of the Gond tribe. Before the Society could act, Captain (now Major-General) Haig, R.E., had employed his spare time in teaching all who cared to learn about the Christian religion. A young Kshatriya, employed in the Commissariat Department, became a convert, and was baptised in 1860. The Mission was soon afterwards commenced, and Razu, the convert referred to, joined in 1863, was ordained in 1872, and is still the resident pastor of the native church in Dummagudem. The place is unhealthy, but the Rev. J. Cain has been able to reside there many years, and makes long tours, accompanied by Mrs. Cain, into the interior, where the Kois principally reside. Mrs. Cain is proficient in the Koi language, and being also clever at medicine, has obtained remarkable influence among the Koi women. The Church of England Zenana Mission has also established a Medical Mission at Dummagudem. Forty-six years ago this Mission was founded, and so recently as 1851 there were in it no Native Clergymen. Then the Agents numbered 13; the native Christians and Catechumens, 60; the Schools 3, and the Scholars 126. Now there are 6 Native Clergymen; 179 Agents; 7,843 Christians and Catechumens; 133 Schools; and 3,160 Scholars. In a recent tour, the Bishop of Madras confirmed no less than 941 persons in the Mission. In each District, a Church Council, composed of native clergy and laity, has been formed. Each of these bodies has certain administrative functions committed to it, and is to a large extent responsible for the financial working of the Mission in its own district. The grant-in-aid given by the Society for pastoral work is slowly decreasing, thus evoking a spirit of self-reliance, evangelistic ardour, and administrative skill, amongst a small but rising church which had no existence forty years ago.

The work of the Society in the District of Tinnevelly is referred to on another page.

It is only within the last twenty years that much progress in the direction of educating Hindu or Musalmani girls in Zenanas has been made. The youngest of all the Societies engaged in this work in Southern India is that known as the Church of England Zenana Mission. It works in connection with the Church Missionary Society. It is now in the seventh year of its existence, and has at work in India 77 lady missionaries, with 48 Eurasian and European assistants, and 349 Bible-women and teachers. Of this body there are at work in South India no less than 22 English ladies, several of whom are honorary workers, 13 assistants, and 147 Bible-women and teachers. The following are the chief stations:—Dummagudem, Ellore, Bezwada, Masulipatam, Madras, Ootacamund, Trichnor, Trevandrum, Palamcottah, and North Tinnevelly. Aid is also given to work carried on by voluntary helpers at Jaggapett, Amalapur, Ponamallee, and Cottayam. Bangalore or Mysore will soon be occupied as a new station. The latest returns show that 1,093 houses are regularly visited, and that there are 60 schools with 2,845 pupils. The income of the Society in England is £25,000, of which about £5,000 is spent in the Diocese of Madras. The sum of £4,500 raised in the Missions themselves is a good evidence of the appreciation that residents in India have of the work done. The Bishop of Madras is the President of the Local Committee, and the Archdeacon the Vice-President. The Rev. H. Arden, M.A., was the first Secretary, and has been succeeded by the Rev. E. Sell, B.D.

The following Missionaries have acted as Secretaries to the Church Missionary Society in Madras, during the last fifty years:—The Rev. J. Tucker, B.D.; T. G. Ragland, B.D.; J. Mondy, B.A.; W. Knight, M.A.; and P. S. Royston, M.A. (now Bishop of Mauritius); Mr. T. J. Ford, now Chief Justice of Singapore; the Revs. W. Gray, M.A.; J. Barton, M.A.; D. J. Barry, B.A.; D. Fenn, M.A.; A. J. Harden, M.A.; and E. Sell, B.D., the present holder of the office.

MISSIONS IN TINNEVELLY.

The S.P.G. Mission in Tinnevelly may be said to date from 1870, when the Mission, already commenced by Swartz, the most memorable name in the history of the Protestant Missions in Southern India, took an organized shape by the formation of a small congregation, at Palamcotta under Swartz's superintendence. He was followed by Jaenicke, Rosen, and Irion, German Missionaries, then by Caemmerer, who had been educated at Bishop's College, Calcutta. He was a man of much energy, and has left his mark in Tinnevelly. There is a brief statement on record of the strength of the Tinnevelly Mission in 1837: baptised members of congregations 4,352, children in schools 269. The number of girls in the schools was only 6. That was a day of very small things. There are at present, in connection with the same Mission, 566 congregations; members of congregations 39,577, of whom 23,656 are baptised, the rest being catechumens. Children in school number 8,517, of whom 2,425 are girls. This includes Ramnad. In Mission Colleges and Schools there are 425 boys; there are 416 girls in boarding schools.

Thus everything connected with the Mission has increased tenfold during the fifty years of Queen Victoria's reign. In the beginning of the year 1841, the Missions in Tinnevelly received a visit from Bishop Spencer, the first visit they had ever received from a Bishop. Towards the close of the same year the Rev. R. Caldwell, afterwards Bishop Caldwell, arrived in Tinnevelly. He commenced his labours at Idaiyangudi, which is still under his special care, but for some years past he has made Tuticorin his head-quarters. In 1843 an Institution was commenced at Sawyerpuram by Dr. G. U. Pope, a name which will always be remembered for the training up of Mission

Agents. This supplied a want which had long been felt. Most of the pupils, as soon as they left were employed in the Mission as Catechists and Schoolmasters, whilst students of superior attainments were drafted to Madras to Sullivan's Gardens, where they enjoyed the advantage of being trained by the Rev. A. R. Symonds, one of the best educationists Southern India has seen. After Dr. Pope left, the Institution came under the care of various Principals, the chief of whom were Mr. Huxtable, afterwards Bishop of Mauritius, and Mr. Brotherton, whose attainments and character were commemorated at Cambridge by the foundation of an Oriental Scholarship bearing his name. During the Principalship of Mr. Sharrock, the present head of the College, the College Department was transferred to Tuticorin, a much more important place than Sawyerpuram, in accordance with a recommendation of the present Bishop of Calcutta, who visited Tinnevelly as Metropolitan in 1881. It has since been raised to the rank of a College of the first grade, teaching up to the B.A. standard, and year by year it is growing in efficiency. It has now the advantage of having a Wrangler as Vice-Principal. It was through the efforts of Bishop Caldwell, after whom the College is named, that the large and commodious College buildings were purchased and presented to the S.P.G. A specialty of the College is the prominence given in it to Christian teaching. It may fairly be described as the most distinctively Christian College in the Presidency. Almost every College and High School in the Presidency has received its Christian Masters from Sawyerpuram, or Tuticorin.

A Girls' Boarding School was commenced at Idaiyangudi by Mrs. Caldwell in 1844, followed by similar schools in other places; she then also introduced lace-making amongst the women, a branch of industry which proved a great success, and is carried on to the present day. This has provided suitable employment for hundreds of native women, especially widows. The Metropolitan of India, Bishop Wilson, visited Tinnevelly in 1841-42.

In 1877 Bishop Caldwell, who had been consecrated at Calcutta as Assistant to the Bishop of Madras, was commissioned to supervise the S.P.G. Missions in Tinnevelly and Ramnad. The number of Native clergy under him is 41, of whom 15 Deacons, and one Priest were ordained by him in one day, the 19th of December, 1886. The number of European Missionaries is three. The first Native ordained was in 1854. In 1877 Southern India was visited by the most terrible famine it has yet known, and in that and the following year there were many accessions to the Christian fold, through gratitude for the help the starving poor received from benevolent Christians. Much of the increase which has taken place, as already mentioned, during Queen Victoria's reign was from this cause. Many of the more ignorant people relapsed, but yet more remained. Church Councils have now been established in every district, and are doing a good work in the organization and consolidation of the Mission. In 1880 a large and beautiful church at Idaiyangudi was opened for Divine service, and in 1885 a similar church was opened at Mudalur. Normal Schools, both for boys and girls, have been established, and the whole Mission will soon be well supplied with trained teachers. Mission Dispensaries have also been established, and every station has now its Post Office.

The S.P.G. Missions in Tinnevelly, including Ramnad, are divided into eleven districts, each of which is under the superintendence of a European Missionary or Native clergyman of superior attainments. To begin with the southern districts in Tinnevelly. There are two of these, Puthiamputhur and Nagalapuram, both under the superintendence of Bishop Caldwell. Puthiamputhur comprises five pastorates, and Nagalapuram six, each of which is under a Native clergyman. Tuticorin town is under the Rev. D. Samuel, B.D., Native Chaplain both to the Bishop of Madras and Bishop Caldwell. Pudukottai and Sawyerpuram are under the care of the Rev. J. A. Sharrock, with three Native clergymen to assist him. As Principal of the College he has spiritual charge of the College also, which with its affiliated schools numbers 925 pupils. Idaiyangudi, with its six pastorates, and Radapuram, with three, are under the care of Bishop Caldwell, whose residence is divided between Idaiyangudi and Tuticorin. The class of 27 candidates for ordination lately held by Bishop Caldwell for three months was held at Idaiyangudi. Sixteen of these candidates were accepted by the Madras Committee and ordained. The ordination of eleven was postponed. The district of Nazareth is under the care of the Rev. A. Margoschis, with three pastorates attached to Nazareth itself, and the districts of Mudalur and Christianagram were lately placed under Mr. Margoschis's care, with four Native clergy. There are Orphanages at Nazareth both for boys and girls, in connection with which there are Industrial Schools. Ramnad follows Tinnevelly, with its one European Missionary in charge, assisted by eight Natives. It has its Orphanages for boys and girls, and its Industrial Schools, and also a Printing Press.

In June 1837 the Church Missionary Society had 4 Missionaries in Tinnevelly, of whom only one was a native. The European element increased at times to 12; now there are only five Europeans, but the Native ordained agents have increased to 64. In June, 1837, missionary operations were carried on in 203 villages; now there are converts in 991 villages and hamlets. In 1837 the number of converts amounted to 8,207; now they exceed 56,380. Then there were 186 communicants only; now there are 11,965. In 1837 there were 3,411 boys learning in the Mission Vernacular Schools, and no English was taught anywhere, except a little in the Palamcottah Boarding School; now there are 15,214 pupils, of whom 3,220 are girls. When, forty years ago, the Zillah Judge was called upon by Government to make a return of the Christians employed in his department, he could mention only one man, the Court sweeper; and it was much the same in the Magisterial and Revenue Departments. Since then there have been a Deputy Collector (now pensioned), a head writer in the Court, five Court Vakils, a Deputy Tahsildar, three Sub Registrars, a Police Inspector, several writers in the Collector's Office, five Overseers in the D. P. W. and Forest Department, besides many other Tinnevelly Christians employed in respectable offices in other parts of the Presidency. There are also a great number of Christians employed as subordinates in the Police and other Government departments. Many Matriculates, F.A.'s, and B.A. Graduates are employed in Colleges and High-Schools.

Education has advanced with rapid strides. The means of culture, at first gratuitously supplied by the Missionary Societies, and subsequently encouraged by grants from Government and Local Boards, has served to show how capable the converts are of mental culture, and the records of the Madras University fully bear out this assertion. Large schools of industry are now the only desiderata required for the extension of material progress. Another appliance has been introduced within the last few years which affects most pleasing results, as it brings Mission work into touch with the domestic life of the Hindus. The Zenana Mission ladies find access to the houses and families of respectable Hindus, and thus, besides their direct teaching, they extend the knowledge of reading, needlework, and in some cases music. They are received kindly, and the most friendly relations exist between the parties. By means of this agency many Hindu families now know far more of English civilisation and literature, manners and customs, than they used to do. Regarding progress generally in Tinnevelly, Bishop Sargent writes:—

"Having come to this District a little more than fifty years ago, I can vouch for the material progress that has been attained. Wherever one goes it is pleasing to see how largely cultivation has been extended. Almost every bit of arable land that could be made productive has been brought under culture, and ownership has been so thoroughly defined by the records of the Revenue Settlement that litigation in such matters has greatly diminished. The people feel greater security in their right as to landed property than they ever did before. Even in larger towns pucka-built houses were very rare, owing to the fact that men were afraid to let it be seen that they were in possession of valuable property, and had the means of living comfortably,—for cases of dacoity were then of constant notoriety. Now, substantial and respectable houses are to be seen on all sides; many of them with upper rooms; and ordinary villages too now show considerable improvements in this way. Fifty years ago it was hardly ever that even a respectable native travelled in any vehicle but a common cart, with a cover of matting, and without springs. Now there are decent-looking coaches on all the main roads for travellers, and men of importance move about in the towns in well-built box-bandies on springs, drawn by good bullocks, and carriages with horses are used by not a few. In short, the people have not only improved their worldly possessions, but they feel so secure in their tenure that they are not afraid to show when they are men of substance, and to emulate one another in demonstrations of prosperity."

ROMAN CATHOLIC PROGRESS.

The Catholic Church in South India has made marked progress during the period embraced in the Queen's reign. The appointment of Vicars Apostolic, whose authority and jurisdiction were confirmed by the Bull *Multa Praeclare* of Gregory XVI. in 1836, gave an impetus to this progress, as it brought in an influx of missionaries, who accompanied the Prelates so appointed. The Abbé Dubois said, in his examination before a Committee of the House of Commons on the 23rd June, 1832, that the native Catholic converts in all Asia might be estimated at 1,200,000; and of these, he added, one half, or 600,000, were to be found in the Peninsula of India. These were governed by four Bishops, and an equal number of Vicars Apostolic—that is, Bishops having a titular See in some other part of the Church. The distribution of Catholics, according to his estimate was, along the coast from Goa to Cape Comorin, excluding Travancore, 330,000; in the Provinces of Mysore, Madura, and Carnatic 120,000; and he placed the other 150,000 in the Island of Ceylon. The *Madras Catholic Directory* of 1855 gives the Catholic population of Ceylon, according to the Government census of 1840, at 150,000: and if this be taken from the total given by the Abbé Dubois, it brings the Catholic population of South India to about 450,000 souls in that year.

Comparing these figures with the *Madras Directory* for 1887,—which is compiled from returns received from the Bishops and Vicars Apostolic of South India,—it is found that the total number of Catholics in South India and Ceylon in 1887 is 1,112,690. Deducting the figures given for the Vicariates of Jaffna, Kandy and Colombo, viz., 207,692, there remains a total of 904,998 for South India, which shows an increase of 454,908 in the half century. It appears on the same authority that there were in 1855 in South India 11 Bishops, 526 Priests, and 629,173 Catholics; in 1865 there were 8 Bishops (two or three Sees being vacant), 554 Priests, and 674,558 Catholics; and in 1875 there were 10 Bishops, 630 Priests, and 791,391 Catholics; whilst in 1887 there are 14 Bishops, 855 Priests (of whom 496 are natives), and 904,998 Catholics. Of the 496 native priests, labouring in the different dioceses of South India, 349 are of the Syrian rite, and belong to the Archdiocese of Verapoly (Cochin). The number of places of Divine worship according to the Roman Catholic ritual, scattered over South India, is 2,292 in 1887. Besides these there are the dioceses of Saint Thomé and Cochin (including Cranganore) directly Suffragan Sees to Goa, which have been vacant, the former since 1818, and the latter since 1816, and which, according to a census taken in 1881, have 20 Missions, 60 Chapels, and 29,073 Christians, and 47 Missions, 222 Chapels, and 82,775 Christians respectively. The number of clergymen ministering to them may be set down at 105, while 3,041 children are in attendance at the schools under their charge. The ecclesiastical governing body has, during this period, vastly increased. In lieu of the few Vicars Apostolic, who were entrusted with this work in 1837, there are now in South India, after the establishment of the Hierarchy—which took place at Bangalore on the 25th January last, by Monseigneur Agliardi, the Papal Delegate—three Archbishops (Madras, Pondicherry, and Verapoly), and seven Suffragan Sees, with 11 Bishops (namely Hyderabad, Vizagapatam, Mangalore, Coimbatore, Mysore, Trichinopoly, and Quilon).

Trichinopoly has had the unique privilege of having only one bishop, who has ruled the Vicariate since its erection in 1846, the Right Rev. Alexis Canoz, S. J. Pondicherry, the oldest but one of the Vicariates Apostolic, erected on the 8th July, 1836, was successively governed, since 1837, by the Right Rev. Clement Bonnand, Bishop of Drusipare in Thracia, by Joseph Isidore Godelle, Bishop of Thermopylæ in Achaia, and by Jean François Laouënan, Bishop of Flaviopolis,—the last named having been promoted to the Archiepiscopate in 1887. Bishop Laouënan had a coadjutor—the Right Rev. Joseph Gandy—appointed in March 1883. The Vicariate of Verapoly (Cochin), originally designated the "Vicariate Apostolic of Malabar," the oldest of the Vicariates of South India, it having been erected by a Papal decree early in 1660, has had for its prelates the Right Rev. Francis Xavier Pescetto, the Right Rev. Ludovico Martini of St. Teresa, the Most Rev. Dr. Bernardino Baccinelli of St. Teresa, Archbishop of Pharsalia, and the Most Rev. Dr. Leonardo Mellano, the present Archbishop under the Hierarchy. The Mission of Vizagapatam, which till 1849 formed part of the Madras Vicariate, was governed from 1849 to 1863 by the Right Rev. Theophilus Sebastian Neyret, who was succeeded by the present Bishop, the Right Rev. John M. Tissot. A coadjutor, in the person of the Right Rev. F. Phillipe, was appointed to Dr. Tissot, in November 1886. The Mission of Hyderabad, though it formed a part of the Madras Vicariate until 1851, was governed from 1846 to 1851 by the Right Rev. Daniel Murphy, as coadjutor to the late Dr. John Fennelly. In 1851 it was separated from Madras, and erected into an independent Vicariate, and was governed by Bishop Murphy till his departure from India in 1864 for the Australian Missions, where he was appointed Bishop of Hobart Town, Tasmania. He was succeeded by the Right Rev. J. M. Barbero, on whose death, on 18th September 1881, at Hyderabad, the present Bishop, the Right Rev. Peter Caprotti was appointed. The Mangalore Vicariate was administered by the Vicar Apostolic of Verapoly till 1853, when it was erected into a separate Vicariate, and had for its Bishops, successively, the Right Rev. Doctors Michael Antony and Mary Ephrem Garrelon, the latter having been translated from the Vicariate of Quilon in 1870. On Bishop Ephrem's death, at Mangalore in 1873, the Vicariate was again administered by Verapoly till the appointment of the present prelate, the Right Rev. Nicholas Pagani, S J., as Administrator in 1878, and Bishop in 1885. The Vicariates of Mysore and Coimbatore were created by the division of the large Vicariate of Pondicherry in 1845. The former had for its first Bishop the Right Rev. Stephen Louis Charbonnaux (for some time coadjutor Vicar Apostolic of Pondicherry and Papal Visitor Apostolic), who was succeeded by the Right Rev. Augustine Chevalier, on whose demise in 1874 the present Bishop, the Right Rev. J. Coadou, succeeded as Bishop of Mysore under the Hierarchy. Coimbatore had a Pro-Vicar Apostolic from 1846 to 1854, the Right Rev. Melchior De Marion Bresillac,—who resigned in 1865, and was succeeded by the Right Rev. Claude Mary Depommier, the mission having in the interim been administered by the Vicar Apostolic of Pondicherry, and was succeeded by the present prelate, the Right Rev. Joseph Louis Bardou in 1874. The Right Rev. Dr. Depommier died at Negapatam in 1873. Quilon was partially separated from the Vicariate Apostolic of Verapoly by Gregory the XVI. in 1845, and raised in 1853 by Pius IX. to a Vicariate Apostolic, the prelates being, successively, the Right Rev. Doctors Bernardino of St. Teresa, Bernardino of St. Agnes, Charles Hyacinth Valerga of St. Elias, and the Right Rev. Mary Ephrem of the Sacred Heart, the last named, on his translation to Mangalore, in 1870, being succeeded by the Right Rev. Ildephonsus of St. John Baptist, who governed it till the arrival of the Right Rev. Ferdinand Rossi, his coadjutor, who was appointed Administrator Apostolic under the Hierarchy.

The Capuchin Fathers, Ephraim and Zeno, who were the founders of the Madras Mission and the first missionaries from the Propaganda, arrived at Madras in 1642. The Capuchins continued their labours in the Madras Mission with varied success until 1836. Pope Gregory XVI. deemed that the interest of religion demanded the appointment of Vicars Apostolic. The Madras Vicariate was created by a Decree in 1832, and confirmed in 1834. The Right Rev. Fre Pedro de Alcantara, nominated Vicar Apostolic *ad interim* of Madras on 5th March, 1833, took charge on the 10th August, 1834, from the Very Rev. Fre John Baptist, the last Prefect of the Capuchin Mission of Madras, but returned to Bombay on the arrival of Dr. O'Connor in August, 1835. Dr. Bede Polding was appointed in 1832 first Vicar Apostolic of Madras, but never reached Madras, having been translated to Van Diemen's Land, Australia. The Right Rev. Dr. Daniel O'Connor, the first British Vicar Apostolic of Madras, governed the Vicariate from 1835 to 1840. The Right Rev. Patrick J. Carew, who was appointed as his coadjutor in 1838, and arrived in Madras in 1839, succeeded him, and governed from December, 1840, to May, 1841, when he was raised to the Archiepiscopal dignity, and translated to Calcutta. The Madras Mission was then provisionally administered by the Very Rev. Dr. William Kennedy until the arrival of Bishop John Fennelly in February, 1842. It was in the time of the latter prelate that the most marked progress was made in the Presidency Town and in the Vicariate generally. Much prejudice had to be lived down, and much up-hill work done, in urging the claims of Catholics to be placed on an equal footing with their co-religionists of other denominations. Bishop John Fennelly died much lamented in January, 1868, after having laboured in the diocese for twenty-six years. The administration then devolved on Bishop Stephen Fennelly, by his appointment in July, 1868, to succeed his brother, and it was characterised by a very steady and sensible progress. The good work (enhanced in its difficulties by the Famine of 1877-8), which he conducted very unobtrusively, he left at his death, 3rd May, 1880, to be largely augmented and advanced by the present prelate, the Most Rev. Archbishop Joseph Colgan, who was, till the 25th January, 1887, Bishop of Aureliopolis and Vicar Apostolic of Madras, and was promoted to the Archiepiscopal dignity under the Hierarchy.

Viewing the progress of Catholic work in the Presidency Town, it appears that, after the Capuchins had handed over charge of the Mission to the Vicar Apostolic, there were very few elementary English schools, and still fewer Vernacular Schools for the education of the rising generation. The *Madras Catholic Expositor* of 1838 states that, "since Dr. O'Connor's arrival, no less than 14 schools have been established in the Vicariate for the education of children in English, Latin, and Tamil," and that "it is gratifying to observe these institutions, though poorly supported, rapidly advancing and numbering 400 scholars." In 1838 there were, besides St. Mary's Seminary, three or four English free schools and an equal number of Tamil schools, supported by the Mission, and the latter were taught principally by Catechists, who had other duties to attend to. Catholic female education may be said to have received its first start in Madras by the advent of the Nuns of the Presentation Order, who came out with Bishop John Fennelly from Ireland in February, 1842. After very successful work during a period of forty-two years in the heart of the Presidency town, the Nuns opened a branch of their House in Vepery in 1884. Both institutions afford the advantages of a high class education, and furnish ample accommodation for the better classes who wish to avail themselves of the Convents as boarding establishments for their children. There are in these two Convents upwards of 500 children receiving a sound religious and secular education. The education of native girls, entrusted till January, 1876, to poorly paid catechists and school mistresses, was in that year committed to a community of Native Nuns from Pondicherry. The Mission has since received auxiliaries in the establishment of four other Native Convents, one in Vepery, one in Royapooram, one in Killacheri (Chingleput District), and one in Feringhipur (Kistna District). Two of these Convents are Tamil, and two Telugu; they have about 400 native children in regular attendance.

There were in the Madras Vicariate in 1886 twenty-two Tamil Schools for boys and girls, and sixteen Telugu Schools with *1862* children in attendance, besides the four native Convent Schools. In 1837 there was, in the Presidency Town, only one Orphanage (with 15 inmates) for Eurasian boys supported by a small subsidy from the Capuchin Funds. It was enlarged, and a Military and Female branch added by Bishop Carew, in 1840. These institutions have rapidly grown under the fostering care of successive Prelates, who have taken a lively interest in their progress, until they are now amongst the largest and most flourishing in Southern India. The number of orphans in these institutions at present is 320. The Famine of 1877-78 brought in a large number of native orphans, who were baptized with their parents during the period of that dire calamity. Native Orphanages,—if a few small ones supported by private benevolence are excepted,—were unknown before that period. Orphanages were opened in 1877 in most of the Vicariates Apostolic of South India, and have continued to be kept up ever since from the resources at the disposal of the various Missions. There are now in all the Catholic Dioceses of South India, forty-six orphanages, supporting and educating 2,914 children. There are now five Catholic Colleges affiliated to the Madras University, and fourteen Seminaries with 1,194 schools, and 34,961 children under instruction, under the management and control of the respective Bishops in South India. These are exclusive of the figures given for St. Thomé and Cochin. Of the other Dioceses in South India, those affording the highest educational advantages are Trichinopoly, Pondicherry, and Mangalore, they having the largest establishments for this purpose. The education of European and Eurasian girls in all the Vicariates is entrusted to European Nuns, but Pondicherry has the pre-eminence in having been the first to open communities of Native Christian women for the training of youth, the first convent of Native Carmelite Nuns having been opened in 1748. In Trichinopoly and Madras alone have attempts been made to form communities of Native men for the education of boys. Madras, Trichinopoly, and Vizagapatam have European monks engaged in education under the supervision of their respective clergy.

In the Madras Diocese there were in 1855 fourteen Missionary head-quarters, with 41 churches and chapels, served by 13 priests. In 1887 there are twenty-eight Missionary districts (seven in Madras and twenty-one scattered throughout the Diocese) with 44 churches and 99 chapels, served by 46 priests, 14 of whom are natives educated for the Ministry in the Diocese itself. The number of adult baptisms in the Vicariate was 15,064, in the forty-seven years ended 30th September last. It has not been possible to ascertain the respective figures under these heads in the other Dioceses of South India, but there is every reason to believe that the progress has been equally rapid in the fifty years under notice.

THE MOHAMMEDANS OF MADRAS.

The first Nawab of the Carnatic who was placed on the musnud under British auspices was Nawab Azim-ud-Dowlah, who was installed at the beginning of the present century by Edward, Lord Clive, the Governor of Madras. His Highness died in 1818, and was succeeded by Nawab Azim Jah, who reigned for six years. Dying in 1824, Azim Jah was succeeded by his infant son, Ghulam Mahomed Ghous Khan, during whose minority his uncle, Prince Azim Jah, was Regent. On the accession of Queen Victoria to the British throne the Regent held a Durbar, and gave a splendid banquet at the Chepauk Palace in the City of Madras. The occasion was one of great rejoicing among the Mohammedans of Southern India, and ever since that time they have proved themselves loyal subjects of the British Crown. There were similar festivities in Chepauk on the occasion of Her Majesty's marriage. In August 1842 Ghulam Ghous Khan was installed as Nawab of the Carnatic by John, Lord Elphinstone, Governor of Madras. He married firstly in 1847 Her Highness Nawab Khair-un-nisa Begum Sahiba, and secondly in 1848 Azim-un-nisa Begum Sahiba. In 1855 he died without issue, and his title and musnud escheated to the Crown. His Begums were granted a monthly allowance of Rs. 12,000, and Rs. 4,000 respectively, and they inherited the greater portion of his jewels, and property of the value of upwards of 25 lakhs of rupees. The creditors of His Highness, however, complained to Government, who, after instituting inquiries into the affairs of the Nawab's family, caused the property to be sold by public auction. The Government purchased the Chepauk Palace for about three lakhs, and converted it into the present Civil Engineering College. The Senior Begum's stipend was in 1859 reduced to Rs. 6,000. At present the two ladies are near neighbours in the City of Madras, the one residing in the Umdah Bagh (McLean's Gardens), and the other in the Bagh-i-Iram (Wood's Gardens), close to the Madras Club.

Prince Azim Jah now claimed the musnud and title of his late nephew, and his claims were strongly urged in Parliament. In 1871 a compromise was effected between the Prince and the then Secretary of State for India, when Lord Napier and Ettrick was Governor of Madras, whereby the title of "Prince of Arcot" was bestowed upon His Highness. This was the first occasion on which Her Majesty exercised her prerogative by conferring the dignity of Prince on a native of India. Prince Azim Jah thus became the First Prince of Arcot, and he was granted an allowance of three lakhs of rupees a year. He took up his residence at the Shadi Mahal, Triplicane, where he was permitted to keep a small battery of Artillery, and a body of armed Guards. He was also declared to be entitled to a personal salute of 15 guns. On his death, which took place in 1875, the stipendiary allowance was reduced by one-half, and the title of Prince of Arcot devolved by patent upon his eldest son, Prince Zahir-ud-Dowlah, who had the honour of being present by invitation at the Imperial assemblage at Delhi in 1877 for the Proclamation of Her Majesty as Empress of India, and of being created in the same year a Knight Grand Commander of the Star of India. He died in 1879, and was succeeded by his next brother, Intizam-ul-Mulk, the present Prince of Arcot, who resides in the Amir Mahal Palace, Pycroft's Road, Royapettah. The other two sons of the First Prince of Arcot died. The title now carries with it an allowance of Rs. 70,000 per annum, while Rs. 80,000 a year is paid towards the maintenance of the other members of the Arcot family. The present Prince of Arcot has not been in the enjoyment of good health for the past three years. His nephew Prince Mahomed Munnover Khan Bahadur is the next heir to the title.

The only members of the Carnatic family who have visited England are the late Hyder Jung Bahadur, and Hafiz Sadrul Islam Khan Bahadur. They each resided in England for a period of ten years, and had the honour of being presented to Her Majesty. The latter gentleman is now in Madras. Sharf-ul-Omara, cousin to the First Prince of Arcot, was created a Knight Commander of the Star of India, and he was the first Mohammedan nominated to the Legislative Council of the Governor of Fort St. George. After him Mir Humayun Jah Bahadur, the great-grandson of Tippu Sultan, was appointed to the Legislative Council. This gentleman has had a seat in the Council for several years, having been re-appointed by Government every second year. A few years ago he was created a Companion of the Order of the Indian Empire. Several Mohammedan gentlemen have had the titles of "Khan Bahadur" and "Khan Sahib" bestowed on them from time to time.

The Prince of Arcot's guards were disarmed about the time of the Mutiny of the Bengal Army, and fears were entertained that the men would revolt. But throughout that very trying period the Mohammedans of Madras remained loyal to the British. Except a few isolated disturbances between Hindus and Mohammedans, and fanatical outbreaks in Malabar, the Mohammedans of the Madras Presidency have been peaceful subjects throughout Her Majesty's reign. As to education, they have been less quick than their Hindu brethren to take advantage of the opportunities afforded them by the State. Fifty years ago very few Mohammedans were acquainted with English; in fact, a dislike prevailed among them to learning that language, and employment in the public service was considered by the better classes to be undignified. The Mohammedans had no public institutions in 1837, and the first of the kind that was started was the Mohammedan Library which was opened in 1850. This institution receives an annual grant of Rs. 420 from the Government.

Shortly afterwards the Madrasa-i-Azam was established—the first Mohammedan School in Madras—by the Nawab of the Carnatic. When Henry Vere, Lord Hobart, became Governor of Madras, he gave special attention to Mohammedan education, and caused several Mohammedan Schools to be established in several districts. A large number of Mohammedan Schools now exist in the Presidency, and they are being largely resorted to by those for whose special benefit they were designed. There are at present about 3,000 Mohammedan boys, and 2,000 girls under instruction. Female education has been greatly encouraged among the Mohammedans, and the "Hobart Girls' School" in Royapettah, under Miss S. Cripps, is doing good work. The Moplahs of Malabar are very enterprising traders, but are, as a rule, indifferent to education. A special Moplah Inspector of Schools was recently appointed by Government, to encourage the people to send their children to school. With the numerous inducements offered by Government, and with the various Scholarships established for their benefit, the Mohammedans of the Madras Presidency will, it is hoped, soon be able to compete with their Hindu fellow-subjects on more equal terms than they now do.

The Presidency produced the first Mohammedan Graduate in Arts in 1872, Mahomed Oosman, who obtained employment in the Government Secretariat. There are now fourteen Mohammedan Graduates in Madras, and three are studying for the B.L. Degree. Orders have recently been passed by the Government directing the employment of qualified Mohammedans in the public service, so as to give the community a *fair* share in the administration of the country. A Mohammedan Graduate is now the Head Master of the Madrasa; several Mohammedans have obtained the appointment of Sub-Registrar; some fill the office of Deputy Collector; one is a Presidency Magistrate; one has been raised to the grade of Honorary Surgeon; one is a Sub-Engineer; and two are Assistant Engineers. There are several Mohammedan Apothecaries, Hospital Assistants, Supervisors, Foresters, and Overseers, and a comparatively large number have found employment in the Revenue Branch of the service. In the Military Department there are a large number who are Subadar Majors, and a few have obtained Commissions as Jemadars.

In regard to trade the Mohammedans are by no means backward. In 1876 the first Mohammedan Association, styled the "Anju-man-i-Islamiah," was started at Madras. Others followed, and one of these started, in October, 1885, an Industrial School in which boys are taught carpentry, weaving, embroidery, and other handicrafts. A few months ago a Central Mohammedan Association was inaugurated, which has for its object the improvement of the Muslim community. Mohammedan Associations have been established in Salem, Trichinopoly, Chittoor, Vizagapatam, Rajamundry, and other places. The first Mohammedan newspaper in Southern India was *Gulshan-i-Akhbar*, which was started about 1843. This was a weekly journal, and was printed in Hindustani. Since that time several other Hindustani weekly papers have been founded, and in 1883 the first Mohammedan newspaper in English, the *Muslim Herald*, came into existence. This also was started as a weekly, but is now a tri-weekly paper, under the editorship of Mr. Ahmad Mohiud-din Khan Bahadur.

TRAVANCORE.

Travancore, the most important Native State subject to the authority of the Government of Madras, is situated at the south-western corner of the Indian Peninsula. It has an area of 6,730 square miles. If the hills, backwaters, and streams, are subtracted from this, there remain about 4,000 square miles of cultivated area (or about half the area of Wales), and this is covered with a network of water communications and roads such as exists in no other part of India. According to the latest census, Travancore has a population of nearly 2½ millions, which gives an average density for the whole country of 357 to a square mile. There are some portions of the country where the population to a square mile is as high as 1,318, 1,170, and 1,135. More than a fifth of the population consists of Christians.

The Royal House of Travancore is an ancient dynasty which exercised sovereign power for some centuries over a very limited tract of country; but for the last century and a half it has reigned over the area comprised in the whole of the present principality. Succession to the Raj goes by the female line. There are no published official reports available to show what Travancore was fifty years ago, though glimpses of the then state of things may be obtained from one or two sources. It appears from a history of Travancore, written by a native of the country in 1878, that Munsiffs' Courts were established for the first time in 1832 for the disposal of petty civil cases; that the reigning Prince at the time invited a Tahsildar from the British district of Malabar to compile a Code of laws for Travancore, after the model of the enactments in force in British territories; that a Code was prepared by the Tahsildar; that this was the first Code of Regulations ever adopted and promulgated in Travancore; that this described the constitution, powers, and procedure of the Civil and Criminal Courts to be established; and that, in order to carry out these laws, and to place a qualified person on the Bench of the Appeal Court, a Munsiff from the Malabar District was invited through the Resident, and appointed Judge of the Appeal Court. It may be concluded therefore that at the time referred to, there were no independent judicial tribunals, but that the executive officials exercised revenue, police, and judicial functions. Whether it was justice or injustice they administered, it had one merit—that of being swift and decisive. It appears that in 1840 a rich and influential native of Madras was appointed by the Maharajah "fourth judge of the Appeal Court," and, at the same time, "Superintendent of the Royal Stables." There were no public schools or hospitals; no attention was paid to Public Works; and the condition of the finances was wretched. At the beginning of 1829 the public treasury was empty; the salaries of the official establishments were in arrears; the revenue was declining; the State was drifting into insolvency; and annexation was imminent. The Rev. Mr. Mateer, of the London Mission, in his *Native Life in Travancore*, published in 1883, states that "men are still alive who remember what Travancore was some thirty years ago—who found it then in the lowest depths of misrule, oppression, and corruption prevalent among all grades of society."

Since the year 1858 oppressive monopolies have been abandoned; hosts of petty and vexatious taxes have been swept away; English and Vernacular Schools have been founded throughout the country, with a Central College at the capital; Hospitals have been established; Public Works have been fostered and extended; the salaries of public servants have been increased, the tone and efficiency of the public service have been raised; the administration of Civil and Criminal Justice has been improved; the reciprocal execution of decrees between the Travancore and British Courts has been allowed; trade has expanded; and the finances have attained a state of much prosperity. Within the last six years, *i.e.* during the *régime* of the late enlightened Maharajah, the judicial machinery was further strengthened and improved; a sound system of Police was established; the different grades of Criminal Courts were reconstructed; the revenue establishments were improved; the old irrigation system in South Travancore was restored and extended; and a systematic survey and settlement was inaugurated, which, by securing a proper demarcation of properties, an accurate registration of titles, and an equitable adjustment of the land assessment, promises to prove of lasting benefit to the State. Since the accession of the present Maharajah, a reform of great practical value has been initiated in connection with the settlement, viz., the abolition of the Vritti service—an ancient institution analogous to what was called the prerogative of purveyance in olden times in Europe—under which a considerable proportion of the agricultural population was bound to find supplies of vegetables and labour at certain fixed rates, greatly below the market prices, for the use of religious and charitable institutions, and of the Royal household.

A few statistics will show better than anything that can be said the beneficial advance which has been made by the State. Just twenty years ago, or in 1864-65, the number of original Civil suits in all the Courts of the State was 13,598, of the value of 18½ lakhs of rupees, whereas it is now 30,388, of the value of upwards of 32 lakhs. If progressive litigation is a necessary result of the increasing wealth and prosperity of a country, the above figures indicate the progress made in this direction in Travancore. On the other hand, under the head of Criminal Justice, where 371 cases, in which 896 persons stood charged with crimes, were committed in 1864-65 to the Sessions Court, in 1884-85 only 139 cases, affecting 246 persons, went before these Courts, showing how much the efficiency of the Police and Magistracy has increased in the interior. The total expenditure on education from public funds in 1864-65 was Rs. 35,000; it is now Rs. 2,17,542. The entire expenditure on Hospitals and Dispensaries was only Rs. 35,000 twenty years ago, whereas it is now not much short of a lakh of rupees; and against 3,128 patients treated at the public expense in 1864-65, there were in 1884-85 111,531. Anterior to the year 1860, Travancore had no Department of Public Works. In the Administration Report for 1865-66, which is the earliest published record available, we are told that the country had long been without an organised and scientifically qualified agency to carry on public works. The reason was twofold; firstly, the importance of public works was not realised, and secondly, the public finances were in such a state of depression that the State could not afford to make any outlay in that direction. In 1864-65, the expenditure on public works was Rs. 4,38,310. Now it is nearly 10 lakhs. At the former date, there were scarcely 200 miles of good road in all Travancore—now there are 1,151 miles of it. The value of the export trade has expanded from Rs. 44,66,312 to Rs. 108,91,337 in the same period. Where the Sirkar Post carried 435,154 private and official covers in 1864-65, it now carries a million of covers. There was no registration of assurances at the time referred to; but, according to the latest Administration Report, more than 70,000 instruments, of the aggregate value of 131 lakhs of rupees, passed through the Registration Offices in 1884-86. Lastly, whereas the total income of the State twenty years ago was Rs. 42,11,140 against an expenditure of of 40,45,734, it was Rs. 66,78,705 against Rs. 64,90,846 in 1884-85. Taking the revenue derived from all sources—land, customs, excise, abkari, opium, salt, and stamps, it is found that the incidence of taxation in Travancore is Rs. 2, against Rs. 2-5-6 in the Madras Presidency. Taking land revenue only, it is Rs. 0-12-1 against Rs. 1-8-8 in Madras.

COCHIN.

The chief physical feature of this State is the backwater, or lagoon, which runs through the greater part of the country. It has an area of 1,361 square miles, more than two-thirds of which are under cultivation. According to the census of February, 1881, it contains a population of 600,728 souls. The average density of population per square mile is 441, but in some parts is as high as 1,430. The population consists of 429,324 Hindus, 136,361 Christians, 33,344 Mahommedans, and 1,249 Jews. The Christians thus form 23 per cent. of the whole population, whereas in Travancore the proportion is 20 per cent., and in the Madras Presidency generally it is only 1·5 per cent. As to the Jews, it is alleged that 10,000 refugees arrived at this part of the Malabar Coast about A.D. 70, or shortly after the final desolation of Jerusalem. 7,000 of these refugees are supposed to have settled down at a place called Mahodranpatna, now Cranganore. Here their industry, thrift, and docility secured for them the respect of the local chiefs. They eventually obtained a grant of various privileges, and had it engraved in Malayalim upon a copper-plate which is still in existence. The actual age of this plate has not been determined, but it is generally supposed to be at least one thousand years old. The community at Cranganore was periodically increased by emigration from Spain, Judea, and other parts, and the colony continued undisturbed until the sixteenth century, when it was subjected to much oppression by the Portuguese, and eventually, in 1565, the Jews fled to Cochin, and sued for the Rajah's protection. This he immediately gave, and he allotted them a site for a new settlement. Their numbers have steadily diminished since then. They are divided into Jerusalem or White Jews, and Black Jews. The former are of pure descent from the refugees from Jerusalem. They have a fair complexion, fine features, and curly black hair. The Black Jews are the descendants of refugees from Jerusalem and of native proselytes, and they claim to be of the sect of the Pharisees. Generally speaking these "children of Israel" are in indigent circumstances; but they are buoyed up by the expectation of the restoration of their race to the Holy Land.

The reigning family of Cochin is of high antiquity. The Rajah claims to hold his territory in right of descent from Cheraman Perumal, who governed the whole country of Keralam, including Travancore and Malabar, as Viceroy, about the beginning of the ninth century of the Christian era, and afterwards established himself as an independent ruler. The Marumakkatayam law, *i.e.* the right of inheritance through the female line, governs the succession to the throne.

There are no authentic records as regards the general history of the country, or the details of the administration until 1863, in which year, for the first time, the working of the Government was regularly recorded and published. During the first half of the fifty years since Her Majesty's accession, there were no properly constituted Courts, and the period does not appear to have been remarkable for any administrative reforms. Of State education, properly so called, there was none. The Public Works Department was in its infancy, and no building of any importance owed its existence to it. The Police officers of the time exercised both Police and Magisterial functions. Though the Judicial Department had its origin as early as 1812, with two Zillah Courts and an Appeal Court for the whole State, the laws and regulations which guided it were of the most primitive kind. The Courts of the period were by no means independent. Even the decisions of the Appeal, or highest Court in matters judicial, were altered, or set aside, by a mere order from the chief of the Executive. It was not until 1860 that a Munsiff's Court was established in the land. The inconvenience arising from the want of tribunals of the latter description had been so greatly felt in 1851, that the Tahsildar of one of the Taluks was specially empowered to hear and dispose of Civil Suits to the value of Rs. 100. In 1862, however, four Munsiffs' Courts were established to meet the increasing demands of litigation, and since that year there have been many other changes of a most important and beneficial character. At first an improved method of procedure in Civil cases was introduced, and at the present time there are in force Civil and Criminal Procedure Codes based on the lines of the British Indian Codes. The Judges have been carefully selected, and a well-educated and competent class of men now occupy the bench. The Bar has likewise been improved by requiring pleaders to qualify themselves by passing special tests. As a token of recognition of the improved efficiency of the Cochin Judicial Service, the Government of India has sanctioned the execution of the decrees of the Courts of the State by the British Courts.

A Police force has been organised according to the system obtaining in the Madras Presidency, which has conduced to the greater safety of person and property, while the Magistracy have been relieved of Police duties. The Registration of Assurances has been brought into practice, and has tended greatly to the security of titles. The Department of Public Works has been thoroughly reorganised, and is one of the most efficient branches of the Administration. It has opened several hundred miles of roads; constructed many important bridges; and has now entered upon a scheme of irrigation on an extensive scale, by opening canals in most of the Taluks, by which large tracts of land will be brought under cultivation. A number of obnoxious taxes on articles of consumption have been abandoned, and the system of exacting forced labour for Sirkar purposes has been abolished. The emoluments of public servants have been liberally increased; hospitals and dispensaries have been established on a scientific basis; and vaccination has been greatly extended. The Anchal, or local post, has received its share of attention. In instituting these reforms the methods pursued by the British Government have been followed as nearly as possible.

The following statistics will show more clearly the various degrees of progress that have already been effected. In 1863-64, the number of original civil suits filed in all the Cochin Courts was 1,998, while in 1885 the number was 7,877. The number of cases committed to the Sessions in 1863-64 was 151, affecting 425 persons; whereas in the year 1885 it was only 46, and involved only 119 persons—a result which testifies to the improved agency, and better working of the police and magistracy. The total expenditure on education in 1863-64 was below Rs. 10,000, but rose in 1885-86 to Rs. 40,826. The number of documents registered in 1885-86 was 17,415, the aggregate value of which was more than 63 lakhs of rupees. The total expenditure on public works for the years 1863-64 was Rs. 1,45,107, while the amount expended in 1885-86 was upwards of three and a half lakhs. The outlay on hospitals and dispensaries in 1863-64 was Rs. 6,231, against Rs. 45,684 expended in 1885-86. The number of patients admitted to the hospitals in 1885-86 was upwards of 10,000, against only 231 in 1863-64. Until 1866 the Unjal, or native post, carried private covers free of charge. In that year a small charge was levied on private letters and parcels. According to the latest reports, upwards of 100,000 official and private covers were carried through this agency as compared with about 15,000 in 1866. Lastly, the revenue of the State has considerably increased during the last fifty years. The entire revenue for the year 1837 was Rs. 6,67,443, with an expenditure of Rs. 6,53,812; while the income in 1885-86 amounted to Rs. 16,56,381, against an expenditure of Rs. 15,23,493.

A system of slavery formerly existed in this State, by which the "Pulayers" or soil-serfs, the lowest class of the people, were held to be the property of the landowner, and were sold, transferred, or mortgaged with the land to which they were attached. The custom was abolished by a proclamation, dated March 24th, 1855. The Government, in addition to abandoning several obnoxious taxes on trade, gave up in 1863 the monopoly on tobacco which had brought no inconsiderable revenue to the State. It further gave effect to the principle of Free Trade by abolishing all the "Chowkeys," or Inland Customs stations, under an interportal convention entered into with the Madras Government in June 1865, which also provided for the duty at the Sirkar ports being equalised with those obtaining in the British Indian ports. The roadstead at Narrakal, five miles north of Cochin, having been found to afford safe anchorage to vessels during the south-west monsoon when the western coast generally is inaccessible to shipping, a port was opened there in 1862, and experience has proved it to be favourable to commerce in the worst periods of the year. It resembles Alleppey in being protected by a mud bank, which ensures comparatively smooth water within the protected area during the height of the monsoon.

It may be mentioned that within the memory of man Cochin has had no experience of drought, famine, or floods—those fruitful causes of great calamity in other parts of Hindustan. The climate is moist, but healthy; the conditions of existence are primitive, but agreeable; the food supplies are large, and relatively cheap; and the Government is paternal and sympathetic. These attractions account for the arrival every year of about 8,000 immigrants from less favoured localities; and they have had much to do with the increase of late years, at the rate of 1·86 per annum, of the total population of the State. This rate of increase has no parallel in Europe, and it promises to double the number of the Rajah's subjects in thirty-nine years. The tendency of the population to collect in towns, and the steady increase in towns of the proportion of tiled to thatched houses, have been very marked of late years.

THE ANNALS OF MADRAS DURING QUEEN VICTORIA'S REIGN.

1837.—Proclamation by the Madras Government on 25th August, that the Princess Alexandrina Victoria had "become our lawful and rightful Liege Lady Queen of the United Kingdom of Great Britain and Ireland, and of the British Territories in the East Indies."—Establishment of the Order of British India for Native officers.—Boat Monopoly at Madras abolished.—Sailors' Home Madras established.—Sir Robert Comyn became Chief Justice.—Dr. Spencer installed Bishop of Madras, 4th November.—General Assembly's Institution opened at Madras, by Rev. Mr. Anderson.—Insurrection in Coorg.—British troops retreated from Puttoor to Mangalore.—Civil Offices and Jail sacked, and records destroyed.—Rebels retired, and dispersed.

1838.—Sir Jasper Nicolls, Commander-in-Chief, arrived 21st December.—Nawab of Kurnool engaged in treasonable preparations; his town and fort captured; he escaped; was subsequently arrested, and interned at Trichinopoly, where he was murdered by one of his servants. His territories were confiscated, and his family pensioned.

1839.—Great storm at Coringa, 20,000 people perished.—Lord Elphinstone issued his scheme for the establishment of a Central College, with provincial colleges and schools in connection with it.—The University Board appointed.

1840.—Madras troops embark for China in April.—The ship *Golconda*, with head-quarters of the 37th Madras Native Infantry, lost at sea.—Public meeting to congratulate the Queen on her marriage, May 4.—The suspension bridge at Chintadrepettah gave way; thirty-one Sepoys injured, June 1.—Eighteen convicts made an attempt to escape from the jail, July 28.—Sir Samuel Whittingham, Commander-in-Chief, arrived August 18.—St. Mary's R. C. Orphanage, Madras, for girls opened.—Coffee cultivation commenced in the Wynaad.

1841.—The High School, now known as the Presidency College, opened at Madras by Lord Elphinstone at the College Hall, April 14.—The 37th N.I. raised to the rank of a Grenadier Regiment for its gallantry in China.—Severe storm at Madras, 16th May.—Mutiny on board the brig *Jumna*, from Moulmein, May 29.—Mutiny on board the *Fetter*.—Poor Schools opened at Vepery, Madras.—Free Church School for Girls, Madras, opened. The School, now known as the Noble College, opened by the Church Missionary Society at Masulipatam.—Sir Hugh Gough, Commander-in-Chief, arrived August 12.

1842.—Pachaiyappa's Central College established under an order of the Supreme Court.—The Marquis of Tweeddale, K.T., arrived 24th September, and assumed the joint offices of Governor and Commander-in-Chief.—The *Hindostan*, the first P. & O. Company's steamer seen in Madras, arrived.—The first Madras Engineers raised to the rank of a Pioneer corps.—Sir R. Comyn, Chief Justice, resigned, and succeeded by Sir Edward Gambier.—Slight mutiny in the Deccan; a company of the 52nd Regiment refused their pay.—Pensions granted to the families of the men lost in the *Golconda*.—Great fire in Black Town.—Storm at Madras in November.

1843.—An *ex-officio* information filed in England against Mr. Archibald Douglas, late Resident at Tanjore, for receiving bribes. He was convicted in 1845.—Hurricane on the Madras Coast in May; several vessels lost.—The new Bank opens, July 1.—Bridge erected across the Tambreparney by Sakecherammi Moodelliar, at a cost of Rs. 50,000.—Memorials transmitted to London for the employment of steamers in India.—The Lying-in-Hospital, Madras, established.—Mr. Conolly, Collector of Malabar, commenced the Teak Plantations at Nellambur.—Neilgherry Hills retransferred from the Malabar to the Coimbatore District.

1844.—The new Lighthouse at Madras opened Jan. 1.—The barque *Potter*, from China, lost on the Prata Shoal.—Mutiny of the 47th Regiment, on board the *John Lane*, when going to Bombay to embark for Aden. Several mutineers executed.—Violent discussions on the subject of religious liberty.—The Wesleyan and American Missionaries opened Chapels.—The members of the Free Church constituted themselves a Presbytery.—The Lutherans and German Missionaries began their labours.—Coffee cultivation commenced on the Neilgherry Hills.

1845.—The King of Denmark transferred Tranquebar and the other Danish settlements in India to the East India Company for the sum of 12½ lakhs of rupees.—A Pier projected at Madras.—The General Assembly's Missionaries commenced their exertions.—The Chief Justice reduced the fees of the Madras bar.—Disturbances in the Northern Circars, and troops sent to suppress them.—The Protestant Collegiate Institution established.—The Eurasians petitioned to have the same rights as the Natives.—The General Assembly Institution at Madras dissolved, and succeeded by the Church of Scotland Institution, and the Free Church of Scotland Mission School: the latter is now known as the Madras Christian College.

1846.—The inhabitants of Madras voted a monument to Major Broadfoot.—Disturbances at Madras in consequence of three youths having asked to be baptized.—In one case the natives appealed to the Supreme Court, which decided that the lad was old enough to act for himself. The mob attacked the carriage in which he was conveyed back to the Missionaries.—The Polytechnic Institution founded.—Great discussion in Madras relative to the suspension by the Government of three judges, viz., Messrs. Lewis, Waters, and Bolleau.—A very large meeting of the natives takes place at Madras, and a strong memorial to the Directors is adopted.—Foundation stone of Patcheappah's Central School building laid Oct. 2.—Madras visited by a great fall of rain and a hurricane, which does unusual damage, Oct. 20.—Many persons lost.—Cyclone at Madras, Nov. 25. Pressure of wind computed at 57lb. per square foot. A pier of Elphinstone Bridge blown away. Several ships injured and lost.—St. Joseph's College, Negapatam, established.—Branch of Patcheappah's School opened at Conjeveram.—The Marquis of Tweeddale visited, and minuted favourably on the Nellambur Teak Plantations.—A descendant of the dispossessed Poligars of Nossam excited a rebellion in Cuddapah district which was promptly suppressed.

1847.—A minute by the Marquis of Tweeddale, advocating the introduction of the Bible as a class-book, excited much discussion in India. The Government Gardens at Ootacamund planned by the Marquis.—The Marquis resigned, Feb. 3. Was succeeded provisionally by Mr. H. Dickinson, Senior Member of Council.—Sir Henry Pottinger arrived April 7, and took his seat as Governor.—Insurrection of Moplahs near Calicut, promptly quelled.—The Madras Polytechnic Institution opened with great formality.—Mr. Malcolm Lewin's nomination to be Provisional Member of Council at Madras is cancelled by the Court of Directors.—Meetings held for relieving the distress in Ireland and Scotland. Collections made.—Disturbances in the Golconda districts.—The Supreme Court disclaimed jurisdiction over the acts of the Company's servants out of Madras.—A boat establishment formed at Madras.—The Commander-in-Chief issued orders that soldiers may attend their own places of worship.—A great inundation at Nellore, eighty tanks having burst their banks.—The Madras University Board dissolved, and succeeded by the Board of General Education.

1848.—The Honourable Sir George Berkeley, Commander-in-Chief, arrived March 13.—The Baptist Meeting House, the Court of Small Causes, and Sullivan's Gardens Seminary, opened.—The Zemindary of Bunganapilly, which had been administered by the Collector of Cuddapah from 1825, in consequence of local disorders, restored to the Jagheerdar.

1849.—The Pier Company dissolved.—Severe gales at Madras.—Dr. Spencer, Bishop of Madras, resigned.—Serious Moplah outbreak near Mungery.

1850.—Dr. Dealtry installed in the Bishopric of Madras, Feb. 3.—Very unusual rain, Feb. 9 to 11.—Disastrous explosion at the Powder Mills, Madras, March 6.—Patcheappah's new School opened, March 20.—Sir Edward Gambier, Chief Justice, resigned. His successor, Sir Christopher Rawlinson, sworn in April 15.—Special mission of Messrs. Morehead and Rohde to Ceylon, April 17.—Madras Railway Meeting in the Banqueting Hall; Sir H. Pottinger, the Governor, in the chair, May 4.—Foundation stone of Mount Road Church laid by the Bishop of Madras, Oct. 5.—The School of Arts, Madras, opened.

1851.—Nomination of a Commission to inquire into the state of Public Works in the Madras Presidency, Feb. 18.—Sir R. Armstrong, Commander-in-Chief, arrived September 29.—The Anamally Hills explored by Captain Michael and Lieutenant Beddome, Oct.—First balloon ascent at Madras, Oct. 20.—Terrific storm at Ootacamund, inundating the roads, and washing away the Segoor Bridge, Nov. 21.—Three native preachers, Messrs. Rajahgopaul, Venkatasamiah, and Etterajaloo, ordained Missionaries by the Madras Presbytery of the Free Church of Scotland, Nov. 26.—Wesleyan Central Institution established at Royapettah, Madras.—Madras Medical College constituted a College.—Detachment of British troops quartered at Malapooram, Malabar, to overawe Moplahs.—Moplah outrages at Colliatoor.

1852.—Madras East Indian Emigration Society formed, Jan. 3.—Breaking out of the Burmese War; embarkation of the Madras Brigade, in March.—Foundation-stone of the Wesleyan Mission Chapel, Royapettah, laid by Mr. H. Bayley, May 1.—Admiral St. Mase, Governor of Pondicherry, arrived at Madras.—Trinity Church at Bangalore opened for Divine Service, July 25.—The first Madras Fusiliers and the Sappers and Miners embarked at Madras for Rangoon, Sept. 7.—Great thunderstorm at Madras, Oct. 17.—Dinner given to the East Indian Emigrants by Sir W. Burton, Puisne Judge, Nov. 4.—Fifty-four East Indian emigrants embarked at Madras for New South Wales, Dec. 10.—Gallant defence of Pegu by Major Hill, 1st Fusiliers, against the attack of the Burmese, Dec. 5–14.—Pegu annexed, Dec. 20.—Consecration of Christ Church in Madras, Dec. 22.—Moplah outrages at Mattanore, near Tellicherry.

1853.—Destruction of the ship *Governor Higginson* by fire in the Madras Roads, Jan. 28.—Defeat of 3,000 Burmese by Captain Rennie near Lamena, Jan. 30.—Rangoon and Bassein declared free ports, Feb. 1.—Wellington Testimonial Meeting in the Banqueting Hall at Madras, Feb. 15.—Brigadier Mayne arrived at Arcot from Hyderabad, to command a Field Force assembled in reference to an apprehended insurrection. He captured 112 Rohillas at Padona, Feb. 27.—Native meeting in honour of Mr. George Norton in Patcheappah's Hall, and Farewell Ball to Mr. and Mrs. Norton in the Banqueting Hall, March 5 and 7.—Dinner to Mr. Norton at the Club, March 11.—Opening of the Exhibition at Madras, March 15.—Disastrous gale and great loss of life in the Madras Roads, March 27.—Railway works commenced at Madras, June 9.—Overflowing of the Godavery caused much distress, and a suspension for several days of communication between that part of the country and Madras, Aug. 11.—First anniversary of the Madras Hindu Debating Society celebrated at Patcheappah's Hall, Aug. 26.—Disastrous inundation at Guntoor in Aug.—Mr. Danby Seymour, Chairman of the India Reform Association, arrived at Madras on a tour of inspection, Oct. 2.—General Staveley, Commander-in-Chief, arrived Oct. 27.—Ceremony at Royapooram of presenting rewards to the boatmen for their services in the late storm, Nov. 16.—Sir Richard Armstrong left Madras Dec. 28.—Drought in the Ceded Districts.—Central School of the London Mission opened at Black Town, Madras.—Moplah Outrage Act passed.

1854.—Electric Telegraph completed between Madras and Poonamallee, Jan. 21.—Fatal epidemic among the Burghers in the Neilgherries, Jan.—New Church at Coonoor consecrated by Bishop Dealtry, March 8.—Sir Henry Pottinger resigned April 24.—Mr. Daniel Elliot becomes Provisional Governor.—Lord Harris assumed office April 28.—Public meeting for setting on foot the Doveton College, May 5.—The Madras Legislative Council met for the first time on May 20.—Completion of the electric telegraph between Madras and Bangalore, May 23.—Madras Exhibition of Agricultural Produce opened July 14.—The College of Fort St. George closed.—Commission appointed to inquire into the alleged employment of torture.—Petition of the East Indians to Lord Harris, July 16.—Frontier duties between the Nizam's and British territories abolished, Aug. 8.—Arrival of the *Nile* 74 days from the Lizard, Sept. 8.—General Anson assumed command of the Madras Army, Sept. 22.—Introduction of uniform cheap postage.—Substitution of the Bengal for the Madras Import Tariff, Oct. 1.—Serious rice riots in Madras, Nov. 9 and 10.—Famine in Bellary.—Meeting in Patcheappah's Hall to forward the views of the Patriotic Fund, Dec. 15.—Government Current Records thrown open to the public.—Despatch received from East India Company, urging the extension of education in India.—Formation of the Education Department, Madras.—Patcheappah's Branch School opened at Chidambaram.—Tea Seed imported into Madras from China, for experimental cultivation on the Neilgherries.

1855.—Discovery of the gutta-percha tree by Colonel F. Cotton in the Wynaad, Jan. 15.—Madras Exhibition opened by Lord Harris, Feb. 20.—Uncovenanted Civil Engineers appointed Feb. 21.—Mr. A. J. Arbuthnot appointed first Director of Public Instruction, March 15.—Moplahs in Malabar disarmed by Mr. Conolly; 7,500 war knives collected, March 30.—Monster native meeting held under pandals erected opposite Patcheappah's Hall, to adopt a petition to the House of Commons, April 3.—Swinging festival at Nellore abolished.—Moplahs in Malabar disarmed.—First locomotive of the Madras Railway landed, June 14.—Madras Medical College recognised by the Royal College of Surgeons, Aug. 9.—Mahomed Ghouse, Nawab of the Carnatic, died without issue, Oct. 7.—Sivajee, Rajah of Tanjore, died Oct. 30, without heirs, and his State lapsed to the East India Company).—The Madras University remodelled.—The Rev. Mr. Anderson of the F. C. of S. Mission School, a distinguished educationist, died.—Mr. Conolly, Collector and Magistrate, murdered in the verandah of his house at Calicut by Moplah fanatics.

1856.—Lord Harris laid the foundation stone of the "Harris School" belonging to the Church Missionary Society at Madras, Jan. 1.—Dinner given to General Anson by the Madras Club, on his departure to assume the chief command in India, Jan. 3.—Visit of Lord Canning, Governor General, to Madras, Feb. 15.—Opening of the Normal School in Madras, March 6.—Agricultural Exhibition opened at Madras, April 8.—Disturbances in Kimedy.—Pegu Medals presented to Madras Fusiliers by Lord Harris, April 25.—News received in Madras of the abolition of the Carnatic Musnud, and of the pensioning of Azeem Jah and family, May 3.—Orders issued stopping the execution of Public Works, May 9.—Sir Patrick Grant, Commander-in-Chief, arrived June 10.—The first portion of the Madras Railway opened for public traffic, June 28.—Mr. Horsley, C.S., murdered at Bellary.—Disbandment of the troops of the late Nawab of the Carnatic, and the late Rajah of Tanjore.—Emigration of Coolies to Mauritius abolished.—Railway from Madras to Arcot opened in July.—Shock of earthquake at Trevandrum, July.—Selection of the Lal Bagh at Bangalore for a Horticultural Garden, July.—Tanjore Fort occupied by the East India Company, Oct. 18.—Eighteen Uncovenanted Deputy Collectors appointed, Nov. 13.—Dispute between the people of Travancore and Cochin respecting the custody of an idol, Nov.—Great Gale at Madras, Nov. 19.—Creation of the Madras Forest Conservancy Department, Dec. 1.—Capture of the Kimedy rebel chief Dunda Sheenah, Dec. 25.

1857.—Railway from Arcot to Vellore opened, May 7.—Madras Exhibition closed, May 16.—Court of Directors sanctioned erection of Iron screw pile Pier at Madras, June 24.—Order issued (consequent on the outbreak of the mutiny of the Bengal Native Army) restraining the expression of opinion by the Press of India, July 2.—Volunteer Corps Act passed, July 9.—Formation of a Volunteer Rifle Corps in Madras sanctioned, July 22.—Mutinous conduct of 8th Madras Light Cavalry, Aug. 18.—The regiment disbanded, Dec. 8.—University of Madras incorporated, Sept. 5.—Fourteen inches of rain fell in Madras on one day, Oct. 25.—Rising in the Dharwar District joined by the Tahsildar of Harpanhully in Bellary.—Insurgents marched upon Ramandroog, were overtaken by British troops at Coppal, and dispersed.

1858.—Captain Biden, Master Attendant at Madras, died, Feb. 25.—First examination for the degree of M.A. held by Madras University, Feb.—Great gale at Madras, May 5.—Colours presented to the Madras Infantry Volunteer Guards by Lady Rawlinson, May 10.—The Rajah of Shorapore, who had been sentenced to transportation for life, shot himself with a revolver on the road from Secunderabad to Chingleput, May 11.—Railway from Vellore to Gudiyattum opened, May 19.—Branch line of Railway to Bangalore sanctioned, Aug. 20.—The Government of India transferred from the East India Company to the Crown, Sept. 1.—New Marine Police Act for Madras came into operation, Oct. 1.—Brilliant Comet visible at Madras, Oct. 5.—Captain Hart shot dead at Vellore by a Mussulman Sepoy, who was drunk with bhang, Oct. 12.—Public Works and Revenue Settlement Departments, and the Inam Commission constituted.—Publication on Nov. 1 of the Queen's Proclamation announcing the transfer of the Government of India from the East India Company to the Crown.—State Ball at Madras to commemorate the assumption of the Government of India by the Queen, with rejoicings on the Island, Nov. 8.—Grain riot and plundering at Combaconum, Nov 16.—Consecration of St. Paul's Church, Vepery, Nov. 18.—Captain Hare, Commandant 5th Regiment Infantry Hyderabad Contingent, shot by a Sepoy, Dec. 1.—Riots at Tinnevelly in consequence of the resistance offered by a mob to the body of a native Christian passing along the street; suppressed with the loss of ten lives, Dec. 11 and 12.—The Lawrence Asylum founded at Ootacamund.—Kurnool, hitherto administered by a Commissioner, constituted a separate Collectorate, with the addition of certain tracts from Cuddapah and Bellary.—A Plantation of Australian Trees commenced near Wellington, Neilgherries.

1859.—Mohammedan and Hindu gentlemen of Madras gave a farewell entertainment to Sir Christopher Rawlinson, Feb. 9.—Sir Henry Davidson, new Chief Justice, arrived.—Return to Madras from active service in Bengal of the 1st Madras Fusiliers; public holiday given in their honour, Feb. 22.—Forty Uncovenanted Deputy Collectors appointed for various districts in Madras, March 25.—Sir Charles Trevelyan arrived as Governor, March 28.—His Minute on the reduction of official correspondence published April 5.—His Minute on the Inam question issued May 24.—Observance of a General Day of Thanksgiving for the restoration of peace in India, July 28.—First screw pile of the Madras Pier turned by Sir Charles Trevelyan, Sept. 17.—Sir Charles Trevelyan communicated to the Press proposals for a Municipality, Dec. 26.—Despatch received from the Secretary of State reaffirming the educational policy expounded in the E. I. Co.'s Despatch of 1854.—The boundaries of the Districts of Guntur, Rajahmundry, and Masulipatam readjusted, and converted into the present Districts of Kistna and Godavery.

1860.—The Governor of Madras visited Pondicherry, Jan. 9.—Completion of the railway bridge over the Palar at Keelmaringly, which delayed the opening of the line beyond Gudiattum, Jan. 13.—Earthquake at Salem, Jan. 17.—Opening of the railway line to Amboor, Jan. 16.—Mr. Wilson announced an Income tax, License tax, and Tobacco tax, in the Viceregal Legislative Council, Feb. 18.—Address presented to Mr. J. B. Norton by the Native Association, in Patchiappah's Hall, Feb. 18.—Madras troops embarked for China, Feb. 28.—Public meeting in Black Town to consider the question of sanitary reform, Feb. 28.—Earthquake at Chandragherry, March 24.—Sir Charles Trevelyan published his Minute opposing Mr. Wilson's scheme of taxation, March 31.—Death of the Right Rev. M. F. Lobo, Episcopal Governor of the Bishopric of Mylapore, April 11.—Native meeting convened by the Sheriff at Patcheappah's Hall, for the purpose of adopting a petition to Parliament on the subject of the Rajah and Ranees of Tanjore, April 12.—Suspension for two years of Mr. Charles Reade, Agent to the Governor at Vizagapatam, April 26.—Public meeting convened by the Sheriff at Patcheappah's Hall, to take into consideration measures of sanitary reform, April 26.—Titles and Khillats conferred by Sir C. Trevelyan on two Native Officials, Messrs. M. Rungacharla and V. Virasama, April 27.—Sword belt from Her Majesty presented to the Maharajah of Travancore, May 2.—Abolition of the Garrison Engineership, May 4.—Native petition adopted in Madras against the new taxes, May 16.—Railway from Gudiattum to Ambur opened Jan. 16; from Ambur to Vaniyambadi, Feb. 1; and from Vaniyambadi to Tirupatur, May 23.—The recall of Sir Charles Trevelyan known in Madras, June 8. His Minute on the Report of the Commissioners on the systems of Judicature in the Madras Presidency published June 16.—Farewell addresses presented to him, June 23.—He left Madras for England, June 24.—Mr. W. Morehead Provisional Governor, June 8 to July 5.—Portraits of Her Majesty presented to the Zemindar of Shevagunga and to a Poligar in the Trichinopoly District, by the Collector of Madras, in the name of Government, July 10.—Presentation of two cases of silver plate to the 1st Regiment of Madras Fusiliers by the inhabitants of Madras, in recognition of the gallantry of the regiment during the Mutiny campaign, July 18.—Income tax came into operation. Aug. 1.—Sir Henry Ward transferred from the Governorship of Ceylon to that of Madras; he arrived July 5, and died of cholera on Aug. 2.—Mr. Morehead again became Provisional Governor, Aug. 2; public meeting held at Madras to petition the Queen to confirm him as Governor, Aug. 13.—Native Testimonial presented to the 1st Madras Fusiliers, Aug. 4.—The Infantry Volunteer Guards converted into a Light Infantry Regiment, August.—Passing of the Bill for abolishing local European Army in India, Aug. 16.—Cinchona introduced into Southern India by Mr. Clements Markham, August; cultivation commenced on the Neilgherry Hills, Oct. 12.—Rifle Club formed in Madras, Sept. 20.—The Arms' Act and the Stamp Act came into operation, Oct. 1.—Order issued disbanding the 5th, 6th, and 7th Regiments of Light Cavalry, and reducing the strength of Infantry Regiments, Oct. 20.—Canara divided into two Districts, North and South Canara, the former being transferred to the Bombay Presidency, October.—The town of Madras transferred for administrative purposes to the Chingleput District, October.—Sir Henry Davidson, Chief Justice of Madras, died, Nov. 3.—Pepper monopoly abolished by the Travancore Government, Nov. 27.—Bhadrachellam and Rekapilly taluks ceded by the Nizam, and attached to the Godavery District, November.

1861.—Sir Charles Trevelyan's defence published, Jan. 17.—The inhabitants of the Madras Presidency held a public meeting, and submitted a petition to Parliament praying for reforms in the mode of administering the Government of India, Jan. 19.—Famine in Travancore, Jan. 26.—Railway from Tirupatur to Salem opened, Feb. 1.—Memorial Hall, Madras, commenced, Feb. 16.—The Bishop of Madras issued a circular to the clergy of the diocese inviting subscriptions for the relief of sufferers from drought in the N. W. Provinces and Travancore, Feb. 16.—Sir William Denison from Tasmania arrived as Governor, Feb. 18.—Public meeting held in Madras for famine relief in N. W. Provinces and Travancore, the Honourable W. A. Morehead in the chair, Feb. 18.—Rama Vurmah, first Prince of Travancore, opened a Fund, with a subscription of Rs. 5,000, for presenting a golden throne to Queen Victoria, Feb. 25.—Departure of Sir Patrick Grant, Commander-in-Chief, Feb. 27.—Railway from Arkonam to Nagari, opened March 4.—Dr. Dealtry, Bishop of Madras, died March 6.—Railway from Beypore to Tirur opened March 12.—Mr. Pogson, Government Astronomer at Madras, discovered a new planet shining as a star of about the eleventh magnitude, and called it "Asia," April 17.—Sir W. Denison left Madras for Calcutta, April 23.—General order by the Governor-

General on the Amalgamation of the Royal and Indian Armies published, April 26.—The strength of the Native Army of India reduced by 110,000 men. The Madras Army to consist of 52 Regiments.—Upwards of 600 Madras Fusiliers volunteered for general service in the Bengal European Infantry and Artillery.—Railway from Tirur to Kuttipuram opened, May 1.—Sir W. Denison returned to Madras from Calcutta, May 13.—Sir Colley H. Scotland, new Chief Justice of the Supreme Court, arrived at Madras, May 23.—The Secretary of State for India introduced a Bill into the House of Commons for reconstituting the Councils in India; he also introduced a Bill for amalgamating the Supreme and Sudder Courts; and another to amend the law relating to the Civil Service. Madras Civilians who have completed twenty-two years service in India, permitted to retire from the service on £500 a year, without waiting for annuity from the Civil Fund, June 7.—Native meeting at Madras to petition Parliament for the restoration of the Nabobship of the Carnatic, June 15.—Large comet visible throughout India, July 2.—The Order of the Star of India created, July 5.—Railway from Negapatam to Tiruvalur opened, July 15.—The Indian Civil Service Bill and Judicature Bill received the assent of Her Majesty, July 6.—Bill for licensing arts, trades, and dealings passed by the Madras Legislative Council, July 13.—Three prizes of £1,000 each, to be awarded for two years in succession in the three Presidencies for the best specimens of cotton.—Brigadier General Sir William Neill's statue at Madras unveiled August 22.—Bill to enable the Banks of Bengal, Madras, and Bombay to undertake the issue &c. of paper currency notes, and certain business hitherto transacted at Government Treasuries, passed in the Viceregal Legislative Council, Aug. 31.—Railway from Kuttipuram to Pattambi opened, Sept. 23.—Minute of Sir W. Denison on the Cotton question published Nov. 14.—Dr. Gell installed as Bishop of Madras, Nov. 27.—Madras Volunteer Guards presented an Address to Colonel Silver, their Commandant, on his retirement from the Corps, Nov. 30.—Madras Screw Pile Pier opened Dec. 1.—Railway from Salem to Sankaridrug opened, Dec. 1.—Railway from Tiruvalur to Tanjore opened, Dec. 2.—Railway from Nagari to Puttur opened, Dec. 8.—The Madras Chamber of Commerce presented an address to Mr. Laing, Finance Minister, on his return from England, Dec. 9.—79 Madras field officers retired from the service on the terms offered by Sir Charles Wood, Dec. 17.—Sir J. Hope Grant, Commander-in-Chief, arrived Dec. 26.—The export of saltpetre except to London or Liverpool prohibited, Dec. 27.

1862.—The Indian Penal Code came into operation, Jan. 1.—A notorious robber chief, named Dharally Wucky, captured and killed at a village near Cochin, Jan. 7.—Colonel Horsley gazetted as Secretary to the Government of Madras in the Public Works Department, Jan. 10.—New Legislative Council assembled for the first time, Jan. 22.—Kumroodeen Khan, one of the Mysore Princes, sentenced to seven years' transportation for forgery, Jan. 23.—The Armenian race, as distinguished from East Indians, pronounced eligible for admission into the Indian Medical Service, Jan. 28.—The Khonds advanced upon Ganjam, destroying several villages, Feb. 1.—Address of condolence to the Queen on the death of the Prince Consort adopted, Feb. 4.—The license tax abandoned, and the money collected ordered to be returned. A deputation from the Madras Trades Association held an interview with Sir W. Denison to claim representation in the new Council, but their request was not entertained, Feb. 20.—North Canara transferred from Madras to Bombay; Saugor and Jubbulpore transferred from Bengal to Madras, Feb. 22.—Sunday trains discontinued on the Great Southern of India Railway; New Paper Currency Bill came into operation, March 1.—Lord Elgin, the Viceroy Designate, arrived at Madras on his way to Calcutta, March 6.—A public meeting held in the Banqueting Hall to adopt a farewell address to Lord Canning, the first Viceroy of India, March 8.—Great Southern of India Railway opened to Trichinopoly, March 11.—Roman Catholic community of Madras held a public meeting to repudiate the Concordat between the King of Portugal and the Pope. A meeting of the East Indian inhabitants of Madras held to petition against their exclusion from the higher grades of the Service, March 22.—First distribution of Mr. Peter Cator's prizes by the Bishop of Madras, April 7.—Emmanuel Church in Black Town consecrated, April 12.—A French Viscount named De Fercy sentenced to 12 months' imprisonment for forgery at Madras, April 17.—Rs. 9,007 presented to the Madras Sailors' Home by the Eden Testimonial Committee, April 23.—The gratuitous issue to the Press of Government telegrams of English news discontinued, May 6.—The South-West line of the Madras Railway completed by the opening of the line to Beypore, May 12.—Minute published by the Government of India abolishing certain distinctions between the Covenanted and Uncovenanted branches of the Service, May 27.—The right of adoption conferred upon the Chiefs of Travancore, Cochin, Poodoocottah, and Sundoor, June 21.—Mr. Breeks, the Governor's Private Secretary, waylaid and robbed near Coimbatore, July 1.—

The Madras Native Association petitioned Parliament respecting the alleged violation of Indian treaties. A general order published at Calcutta authorising a great reduction in the Indian Navy Establishment, July 15.—The Madras Chamber of Commerce held a meeting in aid of the distressed Lancashire operatives, July 30.—Abolition of the Supreme and Sudder Courts, and opening of the High Court of Madras, August 16.—The East India Community of Madras held a public meeting in Patcheappah's Hall to petition Parliament against their exclusion from the higher branches of the Indian Medical Service, August 28.—The Trevelyan gates of Government House erected. A meeting of the Portuguese Catholics of Madras held in Black Town in support of the Pope's Concordat, Sept. 22.—Inauguration of the Normal School, Sept. 26.—Madras Chamber of Commerce presented an address to Mr. Laing, the Finance Minister, on his retirement, Oct. 1.—Public meeting in the Banqueting Hall in honour of Mr. Morehead, Oct. 4.—The Rajah of Travancore contributed Rs. 5,000 as a donation to the Lancashire Relief Fund, Oct. 6.—A succession of gales swept through the Bay of Bengal by which several casualties were occasioned, Oct. 8.—A dramatic and musical entertainment given in the Banqueting Hall in honour of Mr. Morehead. A deputation of gentlemen, representing the Madras community, waited on him with a farewell address, Oct. 25.—Telegram received at Madras of Sir Charles Trevelyan's appointment as Finance Minister in succession to Mr. Laing, Nov. 23.—A prize of Rs. 1,000 and a gold medal presented to Dr. Shortt, Assistant Surgeon of the Madras Medical Establishment, by the Agri-Horticultural Society of India, for an essay on cotton cultivation, Dec. 2.—The Rajah of Travancore arrived at Madras on a visit to the Governor, Dec. 5.—A very numerously attended meeting of the inhabitants of Madras held at the People's Park to adopt a congratulatory address to Sir Charles Trevelyan on his expected arrival from England on his journey to Calcutta, Dec. 22.

1863.—Sir Charles Trevelyan landed at Madras, and received an address from the public of Madras, and one from the Chamber of Commerce, Jan. 8.—Shocks of earthquake felt in the Kistna District, Jan. 10.—M. Bontemps, a godson of the Emperor Napoleon III., arrived in Pondicherry, and assumed the office of Governor, Jan. 15.—The steamer *Burrampooter* ran ashore near Pulicat, Jan. 26.—The *Madras Daily News* started, Feb. 2.—Colonel Fenwick of the 67th Regiment died of cholera in Fort St. George, March 3.—The immediate completion of the Coast Telegraph Line between Madras and Bombay authorised March 7.—Census taken by the Municipal Commissioners shows the population of Madras to be 450,000, March 14.—Meeting held at the Banqueting Hall to congratulate the Queen on the marriage of the Prince of Wales, April 8.—Display of fireworks on the Island in honour of the marriage of the Prince of Wales, April 16.—Dr. Gell, Bishop of Madras, held his first visitation and delivered a charge to the clergy, April 23.—Public Works Department, Madras, reorganised. Abolition of the Indian Navy, May 1.—A fête given at the expense of Government in honour of the marriage of the Prince of Wales to the children of Protestant and Roman Catholic Poor Schools, May 14.—The Restoration of the private property of the Tanjore Royal Family completed, May 18.—The barque *Mahomed Sowdowny* wrecked near the Madras Pier, May 19.—Several new Armstrong guns (110 pounders) arrived in Madras for the protection of the Fort.—A Bill for the reduction of the income-tax brought forward by Sir C. Trevelyan, May 23.—Archbishop Saboh, the Commissary appointed by the Pope to give effect to the Portuguese Concordat, died at Ootacamund, June 6.—The Madras Education Act passed, June 9.—Sir W. Denison proposed the abandonment of the Grand Jury system, July 14.—The case of Prince Azim Jah, claimant of the Nowabship of the Carnatic, again brought before Parliament by Sir Fitzroy Kelly, Aug. 4.—The Secretary of State ruled that in future soldiers' necessaries should be supplied by Government at cost price, Aug. 5.—General Sir J. L. Caldwell, Madras Engineers, the oldest officer of the Indian Army, died, Aug. 6.—The reply from the Queen and Prince of Wales to the Madras Address published, Aug. 12.—The Appellate Branch of the High Court, (late Sudder,) removed to the Beach building, Aug. 15.—The Honourable V. Sadagopah Charlu died, August 19.—The Controller of Military Finance recommended the abolition of the Oossoor Remount Depôt, Aug. 24.—A shock of earthquake felt at Trincomalee, Sept. 4.—The Very Rev. Lord Howard arrived at Madras, Sept. 5.—A grand entertainment given to Mr. H. E. Church, traffic manager of the Madras Railway, Sept. 8.—The ship *New Ville Alfred* wrecked off Calingapatam, Oct. 1.—An accident on the Railway between Avanashy and Erode, Oct. 6.—The construction of a Pier across the Beypore Harbour sanctioned by the Secretary of State, Oct. 8.—A severe gale at Madras; the ship *Percival* and eight Dhonies wrecked, Oct. 19.—The construction of a new road up the Coonoor Ghaut sanctioned, Oct. 23.—A serious murrain prevalent amongst the cattle in Kurnool, destroying them in large numbers, Oct. 29.—Two vessels driven ashore on the coast of

Cochin, thirteen lives lost, Oct. 30.—The Parsees of Bombay subscribed Rs. 80,000 to alleviate the distress among the Madras native weavers, Nov. 5.—Shurf-ool-Oomrah Bahadur appointed a member of the Madras Legislative Council, Nov. 18.—The Metropolitan of India delivered his first visitation charge in St. George's Cathedral.—The Earl of Elgin, Viceroy and Governor-General of India, died at Durmsala in the Kangra Valley, Nov. 20.—The Honourable Sir R. Napier, K.C.B. appointed to act as Governor-General, pending the arrival of Sir W. Denison, Nov. 23.—Ice Company started in Bangalore, Nov. 25.—Sir W. Denison embarked for Calcutta to assume the office of Governor-General of India *pro tem*; the Honourable Mr. Maltby appointed Acting Governor of Madras, Nov 27.—Sir W. Denison acted as Governor-General for seven weeks from Dec. 2.—The Tranquebar Fort ordered to be razed to the ground, Dec. 8.—The murderer of the late Mr. Horsley of the Madras Civil Service captured, Dec 31.

1864.—The Government Alcohol Distillery abolished, Jan. 1.—Thirty-six convicts on their way from Salem to Madras, to be transported, rose upon the Police guard; seven were shot dead, eight were seriously wounded, nine were re-taken, and the rest escaped, Jan 1.—A shock of earthquake felt at Trichinopoly, Jan. 5.—A shock of earthquake felt at Salem, Jan. 7.—Sir John Lawrence, the newly appointed Governor-General of India, arrived off Madras, but did not land, Jan 8.—Sir W. Denison returned to Madras from Calcutta, and resumed the office of Governor of Madras, Jan. 18.—Death of the Rev. J. Devasagayam, the first native of S. India admitted to Holy Orders in the English Church, Jan. 30.—A public meeting of inhabitants of Madras, Sir W. Denison in the chair, adopted an Address of congratulation to the Queen on the birth of a son to the Prince of Wales, March 1.—The title of "Maharajah" conferred as a personal distinction on the Rajah of Vizianagram, March 11.—First meet of the Hockey Club, March 23.—The Elden House started, March 24.—Abolition of the License-tax, and reduction of the Income-tax and Customs tariff, April 1.—Formation of the Sanitary Commission with Mr. R. S. Ellis, C.S., as President, and Dr. Montgomery as Secretary, April 7.—The Hon'ble G. Lutchmenarasu Chetty took his seat as a member of the Legislative Council, April 9.—The Madras Philharmonic Society started, April 9.—Disbandment of the 18th, 42nd, 43rd, and 44th Regiments of Madras Native Infantry, April 30.—Introduction of Fish in the Pycarra and other streams on the Neilgherries, May 4.—Staff Corps rules published, May 23.—A uniform standard of weights and measures introduced throughout India.—Indian Marriage Act came into operation, July 1.—Mr. J. B. Norton appointed Advocate General of Madras, July 19.—Through passenger traffic between Madras and Bangalore opened, Aug. 1.—Sir Charles Trevelyan's Minute on a gold currency for India published, Aug. 1.—Proposed extension of the Railway line from Shoranoor to Narakal and Cochin, Aug. 5.—Bill for the abolition of the Grand Jury published, Aug. 13.—Opening of the Madras Irrigation and Canal Company's Main Canal at Kurnool, Aug. 17.—The Ranee Kuttama Naichiar assumed possession of the Estate and Palace of her father the Istimrar Zemindar of Shivagunga, of which she had been deprived for thirty-five years, Sept. 15.—Mr. Whitley Stokes appointed Secretary to the Calcutta Legislative Council, succeeded in Madras as Law Reporter by Mr. O'Sullivan, Sept. 26.—Railway from Tirupati to Reddipalle opened, Oct. 1.—Loss of the s.s. *Persia*, with all hands on board, from Madras to London, Oct. 5.—Serious inundation at Cuddalore, Oct. 7.—Disastrous Cyclone in Calcutta, great loss of life; and numerous casualties among the shipping, Oct. 10.—Fund opened in Madras for the relief of the sufferers, Oct. 15.—The French ship *Père Anson* stranded on the beach at Madras, Oct. 18.—Loss at Masulipatam of about 30,000 lives from the inflowing of the sea, Nov. 1.—The Maharajah of Vizianagram appointed to a seat on the Viceregal Legislative Council, Nov. 3.—Public Meeting at the Banqueting Hall, the Governor in the chair, for the relief of sufferers from the recent cyclone in the Kistna District, and inundations in Cuddalore, Nov. 16.—Destructive cyclone at Madras 25th Nov.; one ship went to sea and was not heard of again; six were abandoned at sea; four were dismasted.—Agricultural Exhibition at Oossoor, Nov. 29.—"Editors' Room" opened in the Government Office, Dec. 1.

1865.—The Registration Act came into operation Jan. 1.—Transfer of the Hunsur Forest from Madras to Mysore, Jan. 1.—The Memorial Hall completed and opened, Jan. 2.—The Duc de Brabant visited Madras, Jan. 8.—The Royapettah Schools opened, Jan. 9.—Shock of earthquake felt at Venikonda, Kistna District, Jan. 20.—St. George's Cathedral formally re-opened for public worship, several improvements having been made, and a new chancel added, Jan. 22. First public auction sale of Neilgherry tea, Jan. 27.—The Administrator General's Act 1865 passed, Feb. 22.—The Government Forests Act 1865 passed, Feb. 24.—Telegraphic communication between Madras and Europe *via* Turkey opened, March 1.—The Indian Succession Act passed, March 7.—The High Courts Criminal Procedure Amendment Act passed, March 21.

—Arrival in Madras of Sir Hugh Rose, March 27.—Government decided upon amalgamating the Military Male Orphan Asylum with the Lawrence Asylum at Ootacamund, March 30.—Sir W. Denison's letter on Native Agriculture published, April 1.—Railway from Arkonam to Conjeveram opened, May 8.—The Warrant Grade instituted, May 18.—Total subscriptions for the Masulipatam Relief Fund, Rs. 1,60,000, May 20.—Govindu Naick's Primary School formally opened by Sir Colley Scotland, May 22.—Sir Gaspard Le Marchant, Commander-in-Chief, arrived, May 25.—Testimonial presented to Sir Hope and Lady Grant, May 28.—Complimentary dinner to Colonel Impett, Sheriff of Madras, at the Madras Club, in celebration of the fiftieth anniversary of the victory at Waterloo, June 19.—Shock of earthquake felt at Coimbatore, June 24.—The citizens of Madras memorialised the Governor for a share in the management of their municipal affairs, Aug. 9.—Recommendation by the Sanitary Commission for a new General Market in Madras, Aug. 16.—Madras Committee for the International Paris Exhibition of 1867 appointed, with the Hon. H. D. Phillips as President, and Mr. C. A. Lawson as Secretary, Sept. 1.—Railway from Reddipalle to Cuddapah opened, Sept. 1.—Murder of Capt. Gordon on board the *Alarm* in the Madras Roads, Sept. 3.—Rent Recovery Act passed, Sept. 19.—Towns Improvement Act passed, Oct. 14.—Order for the re-organization of the Madras Army promulgated, Oct. 24.—City of Madras Municipality Act came into operation, Nov. 1.—Permission given by the Madras Government to Mr. Sterne to search for gold in various parts of the Presidency, Nov. 15.—Medical Commission appointed, Nov. 22.—Serious drought in Madras, Cuddapah, Bellary, and Kurnool, November.—A rising of the Khonds in Ganjam took place and was soon suppressed, in November.—Railway line opened to Cuddapah, Dec. 6.

1866.—Mutiny Act came into force in India, Jan. 1.—Death of Mr. Steele, First Judge of the Small Cause Court, Jan 21.—Farewell ball in honour of Lady Denison, Jan. 30.—Disturbances among the Khonds in Ganjam suppressed, January.—Public meeting at Madras to protest against the proposed appropriation of a portion of the Park by the Madras Railway Company for the new Central Terminus, Feb. 3. The protest was successful.—Famine in Ganjam, February.—Arrival of the First Prince of Travancore in Madras, Feb. 15.—The Moplah Rajah of Cannanore divested of 22 honorary distinctions hitherto accorded him by Government for alleged complicity in three murders, March 3.—An address presented to the Hon. J. D. Norton by the Hindus on his approaching departure to Europe, March 6.—A Denison Scholarship founded by the Hon. Shurf-Ool-Oomrah Bahadur, March 10.—Farewell dinner given in honour of Sir W. Denison by the Madras Hunt, March 18.—Mohammedan address presented to Sir W. Denison, March 22.—Sir W. Denison succeeded as Governor of Madras by Lord Napier, March 27.—Departure of the former to Europe, March 28.—Distress in Tanjore, March.—South of India Planters' Association formed, April 4.—New Presidency College buildings begun, April 13.—Indian Companies' Act, the Indian Post-Office Act, and the Native Converts' Marriage Dissolution Act came into operation, May 1.—Discovery of a new planet by Mr. Pogson, Government Astronomer, and named by him "Sylvia," May 16.—Adoption of the 1st April as the commencement of the official year in India, June 5.—Presentation of a Testimonial to the Right Rev. Dr. J. Fennelly on the twenty-fifth anniversary of his consecration, June 27.—Famine in Orissa and Ganjam. Lord Napier visits the afflicted districts, July 14.—Distress, resulting from drought, in South Arcot, Salem, Coimbatore, and Bellary. Public meeting to devise means for relieving the distress, July 21.—Railway line from Cuddapah to Mudanur opened, Aug. 1.—The old colours of H.M.'s [illegible], late 1st Madras Fusiliers, placed in St. Mary's Church, Fort St. George, Aug. 28.—The grain [illegible] in Madras looted, Sept. 7.—The Madras Bank Bill passed, Sept. 15.—Shock of earthquake felt at Vellore, Oct. 6.—Serious caste riot in the Kistna District, Oct. 26.—The Rajah of Travancore made a "Maharajah," Nov. 9.—Railway line from Trichinopoly to Caroor opened, Dec. 3.—Colonel Temple, President of the Madras Municipal Board, Captain Hope, and two Misses MacIver, drowned in the river Adyar by the upsetting of a boat, Dec. 23.

1867.—Colonel C. A. Denison appointed President of the Madras Municipal Board, Jan. 6.—Native address presented to Miss Mary Carpenter, Jan. 18.—Opening of the Moorhead Memorial Hall at Chingleput, Jan. 18.—Arrival in Madras of the Maharajah of Travancore, Jan. 24.—The Maharajah invested by Lord Napier, with the G.C.S.I. The Honourable T. Pyer [illegible], the Honourable Shurf-Ool-Oomrah, and Mr. Madava Row, invested with the K.C.S.I.; and the Zemindar of Venkatagiri, Mr. W. R. Robinson, Dr. W. Mackenzie, Mr. E. B. Powell, and the Honourable G. Lakshmiнarasu Chetty with the C.S.I., Feb. 1.—Laying of the foundation stone of the Presidency College with masonic ceremony, Feb. 6.—Lord and Lady Napier left Madras for Calcutta on a visit to the Viceroy, Feb. 16.—They returned March 17.—Arrival of the Right Rev. Dr. Milman, the new Metropolitan of India, March 26.—Violent hailstorm in Kurnool, March 28.—Introduction of a license tax, April 1.—Settlement of H.H. Prince Azim Jah's affairs: £150,000 assigned for the payment of his debts, and an annual allowance granted of £15,000. Her Majesty conferred on him the title of Prince of Arcot, April 8.—Famine in Orissa, April.—Farewell dinner given to Mr. J. G. Coleman, by the Trades Association, April 9.—Madras Petition against the License Tax, April 10.—Rejection by the Madras Bank of the proposed amalgamation of the Presidency Banks, April 10.—Departure of the Right Rev. Dr. J. Fennelly, Roman Catholic Bishop of Madras, to Rome, May 6.—The Rajah of Venkatagiri established a Relief House for the poor of Madras, June 1.—Lord Napier visited Pondicherry, June 7.—Violent thunderstorm at Ramandroog, June 12.—The Trades' Association petitioned against the new Municipal Bill, June 18.—Ceremony of opening the Chilka Lake, or Napier Canal, July 1.—Railway from Karur to Kodumudi opened, July 1.—Madras memorial presented to the Government against the Municipal Act, July 4.—New Central Station, opposite the General Hospital gate, commenced, July 8.—Improved time signals adopted at the suggestion of Mr. Pogson, July 10.—Madras Municipal Bill passed into law, July 13.—Public meeting memorialised the Viceroy against the Municipal Act, July 23.—Major-General W. A. McCleverty appointed to succeed Sir Gaspard Le Marchant as Commander-in-Chief of the Madras Army, July 23.—Riots at Vellore, July 28 and 29.—Appointment of a Committee to report upon the subject of European Vagrancy in the Presidency, Aug. 1.—Provincial School of Combaconum constituted a College, Aug. 1.—The steeple of St. Andrew's Kirk struck by lightning, Aug. 23.—The Public Library buildings at Ootacamund commenced, Aug. 28.—The foundation stone of the new "Biden (Sailors') Home" laid by Lord Napier, Aug. 31.—Serious encroachment of the sea at Cochin in August.—New Police Act came into operation, Sept. 1.—Report of the Cholera Commission published, Sept. 20.—Final Report of the Famine Relief Committee submitted to Government by Mr. Dalyell, Sept. 26.—Shock of earthquake felt at Chitoor, Sept. 29.—Calingapatam visited by a severe gale; two vessels wrecked, Sept. 29.—Table of salutes allowable to the Native Princes and Chiefs of India published, Oct. 1.—New Town Prayer and Reading Room opened, Oct. 12.—Departure of Sir Gaspard Le Marchant from Madras, Oct. 14.—Major-General T. A. Duke acts as Commander-in-Chief pending the arrival of General McCleverty.—"Home" for Destitute Europeans opened at Royapuram, Oct. 20.—Dinner at the Madras Club in honour of Sir Thomas Pycroft on the occasion of his retirement from the Civil Service, Oct. 25.—New Municipal Act came into operation, Nov. 1.—Lieut.-General W. A. McCleverty arrived, Nov. 7.—Return of the Right Rev. Dr. J. Fennelly, from Rome, Nov. 18.—Death of Brigadier General Ireland, Commanding the Malabar and Canara Division, Nov. 23.—The erection of a Central Lunatic Asylum at the Presidency Town sanctioned, Dec. 5.—Arrival of the Rev. Dr. Norman Macleod of Glasgow, on a Mission tour through India, Dec. 21.—Departure of Sir Thomas Pycroft, Dec. 28.

1868.—Railway from Kodumudi to Erode (junction with Madras line) opened, Jan. 1.—Opening of the Chitravutty Bridge, or the Napier Bridge, on the North-West line of Railway, Jan. 8.—Great distress continues in Madras, North Arcot, and Nellore, Jan. 9.—Formation of a Madras Branch of the East India Association, Jan. 10.—Death of the Right Rev. Dr. J. Fennelly, Jan. 23.—Murder of Mrs. MacDougall, widow of the late General MacDougall of the Bombay Army, at Ootacamund, by her horsekeeper, Feb. 4.—Dr. Wyllie bequeathed £4,000 to the city of Madras on behalf of the sick poor, Feb. 12.—Fête at Trichinopoly to celebrate the junction at Erode of the Great Southern of India Railway with the South-West line of the Madras Railway, Feb. 18.—Lord Napier left Madras for Travancore and Cochin, Feb. 20, and returned to Madras March 9.—Appeal made by Archdeacon Dealtry to the public for funds for a peal of bells for the Cathedral, Feb. 28.—Distress in Cuddapah, March.—Retirement of Mr. Justice Holloway, March 31.—License tax abolished, April 1.—Re-organisation of the Subordinate Medical Department, May 1.—Congratulatory address to the Queen on the escape of H.R.H. the Duke of Edinburgh from the attempt made on his life at Sydney adopted at a public meeting in Madras, May 15.—The Neilgherry Hills constituted a separate District, May 22.—Lord Napier laid the foundation stone of the Senate House, Chepauk, May 23.—The Very Rev. Dr. S. Fennelly appointed Roman Catholic Bishop of Madras in succession to his brother, June 1.—The establishment at Madras of a Model Female Normal School by the Maharajah of Vizianagram sanctioned by Government, June 4.—The Madras Mint greatly reduced, June 5.—Wreck of the French barque *Saint Bernard* in the Madras Roads, causing great damage to the Madras Pier, June 6.—The distress in the several districts of the Presidency allayed, in consequence of abundant rain having fallen, June.—The Vepery Hospital converted into a New Civil Female Hospital, and no male out-patients treated there in future, July 4.—Serious floods in Orissa, July 5.—Mr. J. W. Breeks, C.S., appointed the First Commissioner of the Neilgherries, July 6. —Office of Revenue Secretary to Government created, Mr. Dalyell appointed the first incumbent, July 7.—Farewell dinner to Mr J. J. Franklin, the Superintendent of Marine, July 16.—Amalgamation of the Vepery and Royapettah Police Courts, July 20.—The Colar Bridge on the Bangalore branch of the Madras Railway washed away, July 25.—Total Solar Eclipse, Aug. 18.—Dinner given at the Madras Club to the military officers on their return from active service in Abyssinia, Aug. 25.—Railway from Muddoor to Tadpatri opened, Sept. 1.—Extension of the Madras Railway from Coimbatore to Kallar sanctioned by Government, Sept. 2.—New Telegraphic Tariff came into operation, Oct. 1.—Consecration of the new Roman Catholic Bishop of Madras, Oct. 4.—Opening of the first reach of 7½ miles of the East Coast Canal, Oct. 19.—The Earl of Mayo appointed Governor-General of India, Oct. 27.—Shock of earthquake felt at Salem, Nov. 8.—The Biden Home for Sailors at Royapuram opened by Lord Napier, Commodore Sir Leopold Heath being present, Dec. 12.—The *Madras Mail* started, Dec. 15.—Mr. Parkes' Report presented to the Madras Harbour Committee, Dec. 22.—Regatta at the Red Hills during Christmas week.

1869.—Arrival of Lord Mayo from Bombay on a visit to the Governor of Madras, Jan. 2. The Madras Chamber of Commerce presented an address to him, Jan 5. He left for Calcutta on Jan. 7 to succeed Sir John Lawrence as Viceroy of India.—The Saugor division transferred to Madras, Jan. 13.—Sir John Lawrence, late Viceroy, lands at Madras, with Sir James Fergusson, the Governor Designate of Western Australia, and the Marquis of Blandford, Jan. 23.—The Infantry Volunteer Guards' excursion to Conjeveram, Jan. 30.—Establishment of a branch of the Chartered Mercantile Bank at Cocanada, Feb 1.—Office of Consulting Architect to Madras Government created, Feb. 1.—Public Works Commission appointed, Feb. 2. —Henry Thurston sentenced to death for the murder of Captain Page of the barque *Lena*, in Madras, Feb 2, and executed Feb. 11.—Monument erected in Trichinopoly to the memory of Mr. Ronald McDonnell by the native community of the district, Feb. 15.—Laying of the foundation stone of St. Andrew's Native Church, Feb. 24.—The Ootacamund Agri-Horticultural Society established, Feb. 27.—Closing of the Madras Mint, March 5. —Report of the Madras Breakwater Committee published, March 19.—The Madras Repealing Act passed, March 20.—Office of Collector of the Imperial License Tax abolished, and the duties delegated to a Deputy Collector, April 1.—New Income Tax Bill passed, incomes under Rs. 500 per mensem being exempted, in lieu of the License Tax Act, April 1.—Health Office established.—Divorce Act came into operation, April 1.—Arrival of Prince Frederick of Holstein in Madras, April 3.—Harmonic Society formed at Ootacamund, April 15.—The Senate of the Madras University resolved to establish six University Professorships, April 24.—The Maharajah of Vizianagram visited Madras in April.—Abandonment of Kurnool as a Military Station, May 1.—Death of Mr. Chamier, Judge of Salem, May 10.—Archery Club established at Ootacamund, May 21.—Foundering of the s.s. *Carnatic*, in a cyclone in the Bay of Bengal, May 21.—First Neilgherry Agri-Horticultural Exhibition, May 24.—The Indian Articles of War came into operation, June 1.—The armament of Fort St. George reduced, June 1.—Lieutenant and Adjutant Brooking of the 35th N. I. shot on Vepery Parade Ground by a Havildar, who committed suicide, June 7.—Brigadier General Wilde, C.B., C.S.I., Military Secretary to Government, created a K.C.B., June 8.—The British barque *Alexander* wrecked some miles to the south of Madras, July 9.—Railway line opened from Tadpatri to Gooty, Aug. 1.—The demolition of the Chingleput Fort sanctioned, Aug. 6.—Government sanctioned the erection of a screw pile pier at Calicut, Sept. 1.—Shock of earthquake felt at Nellore, Sept. 10.—The Indian Volunteers' Act and the Madras Jails' Act passed, Sept. 30.—Laying of the foundation stone of the Trevandrum College, Oct. 1. —Madras Equitable Assurance Society's Act came into operation, Oct. 13.—The Maharajah of Travancore prohibited the shooting of wild elephants in his territories, Oct. 20.—Departure of the Right Rev. Dr. S. Fennelly to Rome, Oct. 23.—Death of Colonel J. E. Robertson, Adjutant-General of the Madras Army, Nov. 7.—The Rajah of Cochin created a K.C.S.I., Nov. 9.—The opening of the Suez Canal, Nov. 18.—Violent gale and floods at Tinnevelly, Nov. 21.—Explosion of a 64-pounder cannon in Fort St. George, killing a gunner on the spot, Nov. 22.—Soldiers' Industrial Exhibition at the Banqueting Hall, Nov. 29.—Arrival in Madras of Sir Seymour Fitzgerald, Governor of Bombay, Dec. 3.—Departure of Lord Napier and Sir Seymour Fitzgerald to Calcutta to be present there during the visit of the Duke of Edinburgh, Dec. 4.

1870.—Abolition of the Mounted Police, Jan. 1. —The General Stamp Act and the European

Vagrancy Act came into force, Jan. 1.—Installation of Azim Jah, as Prince of Arcot, Jan. 3. —The land opposite Government House transferred to the Municipality for the purposes of a Park, Jan. 8.—Public meeting at Patcheappah's Hall to devise measures for welcoming the Duke of Edinburgh, Jan. 24.—Removal of the Ootacamund Lawrence Asylum children into the new buildings at Lovedale, Jan.—Telegraphic communication between Madras and Europe *viâ* Persia opened, Jan. 31.—Farewell ball to Lady Bittleston at the Banqueting Hall, Feb. 11.—Government restored to the Maharajah of Pudukota the title of "His Excellency," and granted him a salute of thirteen guns, Feb. 27.—Opening of the G.I.P. Railway, the Duke of Edinburgh being present, March 8.—Arrival of the Maharajah of Travancore, March 16.—Arrival of the Governor of Pondicherry, March 20.—Arrival of H.R.H. the Duke of Edinburgh in Madras, March 22.—Addresses presented to the Duke, March 22.—Reception and Ball in honour of the Duke, March 23.—Outbreak in the Central Jail at Trichinopoly, March 23.—Native entertainment to the Duke of Edinburgh, March 24.—The Madras Club Ball to the Duke, March 25.—Opening of the New Presidency College by the Duke, March 25.—Departure of the Duke, March 27.—Departure of the Maharajah of Travancore, March 28.—Arrival of Sir Salar Jung in Madras, April 1.—Death of General William Fenwick, May 8.—Mr. A. J. Arbuthnot, Chief Secretary to the Madras Government, created a C.S.I., June 1.—Telegraphic communication between Madras and Europe *viâ* the Red Sea opened, June 3.—Removal of the Madras High School to the Presidency College buildings at Chepauk, July 1.—Removal of the Royapettah and Vepery Courts to the old High School building in Egmore, the old Royapettah Court being occupied by Prince Azim Jah, July 4.—First meeting of the Council of Fort St. George at Ootacamund, Nilgiri Hills, July 8.—Government sanctioned the proposed junction Canal between the Cooum and the Adyar, July 8.—Transfer to Government of the Madras Medical Fund, July 15.—Inauguration of the Dupleix statue at Pondicherry, July 16.—Abolition of the export duties on rice and indigo, July 23.—Native Memorial to the Duke of Argyll, Secretary of State for India, to extend Lord Napier's time in Madras, July 30.—The opening of the Tinnevelly College, Aug. 1.—Inundation of the Kistna District, Aug. 10.—Dome of the new Roman Catholic Church at Ootacamund fell in, Aug. 29.—The Hindu Wills Act came into operation, Sept. 1.—Arrival in Madras of the Right Rev. Dr. Milman, Metropolitan of India, Sept. 2.—The Indian troops supplied with Snider rifles, Sept. 14.—The new French Republic proclaimed at Pondicherry, Oct. 7.—The Madras Chamber of Commerce undertook to collect subscriptions on behalf of the National Fund for the aid of the sick and wounded in the Franco-Prussian War, Oct. 13.—Consecration of St. Thomas' Church at Ootacamund by the Metropolitan of India, Oct. 16.—Inundation in Cocoanada, Oct. 20.—The Cheyair Bridge on the North West line of the Madras Railway washed away; the Rev. Mr. and Mrs. Seymour and others lost, Oct. 31.—Violent cyclone at Vizagapatam, Nov. 6.—Opening of the St. Thomé College, Nov. 9.—Railway line from Gooty to Toongabudra opened, Dec. 12.—The Submarine Cable between Madras and Singapore completed, Dec. 30.—Return of Bishop Fennelly from Rome, Dec. 31.

1871.—Submarine cable between Penang and Madras opened to the public, Jan. 3.—Departure of General McCleverty to Europe on furlough; Major-General Sandrich acts as Commander-in-Chief of Madras for three months, from March 2.—Opening of the Madras Railway to Raichur, March 15.—Railway from Nundial to Vingpur opened, Jan. 16; from Vingpur to Bellary, March 1; and from Toongabhadra to Raichur (junction with the G.I.P. line), March 15.—Loss of the steamer *Tilly* off Quilandy, March 20.—Durbar at the Banqueting Hall, and Prince Azim Jah presented by Lord Napier with the Letters Patent conferring on him and his successors the title of Prince of Arcot, April 12.—G. I. P. Railway opened to Raichur, April 15.—General McCleverty resigned the command of the Madras Army in consequence of ill-health, and Major-General F. P. Haines nominated to succeed him, April 25.—General Haines arrived in Madras May 20; was created a K.C.B. May 24.—Mr. V. Ramiengar and Mr. Shungoony Menon, Dewan to the Rajah of Cochin, created C.S.I.'s, May 24.—The export duty on pepper abolished, June 1.—Disobedience, on Feb. 13, previous to embarkation for Burmah, and subsequent disbandment June 6, of the 19th Regiment Madras Native Infantry.—Commencement of the General Census of India, July 15.—Bursting of a cast-iron 24 pounder at St. Thomas's Mount, killing one gunner and wounding several others, July 26.—Transfer of the Military Male Orphan Asylum, Madras, to the Lawrence Asylum at Ootacamund, Aug.—Mutiny among the Sepoys at Pondicherry, Sept. 1.—Reorganization of the D. P. W. Madras, Sept. 12.—Lord Napier filed a suit against the *Athenæum and Daily News* for defamation, assessing the damages at Rs. 5,000, Sept. 29.—Reduction of newspaper postage to ½ anna not exceeding ten tolahs weight, Oct. 1.—Mr. J. B. Norton resigned the Advocate Generalship, and succeeded by Mr. J. D. Mayne, Nov. 1.—Native address of farewell to Mr. Norton, and a Scholarship founded in his honour at the University, Nov. 7.—Explosion at the Gunpowder Manufactory, five men killed, Nov. 11.—Arrival of M. Faron, the new Governor of Pondicherry, Nov. 13.—Census concluded, Nov. 14.—Drought in Ganjam in Nov.—Total Solar Eclipse: several observations made by Mr. Lockyer and Mr. Pogson, Dec. 12.—The Towns' Improvement and Local Fund Acts passed.—Sir Colley Scotland resigned the Chief Justiceship of Madras, and succeeded by Sir Walter Morgan.

1872.—Increase of telegraph rates, Jan. 1.—All Saints' Church at Coimbatore consecrated by Bishop Gell, Jan. 27.—Lord Mayo, the Viceroy of India, assassinated at Port Blair by a convict, Feb. 8.—Mr. John Strachey acted as Governor-General pending the arrival of Lord Napier, Governor of Madras.—Lord Napier's defamation suit against the *Madras Athenæum* decided in his favour, Rs. 2,000 being awarded as damages, Feb. 16.—Lord Napier left for Calcutta, Feb. 17, and Mr. A. J. Arbuthnot became Provisional Governor of Madras.—General Thanksgiving Day throughout India for the recovery of the Prince of Wales, Feb. 27.—A public meeting at Madras adopted an address of condolence to Lady Mayo, March 2.—Famine in Ganjam in May, June, July, and August.—Execution at Port Blair of Shere Ali, the murderer of Lord Mayo, March 11.—Departure of Lady Mayo from Bombay to Europe, March 14.—Masonic funeral service at Madras in memory of the late Viceroy, March 16.—Mr. H. S. Cunningham appointed Advocate General, Madras, March 30.—Address and Testimonial presented to the Rev. A. R. Symonds, April 17.—Mr. Seshaya Sastri appointed Dewan of Travancore in succession to Sir T. Madava Row, May 1.—Fearful cyclone swept over Madras; nearly all the shipping was driven ashore, and wrecked, and the pier was again broken, May 2.—Lord Northbrook assumed the office of Viceroy of India, May 3.—The Maharajah of Vizianagram appointed member of the Viceroy's Legislative Council, May 9.—Great floods at Vellore, and loss of about 1,000 lives, May 3.—Major the Hon. F. R. Bourke appointed Postmaster-General of Madras in succession to Col. A. C. Pears, May 6.—Arrival in Madras of Lord and Lady Napier from Calcutta *en route* to Europe, May 12.—Opening of the Madras Water Works by Lord Napier, May 13.—Arrival of Lord Hobart as Governor of Madras, May 15.—Committee appointed by Government to enquire into the late disastrous wrecks, May 22.—The title of Doctor of Divinity conferred on the Rev. H. Bower, of the S.P.G., June 6.—Death of Mr. Breeks, Commissioner of the Neilgherries, June 8.—Mr. Cockerill appointed Commissioner of the Neilgherries, June 9.—H. M.'s 21st Fusiliers, 2nd Battalion and No. 7 Battery, 5th Brigade R.A., paraded at Government House to receive the Testimonials subscribed for by the public at the instance of the Chamber of Commerce, in recognition of gallant services rendered during the late cyclone, June 10.—Native public meeting at Madras to memorialise the Secretary of State against the Marriage Bill recently passed in the Viceroy's Council, June 17.—Extensive forgery of Government currency notes, June 23. Major T. Weldon deputed to trace out the culprits.—Arrest of Venkatachellamiah, the alleged forger, at Tirupati, July 1.—He committed suicide July 21.—Lord Napier raised to the Peerage of the United Kingdom as Baron Napier and Ettrick, July 22.—Madras Municipality accepted the proposal of Sir James Anderson and Mr. William Davis, of London, to establish a system of tramways in Madras, July 26.—The Periyar Project begun, July 31.—Dengue fever prevalent in Madras during the whole of the latter half of the year.—Inspector-General Dr. William Mackenzie's portrait placed in the Medical College, August 30.—Peal of bells hung in the Cathedral, Sept. 18.—Accident on the Madras Railway at the Ballypully Ghaut, nine passengers injured, four seriously, Oct. 1.—Great floods in the southern districts in November.—Sir Richard Temple, Finance Minister, after a short visit, left Madras for Calcutta, Dec. 17.

1873.—Twenty-four persons died from suffocation in a *Pagoda* in Mint Street, Madras, Jan. 8.—Lord and Lady Hobart left Calcutta, Jan. 9.—Fire at Sadagiri, Malabar coast, two lives lost and 183 houses burnt down; estimated loss 5 Lakhs; Jan. 14.—Rev. John Tucker, C.M.S., died Jan. 16.—Shocks of earthquake experienced at Bimlipatam and Vizagapatam, Jan. 24.—The Marquis of Stafford and Lord Lewisham arrived at Madras from Ceylon, Jan. 27.—New Railway Station successfully lighted by Silber's lamps, the Commander-in-Chief and others being present, Jan. 28.—Farewell ball to Colonel Rutherford by the officers of the L. V. G., Jan. 29.—Madras Water Works Town Scheme opened to the public by Colonel Denison, Jan. 31.—Madras Railway line opened from Podanur to Coimbatore town, Feb. 1.—Sir T. Madava Row installed as Dewan of Indore, Feb. 3.—Lord Hobart returned to Madras from Calcutta, Feb. 7.—Dr. Blacklock died at Chittoor, Feb. 12.—Great Hindu festival at Kumbaconum, 200,000 pilgrims present, 2 persons killed under the wheels of the

Car, Feb. 12.—Madras Tramway Company's Prospectus issued in London, Feb. 13.—Napier Water Pandal opened by the Hon. Mr. R. S. Ellis, C.B., March 1.—Madras Civil Courts' Act came into operation, March 1.—Government ordered the publication of Manuals of the Districts of the Presidency, the honorarium to the compilers to be 100 guineas each, March 14.—General H. Pritchard's services of 41 years favourably noticed in G. O by H. E. the Commander-in-Chief of the Madras Army, March 22.—Indian Income Tax abolished, March 31.—Central Station, Madras Railway, which cost £100,000, opened to the public, April 7.—Bishop Ephrem of Mangalore died, April 10.—Foundation stone of Breeks' Memorial School at Ootacamund laid by Mr. J. D. Sim. C.S.I., May 16.—Postage on letters to Australia reduced to six annas per half-ounce, May 19.—Dr. Copperfield died at Madras, May 22.—Mr. A. J. Arbuthnot created a K.C.S.I., May 24.—Important resolution passed by the Government of India for the extension of Mohammedan education, June 14.—Government of India invited applications from native gentlemen who may wish to go to England to give evidence before the E. I. Finance Commission, June 21.—New Medical Warrant for Indian Army published, July 1.—Madras Pier re-opened for traffic, July 31.—Madras Railway line from Coimbatore to Mettapalaiyam opened, Aug. 31.—First Hindu widow re-marriage celebrated in Madras, Sept. 5.—Moplah outrage at Pattamby, two Nairs murdered; 8 Moplahs killed by detachment of the 43rd Foot; 7 Moplahs transported under the Act, Sept. 8.—Colonel R. S. Wilson's offer to compile a History of the Madras Army accepted by Government, Sept. 15.—Madras Female Normal School pronounced a failure, the Director of Public Instruction desired to draw up a new scheme for consideration of Government, Sept. 17.—Bishop of Madras set on foot an Additional Clergy Fund to support five Missionaries, Sept. 20.—Opening of the Kadaru bridge near Kamptee, length 1,300 feet, cost 10 lakhs, Sept. 21.—Elephant Preservation Bill (Madras) came into operation, Oct. 1.—Cosmopolitan Club, Madras, opened Oct. 6.—Tirumala Naick's Palace at Madura struck by lightning, Oct. 7.—Kistna Viaduct opened, length 1,290 yards, cost 14 lakhs, Oct. 9.—Butchers' Strike in Madras, Oct. 17.—Slight Moplah disturbance in Native Cochin, Oct. 22.—First sod of South Indian Railway turned at St. Thomas' Mount, Oct. 29.—The Bishops of Calcutta, Madras, and Bombay met at Nagpore, Nov. 27.—Bishop Depommier of Coimbatore died at Negapatam, Dec. 7.—Madras Port Trust Bill published, Dec. 9.—Musical party at the Banqueting Hall in honour of Her Majesty's birthday, Dec. 9.

1874—Lord Napier of Magdala arrived in Madras from Bombay, Jan. 3.—The Bangalore Camp of Exercise ordered to assemble, Jan. 5.—Lord Napier of Magdala left Madras for Bangalore, Jan. 12.—Volcanic action at Addanki, Nellore District, Jan. 13.—Azim Jah, the first Prince of Arcot, died. Ship *Indian Empire* on fire at Cochin, Jan. 14.—Shock of earthquake experienced in Salem at 12.30 P.M., Jan. 20.—Shocks of earthquake felt at Namakal and Poonagaram, Salem District, Jan. 21.—Earthquake at Ongole, Nellore District, Jan. 31.—Moplah riot in South Travancore, Feb. 5.—Married Women's Property Act and Recruiting Act passed, Feb. 24.—Consecration of Bishop Chevalier as Vicar Apostolic of Mysore, March 1.—Famine Relief Meeting, Madras, subscriptions Rs. 1,10,000, March 2.—Famine Relief Meeting at Cochin, subscriptions Rs. 15,000, March 9.—At a meeting of the Madras Municipality the proposal to elect Commissioners by popular vote was recommended to Government, March 12.—Government made a grant of Rs. 5,000 to Dr. Cornish, Sanitary Commissioner, in recognition of his labours in connection with the Madras Census, March 16.—Government of Madras passed orders for re-organising the School of Industrial Arts, March 25.—Madras Government ordered the abolition of the Palconda Municipality, March 31.—A Crown Prosecutor for Madras appointed, March 31.—Government ruled that public servants are not to receive valedictory addresses, April 4.—Heavy rain and gale in Madras, one Dhony wrecked, 7 inches of rain fell, damage to railway line, May 5.—Ship *Bengal* wrecked off Cocanada, May 9.—Floods on the railway line, trains delayed. Further re-organisation in the D. P. W. upper grades ordered, May 18.—Temperature at Madras 101.8 degrees in the shade.—Fire at Coconada, 200 houses burnt, May 30.—Association of Hindus formed in Madras to encourage widow marriage, June 4.—Railway accident at Papagni bridge, two lives lost; June 15.—Nineteen of the crew of a Chittagong brig lost in the Bay of Bengal, landed at Cochin, June 30.—Amalgamation of the Great Southern and Carnatic Railways sanctioned, July 16.—Madras Tramway line opened, July 20.—Honourable V. Sanjiva Row died at Kumbaconum, July 24.—Madras Government determined upon appointing Honorary Magistrates, and forming benches of Justices in Mofussil towns, July 30.—Free seat system introduced at St. Matthias' Church, Vepery, Aug. 1.—The Bank of Madras proprietors voted £3,000 as gratuity to Mr. McIver, the retiring Secretary and Treasurer, Aug. 3. —The Rev. Mr. Bardou consecrated Vicar Apostolic of Coimbatore, Aug. 23.—Code of Civil Procedure extended to the Madras Court of Small Causes, Aug. 26.—Mar Coorelloos, Syrian Bishop, died at Travancore, Sept. 1.—Deputy Surgeon General C. M. Duff, Madras Service, died in Burmah, Sept. 21.—Mahomed Yusuf Sahib appointed Magistrate of Police, Sept. 22.—Heavy floods in Bezwada, water over the Kistna anicut 19 feet, Sept. 27.—Madras International Ice Company began operations, Sept. 29.—Mr. T. G. Clarke, Senior Magistrate, retired after a public service of 45 years, Sept. 30.—Thirty Colonels of Madras Army retired under new scheme, 18 on commutation, and 12 on annuities, Oct. 6.—Presentation of Khareeta to the Maharajah of Vizianagram, Oct. 14.—Heavy rains in Madras, great damage to railway lines, mails delayed, tanks and bridges injured, Oct. 24.—Heavy floods in Nellore, Pennair rose 19 feet above the anicut, causing much damage to the town, Oct. 25.—Cyclone in Cocanada, 28 lives lost, Oct. 26.—First Industrial School opened in Madras, Nov. 2.—Government sanctioned Rs. 50,000 for the relief of sufferers from floods in Nellore, Nov. 24.—Arrival of Mr. Clarke, Drainage Engineer; new Theatre at College Hall opened, Dec. 12.—Meeting at Vizianagram to lay railway to Raepore, the Maharajah offered 14 lakhs for the purpose, Dec. 14.

1875.—The Government of India issued proclamation deposing Mulhar Rao the Guicowar of Baroda, Jan. 14.—The Maharajah of Travancore arrived in Madras *en route* to Calcutta, Jan. 25.—Madras Government ordered elective principle to be introduced in certain Municipalities, Jan. 27.—Mr. Grant Duff arrived in Madras in the course of a tour through India, Feb. 13.—Honorary Magistrates for the Presidency appointed by Government, Feb. 16.—Second Fine Arts Exhibition in Madras opened, Feb. 27.—Maharajah of Vizianagram's Majority Bill passed in Viceroy's Council, March 2.—Mr. Parkes' Harbour Scheme for Madras sanctioned by the Secretary of State, March 6. —Papal Jubilee Procession in Madras, March 15.—Extra Native Regiment from Madras ordered to Burmah owing to Mission to Mandalay, March 20.—Farewell address presented to Mr. Powell, the retiring Director of Public Instruction, by the Native community of Madras, March 22.—Colonel R. M. Macdonald appointed to succeed him, March 23.—Zenana Mahammedan School opened by Lady Hobart, March 24.—The Princess of Tanjore arrived at Madras, April 7.—Sir A. J. Arbuthnot appointed member of the Viceroy's Council, April 24.—Mulhar Rao, ex-Guicowar of Baroda, arrived at Madras by special train, and was interned at Doveton House, April 25.—Henry Vere, Lord Hobart, died, April 27. Mr. W. Robinson, Senior Member of Council, acted as Governor for seven months.—Public funeral of Lord Hobart, during which an accident occurred at Wallajah Bridge and 5 lives were lost in the Cooum, April 28.—Outbreak in Trichinopoly Jail, 6 convicts wounded, April 28.—High Courts' Procedure Bill came into operation, May 1.—Age for candidates entering the Civil Service raised to 25 years, May 7.—The Duke of Buckingham and Chandos accepted the Governorship of Madras, May 11.—Coffee duty abolished in Travancore, May 13.—The Government of Madras sanctioned formation of a Civil Medical Service, May 18.—Earthquake at Tirupatur, Salem District, June 1.—Secretary of State passed orders for the admission of natives into the Indian Civil Service, July 16.—Lady Hobart left Madras for Europe, July 18.—The Madras Harbour Works commenced, Aug. 3.—New Jury system introduced into Madras High Court Sessions, Aug. 9.—Madras Government sanctioned new degree of L.M.S. in the University, Aug. 23.—South Indian Railway line from Trichinopoly to Madura, and line from Trichinopoly Junction to Trichinopoly Fort, opened, Sept. 1.—Ship *Wildwave* lost off Mulki (S. Canara) with 40 lives, Sept. 2.—Major the Honourable E. R. Bourke, Postmaster General of Madras, resigned Sept. 16.—Foundation stone laid of first Methodist Episcopal Church in Madras, Oct. 1.—Formation of Sanitary Association in Madras, Oct. 9.—Ship *[illegible]* lost by fire off Canara, Oct. 23.—Mr. W. R. Robinson, Provisional Governor of Madras, created K.C.S.I., Nov. 9.—Sir P. P. Haines, Commander-in-Chief, Madras, appointed Commander-in-Chief of India, Nov. 22.—The Duke of Buckingham and Chandos arrived, and assumed office as Governor of Madras, Nov. 23.—The Prince of Wales arrived off Beypore, and left at midnight for Ceylon, Nov. 29.—The Maharajah of Travancore arrived at Madras, Dec. 6.—The Prince of Wales arrived at Tuticorin from Ceylon, Dec. 9; was presented with a Bible by Tamil Christians of Tinnevelly at Maniyachi; travelled in the first passenger train from Tuticorin to Madura; reached Trichinopoly, Dec. 11; left the following day; received loyal welcome in Southern Districts, and reached Madras Dec. 13.—Memorial stone of the Harbour laid by the Prince, Dec. 15.—State Banquet given by the Duke of Buckingham in the Banqueting Hall to the Prince of Wales, followed by a Ball in the Prince's honour at the Madras Club, Dec. 16.—The Prince of Wales at the Children's Fete at People's Park; and public entertainment to the Prince at Royapuram

Railway Terminus, when Address of Welcome was presented, Dec. 17.—The Prince left for Calcutta, Dec. 18.—Farewell dinner to General Haines at the Madras Club: and Sir Neville Chamberlain gazetted Commander-in-Chief and member of Madras Council, Dec. 21.—Lord Hastings died at Tanjore; ball to Colonel Meade at Bangalore, Dec. 22.—Arrival in Madras of Sir W. Gregory, Governor of Ceylon, *en route* to Calcutta, Dec. 23.

1876.—Drought in Bellary, Cuddapah and Nellore. Railway from Madras to Tuticorin opened to the public Jan. 1.—Madras Municipal Bill published.—The Prince of Wales subscribed Rs 10,000 to the Madras charities, Jan. 4.—New Telegraph Bill came into operation, Jan. 6.—Great fire in Cochin, three lakhs of property destroyed, Jan. 7.—The Home Government assented to the appointment of Missionary Bishops in India, Jan. 21.—Court of Wards' Bill passed by Legislative Council, Feb. 3.—Sir Neville Chamberlain, the new Commander-in-Chief, arrived in Madras, Feb. 3.—Earthquake at Vizagapatam, Feb. 5.—The Duke of Buckingham and Chandos left Madras for Calcutta, Feb. 13, and returned March 8.—Native Coinage Act came into operation Feb. 21.—Indian Reformatory Act received assent of the Viceroy, Feb. 29.—The Prince of Wales appointed Honorary Colonel of eight Corps of Indian Army, four to be called "Queen's Own," and four "Prince of Wales' Own" Regiments, March 10.—New Lecture Hall at the Central Museum opened by the Duke of Buckingham and Chandos, March 16.—Bishop Milman, Metropolitan, died at Rawalpindi on March 15, and Bishop Gell was appointed to act as Metropolitan, March 21.—The Assay Office in Madras closed, April 1.—Lord Lytton assumed office as Viceroy of India, in succession to Lord Northbrook, April 12.—Bishop Gell returned from Calcutta, April 21.—Proclamation at Windsor of Her Majesty's assumption of the title of "Empress of India," April 28.—Deputy Surgeon General Stewart died at Trichinopoly, May 4.—Fatal accident on the S.I. Railway, Madras; two lives lost. Meeting held by Bishop of Madras at Ootacamund to further the Milman Memorial Fund, May 13.—Madras Government issued order suppressing lottery advertisements, May 23.—Reduced rates of postage introduced between England and India, July 1.—Heavy rains and floods in Mangalore, July 24.—Dr. Balfour retired from the Surgeon Generalship of the I. M. D., after forty years' service, succeeded by Deputy Surgeon General Geo. Smith, Aug. 16.—Meeting in Dr. Balfour's honour at Patcheappah's Hall, Aug. 26.—Opening of the S.I. Railway between Madras and Tindivanam, Sept. 1.—Suspension for two months of Mr. Weld, C.S., Sept. 4.—The Madras Government sanctioned Rs. 10,000 for relief works in Nellore, Sept. 21.—Merchant Shipping Act 1876, came into operation, Oct. 1.—Archdeacon Johnson appointed Metropolitan of India, Oct. 6.—Cyclone at Vizagapatam, many lives lost, Oct. 7.—Ship *Jules Rose* stranded off Bimlipatam, several lives lost, Oct. 8.—The Duke of Buckingham and Chandos and Sir N. Chamberlain arrived at the Andamans, Oct. 9.—The Governor's Body Guard left Madras for the Delhi Camp, Oct. 10.—Distress reported in parts of Bellary, Cuddapah, and Nellore; one lakh of rupees sanctioned on account of relief works, Oct. 12.—Opening of the Hobart School at Ootacamund, Oct. 17.—Grain riot at Ellore, Oct. 20.—Special meeting of Madras Executive Council in connection with apprehensions of famine, Oct. 24.—Earthquake at Secunderabad, Oct. 25.—Public meeting held at Bangalore on account of the drought, Nov. 2.—The Duke of Buckingham and Chandos and Sir N. Chamberlain returned to Madras from tour in Burmah, Nov. 8.—The Agricultural College at Saidapet opened, Nov. 20.—Earthquake at Chicacole, Nov. 23.—Special Services on account of the famine, Nov. 30.—The Princess of Tanjore arrived at Madras *en route* to Delhi, Dec. 2.—The Duke of Buckingham and Chandos left Madras for Calcutta *en route* to Delhi, Dec. 16.—The Madras Municipality protested against the Junction Canal Works to be carried out by the Madras Government as famine relief measures, Dec. 20.—Collision on Madras Railway, ten lives lost, and twelve persons wounded, Dec. 25.—Address of loyal congratulation voted to Her Imperial Majesty by the Municipality of Madras, Dec. 28.—The Hindus of Madras adopted an Address to Her Majesty, Dec. 30.—The rainfall in Madras for the year was only 21 inches.

1877.—Proclamation of the Assumption of the title of Empress of India by Queen Victoria at the Imperial Assemblage at Delhi. The Order of the Indian Empire founded, Jan. 1.—Railway from Tindivanam to Cuddalore opened, Jan. 1.—The Districts of Bellary, Kurnool, Cuddapah, Kistna, Nellore, Chingleput, North Arcot, Salem, Madura, Coimbatore, Tanjore, and Trichinopoly, with an area of 84,700 square miles, and a population of 19 millions, were afflicted this year by famine, resulting from drought. The monthly number of people employed on relief works varied from a maximum of 1,125,370 in February to a minimum of 628,259 in October. The number gratuitously fed reached a total of 1,603,781 in October.—Sir Richard Temple appointed Famine Commissioner to Bombay and Madras, Jan. 5; he visited Kurnool, Bellary,

Cuddapah, Madura, Trichinopoly, Madras, and Chingleput and North Arcot, in January.—The Duke of Buckingham and Chandos returned to Madras from Delhi, Jan. 18.—S.S. *Duke of Sutherland* grounded at Madras, Jan. 20.—Collision on the Madras Railway at Coimbapore, 9 persons injured, Jan. 23.—Bishop Johnson, the new Metropolitan, arrived at Madras *en route* to Calcutta, Feb. 3.—Conference between Duke of Buckingham and Sir R. Temple at Bellary; Special Health Department appointed in Madras on account of increased death-rate, Feb. 12.—Railway from Tanjore to Mayaveram opened, Feb. 15.—Reductions in Ordnance Depots in the Presidency ordered, Feb. 17.—The question of retention of the Neilgherry Commission settled, Feb. 18.—The Viceroy's despatch acknowledges services of Madras Government in respect to famine, Feb. 21.—Loss of revenue on account of famine in the Madras Presidency estimated at £1,170,000, Feb. 22.—Right Rev. Dr. Caldwell, S.P.G., and Right Rev. Dr. Sargent, C.M.S., consecrated at Calcutta as Missionary Bishops in Tinnevelly, March 11.—Slight disturbance among the Khonds in Ganjam, March 7.—The Madras Government ordered a transfer of certain tracts of Malabar to the Neilgherries, March 8.—New Civil Procedure Bill received the assent of the Viceroy, March 30.—Opium and Registration Acts and Presidency Magistrates Act came into operation, April 1.—The Government of India passed complimentary order about Sir R. Temple's famine mission, April 30.—Sir Richard Temple appointed Governor of Bombay, Feb. 28; he visited Nellore, Coimbatore, and Pondicherry in March, and left for Bombay on April 20.—Specific Relief Act No. 1 of 1877 came into operation. Madras Government appointed sanitary officers to famine districts, May 1.—Heavy rain in Madras, May 18.—Appeal made to the public of Madras on behalf of the sufferers of cyclone, May 19.—Madras Government sanctioned the raising of Municipal house tax to 10 per cent. Society founded at Madras for the Prevention of Cruelty to Animals, May 29.—Canal uniting the rivers Adyar and Cooum at Madras commenced as a relief work in May.—Jubilee of Pope's consecration, June 3.—110,805 poor people fed in Mysore, June 16.—Railway from Cuddalore to Porto Novo opened, July 1.—Railway from Mayaveram to Sheyali opened, July 1.—106 members of the Madras Civil Service memorialised the Secretary of State against the Resolution of the Government of India prohibiting officers in Civil employ from collectively memorialising Government on any subject, July 7.—Madras famine grants up to date 200 lakhs, affairs reported to be very critical, July 10.—Double line of Railway from Madras to Trivellore opened, July 20.—Public meeting at the Banqueting Hall, at which the Duke of Buckingham presided, on behalf of the sufferers from the famine. Telegram despatched to the *Times* soliciting the aid of the public of the United Kingdom, Aug. 4.—Madras Famine Relief Fund opened with Sir William Robinson as chairman, and Mr. William Digby as hon. secretary, Aug. 11.—The Maharajah Holkar held a public meeting and subscribed Rs. 40,000 for Madras Famine Relief Fund, Aug. 8.—Public meeting held at Madras to petition Government against closing the Senior Department of the Medical College, Aug. 20.—Double line of Railway open to Arkonum, Aug. 27.—*Gazette of India* Extra published at Madras setting forth the famine policy to be adopted by the Government, Sept. 3.—Government of France sanctioned 100,000 francs for famine relief in Pondicherry, Sept. 4.—Madras Government sanctioned the establishment of Provincial College at Rajamundry, Sept. 7.—The Duke of Buckingham held a conference at Erode with the Collectors of Coimbatore, Salem, Tanjore, and Trichinopoly, Sept. 19.—Meeting at Calcutta to raise subscriptions for the Madras Famine Relief Fund, Sept. 20.—Lord Lytton arrived in Madras on Aug. 29 to discuss the famine policy with the local Government, and subsequently proceeded to Bangalore and Ootacamund.—Public servants of all grades permitted by Government to assist in the formation of Local Famine Relief Committees, Sept. 24.—Civil Procedure Code came into operation, also the Law of Limitation, Oct. 1.—The Viceroy subscribed £1,000 to the Madras Famine Fund, Oct. 6.—£6,000 received from Australia for the Madras Famine Fund, Oct. 9.—Madras Government sanctioned Rs. 4,55,000 to be advanced to ryots for seed grain, Oct. 17.—Mr. H. S. Cunningham appointed Judge of the High Court of Calcutta, Oct. 24.—The Government of India issued notification prohibiting lotteries and public Derby sweeps, Nov. 3.—Telegram despatched by Famine Relief Committee to Sir Thomas White, Lord Mayor of London: "Your lordship's exertions have brought such liberal aid from all quarters, that under present favourable prospects we gratefully say collections may cease," Nov. 5.—Railway collision at Naggery, 6 lives lost, Nov. 9.—Branch of the National Bank of India opened at Madras, Nov. 13.—Opening of Famine Orphanage at Madras, 44 inmates, Dec. 1.—Madras Famine grants from public funds to date Rs. 4,46,28,627 Dec. 8.—At a meeting of Madras Municipality it was agreed not to accept Mr. Clarke's Drainage Scheme, Dec. 19.—Severe floods in Tinnevelly in December.—Large extension of Lord Mayo's Decentralisation Scheme.

1878.—Continuance of famine. The numbers on relief works fluctuated greatly, sinking to 12,000 in July.—The South Indian Railway line from Sabyali to Coleroon opened, Jan. 1.—H.H. the Prince of Arcot invested by the Duke of Buckingham, at the Banqueting Hall, with the G.C.S.I.; Mr. G. Thornhill, the Rajah of Kalastry, the Nawab of Banganapalle, and Mr. Seshya Sastri with the C.S.I.—The Duke of Buckingham appointed G.C.S.I., Jan. 1. —439,667 poor on the hands of the State, Jan. 4.—Public meeting at Madras to thank the British Nation for relieving the famine-stricken in Southern India, Jan. 28.—Public meeting by native community, Madras, to petition Parliament on Civil Service rules, Jan. 30.—Subscriptions to Madras Famine Relief Fund ceased, Jan. 31. The amounts received were: from the Lord Mayor of London, 57⅓ lakhs; from Lancashire, 8¾ lakhs; from Yorkshire, 2 lakhs; from Scotland, 4½ lakhs; from Australia and New Zealand, 5⅞ lakhs; from Mauritius, Natal, and Gibraltar, ½ lakh; from India, 3 lakhs. Total Rs. 81,53,302.—Sir Andrew Clarke, Public Works Minister, arrived at Madras, Feb. 1.—Mr. Bliss appointed first Salt Commissioner for Madras, Feb. 5.—Madras Municipal Act passed in Council, Feb. 13.—Arrival of the Archbishop of Goa at Madras, Feb. 16.—Sir Andrew Clarke's proposed scheme for the reduction of Public Works expenditure, by the retirement of one hundred engineers, published Feb. 23.—Famine Census of Madras Presidency taken. Meeting at Madras to protest against increased taxation, and adoption of petition to Parliament, March 13.—Vernacular Press Bill passed by the Viceregal Council, March 14.—License Tax Bill passed in Madras Council, March 18.—Madras Salt Act II of 1878 extended to the sea-coast districts of the Presidency, March 21.—General Strachey, President of the Famine Enquiry Commission, arrived in Madras, March 25.—New License Tax and New Customs Acts enforced, April 1. —Mr. O'Sullivan appointed Advocate-General of Madras, April 2.—The Duke of Buckingham inaugurated the Junction Canal, April 7.—Thunderstorm at Mangalore, six lives lost, April 28.—The Pondicherry Railway scheme sanctioned, May 2.—Madura and Tinnevelly removed by order of Government from the list of famine districts, May 10.—Establishment by the Queen Empress of the Order of the Crown of India (for Ladies). Lady Mary Grenville, Lady Pottinger, Lady Napier and Ettrick, Lady Mary Hobart, and Lady Denison appointed thereto, May 29.—With favourable monsoon rains agricultural operations were resumed in the middle of the year.—206,000 persons on relief in the Madras Presidency, June 19.—The mortality attributable directly or indirectly to famine in Madras and Mysore in 1877-78 roughly estimated at 5,000,000. The population of Mysore believed to have been reduced 20 per cent., or from five to four millions.—Accession of 19,304 converts to Christianity between June and July reported from Tinnevelly.—Madras Cinchona Commission appointed by the Government of India, July 24.—Mr. Muthusawmi Iyer appointed a Judge of the High Court, Madras, July 25.—Defensive Works in Madras ordered to be completed, July 26.—Government of India passed a complimentary order acknowledging the services of military officers during the famine, July 27.—South Indian Railway extended to Madras Town, July 30.—Mr. Fawcett presented Madras and Bengal petitions to Parliament in respect to taxation, July 31.—Travancore Government by proclamation ordered vaccination to be generally adopted by the people, Aug. 14.—Sir N. Chamberlain left Madras for Peshawur, Aug. 16.—The South Indian Railway line from Porto Novo to Chidambaram opened, Oct. 1.—New Arms' Act came into operation, Oct. 1.—Cyclone at Vizagapatam and Bimlipatam; three English ships wrecked, and twenty lives lost, Nov. 5.—Government of Madras ordered troops to the Afghan frontier, Nov. 6.—The Native Princes in Northern India offered 3,000 infantry, 1,000 cavalry, and 13 guns to assist in the Afghan expedition, Nov. 13.—The Order of the Crown of India presented to the Princess of Tanjore by the Duke of Buckingham, Nov. 14.—Relief measures in Madras Town stopped, Nov. 25.—Famine Relief Works in Mysore closed, Nov. 30.—Meeting in Madras to raise funds for the relief of the shareholders of the Glasgow Bank, Dec. 2.—Sappers and Miners left Bangalore for Peshawur, Dec. 5.—Sir W. Robinson laid the foundation stone of the Robinson Park, Dec. 6. —Government of Madras ordered famine betts to be stopped, Dec. 7.—Indian Council resolved to increase the Native Indian Army by 15,000 men, Dec. 10.—Public mourning in December for three weeks in Madras for the Princess Alice of Hesse-Darmstadt, from Dec. 19.—Many Native Chiefs sent letters of condolence to the Queen on the death of the Princess.

1879.—Colonel W. S. Drever, Acting Inspector General of Police, and Mr. J. H. Garstin, C.S., Additional (Famine) Secretary to the Government, received the C.S.I. for services during the famine, and were invested by the Duke of Buckingham at the Banqueting Hall. Mr. N. R. Pogson, the Government Astronomer, the Honourable T. Muttusami Aiyer, a Judge of the High Court, Mr. W. Digby, Honorary Secretary of the Madras Famine Relief Fund, and Dr. D. R. Thompson, Madras Medical

Department, appointed C.I.E., Jan. 1.—New Madras Municipal Act came into operation, Jan. 1.—Formation of the "Duke's Own" Volunteer Artillery at Madras, Jan. 10.—Mr. Justice C. A. Turner, of the N.W.P. High Court, appointed Chief Justice of Madras, in succession to Sir W. Morgan, Jan. 15, and knighted March 20.—Madras Government declined to accept proposals for the Neilgherry Railway, Jan. 18.—Sir Neville Chamberlain returned to Madras from Calcutta, Feb. 18.—Opening of the Madras Fine Arts Exhibition, March 7.—Ennore Regatta, March 10.—Outbreak of a rebellion in the Zemindary of Rumpa in March. Insurgents led by several petty chiefs. Vigorous measures taken by Government. The disturbance subsided in November.—New Stamp Act came into operation, April 1.—Lady Mary Grenville laid the foundation-stone of the Hospital Wards, Monegar Choultry, April 8.—Famine Relief Fund Committees dissolved in April. The total number of persons relieved during the famine stated to have been 11,595,341; amount expended Rs. 78,70,020; cost of administration Rs. 40,043.—The Madras Municipality became a semi-elective assembly in April, and 16 members were elected by ballot.—South Indian Missionary Conference started at Bangalore in 1858, met at Ootacamund. The Maharajah of Vizianagram (Vejeeram Gajapati Rao) died at Simla, April 29.—Neilgherry Game Bill passed into law. Sir Charles Turner left Madras to attend the sittings of the Law Commission, May 6.—Cyclone passed over parts of Southern India, and many ships were wrecked on the Western Coast, May 18.—Public meeting at Madras to petition Parliament for the abolition of Import duties, June 2.—Thunderstorm at Guntoor, 3 lives lost, June 10.—The Prince of Arcot, G.C.S.I., son of Prince Azim Jah, the First Prince of Arcot, died at Madras, June 16.—The Hackney Carriage and Police Amendment Acts came into operation in Madras, June 17.—Amended Municipal Bill passed, June 25.—Post-cards introduced into India, July 1.—South Indian Railway opened at Tanjore, July 1.—Railway from Chidambaram to Coleroon opened, July 1.—The Rumpa rebels sunk the steam tug *Shamrock* in the Godavery, July 15.—The Rev. John Speechley consecrated first Bishop of Travancore and Cochin, July 25.—Release in August of 1,204 prisoners in several parts of the Presidency, who had been convicted of offences arising from the famine.—Rules for admitting Natives into the Civil Service published, Aug. 12.—Murder of Sir Louis Cavagnari and the British Embassy in Afghanistan, Sept. 3.—Madras troops ordered to the Afghan Frontier, Sept. 23.—Two Regiments of Madras Infantry, the 14th and the 25th, volunteered for Afghanistan, Sept. 28.—Compulsory Vaccination Bill introduced into the Viceroy's Council, Sept. 30.—Association set on foot in March for providing Eurasian and Anglo-Indian poor with the means of emigrating to British Colonies. Scheme was unsuccessful. Monster meeting was held on the 7th of Oct. to consider the condition of the Eurasian and Anglo-Indian poor; resulted in the formation of the "Eurasian and Anglo-Indian Association of Southern India."—P. & O. steamer *Hindostan* stranded off Madras, Oct. 21.—Accident on the Madras Railway near Chinnampett; 21 lives lost and 48 persons wounded, Oct. 31.—Cyclone passed over parts of the Nellore District, Nov. 17.—Pondicherry Branch Railway opened, Dec. 15.—Railway from Villapuram to Gingee opened, Dec. 16.—Madras Municipality accepted Mr. J. A. Jones' Drainage Scheme. Establishment of Municipalities in Pondicherry, Dec. 17.—Electric light exhibited at People's Park by M. Vernes, a French electrician, whose apparatus was purchased by the Municipality for Rs. 7,000.—Three batteries for Armstrong guns erected on the beach at Madras.

1880.—Further orders passed for the admission of Natives into the Covenanted Service, Jan. 1.—The Metropolitan of India arrived at Madras, Jan. 21.—Telegram received from the Lord Mayor of Dublin asking for subscriptions to relieve the distress in Ireland, Jan. 23.—Meeting at the Madras Club in connection with the Irish distress, Jan. 26.—Sir Andrew Clarke, Public Works Minister, arrived at Madras Jan. 28.—Bishop Speechley installed at Cottayam, Feb. 1.—Public meeting at Madras to raise funds for the Irish distress, Feb. 10.—Meeting at Hyderabad for the relief of the Irish distress, Feb. 13.—Brigadier General F. Jebb, Adjutant General of the Madras Army, died, Feb. 20.—The Metropolitan of India left Madras for Calcutta, Feb. 28.—Opening of the Fine Arts Exhibition at Madras, March 4.—Mr. Irvine, Sessions Judge of Vizagapatam, killed by a cheetah, March 6.—Bishop Chevalier, Vicar Apostolic of Mysore, died, March 25.—Monsieur Laugier, Governor of Pondicherry, arrived at Madras on a visit to the Governor, April 1.—Opening of Mr. P. S. Ramasawmy Mudalliar's Lying-in-Hospital at Madras by the Duke of Buckingham, April 5.—Unveiling of the Statue of Mr. E. B. Powell, late Director of Public Instruction, by the Duke of Buckingham, at the Presidency College, April 13.—Lord Lytton, the Viceroy of India, created an Earl, April 15.—St. Joseph's College at Cochin opened, April 20.—The Marquis of Ripon appointed Viceroy of India, April 27.—The Madras Railway reduced the third class fares to 2 pies a mile, May 1.—The Right Rev. Dr. S. Fennelly, Roman Catholic Bishop of Madras, died, May 3.—The Maharajah of Travancore died, May 30.—The Indian Merchants' Shipping Act came into operation, June 1.—The Marquis of Ripon installed as Viceroy of India, June 8.—Installation of the First Prince as Maharajah of Travancore, June 17.—The Opium Act came into operation in the Madras Presidency, July 1.—Compulsory Vaccination Bill passed by the Viceroy's Council, July 10.—Captain Mahomed Hussain, A.D.C. to Sir Neville Chamberlain killed on the S. I. Railway line, Egmore, July 20.—Public Meeting at Patcheappah's Hall in honour of Colonel Macdonald, the retiring Director of Public Instruction, July 26.—Madras Government ordered the admission of private students into the Medical College, Second Department, Aug. 18.—Sir Frederick Roberts appointed Commander-in-Chief, Madras Army, in succession to Sir N. Chamberlain, Sept. 5.—Royal salutes fired at Military Stations in honour of General Roberts' victory at Kandahar three days previously, Sept. 6.—A scare at Ootacamund Sept. 7.—Mr. Elliot appointed Census Commissioner for all India, Sept. 10.—Mr. V. Ramiengar appointed Dewan of Travancore, Sept. 18.—Mr. W. P. Adam, M.P. appointed Governor of Madras, Sept. 26.—Bicentenary of St. Mary's Church, Fort St. George celebrated Oct. 28.—The Rev. Mr. Sloan drowned at Negapatam, Nov. 1.—Native meeting held in honour of the Duke of Buckingham, Nov. 8.—Sir Neville Chamberlain's order published welcoming the Madras troops that served in Afghanistan, Nov. 12.—Heavy rains and floods in Southern districts; loss of 7 lives in the Madras Harbour, Nov. 21.—Mr. Runganatha Sastry appointed Member of the Legislative Council, Nov. 23.—The Bill to abolish the Neilgherry Commission passed in the Legislative Council, Nov. 27.—Mohammedan Entertainment to the Duke of Buckingham, Nov. 29.—Eurasian addresses presented to the Duke of Buckingham, Dec. 14.—Native Entertainment given to the Duke of Buckingham at Patcheappah's Hall, Dec. 15.—The S. I. Railway line opened from Chingleput to Conjeveram, Dec. 16.—Arrival of Mr. W. P. Adam, the new Governor of Madras; the Duke of Buckingham resigned, and left Madras for Europe Dec. 20.—Mohammedan address of welcome presented to the Governor, Dec. 30.

1881.—The South Indian Railway line from Maniyachi Junction to Tinnevelly opened, Jan. 1.—Madras Municipal address presented to the Governor, Jan. 24.—Opening of the first section of the Mysore State Railway, Feb. 1.—Sir Neville Chamberlain embarked for England, Feb. 3.—Industrial School opened at Pondicherry, Feb. 14.—Madras Field Games Association established, Feb. 17.—Fireworks explosion at Bangalore, 14 lives lost, Feb. 28.—Sir Frederick Roberts created a Baronet, March 2.—Madras Fine Arts Exhibition opened, March 4.—The Senior Ranee of Travancore appointed to the Order of the Crown of India, March 5.—The Press Commissionership of India abolished, March 16.—Chamarajendra Wodiyar, adopted son of the late Maharajah Krishnaraj Wodiyar, installed at the town of Mysore as Maharajah, by Mr. Adam, Governor of Madras, on behalf of the Viceroy, March 25.—Eurasian deputation waited on the Governor, March 31.—The Rev. Dr. Johnson, Bishop of Calcutta and Metropolitan of India, visited the Madras Presidency in March.—Probate and Administration Act came into operation, April 1.—Mr. W. P. Adam, Governor of Madras, died at Ootacamund, May 24. The Honourable W. Hudleston, Senior Member of Council, officiated as Governor for six months.—Regatta in the Madras Harbour, June 11.—Mr. M. E. Grant Duff, M.P., appointed Governor of Madras, June 22.—Mr. Handley appointed Chief Judge of Small Cause Court, Madras, June 28.—Reduced rates for telegraph messages introduced, June 30.—Deputation of the Eurasian and Anglo-Indian Association waited on the Maharajah of Mysore, July 29.—Much attention given to the auriferous resources of Mysore and Wynaad. In July forty-four Mining Companies, with a nominal capital exceeding five millions sterling, were in existence.—Mr. H. E. Sullivan appointed to the Madras Council; Mr. Davidson, who had been provisionally appointed, reverted to Chief Secretaryship, Aug. 2.—Maharajah of Mysore inspected Kolar Gold Fields, Sept. 3.—Population of India returned by census at 316,554,918 in 1881, against 204,751,851 in 1871, Sept. 9.—Census returns show that the Madras Presidency had a population of 30,800,000, being a decrease (consequent on the late famine) of 2·4 per cent. as compared with the census of 1871.—Installation of the Maharajah of Vizianagram, Oct. 19.—Mr. Grant Duff arrived from England, and assumed office as Governor of Madras, Nov. 5.—Post Office Savings Banks opened, Nov. 11.—Storm of some violence at Madras; eastern arm of the Harbour Works washed away; two hopper barges foundered in the harbour, and 15 lives lost, Nov. 12.—Reduced rates of newspaper postage introduced, Nov. 15.—Mohammedan deputation waited on the new Governor, Nov. 19.—Sir Frederick Roberts, Bart., G.C.B., V.C., took his seat as second Member of Council, Nov. 25.—Sham fight at Pallaveram, Sir F. Roberts present, Dec. 9.—Opening of the

Agricultural College buildings, Saidapet, by the Governor, Dec. 21.—Address presented to the Governor by the Eurasian Association, Dec. 26. —Shocks of Earthquake at Madras, Dec. 31.

1882.—Address presented by the Nilgiri Planting and Mining Association to the Governor, at Devala, Jan. 12.—Repeal of the Indian Vernacular Press Act, Jan. 19.—Opening of the Telephone Exchange at Madras, Jan. 28.—The Nilgiri Commission abolished, and a Collectorate established, Feb. 1.—Mr. W. E. Baxter, M.P., arrived at Madras, Feb. 2.—Hindu and Mohammedan deputation waited on Mr. Baxter at Guindy to deprecate Indian ecclesiastical expenditure, Feb. 4.—Formation of the Indian Evangelisation Society at Madras, Feb. 13.—Indian Trusts and Negotiable Instruments Acts came in operation, March 1.—Admiral Gore Jones arrived at Madras, March 5. —Public meeting at Madras to arrange for the erection of a Town Hall, March 19.—Colonel Dyer, Deputy Adjutant General of the Madras Army, died from the results of an accident, March 19.—Abolition of Import duties in India, March 11.—Madras Municipality voted an address to the Queen, March 24.—Post Office Savings Banks established in India, April 1.—Earthquake shocks at Bangalore, Coonoor, and Ootacamund, April 13.—Colonel Olcott and Madame Blavatsky, Theosophists, arrived at Madras, April 23.—Orders issued for the reorganization and reduction of the Indian Army, April 25.—Sir Ashley Eden, late Lieutenant-Governor of Bengal, arrived at Madras, April 28.—The Indian Companies' Act came into operation, May 1.—Mr. Plumer, late M.C.S., appointed Chief Judge of Mysore, May 2.—Mrs. Adam raised to the rank of a Baronet's widow, and her eldest son created a Baronet, May 23. —The Maharajah of Travancore created a G.S.C.I., and Mr. W. Hudleston a C.S.I., May 24.—Prohibition of lotteries ordered by the Government of India, May 31.—Madras Presidency recovering from the effects of the late famine. Gross revenue amounted to 984 lakhs; and gross expenditure to 750 lakhs, leaving a surplus of 234 lakhs, May.—New Civil Procedure Code came into operation, June 1.—Government of India Stock Notes ordered to be issued, June 6.—Honorary Grade of Assistant Engineers created June 8.—New Quarantine Rules enforced, June 16.—Heavy floods in the Cauvery and Coleroon, June 18.—Congratulatory addresses presented to the Very Rev. J. Colgan, on his being appointed R. C. Bishop of Madras, June 23.—Consecration of Bishop Capretti of Hyderabad; St. Aloysius' College at Mangalore established, June 29.—Transfer of Property Act, Indian Easements Act, and Presidency Small Cause Courts Acts, and new organization scheme of the Indian Army came into operation, July 1.—Railway line from Bangalore Cantonment to Bangalore City opened, July 1.—Installation of Rev. Dr. Strachan as Bishop of Rangoon, July 2.—Madras troops, the 4th, 30th, and 31st Regiments, ordered to Egypt, July 5.—Comet (of 1812) visible at Madras, July 24.—Riots at Salem arising out of disputes between Hindus and Mohammedans, July 28.—Consecration of Bishop Colgan, at the R.C. Cathedral, Madras, Aug. 24.—Formation of a Total Abstinence League at Madras, Sept. 4.—The Maharajah of Mysore turned the first sod of the Bangalore-Toomkoor Railway, Sept. 11.—Imperial salutes fired in honour of the success of the British in Egypt, Sept. 18.—The Education Commission began its sittings in Madras, Oct. 4, closed on Oct. 18.—The principal offenders in the Salem riots sentenced, some to imprisonment in India, and others to transportation to the Andamans, Oct. 21.—Deputation of members of the Madras Chamber of Commerce waited on Major Baring, the Finance Minister, at Government House, Nov. 30.—Mrs. Grant Duff laid the foundation stone of the fountain at Robinson Park, Dec. 22.—Deputation of Tinnevelly merchants waited on the Governor, Dec. 23.

1883.—The Madras Jails' Act, the Madras Forest Act, the New Code of Criminal Procedure, alterations in the Train Service on the Madras Railway, and reduced rates on the S.I. Railway came into operation Jan. 1.—Muttom Light House (Travancore coast) first lighted; Indian Postal Notes issued, Jan. 1.—Dr. Bidie, Superintendent, Central Museum, Madras, appointed C.I.E., Jan. 1.—Pallavaram Camp of Exercise opened, Jan. 8.—Presentation of the Star of India to the Maharajah of Travancore, Feb. 1. —Afghan War Medals presented to the Sappers and Miners at Bangalore by Sir F. Roberts, Feb. 3.—Nawab Sir Salar Jung, G.C.S.I., Prime Minister of Hyderabad, died, after having held that office for thirty years with great distinction, Feb. 8.—Bill introduced Feb. 9 by Mr. Ilbert, Law Member, into the Viceregal Legislative Council, proposing to concede criminal jurisdiction over European British subjects to Native Magistrates; this excited much opposition among Europeans in the Madras Presidency, as elsewhere throughout India. The project was modified in December, and the right of European British subjects to be tried by a jury, the majority of whom shall consist of European British subjects, was admitted.—Mr. Ranga Charlu, C.I.E., the first Dewan of Mysore, since the rendition of the State to native rule, died Jan. 23; succeeded by Mr. Seshadri Aiyar, another native of

Madras, Feb. 12.—Opening of the Madras Agricultural Exhibition, Feb. 15.—Public meeting at Madras in the Chamber of Commerce to protest against Mr. Ilbert's Bill, Feb. 23.—The Revenue Board Bill passed the Legislative Council, March 16.—The Flagship *Euryalus* arrived at Madras from Calcutta, March 18.—Formation of the Anglo-Indian Defence Association in Calcutta, March 19.—Formation of a Ladies' Defence Association at Calcutta, March 26.—Arrival of a Contingent of the Salvation Army at Madras, April 28.—Native Entertainment at Patcheappah's Hall in honour of Mr. Justice Innes, of the High Court Bench, May 5.—Mr. Innes left for Europe, May 8.—First Anniversary meeting of Local Self-Government scheme at Madras, May 18.—The Order of the Crown of India conferred on Mrs. Grant Duff, wife of the Governor of Madras, May 24.—Colonel T. Rose Church, Commandant, Madras Volunteer Guards, appointed a C.I.E., May 24.—The Bombay Government gave up Madras time, and adopted local time in all public offices, June 1.—Madras Deputy Collectors graded, June 26.—Colonel Drever, C.S.I., Commissioner of Madras City Police, died, July 12.—Death in England of Mr. J. B. Norton, formerly Advocate General of Madras, who achieved eminence as a journalist, a politician, a scholar, and a jurist, July 15.—Hindu Musical Society formed at Madras, Aug. 18.—Mr. Justice Muthusamy Aiyar confirmed as a Judge of the Madras High Court, Aug. 24.—Mr. T. T. Shungunni Menon, C.S.I., ex-Dewan of Cochin, died in Travancore, Aug. 28.—Mr. J. Wallace, Acting District Judge of Cuddapah, removed by the Secretary of State from the Madras Civil Service, for attributing his retention at Cuddapah to his not having given handsome wedding presents to the two daughters of Mr. Carmichael, Senior Member of Council, Aug.—Shocks of earthquake at Tirupatur, Salem, Sept. 5.—Consecration of Dr. Gandy, Coadjutor to Vicar Apostolic of Pondicherry, Sept. 9.—1st Madras Pioneers left Secunderabad for the Bolan Pass, Sept. 28.—The phenomenal appearance of the Sun in September excited much speculation. It was attributed to sulphurous vapours that emanated from great volcanic disturbances which had occurred in August in Java.—Opening of the Tanjore Medical School, established in honour of the Prince of Wales's visit, Oct. 1.—Mr. Havell, of the South Kensington Museum, appointed Superintendent of the Madras School of Arts, Nov. 11.—Public meeting at Madras in honour of Mr. D. F. Carmichael, Dec. 1.—Mr. Carmichael vacated office as Senior Member of Council on Dec. 10; was entertained by the native community at the Banqueting Hall on Dec. 18, and presented with farewell Addresses.—Mr. J. G. Coleman, a philanthropist, the first Eurasian admitted to the Madras Legislative Council, died Dec. 14. He joined the Madras Volunteer Guards in 1857, and rose to the rank of Lieutenant Colonel.—The foundation stone of the Madras Town Hall laid at the People's Park by the Maharajah of Vizianagram in the presence of a very large gathering, Dec. 17. The name of the building was subsequently changed to that of the Madras People's Victoria Hall.—Surgeon General Cornish appointed to the Legislative Council, Dec. 21.—Compromise effected in Calcutta between the Government of India and the Defence Association in respect to Mr. Ilbert's Jurisdiction Bill, Dec. 22.—Outbreak of epidemic among fish on the Coromandel coast, Dec.—Madras made liberal contributions to the Calcutta Exhibition, Dec.

1884.—Camp of Exercise at Krishnarajpuram, near Bangalore, opened, Jan. 5.—General Hardinge, Commander-in-Chief of Bombay, arrived at Madras from Bombay, Jan. 12.—Sir Donald Stewart, Commander-in-Chief of India, arrived at Madras, Jan. 13.—Native meeting at Madras in honour of Lord Ripon, Viceroy of India, Jan. 19.—Mr. Grant Duff proceeded to the Camp of Exercise, Jan. 22.—The Madras Municipality voted an address to Lord Ripon; Archdeacon G. Warlow died; Native Jurisdiction Bill passed the Viceroy's Council, Jan. 25.—Arrival of Lord and Lady Ripon at Madras from Calcutta, Jan. 31.—Induction of Archdeacon Browne at St. George's Cathedral, Feb. 3.—Mr. Justice Kindersley retired from the service, and was succeeded by Mr. F. Brandt as Judge of the High Court, Feb. 4.—Lord Ripon installed the young Nizam at Hyderabad on Feb. 5.—The Princess of Tanjore arrived at Madras on a visit to the Viceroy, Feb. 8.—The Maharajah of Mysore arrived at Madras, Feb. 11.—The Marquis of Ripon left Madras, after receiving 27 deputations, Feb. 13.—Army Head-Quarters permanently established at Ootacamund, March 6.—Foundation stone of the first large cotton mill in Malabar laid by Mr. F. Wilkinson, C.S., March 9.—The Maharajah of Vizianagram took his seat in the Madras Legislative Council, March 25.—Opening of the Madras Water Works, March 31.—City of Madras Municipal Act of 1884 came into operation, April 1.—Madras Harbour Dues Act came into operation; Pilotage dues abolished in the Suez Canal, April 1.—Madras Municipality voted telegram of condolence to the Queen on the death of Prince Leopold, April 2.—Special Health Officer appointed for Madras Town, April 6.—Travancore Agricultural Exhibition opened, April 17.—A public meeting in Madras voted an address of condolence to the Queen, April 18.—Madras New Post and Telegraph Office Buildings opened, April 26.—Compulsory Vaccination introduced, May 1.—Action brought by Mr. Vijiaraghava Chari of Salem against the Secretary of State for Rs. 10,000 damages for alleged wrongful removal from the office of Municipal Commissioner; Madras High Court awarded him Rs. 100 damages, and costs, May 2.—The Oriental Bank Corporation suspended payment, May 3.—The Maharajah of Mysore created G.C.S.I. and the Rev. W. Miller C.I.E., May 24.—The New High Court of Mysore formally opened, May 28.—The British ship *Riversdale* wrecked near Point Divi, in May.—Government decided to extend the Madras Municipal franchise to 24 out of 32 Commissioners, June 10.—Arrest of the Burmese Meingoon Prince at Colombo, June 25. He returned to Pondicherry and remained under French protection.—New Drainage Works of Madras City opened by the Governor, June 30.—Mass meeting at Madras to petition Parliament and the Viceroy against the removal from Madras of the seat of Government to Ootacamund, and of the Military Accounts Offices to Bangalore, July 3.—District Municipalities Bill and the Local Fund Bill passed in the Viceroy's Council, July 21.—Government deputed Colonel Weldon, Chief Presidency Magistrate, to proceed to Tinnevelly to inquire into charges brought against Mr. A. J. Brooke Atkinson, of the Madras Civil Service, Acting Collector of Tinnevelly, of having borrowed money in the district. The inquiry began on the 11th July. Mr. Atkinson was eventually removed from the service.—The Bangalore Toomkur Railway opened, July 28.—The Madras High Court refused to grant Mr. John Wallace, formerly of the Madras Civil Service, permission to institute a criminal prosecution of the members of the Madras Government, July.—The s.s. *Golconda* wrecked off Tuticorin in July.—Re-organisation of the Subordinate Medical Department, Aug. 4.—East Deccan Section, Southern Mahratta Railway, Hotgi to Gadag, opened, Aug. 6.—Government of Madras decided to abandon the scheme for locating the Military Accounts Offices in Bangalore, Aug. 7.—Madras Government created the appointment of Commissioner for Salt and Abkari, Aug. 26.—Earl of Dufferin appointed Viceroy of India in succession to Lord Ripon, Sept. 10.—Butchers' strike at Madras, Oct. 26, terminated Nov. 6.—Nizam of Hyderabad appointed G.C.S.I., Nov. 5.—Cyclone at Madras; Red Hills Tank breached, and the City of Madras threatened with the loss of its entire water supply, Nov. 20. Damage repaired in ensuing months.—Mr. S. Subramanya Aiyar appointed to the Legislative Council, Madras, Nov. 26.—All prisoners in the Andamans and in India connected with the Salem riots of July, 1882, received a free pardon, Nov. 27.—Lord Radstock arrived at Madras, on a preaching tour, Dec. 10.—Lord Dufferin arrived in Calcutta, and took his seat as Viceroy of India, Dec. 13. Mr. James Darragh's Mill at Quilon, Travancore, opened by the Maharajah, Dec. 16.—Public Conference of the Madras Mahajana Sabha, Dec. 29.—Public meeting to discuss the Hindu Widow Marriage Question, Dec. 30.

1885.—The Porter Town Hall at Combaconum was opened Jan. 17. It was designed as a memorial of the services rendered by Mr. W. A. Porter, for many years Principal of the Combaconum College.—Mr. Grant Duff, Governor of Madras, paid a State visit to the Governor of Pondicherry at Pondicherry in February, staying there for three days.—Lord Reay, Governor of Bombay, arrived in Madras on a visit to the Governor.—The Students' Home, erected by the Rev. Dr. W. Miller for the use of Brahmin students attending the Madras Christian College, opened March 1.—The foundation stone of the Jenkins' School, Royapettah, laid in the presence of the Rev. R. B. Jenkins, Secretary to the Wesleyan Missionary Society, who was in Madras on a tour through the East, March 21.—Discovery of a new planet by Mr. Pogson, Government Astronomer, March 23.—Two memorials erected in March in Madras to the memory of the late Colonel W. S. Drever, C.S.I., Commissioner of Police.—An Association of Graduates in Madras formed at a public meeting, April 11.—The Madras Mounted Infantry organised in April.—Colonel E. H. C. Bradford, C.S.I., Madras Staff Corps, appointed K.C.S.I.; Dep. Surgeon-General F. Day, Madras Establishment (retired), Mr. G. Hammett, and Mr. P. S. Ramasawmy Mudelliar appointed C.I.E.'s, June 6.—Separate Railway Volunteer Regiment, in connection with the Madras Railway Company, formed, June 23.—Sir Charles Turner, C.I.E., Chief Justice, resigned June 30.—The Jubilee of British Sargent, L.M.S., celebrated at Palamcottah in July.—Sir Frederick Roberts resigned the command of the Madras Army on Aug. 14, and proceeded to England before assuming the chief command in India.—The Maharajah of Travancore, G.C.S.I., died at Trevandrum in August, and was succeeded by his nephew.—The Nizam of Hyderabad passed a few weeks at Ootacamund in September.—The Governor and Mrs. Grant Duff paid a visit in September to Lord Reay at Poona, and to the Viceroy at Simla, and returned to Madras Oct. 24.—Sir Herbert Macpherson appointed to the command of the Madras Army,

November.—In connection with the general election in the United Kingdom three Native Associations in Calcutta, Madras, and Bombay sent three native delegates, Messrs. Manmohun Ghose, Salem Ramaswamy Mudelliar, and N. E. Chandavarkar respectively, to England in order to interest the electors of the United Kingdom in important Indian questions.—Sir Arthur Collins, Q.C., arrived, and was sworn in as Chief Justice, Nov. 26.—Lady Dufferin inaugurated a fund for supplying medical aid to the women of India. A movement for providing medical aid for native women was stimulated in Madras by the active support of Mrs. Grant Duff, C.I., under whose auspices the Victoria Hospital for Gosha and Caste Women was started. Towards these institutions the Rajah of Venkatagiri subscribed Rs. 40,000, and the Maharajah of Vizianagram Rs. 25,000.—Expedition fitted out at Madras for service in Upper Burmah, the command being conferred on Major General Harry Prendergast, C.B., V.C., an officer of the Royal (late Madras) Engineers. A large portion of the force consisted of Madras native regiments. General Prendergast arrived in Rangoon on Nov. 7, captured Minhla on the 17th, reached Ava on the 26th, occupied Mandalay on the 27th, and accepted the personal surrender of King Theebaw on the 29th. The King, his two Queens, and suite, were sent to Madras, where they arrived on Dec. 15. General Prendergast received the K.C.B.—M. Richaud, Governor of Pondicherry, paid the return State visit to the Governor of Madras on Dec. 24, and remained four days.

1886.—Mr. H. E. Sullivan, senior member of the Madras Executive Council, created a C.S.I., Jan. 1.—Mr. Grant Duff paid a State visit to the Rajah of Pudukota on the 1st Feb., and stayed there two days.—Mr. C. S. Crole, Collector of Madura, suspended by Government for one year from the 4th Feb., for alleged insubordination, in having brought to the notice of Government that Mr. Sullivan, one of its members, was concerned in certain irregular land transactions. He petitioned the Secretary of State, and was eventually reinstated, the period of his suspension being allowed to count towards pension, and full salary being paid in arrears to him. Mr. Sullivan resigned in Dec.—Madras Fine Arts Exhibition opened, Feb. 17.—Opening of the Robinson Park Fernery, presented by Mr. A. Dhanakoti Mudelliar, Feb. 20.—Mr. Chisholm, Consulting Architect to the Government of Madras, retired from the public service in Feb. He was succeeded by Colonel J. L. L. Morant, who, however, died shortly afterwards in Melbourne.—A new school fee notification issued by Government in Feb. caused great agitation throughout the Presidency. Public meetings were held, and in May the Government withdrew the notification.—A Finance Committee for the reduction of expenditure, formed in Feb. by the Government of India, visited Madras, and advised numerous retrenchments.—Lord Dufferin, Viceroy, Lady Dufferin, and Sir Frederick Roberts arrived in Madras on the 1st March from Mandalay, and after a stay of two days left for Calcutta.—Sir Herbert Macpherson assumed command of the Madras Army, March 1.—The Nizam arrived at Madras on a visit to the Viceroy, March 2.—Amalgamation of District and Post Office Savings Banks, April 1.—Opening of the Warangal extension of the Nizam's guaranteed State Railway took place on April 3.—Theebaw, ex-King of Burmah, was removed from Madras to Ratnagherry, April 10.—Ramachendra Tondaman, Rajah of Pudukota, died in April.—Opening of the Colonial and Indian Exhibition at South Kensington, London, May 4. Colonel Le Messurier, Commissioner at the Exhibition for the Maharajah of Mysore, and Major Nevill, Commissioner for the Nizam of Hyderabad, appointed C.I.E.'s.—The Zemindar of Bodinayakanur and 17 others charged with insulting Mr. J. H. Garstin, Second Member of the Board of Revenue. The case was committed for trial to the High Court, Madras, and the prosecution failed, May 9.—The Governor General issued a General Order recording his cordial recognition of the admirable manner in which General Sir H. N. D. Prendergast, V.C., K.C.B., and the troops under his orders, had carried out the task set before them, May 14.—Mr. Grant Duff appointed G.C.S.I., May 24.—The Madras Harbour Trust Act came into operation, June 1.—Great fire at Tinnevelly, about 130 persons lost their lives, and a large number were injured, July 26.—Exchange fell to 1s. 4½d. in August.—Sir Herbert Macpherson left Madras to assume the chief command in Burmah, Sept. 2.—Lady Grant Duff laid the foundation stone of the new Gosha Hospital at Chepauk, Sept. 18.—The Pope issued an Encyclical Letter, in Sept., establishing the R. C. Hierarchy in India.—The Bellary-Kistna State Railway from Guntakul to Nandyal opened, Oct. 9.—Sir Herbert Macpherson died of fever when returning from Mandalay to Rangoon, Oct. 20.—Prince Louis Napoleon visited Madras in Oct.—Storm at Madras, Nov. 9.—Great encroachment of the sea to the north of the harbour in Nov.—Sir M. E. Grant Duff vacated the office of Governor, Dec. 7. Mr. Robert Bourke, late M.P., arrived Dec. 7, and assumed the office of Governor, Dec. 8.—Sir Charles Arbuthnot, late Commander-in-Chief, Bombay, arrived in Madras, and assumed command of the Madras Army, Dec. 9.—Lord Dufferin, the Viceroy, paid a private visit to Madras, on his way to Calcutta, after a tour from Simla to Hyderabad, Mysore, Southern Districts, and Pondicherry, Dec. 11.—Mr. H. E. Church, Traffic Manager of the Madras Railway, died Dec. 17.—The Madras Chamber of Commerce celebrated its Jubilee by a banquet at the Madras Club, Dec. 18.—Sir Robert Fowler, ex-Lord Mayor of London, visited Madras, Dec. 30.—Terrible catastrophe at the Madras People's Park Fair; over four hundred people were burnt, or suffocated; others subsequently died from injuries received, Dec. 31.

1887.—Telegram of sympathy regarding the fire received by the Governor from the Viceroy, Jan. 1.—Telegram received from the Secretary of State expressing Her Majesty's sympathy with the sufferers, Jan. 2.—Dewan Bahadur Ragunath Row, Deputy Collector of Madras, invested as Prime Minister of Indore, Jan. 4.—The Oriental Library at the Head Quarters of the Theosophical Society, Adyar, opened Jan. 4.—The Nilgiris Cricket Club started, Jan. 8.—Government ordered a full inquiry into the cause of the fire at the People's Park, Jan. 9; after an exhaustive inquiry before the Coroner and a special jury, a verdict was brought in that the fire was attributable to accident.—Bishop Wilson, of the South American Episcopal Church, arrived in Madras, Jan. 9.—Mr. V. Ramiengar, C.S.I., retired from the Dewanship of Travancore, and was succeeded by Mr. T. Rama Row, Jan. 10.—Opening of the Nerbudda Railway, Jan. 15.—Arrival in Madras, from Colombo, of Monseigneur Agliardi, Papal Delegate Apostolic, Jan. 17.—Mohammedan Address of Welcome presented to the Governor, Jan. 18.—Sheriff's meeting at the Banqueting Hall, the Governor in the chair, to concert measures for the celebration of the Queen's Jubilee, Jan. 24.—The Right Rev. Dr. J. Colgan, Roman Catholic Bishop of Madras, installed as Archbishop by the Papal Delegate Apostolic, Jan. 25.—Synod of Roman Catholic Bishops of Southern India met Monseigneur Agliardi at Bangalore, and the Roman Catholic Hierarchy, established on the terms of the Concordat, was publicly proclaimed, Jan. 25.—Prince Frederick Leopold of Prussia arrived in Madras, Jan. 27.—The Public Service Commission commenced its sittings at Madras, Jan. 31, and closed them Feb. 12.—Eurasian Address of Welcome presented to the Governor, Feb. 14.—The Centenary of the Military Female Orphan Asylum celebrated, Feb. 15.—Celebration of the Queen's Jubilee throughout the Presidency of Madras.—The Honourable C. G. Master, Member of Council, and Mr. K. Sheshadri Iyer, Dewan of Mysore, appointed Companions of the Star of India; the Maharajah of Vizianagram, and Mr. R. A. Dalyell, C.S.I. (late Madras), Member of the Council of India, appointed Knights Commander of the Indian Empire; Mr. P. Chentsal Row Pantalu appointed Companion of the Indian Empire; and Mr. P. S. Ramasawmy Mudelliar, Sheriff of Madras, appointed Knight Bachelor, Feb. 16.—The Honourable P. O'Sullivan, Advocate General of Madras, died Feb. 25.—The Earl and Countess of Aberdeen arrived in Madras on a visit to the Governor, March 1.—The portrait of the late Mr. Adam unveiled in the Banqueting Hall, March 2.—The Finance Commission brought its labours to a close, March 18.—Jubilee Anniversary of Bishop Corrie's Grammar School, Madras, celebrated, March 22.—Orders arrived in Madras from the Secretary of State for the immediate closing of the Gunpowder Factory, but the execution of those orders was suspended, March 23.—Re-organization of the Madras Board of Revenue, April 1.—The Mahajana Sabha Conference held at Combaconum, April 16.—Mr. V. Ramiengar, C.S.I., late Dewan of Travancore, died May 10.—Mr. Robert Bourke, Governor of Madras, raised to the Peerage as Lord Connemara, May 13.—Conclusion of the celebration of the Jubilee of the Queen's reign in the City of Madras. A Statue of Her Majesty, the gift of Rajah Gajapathi Row to the City of Madras, unveiled by Lord Connemara, June 20.—Celebration of the Jubilee in the United Kingdom. Lord Connemara appointed a Knight Grand Commander of the Order of the Indian Empire, June 21.—Presentation of the Madras Presidential Address to H. M. the Queen Empress at Windsor Castle by Mr. Charles Lawson, the Madras Delegate. Mr. Lawson received the honour of Knighthood, June 30.

OFFICIAL PERSONNEL OF MADRAS.

1837 to 1887.

THE GOVERNMENT.

THE GOVERNORS OF FORT ST. GEORGE.

	ASSUMED CHARGE
The Right Hon'ble John, Lord Elphinstone, G.C.H.	6th Mar. 1837
Lieut.-General George, Marquis of Tweeddale, K.T., C.B.	24th Sept. 1842
Major-General the Right Hon'ble Sir Henry Pottinger, Bart., G.C.B.	7th Apr. 1848
The Right Hon'ble George, Lord Harris	28th Apr. 1854
The Right Hon'ble Sir Charles Edward Trevelyan, K.C.B.	28th Mar. 1859
His Excellency Sir Henry Ward, G.C.M.G.	5th July 1860
His Excellency Colonel Sir William Denison, K.C.B.	18th Feb. 1861
The Right Hon'ble Francis, Lord Napier, K.T.	27th Mar. 1866
The Right Hon'ble Henry Vere, Lord Hobart	15th May 1872
His Grace the Duke of Buckingham and Chandos, G.C.S.I., C.I.E.	23rd Nov. 1875
The Right Hon'ble William P. Adam	20th Dec. 1880
The Right Hon'ble Sir Mountstuart Elphinstone Grant Duff, G.C.S.I., C.I.E.	5th Nov. 1881
The Right Hon'ble Robert Bourke, Lord Connemara, G.C.I.E.	8th Dec. 1886

[Sir Henry Ward, Lord Hobart, and Mr. Adam died in office. Sir William Denison acted as Viceroy and Governor-General of India from December 1863 to 12th January 1864, and Lord Napier from February to March 1872. Mr. Henry Dickinson, C.S., acted as Governor from 23rd Feb. to 7th April 1848. Mr. Daniel Eliott, C.S., from 20th to 28th April 1854. Mr. William A. Morehead, C.S., from 8th June to 5th July 1860, and from 18th Aug. 1860 to 18th Feb. 1861; Mr. Edward Maltby, C.S., from 26th Nov. 1863 to 18th Jan. 1864; Mr. (afterwards Sir) Alexander J. Arbuthnot, C.S., from 19th Feb. to 15th March 1872; Mr. (afterwards Sir) William R. Robinson, C.S., from 29th April to 23rd Nov. 1875; and Mr. William Hudleston, C.S., from 24th May to 5th Nov. 1881.]

THE COMMANDERS-IN-CHIEF.

		ASSUMED CHARGE
Lieut.-General	Sir Peregrine Maitland, K.C.B.	11th Oct. 1836
" "	Sir Jasper Nicolls, K.C.B.	21st Dec. 1838
" "	Sir Samuel F. Whittingham, K.C.B., K.C.H.	1st Aug. 1840
" "	Sir Hugh Gough, G.C.B.	12th Aug. 1841
" "	George, Marquis of Tweeddale, K.T., C.B.	24th Sept. 1842
" "	the Hon'ble Sir George Henry Berkeley, K.C.B.	13th Mar. 1848
" "	Sir Richard Armstrong, C.B., K.T. & S.	29th Sept. 1851
" "	William Staveley, C.B.	27th Oct. 1853
" "	the Hon'ble George Anson	25th Sept. 1854
" "	Sir Patrick Grant, G.C.B.	10th June 1856
" "	Sir James Hope Grant, G.C.B.	26th Dec. 1861
" "	Sir John Gaspard Le Marchant, G.C.M.G., K.C.B.	25th May 1865
" "	William Anson McCleverty	8th Nov. 1867
" "	Sir Frederick Paul Haines, G.C.B.	30th May 1871
" "	Sir Neville Bowles Chamberlain, G.C.B., G.C.S.I.	3rd Feb. 1876
" "	Sir Frederick Sleigh Roberts, Bart., G.C.B., K.C.I.E., V.C. ...	28th Nov. 1881
" "	Sir Herbert Taylor Macpherson, K.C.B., K.C.S.I., V.C. ...	1st Mar. 1886
" "	Sir Charles George Arbuthnot, K.C.B.	9th Dec. 1886

THE CIVILIAN MEMBERS OF COUNCIL.

The Hon'ble	G. E. Russell	1833	The Hon'ble	H. D. Phillips	1864
"	John Sullivan	1837	"	Sir Alex. J. Arbuthnot, K.C.S.I.	1867
"	C. M. Lushington	1838	"	Robert S. Ellis, C.B.* ...	1869
"	John Bird	1840	"	James D. Sim, C.S.I. ...	1870
"	Henry Chamier	1843	"	Robert S. Ellis, C.B. ...	1872
"	Henry Dickinson	1845	"	Sir Wm. R. Robinson, K.C.S.I.	1873
"	Daniel Eliott	1848	"	William Hudleston, C.S.I. ...	1877
"	J. F. Thomas	1850	"	David F. Carmichael ...	1878
"	Walter Elliot	1854	"	Henry E. Sullivan, C.S.I. ...	1882
"	Sir Henry C. Montgomery, Bart	1855	"	Charles G. Master, C.S.I. ...	1884
"	William A. Morehead ...	1857	"	E. Foster Webster*	1886
"	Edward Maltby	1859	"	Philip P. Hutchins*	1886
"	Sir Thomas Pycroft, K.C.S.I.	1862	"	Philip P. Hutchins	1887

* Acting.

ADDITIONAL MEMBERS OF THE LEGISLATIVE COUNCIL.

Mr. T. Sydney Smith ... — 1862
" Charles Pelly, C.S. — 1862
" W. Reierson Arbuthnot — 1862
" Robert O. Campbell — 1862
" V. Sadagopah Charlu — 1862
" John Bruce Norton — 1863
" Alex. J. Arbuthnot, C.S. — 1865
Sir Sharfool Oomrah, K.C.S.I. — 1865
Mr. G. Lutchmanarasu Chetty, C.S.I. 1863
" R. S. Ellis, C.S. ... — 1866
" J. Dawson Mayne... — 1867
" A. Forrester Brown — 1867
" John Young... — 1867
" Thomas Clarke, C.S. — 1868
" John C. Loch — 1868
" V. Ramiengar, C.S.I. — 1870
Mir Humayun Jah ... — 1870
Rajah G. N. Gajapathi Row — 1870
Mr. Patrick Macfadyen ... 1870
" Alexander Mackenzie — 1872
" William Hudleston, C.S. — 1872
" Vencum Sanjiva Row — 1872
" Henry S. Cunningham ... 1872
" G. S. Forbes, C.S. — 1873
" David F. Carmichael, C.S. 1874
" James G. Coleman... — 1875
" Patrick O'Sullivan... — 1877
The Rajah of Pittapore... ... 1876
Mr A. Seshayya Sastri, C.S.I. ... 1878
" R. Davidson, C.S., C.S.I. 1880
" K. V. Rangasamia Sastri ... 1880
" Henry E. Sullivan, C.S. ... 1881
Rajah T. Rama Row — ... 1880
Mr. Charles G. Master, C.S. ... 1883
Major-Gen'l R. H. Sankey, C.B. 1883
Colonel J. H. M. Shaw Stewart 1884
Mr. E. Forster Webster, C.S. ... 1884
Surgn.-Gen. W. R. Cornish, C.I.E. 1884
Maharaja of Vizianagram, K.C.I.E. 1884
Mr. Hale H. Shephard ... — 1885
" John A. Boyson — — 1885
" William Wilson, C.S. — 1885
" Richard W. Barlow, C.S. ... 1886
" S. Subrahmanya Aiyar ... 1886
" Henry E. Stokes, C.S. ... 1886
" Stewart R. Turnbull ... 1887
" James H. Spring Branson... 1887
" P. Chentsal Row, C.I.E. ... 1889

[N.B.—Re-appointments are not included in the above list.]

MADRAS MEMBERS

VICEREGAL LEGISLATIVE COUNCIL.

Mr. Henry Forbes, C.S. ... 1862
" Robert S. Ellis, C.B., C.S. ... 1866
The Maharajah of Vizianagram 1864
Mr. Gordon Forbes, C.S. — 1868
" W. R. Robinson, C.S.I., C.S. 1870
" Robert A. Dalyell, C.S. — 1873
reappointed — — 1875
reappointed ... — 1877
" A. Seshiah Sastri, C.S.I. — 1879
" Louis Forbes, C.S. ... 1881
" Henry S. Thomas, C.S. ... 1880
" H. St. A. Goodrich, C.S. — 1882
" Wm. S. Whiteside, C.S. — 1884

SUPREME COUNCIL OF INDIA.

Mr. G. N. Taylor, M.C.S. 1865-1870
Sir A. J. Arbuthnot, K.C.S.I., M.C.S. — — — 1875-1880

SECRETARY OF STATE'S COUNCIL.

The Right Hon. Sir Henry Montgomery, Bt., late C.S. 1858
General Sir Robert Vivian, K.C.B., late Madras Army 1858
Mr. W. Urquhart Arbuthnot, late C.S., then of Messrs. Arbuthnot & Co., Madras. 1858
General Sir Alfred Wilde, K.C.B., late Madras Army 1876
Robert [illegible] Ellis, C.B., late C.S. — — — 1877
Sir Robert A. Dalyell, K.C.I.E., C.S.I., late C.S. — 1877

THE SECRETARIAT.

CHIEF SECRETARIES.

Mr. H. Chamier ... — — 1827
" R. Clerk* ... — — 1842
" G. D. Drury — — 1843
" J. F. Thomas* — — 1840
" J. F. Thomas — — 1845
Sir H. C. Montgomery, Bt. — 1850
Mr. T. Pycroft ... — ... 1855
" A. J. Arbuthnot — — 1862
" R. S. Ellis, C.B. — — 1867
" J. I. Minchin* — — 1868
" R. S. Ellis, C.B. — — 1870
" W. Hudleston ... — 1868
" D. F. Carmichael* — — 1870
" W. Hudleston — — 1873
" D. F. Carmichael — — 1877
" C. G. Master* ... — 1878
" R. Davidson, C.S.I. — 1880
" C. G. Master — — 1882
" E. F. Webster* — — 1883
" E. F. Webster — — 1884
" W. Wilson* — — 1885
" E. F. Webster — ... 1886
" H. E. Stokes* 1886

SECRETARIES REVENUE DEPART.

Mr. R. Clerk ... — — 1837
" Walter Elliot* — — 1846
" J. F. Thomas ... — 1843
" J. F. Thompson ... — 1845
Sir H. C. Montgomery, Bt. — 1847
Mr. T. Pycroft ... ... — 1850
" J. D. Bourdillon ... — 1855
" H. Forbes* ... ... — 1857
" W. H. Bayley* — — 1858
" J. D. Bourdillon ... — 1859
" J. D. Sim* — — — 1860
" J. D. Sim — — — 1862
" W. Hudleston — ... 1865
" R. A. Dalyell* — — 1868
" W. Hudleston — — 1870
" D. F. Carmichael — — 1872
" C. G. Master* ... — 1874
" D. F. Carmichael — — 1875
" C. G. Master — — 1877
" H. S. Thomas* — — 1878
" J. H. Garstin, C.S.I.* ... 1879
" C. G. Master ... — 1880
" E. F. Webster ... — 1880
" H. E. Stokes* — — 1883
" H. E. Stokes ... — 1884
" J. F. Price* ... ... — 1885

SECRETARIES MILITARY DEPART.

Lieut.-Col. R. W. Steel, C.B. ... 1837
" G. Fryer* ... — 1844
" C. A. Browne — 1845

Colonel H. Marshall* ... — 1850
" H. Marshall ... — 1860
" Sir A. T. Wilde, K.C.B.* 1863
Maj.-Gen'l Sir A. T. Wilde — 1867
Colonel A. C. Silver* ... — 1871
" A. C. Silver ... — 1873
" J. Michael, C.S.I. ... 1874
Lieut.-Col. G. A. Arbuthnot* — 1878
Colonel J. Michael, C.S.I. — 1879
" E. L. Hankin* ... — 1880
" E. L. Hankin ... — 1883
Lieut.-Col. A. R. Kenney-Herbert* 1884
" A. R. Kenney-Herbert — 1885

SECRETARIES P. W. DEPART.

Colonel A. C. Orr — — 1862
" J. Carpendale — — 1871
" G. W. Walker — — 1872
" R. A. Fuart — — 1877
" R. H. Sankey, C.B. — 1879
" J. H. M. Shaw Stewart 1883
" J. O. Hasted — — 1886

JOINT SECRETARIES P.W.D.

Lieut.-Col. J. C. Anderson — 1867
Major J. Mullins* — — 1869
Captain R. F. Oakes* — ... 1871
Lieut.-Colonel J. Mullins* — 1872

JOINT SECRETARIES IRRIGAT. P. W. D.

Lieut.-Col. J. Mullins — ... 1877
Colonel J. O. Hasted* — ... 1880
" J. O. Hasted — ... 1884
Lieut.-Colonel J. Pennycuick* 1886

JOINT SECRETARIES RAIL. P.W.D.

Col. J. H. M. Shaw Stewart ... 1879
Colonel C. J. Smith* — ... 1883
" C. J. Smith — ... 1884

THE BOARD OF REVENUE.

PRESIDENTS.

Mr. John Sullivan — — 1830
" John Bird — — 1840
" C. M. Lushington ... — 1842
" Henry Chamier — — 1843
" Daniel Eliott — — 1847
" Walter Elliot ... — 1854
" Edward Maltby — — 1858
" Thomas Pycroft — — 1862
" Henry D. Phillips — — 1864

FIRST MEMBERS.

Mr. James D. Sim (on leave) 1862
" William Robinson* — 1869
" Gordon S. Forbes 1870
" G. Thornhill... 1877
" G. A. Ballard (other duty) 1878
" Henry E. Sullivan* — 1878
" H. E. Sullivan (other duty) 1879
" R. Knyvet Puckle, C.I.E.* ... 1879
" Henry E. Sullivan — 1880
" Robert Davidson, C.S.I. ... 1880
" John H. Garstin, C.S.I.* ... 1883
" Henry S. Thomas ... — 1884

THE JUDICATURE.

CHIEF JUSTICES OF SUPREME (NOW HIGH) COURT.

The Hon'ble Sir Robt. B. Comyn 1831
" Sir Edward J. Gambier 1842

* Acting.

The Hon'ble Sir Chrs. Rawlinson ... 1865
" Sir Henry Davidson ... 1869
" Sir Colley H. Scotland ... 1861
" Sir Walter Morgan ... 1871
" Sir Charles A. Turner ... 1879
" Sir Arthur J. H. Collins ... 1885

[Mr. Justice Holloway acted as Chief Justice, December 1870, and January 1872, February 1873, March to August, 1873; Mr. Justice Innes from August to November 1877, October and November 1878, July to September 1879, July to September 1882; and Mr. Justice Kernan from July to November 1885.]

Puisne Judges Supreme Court.

The Hon'ble Sir Ed. J. Gambier ... 1838
" Sir John D. Norton ... 1842
" Sir William W. Burton ... 1844
" Sir Henry Davidson ... 1857
" Sir Adam Bittleston ... 1858

Judges of the late Sudr and Foujdaree Adalat.

The Hon'ble G. E. Russell (Ch.) ... 1830
" C. M. Lushington ... 1832
" John Bird ... 1832
" W. Hudleston ... 1832
" Thomas A. Oakes ... 1832
" A. Duncan Campbell ... 1835
" H. Dickinson ... 1840
" G. J. Casamajor ... 1840
" M. Lewin ... 1840
" A. Maclean ... [illegible]
" G. J. Waters ... [illegible]
" W. A. Morehead ... [illegible]
" E. K. J. Bellew ... [illegible]
" C. S. Harper ... 1847
" E. P. Thompson ... 1847
" J. F. Thomas (Ch.) ... 1850
" T. L. Strange ... 1850
" F. Anderson ... 1852
" Sir H. Montgomery (Ch.) ... 1855
" T. W. Goodwyn ... 1856
" G. A. Harris ... 1856
" C. R. Baynes ... 1857
" M. D. Phillips ... 1858
" Harley Frere ... 1859
" G. T. Beauchamp ... 1859

Puisne Judges of High Court.

The Hon'ble W. Holloway ... 1863
" L. C. Innes ... 1863
" C. Collett ... 1866
" G. H. Ellis* ... 1866
" D. F. Carmichael ... 1869
" J. Kernan, Q.C. ... 1870
" J. R. Kindersley* ... 1872
" J. R. Kindersley ... 1877
" L. Forbes* ... 1873
" L. Forbes* ... 1876
" L. Forbes* ... 1880
" T. M. Boswed* ... 1873
" H. J. Tarrant* ... 1877
" H. J. Tarrant* ... 1880
" H. J. Tarrant* ... 1876
" T. Muthusamy Aiyar ... 1878
" R. P. Hutchins* ... 1882
" P. P. Hutchins ... 1883
" F. Brandt* ... 1884
" F. Brandt ... 1884
" J. W. Handley* ... 1885

The Hon'ble C. A. Parker* ... 1885
" C. A. Parker ... 1887

Advocates-General.

The Hon'ble George Norton ... 1828
" Richard Sargent ... 1853
" T. Sydney Smith ... 1853
" John Bruce Norton* ... 1853
" John Bruce Norton ... 1863
" John Dawson Mayne* ... 1871
" Henry S. Cunningham ... 1872
" Patrick O'Sullivan ... 1877
" Hale H. Shephard* ... 1885
" J. H. Spring Branson* ... 1887

Sheriffs.

Mr. John Young Fullerton ... 1837
" Arthur John Mackenzie ... 1838
" John Young Fullerton ... 1839
" John Loco Johnson ... 1840
" Duncan Montgomerie ... 1841
" William Gardiner Burn ... 1842
" Christopher Biden ... 1843
" John Bruce Norton ... 1844
" John Fendley McKennie ... 1845
" Leonard Cooper ... 1846
" Mars Shepherd ... 1847
" John James Franklin ... 1848
" Richard Burgess ... 1849
" Arthur Macdonald Ritchie ... 1849
" Leonard Cooper ... 1850
" Arthur Macdonald Ritchie ... 1851
" Leonard Cooper ... 1852
" Richard Burgess ... (Actg.) 1852
" Richard Burgess ... 1853
" Edward Salmon ... (Actg.) 1853
" Christopher Biden ... 1854
" H. D. E. Dalrymple ... 1855
" Frederick Orme ... 1856
" John Findley McKennie ... 1857
" John James Franklin ... 1858
" William Sydney Wright ... 1859
" Eyre Burton Powell ... 1860
" H. D. E. Dalrymple ... 1860
Colonel John Impett ... 1860
Mr. H. D. E. Dalrymple ... 1867
" John Charles Loch ... (May) 1870
" H. D. E. Dalrymple ... 1871
" John Charles Loch ... 1874
" Clement Simpson ... (May) 1875
" William Walter Mundy ... 1877
" Robt. Collingwood Waller ... 1879
" Basil Lowry ... 1881
" E. J. Firth ... 1883
Lieutenant J. H. Taylor, R. N. R. ... 1885
Sir S. Ramasawmy Mudeliar, C.I.E. ... 1887

MEDICAL OFFICERS.

First Members Medical Board.

Dr. J. Annesley ... 1837
" R. Macaulay ... 1838
" J. Cuddy ... 1841
" L. G. Ford ... 1840
" G. Adams* ... 1840

Physicians-General.

Dr. L. G. Ford ... 1843
" G. Adams* ... 1843
" G. Adams ... 1845
" R. Bladen ... 1846
" C. Currie ... 1847
" R. Davidson ... 1850
" J. W. Sherman ... 1853
" J. B. Bunsen ... 1855

* Acting.

Director-General.

Dr. A. N. Magrath ... 1858

Principal Inspectors-General.

Dr. G. Pearse ... 1860
" Robert Cole ... 1862
" James Shaw ... 1867

Inspectors-General (British).

Dr. S. M. Hadaway ... 1868
" E. Currie, C.B. ... 1870

Surgeons-General (British).

Dr. S. Currie, C.B. ... 1874
" Charles A. Gordon, C.B. ... 1878
" Thomas Crawford ... 1880
" Sir A. D. Home, V.C., K.C.B. ... 1881
" Charles D. Madden ... 1883
" John Irvine ... 1886

Inspectors-General (Indian).

Dr. Wm. Mackenzie, C.B., C.S.I. ... 1868
" Edward Green Balfour ... 1872

Surgeons-General (Indian).

Dr. Edward Green Balfour ... 1874
" George Smith ... 1877
" Wm. Robert Cornish, C.I.E. ... 1880
" Michael Cudmore Furnell* ... 1885
" Michael C. Furnell, C.I.E. ... 1885
" George Bidie, C.I.E. ... 1886

Sanitary Commissioners.

Mr. Robert S. Ellis, C.B. ... 1864
Insp.-Gen. D. Macpherson, C.B.* ... 1866
Surgeon-Major J. L. Ranking ... 1867
" W. R. Cornish, C.I.E. ... 1870
" H. King* ... 1876
Dep.-Surg.-Gen'l. Furnell, C.I.E. ... 1880
" G. Bidie, C.I.E. ... 1883
" W. Farquhar ... 1886
Surgeon-Major J. Laing ... 1887

ORDNANCE OFFICERS.

Principal Commissaries of Ordnance.

Lieut.-Colonel J. H. Frith ... 1833
" P. Montgomerie, C.B. ... 1839
" F. Derville ... 1844
" F. P. Whinyates ... 1849
Colonel F. Blundell ... 1850
" F. Hammond ... 1856

Inspect.-Gen. of Ordnance, &c.

Lieut.-Col. George Balfour, C.B. ... 1857
Colonel G. W. Sington ... 1860
" J. L. Barrow ... 1868
" Alexander T. Cadell* ... 1869
" A. Stewart* ... 1870
" A. Stewart ... 1871
" Robert Cadell, C.B. ... 1876
Major-Gen. Robert Cadell, C.B. ... 1880
" S. H. E. Chamier, C.B. ... 1881
" Henry McLeod ... 1886

COMMISSARIAT.

Commissaries-General.

Colonel W. Cullen ... 1830
" A. Tulloch ... 1840
" A. McCally ... 1850

Colonel J. Hill ... — — [illegible]
" E. B. Miller — — 1880
" John Loudon ... — 1873
" Charles Sones-Ellis — [illegible]
" Richard A. Moore* — 1879
" B. H. W. Magrath — 1883
" Henry P. Hawkes* — 1883
" Henry P. Hawkes — [illegible]
" John Campbell Gorming 1887

PUBLIC INSTRUCTION

Directors.

Mr. (now Sir) A. J. Arbuthnot, C.S. 1855
" Eyre B. Powell, M.A., C.S.I. 1862
" E. Thompson, M.A.* (3 mos.) 1875
Col. R. M. Macdonald, M.S.C. 1875
Mr. E. Thompson, M.A.* (3 mos.) [illegible]
" H. B. Grigg, M.A., C.S. — 1880
" J. Townshend Fowler* (2 mos.) [illegible]
Dr. D. Duncan, M.A., D.Sc.* 1885–1887

Principals Presidency College.

Mr. E. B. Powell, M.A., C.S.I. 1847
" Edmund Thompson, M.A. 1862
Dr. David Duncan, M.A., D.Sc. 1883

[Mr. Henry Fortey, M.A., Mr. William A. Porter, M.A., and Mr. Francis S. Evans, M.A., acted from time to time as Principal.]

MARINE

Superintendent of Marine.

J. J. Franklin — — 1858–1880

Master Attendant Madras.

Captain C. Dalrymple — — [illegible]
" C. Biden — — [illegible]
" H. D. E. Dalrymple ... [illegible]
" J. H. Taylor ... — 1870

ASTRONOMERS.

Mr. Thomas Glanville Taylor ... 1830
Captain W. S. Jacob, Bom. E. ... 1849
Major J. F. Tennant, R.E. — 1859
" W. K. Worster, R.A.* ... 1859
Mr. Norman R. Pogson, C.I.E. 1861

POLICE AND JAILS

Inspectors-General of Police.

Mr. William R. Robinson, C.S. 1859
Colonel Charles S. Hearn, C.I.E. 1869
" Henry Daniel Chase ... 1881
" Thomas Kay Guthrie ... 1883

Commissioners of City Police.

Mr. E. F. Elliot ... — — 1834
Colonel Boulderson — — 1856
" Wilson — — — 1861
" Charles S. Hearn, C.I.E. 1866
" William S. Drever, C.S.I. 1869
" Thomas Kay Guthrie ... 1873
" Thomas Weldon — 1885

Inspectors-General of Prisons.

Mr. J. Rohde, C.S. — — 1855
Lieut.-Colonel W. J. Wilson ... 1866
Colonel Thomas H. E. Tennant 1874
Mr. Henry R. Grimes, U.C.S. 1884

REGISTRATION.

Inspectors-General.

Colonel Robt. M. Macdonald ... 1864
Mr. V. Ramiengar, C.S.I. ... 1875
Mr. George Hammett, C.I.E. ... 1880

FORESTS.

Conservators of Forests.

Dr. Hugh Cleghorn, M.D. ... 1856
Lieut.-Colonel R. H. Beddome 1867
Lieut.-Colonel Campbell Walker 1881

POST OFFICE.

Postmasters-General.

Mr. W. N. Taylor, M.C.S. ... 1837
" A. F. Bruce, M.C.S. — 1838
" C. P. Brown, M.C.S. — 1840
" A. F. Bruce, M.C.S. — 1843
" C. P. Brown, M.C.S. — 1846
" D. H. Williamson, M.C.S. 1853
" E. Fane, M.C.S. ... — 1858
" C. A. Roberts, M.C.S. ... 1859
" R. H. Williamson, M.C.S. 1860
Colonel A. C. Fraser ... [illegible]
Mr. C. W. Hutchinson, U.C.S.* 1864
Colonel A. C. Fraser* ... 1869
Maharaja the Hon'ble E. R. Bourke 1870
Mr. H. G. Turner, M.C.S. — 1873
" Temple Scott, U.C.S.* — 1876
" H. E. Tennant, M.C.S. — 1876
" C. W. Hutchinson, U.C.S.* 1880
" R. R. Douglas, U.C.S.* — 1882
" C. F. McCartie, M.C.S.* — 1883
" C. W. Hutchinson, U.C.S. 1884
" M. Hammick, M.C.S.* — 1886
" S. Dalton, U.C.S.* — 1886
" M. Farren, B.C.S. — 1886

ECCLESIASTICAL.

Anglican Bishops.

Right Rev. Daniel Corrie, D.D. 1835
" J. G. T. Spencer, D.D. 1838
" Thos. Dealtry, D.D. 1850
" Frederick Gell, D.D. 1861

Anglican Missionary Bishops.

Right Rev. R. Caldwell, D.D. (Tinnevelly, S.P.G.) 1877
" J. Sargent, D.D. (Tinnevelly, C.M.S.) 1877
" J. M. Speechly, D.D. (Travancore and Cochin.) 1879

Anglican Archdeacons.

The Ven. H. Harper, M.A. ... 1836
" V. Shortland, M.D. — 1847
" Thos. Dealtry, M.A. 1861
" John Garrett, M.A. ... 1871
" Chas. R. Drury, M.A. 1875
" George Warlow, M.A. 1881
" Jas. F. Browne, B.D. 1884

(R.C.) Vicars Apostolic.

Right Rev. F. P. de Alcantara* 1834
" D. O'Connor, D.D. 1835
" P. J. Carew, D.D. 1840
Very Rev. W. Kennedy, D.D.* 1841
Right Rev. John Fennelly, D.D. 1842
" S. Fennelly, D.D. — 1868
" Joseph Colgan, D.D. 1880

(R.C.) Archbishop.

Most Rev. Joseph Colgan, D.D. 1887

RAILWAYS.

Consulting Engineers.

Major T. T. Pears, C.B., R.E. 1850
Captain C. C. Johnston, R.E. ... 1857
" P. P. L. O'Connell, R.E. 1860
Lieut.-Col. J. C. Anderson, R.E. 1865
Col. J. H. M. Shaw Stewart, R.E. 1867
" H. L. Prendergast, R.E.* 1870
" J. H. M. Shaw Stewart, R.E. 1872
" C. J. Smith, R.E. — — 1883

Agents, Madras Railway.

Mr. E. Smalley — — — 1845
Major Jenkins — — — 1854
Mr. N. B. Acworth — — 1857
" H. A. Fletcher — — 1860
" Robert H. Elwin — — 1860
" Arthur M. Brandon — 1868
" W. R. Rolleston* — — 1883

Agents, Great Southern Ry.

Mr. J. T. Martagon — — 1856
" W. S. Irvine ... — — 1868

Agent, Carnatic Railway.

Mr. J. T. Pickett — — 1873

Agents, South Indian Ry.

Mr. W. S. Irvine ... — — 1874
" David Logan* — — 1869
" W. R. Bell ... — — 1880

THE UNIVERSITY.

Chancellors.

H.E. Lord Harris — — 1857
H.E. Sir Charles Trevelyan ... 1859
The Hon'ble W. A. Morehead. 1860
H.E. Sir Henry Ward ... — 1860
The Hon'ble W. A. Morehead. 1860
H.E. Sir William Denison — 1861
The Hon'ble E. Maltby — 1865
H.E. Sir William Denison — 1866
H.E. Francis, Lord Napier, K.T. 1866
The Hon'ble Alex. J. Arbuthnot 1872
H.E. Vere Henry, Lord Hobart 1872
The Hon'ble W. R. Robinson 1875
The Duke of Buckingham, &c. 1875
H.E. William P. Adam ... Nov. 1880
The Hon'ble W. Hudleston, May 1881
H.E. M. E. Grant Duff ... Nov. 1881
H.E. Lord Connemara ... Nov. 1886

Vice-Chancellors.

The Hon'ble Sir C. Rawlinson. 1857
" W. A. Morehead ... — 1860
" Sir Colley H. Scotland ... 1860
" A. J. Arbuthnot, C.S.I. ... 1871
" Mr. Justice Holloway — 1872
" Mr. Justice Innes ... 1874
" Sir Charles A. Turner, C.I.E. 1880
" Mr. Justice Kernan, M.A., Q.C. 1885

Registrars.

The Rev. P. Percival — — 1857
Mr. A. A. Gordon, M.A. ... 1860
" D. Duncan, M.A. ... — 1879
" F. S. Evans, M.A. — 1884

* Acting.

Dr. D. Duncan, M.A., D.Sc. ... [illegible]
„ W. H. Wilson, Ph.D. ... [illegible]

Fellows (June, [illegible].)

Mr. John Adam, M.A.
Mr Ameenuddin Sahib Bhdr.
Lt.-Genl. Sir C. Arbuthnot, K.C.B.
Mr. A. T. Arundel, B.A.
Rev. A. W. Atkinson, M.A.
Mr B. Balaji Rao, B.L.
Mr Cecil M. Barrow, M.A.
Rai Bhdr. V. Bhashyam Aiy. B.A.
Mr. O. Beauchamp
Surg. Genl. G. Bidie, M.B., C.I.E.
Mr. J. R. Bilderbeck, B.A.
Mr. H. W. Bliss, B.A.
Dr. A. G. Bourne, D.Sc., F.L.S.
Dr. J. Adam Bradshaw, M.A., LL.D.
The Hon'ble F. Brandt, B.A.
Ven'ble. Archd. J. F. Browne, B.D.
Surg. Major A. M. Branfoot, M.B.
Rt. Rev. R. Caldwell, D.D., Bishop.
The Zamorin of Calicut.
Mr. P. Chentsal Rao, C.I.E.
Mr. R. F. Chisholm, F.R.I.B.A.
Major W. H. Coghlan, R.E.
Most Rev. J. Colgan, D.D., Archbp.
Hon'ble Sir Arthur Collins, Q.C., C.J.
Mr. J. Cook, M.A.
Rev. James Cooling, M.A.
Mr. C. Chandrasekharam, B.A.
Rev. Charles Cooper, M.A.
Dr. W. E. Dhanakoti Raju, M.D.
Surg. Maj. Drake-Brockman, F.R.C.S.
Dr. David Duncan, M.A., D.Sc.
Mr. C. C. Flanagan, M.A.
Mr R. Bruce Foote.
Rev. T. Foulkes, F.L.S., F.R.G.S.
Mr. J. Townshend Fowler, F.R.G.S.
Rajah G. N. Gajapathi Rao
Mr. J. S. Garabin, M.A.
„ J. H. Garstin, C.S.I.
„ L. Garthwaite, B.A.
Rt. Rev. F. Gell, D.D., Bishop.
Mr. Abdul Ghani Khan Bhdr.
Dr. Michael Gould, M.A., LL.D.
Mr. H. B. Grigg, M.A.
„ James Gross, M.A.
„ S. Gopalaswami, M.A.
Lt.-Col. W. Hughes-Hallett.
Mr. J. G. Handley, M.A.
„ F. B. Horne, M.A., M.E.
Dr. R. Harvey, M.A., LL.D.
Colonel J. H. Hasted, R.E.
„ H. P. Hawkins.
Rev. Dr. John Hay, M.A., D.D.
Mr. J. R. Henderson, M.B., C.M.
Hon'ble Mir Humayun Jah, C.I.E.
The Hon'ble P. P. Hutchins.
R. Bhdr. V. Jagannatha Row Pant.
Rev. A. Jean, B.A., D.D.
Surg. Ferguson J. Keane, M.D.
V. T. Kerala Varma.
The Hon'ble J. Kernan, M.A., Q.C.
Dr. William King, D.Sc.
Mr. V. Krishnamachariyar.
Mr. K. Krishnaswami Rao.
Sir Charles Lawson.
Mr. M. A. Lawson, M.A.
Mr. H. Logan, M.I.C.E.
Mr. W. Logan.
Captain H. D. Love, R.E.
Mr. Basil Lovery.
Mr. Patrick Macfadyen.
Dr. C. D. Mackenzie, M.A., Mus. D.

Surg. Major C. J. McNally, M.D.
Rajah Sir T. Madava Rao, K.C.S.I.
Mr. E. Marsden, B.A.
The Hon'ble C. G. Master, C.S.I.
Mr. E. P. Metcalfe, M.A.
Mr. R. B. Michell, M.A.
Rev. Dr. W. Miller, M.A., LL.D., C.I.E.
Mr. A. Moore, M.A., B.C.L.
Hon'ble T. Muttusawmy Aiyar, C.I.E.
Dr. Gustav Oppert, Ph. D.
Rev. G. Patterson.
Mr. N. R. Pogson, F.R.A.S., C.I.E.
Brig. Surg. A. Porter, M.D., F.R.C.S.I.
Rev. G. Milne Rae, M.A.
Rajah Hon'ble T. Rama Row, B.A.
Mr. A. Ramachandra Aiyar, B.L.
Mr. T. Rama Row.
Mr. S. Ramaswami Mudelli, M.A.
Rai Bhdr. P. Rangenatha Mudali, M.A.
Mr. P. Ragunatha Row D. Bhdr.
Surg. Major J. J. L. Ratton, M.D.
Mr. J. D. Rees, F.R.G.S., M.R.A.S.
Mr. L. Rees, C.I.E.
Mr. W. R. Robertson, M.R.A.C.
Rev. W. T. Satyanathan, B.D.
Mr. A. Sankara Aiyar, B.A.
Rt. Rev. E. Sargent, D.D., Bishop.
Mr. A. F. Seely, M.A.
Hon'ble. A. Seshayya Sastry, C.S.I.
Mr. M. Seshagiri Sastriyar, M.A.
Mr. E. Sedgwick, B.A.
Rev. E. Sell, B.D.
Mr. K. Seshadri Aiyar, B.A., C.S.I.
Rev. J. D. W. Sewell, S.J.
Mr. R. Sewell.
Mr. H. H. Shepherd, M.A.
Dr. Mohideen Sheriff, Khan Bhdr.
Dep. Surg. Genl. J. Shortt, M.D.
Mir Shujaat Ali Khan.
Brig. Surg. C. Sibthorpe, F.R.Q.C.P.
Mr. D. Sinclair, M.A.
Mr. C. Michie Smith, B.Sc., F.R.S.E.
Rt. Rev. J. M. Spratling, D.D., Bp.
Mr. P. Srinivasa Rao, Dewan Bhdr.
Mr. H. S. Stokes, B.A.
Rt. Rev. J. M. Strachan, M.D., Bishop.
Mr. G. H. Stuart, M.A.
Rai Bhdr. Hon. S. Subramanya Aiyar.
Mr. C. W. Tamotharam Pillay, B.A.
Mr. H. S. Thomas, F.L.S., F.Z.S.
Mr. E. Thurston, L.R.C.P., L.S.A.
Mr. F. H. Trevelyan.
Mr. P. Vijayaranga Mudaliar.
Hon. Maharajah of Vizianagram, K.C.I.E.
Rev. Dr. J. A. Willy, D.D.
Mr. W. Wilson, M.A.
Dr. W. H. Wilson, Ph.D., F.C.S., F.G.S.
Mr. G. K. Winter.

CHAMBER OF COMMERCE.

Chairmen.

Mr. J. A. Arbuthnot ... Sept. [illegible]
„ J. W. Dare ... July [illegible]
„ W. S. Binny ... July [illegible]
„ J. Line ... July [illegible]
„ F. Scott ... July [illegible]
„ J. U. Ellis ... July [illegible]
„ J. Ouchterlony ... July [illegible]
„ J. Thompson ... July [illegible]
„ J. B. Kay ... July [illegible]
„ G. Arbuthnot ... July [illegible]
„ J. Ouchterlony ... — [illegible]
„ H. Nelson ... — [illegible]
„ W. McTaggart ... Jan. [illegible]

* Acting.

Mr. W. G. Arbuthnot ... April [illegible]
„ J. Ouchterlony ... — [illegible]
„ J. Gowlden ... — [illegible]
„ J. Ouchterlony ... — [illegible]
„ J. Scott ... July [illegible]
„ R. O. Campbell ... July [illegible]
„ J. Ouchterlony ... — [illegible]
„ J. B. Kay ... July [illegible]
„ W. H. Crake ... — [illegible]
„ J. Vans Agnew ... — [illegible]
„ H. Nelson ... — [illegible]
„ A. J. Byard ... — [illegible]
„ W. R. Arbuthnot ... July [illegible]
„ R. O. Campbell ... — [illegible]
„ W. H. Crake ... Oct. [illegible]
„ A. J. Byard ... — [illegible]
„ H. Tolputt ... July [illegible]
„ J. Young ... April [illegible]
„ A. F. Brown ... Oct. [illegible]
„ W. R. Arbuthnot ... — [illegible]
„ J. C. Loch ... Jan. [illegible]
„ A. J. Byard ... April [illegible]
„ P. Macfadyen ... — [illegible]
„ R. C. Walker ... — [illegible]
„ A. F. Brown ... — [illegible]
„ P. Macfadyen ... — [illegible]
„ C. Simpson ... — [illegible]
„ P. Macfadyen ... — [illegible]
„ L. Jones ... April [illegible]
„ A. Mackenzie ... — [illegible]
„ P. Macfadyen ... April [illegible]
„ C. Simpson ... — [illegible]
„ J. C. Shaw ... — [illegible]
„ J. A. Boyson ... — [illegible]
„ P. Macfadyen ... — [illegible]
„ G. G. Arbuthnot ... April [illegible]
„ S. H. Turnbull ... — [illegible]

Secretaries.

Mr. A. J. Madison ... [illegible]
Vacant ... [illegible]
Mr. R. Cardew ... [illegible]
„ R. W. Harler ... [illegible]
„ C. A. Lawson ... [illegible]

BANK OF MADRAS.

Presidents.

Mr. J. C. Morris, C.S. ... [illegible]
„ J. U. Ellis ... Mar. [illegible]
„ J. G. Kay ... Aug. [illegible]
„ T. Stevenson, C.S., Dec. [illegible]
„ J. B. Kay ... — [illegible]
„ J. Thompson ... — [illegible]
„ W. U. Arbuthnot ... — [illegible]
„ J. Thompson ... — [illegible]
„ G. Arbuthnot ... — [illegible]
„ J. B. Kay ... — [illegible]
„ S. D. Birch, C.S. ... Feb. [illegible]
„ H. Nelson ... July [illegible]
Major J. T. Smith, R.E. Feb. [illegible]
Mr. H. Nelson ... — [illegible]
„ J. B. Kay ... — [illegible]
„ J. Gowlden ... — [illegible]
„ H. Nelson ... — [illegible]
„ R. O. Campbell ... — [illegible]
„ W. R. Arbuthnot ... — [illegible]
„ R. O. Campbell ... — [illegible]
„ J. Young ... — [illegible]
„ A. F. Brown ... — [illegible]
„ W. R. Arbuthnot ... — [illegible]
„ A. F. Brown ... — [illegible]
Colonel C. A. Orr, R.E. ... — [illegible]
„ J. Carpendale, R.E. May [illegible]

Mr. A. Mackenzie	April	1870
" A. F. Brown	Dec.	1870
" W. R. Arbuthnot	May	1870
" A. Mackenzie	May	1873
" C. A. Ainslie	...	1878
" M. Gould	...	1879
" P. Macfadyen	...	1880
" J. C. Shaw	...	1881
" R. C. Walker	April	1882
" C. A. Ainslie	...	1882
" R. C. Walker	...	1883
" J. C. Shaw	...	1884
" R. C. Walker	...	1885
" P. Macfadyen	Aug.	1885
" R. C. Walker	...	1886
" G. O. Arbuthnot	...	1887
" R. C. Walker	April	1887

SECRETARIES AND TREASURERS.

Mr. S. D. Birch, C.S.	June	1843
" J. Haynes	...	1844
" J. E. Spencer*	Aug.	1842
" R. Hunter	Nov.	1845
" J. Maltby	Feb.	1851
" T. E. French	...	1873
" J. L. Duffield*	April	1881
" D. A. J. Cruickshank	...	1880

AGRI-HORTICULT. SOCIETY.

HONORARY SECRETARIES.

Mr. Haynes	1835
" Ouchterlony*	1835
Lieutenant Thompson	1835
Mr. Liddle	1836
" W. B. Underwood	1838
Dr. R. Robert Wight	1850
Captain F. A. Reid, C.B.	1861
" F. H. Seaton	1860
Mr. G. M. Swinton	1863
Captain F. S. Gabb	1863
" Hayne	1866
" W. K. Worster	1867
Major F. A. Reid, C.B.	1868
Captain W. K. Worster*	1870
Dr. H. F. C. Cleghorn, M.D.	1850
Colonel F. A. Reid, C.B.	1852
Mr. J. T. Maclagan	1857
Dr. H. H. Montgomery, M.D.	1858
Rev. J. R. Macfarlane	1860
Dr. Alexander Hunter, M.D.	1860
" George Bidie, M.D.	1866
" Alexander Hunter, M.D.*	1867
Mr. William R. Liddle	1868
" William W. Moore	1870
Colonel Robert Beddome, F.L.S.	1873
Mr. John Shaw	1873
" Joseph Stevenson, B.A.	1877

TRAVANCORE.

THE MAHARAJAHS.

H.H. Rama Varma	1830
H.H. Martanda Varma	1846
H.H. Rama Varma, G.C.S.I.	1860
H.H. Rama Varma, G.C.S.I.	1880
H.H. Rama Varma	1885

THE DEWANS.

M. R. Ry. Ranga Rao*	1837
M. R. Ry. Venkata Rao	1838
M. R. Ry. Subba Rao	1839
M. R. Ry. V. Krishna Rao*	1842
M. R. Ry. Venkata Rao	1843
M. R. Ry. Srinivasa Rao*	1845
M. R. Ry. V. Krishna Rao	1847
Sir T. Madava Row, K.C.S.I.	1858
M. R. Ry. Seshiah Sastri, C.S.I.	1872
M. R. Ry. Nanoo Pillai	1877
M. R. Ry. V. Ramiengar, C.S.I.	1880
M. R. Ry. T. Rama Rao	1887

COCHIN.

THE MAHARAJAHS.

H.H. Rama Varma	1839
H.H. Rama Varma	1844
H.H. Vira Kerala Varma	1851
H.H. Ravi Varma	1853
H.H. Rama Varma, K.C.S.I.	1864

THE DEWANS.

M. R. Ry. Venkata Subba Iyer	1837
M. R. Ry. Sankara Variar	1845
M. R. Ry. Venkata Rao	1856
M. R. Ry. Shungoonny Menon, C.S.I.	1860
M. R. Ry. T. Govinda Menon	1880

* Acting.

www.ingramcontent.com/pod-product-compliance
Lightning Source LLC
Chambersburg PA
CBHW050848300426
44111CB00010B/1182
9783742831934